Cognitive-Behavioral Procedures with Children and Adolescents

A Practical Guide

Edited by

A. J FINCH, JR., Ph.D.
The Citadel

W. MICHAEL NELSON III, Ph.D.
Xavier University

EDITH S. OTT, Ph.D.
Independent Practice of Clinical Psychology

ALLYN AND BACON
Boston   London   Toronto   Sydney   Tokyo   Singapore

Library of Congress Cataloging-in-Publication Data

Cognitive-behavioral procedures with children and adolescents : a
   practical guide / edited by A. J Finch, Jr., W. Michael Nelson III,
   Edith S. Ott.
        p.   cm.
   Includes bibliographical references and indexes.
   ISBN 0-205-13435-1 (cased)
   1. Cognitive therapy for children. 2. Cognitive therapy for
teenagers. I. Finch, A. J,   . II. Nelson, W. Michael.
III. Ott, Edith S.
RJ505.C63C64 1993
618.92′89142 – dc20   92-4946
                                          CIP

Printed in the United States of America
10 9 8 7 6 5 4 3 2   96 95

Contents

List of Contributors   ix
Preface   xi

PART ONE
General Issues in Cognitive-Behavioral Treatment of Children and Adolescents

Chapter One • *Cognitive-Behavioral Procedures with Children: Historical Context and Current Status*   1
    by Kathleen J. Hart and John R. Morgan

    Historical Considerations   2

    Defining Cognitive-Behavioral Interventions   5

    The Development of Cognitive-Behavioral Procedures with Children   11

    The Efficacy of Cognitive-Behavioral Interventions   15

    The Direction of Cognitive-Behavioral Interventions with Children   17

    Conclusions   18

    References   19

Chapter Two • *The Role of Developmental Variables in Cognitive-Behavioral Interventions with Children*   25
    by William Kimball, W. M. Nelson III, and P. M. Politano

    The Relation of Developmentally Based Variables to Social Behavior   26

    Comprehending Social Information: Attention and Retention   31

    Evaluating Social Acts: Role Taking and Moral Reasoning   34

    An Example of a Developmentally Based Intervention Plan   51

Conclusions   58

References   59

Chapter Three • *Children and the Use of Self-Monitoring, Self-Evaluation, and Self-Reinforcement   67*
   by Helen L. Evans and Maureen A. Sullivan

   Theoretical Considerations   68

   Self-Monitoring Skills   70

   Self-Evaluation Techniques   74

   Self-Reinforcement   75

   Classroom Application   77

   Case Studies   79

   Summary   86

   References   87

Chapter Four • *Cognitive-Behavioral Assessment of Children: A Review of Measures and Methods   90*
   by David S. Pellegrini, Cynthia L. Galinski, Kathleen J. Hart, and Philip C. Kendall

   Beginning the Assessment   91

   From Referral to Specifics   92

   Specific Dimensions of Assessment   104

   Closing Comments   128

   References   129

PART TWO
Treatment Applications for Cognitive-Behavioral Procedures with Children and Adolescents

Chapter Five • *Childhood Aggression: Cognitive-Behavioral Therapy Strategies and Interventions   148*
   by A. J Finch, Jr., W. M. Nelson III, and Jon H. Moss

   Assessment of Anger   152

   Cognitive-Behavioral Techniques   163

   Session-by-Session Guidelines   169

   Case Presentation   178

   The Stress Inoculation Approach Within a Problem-Solving Framework   192

   References   201

Chapter Six • *Social Skills Training with Physically Aggressive Children   206*
by James Polyson and William Kimball
Literature Review and Key Issues   207
Treatment Approaches   214
The Training Manual   216
Summary   228
References   228

Chapter Seven • *Cognitive Self-Instruction for Impulse Control in Children   233*
by A. J Finch, Jr., Anthony Spirito, Pamela S. Imm, and Edith S. Ott
Background Review   234
Training Materials   242
Verbal Self-Instructions   244
Response-Cost Component   245
Training Setting   246
Training Sessions   246
Final Thoughts   252
References   254

Chapter Eight • *Coping Skills for Anxiety Control in Children   257*
by Nancy Grace, Anthony Spirito, A. J Finch, Jr., and Edith S. Ott
Coping Approaches to Anxiety Management   258
Coping Skills Guidelines   266
Appendix A: Videotape Script   283
References   284

Chapter Nine • *Child and Adolescent Depression: Cognitive-Behavioral Strategies and Interventions   289*
by Michael P. Carey
Assessment of Childhood and Adolescent Depression   292
Cognitive-Behavioral Intervention Models of Depression   295
Efficacy of Cognitive-Behavioral Intervention Strategies   305
Summary and Conclusions   310
References   311

Chapter Ten • *Cognitive-Behavioral Intervention for Adolescent Drug Abuse   315*

    by W. Robert Nay and George R. Ross

    Drug Abuse Myths   316

    Recognition of the Problem   317

    From Conceptualization to Assessment   320

    Intervention Targets and Cognitive Treatment Alternatives   323

    An Application: The L.I.F.E. Program   339

    References   342

Chapter Eleven • *Children and Coping with Pain: A Cognitive-Behavioral Management Approach   344*

    by W. M. Nelson III

    What Is Pain?   344

    Assessment of Pain in Children: A Brief Overview   349

    Intervention Techniques: Other Management Strategies   351

    Intervention Techniques: Cognitive-Behavioral Strategies   353

    Assessment: Cognitive-Behavioral Procedures   354

    Treatment: Stress Inoculation and the Management of Pain   358

    Case Study   362

    References   367

PART THREE
Integrative Issues

Chapter Twelve • *A Conceptualization of Psychotherapy with Children and Adolescents   372*

    by P. M. Politano

    Historical Perspective   372

    Differences: Young People and Adults   375

    Goals and Givens   379

    Conceptual Framework for Therapy   381

    The Process of Change   386

    Summary   390

    References   390

Author Index   393
Subject Index   402

List of Contributors

Michael P. Carey, Ph.D.
Department of Psychiatry
Child & Adolescent Psychiatric
   Hospital
3000 Arlington Avenue, CS 10008
Toledo, Ohio 43699

Helen Evans, Ph.D.
Illinois School of Professional
   Psychology
220 South State Street
Chicago, Illinois 60604-2276

A. J Finch, Jr., Ph.D.
Psychology Department
The Citadel
Charleston, South Carolina 29409

Cynthia L. Galinski
Department of Psychology
Catholic University of America
Washington, D.C. 20064

Nancy Grace, Ph.D.
Child and Family Psychiatry
Rhode Island Hospital
593 Eddy Street
Providence, Rhode Island 02902

Kathleen J. Hart, Ph.D.
Department of Psychology
Xavier University
Cincinnati, Ohio 45207

Pamela Imm, M.A.
University of South Carolina
Columbia, South Carolina 29201

Philip C. Kendall, Ph.D.
Department of Psychology
Temple University
238 Meeting House Lane
Marion, Pennsylvania 19066

William Kimball, Ph.D.
Mercy Hospital, Community Mental
   Health Center
218 Stone Street
Watertown, New York 13601

John R. Morgan, Ph.D.
Box 82
Chesterfield Mental Health and
   Mental Retardation Department
Chesterfield, Virginia 23832

Jon Moss, Ph.D.
Child and Adolescent Services
501 North Street, 2nd Floor
Richmond, Virginia 23219

W. Robert Nay, Ph.D.
McLean Psychological Center
7601 Lewinsville Road, Suite 203
McLean, Virginia 22102

W. Michael Nelson III, Ph.D.
Department of Psychology
Xavier University
Cincinnati, Ohio 45207-6511

Edith S. Ott, Ph.D.
500 Libbie Avenue, Suite 2-B
Richmond, Virginia 23226

David S. Pellegrini, Ph.D.
Life Cycle Institute
Catholic University of America
Washington, D.C. 20064

P. Michael Politano, Ph.D.
Psychology Department
The Citadel
Charleston, South Carolina 29409

James Polyson, Ph.D.
4826 Kellywood Drive
Glen Allen, Virginia 23060

George R. Ross
McLean Psychological Center
7601 Lewinsville Road, Suite 203
McLean, Virginia 22101

Anthony Spirito, Ph.D.
Child and Family Psychiatry
Rhode Island Hospital
593 Eddy Street
Providence, Rhode Island 02902

Maureen A. Sullivan, Ph.D.
Department of Psychology
Oklahoma State University
Stillwater, Oklahoma 74076

Preface

This book is designed to serve as a guide for mental health professionals and educators who use cognitive-behavior therapy procedures in their work, or who are interested in exploring the possibility of using this treatment modality, or who want to expose their students to this approach. In other words, this volume is for clinicians and teachers who appreciate the usefulness of a cognitive-behavioral approach in the treatment of children and adolescents with a wide range of presenting problems. Rather than providing an exhaustive review of the literature, we have brought together the information gathered by various authors who have used cognitive-behavioral procedures in their practice of clinical psychology with young people.

The authors have contributed to the advancement of the cognitive-behavioral movement through their scientific publications; however, in the literature there is usually a gap between research and actual clinical practice. In this volume we attempt to bridge that gap by emphasizing the practical application of research findings in clinical practice. Because the contributors are all clinical practitioners in the field of child and adolescent therapy, each is aware of the special considerations that apply to the assessment and treatment of children. Also, the authors of these chapters have spent a large part of their professional lives teaching and supervising other clinicians, clarifying and sharpening their understanding of cognitive-behavioral approaches in the process.

Thus, this book is different from those in which authors are typically presented with an outline into which their chapter must "fit." Indeed, the authors have not been given a format with plans and suggestions for consistency across chapters. Instead, they have been asked to "tell of your own experience in conducting and teaching a cognitive-behavioral approach." Therefore, the authors have developed the individual chapters independently to reflect their own clinical experience as well as the methods that have been most helpful for them in their teaching and supervision of others. Each chapter in this volume stands alone and presents the views and experiences of the contributors.

Although common theoretical tenets are discussed throughout the book, specific treatment recommendations are geared for the particular area of psychopathology addressed in each chapter. Thus, the presentation of important conceptual issues and treatment recommendations is the singular reflection of the authors' clinical and teaching experience. Many of the chapters provide actual treatment manuals and case examples that have evolved from this experience and have guided the application of various cognitive-behavioral treatment programs.

The text does not attempt to offer treatment procedures for the entire spectrum of childhood psychopathology; however, it does address many of the common problems encountered in clinical practice — such as depression, anxiety, aggression, and substance abuse. Throughout this volume we emphasize that the most successful treatment interventions with children and adolescents are those that involve a clearly articulated theoretical orientation as a foundation for a clearly articulated assessment of the presenting problem. We maintain that a thorough assessment is always an essential prerequisite for treatment. Assessment is an exploratory hypothesis-testing process that employs a variety of procedures to understand a particular child and to formulate and evaluate specific intervention strategies. Cognitive-behavioral assessment entails more than operationalizing and observing highly discrete behaviors and their controlling variables. Many of the newly developed assessment procedures are described in Chapter 4, and many of the treatment chapters present novel ways to determine controlling and contributing variables to the problems that arise in childhood and adolescence. In a global sense, it is clear from the experience of the authors that assessment needs to be multimethod in nature and that it must also be sensitive to developmental changes as they affect specific assessment procedures.

This volume is organized in three sections: general issues, application of therapeutic procedures for specific problems of children and adolescents, and integrative considerations. The first section addresses the historical basis and the current status of cognitive-behavioral approaches with children and the role of developmental variables in their therapeutic application. Self-monitoring, self-evaluation, and self-reinforcement strategies for children and adolescents are then described, and the final chapter in this section focuses on cognitive-behavioral assessment techniques. The second section addresses issues and procedures in the treatment of children who have problems with aggression, impulse control, anxiety, depression, and substance abuse. These areas were selected for inclusion because multivariate statistical approaches clearly indicate that the construction of a descriptive behavioral taxonomy for childhood and adolescent disorders must include the dimensions of externalizing (undersocialized and socialized conduct disorders, immaturity, and attention deficit disorders) and internalizing (anxiety, withdrawal, and dysphoria). An additional chapter on the use of cognitive-behavioral procedures with children who experience pain was included because of the rising referral rate for children with significant medical problems. Finally, the last section presents a view of general therapeutic issues in dealing with children and adolescents.

This volume is intended to interest and to guide individuals who work with children in mental health settings or in related applied settings such as special education, nursing, rehabilitation, and counseling. As a text or supplement for practicum experiences and courses in child and adolescent psychotherapy, the book offers a broad view of the cognitive-behavioral approach for students and professionals in the areas of clinical, counseling, and school psychology as well as special education, social work, and psychiatry.

CHAPTER ONE

Cognitive-Behavioral Procedures with Children

Historical Context and Current Status

KATHLEEN J. HART   JOHN R. MORGAN

When descriptions of cognitive-behavior modification techniques first appeared in the psychology literature in the mid- to late 1970s, there was a great deal of enthusiasm about the techniques being described. Empirical support for these interventions was sparse at that point, however. The intervening decades have been marked with continued research of these techniques, and this has led to a stronger empirical basis for the initial claims, thus making cognitive-behavioral interventions much more than a "flash in the pan" of therapeutic trends.

This volume is designed to address the use of cognitive-behavioral interventions for the problems of children and adolescents. In order to understand the applications of these interventions, this chapter is designed to review the conceptual and research trends that have contributed to the current status of the cognitive-behavioral approach for this population. The chapter includes an overview of the historical and philosophical trends that led to the "cognitive-behavioral revolution" and of the evolution of cognitive-behaviorism since it emerged 20 years ago. We begin by setting the background for cognitive-behaviorism and continue by discussing the evolving "definition" of this approach from both a theoretical and a practical perspective. We also provide an overview of the current empirical support for the theoretical underpinnings of cognitive-behaviorism.

Historical Considerations

Over the course of the last 20 years, the orientation of many subspecialties in psychology—including human experimental, animal experimental, developmental, and even clinical—has undergone a shift toward greater acknowledgment of and interest in cognitive activity. After a 50-year domination by behaviorism as the most influential philosophy of American psychology, psychologists reoriented themselves to address research and clinical questions with new emphasis on constructs such as thinking, feelings, motives, plans, purposes, images, and knowledge—ideas that were denied legitimacy in behaviorism (Baars, 1986).

Although this reorientation was described initially as an abrupt change in theory, the tides of change long preceded the alleged "dramatic" shift. For example, the roots of cognitive-behaviorism can be found in the work of Edward C. Tolman in the 1930s. Although he is remembered primarily for his studies on learning, Tolman (unlike the behaviorists who followed him) postulated cognitive "intervening variables" and mental representations in the learning process and proposed that these were legitimate areas of empirical study (Baars, 1986).

In the clinical arena the work of George Kelly (1955) espoused a cognitive focus as early as the 1950s. In his personal constructs theory, Kelly (1955) focused on the individual's interpretation of life events and on the behavioral patterns that reflect the assumptions and interpretations of events. These notions were expanded in the later work of noted cognitive therapists such as Albert Ellis (1962).

In the 1960s, Bandura's (1969) studies on observational learning acknowledged covert (cognitive) events in the learning process and allowed for a shift from the simplistic S-R model based on animal conditioning models to an S-O-R model in which the O represented cognitive-mediational processes in the acquisition and regulation of behavior. This new model, in turn, paved the way for an increased emphasis on cognition in the therapeutic process.

As the basic research evolved into theoretical formulations, most notably represented by Bandura's social learning theory, attempts were made to apply these ideas to the clinical realm. Labeled *cognitive-behaviorism,* these approaches were designed to preserve the best of clinical behavioral interventions while recognizing the "inner" (cognitive) experiences of the individual. In contrast to existing behavioral interventions, these new therapies not only recognized the role of cognitive events but also targeted these events as the foci of change. Although in the early 1970s some saw the cognitive-behavioral approach as a major paradigm shift in clinical psychology, others (e.g., Wilson, 1978) recognized the work of individuals such as Beck, Mahoney, and Meichenbaum as extensions and clinical applications of earlier theorists such as Kelly and Bandura. In addition to these trends, the theoretical and empirical contributions of developmental psychology also exerted a strong influence on cognitive-behavioral interventions with children, particularly in the areas of the development of self-control, social cognition, memory, and meta-cognitive skills (Braswell & Kendall, 1988).

In addition to the general theoretical changes that contributed to the development of cognitive-behavioral interventions, several forces within clinical psychology and behavior therapy coalesced to provide impetus for the rapid adoption of cognitive-behaviorism. These are briefly described below.

1. *Dissatisfaction with "radical behaviorism" and a shift to "methodical behaviorism"* (Craighead, Wilcoxin-Craighead, & Meyers, 1978). Early behavior modifiers seemed to adopt, at least implicitly, a radical behaviorism that held that all behaviors were a result of near or remote environmental contingencies. Private events, being unobservable, were not legitimate targets for inquiry. This doctrinaire stand may have been a necessary one for the early development of behavioral approaches (Mahoney, Kazdin, & Lesswing, 1974), but many criticisms of the radical view and much evidence pointing out its shortcomings contributed to broadening the definition of behavior therapy's subject matter to include cognitive events. This expansion in subject matter has not led to a "softening" of the procedures and methodology employed by the new breed of cognitive behaviorist. Operational definitions of procedures and of outcomes, controlled experimentation, and replication of results are all cardinal tenets of methodological behaviorism and have been, or at least should be, preserved in cognitive-behavioral investigation.

2. *Evidence that thought processes influence behavior and learning and that strict S-R formulations cannot account for all outcomes as well as mediational models can.* As previously mentioned, this evidence stems from the work on vicarious learning (other evidence is reviewed extensively by Mahoney, 1974). The work of Bandura (1969, 1986) and colleagues documents that observers can acquire a wide range of new behaviors by simply watching someone performing these behaviors in the absence of rewards for the observer (or the model). Nonmediational conceptions of the imitation process (Gewirtz, 1971) have not proved as adequate as Bandura's mediational, social learning model in accounting for the results. Evidence from this area has provoked a consideration of cognitive, mediational variables in behavioral change formulations.

3. *Role of cognitions in operant and classical conditioning.* Studies have demonstrated that cognition can influence behavior previously thought to derive from "pure" conditioning (see Kazdin, 1978, for extensive review). That is, if information about a classical conditioning situation is

provided to the subject, the results predicted by a strict conditioning model are altered. For example, being informed of the role of the bell-and-pad device in classically conditioned waking to a full bladder can decrease the number of trials required to reach optimal response. In operant conditioning studies, cognitive factors may have an even greater role. Subjects who are informed of the stimulus-response contingencies demonstrate accelerated learning, and although some learning may not involve awareness of contingencies, cognitions seem to have central importance in operant conditioning. Instructions and the "information value" provided by reinforcement (i.e., the subject may engage in active, cognitive interpretations of reinforcement) may exert more influence on behavior than the reinforcement value of the reward. The literature concerning cognitive factors in human learning is extensive (see Weiner & Palermo, 1974, for a more complete discussion). The evidence for cognitive factors in operant and classical conditioning was another major influence in the genesis of cognitive-behavioral approaches to therapy.

4. *Application of conditioning techniques to private events.* In 1965, Lloyd Homme authored a seminal paper in which he envisioned the possibility of addressing cognitive events with behavioral strategies. Viewing thoughts as "coverants" (covert operants), he reasoned that although these coverants were unobservable, the client could directly influence the coverants by "self consequating" them—that is, by applying operant-behavior technology to the task of increasing or decreasing private events. He stated that the client could systematically alter private events, even if this process could not be verified by an observer. Homme's blending of cognitive subject matter with self-control techniques was the first clear demonstration that the influence of thoughts on behavior could have some applied relevance when systematically integrated into a behavioral perspective. Homme's analysis gave impetus to the pioneering work of Cautela and colleagues (e.g., Cautela, 1967) in the development of "covert" techniques and to much of the self-control literature.

5. *Theoretical analyses of the role of cognitions in behavior and behavior change.* Theoretical formulations (Bandura, 1986; Kanfer, 1970; Mahoney, 1974; Meichenbaum, 1977) have accelerated the adoption of cognitive-behavioral approaches by providing schemas with which to organize the diversity of data and by stimulating further research to test the predictions of these similar viewpoints. Currently there is a better understanding of how thought processes might influence behavior change, and some of these formulations have even resulted in recommendations with therapeutic relevance (Meichenbaum, 1977).

6. *Failure of operant procedures to produce generalization and maintenance.* As evidence mounted that the impressive demonstrations of behavior modification were not permanent or widely generalized beyond the

therapeutic target or milieu (Kazdin, 1979; Kazdin & Wilson, 1978; Keeley, Shemberg, & Carbonell, 1976), researchers and clinicians began to consider the potential of cognitive techniques for promoting generalization and maintenance. It seemed reasonable that cognitive changes could mediate stable and generalized behavior change, because these cognitions could be available as coping techniques in a wide variety of situations beyond the therapeutic (training) setting.

Defining Cognitive-Behavioral Interventions

Generally speaking, cognitive-behavioral interventions "emphasize the complex interaction among cognitive events, processes, products, and structures, affect, overt behavior, and environmental context and experiences as contributing to various facets of dysfunctional behavior" (Braswell & Kendall, 1988, p. 167). Although cognitive-behavior therapy encompasses a variety of strategies and procedures, all share the tenet that learning plays a central role in the acquisition and maintenance of behavior, whether adaptive or dysfunctional. Further, cognitive-behavioral approaches recognize that learning involves more than just the environmental consequences of behavior; learning involves the manner in which the individual processes information cognitively (Foster, Kendall, & Geuvremont, in press). As such, it should be understood that "cognition" and "behavior" are not dichotomous concepts when used in the context of describing therapeutic interventions. Indeed, all therapeutic approaches can be classified on a continuum with varying degrees of cognitive and/or behavioral elements (Ledwidge, 1978). Thus, the labels that distinguish "cognitive" from "behavioral" and from "cognitive-behavioral" are somewhat deceiving. There are often cognitive elements in the most "behavioral" operant and classical conditioning procedures as well as behavioral elements in traditional semantic therapies (including, at minimum, subtle therapist reinforcement of certain client behaviors).

In the decade since the inception of cognitive-behavior therapies, many therapeutic strategies used with adult disorders have dropped "behavior" from the label and are described simply as "cognitive therapies." Although little clear distinction is made between those interventions or therapy approaches that are cognitive-behavioral and those that are cognitive, the labels seem to reflect the deemphasis of operant components of the intervention. Cognitive-behavioral interventions for adults were strongly influenced by Ellis's (1962) Rational Emotive Therapy and Beck's cognitive theory of depression (Beck, Rush, Shaw, & Emery, 1979). The first application of cognitive-behavioral therapy for children is credited to the important work of Donald Meichenbaum. Drawing upon the work of Soviet psychologists Luria (1959, 1961) and Vygotsky (1962), Meichenbaum became interested in the degree to which internalized verbal commands guide overt behavior. Both Luria and Vygotsky had studied the relationship among behavior, thought, and language from a developmental perspective, and they postulated that voluntary control over behavior developed as a gradual progression from external regulation by others (e.g., instructions given by parents) to internalized verbal commands that serve a self-regulatory function. Meichenbaum and Goodman (1971) developed Self-Instructional Training (SIT) to remediate the "mediational deficiencies" of behaviorally impulsive children. This program aimed to teach impulsive children to generate guiding verbal self-commands that would bring their behavior under their own control. The sequence of SIT was designed to replicate the developmental stages described by Luria (1961) and Vygotsky (1962).

Since its original application, SIT has been widely researched, refined, and applied to disorders ranging from schizophrenia to anxiety and phobias (e.g., Meichenbaum & Cameron, 1973; Meichenbaum & Turk, 1976). Although theorists may dispute minor aspects, there is a rather remarkable consistency among procedures used for children. Table 1-1 outlines the key aspects of cognitive behavioral interventions for children. The first characteristic is obvious: The approach represents combinations of what typically are called behavioral or learning approaches with features of what traditionally have been termed cognitive or "semantic" therapies (Kendall & Hollon, 1979; Mahoney, 1974; Meichenbaum, 1977). As noted previously, most procedures entail at least some degree of both behavioral and cognitive elements, but cognitive-behavioral therapies involve a very deliberate amalgam — one that is thought to provide more relevance or potency than either option used alone (Kendall & Hollon, 1979). There is relative consensus about the content of this amalgam, as the second characteristic illustrates. On the one hand, cognitive variables (beliefs, cognitions, attri-

---

TABLE 1-1 • General Characteristics of a Cognitive-Behavioral Approach

1. Deliberate attempt to combine concerns of theretofore opposing approaches — cognitive, semantic therapies, and behavior therapies.
2. Cognitions (private events) held to be legitimate and even necessary concerns for the therapist.
3. Methodological behaviorism perceived as the most appropriate methodology for studying these private events.
4. Assertion that cognitions mediate behavior and learning.
5. Assertion that human functioning is "reciprocally determined," i.e., that cognitions and behavior are functionally related, that changing one can change the other.
6. Attempt to apply "learning-based" techniques — previously used to alter overt behaviors — to cognitive events as well.

---

butions, expectancies, images), previously outside the domain of behavioral approaches, are considered legitimate and, in fact, necessary concerns of the cognitive-behavioral clinician. There are several sources of empirical work that have influenced this trend, including data indicating that cognitions influence behavior and the behavior change process (Bandura, 1969, 1977b, 1986; Mahoney, 1974) and that a strict conditioning model cannot account for all outcomes in research or in clinical practice.

A third characteristic is the consensus that the most appropriate methodology with which to consider and to examine unobservable private events is a behavioral one—that is, cognitions should be analyzed in the same empirical fashion that characterizes the investigation of motor behaviors in the behavior modification literature. This shift toward the use of "methodological" rather than "radical" behaviorism has been highlighted by many as the major factor in prompting the development of cognitive-behavioral approaches (Craighead et al., 1978). Cognitive-behavioral researchers insist on the same operational clarity in defining target behaviors and procedures and on the same empirical demonstration of effectiveness that have characterized the behavioral modification literature.

The fourth distinguishing characteristic of a cognitive-behavioral approach is the explicit acknowledgment of a mediational viewpoint in cognitive-behavioral analyses—a contention that cognitive events mediate behavior and learning (Bandura, 1977a; Karoly, 1977; Meichenbaum, 1977). As a consequence, cognitions themselves become appropriate targets for intervention and can be deliberately and systematically altered to produce behavior change. Of course, traditional semantic therapies also attempt to change behaviors by altering cognitions, but often they do so in an unsystematic fashion, and usually to the exclusion of environmental manipulations that might influence behavior directly. The cognitive-behavioral therapist systematically attempts to alter both internal and external environments to produce desired behavior change, with the belief that the "reciprocal determinism" (Bandura, 1969, 1986) that characterizes human functioning can best be served by this combination.

The assertion that cognitions and behaviors influence one another reciprocally is the fifth characteristic of the approach. The frequent claim of behavior therapists that changes in behavior lead to changes in attitudes, beliefs, and emotions has ample supporting evidence, as reviewed by Bandura (1969, 1986). However, as Mahoney (1974) emphasized, other evidence demonstrates that cognitive changes can produce behavioral ones. Cognitive-behavioral theorists comfortably assert that both strategies have credence.

A final distinguishing characteristic of a cognitive-behavioral approach concerns the clinical application of the assertions already outlined. If cognitions are functionally related to behavior change (learning), then these private events should be amenable to change using the techniques that also influence overt behaviors—namely, techniques based on principles of learning. No unitary set of principles can be labeled "principles of learning," and there is no one theory that can be termed "learning theory." Likewise, there is no longer a claim that behavior modifiers apply these "principles" with strict adherence to their application in laboratory settings (Kazdin, 1979). However, conditioning techniques that are at least loosely based on the learning literature and are applied effectively to overt behaviors might be applied to the task of altering cognitions (Cautela, 1967; Homme, 1965). In other words, applied behavioral technology can be extended to private events, and the results predicted by learning theory can be predicted and evaluated with private events as well.

In the application of these characteristics of cognitive-behavioral treatments, a fundamental difference exists between children and adults. Adult approaches presume that maladaptive behavior or negative emotion arises from a distortion in the cognitive representations of events. Cognitive-behavioral treatments for children, in contrast, are frequently designed to remediate a deficiency in the child's cognitive abilities. Impulsiveness, hyperactivity, and attentional difficulties, for example, may reflect an absence of effective mediational strategies for regulating behavior. This difference is more than just a matter of semantics; therapy is often designed to assist in the unfolding of an unrealized developmental potential. As such, issues concerning the development of memory and other cognitive skills are paramount in interventions for children.

These major characteristics assist in defining the conceptual foundation of the cognitive-behavioral approach; a descriptive view can help to further illustrate these characteristics. A typology of cognitive-behavioral interventions is presented in Table 1-2; however, not all the interventions have been evaluated with child populations. This typology is neither exhaustive nor composed of mutually exclusive categories. It is not necessarily concordant with other organizational schemes (Abikoff, 1979; Mahoney, 1974; Meichenbaum, 1977), and arbitrary exclusions and assignments have been made. For example, techniques that are typically labeled "self-reward" or "self-punishment" have been included under a "self-conservation" heading. These former techniques have been developed under a "self-control" or "self-management" rubric (Kanfer, 1970; Thoresen & Mahoney, 1974), and although similarities exist among these techniques and approaches, some self-control techniques are not primarily cognitive in focus (e.g., environmental planning; Thoresen & Mahoney, 1974).

Another exclusion may require some justification. For rather arbitrary reasons that might be persuasively debated by others, systematic desensitization and other behavior therapy procedures using extensive imagery have not been included. Because these procedures typically involve no

TABLE 1-2 • Typology of Cognitive-Behavioral Interventions

Technique	Representative Work	General Characteristics of Intervention	Typical Behavior Targets
Self-Consequation (self-reward, self-punishment)	Bolstad & Johnson (1972) Glynn (1970) Hinshaw, Whalen, & Henker (1984) Kanfer & Gaelick (1986)	Train client through modeling or reinforcement to evaluate in comparison to a standard and then to make rewarding or critical self-statement, or to deliver rewarding or punishing consequences.	Academic performance, disruptive classroom behavior
Covert Conditioning Techniques (covert reinforcement, covert punishment, etc.)	Cautela (1967) Wisocki (1970)	Teach client to consequate own behavior using cognitive representation (image) of reinforcement or punishing event, i.e., "Imagine yourself getting this reward."	Habit disorders, obsessive-compulsive disorders
Cognitive Modeling	Meichenbaum & Goodman (1971) Bandura (1986)	Train client to change cognitions (e.g., self-statements, self-reward patterns) by observing a model demonstrating adaptive cognitions (model "thinks out loud").	Fears, phobias, anxiety, impulsive behavior
Covert Modeling	Kazdin (1973) Bandura (1986)	Train client to imagine someone else performing adaptive behavior	Nonassertive behaviors, phobias, anxiety

Continued

9

TABLE 1-2 • Continued

Technique	Representative Work	General Characteristics of Intervention	Typical Behavior Targets
Coping Imagery	Lazarus & Abramowitz (1962)	Train client to imagine pleasing, rewarding, distracting, or coping scene in presence of anxiety-provoking stimuli.	Anxiety, phobic states, pain, anger
Self-Instruction	Meichenbaum & Goodman (1971) Kendall & Finch (1978) Kendall & Braswell (1985) Nelson & Behler (1990) Meichenbaum (1985)	Train client, using contingent consequences or modeling, to alter self-statements before and during difficult tasks or situations, substituting coping self-statements for maladaptive ones.	Hyperactivity, impulsivity, aggressive behaviors, academic difficulties
Cognitive Restructuring/ Attrition Retraining	Shaw (1977) Dweck (1975) Pearl (1985)	Train client to change irrational beliefs and expectancies, or faulty thinking styles, by demonstrating through logical analysis how they are maladaptive.	Depression, anxiety, phobias, anger
Cognitive Problem-Solving	Peterson & Shigetomi (1981) Lochman & Curry (1986) Spivak, Platt, & Shure (1976) Haaga & Davison (1986)	Teach client how to deal with stressors by engaging in several modes of cognitive preparation and/or coping, including self-instruction, self-monitoring, cognitive rehearsal, distracting imagery, etc.	Anger, pain, fears, phobias

deliberate attempt to alter client cognitions and to render them more adaptive (the cognitions are not the change targets), it seems that imagery is a procedural tool used to produce physiological arousal to be counter-conditioned rather than a mediator of behavior change. We consider these techniques to be "affect-mediated," and, therefore, not consistent with cognitive-behavioral approaches.

In addition, typical modeling or vicarious learning procedures have been excluded, although a more specific category called "cognitive modeling" is included. It is clear that the mediational properties of images are central to modeling techniques; theoretically, observing a model produces lasting images that can be retrieved later to guide performance (Bandura, 1977b, 1986). However, it is usually assumed (clinically) that mere observation engenders an adequate image for later retrieval, and there are no attempts to provide the client with cognitive skills or operations that might enhance this imagery (see Gerst, 1971; Bandura & Jeffery, 1973; and Morgan, 1976, for nonclinical exceptions). However, some researchers have employed cognitive modeling (Meichenbaum & Goodman, 1971; Kendall & Finch, 1978; Nelson, 1976), in which observers watch a model emit self-statements that make overt the usually covert cognitive processes of the model. For example, the model may engage (out loud) in coping self-instructions that the observer can imitate with the intent to systematically influence the cognitive operations of the observer. This specialized adaptation of modeling procedures has been included in the typology.

As will be evident, some of the techniques listed have not been systematically evaluated with children. Self-instruction training, problem-solving skills training, and to a lesser extent the self-conservation procedures are the only techniques with a significant number of investigations.

The Development of Cognitive-Behavioral Procedures with Children

The application of cognitive-behavioral interventions with children has focused on specific areas that embody what are believed to be the foci of many children's maladaptation. These targets of intervention have been strongly influenced by research and theoretical trends in developmental psychology.

Verbal Control of Behavior

Pioneering work by Russian psychologists Luria (1959, 1961) and Vygotsky (1962) suggested that children develop verbal control of behavior in sequential fashion. Initially, behavior is controlled externally by the words and actions of adults. Gradually the child's speech begins to direct and control his or her own behavior, as demonstrated by observational studies (Meichenbaum, 1971) showing that the talk-to-self-out-loud technique served to initiate but not to inhibit motor behaviors. In a third stage the direction and inhibiting nature of self-talk becomes internalized and begins to take on an automatic quality.

The proposed developmental sequence has not been supported in attempts to replicate Luria's findings (e.g., Towell, 1977). Research does indicate that as children grow older their self-talk becomes more internalized and directive (Meichenbaum, 1971), although there are wide individual variations in the ability to employ verbal self-statements to direct motor behavior. In particular, Meichenbaum and Goodman (1969) demonstrated that the self-talk of cognitively impulsive preschoolers was less mature and less directive than that of cognitively reflective children. On a laboratory motor task, 85% of the reflective children, but only 40% of the impulsive children, could attain 90% correct responding using the self-instructions taught to subjects. Naturalistic observation also confirmed that the private speech of impulsive children was less mature. Reflective children used private speech in a more instrumental fashion; their self-directed speech increased by 14% when they were confronted with a specific problem-solving situation. Impulsive children showed no corresponding increase (Meichenbaum, 1971).

These developmental studies were provided clinical relevance by Meichenbaum and his associates (Meichenbaum & Goodman, 1971). Using Luria's proposed developmental sequence, they employed a cognitive Self-Instruction Training program to modify impulsive behavior. Because these children had demonstrated an inability to employ verbal self-instructions to direct behavior, the investigators taught impulsive children by first having a model demonstrate self-instructions (talking out loud) and then having the child talk out loud while performing the task. When the verbal self-instructions were mastered, the model began whispering instead of talking out loud, and finally the child was instructed to talk silently while doing the task. The self-instructions included cognitive rehearsal and planning of relevant task aspects, self-instructions about efficient ways to accomplish the task, self-statements to cope with frustration and failure, and self-reinforcement. Results indicated that relative to attention-placebo and assessment-only control groups, those receiving self-instructional training improved significantly on the Porteus Maze Test, on the WISC Performance IQ, and on the Matching-Familiar Figures Test. Results were maintained at one-month follow-up.

Verbal control investigations and the resulting investigation of self-instructional procedures have proved to be an enduring focus of interest and concern. The self-instructional procedures originally developed by Meichenbaum and extended by others (Camp, Blom, Herbert, & van Doornick, 1977; Douglas, Parry, Marton, & Garson, 1976) remain the most extensively evaluated of the cognitive-behavioral approaches applied to children.

Children's Self-Regulation

Also termed *self-control,* the self-regulatory function is usually defined as the ability to choose, in the absence of external constraints, a previously low-probability behavior when the higher-probability behavior is still freely available (Thoresen & Mahoney, 1974).

The development of self-control in children has been investigated extensively, primarily from two separate laboratory paradigms—the directed-learning paradigm of Kanfer and associates (Kanfer, 1966; Kanfer & Duerfeldt, 1967) and the social learning model of Bandura and colleagues (Bandura & Kupers, 1964; Liebert & Allen, 1967). In the directed-learning paradigm a reinforcer is freely available to the child, who is instructed to self-reward (or self-criticize) after each performance. The subject is trained to perform a very ambiguous perceptual learning task, and because of the task's ambiguity the child is never certain of the correctness of the responses. After initial training the subject is instructed to begin self-rewarding whenever he or she decides that the response is correct. A representative study (Kanfer & Marston, 1963) manipulated the strictness or liberality of experimenter rewards. One group was rewarded liberally, a second group was rewarded liberally for ambiguous performance, and a third group was rewarded much less liberally. The subsequent self-reward patterns of the subjects reflected previous training; those rewarded liberally judged themselves correct more often and, hence, rewarded themselves more frequently than those trained with stricter criteria. In short, results from this and other studies demonstrate that self-regulation (i.e., self-reward patterns) can be invalidated by external reinforcement.

The social learning paradigm demonstrates that self-reward patterns can be influenced by observations of the patterns and criteria exhibited by models. In the typical experiment the child observes a model playing a game and self-rewarding according to certain criteria. These criteria are made explicit to the observer through the model's verbalizations. The child then plays the game, receives prearranged scores similar to the model's, and is asked to self-reward. Bandura and Kupers (1964) investigated the transmission of patterns of self-reward with this methodology and found that subjects rewarded themselves according to the criteria of the model they observed (high or low criterion) in the absence of external reinforcement for adhering to a certain standard. Later studies have made more explicit the relation between modeled and acquired patterns.

Liebert and Allen (1967) compared directed-learning (external reinforcement) and modeling approaches and found no difference in self-reward criteria between the two experimental groups. However, in a laboratory study with potential clinical relevance, Bandura and Perloff (1967) compared self-imposed and experimenter-imposed standards on a wheel-turning task. Children in the self-reinforcement group selected their own standards and rewarded themselves accordingly, even choosing the magnitude of each reward. Experimenter-imposed subjects were yoked with self-imposed subjects, receiving the same frequency and magnitude of reinforcement. The self-reward subjects chose very strict reinforcement criteria (in a permissive atmosphere with no social pressure to do so), and they maintained effort and performance equal to subjects who received experimenter-determined rewards.

These studies of the development of self-regulation in children fostered several early attempts to apply the findings clinically. For example, Bolstad and Johnson (1972) used self-determined reward criteria to reduce disruptive classroom behavior. Children who were allowed to determine their own reward criteria reduced disruptive behavior slightly more than those who were rewarded according to teacher-determined criteria. The self-determined subjects also showed slightly greater resistance to extinction than did the external reward subjects. Neither result was statistically significant, however. Glynn (1970) demonstrated that self-determined criteria were as effective as externally imposed standards in improving academic performance.

Children's Cognitive Style and Problem-Solving Abilities

Beginning with Kagan's (1966) influential investigations of children's thinking styles, there have been attempts to classify children along a dimension labeled "conceptual tempo" or "cognitive style." Early studies placed cognitive style on a reflective–impulsive continuum. Children who were classified as "reflective" evaluated alternatives before responding and delayed responding until they considered the consequence of actions. "Impulsive" children, on the other hand, characteristically responded quickly and with little or no regard for the consequences of their actions. Research using measures such as the Matching Familiar Figures Test found that impulsive children do not employ verbal self-instructions as often or as maturely as reflective children (Meichenbaum & Goodman, 1971), spend less time viewing the stimulus (choice) array, make decisions with less information than reflective subjects (Messer, 1976), and use less efficient information-seeking strategies (Finch & Montgomery, 1973). It remains unclear whether this cognitive style is a relatively stable temperamental characteristic (Buss & Plomin, 1975), a learned pattern of cognitive and behavioral responses (Ainslie, 1975), or, most likely, an interactive result of these two influences.

A parallel line of investigation documented individual differences in children's cognitive problem-solving strategies. Spivack and Levine (1963) found that emotionally disturbed children were less successful than their peers in generating alternative solutions to interpersonal problems. Further studies also indicated deficits in means–end thinking (evaluating consequences of alternative solutions). Emotionally disturbed children generate fewer alternatives, fewer statements about likely consequences, and qualitatively more aggressive or impulsive solutions (Shure & Spivack, 1978; Shure, Spivack, & Jaeger, 1971).

These and other studies have had an impact on formulations of childhood social competence and psychopathology. Indeed, a number of child psychologists now emphasize the role of social cognitive skills in contributing to dysfunctional behavior (e.g., Asarnow & Callahan, 1985; Kendall, 1985). Social cognitive skills are described as a variety of processes that influence a child's attention to, interpretation of, and organization of social information (see Spivack & Shure, 1974). Social or interpersonal problem solving is one area of social-cognitive functioning that has been employed in the treatment of a variety of childhood disorders including antisocial behavior (e.g., Kazdin, Esveldt-Dawson, French, & Unis, 1987) and depression (e.g., Nezu, 1987) and as a preventative intervention (e.g., Weissberg, Gesten, Rapkin, et al., 1981; Weissberg, Gesten, Carnirike, et al., 1981).

The Efficacy of Cognitive-Behavioral Interventions

The numerous studies have demonstrated that cognitive-behavioral interventions promote behavior and affective change (e.g., Miller & Berman, 1983); the legitimacy of cognitive-behavioral therapies is established. However, a more difficult issue is the relative efficacy of cognitive-behavioral therapies compared to other interventions such as behavior therapy or pharmacotherapy. In the first attempt to address this question, Ledwidge (1978) critically reviewed 13 controlled studies that had contrasted cognitive-behavioral therapies with behavioral interventions. All of these studies utilized analogue patient samples, and the targets of change were also analogue—such as test anxiety, snake phobia, and speech anxiety. Ledwidge concluded that cognitive-behavior treatment had not been shown to be superior to behavior therapy. Specifically, he found that 3 of the 13 studies produced greater behavioral treatment effects, 2 found greater cognitive-behavioral treatment effects, 3 reported "mixed results," and 5 found no differences between the therapy approaches on the measures of treatment outcome. Hollan and Kendall (1979) updated Ledwidge's analysis and found several additional studies that favored the cognitive-behavioral approach, particularly in the treatment of adult depression. Miller and Berman (1983) also addressed the issue of the efficacy of cognitive-behavior therapy by conducting a quantitative review of 48 studies. They concluded that although cognitive-behavior therapies were superior to no treatment, there was no firm evidence to suggest that these interventions were superior to other psychotherapeutic interventions.

In a study designed to address the general question of the relative efficacy of a variety of treatment modalities, Shapiro and Shapiro (1982) conducted a meta-analysis of 143 treatment outcome studies in which two or more treatments were compared. Although their overall conclusion suggested that it was difficult to separate the impact of treatment from other variables related to change, direct comparison analyses between pairs of treatments suggested some superiority of cognitive- and certain multimodal-behavioral treatment methods. They cautioned against overinterpretation of their findings, however, in light of factors such as the patient populations in these studies.

The comparison of therapeutic methods limited to child populations is sparse, and most of these studies compare cognitive-behavioral interventions with "strictly" behavioral methods, a comparison that might have little meaning. For example, Urbain and Kendall (1981) compared interpersonal problem-solving training, perspective-taking training, and behavioral contingency management. They found that although all three conditions resulted in improvement on problem-solving and perspective-taking measures, there was no significant change in teacher ratings of classroom behavior. Similarly, Stark, Kaslow, and Reynolds (1985) compared a self-control (cognitive) intervention with a behavior therapy program in a group of 9- to 12-year-old depressed children. Relative to the waiting list control group, both groups showed improvement of depressive symptoms after the 12-session program. In this study the positive results seemed to be more pronounced for the self-control therapy group, although these did not reach statistical significance. Studies by Friedling and O'Leary (1979), Peterson and Shigetomi (1981), and Forman (1980) yielded similar conclusions.

The general conclusion, then, is that children appear to benefit from involvement in cognitive-behavioral intervention programs. However, there is a lack of clear-cut evidence for the superiority of cognitive-behavioral therapy over other therapies, particularly as applied to children. As previously mentioned, most available studies on the relative efficacy of cognitive-behavioral interventions with children have involved the comparison of these techniques with "pure" behavioral interventions, yielding generally equivocal results. It may be that the differences between these interventions are not sufficiently pronounced to produce consistent superiority of either method. Rather than continued comparison of these effective interventions, research might optimally focus on finding the best match between intervention strategy and target of change.

The Direction of Cognitive-Behavioral Interventions with Children

Although much of the present emphasis in cognitive-behavioral interventions with children can be traced directly or indirectly to Meichenbaum's Self-Instructional Training, these strategies have been enhanced by work in the areas of children's meta-cognitive skills, memory, and attributional processes. Indeed, more recent work has highlighted the need to understand such areas as a child's attentional and memory capacities, for these bear directly on the ability to benefit from specific interventions. Verbal fluency, language development, and the capacity for conceptual reasoning are other factors that should be considered when designing a therapeutic intervention with an individual child. It seems safe to speculate that elementary school-age children would have difficulty making the conceptual distinctions required of interventions such as Rational Emotive Therapy (Ellis, 1962), for example; however, there is little empirical research addressing the means by which the clinician can assess a child's ability to manage the cognitive requirements of specific interventions. Indeed, there is inadequate information about questions such as the age at which children generally acquire the requisite skills for various interventions. A review of available information regarding developmental changes and cognitive-behavioral interventions is found in Chapter 2. In light of the recent clinical attention to these basic cognitive processes, it is likely that the refinement of cognitive-behavioral interventions for children will come from a strong alliance with developmental psychology.

Cognitive-behavior therapists have increased their focus on concepts such as attribution and self-efficacy. In the adult literature the description of a "depressogenic" cognitive style (Dobson & Shaw, 1986; Hollon, Kendall, & Lumry, 1986) has helped in the development of cognitive interventions for this population. Although in the child literature a consensus has not been reached regarding a consistent cognitive style, there is growing curiosity about the extent to which children engage in attributional styles that reflect specific disorders such as depression. In particular, Bandura's description of the concept of self-efficacy expectations (Bandura, 1977a) appears to be a particularly promising area of study. *Self-efficacy* is described as the extent to which the individual feels capable of behaving in a manner that will result in successful achievement of desired goals. Bandura believes that all changes in behavior share the common underlying cognitive process of self-efficacy. Along these lines, Keyser and Barling (1981) have developed and replicated (Barling & Snipelisky, 1983) a self-report scale designed to measure children's self-efficacy beliefs regarding academic tasks. These and other instruments, although still in their infancy, will be vitally important as therapy focuses more directly on this dimension.

Unlike self-efficacy, which involves a prediction about future behavior, the concept of *attribution* describes the manner in which one interprets or explains an event after it happens. Several investigations with children have attempted to understand the role that attribution plays in the child's cognitive and behavior patterns (e.g., Asarnow & Callahan, 1985), and assessment instruments such as the Cognitive Bias Questionnaire for Children (Haley, Fine, Marriage, Mozetti, & Freeman, 1985) and the Children's Attributional Style Questionnaire (Kaslow, Tannenbaum, & Seligman, 1978) will aid in assessing the relevance of this concept.

Conclusions

What should we say to ourselves about the status of cognitive-behavioral approaches for children? Our internal monologue might include statements like: "These are very interesting techniques, but let me be careful. Don't just jump in and use them blindly. Stand back, slow down, take a good look first. If I use a technique, how will I evaluate outcome? Is there evidence to show its effectiveness with this particular problem? I'll apply this technique, but I'll do it cautiously with every effort to evaluate it well. I think it will work, but I have to keep my cool and try to remain objective. That's it, I'm doing a good job!"

The caution proposed herein is directed primarily toward those in the "real" world where practitioners can become excited about new developments in the field. Here the "fad" aspects of the cognitive-behavioral approach may present the greatest dangers, because the intuitive, face validity of the techniques is very high. Further, although reading about cognitive-behavioral approaches can be very enlightening, it does not make them easy to apply. As with other approaches, creativity, flexibility, communication, rapport, effective rationale in delivery, and (especially) clinical competence in working with children are necessary components of the therapy enterprise. The ability and motivation to engage children effectively in this enterprise are crucial and are emphasized by various clinical researchers (e.g., Craighead et al., 1977; Kendall, 1977; Kendall & Finch, 1979; Meichenbaum, 1977).

As illustrated in our review of the historical context, cognitive-behaviorism has descended from influential and enduring forces in psychology, introducing new features while retaining preexisting ideas. The approach is new in that it reflects a shift toward a more integrative, reciprocal, and holistic picture of behavior change. It is old in that it reflects a consistent and rational extension of the scope of behavior therapy to include findings and subject matter from distinct and valid traditions. In this sense, cognitive-behaviorism is not a fad, but rather a significant and exciting endeavor in its early stages of development. Within this context, the ensuing chapters should provide an indication of the extensions, refinements, and clarifications that can be anticipated as the field continues to grow and to develop.

References

Abikoff, H. (1979). Cognitive training interventions in children: Review of a new approach. *Journal of Learning Disabilities, 12,* 123–135.

Ainslie, G. (1975). Specious reward: A behavioral theory of impulsiveness and impulse control. *Psychological Bulletin, 82,* 463–496.

Asarnow, J. R., & Callahan, J. W. (1985). Boys with poor adjustment problems: Social cognitive processes. *Journal of Consulting and Clinical Psychology, 53,* 80–87.

Baars, B. J. (1986). *The cognitive revolution in psychology.* New York: Guilford Press.

Bandura, A. (1969). *Principles of behavior modification.* New York: Holt, Rinehart & Winston.

Bandura, A. (1977a). Self-efficacy: Toward a unifying theory of behavioral change. *Psychological Review, 84,* 191–215.

Bandura, A. (1977b). *Social learning theory.* Englewood Cliffs, NJ: Prentice-Hall.

Bandura, A. (1986). *Social foundations of thought and action: A social cognitive theory.* Englewood Cliffs, NJ: Prentice-Hall.

Bandura, A., & Jeffery, R. W. (1973). Role of symbolic coding and rehearsal processes in observational learning. *Journal of Personality and Social Psychology, 26,* 122–130.

Bandura, A., & Kupers, C. J. (1964). The transmission of patterns of self-reinforcement through modeling. *Journal of Abnormal and Social Psychology, 69,* 1–9.

Bandura, A., & Perloff, B. (1967). Relative efficacy of self-monitored and externally-imposed reinforcement systems. *Journal of Personality and Social Psychology, 7,* 111–116.

Barling, J., & Snipelisky, B. (1983). Assessing the determinants of children's academic self-efficacy beliefs: A replication. *Cognitive Therapy and Research, 7,* 371–376.

Beck, A. T., Rush, A. J., Shaw, B. F., & Emery, G. (1979). *Cognitive therapy of depression.* New York: Guilford Press.

Bolstad, O. D., & Johnson, S. M. (1972). Self-regulation in the modification of disruptive classroom behavior. *Journal of Applied Behavior Analysis, 5,* 443–454.

Braswell, L., & Kendall, P. C. (1988). Cognitive-behavioral methods with children. In K. C. Dobson (Ed.' *Handbook of cognitive-behavioral therapies.* New York: Guilford Press.

Buss, A. H., & Plomin, R. (1975). *A temperament theory of personality development.* New York: Wiley.

Camp, B., Blom, G., Herbert, F., & van Doornick, W. (1977). "Think aloud": A program for developing self-control in young aggressive boys. *Journal of Abnormal Child Psychology, 5,* 157-169.

Cautela, J. R. (1967). Covert sensitization. *Psychological Reports, 20,* 459-468.

Craighead, W. E., Wilcoxon-Craighead, L., & Meyers, A. (1978). New directions in behavior modification with children. In M. Hersen, R. Eisler, & P. Miller (Eds.), *Progress in behavior modification* (Vol. 6). New York: Academic Press.

Dobson, K. S., & Shaw, B. F. (1986). Cognitive assessment with major depressive disorders. *Cognitive Therapy and Research, 10,* 13-29.

Douglas, V. I., Parry, P., Marton, P., & Garson, C. (1976). Assessment of a cognitive training program for hyperactive children. *Journal of Abnormal Child Psychology, 4,* 389-410.

Dweck, D. S. (1975). The role of expectations and attributions in the alteration of learned helplessness. *Journal of Personality and Social Psychology, 25,* 109-116.

Ellis, A. (1962). *Reason and emotion in psychotherapy.* New York: Stuart.

Ellis, A., & Greiger, R. (1977). *Handbook of Rational Emotive Therapy.* New York: Springer.

Finch, A. J, & Montgomery, L. E. (1973). Reflection–impulsivity and information seeking in emotionally disturbed children. *Journal of Abnormal Child Psychology, 1,* 358-362.

Forman, S. G. (1980). A comparison of cognitive training and response cost procedures in modifying aggressive behavior of elementary school children. *Behavior Therapy, 11,* 594-600.

Foster, S. L., Kendall, P. C., & Geuvremont, D. (in press). Cognitive and social learning theory and therapy. In J. Matson (Ed.), *Handbook of treatment approaches in childhood psychopathology.* New York: Plenum Press.

Friedling, C., & O'Leary, K. D. (1979). Effects of self-instruction training on 2nd and 3rd grade hyperactive children: A failure to replicate. *Journal of Applied Behavior Analysis, 12,* 211-220.

Gerst, M. S. (1971). Symbolic coding processes in observation learning. *Journal of Personality and Social Psychology, 19,* 7-17.

Gewirtz, J. L. (1971). The roles of overt responding and extrinsic reinforcement in "self-" and "vicarious-reinforcement" and in "observational learning" and imitation. In R. Glaser (Ed.), *The nature of reinforcement.* New York: Academic Press.

Glynn, E. L. (1970). Classroom applications of self-determined reinforcement. *Journal of Applied Behavior Analysis, 3,* 123-132.

Gottman, J., Gonso, J., & Schuler, P. (1976). Teaching social skills to isolated children. *Journal of Abnormal Child Psychology, 4,* 179-197.

Haaga, D. A., & Davison, G. C. (1986). Cognitive change methods. In F. H. Kanfer & A. P. Goldstein (Eds.), *Helping people change: A textbook of methods.* New York: Pergamon Press.

Haley, G. M., Fine, S., Marriage, K., Mozetti, M. M., & Freeman, R. J. (1985).

Cognitive bias and depression in psychiatrically disturbed children and adolescents. *Journal of Consulting and Clinical Psychology, 53,* 535–537.

Hinshaw, S. P., Whalen, C. K., & Henker, B. (1984). Cognitive-behavioral and pharmacologic interventions for hyperactive boys: Comparative and combined effects. *Journal of Consulting and Clinical Psychology, 52,* 739–749.

Hollon, S. D., & Kendall, P. C. (1979). Cognitive-behavioral interventions: Theory and procedure. In P. C. Kendall & S. D. Hollon (Eds.), *Cognitive-behavioral interventions: Theory, research, and procedures.* New York: Academic Press.

Hollon, S. D., Kendall, P. C., & Lumry, A. (1986). Specificity of depressotypic cognition in clinical depression. *Journal of Abnormal Psychology, 95,* 52–59.

Homme, L. E. (1965). Perspectives in psychology, XXIV: Control in coverants, the operants of the mind. *Psychological Record, 15,* 501–511.

Kagan, J. (1966). Reflection–impulsivity: The generality and dynamics of conceptual tempo. *Journal of Abnormal Psychology, 71,* 17–24.

Kanfer, F. H. (1966). Influence of age and incentive conditions on children's self rewards. *Psychological Reports, 19,* 263–274.

Kanfer, F. H. (1970). Self-regulation: Research, issues, and speculations. In C. Neuringer & J. L. Michael (Eds.), *Behavior modification in clinical psychology.* New York: Appleton.

Kanfer, F. H., & Duerfeldt, P. H. (1967). Effects of pretraining on self-evaluation and self-reinforcement. *Journal of Personality and Social Psychology, 2,* 164–168.

Kanfer, F. H., & Gaelick, L. (1986). Self-management methods. In F. H. Kanfer & A. P. Goldstein (Eds.), *Helping people change: A textbook of methods.* New York: Pergamon Press.

Kanfer, F. H., & Marston, A. R. (1963). Determinants of self-reinforcement in human learning. *Journal of Experimental Psychology, 66,* 245–254.

Karoly, P. (1977). Behavioral self-management in children: Concepts, methods, issues, and directions. In M. Hersen, R. Eisler, & P. Miller (Eds.), *Progress in behavior modification* (Vol. 5). New York: Academic Press.

Kaslow, N. J., Tanenbaum, R. L., & Seligman, M. E. (1978). *The KASTAN; A children's attributional style questionnaire.* Unpublished manuscript, University of Pennsylvania, Philadelphia.

Kazdin, A. E. (1973). Covert modeling and reduction of avoidance behavior. *Journal of Abnormal Psychology, 81,* 87–95.

Kazdin, A. E. (1978). *History of behavior modification: Experimental foundations of contemporary research.* Baltimore, MD: University Park Press.

Kazdin, A. E. (1979). Fictions, factions, and functions of behavior therapy. *Behavior Therapy, 10,* 629–654.

Kazdin, A. E., Esveldt-Dawson, K., French, N. H., & Unis, A. S. (1987). Problem-solving skills training and relationship therapy in the treatment of antisocial child behavior. *Journal of Consulting and Clinical Psychology, 55*(1), 76–85.

Kazdin, A. E., & Wilson, G. T. (1978). *Evaluation of behavior therapy: Issues, evidences, and research strategies.* Cambridge, MA: Ballinger.

Keeley, S. M., Shemberg, K. M., & Carbonell, J. (1976). Operant clinical interventions: Behavior management or legend? Where are the data? *Behavioral Therapy, 7,* 292–305.

Kelly, G. A. (1955). *The psychology of personal constructs.* New York: Norton.

Kendall, P. C. (1977). On the efficacious use of verbal self-instructional procedures with children. *Cognitive Therapy and Research, 1,* 331–341.

Kendall, P. C. (1985). Toward a cognitive-behavioral model of child psychopathology and a critique of related interventions. *Journal of Abnormal Child Psychology, 13,* 357–372.

Kendall, P. C., & Braswell, L. (1985). *Cognitive-behavioral therapy for impulsive children.* New York: Guilford Press.

Kendall, P. C., & Finch, A. J (1978). A cognitive-behavioral treatment for impulse control: A group comparison study. *Journal of Consulting and Clinical Psychology, 46,* 110–118.

Kendall, P. C., & Finch, A. J (1979). Developing nonimpulsive behavior in children: Cognitive-behavioral strategies for self-control. In P. C. Kendall & S. D. Hollon (Eds.), *Cognitive-behavioral interventions: Theory, research, and procedures.* New York: Academic Press.

Kendall, P. C., & Hollon, S. D. (1979). Cognitive-behavioral interventions: Overview and current status. In P. C. Kendall & S. D. Hollon (Eds.), *Cognitive-behavioral interventions: Theory, research, and procedures.* New York: Academic Press.

Keyser, V., & Barling, J. (1981). Determinants of children's self-efficacy beliefs in an academic environment. *Cognitive Therapy and Research, 5,* 29–40.

Lazarus, A., & Abramowitz, A. (1962). The use of "emotive imagery" in the treatment of children's phobias. *Journal of Mental Science, 108,* 191–195.

Ledwidge, B. (1978). Cognitive behavior modification: A step in the wrong direction? *Psychological Bulletin, 85,* 353–375.

Liebert, R. M., & Allen, M. K. (1967). Effects of rule structure and reward magnitude on the acquisition and adaptation of self-reward criteria. *Psychological Reports, 21,* 445–452.

Lochman, J. E., & Curry, J. F. (1986). Effects of social problem-solving training and self-instruction training with aggressive boys. *Journal of Clinical Child Psychology, 15,* 159–164.

Luria, A. R. (1959). The directive function of speech in development and dissolution. *Word, 15,* 341–352.

Luria, A. R. (1961). *The role of speech in the regulation of normal and abnormal behavior.* New York: Liveright.

Mahoney, M. J. (1974). Reflections on the cognitive-learning trend in psychotherapy. *American Psychologist, 32,* 5–13.

Mahoney, M. J., Kazdin, A. E., & Lesswing, N. J. (1974). Behavior modification: Delusion or deliverance? In C. M. Frank & G. T. Wilson (Eds.), *Annual Review of Behavior Therapy and Practice* (Vol. 2). New York: Brunner/Mazel.

Meichenbaum, D. (1971). *The nature and modification of impulsive children.* Paper presented at the meeting of the Society for Research in Child Development. Minneapolis, MN.

Meichenbaum, D. (1977). *Cognitive behavior modification: An integrative approach.* New York: Plenum Press.

Meichenbaum, D. (1985). *Stress inoculation training.* Toronto: Pergamon Press.

Meichenbaum D., & Cameron, R. (1973). *Stress inoculation: A skills training approach to anxiety management.* Unpublished manuscript, University of Waterloo.

Meichenbaum D., & Goodman, J. (1969). Reflection–impulsivity and verbal control of motor behavior. *Child Development, 40,* 785–797.

Meichenbaum, D., & Goodman, J. (1971). Training impulsive children to talk to themselves: A means of developing self-control. *Journal of Abnormal Psychology, 77,* 115–126.

Meichenbaum, D., & Turk, D. (1976). The cognitive-behavioral management of anxiety, anger, and pain. In P. Davidson (Ed.), *The behavioral management of anxiety, depression and pain.* New York: Brunner/Mazel.

Messer, S. B. (1976). Reflection–impulsivity: A review. *Psychological Bulletin, 83,* 1026–1052.

Miller, R. C., & Berman, J. S. (1983). The efficacy of cognitive behavior therapies: A quantitative review of research evidence. *Psychological Bulletin, 94*(1), 39–53.

Morgan, J. R. (1976). *The role of symbolic coding strategies in the long-term retention of model content.* Paper presented at the meeting of the Southeastern Psychological Association, New Orleans.

Nelson, W. M., III. (1976). *Cognitive-behavioral strategies in modifying an impulsive cognitive style.* Unpublished doctoral dissertation, Virginia Commonwealth University, Richmond.

Nelson, W. M., III, & Behler, J. (1990). Cognitive impulsivity training: The effects of peer teaching. *Journal of Behavior Therapy and Experimental Psychiatry, 20,* 303–309.

Nezu, A. (1987). A problem-solving formulation of depression: A literature review and proposal of a pluralistic model. *Clinical Psychology Review, 7,* 121–144.

Pearl, R. (1985). Cognitive-behavioral interventions for increasing motivation. *Journal of Abnormal Child Psychology, 13,* 443–454.

Peterson, L., & Shigetomi, C. (1981). The use of coping techniques to minimize anxiety in hospitalized children. *Behavior Therapy, 12,* 1–14.

Shapiro, D. A., & Shapiro, D. (1982). Meta-analysis of comparative therapy outcome studies: A replication and refinement. *Psychological Bulletin, 92*(3), 581–604.

Shaw, K. C. (1977). Comparison of cognitive therapy and behavior therapy in the treatment of depression. *Journal of Consulting and Clinical Psychology, 45,* 543–551.

Shure, M. B., & Spivack, G. (1978). *Problem-solving techniques in child-rearing.* San Francisco: Jossey-Bass.

Shure, M. B., & Spivack, G. (1980). Interpersonal problem solving in young children. A cognitive approach to prevention. *American Journal of Community Psychology, 10,* 341–356.

Shure, M. B., Spivack, G., & Jaeger, M. (1971). Problem solving thinking and adjustment among disadvantaged preschool children. *Child Development, 42,* 1791–1803.

Spivack, G., & Levine, M. (1963). *Self regulation in acting-out and normal adolescents.* Report M-4531. Washington, DC: National Institute of Health.

Spivack, G., Platt, J., & Shure, M. (1976). *The problem-solving approach to adjustment.* San Francisco: Jossey-Bass.

Spivack, G., & Shure, M. B. (1974). *Social adjustment of young children.* San Francisco: Jossey-Bass.

Stark, K. D., Kaslow, N. J., & Reynolds, W. M. (1985). A comparison of the relative efficacy of self-control and behavior therapy for the reduction of depression in children. Paper presented at the Fourth National Conference on the Clinical Application of Cognitive Behavior Therapy, Honolulu.

Thoresen, C. E., & Mahoney, M. J. (1974). *Behavioral self-control.* New York: Holt, Rinehart & Winston.

Urbain, E. S., & Kendall, P. C. (1981). *Interpersonal problem-solving, social perspective-taking, and behavioral contingencies: A comparison of group approaches with impulsive-aggressive children.* Unpublished manuscript, University of Minnesota.

Vygotsky, L. (1962). *Thought and Language.* New York: Wiley.

Weiner, W. B., & Palermo, D. S. (1974). *Cognition and the symbolic processes.* Hillsdale, NJ: Erlbaum.

Weissberg, R. P., Gesten, E. L., Carnirike, C. L., Toro, P. A., Rapkin, B. D., Davidson, E., & Cowen, E. L. (1981). Social problem-solving skills training: A competence-building intervention with second- to fourth-grade children. *American Journal of Community Psychology, 9,* 411–424.

Weissberg, R. P., Gesten, E. L., Rapkin, B. D., Cowen, E. L., Davidson, E., Flores de Apodaca, R., & McKim, B. J. (1981). The evaluation of a social problem-solving training program for suburban and inner-city third grade children. *Journal of Consulting and Clinical Psychology, 49,* 251–261.

Wilson, G. T. (1978). Cognitive behavior therapy: Paradigm shift or passing phase. In J. P. Foreyt & D. P. Rathjen (Eds.), *Cognitive behavior therapy.* New York: Plenum Press.

Wisocki, P. (1970). The treatment of obsessive-compulsive behavior by covert sensitization and covert reinforcement: A case report. *Journal of Behavioral Therapy and Experimental Psychiatry, 1,* 233–239.

CHAPTER TWO

The Role of Developmental Variables in Cognitive-Behavioral Interventions with Children

WILLIAM KIMBALL   W. M. NELSON III

P. M. POLITANO

In light of the recent advances in cognitive-behavioral interventions with children and adolescents, it is important to consider the potential therapeutic implications of developmental differences in cognitive capacity across ages. Adolescents are not merely smaller versions of adults, nor are grade-school children smaller versions of adolescents, preschoolers smaller versions of grade-school children, and so forth. There are age-related changes in the important cognitive skills involved in helping a child deal with a wide variety of problem situations (Sollod & Wachtel, 1980). However, within a cognitive-behavioral framework, the importance of developmental differences often has been overlooked. This oversight is a function of the radical behavioral roots of modern-day cognitive behaviorism. The early behaviorists emphasized the "continuous" aspects of development in which the formation of personality throughout the life-span was viewed solely as a result of shaping processes that gradually determined the rates at which various types of behavior were manifested. "Personalities" were viewed simply as verbal labels for specific behaviors rather than as something that existed in the personality structure as a trait. On the other hand, stage theorists such as Freud and Piaget focused on universal, natural progressions through a series of "discontinuous" stages. The purpose of this chapter is to sensitize the reader to certain developmental issues and to suggest ways to conceptualize the role of age-related changes in *cognitive* capacities within a cognitive-behavioral framework. In addition, evidence will be presented to demonstrate that, because of the age-related nature of these cognitive skills, cognitive-behavioral treatment procedures need to be tailored to the developmental level of the individual, either child or adolescent.

The literature of the social learning and cognitive-developmental traditions presents several suggestions concerning important age-related cognitive skills involved in helping a child or adolescent deal with a wide variety of problem situations. These skills involve age-related changes in the ability to comprehend social information, to evaluate social acts through role taking and moral reasoning, and to use verbal self-regulation and problem-solving skills in interpersonal conflict situations.

This chapter is organized as follows. First, a theoretical discussion will provide a foundation for conceptualizing developmental changes in these different areas. An in-depth analysis of various developmental processes will not be presented; instead, we will discuss briefly several developmental issues that have a direct bearing on treatment strategies that are important to the practicing clinician. Second, the important age-related cognitive skills, their developmental progression, their relation to social behavior, and associated training methods will be described. Finally, potential intervention strategies tailored to appropriate developmental levels will be presented.

The Relation of Developmentally Based Variables to Social Behavior

Professionals who have worked with children and adolescents know that their clients are constantly changing. This change seems, at times, to be systematic and at other times rather erratic, but it is inexorable. In recent years, professionals have come to realize the importance of attending to developmental variables in child and adolescent psychopathology, because the same behaviors (e.g., enuresis, negativism) are "normal" for children at one stage of development and "abnormal" for children at another (Achenbach & Edelbrock, 1981; Kazdin, 1989). In dealing with such behaviors it is important to have knowledge of developmental trends (e.g., physical, cognitive, linguistic, moral, social), for there is a dynamic interplay between normal and abnormal processes. The view that psychopathology involves normal developmental process "gone awry" is gaining more support (Wenar, 1982, 1983).

In understanding particular emotional/behavioral difficulties, it is important to specify the precise nature of the developmental disturbance, the factors causing it, and the way these factors interact. Theories of development assist us in this endeavor. Whether these theories are based on stage (qualitative) or nonstage (continuous) models, they all recognize a number of ways in which development increases quantitatively—in degree, frequency, or amount. For example, with increasing age, children and adolescents strengthen and generalize their cognitive skills (Piaget), increase their ego strength (Freud and Erikson), imitate more accurately (social learning theory), process information more efficiently (information processing), refine the interweaving of learned and innate components (ethology), and detect more distinctive features (Gibson). Although all of these theories acknowledge at least minor qualitative changes, the stage advocates make change a central part of their theories. Other theorists view common qualitative changes more as a new strategy of learning or problem solving.

No one theory has thoroughly explained the fact that development proceeds on several levels and in many content areas simultaneously. Different theories focus on different levels of behavior and select different content areas. The stage theorists operate at a very general level that focuses on establishing general laws that pertain to groups of individuals. In their view the most important developments are cognitive structures (Piaget) or personality structures (Freud and Erikson). Other theorists focus more on specific acquisitions — rules (social learning theory and information processing), distinctive features (Gibson), and adaptive behavior (ethology).

The two major theoretical views on the relationship between cognitive and social development that will be examined here are social learning theory (Bandura, 1977, 1986; Mischel, 1973, 1979; Rosenthal & Zimmerman, 1978) and cognitive developmental theory (Kohlberg, 1969, 1976; Selman, 1976a, 1976b). Cognitive-behavioral interventions have been most heavily influenced by social learning theory. These two contrasting theoretical views integrate around the activity of cognition (thinking and knowing) within the context of social influences across the developmental spectrum (Belmont, 1989; Vygotsky, 1978). Thus, while the present authors are heavily influenced by social learning theory, the knowledge gained from research conducted from both theoretical perspectives can be profitable.

Cognitive developmental theorists (Kohlberg, 1976; Selman, 1976a, 1976b) place a primary focus on *stages* of development, and changes in behavior are viewed as a function of development. By implication, stages are discontinuous—that is, they are clearly differentiated from what came before and from what will follow (as in Piaget's theory of cognitive development, Freud's psychosexual stages of development, and Erikson's eight stages of man). Individual differences are relegated to secondary importance in the attempt to establish the existence of invariant stage sequences. Individual differences, thus, are often overlooked from the stage-theory viewpoint and are considered as "error variance." In regard to cognitive-developmental stage theory, it is postulated that underlying cognitive structures mature in an unchanging sequence of stages. Although experience provides the symbolic content for the structure, it cannot create the structure. As a result, the role of experience is delineated by the structure that the child or adolescent possesses.

In social learning theory (Bandura, 1977, 1986; Rosenthal & Zimmerman, 1978), behavior is seen as a product of both person and situational factors (Lewin, 1951). Children and adolescents do not just generate behavior; they also categorize, evaluate, and judge it (Mischel & Mischel, 1976). Person variables include such factors as attention, retention, and encoding strategies (Mischel, 1973) as well as current cognitive variables (e.g., self-talk, belief system). Situational factors include variables such as available models, the type of task, the reinforcement variables, and the learning history. A heavy emphasis placed on "reciprocal determinism" behavior is seen as a product of the ever-changing interaction between person and environmental factors (Bandura, 1977, 1986). Behavior develops through a process of maturation and interaction with the environment (Harris, 1985).

Social learning theorists do not view development as being composed of relatively rapid qualitative changes involving movement from one stage to the next with massive cognitive reorganization. Although they do not deny that stages exist, they consider emphasis on stages as counterproductive in a social learning model because stages "tend to cast people into prefix types, thus lending themselves readily to stereotyping people by stage classification" (Bandura, 1977, p. 183). Thus, an analysis of subskills and of what is needed to produce certain behaviors or knowledge is considered more fruitful. Children and adolescent thinking is viewed as much too flexible and complex to be categorized into homogenous stages. Moreover, children and adolescents can operate at different levels depending upon the motivational and task characteristics present in the situation (Dweck, 1986; Rosenthal & Zimmerman, 1978). In social learning theory the emphasis is placed on the development of cognitive skills (e.g., attention, retention skills, retrieving, encoding, and decoding strategies) rather than on the categorization of children and adolescents into uniform stages. Consequently, when analyzing the developmental determinants of performance, it is essential to analyze not only cognitive abilities but also task requirements and motivational factors. This approach implies that a researcher who wants to predict performance should conduct a component analysis of the cognitive abilities required to perform a task, as those abilities interact with situational demands (Bandura, 1977; Chandler, 1976).

Although a child's or adolescent's prior cognitive skill level places limits on what he or she can understand, research evidence suggests that performance levels of these skills can be advanced through modeling, appropriate reinforcement, cognitive conflict, discussion, and role playing (Selman & Lieberman, 1975; Chandler, 1973; Peterson & Skevington, 1988)—essential techniques in the therapist's clinical repertoire. However, there are limits on how far progress can be pushed in a particular situation, because not *any* skill can be learned at *any* age. Hence, the clinician/researcher needs to reach a balance between assuming that a child or adolescent can learn any skill at any age and assuming that failures in cognitive learning are readily attributable to lack of "readiness." It is crucial for future researchers within the social learning tradition to identify the developmental progression of cognitive skill acquisition in relation to situational variables, even though qualitative changes are viewed as the gradual development of a new strategy of learning or problem solving.

At this point it is important to examine the way in which age-related changes in cognitive capacities influence child and adolescent social behavior. By influencing perceptions of environmental events, age-related factors (comprehension and evaluation of social acts, attention, storage and recall, problem solving, verbal self-regulation) may influence overt behavior and place limits on the ability to interpret and organize the social world. For example, as the child or adolescent matures, there is development of a more mature and complex understanding of the rights and feelings of others. However, the interactional nature of cognitive processes defies a search for simple relationships between perceptions and actions. For instance, behavior is much too complex for there to be a simple relationship between moral reasoning and moral behavior (Gerson & Damon, 1978). To make sophisticated predictions about a child's or adolescent's conduct, it is necessary to understand fully their capacities and goals in relation to the particular context in which the behavior occurs. These predictions should be less concerned with identifying a stage in which to categorize thinking than with identifying the interpretation of the particular situation and the various motivational factors present (Damon, 1977; Dweck, 1986; Gerson & Damon, 1978). As suggested by Chandler (1976) and Gerson and Damon (1978), different kinds of knowledge are gradually formed in different settings. As a result, children and adolescents tailor their interpretations to meet the specific demands of different social contexts. Thus, the situation and the specific nature of cognitions are important to consider in explaining behavior, especially from a cognitive-behavioral viewpoint.

This discussion is not intended to suggest that there is no consistency across children's or adolescents' perceptions of situations, for this would ignore the wealth of data amassed by the stage theorists. Children and adolescents do not always come into a situation as if it were a new one. Rather, they build on prior constructions of situations; Piaget (1970) described these processes in terms of "assimilation" and "accommodation." Stability can be expected whenever there is recognized similarity between present and past social experiences. When this recognition exists, there is a high likelihood of drawing upon representations already worked out in the past, although significant variability is evident from individual to individual and situation to situation.

The reciprocal relationship between a child's or adolescent's goal and his or her conceptualizations of situations is also important. A more mechanistic or radical behavioral view proposes that children and adolescents try to mold an understanding of a situation that is in accord with their goals. In such a one-way analysis of behavior, an explanation will be made up to meet these goals. However, an interactional view proposes that "in many cases . . . the understanding will itself influence the objectives, just as objectives may influence understanding . . . therefore, objectives and understanding have a mutual influence" (Gerson & Damon, 1978, p. 49).

The reciprocal nature of the relationship between age-related cognitive skills and situational variables has important clinical implications. When assessing cognitive skills, a clinician must be careful to examine them in relation to the situation of interest rather than to assume that the child's or adolescent's cognitive skills in hypothetical situations will be equivalent to those in real-life situations. For instance, Keller (1976) found that role-taking skills in school situations were not equivalent to those in home situations. Behavior therapists have traditionally referred to this as "response specificity." Consequently, when assessing a child or adolescent who exhibits disruptive behavior, a clinician first needs to identify the types of situations that are problematic and then to assess cognitive skills in relation to the problem-eliciting situations. Moreover, the cognitive demands on the child or adolescent in the assessment situation need to be related to the demands that they might encounter in real-life problem situations. Because much of the research on person variables has been directed toward describing their developmental progression rather than toward relating them to behavior, it is necessary to modify the typically used assessment devices to include more relevant content areas. To predict behavior accurately a clinician must consider cognitive abilities in relation to particular content areas and to the important social variables present in the situation (Mischel & Mischel, 1976).

This point is further emphasized when one examines the discrepancy principle, which suggests that children or adolescents will be most attracted to events within the social sphere that are partially dissimilar to past social events, rather than to events that are opposed to, completely dissimilar to, or not at all similar to past social events (McCall, Kennedy, & Appelbaum, 1977; Resnick, 1982). The discrepancy principle reemphasizes the need to consider the context within which cognitive processes take place.

Following this brief review of social learning theorists (Bandura, 1977, 1986; Rosenthal & Zimmerman, 1978), we move to an evaluation of the relevant literature, which is important in understanding developmentally based variables in regard to the comprehension of social acts, the evaluation of social acts through role taking and moral reasoning, interpersonal problem solving, and self-instructional training.

Comprehending Social Information: Attention and Retention

Definition and Assessment

Because the basis of observational learning requires observation of the world and, in the process, gathering and organizing new knowledge, the way in which this process occurs is significant. Children's and adolescents' learning of material presented through modeling is certainly influenced by the development of attentional and retentional factors. These aspects of observational learning research will be considered here, because observational learning is involved in the clinical treatment for many of the problem areas to be discussed. Although attentional and retentional processes will be examined in isolation from other processes, the reader should always be cognizant of the fact that development proceeds on several levels and in many areas.

Attention and retention are measured in a variety of ways. In regard to modeling procedures, selective attention has been assessed primarily by observing subjects who are viewing a model in order to determine precisely how they attend to central rather than to peripheral information (Yussen, 1974). The ability to connect sequences has been assessed by presenting modeled sequences and asking subjects to relate the content and themes of the sequences (Collins, Berndt, & Hess, 1973). For example, the ability to associate content cues has been examined by inserting motives into an aggressive scene and observing the effects of laboratory measures of aggression (Collins, 1973). To assess developmental differences in retention, several investigators have explored the effects of overt responding or labeling on retention (Yussen & Santrock, 1974; Coates & Hartup, 1969).

Developmental Changes

As children develop, information in modeling films is perceived less as static and more as a process composed of both central and peripheral information (Yussen, 1974). The young child is able to attend to only one aspect of a problem without connecting sequences (Collins et al., 1973). Consequently, if a complicated modeling program is employed, the young child may remember disconnected segments of what has been viewed, while older children will remember the various plots and themes. For example, the young child may be less able to associate context cues, such as negative motives, with violent acts (Collins, 1975; Collins, Wellman, Keniston, & Westby, 1978; Rubinstein, 1983). This has contributed to distorted perceptions of "messages" in violent televised programming (National Institute of Mental Health [NIMH], 1982). Adolescents, however, demonstrate the ability to differentiate central from peripheral information and to integrate both, and thus are less prone to distortions based on static perceptions. However, the adolescent's apparent stability relative to learning from models is undermined by a wider and more varied range of models in the everyday world, thus countering cognitive stability and reintroducing instability.

Developmental differences have also been found for the effects of summary or verbal labels on learning and retention. Coates and Hartup (1969) demonstrated that the use of structured verbalizations increased learning of filmed sequences for 4-year-olds but not for 7-year-olds. Yussen and Santrock (1974) found that providing verbal labels increased retention for preschool and second-grade children but that verbally describing the model's ongoing actions increased retention only for the preschoolers. Denney (1975) compared the effects of cognitive modeling (the model verbalized a strategy for asking constraint-seeking questions) to exemplary modeling (the model merely demonstrated constraint-seeking questions). Cognitive modeling was a more successful training technique for all children, but the difference between cognitive and exemplary modeling was most notable among the youngest children, who appeared to require the additional guidance afforded by the verbalization of the cognitive model (it should be noted that such developmental differences may be due to the fact that older children may already possess the modeled behavior in their repertoire and that in this study it was only necessary to elicit the behavior). Additionally, Rogoff and Gardner (1984) suggested that learning through modeling is enhanced when there is a perceived shared responsibility between the observer and model relative to attaining goals, and this effect cuts across all ages. Therefore, when teaching a new behavior, it is probably necessary to include more explicit cues for young children and to foster a shared sense of responsibility for all ages. Clinicians need to be particularly aware of possible behavioral/response repertoire deficiencies and to assess this possibility carefully prior to initiating treatment.

Implications for Observational Learning Training Program

These results have several implications for observational training programs. First, because the young child is less able to connect sequences, the modeled behavior should be less complex. Also, because the young child is less able to focus on multidimensional cues, the clinician must be careful to ensure that the important cues are salient. If improper cues are salient, a child is much more likely to interpret a scene incorrectly. The saliency of various cues, however, is directly related to various developmental processes — especially to attention and to the organization of cues for memory and recall. Prior to age 5 or 6, children's attention (as well as their problem-solving abilities, memory, and reasoning) seem "captured" by the characteristics of the stimuli, and children rarely impose an organization on tasks as an attempt to guide and regulate their behavior (Paris & Lindauer, 1982). Although development is continuous between 5 and 7 years of age, there seems to be a marked shift that enables children to engage in more self-controlled, intentional, and systematic problem solving. Thus, what is observed (via models) can be processed in a rather "different" fashion at this age, with different consequences for overt behavior. Studies that address the saliency issue in respect to moral judgment demonstrate that younger children can focus on intention cues if these cues are made more salient than the consequence cues (Chandler, Greenspan, & Barenboim, 1973; Nummedal & Bass, 1976). In addition, because young children are less able to connect sequences, especially if time lags occur (Collins, 1973), it is important to put context cues temporally close to their associated behaviors. It may also be important to avoid including divergent cues and contrast models with young children when right and wrong behaviors are shown (Collins, 1975, 1983). And, finally, to enhance young children's learning of modeled behavior, the clinical use of structured verbal labeling as *symbolic coding* (term used to describe any sort of procedure that reduces an observable behavior to a form that can be easily retained) is very helpful.

By adolescence, thinking is characterized by a greater degree of flexibility, more accurate mental representations of the environment, and more efficient information-gathering strategies, all of which affect observational learning capabilities. Additionally, observational learning is enhanced at all ages by reattributing failures to levels of effort and/or to chosen strategies rather than to ability (Fowler & Peterson, 1981). Indeed, "programmed success" using high repetitions of task behaviors may be counterproductive to the development of persistence and confidence in ability (Dweck, 1975). Research by Csikszentmihalyi and Larson (1984) suggests that, particularly for adolescents, repetitive and easy tasks result in rapid levels of skill acquisition to the level of the task, followed by boredom.

Evaluating Social Acts: Role Taking and Moral Reasoning

Role Taking

Definition and Assessment
Role taking was initially defined by Mead (1934) as learning to take the role of another. Kurdek (1978a, 1978b) added a social dimension that incorporated social perspectives and their influence on others' behaviors. Additionally, role taking refers to the ability to take the perspective of others and to make inferences about their inner, psychological experiences (Shantz, 1975). As such, role taking involves understanding of the knowledge base upon which others operate (Chandler & Boyes, 1982) and is instrumental in the development of social relations and moral development (Mead, 1934). Role taking is a key cognitive element in children's and adolescents' understanding of relationships. Because clinicians are called upon to assist in the acquisition of social capabilities and skills, this area of research is potentially very fruitful in regard to developing effective treatment strategies across age groups.

Role taking can be assessed in a variety of ways. For instance, a young child may be presented with a story about an affective situation and asked to identify the emotions of the characters. At later ages a child may be presented with a story and asked to tell the story either from the perspective of each character involved or from the perspective of an individual who has less information about the situation (see Shantz, 1975, for a more thorough description of other measures). It is important for the clinician to note that there are low intercorrelations among the various measures of role taking (Zahn-Waxler, Radke-Yarrow, & Brady-Smith, 1977; Rubin, 1978; Piche, Michlin, Rubin, & Johnson, 1975; Kurdek & Rogdon, 1975) and that the existence of a unitary skill of role taking cannot be assumed. Moreover, even with the same role-taking measure, performance levels may not necessarily progress at the same rate in different content areas (e.g., home vs. school) (Keller, 1976). Consequently, it is important for the clinician to assess role taking in relation to situational variables.

Developmental Trends

An abundance of evidence demonstrates that age trends exist in the growing understanding of relationships, especially in the cognitive element of this ability (i.e., role taking) (e.g., Selman, 1971, 1980; Rubin, 1972; Kurdek & Rogdon, 1975). In Selman's (1976a, 1980) model of role taking (heavily influenced by Mead's and Piaget's theories), young children (ages 3 to 6) are not yet aware that others do not feel or think as they do (egocentric viewpoint). Just as they do not differentiate points of view, they do not relate perspectives. Young children can recognize other people's feelings, such as knowing that yelling and cursing mean that someone is "angry," but they have not connected this external event to their own internal experience of anger. As age increases, there is increased ability to differentiate between one's own feelings and the feelings of others (Nannis & Cowan, 1987). These children base their judgments of others on observable actions rather than on covert psychological data; therefore, they judge the actions of others by the consequences rather than by the intention of the actor. From ages 6 to 8, children begin to see themselves and others as actors with potentially different ideas and feelings about the same situation (social-informational role taking). They begin to understand the differences between what people do and what they think and feel and, therefore, begin to distinguish between intentions and consequences. However, at this developmental stage, children still tend to focus on one perspective, for they are unable to maintain their own perspective while simultaneously understanding the perspective of others. These children have yet to consider that their view of the other is influenced by their understanding of the other's view of them — or the next step, which is "I know that you know that I know." Older children (ages 8 to 10) realize that individuals can "read" or be aware of the other's perspective and that this awareness influences how people view each other (self-reflective role taking). These reflections occur sequentially rather than simultaneously, however. At this age the child begins to think of others as multimotivated rather than as unimotivated, and, thus, the child can now conceive of persons doing things that others may not want to do. The child realizes that people can be both angry and loving and that they might do things that they did not intend or want to do. At later ages (10 to 12), children begin to discover that both they and others can consider each party's point of view simultaneously (mutual role taking). They can put themselves in the other's place before deciding how to act. As adolescents (age 13 and above), consideration is given to the position of "generalized others" as members of the larger social fabric (social and conventional system role taking).

Hoffman (1977), however, took a somewhat different view and equated role taking to a cognitive sense of others, designated as *cognitive perspec-*

tive taking. Four levels of perspective taking are described: fusion as an infant; differentiation during early childhood; the notion in middle childhood that others have thoughts and feelings; adolescent awareness that others come from different life experiences that will influence their perspectives.

Relationship to Social Behavior

It appears that a child's or adolescent's role-taking level has an important impact on social behavior. Through taking the perspective of the other, they may be able both to predict another's behavior and to recognize the consequences of their behavior on the other (Shantz, 1975).

Eisenberg and Neal (1979) demonstrated that with or without induction, explicit modeling is most effective in inducing prosocial behavior in children and adolescents and insulating them against antisocial behavior. Using a variety of assessment devices, several investigators have correlated children's role-taking scores with social behavior indices. These studies demonstrated that role taking is correlated significantly with young children's peer popularity (Rubin & Maioni, 1976; Rubin, 1972; Deutsch, 1974; Gottman, Gonso, & Rasmussen, 1975; Jennings, 1975; Spence, 1987), decreases in egocentricism (Gollins & Sharp, 1987), sophistication of children's play (Rubin, 1976), middle children's cooperative behavior (Johnson, 1975a, 1975b), sharing or altruistic behavior (Rubin & Schneider, 1973; Jennings, Fitch, & Suwalsky, 1987; Olejnik, 1975; Buckley, Siegel, & Ness, 1979), children's classroom adjustment as determined by teacher ratings (Burka & Glenwick, 1978; Elarado, Caldwell, & Webb, 1976), adolescents' nondelinquent behavior (Chandler, 1973; Selman, 1976b), and adolescents' and adults' social adjustment (Spivack, Platt, & Shure, 1976). However, others have failed to find significant relationships between role taking and cooperative or helping behaviors in young and middle children (Zahn-Waxler et al., 1977; Rushton & Weiner, 1975; Ceresnie, cited by Shantz, 1975), aggressive behavior in middle children (Iannotti, 1978; Kurdek, 1978b; MacQuiddy, Maise, & Hamilton, 1987), or peer popularity of middle children (LeMare & Rubin, 1987; Rothenberg, 1970).

The following studies further highlight the complexities involved in relating role taking and social behaviors. Rubin (1972) found significant correlations between role taking and sociometric popularity for kindergarteners and second-graders, but not for fourth- and sixth-graders. Spence (1987) found positive correlations for kindergarteners; LeMare and Rubin (1987) found positive correlations only for third-graders. One possible explanation of these results is that effective social interaction requires a minimal level of role taking that not all young children have acquired. Accordingly, most of the older children may have developed the minimal level of role taking required for effective social interaction, and social abilities other than role taking may differentiate high- and low-popular fourth- and sixth-graders. Research by Shirk (1987) indicated a negative relationship between self-doubt and role taking, with both showing a developmental trend. Although this area is still open to study, it illustrates the possibility that other social abilities influence role taking and associated positive attributes. A second speculation is that a ceiling effect occurred with the older children and prevented strong correlations. Whatever the explanation, it is clear that when a clinician or researcher examines the relationship between social behavior and role taking, the social context of the behavior as well as the developmental level must be carefully considered.

A study by Johnson (1975b) illustrated the point that the content of the role-taking task and the predicted social behavior may need to be closely related. Johnson found that affective role taking (the ability to recognize how another is feeling), but not perceptual role taking (knowing how another perceives physical objects), correlated significantly with cooperative behavior. It is apparent that knowing how another feels is more closely related in content to cooperative behavior than knowing how another perceives physical objects.

Overall, the studies correlating role taking and social behaviors indicate moderate positive relationships between role taking and prosocial behaviors and moderate negative relationships between role taking and antisocial behavior. To predict social behavior accurately, it may be necessary for the content and cognitive demands of the role-taking task to be related to the types of situations in which a child is having difficulty. It is also important for researchers and clinicians to examine further and to consider the environmental contingencies operating in the situations causing problems for the child or adolescent.

Training in Role Taking

Although the implications for actual therapeutic procedures for children and adolescents have not been clearly defined, the developmental research on role taking provides several suggestions for the practicing clinician to consider. To foster role-taking skills, a clinician should provide the child or adolescent with a wide range of role-play and peer group opportunities. The types of activities that are important will vary with age. Rosen (1974) advanced young children's role taking by enhancing their sociodramatic play—play that occurs when several children take on different roles and interact with each other in terms of a situation that they have spontaneously created (e.g., a doctor's office with doctors, nurses, patients). When enacting a role, the child draws upon observations of situations and people and then expresses these experiences through actions and verbalizations. In Rosen's intervention program the experimenter entered into the child's play activity and acted as a role model by engaging in sociodramatic play. The experimenter then encouraged the child to mimic the behavior. Peterson and Skevington (1988) suggested that cognitive conflict-reducing childrearing methods can stimulate cognitive role taking. The clinical application of such a technique is obvious.

With older children and adolescents, Chandler (1973) recommended the use of a series of role-play experiences. In Chandler's intervention plan, delinquents played the roles of others in situations simulating interpersonal problem situations. A key aspect of this role-taking intervention program is role reversal. Presumably, through assuming the role of others, the delinquent learns that others have different viewpoints and feelings. Chandler's program was successful in reducing the recidivism rate of juvenile delinquents. Other important therapeutic strategies come from a program entitled "Project Aware" (Elarado & Caldwell, 1979; Elarado & Cooper, 1978). Teachers of elementary school children were trained in activities designed to facilitate the development of role taking and interpersonal problem solving. Over a 6-month period the classroom teachers conducted a program that included 72 discussion activities and over 200 activities designed to incorporate role taking and problem solving into the curriculum. The discussion periods provided opportunities for children to exchange ideas and feelings and to be exposed to the thoughts and feelings of others. In the discussions, problem situations were presented, and the children were encouraged to think of alternative solutions. Teachers were encouraged to include the skills in their daily activities with the children. After the program's conclusion it was found that teachers rated the children as better adjusted on the basis of the Devereux Scale. However, the ratings were not "blind," as they were made by the teachers who carried out the program. Nevertheless, the results were encouraging, especially in light of the fact that the students and teachers appeared to enjoy the program and that the teachers rated themselves as more comfortable in handling conflict situations following the training program.

Still other role-taking training studies conducted by Cooney (1977) and Enright, Colby, and McMullen (1977) have produced advances in school-age children's conceptualizations of interpersonal relationships. However, systematic evaluations of the effects of these programs on actual behavior are not available, and, therefore, their therapeutic effectiveness can only be speculated upon at this time.

Summary
The evidence for a relationship between role taking and social behavior and for the effects of role-taking training on social behavior is inconclusive but encouraging. Age trends in role taking do exist, and role taking appears to be an important correlate of social behavior. However, because

of the low intercorrelations between the various role-taking measures and the inconsistent correlations between role taking and social behavior, future researchers and clinicians need to consider carefully the situation-specificity of children's and adolescents' developing cognitive skills rather than to assume that a clear stagelike progression exists. When trying to predict, understand, or influence behavior, the content and context of role-taking tasks need to be related to the behavior to be predicted. Moreover, in all cases, other environmental factors, such as motivational variables, need to be examined.

Moral Reasoning

Definition and Assessment

The previous section focused on understanding of *relationships* with others; social understanding also requires the child or adolescent to think about or explain other people's *actions*. The facet of this process that has intrigued developmental researchers is the judgment of the "morality" of actions. *Moral reasoning* refers to how an individual evaluates an act ("good-bad") and how he or she decides what "ought to be done" about it (Mischel & Mischel, 1976). Traditionally, moral reasoning has been assessed by either Piaget's (1932) or Kohlberg's (1976) clinical interview technique.

In Piaget's procedure, subjects are given a series of two story items in which the intentionality and magnitude of the consequences are altered systematically, and the task is to evaluate the appropriateness of a child's actions. It has generally been found that, in judging the goodness or badness of others' actions, younger children (moral realism stage) focus more heavily on consequences, while older children and adolescents (moral relativism stage) focus more heavily on intentions (Piaget, 1932, 1965).

Kohlberg's test consists of nine structured hypothetical moral dilemmas, and the subject is asked to relate the reasons for his or her behavioral choice. Moral reasoning, according to Kohlberg (1975), is tied to logical or cognitive reasoning. Thus, a child in the concrete operational period would not progress further than preconventional moral reasoning, while early formal operations in adolescents should place them into conventional moral reasoning. A cautionary note (Kurtines & Greif, 1974) is in order, however, as methodological deficiencies present in Kohlberg's procedure have made it somewhat difficult to interpret his results; there is a lack of standard statistical information such as temporal stability, internal consistency, and the standard error of measurement. In this regard it should be noted that Kohlberg (1978) has modified his theory, and attempts have been made to standardize the scoring procedure. Presumably, future research will reflect this improved methodology.

To overcome the methodological problems and the practical problems (e.g., length of administration) in Kohlberg's procedure, Rest (1975) developed an objective moral reasoning test. In Rest's test a subject reads a series of six moral dilemmas, is presented with 12 statements that define the issue of the dilemma in various ways, and is asked to rate the statements in terms of their perceived importance. For the practicing clinician, however, there is a problem with the tests of moral reasoning in that the content of the moral dilemmas is often far removed from the situations that children and adolescents actually encounter. For clinical assessment purposes it is desirable to have a quick, easily interpretable measure that assesses the evaluation of the appropriateness of actions relevant to the child's or adolescent's life.

Developmental Trends

It is clear that there are age trends in the development of moral reasoning. Piaget (1932) found that before the age of 8 or 9, children tend to focus on consequences rather than on intentions. However, recent research studies have found that apparent deficiencies in 6- or 7-year-olds' perception of intention cues is partly an artifact of the assessment procedure. As mentioned earlier, two studies (Chandler et al., 1973; Nummedal & Bass, 1976) found that children as young as 6 or 7 can focus on intention cues if these cues are made more salient than the consequence cues.

Kohlberg (1976) outlined six stages of moral reasoning. In the "preconventional" level or earliest stages (1 and 2), the child tends to focus on the immediate and concrete consequence of punishment or the lack of punishment. "Right" is defined according to what is valued by the child. The next two stages have been labeled "conventional" thinking. In Stage 3, right is defined by the Golden Rule, as the child seeks to win the approval of the immediate group. In Stage 4 the child respects and upholds social standards out of a concern for law and order. Moral judgments are based on the expectations of the group or society, and the emphasis is on conformity and approval from those in authority. Finally, in the "postconventional" stages the arbitrary nature of social and legal conventions is recognized, and external social definitions of right or wrong give way to "rational" considerations. Children in these last two stages (5 and 6) tend to focus on temporally distant and abstract cues. According to Kohlberg (1976), few people ever reach the last two stages, and he revised the theory to include a five-stage model (Kohlberg, 1978).

Although it has been shown that age trends exist in both Kohlberg's (Holstein, 1976; Kuhn, 1976) and Rest's tests (Rest, 1975), it has not been shown that moral reasoning develops in uniform stages or in an invariant sequence (Rosenthal & Zimmerman, 1978). According to Rosenthal and

Zimmerman (1978), the extensive stage variability shown by children and adolescents and the fact that moral reasoning can be altered through modeling and reinforcement argue against a stage model.

The Relationship to Moral Behavior

Kohlberg (1975) suggested that moral reasoning was a necessary but not sufficient condition for moral action. Higher levels of moral reasoning should entail more genuine and profound awareness and consideration of the welfare of others and activate behavior that may be unselfish, compassionate, and socially beneficial. However, Kohlberg (1975) did not propose that an advanced moral reasoning level is *always* associated with advanced moral action. Moral reasoning is seen as a powerful predictor of moral action only when the different levels of reasoning are evaluated relative to the situation, environmental pressures, and individual motives.

Although knowing the level of reasoning does not make it possible to predict *precisely* what a child or adolescent will actually do in a real-life situation, researchers have found significant correlations between moral reasoning and middle children's and adolescents' honesty (Harris, Mussen, & Rutherford, 1976; Schwartz, Feldman, Brown, & Heingartner, 1969), middle children's generosity (Rushton, 1975; Emler & Rushton, 1974; Rubin & Schneider, 1973; Olejnik, 1975), older children's "communicative competence" (Selman, Schorin, Stone, & Phelps, 1983), and "social competence" (Ford, 1982). The findings of Jurkovic and Prentice (1977) and Selman (1976b) also support the view that children and adolescents who exhibit antisocial behavior have lower levels of moral reasoning. In addition, Kurdek (1980) found that elementary school children who score relatively high on moral reasoning are rated by their parents as better behaved. Although the correlations between prosocial behavior and moral reasoning are often statistically significant, these correlations are often relatively low (Kurdek, 1978a). For example, Harris et al. (1976) correlated scores on Kohlberg's test with resistance to temptation in a situation in which it was easy to cheat and not be detected. The correlation between honesty and scores on the moral reasoning test was .45; however, with IQ partialed out, the correlation dropped to .27 (not statistically significant). There was great variability in the correlations between moral reasoning and moral conduct as judged by peer ratings. Correlations ranged from .63 on a question asking "Who can everyone count on to lend a helping hand?" to .06 on "Who would never lie to the teacher?" It is clear that many of the correlations are statistically but not clinically significant.

In another study, Fodor (1972) examined differences in the moral reasoning of delinquent and nondelinquent youth. Although significant group differences were found, they were small. Furthermore, both groups obtained average scores within the conventional level (Stage 3) of moral reasoning on Kohlberg's test; thus, moral reasoning level alone would seem to be a poor predictor of delinquent behavior.

In the studies that have been discussed, a stage model of moral reasoning was used to examine the relationships between reasoning and conduct. In most cases the correlations were relatively small and/or inconsistent. As an alternative to the stage model, Damon (1977) and Gerson and Damon (1978) developed an interactional model of the relationship between children's and adolescents' developing thought and moral conduct. This model assumes that a simple concordance between moral thought and moral conduct does not exist. To make sophisticated predictions about conduct, it is necessary to examine situational factors as well as the developing nature of thought processes. Children's and adolescents' thinking should be explored in the context of the designated situation rather than solely in hypothetical situations. Social knowledge is better seen as an "interaction between the child's constructive activities and the salient details of a situation" (Gerson & Damon, 1978, p. 52).

One example of Damon's (1977; Gerson & Damon, 1978) research is the study of the distribution of rewards in relation to reasoning about fairness. The experimental situation required children to distribute a reward among themselves for making bracelets, and each of four children had a claim to the reward of 10 candy bars. The four children, among whom each child could be any of the first three, were (a) a child who had made the most and best bracelets, (b) a child who was the biggest, (c) a child who simply did a "nice job," and (d) a younger child who did poorly and was absent during the reward distribution. The "conduct" of each child was the decision about how to split up the candy. Moral reasoning of the children was assessed by means of an interview about hypothetical justice problems. The actual reasoning used to justify the child's own conduct in the experimental situation was also assessed.

The relationship between the children's conduct and their thinking in the hypothetical and "real-life" (experimental) situations was intriguing. From prior research, Damon (1977) had found that children's justice conceptions progressed: from primitive levels, in which fairness is what the person wants; to intermediate levels, in which equality and deservingness are emphasized; to advanced levels, in which a fair solution is based on the particular nature of the situation. From a stage model it would be predicted that a child's positive justice reasoning as measured in a hypothetical situation will place limits on his or her conduct in the experimental situation. Thus, children at the lowest levels would prefer themselves, children at the intermediate level would focus on equal distributions or merit, and children at the advanced level would focus on special considerations.

The results confirmed some, but not all, of Damon's (1977) predictions based on the stage model. For example, children at the lowest level of moral reasoning rewarded themselves more than did the advanced reasoners, and the most advanced reasoners were the most considerate of the younger child. Interestingly, the intermediate children were not the most likely to reward everyone equally or to favor the "meritorious" child. However, there was a striking interaction between situational and cognitive factors. Unlike children at the lower levels, the intermediate children gave more candy bars to children in the "merit" position when they themselves were in that position. Thus, the child's level of reasoning and the child's position in the experiment were interrelated.

By comparison, adolescent moral reasoning may be more complex than simple stage theories suggest due to the interaction of different developmental processes. For example, adolescents are often caught between the drive for independence (individuation and separation) from the family and the need for dependence. Thus, moral decisions of adolescents appear to center around individual rights that protect individuation and separation contrasting with acknowledged responsibilities that sustain connections counter to the separation-individuation process (Gilligan, 1982).

Given the developmental research, the following tentative conclusions can be drawn for the practicing clinician. First, a child's or adolescent's varying abilities during development establish limits on his or her organization of the social world. The evidence supporting this position (as in the Gerson and Damon study) is that the least advanced children were most likely to prefer themselves in the candy bar distribution situation, while the advanced reasoners were the most considerate of the disadvantaged younger child. Second, although reasoning in hypothetical situations was related to behavior, the actual reasoning used to justify conduct in the experimental situation was more closely related to conduct than to the hypothetical reasoning. Third, while a strong correlation existed between reasoning in the hypothetical and real-life situations, half of the children differed in their reasoning in the two situations, and half of the children differed in their reasoning in the two contexts (usually by one level only). Most importantly, children and adolescents reason at different levels in hypothetical and real-life situations. Fourth, the child's position interacted with moral considerations to influence behavior. Additional evidence for the importance of situational factors is the finding that the longer a child was exposed to peers in the experimental situation, the more the child tended to agree to an equal distribution. It appears that getting along with peers became a primary objective.

In summary, to predict behavior accurately "we must consider how children at different developmental levels organize both the general and specific aspects of their moral knowledge, as well as how moral knowledge itself interacts with other types of social knowledge as the child reasons and acts in a particular social context" (Damon, 1977, p. 44). Three factors seem to be particularly important in understanding the relationship between moral reasoning and behavior: "habitual" moral reactions (Gerson & Damon, 1978), the peer group, and developmental patterns. As a result of facing small moral decisions every day, each person learns to handle the decisions in a relatively automatic way. Sometimes these "habitual" choices may be made at a lower level of reasoning than one might use if the decision were considered in more detail. Probably of much more importance, however, is the group with which the child or adolescent is affiliated. It is likely that when the impact of the peer group is particularly strong — as in early adolescence — the effect on moral actions is also strong. Youngsters at this age are especially susceptible to group decisions to sneak a beer into a party, to go joyriding, or to soap a teacher's car windows on Halloween (Berndt, 1979). However, all children are not equally vulnerable to group pressure (Kohlberg, 1969), and we do not completely understand the factors that lead children, as well as ourselves, to behave in ways that are less thoughtful, considerate, or fair than we "know how" to do.

Training in Moral Reasoning

Three basic conditions appear to be involved in movement across moral reasoning stages and, thus, have implications for training in moral reasoning (Kohlberg, 1975). First, the child or adolescent must feel some conflict or indecision about the "right" or moral action. Second, the child or adolescent must be exposed to moral reasoning that is slightly more advanced than the present level of reasoning. And, third, the child or adolescent must be given the opportunity to air his or her conflicts in open dialogue with others.

Two important studies illustrate the application of these conditions to influencing moral reasoning. In a role-play format, Turiel (1966) presented 12- to 13-year-old subjects with moral arguments either one stage lower, one stage higher, or two stages higher than their own. Turiel found that subjects who were exposed to arguments one stage higher than their own changed in that direction. In another study, Selman and Lieberman (1975) developed a combined circumstance and discussion program. They presented a series of moral dilemmas involving a conflict between two or more values understood by primary school children (e.g., truth telling, sharing, taking turns, promise keeping, property rights, and rules). Following the presentation of the dilemmas, open-ended discussions were held in which different viewpoints were expressed concerning the resolution of the dilemmas. The group leaders made sure that a range of reasoning levels was included. It is important to present reasoning below, at, and slightly above the level of most children to stimulate them to advance their reasoning level. Selman and Lieberman (1975) found that their intervention program led to more sophisticated levels of moral reasoning, but, unfortunately, no data were presented on actual behavioral changes in moral conduct. The authors speculated that the advances in moral development may have been partially due to the fact that several teachers continued to use the methods of small-group discussion throughout the year to resolve interpersonal and moral conflicts that arose in the classroom. Together the two studies suggest a tendency for children to move upward in their moral reasoning, rather than downward, when they are confronted with models in both directions.

Various studies have focused on helping parents provide a family atmosphere in which there are role-taking opportunities to facilitate the development of moral reasoning. As discussed by Selman (1976a), an "inductive environment" should advance role-taking opportunities and thus promote the development of moral reasoning. In such an environment the *reason* or the "why" a particular behavior is "bad" or "good" is explained to the individual, and the motives, feelings, and consequences of actions are discussed. Bunzl, Coder, and Wirt (1977) and Stanley (1978) found that in parent education groups that focused on how to develop "inductive" home environments, participants were able to advance their children's moral reasoning. Again, however, the clinical utility of these findings cannot be determined, as there were no measures of the children's conduct. Nevertheless, it appears useful to encourage the use of "inductive discipline," as it seems not only to work better than physical punishment or withdrawal of love but also to foster resistance to temptation and to increase helpfulness and compassion.

Interpersonal Problem Solving

Definition and Assessment

Interpersonal problem solving is defined as a series of interpersonal skills that emerge at different ages depending upon task characteristics rather than as a unitary trait and that overlap with social cognition—that is, cognitions about others and what they do and why. Spivack and Shure and their colleagues (Spivack & Shure, 1974; Spivack et al., 1976; Shure & Spivack, 1978) suggest that it is crucial to understand the way a child or adolescent thinks about and works through interpersonal problems. Alternative thinking, consequential thinking, means–end thinking, and causal thinking are the four major interpersonal skills involved in problem solving. Underlying these interpersonal skills are the social cognitive skills of existence, need, and inference.

First, *alternative thinking* is assessed with young children (ages 4–5) by presenting a series of stories depicting two types of age-relevant problem situations and then eliciting an alternative solution for as many stories as possible. Because young children lose interest or are unable to respond with more than one idea to the same question, a series of brief stories serves as the stimulus in the assessment of alternative thinking. Reflecting the fact that the assessment of alternative thinking is tailored to children's developmental level, middle children (ages 9–12) are presented with more sophisticated stories and are required to give as many alternative solutions as possible to each problem.

Second, *consequential thinking* is assessed by presenting young children with solutions to problems (different problems than those used to assess alternative thinking) and asking them to tell what might happen next in the situation. With middle children, consequential thinking entails more than the ability to name alternative consequences; it includes the ability to consider how one's actions may affect other people and oneself. To assess this ability, middle children are asked to complete a story depicting interpersonal problems and to indicate what the hypothetical person is thinking about before deciding what to do. In addition, these children are asked to state what will happen next.

Third, *means–end thinking* is the recognition of the obstacles involved in solving a problem and of the step-by-step process that is necessary to solve it. It is measured with middle and older children (few studies have assessed it with young children) by presenting an interpersonal problem and noting the steps that are enumerated and the obstacles that are noted in solving the problem. Means–end thinking can also be measured by presenting several means and then asking the older child/adolescent to choose the most appropriate one.

Fourth, *causal thinking* is the ability to relate two events to one another over time with regard to the "why" (the cause) that may have precipitated an act. With children of all ages it is measured by presenting two related events and asking the child to determine the connection between the two.

However, before problem solving can take place, it is necessary to recognize the existence of a problem, and when such awareness occurs, there must be an experienced need to act in some way within that situation. The success or quality of the act (execution of need) will depend on the sophistication of the cognitive process (thinking) available to the individual. Thus, interpersonal problem solving will change as the developmental level of cognitive abilities changes—that is, problem solving in particular follows cognitive development in general (Flavell, 1985).

Developmental Changes and Their Relationship to Social Behaviors

Spivack et al. (1976) proposed that interpersonal problem-solving skills are important mediators of social adjustment because they help to provide generalized strategies for coping with the difficulties encountered in everyday life. Because these skills are measured with different instruments at different ages, however, it is difficult to compare performance according to levels of development. Several age-related differences can be noted in causal thinking, which is assessed similarly at different ages.

As measured by parental, teacher, and other adjustment ratings, the significance of interpersonal problem-solving skills in mediating social adjustment varies as a function of development level. According to Spivack and his colleagues, the most important skill for young children is the ability to generate alternative solutions (regardless of their content), followed by the ability to generate alternative consequences. In the middle childhood years the ability to generate alternative solutions and to engage in means-ends thinking are also important correlates of social adjustment. Causal thinking and consequential thinking do not appear to be important mediators of adjustment at this age. During adolescence, means–end thinking is the most important skill affecting social adjustment. The generation of alternative solutions and consequential thinking are also important correlates of social adjustment for adolescents. The findings of Spivack's research make it clear that developmental level is an important factor to consider when examining the relationship between interpersonal problem-solving skills and social adjustment.

Training in Interpersonal Problem Solving

The results of training studies — especially with young children — support the view that interpersonal problem-solving skills are important correlates of social adjustment. Spivack and Shure (1974) found that the training of alternative thinking led to improvements in young children's social adjustment as measured by teacher ratings. Consequential thinking also improved through training programs for both 4- and 5-year-olds, but the program was more successful for 5-year-olds (Spivack et al., 1976). Spivack and his colleagues found that their interpersonal problem-solving training program focusing on both alternative and consequential thinking led to improved social adjustment even at a one-year follow-up. It is possible that critical developmental differences exist between the ages of 4 and 5 years. Shantz (1983) suggested that there is a developmental variation in how young children perceive what others perceive. At Level I, children (usually under age 4) assume that others see things in the same way that they do. At Level II, children begin to be aware that others may see things differently from themselves. This change in awareness has important implications for social cognition in that the child moves from surface observation of others' perspectives to a more in-depth recognition of how others' views may differ given similar stimulus material.

Other interpersonal problem-solving training studies have focused on middle children. Allen, Chinsky, Larcen, Lochman, and Selinger (1976) found that their training program did not lead to maintained gains in interpersonal problem solving or in the children's conduct. As discussed earlier, "Project Aware" (Elarado & Caldwell, 1979; Elarado & Cooper,

1978) included training in interpersonal problem solving as well as in role taking. On the basis of "nonblind" teacher ratings, middle children's behavior improved following training. A study by Gesten, deApodace, Rains, Weissberg, and Cowen (1979) provided further preliminary support for the efficacy of interpersonal problem-solving training with middle children, and a long-term follow-up on the children's behavioral adjustment supported the finding that the training program led to improved problem solving. Asher and Renshaw (1981) used social skills training to improve popularity of unpopular children, with gains in popularity still evident one year later.

Training techniques vary with age and reflect clinical sensitivity to developmental differences. With young children, training may best take place in a play (Rosen, 1974) or game (Spivack & Shure, 1974) format. At first the young child learns relevant language skills and the identification and labeling of emotions. Then the focus is placed on having the child generate as many alternative solutions as possible when problem situations are presented. The emphasis is on the number of solutions that are generated rather than on the appropriateness or rightness of a solution. Although alternative thinking is considered most important, there is emphasis on consequential thinking as well. With older children and adolescents, role-playing and discussion formats replace the game format. Some attention is given to the generation of alternatives; however, special emphasis is placed on means-end, consequential, and causal thinking. At all ages it is important to present situations relevant to the child's or adolescent's life (Spivack & Shure, 1974).

In their studies with parents, Shure and Spivack (1978) found significant parental correlates of interpersonal problem-solving skills. Effective parents model and reinforce the various steps. They elicit thinking processes (e.g., "Tell me what happened. How else could you have done that?"). Effective parents also ask about the sources of actions and the perspectives of others. The parents' questions are tailored to the level of the child's or adolescent's comprehension. In addition to their training manual for teachers, Shure and Spivack (1978) have written a parents' manual that can also be useful to therapists.

Verbal Self-Regulation

Definition and Assessment

Verbal self-regulation consists of the ability to talk to oneself in a relevant manner when confronted with a problem to be solved. It has been suggested that when children or adolescents learn to employ language in a self-regulating fashion, they are better able to inhibit first available responses to a stimulus, and they are better able to maintain attention to a task (Camp, 1977).

Verbal self-regulation has been assessed in two basic ways. One strategy is to observe performance on a nonverbal task, noting the use of appropriate private speech. For example, Camp (1977) recorded spontaneous verbalizations on nonverbal intelligence tests. The verbalizations were rated as (a) guiding behavior, (b) making irrelevant comments to the experimenter, or (c) commenting about success or failure. A further example of this strategy is Meichenbaum's (1971) recording of young children's private speech in play situations. A second assessment strategy is to provide the child or adolescent with verbal self-regulatory plans and to assess the effects of the plans on behavior (Patterson & Mischell, 1975, 1976).

Developmental Trends

Clear developmental differences exist in verbal self-regulation. Luria (cited by Meichenbaum & Goodman, 1971) proposed three stages in which the inhibition of voluntary motor behavior comes under verbal control. During the first stage ("other-external") the speech of others—usually adults—controls and directs behavior. The second stage ("self-external") is characterized by the self-regulation of behavior through overt speech. In the final stage ("self-internal"), covert or inner speech assumes a self-governing role. Luria also proposed age-related changes in the form of self-regulation. For children younger than age 3, any combination of motor and verbal responding is difficult and is of no regulatory value. With 3- to 4-year-old children, a clear regulation of motor reactions is attained when a verbal accompaniment corresponds rhythmically to the motor task—regardless of the meaning of the word employed. For older children the meaning of the verbal accompaniment begins to predominate over its rhythmic aspect. Although these results have not always been replicated (e.g., Flavell, 1977), Rondal (1976) supported Luria's basic findings regarding regulation by the rhythmic aspects of speech. However, results did not confirm predictions derived from the portion of Luria's hypotheses that related to the regulatory function of speech in its meaningful aspect.

Researchers have found age-related changes in the use of speech and other rehearsal strategies to regulate a child's behavior, attention, and retention. The young child spontaneously produces and utilizes fewer relevant verbal mediators (Meichenbaum & Goodman, 1971). Although recall of tasks improves when children are instructed to rehearse material, only older children (i.e., 9 to 10 or older) typically rehearse spontaneously when asked to remember something over a brief delay (Flavell, Beach, & Chinsky, 1966; Keeney, Cannizzo, & Flavell, 1967).

Relationships to Social Adjustment

It is likely that verbal mediations are used to inhibit first available responses to a stimulus and that this ability is lacking in impulsive children and adolescents. Meichenbaum and Goodman (1971) reported that reflective preschoolers used their private speech in a more instrumental self-guiding fashion than did impulsive children. A study by Camp (1977) indicated that aggressive boys use verbal self-regulation less appropriately than do nonaggressive boys.

Training in Verbal Self-Regulation

Verbal mediation or self-instructional training for impulsivity is discussed in Chapter 7, and a considerable body of literature points to the potential therapeutic effectiveness of these procedures. Meichenbaum and Goodman (1971) and Douglas, Parry, Marton, and Garson (1976) found that self-instructional training with hyperactive children led to improvements on cognitive measures of success but did not lead to improved classroom behavior. A program by Bornstein and Quevillon (1976) produced dramatic decreases in the disruptive behaviors of overactive preschoolers, but these results have not been replicated with school-age children (Friedling & O'Leary, 1979; Varni & Henker, 1979). Kendall and Finch (1976, 1978) found that a self-instructional program led to improved behavior in overactive emotionally disturbed children. The training program conducted by Camp, Blom, Herbert, and van Doornick (1977) led to improvement in the prosocial behavior of second-grade aggressive boys but not to a decrease in their aggressive behaviors. Through training in verbal self-regulation, Siegel and Peterson (1981) decreased dental anxiety in children, and Spivak and Shure (1982) taught interpersonal problem-solving skills to young children. Overall, the results of these findings are variable yet encouraging.

Other studies are worthy of special attention because of their developmental implications. Bugental, Whalen, and Henker (1977) compared the relative effectiveness of self-instructional training and social reinforcement procedures. Supporting an interactionist position, their findings demonstrated that children with high perceived personal causality (self-efficacy, Bandura, 1989) responded best to self-instructional training, whereas children with low perceived sense of personal causality responded better to social reinforcement. Self-efficacy is seen as the foundation of arousal, thinking patterns, motivation, affect, and action (Bandura, 1989). Snyder and White (1979) implemented self-instructional training with adolescent delinquents and found that there were improvements in behavior compared to individuals who received the standard reinforcement program. This training program was similar to the anger-control training package described in Chapter 5.

For older children, self-instructional procedures have become more effective and sophisticated (see Kendall & Braswell, 1985). For example, Kendall and Wilcox (1980) compared the effectiveness of concrete labeling versus conceptual labeling in self-instructional training. Concrete labeling focused on the specific task at hand (e.g., "I have to find a picture that doesn't match this one."), while conceptual labeling focused on the task at hand as well as on a general strategy (e.g., "My first step is to make sure I know what I am supposed to do. Well, I should look at all the possibilities."). It was hypothesized that conceptual labeling would promote enhanced generalization because it focused on a general strategy. With 8- to 12-year-old children exhibiting behavior problems in school, Kendall and Wilcox (1980) found that the conceptual labeling group maintained posttreatment gains, while the concrete labeling group did not. It would be interesting to test this hypothesis with younger children, who may need a greater degree of concreteness than older children who can comprehend abstract plans more readily. Future researchers also need to examine age differences and the effects of situational factors such as task characteristics. The reader is referred to Kendall and Braswell (1985), who thoroughly outline cognitive-behavioral impulsivity training for treatment of children with behavioral, emotional, and academic problems.

Summary

It is apparent that developmentally based variables of role taking, moral reasoning, interpersonal problem solving, and verbal self-mediation are important correlates of social adjustment. Through the development of skills in these areas, a child or adolescent may learn how to be more effective in a wide variety of social and interpersonal situations. Therefore, treatment programs designed to develop these skills may prove to be very useful clinically. In light of some "conflicting" and "inconsistent" findings, it is necessary to examine critically the effectiveness of such programs before recommending or advocating large-scale intervention programs in educational or psychological settings. As emphasized throughout this review, it is crucial for clinician and researcher alike to examine and promote these skills in the context of a wide variety of situations and to pay close attention to motivational factors that influence behaviors. To illustrate the potential clinical usefulness of this interactional approach, we will describe an intervention plan for disruptive children of different ages. As suggested by the literature review, the plan emphasizes the importance of both cognitive skill development and situational factors.

An Example of a Developmentally Based Intervention Plan

Assessment

As recent attention to cognition in clinical treatment has developed as a result of cognitive-behavioral procedures, so has the need to assess cognitive changes in a reliable and valid manner. Thus, it is possible to assess the potential role of cognitive change in mediating or contributing to behavioral change. As in other areas, most research has been conducted with adult populations (see Merluzzi, Glass, & Genest, 1981). Although many techniques have been designed primarily for adults, it is possible to adapt these for use with children and adolescents. Chapter 4 addresses cognitive-behavioral assessment techniques with children in detail and reviews the specific attempts that have been made to tap into the cognitive domain of children. Before embarking on a treatment plan, it is essential to assess the level of inappropriate and appropriate behaviors and to keep in mind the skill levels on specific developmental variables. Furthermore, it is essential to assess developmental factors in the particular situations identified as problematic. When possible, it is important to include observational measures of the behavior as well as teacher and/or parent ratings. While observing the child or adolescent, it is critical to note the type of situations in which difficulties are experienced and the environmental contingencies that influence behavior.

Also, it is important to identify the specific environmental antecedents and/or consequences that often have a dramatic influence on behavior (Bandura, 1977, 1989). For instance, the child or adolescent may gain little peer or teacher attention through appropriate behavior but may achieve notoriety through negative behavior. Likewise, cognitive assessment of potential success or failure in anticipated social environments may lead to deselection of those environments (Bandura, 1989). Possible treatment options can be identified through assessing the motivational factors that influence the child's or adolescent's behavior.

When assessing cognitive skill levels it is crucial to try to see situations and problems through the eyes of the child or adolescent. Knowledge of viewpoints helps the clinician understand how the child or adolescent looks at the world and may help make it possible to avoid expectations of abilities that have not yet developed. This approach emphasizes assessing cognitive skill levels in a wide variety of situations (Selman, 1976a).

In light of the various developmentally based variables (some of which have been addressed in this chapter), it is often difficult to know what to assess and when to assess it. A "shotgun" approach would involve a routine assessment of these variables with all deviant children or adolescents. However, a battery of tests demonstrates only that a child or adolescent is performing differently from normal counterparts on a particular task. The deficient performance can arise from a variety of different reasons; therefore, the shotgun approach provides little useful information about the subprocesses contributing to the deficient performance (Meichenbaum, 1976).

A cognitive-functional approach is proposed as a more efficient and effective alternative to the shotgun approach. The purpose of cognitive-functional assessment is to determine which abilities, under what circumstances, contribute to or interfere with adequate conduct. To this end the clinician examines the cognitive skills that are needed for success in typical problem situations. In addition, it is necessary to pinpoint the environmental antecedents and consequences related to performance. The child or adolescent might utilize certain cognitive skills in some situations on some tasks but then abandon these skills in other situations or tasks. Diagnostically, it is very useful to alter motivational and other situational factors to determine their impact on the utilization of cognitive skills. It is also important to obtain data from several sources. The spontaneous use of certain strategies, the description of the use of these strategies, and the effects of teaching these strategies to the child or adolescent are all useful sources of data (Meichenbaum, 1976).

The format of the assessment will depend upon age. To assess the young child's cognitive skills, situations that create difficulties for the child may be acted out in a game and/or puppet format. The clinician may assess role taking in a specific situation by asking the child to play different parts in a puppet play in order to discover the circumstances in which the child does or does not take the role of the other. In this way the clinician can partially determine if the perspective-taking skills are important determinants of the child's maladaptive behavior. Similarly, to assess the child's interpersonal problem-solving skills—particularly the ability to generate alternatives—the therapist may ask the child to think of different solutions to a wide variety of problem situations. In an effort to gain the child's participation and compliance, the clinician may model or "think out loud" some examples of the strategies that are of interest. The clinician should systemically alter environmental factors, such as the motivation present in the situation, the length of time the child has to respond, and the effects of success and failure. For example, it may be that the child's cognitive skill level is different after a success experience rather than after a failure experience, and the skill level may be influenced by the degree to which peer acceptance is important. These situational and cognitive skill factors need to be assessed in an interactional fashion.

Ravenette (1975, 1977) developed an interesting technique for eliciting important cognitive strategies/variables with preadolescent children. Although he described several assessment techniques (see Ravenette, 1980), one of the most interesting is the "Troubles with School" strategy, which requires the preadolescent to choose three from a selection of eight drawings pertaining to situations in school. While each drawing is loosely detailed, it is well structured thematically. Each selected situation serves as the focus of a detailed, semistructured inquiry during which the following six questions are posed:

1. What do you think is happening?
2. Who do you think is troubled or upset and why?

3. How do you think this came about?
4. If that child were you, what would you think/feel/do? What difference would that make to anyone? As a result of this, would you feel good or bad and why?
5. If the child were not you, what sort of boy/girl would you say he/she was?

In this way the clinician can discover how a preadolescent makes sense of problematic situations and can determine the degree of awareness concerning his/her own thoughts, feelings, and actions, as well as their perceived degree of impact on others.

The assessment of older children also must be tailored to meet their individual needs. For adolescents a discussion or role-play format may replace a game format. Adolescents may be more insightful and better able to relate their cognitive strategies directly. In role-play situations they should be encouraged to "think out loud" and to explain the cognitive strategies that are being used (see Genest & Turk, 1981, for more information). Also, they should be encouraged to play alternative roles in a variety of situations. Again, the situational factors need to be altered systematically to examine their effects on cognitive skills.

Nelson and Cholera (1986) developed a projective-cognitive technique to assess problem-solving strategies, coping repertoire, and self-instructional styles of adolescents undergoing various dental procedures. In this format, adolescents were shown five TAT-like cards depicting a child's visit to the dentist and were asked specific questions addressing thinking processes, feelings, and actions. Responses were utilized to tap into important cognitive factors.

Although this discussion provides only a brief outline of assessment examples using a cognitive-functional approach (Meichenbaum, 1976), some tentative guidelines have been established. The clinician needs to sample directly relevant problem situations and to identify the behavioral and cognitive skills that contribute to problematic behavior.

Implementation

Following a cognitive-functional assessment the cognitive-behavioral approach attempts to implement a systematic program involving a combination of environmental contingencies and cognitive skills training. The remainder of this chapter will describe potential intervention strategies from a cognitive-behavioral viewpoint. Two hypothetical children will be used to illustrate these strategies—a 4-year-old boy and a 9-year-old boy, both of whom exhibit disruptive, acting-out conduct problems such as destroying property, fighting with peers, and an inability to maintain attention to school tasks. It is recommended that the described cognitive skill intervention procedures be incorporated within the context of an environmental contingency program using positive reinforcement and punishment techniques. Although the primary focus of this discussion is on cognitive skills training, we also emphasize environmental contingencies (O'Leary & O'Leary, 1976) and self-control procedures such as self-observation and self-reinforcement (Drabman, Spitalnik, & O'Leary, 1973; Meichenbaum, 1979).

Punishment

Although the "pros and cons" of punishment will not be discussed here, the fact remains that punishment procedures are frequently employed by adults in their management of children's behavior. Typically, in disciplining children, punishment consists of loss of privileges, time out, loss of points, or loss of attention. When employing mild aversive techniques, it is important for the adult to be cognizant of cognitive-developmental variables. Our information concerning moral reasoning highlights the importance of providing reasons for the punishment, and this reasoning should be based on developmental level. For instance, with the 4-year-old who is discovered carelessly handling an object, the use of object-oriented appeals ("The toy is fragile and might break") may be effective. This emphasis on the immediate physical consequences of an action is similar to the types of justificatory rationales that young children use on tests of moral judgment. With the older child in the same situation, the use of a property rule rationale ("The toy belongs to another child") stresses the ethical norms of ownership and may be more effective. The property rule is more abstract, assumes that the child understands the rights of other children, and represents a more sophisticated moral judgment level (Parke, 1974). With older children it might also be important to use rationales that include the long-term rather than just the immediate consequences of an action ("If you break that toy, the cost will come out of your next allowance"). The use of justificatory rationales may help to promote advances in the evaluation of social acts, help to create understanding of the validity of the punishment, and help to generalize more appropriate behavior to future situations.

When using punishment it is also important to help the child attend to the perspectives of other children. Consider the example of the hypothetical 4-year-old fighting with a smaller child. With this young child, whose role taking is very limited, the teacher/parent may need to model perspective taking at a very low level ("Your doing that makes him feel bad"). Verbal labeling might promote and enhance retention of these skills (e.g., the child could draw a picture of how the other child feels and then label it). Also, as the young child may be able to focus on only one aspect of the sequence

("But Johnny hit me first!"), the teacher/parent should make other situational cues salient. For instance, if the child has instigated a fighting incident by calling the other child a name or if the other child unintentionally struck the first blow, the focus should be switched to the behaviors leading up to the aggression. The young child still may be unable to coordinate multidimensional cues, but by focusing on different cues than usual, it may be possible to develop a better understanding of the effects of one's actions on others.

For the older child with a repertoire of elementary role-taking skills, the focus needs to be on eliciting and further advancing available skills. Following the 9-year-old's involvement in a fighting incident, the teacher/parent should encourage role taking by asking questions such as "How did Johnny feel when you did that?" or "Now, how would you feel if you were in his shoes?" The teacher/parent should model role-taking skills that are slightly more advanced than those of the child. For example, with the child who is just beginning to coordinate perspectives, the teacher/parent may focus on how the child's behavior affects long-term trust and friendship with others. In contrast with a younger child, the 9-year-old may have begun to perceive that consistent actions by each person over time are necessary for the establishment of mutual relationships (Selman, 1976a). Because the older child may be able to attend to multidimensional cues, it is important to relate the entire fighting incident, noting the relationship between intention and consequence cues. Although the focus on role taking may help generalize behavior to future situations, contingencies (e.g., loss of privileges or points) may also need to be in effect to discourage fighting.

In addition, after a fighting incident, positive practice procedures may be included. In this type of procedure, inappropriate behavior may be punished, but, more importantly, the child or adolescent is subsequently required to practice correct behavior (Azrin & Powers, 1975). Moreover, it is important to include reinforcement for the prosocial alternative way of behaving and thinking (Perry & Parke, 1975). In addition to positively practicing the correct overt behavior, the child or adolescent should be encouraged to practice appropriate cognitive skills and should be contingently reinforced for such behavior. The child or adolescent may be encouraged to utilize appropriate interpersonal problem-solving skills before choosing an appropriate behavior. For the 4-year-old, positive practice may take the form of games of sociodramatic play, as described by Rosen (1974). Also, exercises described by Spivack and Shure (1974) may be used. For instance, a teacher/parent may recreate the fighting incident in a puppet play situation. Initially the teacher/parent may act as a "cognitive model" and verbalize interpersonal problem-solving skills. With the 4-year-old the primary focus should be on the generation of alternatives and consequences. The trainer should encourage the child by asking questions such as "What else could you do?" or "What might happen next?" It is helpful to create a variety of situations related to the general problem area, and the child should be encouraged to generate alternatives and consequences in each of them.

For the older child, following the fighting incident, positive practice may take the form of role playing or of verbal mediation essays (MacPherson, Candes, & Hohman, 1974). The fighting situation and other related incidents are recreated, and the older child is encouraged to generate alternative behaviors and to recognize the consequences of actions taken. When attempting to foster problem solving, it is important to focus also on the development of means–end thinking. The older child should be encouraged to develop specific plans for overcoming the obstacles involved in an interpersonal problem situation and to enumerate the steps necessary to solve the problem.

When the young child demonstrates an inability to attend to school tasks, positive practice in the form of self-instructional training may be appropriate. At first the teacher/parent may model the task while thinking aloud. Self-instructions may take the form of four verbalizations: (a) questions about the task ("What does the teacher/parent want me to do?"); (b) answers to the question in the form of cognitive rehearsal ("Oh, that's right, I'm supposed to copy the picture."); (c) self-instructions that guide the child through the task ("OK, first I draw a line here . . ."); and (d) self-reinforcement ("That's the way to go!") (Bornstein & Quevillon, 1976). The focus should be on helping the child maintain attention to one aspect of the problem at a time.

With the older child who often does not pay attention to school tasks, self-instructional training is similar to the previous format, but the complexity of the self-instructions is increased. For example, the self-instructions may take the form of attending to multidimensional cues and to sequences of events.

Positive Reinforcement

It is important to note that the main focus of any intervention strategy should never be solely aversive or punitive. On the contrary, the main focus should be on positive reinforcement of appropriate behavior, supplemented by the use of appropriate cognitive strategies. For example, when the teacher recognizes that a child or adolescent is "thinking before acting," the teacher should reinforce both the behavior and the use of cognitive skills. Similarly, when the child or adolescent appears to be engaged in role taking, the teacher/parent should both label the cognitive strategy and reinforce its use. In addition, specification of adaptive reasoning should be included when reinforcing appropriate behaviors. The reasoning process that is highlighted by the teacher/parent needs to be based on the child's or adolescent's developmental level. For instance, with a young child the reasons should be concrete, immediate, and object-oriented (e.g., "When you didn't hit him and asked him to give you the ball back, you can see he didn't hit you and gave the ball back to you. That's great!"). With the older child the reasons can be more abstract (e.g., "It's important to build trust in a relationship, and it's great that you are trying to do so."). The purpose of focusing on long-term consequences is to provide reasons for developing competencies and to help focus on naturally sustaining reinforcements.

Teacher/Parent Modeling of Appropriate Strategies

Even when specific behaviors are not being intentionally reinforced or punished, the teacher/parent can act as an appropriate model for the child or adolescent. The teacher/parent may model flexible interpersonal problem-solving strategies and should explain reasons for behavior at understandable levels. Perspective-taking skills might also be modeled (e.g., "I know you do not enjoy this and that doing it makes you unhappy, but I feel that doing it will help you make friends."). When the teacher/parent is confronted with an interpersonal problem affecting the child or adolescent, appropriate problem-solving skills should be explicitly modeled and labeled, and contributions from the child or adolescent should be encouraged and valued.

There are a wide variety of potentially troublesome situations in which the use of these skills may prevent difficulties. In these situations the adult can help promote developmentally appropriate cognitive skills. Samples of such situations include: when a child or adolescent seems bored or unhappy (e.g., "What else could you do now to make things better?"); when requests are being made of the parent/teacher, but the parent/teacher is too busy (e.g., "I am too busy now. What else could you do until I have time to be with you?"); when a teacher/parent anticipates that a conflict or fight will occur between two children over a toy (e.g., "Now, what can you do besides fighting to get the toy?"); when a child is left out by other children (e.g, "What can you do to get the others to play with you?"). A sensitive and skilled adult may be able to prevent problems from occurring and to foster age-related cognitive skills by anticipating troublesome situations and by talking appropriately to the child or adolescent at those times.

Conclusions

This chapter represents an attempt to illustrate how cognitive-behavioral programs can be tailored to developmental levels. In conjunction with operant procedures, the utilization of these techniques can promote generalization and maintenance of behavioral gains. Throughout this chapter, emphasis has been placed on considering how children and adolescents organize social knowledge, as well as how social knowledge itself is affected by a wide variety of situational factors. Identifying and promoting the development of cognitive skills may lead to therapeutic gains in children's behavior.

References

Achenbach, T. M., & Edelbrock, C. S. (1981). Behavioral problems and competence reported by parents of normal and disturbed children age 4 through 16. *Monographs of the Society for Research in Child Development, 46.*

Allen, G., Chinsky, J., Larcen, S., Lochman, J., & Selinger, H. (1976). *Community psychology and the schools.* Hillsdale, NJ: Erlbaum.

Asher, S. R., & Renshaw, P. D. (1981). Children without friends: Social knowledge and social skills training. In S. R. Asher & T. M. Gottman (Eds.), *The development of children's friendships.* New York: Cambridge University Press.

Azrin, N., & Powers, M. (1975). Eliminating classroom disturbances of emotionally disturbed children by positive practice procedures. *Behavior Therapy, 6,* 525–534.

Bandura, A. (1977). *Social learning theory.* Englewood Cliffs, NJ: Prentice-Hall.

Bandura, A. (1986). *Social foundations of thought and action: A social cognitive theory.* Englewood Cliffs, NJ: Prentice-Hall.

Bandura, A. (1989). Human agency in social cognitive theory. *American Psychologist, 44,* 1175–1184.

Belmont, T. M. (1989). Cognitive strategies and strategic learning. *American Psychologist, 44,* 144–148.

Berndt, T. J. (1979). Developmental changes in conformity to peers and parents. *Developmental Psychology, 15,* 608–616.

Bornstein, P., & Quevillon, R. (1976). The effects of a self-instructional package with overactive pre-schoolers. *Journal of Applied Behavior Analysis, 9,* 179–188.

Buckley, N., Siegel, L., & Ness, S. (1979). Egocentrism, empathy, and altruistic behavior in young children. *Developmental Psychology, 15,* 329–336.

Bugental, D., Whalen, C., & Henker, B. (1977). Causal attribution of hyperactive children and motivational assumptions of two behavior change approaches: Evidence for an interactionist position. *Child Development, 48,* 874–884.

Bunzl, M., Coder, R., & Wirt, R. (1977). Enhancement of maturity of moral judgments by parent education. *Journal of Abnormal Child Psychology, 5,* 177–186.

Burka, A., & Glenwick, D. (1978). Egocentrism and classroom adjustment. *Journal of Abnormal Child Psychology, 6,* 61–70.

Camp, B. (1977). Verbal mediation in young aggressive boys. *Journal of Abnormal Psychology, 86,* 145–153.

Camp, B., Blom, G., Herbert, F., & van Doornick, W. (1977). "Think Aloud": A program for developing self-control in young aggressive boys. *Journal of Abnormal Child Psychology, 5,* 157–169.

Chandler, M. (1973). Egocentrism and antisocial behavior: The assessment and training of social perspective-taking skills. *Developmental Psychology, 9,* 326–332.

Chandler, M. (1976). Social cognition and life span approaches to the study of child development. In H. Reese (Ed.), *Advances in child development and behavior* (Vol. 11). New York: Academic Press.

Chandler, M., & Boyes, M. (1982). Social-cognitive development. In B. Wolman (Ed.), *Handbook of developmental psychology.* New York: Wiley.

Chandler, M., Greenspan, S., & Barenboim, C. (1973). Judgments of intentionality in response to videotaped and verbally presented moral dilemmas: The medium is the message. *Child Development, 44,* 315–320.

Coates, B., & Hartup, W. (1969). Age and verbalization in observational learning. *Developmental Psychology, 1,* 556–562.

Collins, W. (1973). Effects of temporal separation between motivation, aggression, and consequences: A developmental study. *Developmental Psychology, 8,* 215–221.

Collins, W.A. (1983). Interpretation and inference in children's television viewing. In J. Bryant & D.R. Anderson (Eds.), *Children's understanding of television: Research on attention and comprehension.* New York: Academic Press.

Collins, W. (1975). The developing child as viewer. *Journal of Communications, 25,* 35–44.

Collins, W., Berndt, T., & Hess, V. (1973). *Social influences about motives and consequences for televised aggression: A developmental study.* Paper presented at meeting for the Society for Research in Child Development, Philadelphia.

Collins, W. A., Wellman, H., Keniston, A.H., & Westby, S. D. (1978). Age-related aspects of comprehension and inference from a televised dramatic narrative. *Child Development, 49,* 389–399.

Cooney, E. (1977). Social cognitive development: Application to intervention and evaluation in the elementary grades. *The Counseling Psychologist, 6,* 6–9.

Csikszentmihalyi, M., & Larson, R. (1984). *Being adolescent: Conflict and growth in the teenage years.* New York: Basic Books.

Damon, W. (1977). *The social world of the child.* San Francisco: Jossey-Bass.

Denney, D. (1975). The effects of exemplary and cognitive models and self-rehearsal on children's interrogative strategies. *Journal of Experimental Child Psychology, 19,* 476–488.

Deutsch, F. (1974). Observational and sociometric measures of peer popularity and their relationship to egocentric communication in female pre-schoolers. *Developmental Psychology, 10,* 745–747.

Douglas, V., Parry, P., Marton, P., & Garson, C. (1976). Assessment of cognitive training program for hyperactive children. *Journal of Abnormal Child Psychology, 4,* 389–410.

Drabman, R., Spitalnik, R., & O'Leary, L. (1973). Teaching self-control to disruptive children. *Journal of Abnormal Psychology, 82,* 10–16.

Dweck, C. S. (1975). The role of expectations and attributions in the alleviation of learned helplessness. *Journal of Personality and Social Psychology, 31,* 674–685.

Dweck, C. S. (1986). Motivational processes affecting learning. *American Psychologist, 41,* 1040–1048.

Eisenberg-Berg, N., & Neal C. Children's moral reasoning about their own spontaneous prosocial behavior. *Developmental Psychology,* 1979, *15,* 228–229.

Elarado, P., & Caldwell, B. (1979). The effects of an experimental social development program on children in the middle childhood period. *Psychology in the Schools, 16,* 93–100.

Elarado, P., Caldwell, B., & Webb, R. (1976). *An examination of the relationship between role taking and social competence.* Revision of a paper presented at the Southeastern Conference on Human Development, Nashville, TN.

Elarado, P., & Cooper, M. (1978). Project Aware: A developmental approach to humanistic education. *Elementary School Guidance and Counseling,* December, 112–122.

Emler, N., & Rushton, J. (1974). Cognitive developmental factors in children's generosity. *British Journal of Social and Clinical Psychology, 13,* 277–281.

Enright, R., Colby, S., & McMullen, I. (1977). A social cognitive developmental intervention with sixth and fourth graders. *The Counseling Psychologist, 6,* 10–12.

Flavell, J. H. (1977). *Cognitive development.* Englewood Cliffs, NJ: Prentice-Hall.

Flavell, J. H. (1985). *Cognitive development* (2nd ed.). Englewood Cliffs, NJ: Prentice-Hall.

Flavell, J. H., Beach, D. R., & Chinsky, J. M. (1966). Spontaneous verbal rehearsal in a memory task as a function of age. *Child Development, 37,* 283–299.

Fodor, E. (1972). Delinquency and susceptibility to social influence among adolescents as a function of moral development. *Journal of Social Psychology, 86,* 257–266.

Ford, M. E. (1982). Social cognition and social competence in adolescence. *Developmental Psychology, 18,* 323–340.

Fowler, J. W., & Peterson, P. L. (1981). Increasing reading persistence and altering attributional style of learned helpless children. *Journal of Educational Psychology, 73,* 251–260.

Friedling, C., & O'Leary, S. (1979). Effects of self-instructional training in second and third grade children: A failure to replicate. *Journal of Applied Behavior Analysis, 12,* 211–220.

Genest, M., & Turk, D. C. (1981). Think aloud approaches to cognitive assessment. In T. V. Merluzzi, C. R. Glass, & M. Genest (Eds.), *Cognitive assessment.* New York: Guilford Press.

Gerson, R., & Damon, W. (1978). Moral understanding and children's conduct. *New Directions for Child Development, 2,* 41–59.

Gesten, E., deApodace, R., Rains, M., Weissberg, R., & Cowen, E. (1979). Promoting peer-related social competence in schools. In M. Kent & J. Rolf (Eds.), *Primary prevention of psychopathology* (Vol. 3). Hanover, NH: University Press of New England.

Gilligan, C. In a different voice: Psychological theory and women's development. Cambridge, Mass.: Harvard University Press, 1982.

Gollins, E. S., & Sharp, M. T. (1987). Visual perspective-taking in young children: Reduction of egocentric errors. *Bulletin of the Psychonomic Society, 25,* 435–437.

Gottman, J., Gonso, J., & Rasmussen, B. (1975). Social interaction, social competence, and friendship in children. *Child Development, 46,* 709–718.

Harris, K. R. (1985). Conceptual, methodological, and clinical issues in cognitive-behavioral assessment. *Journal of Abnormal Child Psychology, 13,* 373–380.

Harris, S., Mussen, P., & Rutherford, E. (1976). Some cognitive, behavioral, and personality correlates of maturity of moral judgment. *Journal of Genetic Psychology, 128,* 123–185.

Hoffman, M. L. (1977). Personality and social development. *Annual Review of Psychology, 28,* 259–331.

Holstein, C. (1976). Irreversible, stepwise sequence in the development of moral judgment: A longitudinal study of males and females. *Child Development, 57,* 51–61.

Iannotti, R. (1978). Effects of role taking experiences on role taking, empathy, altruism, and aggression. *Developmental Psychology, 14,* 119–124.

Jennings, K. (1975). People versus object orientation, social behavior, and intellectual abilities in preschool children. *Developmental Psychology, 11,* 511–519.

Jennings, K. D., Fitch, D., & Suwalsky, J. T. (1987). Social cognition and social interaction in three-year-olds: Is social cognition truly social? *Child Study Journal, 17,* 1–14.

Johnson, D. (1975a). Affective perspective taking and cooperative pre-disposition. *Developmental Psychology, 11,* 869–870.

Johnson, D. (1975b). Cooperativeness and social perspective taking. *Journal of Personality and Social Psychology, 31,* 241–244.

Jurkovic, G., & Prentice, N. (1977). Relation of moral and cognitive development to dimensions of juvenile delinquency. *Journal of Abnormal Psychology, 86,* 414–420.

Kazdin, A. E. (1989). Developmental psychopathology: Current research, issues, and directions. *American Psychologist, 44,* 180–187.

Keeney, T. J., Cannizzo, S. R., & Flavell, J. H. (1967). Spontaneous and induced verbal rehearsal in a recall task. *Child Development, 38,* 953–966.

Keller, M. (1976). Development of role taking ability: Social antecedents and consequences for school success. *Human Development, 19,* 120–132.

Kendall, P. C., & Braswell, L. (1985). *Cognitive-behavioral therapy for impulsive children.* New York: Guilford Press.

Kendall, P., & Finch, A. (1976). A cognitive-behavioral treatment for impulse control: A case study. *Journal of Consulting and Clinical Psychology, 44,* 852–857.

Kendall, P., & Finch, A. (1978). A cognitive-behavioral treatment for impulsivity: A group comparison study. *Journal of Consulting and Clinical Psychology, 46,* 110–118.

Kendall, P., & Wilcox, L. (1980). A cognitive-behavioral treatment for impulsivity: Concrete versus conceptual labeling with nonself-controlled problem children. *Journal of Consulting and Clinical Psychology, 48,* 80–91.

Kohlberg, L. (1969). Stage and sequence: The cognitive developmental approach. In D. Goslin (Ed.), *Handbook of socialization theory and research.* Chicago: Rand McNally.

Kohlberg, L. (1975). The cognitive-developmental approach to moral education. *Phi Delta Kappan, 56,* 670–677.

Kohlberg, L. (1976). Moral stages and moralization: The cognitive developmental approach. In T. Lickona (Ed.), *Moral development and behavior.* New York: Holt, Rinehart & Winston.

Kohlberg, L. (1978). Revisions in the theory and practice in moral development. *New Directions for Child Development, 2,* 83–87.

Kuhn, D. (1976). Short term longitudinal evidence for the sequentiality of Kohlberg's early stages of moral judgment. *Developmental Psychology, 12,* 162–166.

Kurdek, L. (1978a). Perspective taking as the cognitive basis of children's moral development: A review of the literature. *Merrill-Palmer Quarterly, 24,* 3–28.

Kurdek, L. (1978b). Relationship between cognitive perspective taking and teacher's ratings of children's classroom behavior in grades one through four. *Journal of Genetic Psychology, 132,* 21–27.

Kurdek, L. (1980). Developmental relations among children's perspective taking, moral judgment, and parent rated behaviors. *Merrill-Palmer Quarterly, 26,* 103–121.

Kurdek, L., & Rodgon, M. (1975). Perceptual, cognitive, and affective perspective taking in kindergarten through sixth grade children. *Developmental Psychology, 11,* 643–650.

Kurtines, W., & Greif, E. (1974). The development of moral thought: Review and evaluation of Kohlberg's approach. *Psychological Bulletin, 81,* 453–470.

LeMare, L. J., & Rubin, K. H. (1987). Perspective taking and peer interaction: Structural and developmental analysis. *Child Development, 58,* 306–315.

Lewin, K. (1951). *Field theory and social science.* New York: Harper & Row.

MacPherson, E., Candes, B., & Hohman, B. (1974). A comparison of three methods for eliminating disruptive lunchroom behavior. *Journal of Applied Behavior Analysis, 7,* 287–297.

MacQuiddy, S. L., Maise, S. J., & Hamilton, S. B. (1987). Empathy and affective perspective-taking skills in parent-identified conduct-disordered boys. *Journal of Clinical Child Psychology, 16,* 260–268.

McCall, R. B., Kennedy, C. B., & Appelbaum, M. I. (1977). Magnitude of discrepancy and the direction of attention in infants. *Child Development, 48,* 772–785.

Mead, H. (1934). *Mind, self and society.* Chicago: University of Chicago Press.

Meichenbaum, D. (1971). *The nature and modification of impulsive children: Training impulsive children to talk to themselves.* Paper presented at the Society for Research on Child Development, Minneapolis, MN.

Meichenbaum, D. (1976). A cognitive behavior modification approach to assessment. In M. Hersen & A. Bellack (Eds.), *Behavioral assessment: A practical approach.* New York: Pergamon Press.

Meichenbaum, D. (1979). Teaching children self-control. In B. Lahey & A. Kazdin (Eds.), *Advances in clinical child psychology* (Vol. 12). New York: Plenum Press.

Meichenbaum, D., & Goodman, J. (1971). Training impulsive children to talk to themselves: A means of developing self-control. *Journal of Abnormal Psychology, 77,* 115–126.

Merluzzi, T. V., Glass, C. R., & Genest, M. (1981). *Cognitive assessment.* New York: Guilford Press.

Mischel, W. (1973). Toward a cognitive social learning reconceptualization of personality. *Psychological Review, 80,* 252–283.

Mischel, W. (1979). On the interface of cognition and personality. *American Psychologist, 34,* 740–754.

Mischel, W., & Mischel, H. (1976). A cognitive social-learning approach to morality and self-regulation. In T. Lickona (Ed.), *Moral development and behavior.* New York: Holt, Rinehart & Winston.

National Institute of Mental Health (NIMH). (1982). *Television and behavior: Ten years of scientific progress and implications for the eighties* (vols. 1 & 2). Washington, DC: U.S. Government Printing Office.

Nannis, E. D., & Cowan, P. A. (1987). Emotional understanding: A matter of age, dimension, and point of view. *Journal of Applied Developmental Psychology, 8,* 289–304.

Nelson, W. M. III, & Cholera, S. (1986). Projective-cognitive assessment of thoughts and feelings and their relationship to adaptive behavior in a dental situation. *Adolescence, XXI*, 855–862.

Nummedal, S., & Bass, S. (1976). Effects of the salience of intention and consequences on children's moral judgments. *Developmental Psychology, 12*, 475–476.

Olejnik, A. (1975). *Developmental changes and interrelationships among role taking, moral judgment, and children's sharing.* Paper presented at the Biennial Meeting of the Society for Research in Child Development, Denver, CO.

O'Leary, S., & O'Leary, K. (1976). Behavior modification in the schools. In H. Leitenberg (Ed.), *Handbook of behavior modification and behavior therapy.* Englewood Cliffs, NJ: Prentice-Hall.

Paris, S. G., & Lindauer, B. K. (1982). The development of cognitive skills during childhood. In B. Wolman (Ed.), *Handbook of developmental psychology.* Englewood Cliffs, NJ: Prentice-Hall.

Parke, R. (1974). Rules and resistance to deviation: Recent advances in punishment, discipline, and self control. In A. Pick (Ed.), *Minnesota symposium on child psychology* (Vol. 8). Minneapolis, MN: University of Minnesota Press.

Patterson, C., & Mischel, W. (1975). Plans to resist distractions. *Developmental Psychology, 11*, 369–378.

Patterson, C., & Mischel, W. (1976). Effects of temptation-inhibiting and task-facilitating plans on self-control. *Journal of Personality and Social Psychology, 33*, 209–217.

Perry, D., & Parke, R. (1975). Punishment and alternative response training as determinants of response inhibition in children. *Genetic Psychology Monographs, 91*, 257–279.

Peterson, C., & Skevington, S. (1988). The relation between young children's cognitive role taking and mothers' preference for a conflict-inducing child-rearing method. *Journal of Genetic Psychology, 149*, 163–174.

Piaget, J. (1932). *The moral judgment of the child.* London: Kegan Paul.

Piaget, J. (1965). *The moral judgment of children.* New York: Free Press.

Piaget, J. (1970). Piaget's theory. In P. H. Mussen (Ed.), *Carmichael's manual of child psychology* (3rd ed.). New York: Wiley.

Piche, G., Michlin, R., Rubin, D., & Johnson, F. (1975). Relationships between fourth graders' performance on selected role taking tasks and referential communication accuracy tasks. *Child Development, 46*, 965–969.

Ravenette, A. T. (1975). Good techniques for children. *Journal of Child Psychology and Psychiatry, 16*, 79–83.

Ravenette, A. T. (1977). Personal construct theory: An approach to the psychological investigation of children and young people. In D. Bannister (Ed.), *New perspectives in personal construct theory.* New York: Academic Press.

Ravenette, A. T. (1980). The exploration of consciousness: Personal construct intervention with children. In A. W. Landfield & L. Leitner (Eds.), *Personal construct psychology: Psychotherapy and personality.* New York: Wiley.

Rest, J. (1975). Longitudinal study of the defining issues test of moral judgment: A strategy for analyzing developmental change. *Developmental Psychology, 11*, 738–748.

Resnick, J. S. (1982). *The development of perceptual and lexical categories in the human infant.* Unpublished doctoral dissertation, University of Colorado.

Rogoff, B., & Gardner, W. (1984). Adult guidance of cognitive development. In

B. Rogoff & J. Lave (Eds.), *Everyday cognition: Its development in social context* (pp. 95-116). Cambridge, MA: Harvard University Press.

Rondal, J. A. (1976). Investigation of the regulatory power of the impulsive and meaningful aspects of speech. *Genetic Psychology Monographs, 94,* 3-33.

Rosen, C. (1974). The effects of sociodramatic play on problem-solving behavior among culturally disadvantaged preschool children. *Child Development, 45,* 920-927.

Rosenthal, T., & Zimmerman, B. (1978). *Social learning and cognition.* New York: Academic Press.

Rothenberg, B. (1970). Children's social sensitivity and the relationship to interpersonal competence, intrapersonal comfort, and intellectual level. *Developmental Psychology, 2,* 335-350.

Rubin, K. (1972). Relationships among egocentric communication and popularity among peers. *Developmental Psychology, 7,* 364.

Rubin, K. (1976). Relation between social participation and role taking skill in preschool children. *Psychological Reports, 39,* 823-826.

Rubin, K. (1978). Role taking in children: Some methodological considerations. *Child Development, 49,* 428-433.

Rubin, K., & Maioni, T. (1976). Play preference and its relationships to egocentrism, popularity, and classification skills in preschoolers. *Merrill-Palmer Quarterly, 21,* 171-179.

Rubin, K., & Schneider, F. (1973). The relationship between moral judgment, egocentric, and altruistic behavior. *Child Development, 44,* 661-665.

Rubinstein, E. A. (1983). Television and behavior: Research conclusions of the 1982 NIMH Report and their policy implications. *American Psychologist, 38,* 820-825.

Rushton, J. (1975). Generosity in children: Immediate and long term effects of modeling, preaching, and moral judgment. *Journal of Personality and Social Psychology, 31,* 459-466.

Rushton, J., & Weiner, J. (1975). Altruism and cognitive development in children. *British Journal of Social and Clinical Psychology, 14,* 341-349.

Schwartz, S., Feldman, K., Brown, M., & Heingartner, A. (1969). Some personality correlates of conduct in two situations of moral conduct. *Journal of Personality, 37,* 41-57.

Selman, R. (1971). Taking another's perspective: Role taking in early childhood. *Child Development, 42,* 79-91.

Selman, R. (1976a). Social cognitive understandings: A guide to educational and clinical practice. In T. Lickona (Ed.), *Moral development and behavior.* New York: Holt, Rinehart & Winston.

Selman, R. (1976b). Toward a structural analysis of developing interpersonal relations concepts: Research with normal and disturbed preadolescent boys. In A. Pick (Ed.), *Minnesota symposium on child development* (Vol. 10). Minneapolis, MN: University of Minnesota Press.

Selman, R. L. (1980). *The growth of interpersonal understanding.* New York: Academic Press.

Selman, R., & Lieberman, M. (1975). Moral education in the primary grades: An evaluation of a developmental curriculum. *Journal of Educational Psychology, 67,* 712-716.

Selman, R. L., Schorin, M. Z., Stone, C. R., & Phelps, E. (1983). A naturalistic study of children's social understanding. *Developmental Psychology, 19,* 82-102.

Shantz, C. (1975). The development of social cognition. In E. Hetherington (Ed.), *Review of child development research* (Vol. 5). Chicago: University of Chicago Press.

Shantz, C. U. (1983). Social cognition. In J. H. Flavell & E. M. Markman (Eds.), *Handbook of child psychology: Cognitive development* (Vol. 3). New York: Wiley.

Shirk, S. R. (1987). Self-doubt in late childhood and early adolescence. *Journal of Youth and Adolescence, 16,* 59–68.

Shure, M., & Spivack, G. (1978). *Problem-solving techniques in childrearing.* San Francisco: Jossey-Bass.

Siegel, L. J., & Peterson, L. (1981). Maintenance effects of coping skills and sensory information on young children's response to repeated dental procedures. *Behavior Therapy, 12,* 530–535.

Snyder, J. J., & White, M. J. (1979). The use of cognitive self-instruction in the treatment of behaviorally disturbed adolescents. *Behavior Therapy, 10,* 227–235.

Sollod, R., & Wachtel, P. (1980). A structural and transactional approach to cognition in clinical problems. In M. Mahoney (Ed.), *Psychotherapy process.* New York: Plenum Press.

Spence, S. H. (1987). The relationship between social-cognitive skills and peer sociometric status. *British Journal of Developmental Psychology, 5,* 347–356.

Spivack, G., Platt, J., & Shure, M. (1976). *The problem solving approach to adjustment.* San Francisco: Jossey-Bass.

Spivack, G., & Shure, M. (1974). *Social adjustment of young children: A cognitive approach to solving real-life problems.* San Francisco: Jossey-Bass.

Spivack, G., & Shure, M. B. (1982). The cognition of social adjustment: Interpersonal cognitive problem-solving training. In B. B. Lahey & A. E. Kazdin (Eds.), *Advances in clinical child psychology* (Vol. 5). New York: Plenum Press.

Stanley, S. (1978). Family education to enhance the moral atmosphere of the family and the moral development of adolescents. *Journal of Counseling Psychology, 25,* 110–118.

Turiel, E. (1966). An experimental test of the sequentiality of developmental stages in the child's moral judgments. *Journal of Personality and Social Psychology, 3,* 611–618.

Varni, J., & Henker, B. (1979). A self-regulation approach to the treatment of three hyperactive boys. *Child Behavior Therapy, 1,* 171–192.

Vygotsky, L. S. (1978). *Mind in society: The development of higher psychological processes.* Cambridge, MA: Harvard University Press.

Wenar, C. (1982). Developmental psychopathology: Its venture and models. *Journal of Clinical Child Psychology, 11,* 192–201.

Wenar, C. (1983). *Psychopathology from infancy through adolescence.* New York: Random House.

Yussen, S. (1974). Determinants of visual attention and recall in observational learning by preschoolers and second graders. *Developmental Psychology, 10,* 93–100.

Yussen, S., & Santrock, J. (1974). Comparison of the retention of pre-school and second grade performers and observers under three verbalization conditions. *Child Development, 45,* 821–824.

Zahn-Waxler, C., Radke-Yarrow, M., & Brady-Smith, J. (1977). Perspective taking and prosocial behavior. *Developmental Psychology, 13,* 87–88.

Children and the Use of Self-Monitoring, Self-Evaluation, and Self-Reinforcement

HELEN L. EVANS   MAUREEN A. SULLIVAN

Research in the area of cognitive behavior management of children's academic and social behavior has demonstrated the effectiveness of self-management programs (Gross & Wojnilower, 1984; Jones, Nelson, & Kazdin, 1977; O'Leary & Dubey, 1979). Self-management techniques such as self-monitoring, self-evaluation, and self-reinforcement have been used to promote behavior change, to increase the client's role in treatment (thereby enhancing behavior change), and to facilitate maintenance of behavior change following the withdrawal of external reinforcement. Teaching children to sustain behavior in the absence of continuous external reinforcement is a critical process for the successful socialization of children in our society (Thoresen & Mahoney, 1974). However, many children referred for behavioral, academic, and emotional problems often lack the necessary skills to manage their own behavior. A child may fail to acquire and/or to utilize self-management skills for a variety of reasons. For example, a child's parents or teachers may not have modeled self-management skills and/or may not have provided the necessary external reinforcement. Alternatively, a child may have difficulty learning or utilizing self-management skills because of limited cognitive abilities. In these cases, direct instruction in and reinforcement for self-monitoring, self-evaluation, and self-reinforcement may be effective tools for teaching a child to manage behavior and for increasing use of these skills.

Self-monitoring, self-evaluation, and self-reinforcement have been used in the treatment of a variety of children's problem behaviors. These techniques have been used most often in treating behaviors relevant to children's successful school performance, either by focusing on appropriate classroom deportment or by focusing on improved academic performance (i.e., increased accuracy and productivity). Self-management techniques have also been used as components in behavior management programs for treating more serious problems such as enuresis (Houts, Liebert, & Padawer, 1983), childhood obesity (Brownell & Venditti, 1982), or noncompliance with medical regimens (Gross, 1983). Thus, self-management techniques can be useful tools for the clinician working with children who exhibit a variety of difficulties.

This chapter focuses on the use of self-management techniques with children. A brief overview of relevant theoretical issues is presented first. The remainder of the chapter addresses the use of self-management techniques in clinical practice. Two case studies are also presented to illustrate the use of these techniques with individual clients and with groups.

Theoretical Considerations

Several behaviorists (e.g., Thoresen & Mahoney, 1974) have argued that many responses occur in the relative absence of concrete rewards. According to Rachlin (1974), self-reinforcement is a secondary reinforcement process that allows an individual to bridge the temporal gap between an initial response and its ultimate long-term consequences. Thus, as a child matures, motivation for actions becomes less concrete, and symbolic rewards are presented by the child to consequate his or her own behavior.

According to Kanfer (1971), self-reinforcement is a three-step process. First, an individual must self-monitor behavior in order to attend to and record the occurrence of some response. Next, in self-evaluation of performance the individual compares his or her behavior with a self-selected criterion or standard. The standard or criterion is based on direct training, social norms, previous external reinforcement, and/or expectations for success (Bandura, 1977, 1978; Karoly, 1977). If the behavior adequately meets the standard, then in the third step the individual rewards his or her performance. According to Bandura (1977, 1978, 1986), these self-administered rewards include both concrete and symbolic reinforcement.

Children gradually learn the component behaviors of self-reinforcement as they mature and are socialized (Bandura, 1977). Bandura (1986) emphasized the necessity of numerous childhood experiences in order for children to learn to define their own capabilities, to develop self-standards, and to become motivated to monitor their own behavior and to reward or punish their accomplishments. Although from a social learning perspective, specific age changes are not emphasized, Bandura (1986) recognized the fact that very young children lack the required ability to encode information, to problem solve, and to conceptualize a sense of self in order to utilize self-management skills. A sense of self allows the child to identify which aspect of behavior to self-evaluate and to determine the adequacy of performance. Bandura (1986) also emphasized that a child's self-efficacy—the belief in the ability to perform and to attain goals—is a critical factor in children's utilization of self-management skills.

Children begin developing component self-reinforcement behaviors as their parents begin to use concrete rewards to increase their children's responses. Later, social reactions replace concrete reinforcers in teaching the child to respond appropriately. Parents begin to instruct their children on how to set their own standards, how to self-observe, and how to self-reward or punish (Bandura, 1986). Usually parents—and later other adults and peers—urge the child to adopt standards similar to their own by the use of verbal instructions and by positively reinforcing the adoption of these standards. According to Bandura (1986), the child's observation of parents' and others' self-management responses and their consequences has a major influence upon the child's use of self-reinforcing responses. Once established, self-prescribed standards, self-evaluation, and self-reward are maintained by periodic external reinforcement.

Within the theoretical literature there has been debate about why self-reinforcement techniques result in behavior changes. Behaviorists (Catania, 1976; Jones & Evans, 1980; Rachlin, 1974; Stuart, 1972) questioned whether self-reinforcement occurs without the immediate presence of external limitations on the availability of reinforcers and the standards for self-reward. According to Gross and Wojnilower (1984), the available research has failed to examine children's use of self-reinforcement in the absence of any externally imposed contingencies. However, self-reinforcement may entail a process that is different from external reinforcement. Alternative explanations include describing self-reinforcement as self-awareness, self-monitoring, and self-evaluation, but not reinforcement (Catania, 1976; Rachlin, 1974). Rachlin (1974) described self-evaluation as secondary reinforcement. However, no one has argued against the presence of some type of covert process that allows one to maintain responses in the absence of immediate external reinforcement. Future controlled research is necessary to determine the mechanisms inherent in self-reinforcement techniques.

Throughout the remainder of this chapter, the terms *self-monitoring, self-evaluation,* and *self-reinforcement* will be used to refer to various self-controlling responses defined in the research literature and in the theoretical models of Bandura (1977, 1986) and Kanfer (1971).

Self-Monitoring Skills

Research indicates that self-monitoring is an effective assessment technique for evaluating problem behaviors (Kazdin, 1974; Thoresen & Mahoney, 1974). Also, the available research shows that self-monitoring often has the effect of improving performance (Kazdin, 1974; Nelson & Hayes, 1981) and, therefore, may be effective in treatment as well.

The clinician's first task is to decide when self-monitoring is an appropriate method to utilize with a child. This decision may be made in situations that include (a) assessing the client's behavior prior to beginning a therapy program, (b) beginning a self-management program (either alone or as a component of a behavior management program) to modify an identified behavior, and (c) attempting to maintain behavior change after the removal of a program using external reinforcement. In all three situations, self-monitoring will be effective only if significant others in the child's environment are cooperative (Karoly, 1977; Thoresen & Mahoney, 1974). The child's maintenance of self-monitoring responses is partially dependent upon the external reinforcement provided by significant others. It is crucial that the clinician ascertain that parents and others have the required skill and motivation to provide effective external reinforcement of the child's behavior. Through interviews with the child, parents, or others, it is possible to assess the adults' skills and motivation for helping the child learn to carry out the program. Often parents are unaware of the influence of their behavior and verbal communication on their children. It is important to assess whether the child's environment includes models who have adopted prosocial standards and who utilize self-monitoring and self-reinforcement to accomplish goals and to receive positive external reinforcement.

The clinician should also assess the child's motivation to change, and the child's skill in monitoring behavior (Karoly, 1977). For example, "incomplete sentences" related to the problem behavior may reveal the type of self-statements the child makes that relate to achieving improvement in the target behavior and the standards used by the child to monitor his or her behavior. In teaching or evaluating the child's skill in monitoring behavior, the clinician also might utilize a behavioral game that requires the child to count a specific behavior of the clinician during a therapy session. For example, the first author has used a game in which the therapist asks the child to count the number of times the clinician uses the word "I." Next, the child is required to count the same behavior emitted by himself or herself. This behavioral game provides some information about the child's willingness and ability to self-monitor and may provide valuable information about the probable success in monitoring the problem behavior.

Throughout the assessment of the child's self-monitoring skills, it is essential to consider limitations in the child's ability to self-monitor as a result of age and inexperience (Karoly, 1977). Clearly, the child needs to be developmentally capable of following simple directions, of self-observing the occurrence of the targeted behavior, and of recording the occurrence of the targeted behavior. With children younger than school age, counters may be more useful than diaries or other written records of behavior. However, there is limited research concerning methods that are most effective with younger children. Below school age it is likely to be very difficult for the child to maintain the focused attention necessary to self-observe and to self-monitor behavior.

In addition to referring to the literature on child development, it is helpful for the therapist to compare the client's behavior and skill to those of a peer to determine the child's ability to participate in a self-control program. For instance, if several children are seen in a group setting (e.g., classroom or inpatient group), the behavior of the child targeted for the change program could be compared to the behaviors of same-age children in terms of accuracy of self-monitoring and ability to self-monitor over a period of time (e.g., 2 hours).

If self-monitoring is identified as one of the viable methods of assessing and changing the child's behavior, then the clinician must provide instruction in monitoring the specific targeted behaviors. First, the behaviors to be monitored must be defined as precisely as possible in order to maximize the child's understanding of what responses to record. Second, the recording methods should be tailored to the child's cognitive level and should be as nonintrusive as possible. A variety of counters—such as golfer counters—have been utilized in self-monitoring approaches (Thoresen & Mahoney, 1974). These devices can often be worn by the child, thus making them less intrusive. Index cards, notepads, and small notebooks also have been used effectively. When using written records, the therapist may find it helpful to create a form that requires that the child check each occurrence of the behavior or circle a letter indicating the occurrence of the incident. Also, it is important to include the specific time interval for the recording. Table 3-1 illustrates a simple frequency check for a 7-year-old girl. This procedure can be augmented by the use of "countoons" (Kunzelman, 1970), which picture simple stick figures that demonstrate the behaviors targeted for self-monitoring. The child is instructed to place a check next to the picture when the behavior occurs. For example, to enhance memory if there is difficulty recalling the specific targeted behavior, the frequency check (Table 3-1) might include a picture or stick figure of a girl sucking her thumb. Such additional prompts seem to be useful for younger children. With older children more detailed information can be gathered. In addition to a simple frequency count, the older child might be asked to provide qualitative information such as antecedent events, feelings surrounding the behaviors, and consequences of the behavior. The older child is more likely to have the

TABLE 3-1 • Self-Monitoring Chart for a 7-Year-Old Girl's Thumbsucking: A Frequency Check

Date: _____

Count of Thumbsucking

Morning before school (the child circles the next number each time he or she sucks thumb)

1	2	3	4	5	6	7	8
9	10	11	12	13	14	15	16

School — morning

1	2	3	4	5	6	7	8
9	10	11	12	13	14	15	16

School — afternoon

1	2	3	4	5	6	7	8
9	10	11	12	13	14	15	16

Before dinner

1	2	3	4	5	6	7	8
9	10	11	12	13	14	15	16

After dinner

1	2	3	4	5	6	7	8
9	10	11	12	13	14	15	16

ability to describe the behavior sequence in detail. Table 3-2 illustrates a self-monitoring chart used with a 13-year-old boy who wanted to increase the varieties of foods he ate.

Third, the clinician must decide if accuracy of self-monitoring is a critical issue. There is some evidence to suggest that treatment benefits exist even if self-monitoring is inaccurate (Broden, Hall, & Mitts, 1971; Rosenbaum & Drabman, 1979). However, a rather high degree of accuracy is desirable when utilizing self-monitoring information for planning a self-management treatment program or for evaluating a behavioral maintenance program. Research (see Rosenbaum & Drabman, 1979, for a review) has shown that level of accuracy can be increased by first providing external rewards for matching or for being within a range of a significant other's (e.g., teacher's) recording of the targeted behavior. This type of training has resulted in high levels of accuracy. When the external reward is withdrawn

TABLE 3-2 • Self-Monitoring Chart for a 13-Year-Old Boy's Food Intake

Name:

Date:

Food	Yes	No	Breakfast Type	Number of Servings (1, 2, 3, etc.)
Meats				
Eggs				
Beverages				
Breads				
Cereals				
Pastries				
Other				

Food	Yes	No	Lunch Type	Number of Servings (1, 2, 3, etc.)
Beverages				
Breads				
Sandwiches				
Meats				
Fruits				
Vegetables				
Desserts				
Other				

Food	Yes	No	Dinner Type	Number of Servings (1, 2, 3, etc.)
Beverages				
Breads				
Sandwiches				
Meats				
Fruits				
Vegetables				
Desserts				
Other				

abruptly, there may be a return to inaccurate self-monitoring if the child has a history of severe social and behavioral problems (Santogrossi, O'Leary, Romanczyk, & Kaufman, 1973). When external reinforcement for accuracy is decreased gradually, however, accuracy of self-monitoring is likely to be maintained (Drabman, Spitalnik, & O'Leary, 1973; Turkewitz, O'Leary, & Ironsmith, 1975). Thus, external reinforcement should be decreased gradually in order to facilitate maintenance of accuracy. For situations in which self-monitoring is utilized as a beginning step in a self-management program or as a part of a behavioral maintenance program, monitoring will need to be continued throughout therapy, with training in self-evaluation and self-reinforcement included when appropriate. In therapy the clinician may observe some initial treatment effects as a result of self-monitoring, even if the self-monitoring is inaccurate (Kazdin, 1974; Rosenbaum & Drabman, 1979).

The clinician must also address the type of behavior to be monitored. Self-monitoring of both positive and negative behaviors typically results in behavior change in the desired direction. However, there is some evidence (Gottmann & McFall, 1972; Kirschenbaum & Karoly, 1977) that monitoring negative behaviors may result in an increase in those behaviors. Also, when the focus is on self-monitoring of negative behaviors, there may be a tendency for the child to develop negative associations with treatment. Clearly, ongoing evaluation is necessary to determine whether the self-monitoring program is having the expected treatment effect.

Finally, even if behavior improves following self-monitoring, research (Rosenbaum & Drabman, 1979) indicates that, as a single treatment method, self-monitoring is not sufficient to help children change behaviors such as academic performance or behaviors that are highly resistant to change (Bandura, 1986).

Self-Evaluation Techniques

Self-evaluation seems to be a key element for behavior change even though, as a single treatment method, it does not appear to improve behavior (Bandura & Perloff, 1967; Gross & Drabman, 1982). It is the second step in the self-reinforcement process, because one must evaluate his or her behavior prior to self-administering a reward. In therapy, self-evaluation involves teaching the client to set a standard for a particular behavior and to use self-monitored information to decide if the behavior meets the standard and deserves to be reinforced. There is some evidence to suggest that it is important to encourage children to set high standards for self-evaluation (Evans, 1981; Jones & Evans, 1980; Masters, Furman, & Barden, 1977; O'Leary & Dubey, 1979). Instructions to set high standards for self-evaluation and for praise have been used effectively to help children maintain stringent criteria for behavioral improvement (Jones & Evans, 1980). However, it may be important to evaluate skill level in order to encourage the child to set reasonable performance criteria for self-consequating behavior.

As in any behavioral program, it is often beneficial to utilize a shaping process that urges the child to set more stringent performance criteria as the behavior improves.

Without the support of the therapist, the child is likely to self-evaluate with more lenient performance criteria over time and, thus, may not benefit from the self-management program (Felixbrod & O'Leary, 1973, 1974; Winston, Torney, & Labbee, 1978). Through playing a self-evaluation game in which the therapist models self-administered rewards for meeting high standards (Hildebrandt, Feldman, & Ditrichs, 1973), the child observes a model for rewarding stringent and reasonable performance standards. The child who has previously received reinforcement for lenient or antisocial standards will need a period of external reinforcement for conforming to the standards defined by the therapist and significant others.

The available research is unclear about the effect of adding self-evaluation to self-monitoring techniques (Kazdin, 1974; Sagotsky, Patterson, & Lepper, 1978). However, this addition seems to be a logical step in teaching a child to self-consequate behavior. In order to self-reward or to self-punish, the child must compare behavior to an established standard. Self-evaluation helps sustain continued performance if the child considers his or her behavior as satisfactory in relation to a prescribed standard (Bandura, 1986).

Self-Reinforcement

The use of self-administered rewards has been shown to increase children's appropriate behavior in a variety of settings (O'Leary & Dubey, 1979). Although it is a clinical tool with established effectiveness, there is a great deal of controversy about why self-reinforcement changes behavior. The theoretical controversy surrounding self-administered rewards is relevant to its clinical application because it implies that the therapist needs to monitor the client's responses to ensure adherence to the selected criteria for self-reward. An initial step in ensuring adherence to these criteria is the examination of the child's history of external reinforcement. If the child has received inconsistent reinforcement for appropriate behavior, the therapist needs to develop a program of external reinforcement that provides consistent rewards for these appropriate responses (O'Leary & Dubey, 1979). This external reinforcement program might consist of either a token economy or an immediate reward system. In training the child to use self-reward, the clinician may first include reinforcement for positive self-verbalizations prior to beginning a self-reward program based on the child's performance.

Several steps are involved in developing a self-reward program. First, the clinician must provide direct instruction so that the child learns to identify the response to evaluate prior to self-administering a reward. Next, the clinician must teach the child to monitor and evaluate performance in order to decide to follow it with a positive consequence or to remove some negative stimulus. The clinician should also provide periodic external checking and/or external cues for stringent criteria-setting (O'Leary & Dubey, 1979) to ensure that the child adheres to performance criteria for self-rewarding. Eventually these external checking procedures should be faded and eliminated.

The next step involves teaching children to provide consequences for their own behavior. In individual or group sessions the therapist might utilize modeling techniques to demonstrate how to self-consequate behavior. The research of Bandura and his colleagues (Bandura & Kupers, 1964; Bandura & Whalen, 1966; Mischel & Liebert, 1966; Bandura, Grusec, & Menlove, 1967) suggests that self-reward is learned as a result of observing a therapist who adopts stringent performance criteria, who is consistent in the criteria for self-reward, and who shows mastery behavior rather than being overly competent. For example, on a math test the therapist might self-reward for correcting an error as well as for being correct.

The therapist can further enhance the utility of the self-reward program by involving the child's parents. Parents can learn to provide instructions and external reinforcement for the child's self-reward program. Also, parents can play games with the child in which they model self-monitoring, goal setting, self-evaluation, and self-reward for correcting an error. In this way the child receives additional instruction, gains additional models to observe, and receives external reinforcement for appropriate self-management.

In planning a self-reward program it is essential to assess the child's behavioral repertoire to predict responsiveness to this type of program. Academic achievement and age have been shown to affect outcome for self-reinforcement programs in some studies (Kanfer & Duerfeldt, 1968; Evans, 1981), but this is not always the case (Tiedmann & McMahon, 1985). Age may influence outcome because of the younger child's more limited sense of self and limited cognitive ability to evaluate performance and encode information. Research has indicated that it may be more difficult to develop effective self-reward programs with children who have behavioral problems that limit their compliance with adult instructions (Santogrossi et al., 1973). These variables may be related to a history of inconsistent external reinforcement for adhering to performance criteria. When developing a self-reward program, the instructions for this behavior must include more details regarding performance criteria to self-consequate if the child has person variables such as low academic achievement related to the behavior targeted for self-reward. The therapist should monitor and reinforce adherence to the performance criteria if person variables suggest that these factors are affecting the child's ability to use self-reward.

Classroom Application

The use of self-management techniques in the classroom provides teachers with a method for increasing students' academic performance without having to give unusual amounts of individual attention. Although the development of a self-management program initially may require extensive time from the teacher, eventually students will learn to manage their own behavior, and the teacher's time and efforts can be directed to other areas.

In a classroom setting there are many opportunities to utilize self-monitoring, self-evaluation, and self-reward to improve children's academic performance and deportment. When developing a classroom self-management program, the first task is to decide whether to focus on academic performance (i.e., increased accuracy and productivity) or on classroom deportment (i.e., attending to the teacher, sitting quietly while doing independent seat work, and not talking without permission). The available research suggests the importance of focusing on academic behavior rather than on classroom management when the goal is to improve academic performance (Jones & Kazdin, 1981). If academic performance is targeted for the self-management program, it may also produce an increase in attentive behavior (Lloyd, Bateman, Landrum, & Hallahan, 1989). However, it is unlikely that a focus only on changing disruptive classroom behaviors will improve academic performance (Jones & Kazdin, 1981). Ideally a classroom self-management program will include behaviors to increase attention to classroom activities as well as to improve specific academic performance.

Once behaviors are identified for a self-management program, it is important to do a functional analysis of the children's targeted behaviors. This involves examining the problem behavior in the context of antecedent and consequent events in order to understand what function the behavior serves for the child. This information is used to develop an appropriate intervention. These targeted behaviors need to be specified and clearly explained to the children. As previously indicated, some type of visual display of the targeted behaviors is helpful, especially to elementary school children. For example, if a child is trying to increase time in seat, a picture of a child sitting at a desk may be placed in front of the child when the class activity requires sitting. For on-task behavior a chart can indicate if the children should be working on assignments or listening to the teacher (Glynn & Thomas, 1974). Self-monitoring can be utilized as part of the assessment of the children's classroom behavior and academic performance. Because self-monitoring has a reactive effect, this may produce some improvement in behavior. Thus, this data may not accurately reflect preassessment levels of the targeted behaviors.

In the classroom setting the frequency of children's self-monitoring of time on task, of completion of academic work, or of another targeted behavior can be increased by the use of a cue to remind them to self-record the targeted behavior. A tape-recorded "beep" sound or a bell might be used to signal the students to evaluate and record their behavior. This method of cueing frequently has been used to remind students to record attention to their school work (e.g., Glynn & Thomas, 1974; Lloyd et al., 1989). When teaching children to self-monitor academic performance, it may be helpful to use a form that is marked each time a step in the particular lesson is completed. Another method found to be effective with junior high school children is to mark slips of paper provided by the teacher (Broden, Hall, & Mitts, 1971). There is some evidence that monitoring study time may increase academic performance (Gottman & McFall, 1972; Sagotsky et al., 1978). In most classroom settings, children who have a history of poor academic task performance will require a self-management program that includes more information about inconsistent external reinforcement of academic and self-control behaviors. Classroom research (see Rosenbaum & Drabman, 1979) suggests that a history of inconsistent external reinforcement impairs the ability to utilize self-control behaviors.

One method of enhancing the success of a classroom self-management program is the initial use of an external reinforcement program (such as a token economy system), followed by the gradual introduction of self-management responses. In the typical token economy program, self-evaluation and/or self-monitoring procedures are gradually added to the classroom procedures (Drabman, Spitalnik, & O'Leary, 1973; Kaufman & O'Leary, 1972; Rosenbaum & Drabman, 1979). To institute self-monitoring of classroom performance and behavior, children are required to match the teacher's record of their responses. Praise, tokens, or extra back-up rewards can be used to reinforce accurate self-monitoring, and loss of reward can be used as punishment. External reinforcement is based on the number of tokens earned for the child's self-monitored behavior. Gradually accuracy checks are eliminated.

An effective way to teach children to self-evaluate and to self-monitor their classroom behavior is to have them monitor and rate specific classroom behaviors (Turkewitz et al., 1975; Drabman et al., 1973). Initially students are required to match teacher ratings of their performance during short time intervals (e.g., 15-minute periods). Eventually matching is faded either by decreasing the number of intervals checked for accuracy or by decreasing the number of students required to match the teacher's ratings.

Although matching of self-ratings is faded, the teacher should continue to praise self-monitoring and self-evaluation of behaviors.

In addition to self-monitoring and self-evaluating behavior, some classroom programs have allowed children to determine the size or number of reinforcers for their performance. Bowers, Clement, Fantuzzo, and Sorensen (1985) demonstrated that making choices available to children enhanced the effectiveness of a self-management program. In programs including choices it is important to use external cues for setting high standards for self-reward. This can be accomplished through the use of instructions suggesting self-reward standards, by public reporting of self-reward standards as a way to facilitate peer reinforcement, and by limiting the range of the size or number of reinforcers (Wall, 1983). Without any external cues as guidelines, children are apt to self-reward according to very lenient standards of academic and classroom behavior (Jones & Kazdin, 1981).

Case Studies

Two case studies—one involving a 12-year-old boy and another involving a group of inpatient children—are presented to illustrate the use of self-monitoring in therapy. It is hoped that through reading these cases the clinician will see the therapeutic potential of self-monitoring procedures with children. As previously indicated, these procedures have been found to be applicable to a wide range of childhood behavior problems in various settings such as home, school, and institutions. The procedures are potentially useful for child clinicians, for they offer practical, efficient means of collecting data and of evaluating the progress of therapeutic interventions.

Individual Case Study*

Paul, a 12-year-old boy, was referred because of excessive thumbsucking. His dentist had informed his parents that this behavior was having a destructive effect upon his teeth. According to Paul and his parents, his friends had begun to tease him more frequently about sucking his thumb.

According to school reports and clinical interviews, excessive thumbsucking appeared to be Paul's only major problem. Previous psychological reports indicated above average intellectual functioning. His social skills

*This case study is a modification of a project conducted by Patricia Minzer of Xavier University (Ohio) under the first author's supervision.

seemed to be adequate. For example, he had friends who often came to his house, and he enjoyed playing soccer and other games.

Because Paul was eager to stop sucking his thumb, a self-control program was initiated after the first interview. To assess the frequency of thumbsucking and the antecedent events for this behavior, a self-monitoring program was instituted. Paul was instructed to record the number of times thumbsucking occurred in specified periods before school, during morning time in school, during afternoon time in school, and after school. In addition, Paul recorded place and activity when thumbsucking occurred. In order to estimate the accuracy of Paul's self-recordings, his father recorded the thumbsucking behavior during the periods when Paul was not in school. Whenever Paul's recordings for the day matched his father's within two instances, he was reinforced with food or money (5¢). During this self-monitoring phase, Paul reported a decrease in the length of time he sucked his thumb. However, although the frequency of thumbsucking decreased initially, it increased after the first four days. As with most behaviors, self-monitoring had the initial effect of decreasing the maladaptive behavior, but this reactivity effect decreased over time.

After examining the self-monitoring records of two weeks, it was apparent that Paul's thumbsucking occurred more frequently in the evenings while he watched T.V., read a book, or played a sedentary game (e.g., cards) with friends. Therefore, the treatment program initially focused on evenings — the time period in which Paul had the most difficulty with thumbsucking. For the first week of treatment, Paul was allowed to suck a lollipop if he did not suck his thumb. Examination of the self-monitoring records indicated that this procedure had no effect upon thumbsucking. Next, Paul was taught to use an aversive imagery technique. Whenever he started to suck his thumb, he was instructed to imagine that it was swelling, cracking, and having pus run out of it. When he had mastered this imagery technique, Paul was instructed to use imagery after school. At first his father would say the word "pus" to cue him to use the procedure. After the third day of receiving cues, Paul reported being able to visualize the scene without being reminded. By the 14th day of treatment, self-monitoring records revealed that Paul had stopped sucking his thumb. It was not necessary to develop a treatment phase for other parts of the day because Paul reported using the aversive technique in each time period and situation.

In this case, self-monitoring was used to assess the problem behavior prior to designing a behavior change program. Self-monitoring records were also used to evaluate the effectiveness of the behavior change program. These records indicated that the initial treatment with the lollipop was ineffective. Self-monitoring records collected while the second treatment was in effect documented the success of the imagery technique.

Furthermore, these records indicated that it was unnecessary to expand treatment to nontargeted time periods and situations because generalization had occurred spontaneously.

Group Case Study

In a residential psychiatric center for children, "self-control groups" were formed in order to teach residents ways of improving their ratings on the hospital-wide token economy system and to enhance the maintenance and generalization of behaviors learned in the groups. The group therapy format was chosen over an individual treatment approach because (a) role playing of difficult situations was planned to increase skills necessary for effective use of self-control methods, (b) the use of a group gave each child a chance to practice behavior in a setting more similar to the natural environment, and (c) peers were expected to serve as role models for each other and to provide reinforcement of appropriate behavior (Edelson, 1981). Also, a group approach allowed the use of activities that either required or were enhanced by a group setting. The following description is a composite of several groups conducted by the first author or psychology trainees under her supervision.

When organizing the groups the initial individual interviews with the potential group members were aimed at identifying children who would be able to improve their cognitive and overt behavior through the use of self-monitoring, self-evaluation, and self-reinforcement. During the interviews the group leaders assessed the child's interest in participating in the group and the child's basic understanding of the token system. Children were identified for the interview screening process according to the following criteria: (a) having at least average cognitive ability as measured on intelligence tests, (b) having been on the token system for at least one month, (c) having attained levels above the lowest on the token economy system (the token system was divided into four levels according to points earned for working three "target behaviors" determined by the child's hospital treatment team), and (d) having sufficient social skills to be able to participate in group sessions without engaging in physical fights (as determined by points lost on the token system for fighting).

The boys who met these criteria ranged in age from 9 to 12. Each group included boys who were from the same hospital unit and who were of similar age. The groups varied both racially (including both blacks and whites) and socioeconomically (although most were from lower to lower-middle income families). All group members had been in psychiatric treatment for at least 3 months. Their performance on the token system was sporadic; most of the boys had attained weekly levels varying from the lowest to the highest level. These variations indicated problems in being able to work consistently on three "target behaviors." Included among the target behaviors were responses such as playing with another peer for 15 minutes per day without fighting, cooperating with staff requests, slowing down and thinking before answering, talking to staff when angry rather than hiding in the bedroom, and talking without cursing. On each shift the boys received ratings on their target behaviors from the staff. These ratings were later converted into points for which the boys received various privileges and rewards.

In organizing the groups an effort was made to maximize the similarity in behavioral repertoires (i.e., token system levels and personal characteristics such as age and unit placement). It was felt that the impact of observational learning upon group members' behavior would be enhanced by similarity of their behavioral repertoires. Similar behavioral repertoires were expected to increase the likelihood that the boys would model each other's behavior. Previous research (see Rimm & Masters, 1979) has shown that behavior is more likely to be modeled if the model and observer have similar characteristics. Also, a coping model (one with a less than perfect performance) is more apt to be imitated than a mastery model (one with a perfect performance).

The self-control groups met once a week for 50-minute sessions over a 4-month period. The therapy program was divided into an orientation phase (sessions 1–4) devoted to developing rapport and ensuring an understanding of the token system, a teaching phase (sessions 5–12) aimed at teaching self-monitoring, self-evaluation, and self-reinforcement skills, and a practice phase (sessions 13–16) devoted to reports of completion of homework assignments and to further practice.

Session 1

The first session focused on getting the boys acquainted with the group therapist and on helping them understand the group's purpose. Initially the therapist explained that the group members would learn skills to help them obtain higher levels on the token system (and, subsequently, to earn more privileges and rewards). Each group member was encouraged to verbalize his targeted behaviors, his level, and something that happened during the previous week about which he was pleased. This activity was designed to help the boys understand the relationship between behavior and its consequences. To foster a sense of "groupness," the boys developed a name for their group and drew a picture that they described to the group.

Each session ended with concrete reinforcers for group participation. In the first session the therapist gave each child a token check for 20 points to be exchanged at the token store for rewards such as toys, clothes, and toiletries. Also, each group member received a small piece of candy.

Session 2

Approximately half of this session was devoted to developing rules for group behavior (extremely important in dealing with hospitalized youngsters). The rules focused on specific behaviors that would be used later in the self-control training sessions. For example, one group agreed to rules that stated that only one person at a time could talk and that members must stay seated unless the activity required a person to stand. The boys were told that the therapist would deduct points from their 20-point token check for violations of the rules. This response-cost method was utilized to maintain order in the group and to help each boy understand the importance of rule compliance. After the development of rules the remainder of this session focused on identifying reinforcers (such as foods, activities, and small toys) to use in future sessions. In this group, as well as in other groups conducted in this particular psychiatric setting, the first author found that the children needed encouragement in order to think of rewards other than foods such as candy; these types of sweets were seldom available to the children.

In most of the groups it was difficult for children to understand the concept of reinforcement. It might have been helpful to demonstrate how reinforcers or rewards influence behaviors. For example, a simple response such as asking questions could have been reinforced with candy during a 10-minute period, and the therapist could have kept a count of questions asked per 2-minute period, demonstrating that this behavior increased with reinforcement.

Session 3

The group therapist introduced the idea of monitoring targeted behaviors and keeping up with daily ratings. Each group member was asked to state his target behaviors and to guess what level (i.e., points earned) he had reached during the past week. (The boys did not know their final rating for the week prior to the meeting.) Each boy was given an extra bonus of five token points if he guessed his level and/or stated an accurate reason for having lost points. These methods were utilized to reinforce group members for accurately reporting their behavior during group sessions and for increasing self-monitoring and self-evaluation of their behavior on a daily basis.

In each session the boys were given a homework assignment that required that they come to the next session prepared to name one behavior for which they earned high ratings during the week and to identify a behavior for which they earned low ratings. This homework assignment was designed to help each boy identify areas needing improvement and areas deserving of self-reinforcement.

As the last activity, group members received the right to choose a reward for group participation if they had earned 15 or more points for compliance with group rules. The rewards included the right to play games such as Candyland, as well as material rewards such as bubble gum. At the end of the session, the group therapist reviewed the points earned by each person for rule compliance and wrote a token check for each boy to exchange in the Token Economy Store.

Session 4

The group members read the group rules and were reminded of the penalties for not complying with the rules. Next, the group members discussed their targeted behaviors and guessed their levels. The group therapist once again gave extra tokens for accuracy of token system information. Each boy reported on his homework by identifying a behavior for which he earned high ratings and identifying a behavior needing improvement. The boys role played one or two problem behaviors, which were suggested by several group members. This process allowed the boys to receive feedback from other group members and from the group therapist concerning alternative ways of responding.

In this session the group therapist allowed members to read through their actual rating sheet for the previous week. Group members were encouraged to discuss their rating sheets and to identify their rating successes. The group clapped and cheered for ratings that group members identified as worthy of praise.

This session ended with a game, and the boys received candy for group participation if they had maintained 15 or more token points for rule compliance. During these early sessions a boy occasionally would refuse to participate in the group and would lose his rewards. At the very end of each session, each boy was given a token check based on points earned for rule compliance.

Sessions 5–12

These sessions focused on increasing the boys' skill in self-monitoring, self-evaluation, and self-reinforcement. The group continued to discuss performance on the token system, and the therapist introduced the idea of graphing weekly performance level. The concept of mountains and valleys was used to help the boys understand when their appropriate behavior was increasing or decreasing according to their graphs. Homework assignments gradually changed to guessing daily ratings and writing them down in order to receive token points for bringing this information to the group sessions and for estimating it accurately. Also, an incentive of a group reward (going to McDonald's) was added for maintaining high levels (3 and 4) on the token system. This incentive was introduced to try to make the boys' performance of targeted behaviors more consistent.

During the fifth session the group therapist introduced the idea of self-monitoring by having each boy count the number of times he said "I" while telling about his favorite leisure activities. Each boy told the group about something that he had enjoyed doing, and as he made his report he and the group counted the number of times he used the pronoun "I." The therapist went over the differences in number of "I's" recorded and explained these differences by pointing out how hard it is to monitor behavior accurately. In sessions 6 through 12 the boys continued to play some type of self-monitoring game (e.g., in one session they counted the number of times the group leader said "uh huh"). Eventually the boys were required to monitor compliance with the rules developed at the beginning of the group sessions. Also, they were allowed to determine how many tokens they would receive. When their self-reward standard was within two points of the group therapist's standard, they received a token check for this number of points. Whenever their self-reward standard was more than two points from the group therapist's assessment, they were given a token check for five points less than their estimate. The boys' ratings were always within two points of the therapist's assessment of points earned.

Sessions 13–16 and Beyond

The last month of group training focused on helping the boys use self-control techniques outside of the group. They were encouraged to monitor one of their target behaviors by rating it the same way staff did. The boys received bonus points and concrete rewards for bringing their completed diaries to group sessions and were rewarded for accuracy of rating their targeted behaviors by receiving extra token points and extra concrete rewards (e.g., time to play games or candy).

The groups were disbanded after the 20th session. Most of the group members were able to increase their appropriate functioning in the targeted behaviors. However, because of administrative problems and the discharge of some of the group members, it was not possible to gradually fade out the accuracy checks of self-ratings of targeted behaviors. In one group it was possible to fade out material reinforcers (e.g., candy) and to use only activity reinforcers and praise. Ideally the groups would have had three or four more sessions to focus on gradual elimination of the group reinforcers for self-evaluation. Also, the boys could have been taught to self-reward covertly rather than to self-reward with materials and token rewards. Within a different setting it might have been possible to move children in the self-control groups from the hospital-wide token system to a self-reinforcement system.

In this example, self-management techniques were included in a behavior change program designed to enhance children's performance on a token system. Self-monitoring was introduced, and accurate recording was achieved by providing direct instruction, modeling, feedback on accuracy, and external reinforcement. Self-evaluation and self-reinforcement were also added, and the adoption of high performance standards was fostered in order to facilitate optimal behavior change. Thus, in this example, self-management techniques served primarily to enhance the effectiveness of a behavior change program.

Summary

Self-monitoring, self-evaluation, and self-reinforcement can be successful techniques for helping children control their behavior. These strategies can be used either alone or in conjunction with behavior management programs designed to increase appropriate behavior and/or to facilitate maintenance of appropriate behavior following the withdrawal of external reinforcement. Theories of self-control have focused on the mechanism by which responses occur in the absence of external reinforcement and on the development of self-control through socialization. However, research in self-management has focused primarily on the use of self-monitoring, self-evaluation, and self-reinforcement to treat behavior problems. This research has demonstrated the effectiveness of self-management programs with a variety of behavior problems in children. A review of the self-management literature indicates that the child-clinician may enhance the effectiveness of clinical interventions by including self-monitoring, self-evaluation, and self-reinforcement in behavior change programs. Through direct instruction, modeling, and reinforcement, the clinician can teach a child to use self-management skills. Self-monitoring is useful in assessment of problem behaviors, in evaluating effectiveness of treatment, and in promoting behavior change. Successful use of self-monitoring depends on the child's willingness and ability to record behavior, on the choice of appropriate recording methods (based on the child's skill level), and on the accuracy of recording. In self-evaluation, children compare their behavior to a standard and determine whether their behavior matches or exceeds that standard. In order to obtain optimal performance, the clinician must encourage children to adopt high standards. If the behavior evaluated matches or exceeds the chosen standard, the child self-rewards. Clinicians should also encourage stringent criteria in the selection of rewards. Finally, it is important for clinicians to consider factors that may affect a child's ability to use self-control skills. These factors include the supportiveness of the child's environment and person variables such as age, cognitive ability, and history of inconsistent reward for appropriate behavior.

References

Bandura, A. (1977). *Social learning theory.* Englewood Cliffs, NJ: Prentice-Hall.

Bandura, A. (1978). The self system in reciprocal determinism. *American Psychologist, 33,* 344–358.

Bandura, A. (1986). *Social foundations of thought and action: A social cognitive theory.* Englewood Cliffs, NJ: Prentice-Hall.

Bandura, A., Grusec, J. E., & Menlove, F. L. (1967). Some determinants of self-monitoring reinforcement systems. *Journal of Personality and Social Psychology, 5,* 449–455.

Bandura, A., & Kupers, C. J. (1964). Transmission patterns of self-reinforcement through modeling. *Journal of Abnormal and Social Psychology, 69,* 1–9.

Bandura, A., & Perloff, B. (1967). Relative efficacy of self-monitored and externally imposed reinforcement systems. *Journal of Personality and Social Psychology, 7,* 111–116.

Bandura, A., & Walen, C. K. (1966). The influence of antecedent reinforcement and divergent modeling cues on patterns of self-reward. *Journal of Personality and Social Psychology, 3,* 373–382.

Bowers, D. S., Clement, P. W., Fantuzzo, J. W., & Sorensen, D. A. (1985). Effects of teacher-administered and self-administered reinforcers on learning disabled children. *Behavior Therapy, 16,* 357–369.

Brigham, T. A. (1979). Some effects of choice on academic performance. In L. Perlmuter & R. Monty (Eds.), *Choice and perceived control* (pp. 131–141). New York: Erlbaum.

Broden, M., Hall, R. V., & Mitts, B. (1971). The effect of self-recording on the classroom behavior of two eighth grade students. *Journal of Applied Behavioral Analysis, 4,* 191–199.

Brownell, K. D., & Venditti, E. M. (1982). The etiology and treatment of obesity. In W. E. Fann, I. Karacan, A. D. Pokorny, & R. L. Williams (Eds.), *Phenomenology and the treatment of psychophysiologic disorders.* New York: Spectrum.

Catania, C. A. (1976). Self-reinforcement revisited. *Behaviorism, 4,* 157–162.

Drabman, R. S., Spitalnik, R. S., & O'Leary, K. D. (1973). Teaching self-control to disruptive children. *Journal of Abnormal Psychology, 82,* 10–16.

Edelson, J. L. (1981). Teaching children to resolve conflict: A group approach. *Social Work, 37,* 488–493.

Evans, H. L. (1981). *The role of instructions, criterion-setting and tangible rewards in self-reinforcements.* Unpublished doctoral dissertation. University of Pittsburgh.

Felixbrod, J. J., & O'Leary, K. D. (1973). Effects of reinforcement on children's academic behavior as a function of self-determined and externally imposed contingencies. *Journal of Applied Behavior Analysis, 6,* 241–250.

Felixbrod, J. J., & O'Leary, K. D. (1974). Self-determination of academic standards by children. *Journal of Educational Psychology, 66,* 845–850.

Glynn, E. L., & Thomas, J. D. (1974). Effects of cueing on self-control of classroom behavior. *Journal of Applied Behavior Analysis, 7,* 299–306.

Gottman, J. M., & McFall, R. M. (1972). Self-monitoring effects in a program for potential high school dropouts: A time-series analysis. *Journal of Consulting and Clinical Psychology, 39,* 273–281.

Gross, A. M. (1983). Self-management training and medication compliance in young diabetics. *Child & Family Behavior Therapy, 4,* 47–55.

Gross, A. M., & Drabman, R. S. (1982). Teaching self-recording, self-evaluation, and self-reward to nonclinic children and adolescents. In P. Karoly & F. H. Kanfer (Eds.), *Self-management and behavior change: From theory to practice* (pp. 285–314). New York: Pergamon Press.

Gross, A. M., & Wojnilower, D. A. (1984). Self-directed behavior change in children: Is it self-directed? *Behavior Therapy, 15,* 501–514.

Hildebrandt, D. E., Feldman, S. E., & Ditrichs, R. (1973). Rules, models, and self-reinforcement in children. *Journal of Personality and Social Psychology, 25,* 1–5.

Houts, A. C., Liebert, R. M., & Padawer, W. (1983). A delivery system for the treatment of primary enuresis. *Journal of Abnormal Child Psychology, 11,* 513–519.

Jones, R. T., & Evans, H. (1980). Self-reinforcement: A continuum of external cues. *Journal of Educational Psychology, 72*(5), 625–635.

Jones, R. T., & Kazdin, A. (1981). Childhood behavior problems in the school. In S. M. Turner, K. S. Calhoun, & H. E. Adams (Eds.), *Handbook of clinical behavior therapy* (pp. 568–606). New York: Wiley.

Jones, R. T., Nelson, R. E., & Kazdin, A. (1977). The role of external variables in self-reinforcement: A review. *Behavior Modification 1,* 147–178.

Kanfer, F. H. (1971). The maintenance of behavior by self-generated stimuli and reinforcement. In A. Jacobs & L. B. Sachs (Eds.), *The psychology of private events* (pp. 39–59). New York: Academic Press.

Kanfer, F. H., & Duerfeldt, P. H. (1968). Age, class standing, and commitment as determinants of cheating in children. *Child Development, 39,* 545–557.

Karoly, P. (1977). Behavioral self-management in children: Concepts, methods, issues, and directions. In M. Hersen, R. M. Eisler, & P. M. Miller (Eds.), *Progress in behavior modification* (Vol. 5). New York: Academic Press.

Kaufman, K. F., & O'Leary, K. D. (1972). Reward, cost, and self-evaluation procedures for disruptive adolescents in a psychiatric hospital school. *Journal of Applied Behavior Analysis, 5,* 293–309.

Kazdin, A. E. (1974). Reactive self-monitoring: The effects of response desirability, goal-setting, and feedback. *Journal of Consulting and Clinical Psychology 42*(5), 704–716.

Kirschenbaum, D., & Karoly, P. (1977). When self-regulation fails: Tests of some preliminary hypotheses. *Journal of Consulting and Clinical Psychology, 45,* 1116–1125.

Kunzelman, H. D. (Ed.). (1970). *Precision teaching.* Seattle, WA: Special Child Publishers.

Lloyd, J. W., Bateman, D. F., Landrum, T. J., & Hallahan, D. P. (1989). Self-recording of attention versus productivity. *Journal of Applied Behavior Analysis, 22,* 315–323.

Masters, J. C., Furman, W., & Barden, R. C. (1977). Effects of achievement standards, tangible rewards, and self-dispensed achievement on children's task mastery. *Child Development, 48,* 217–224.

Mischel, W., & Liebert, R. M. (1966). The role of power in the adoption of self-reward patterns. *Child Development, 38,* 673–683.

Nelson, R., & Hayes, S. (1981). Theoretical explanations for reactivity in self-monitoring. *Behavior Modification, 5,* 3–14.

O'Leary, S. G., & Dubey, D. R. (1979). Applications of self-control procedures by children: A review. *Journal of Applied Behavioral Analysis, 12,* 449–465.

Rachlin, H. (1974). Self-control. *Behaviorism, 2,* 94–107.

Rimm, O., & Masters, J. (1979). *Behavior therapy.* New York: Academic Press.

Rosenbaum, R. S., & Drabman, R. S. (1979). Self-control training in the classroom: A review and critique. *Journal of Applied Behavior Analysis, 12,* 467–485.

Sagotsky, G., Patterson, C. J., & Lepper, M. R. (1978). Training children's self-control: A field experiment in self-monitoring and goalsetting in the classroom. *Journal of Experimental Child Psychology, 25,* 242–253.

Santogrossi, D. A., O'Leary, K. D., Romanczyk, R. G., & Kaufman, K. F. (1973). Self-evaluation by adolescents in a psychiatric hospital school token program. *Journal of Applied Behavior Analysis, 6,* 277–287.

Stuart, R. B. (1972). Situational versus self-control. In R. D. Rubin, H. Fensterheim, J. D. Henderson, & L. P. Ullman (Eds.), *Advances in behavior therapy.* New York: Academic Press.

Thoresen, C. E., & Mahoney, M. J. (1974). *Behavioral self-control.* New York: Holt, Rinehart & Winston.

Tiedmann, G. L., & McMahon, R. J. (1985). Individual differences in children's responses to self- and externally-administered reward. *Behavior Therapy, 16,* 516–523.

Turkewitz, H., O'Leary, K. D., & Ironsmith, M. (1975). Generalization and maintenance of appropriate behavior through self-control. *Journal of Consulting and Clinical Psychology, 43*(4), 577–583.

Wall, S. M. (1983). Children's self-determination of standards in reinforcement contingencies: A reexamination. *Journal of School Psychology, 21,* 123–131.

Winston, A. S., Torney, D., & Labbee, P. (1978). Children's self-reinforcement: Some evidence for maximization of payoff and minimization of effort. *Child Development, 49,* 882–884.

CHAPTER FOUR

Cognitive-Behavioral Assessment of Children
A Review of Measures and Methods

DAVID S. PELLEGRINI   CYNTHIA L. GALINSKI

KATHLEEN J. HART   PHILIP C. KENDALL

Just as cognitive-behavioral therapies combine behavioral interventions with techniques that attempt to alter internal, cognitive events, cognitive-behavioral assessment attempts to measure both of these domains. Whereas the aim of "traditional" psychological assessment is to identify underlying personality characteristics, cognitive-behavioral assessment attempts to achieve something different: a description of both current behavior (including specific environmental conditions that reinforce behavior) and the affective and cognitive events (including thoughts, ideas, beliefs, self-statements, and experiences) that mediate that behavior.

To reach a complete description of a child's current functioning, cognitive-behavioral assessment utilizes multiple assessment strategies. These include the clinical interview, standardized testing, behavioral observation, rating forms completed by the child and/or by significant others in the environment, and self-report measures. The multimethod approach to assessment (i.e., some combination of the aforementioned strategies) has been espoused by numerous researchers and clinicians (e.g., Ollendick & Hersen, 1984; Ross, 1980).

Many clinicians question the "cost-benefit ratio" of time spent in assessment. Hayes, Nelson, and Jarrett (1987) called for a direct evaluation of the "treatment utility of assessment" (p. 963) in future research development of assessment strategies, while Bellack and Hersen (1988) stated that the ultimate value of assessment lies in its usefulness in the treatment process.

From our perspective a clinician's time is well spent in assessment when there is a focus to the assessment and when the clinician knows how to utilize the data generated by the assessment. Furthermore, a complete assessment provides information for four important areas relevant to treatment. First, assessment allows for thorough evaluation of the presenting problem(s). Second, the generated data allow the clinician to formulate a working hypothesis about the antecedent and consequent events or factors that promote or maintain the presenting problem. These events or factors include environmental as well as cognitive components. Third, this formulated hypothesis is used to guide the selection and focus of intervention strategies. Finally, assessment before and after treatment allows the clinician to evaluate treatment outcome in an objective manner.

In this chapter we will describe and review a variety of assessment procedures pertinent to cognitive-behavioral interventions with children. We will not directly concern ourselves with diagnostic issues or nosological inquiries, nor will we attempt to cover the cognitive assessment methods related to intelligence or projective testing. These procedures are described in great detail in other volumes.

Beginning the Assessment

This chapter will present a wide range of assessment approaches and instruments. Clearly, it would be impractical and inefficient to incorporate every one of these instruments into an assessment battery. A successful assessment begins with the thoughtful selection of appropriate techniques and approaches for the individual client. In making this selection it is useful to view the assessment process as operating at two levels: global and specific. Most treatment referrals take the form of nonspecific and global descriptions of a child's difficulty (e.g., "he never listens to what he's told") or general dispositions (e.g., "he seems unhappy") that do not translate readily into a viable treatment plan. Thus, the first step in the assessment process is to "concretize" exact behaviors in specific situations from the referral source's general statements about the child. The most popular methods at this stage are the clinical interview, behavioral observations, behavioral ratings scales, and self-report measures of general cognitive style. These will be described in greater detail in the next section of the chapter. On the basis of the initial data gathered from these sources, hypotheses can be generated about the specific nature of a child's difficulty. For example, do these data suggest that the child is experiencing peer relationship problems? Is this child depressed or anxious? At this point the clinician may choose among various measures that assess specific dimensions. In the latter part of the chapter, assessment of some of the dimensions common to childhood — social skills deficits, ADHD/impulsivity, depression, and anxiety — will be described.

From Referral to Specifics

Global Techniques

The Clinical Interview

By far the most widely used assessment procedure is the clinical interview. Regardless of theoretical orientation, the clinical interview typically is used as the first source of information. It provides historical and contextual data about the person(s) seeking treatment and about the areas identified as problems. When the assessment is a prelude to psychotherapy, the interview can also provide an opportunity for the development of clinician–client rapport and can enhance both the assessment process and the upcoming therapy (Perry, 1990).

In the majority of referrals for problems with children, the initial interview is conducted with the parents. Usually the purpose of this contact is to identify the parents' concerns about the child's behavior and to understand their goals for intervention. Information about family members, family structure, and parental behavioral management style is obtained, and the clinician attempts to identify the situations in which the problem behaviors occur, the antecedent events, and the way parents respond to the problem behavior. Although some clinicians view the parent interview as the source of *all* relevant information, it is probably best seen as a means to generate hypotheses that will be "tested" through further assessment and treatment. Specifically, this interview helps the clinician decide whether or not other important individuals should be contacted (e.g., day care providers, teachers, grandparents) and which assessment techniques might yield the most pertinent information (e.g., behavioral observation, behavioral checklists, self-report measures).

Interviews with the child can also assist in rapport building, problem identification, and increased understanding of antecedent and consequent events. The child, however, is the primary source of information about "private" cognitive events that are generally unknown to parents or significant others. Therefore, in a cognitive-behavioral approach to assessment, there is an effort throughout the interview process to help the child describe thoughts, feelings, and self-statements that mediate specific behaviors. For example, a child whose difficulties with anger control lead to frequent fist-fights can (with assistance) describe the thoughts that contribute to his or her anger. Identification of these unique thought patterns and self-statements may play a pivotal role in the development of an individualized intervention program.

Although clinicians typically interview parents and child separately, many stress the importance of a clinical interview with parents and child together—a rich opportunity to gather additional information, to observe interactional patterns among family members, and to broaden the basis for hypothesis generation.

Behavioral Observations

Direct observation has a long tradition in the behavioral assessment of children (for example, see Dodge, Pettit, McClaskey, & Brown, 1986; Gottman, Gonso, & Rasmussen, 1975; Hartup, Glazer, & Charlesworth, 1967; Marshall & McCandless, 1957). However, the number and types of target behaviors, as well as the complexity of the observational systems employed, have varied considerably. Assessments have ranged from the observation of a single, narrowly defined behavior such as excessive crawling in a 3-year-old child (e.g., Harris, Johnston, Kelley, & Wolf, 1964) to complex codes designed to capture the richness of family interactions (e.g., Patterson, Ray, Shaw, & Cobb, 1969).

Careful observational assessment has much to commend its use. For example, whereas global ratings of behavior or adjustment can be vulnerable to rating bias, observational codes appear to be much less vulnerable, as behavioral codes can be defined with precise operational criteria (Kent, O'Leary, Diament, & Dietz, 1974). Observational codes also provide a clear picture of children's ongoing sequential behavior patterns—a picture that permits more accurate description and classification (Reid, Baldwin, Patterson, & Dishion, 1988).

Observational assessment may play a particularly vital role in treatment evaluation, for it provides a measure of treatment effect independent of the agent of change. For this purpose, Gottman, Gonso, and Schuler (1976) recommended that observers be kept "blind" to treatment. Also, rather than making repeated observations of target children to the exclusion of their peers (as is typical of most interventions), these investigators recommended the more stringent (and costly) procedure of observing several children throughout the assessment process. Further, the inclusion of a child's social system in the collection of observational data allows for the generation of a data base that may serve in the construction and advancement of theoretical models (McFall, 1986; Patterson, 1982; 1986).

Clearly, however, behavioral observation is not the simple or straightforward task that it was once thought to be, nor is it an easy answer to the reliability and validity shortcomings of other assessment methods. It is beyond the scope of this chapter to review all of the concerns of observational assessment (see Foster & Cone, 1986; Reid et al., 1988) or the wide variety of assessment schemes that have been devised (see Cone & Hawkins, 1977; Haynes, 1978; Mash & Terdal, 1988; Nay, 1979; Nelson & Hayes, 1979). However, because behavioral observation is an important feature of any cognitive-behavioral assessment battery, some of these issues will be reviewed briefly.

Perhaps the most important methodological issue related to behavioral observation is that the very act of observation changes or affects the actual behavior being observed (e.g., Mercatoris & Craighead, 1974; Roberts & Renzaglia, 1965). Moreover, unless observers are continually checked for agreement, interrater reliability tends to drop precipitously after initial training (Reid, 1970). To overcome these problems, Kazdin (1977) suggested continuous retraining of observers through the use of training tapes that allow observers to compare their recordings with preestablished, standard behavioral codes. Furthermore, random and periodic spotchecking of observers has been found to prevent observer drift (Taplin & Reid, 1973), and observer effects on behavior can be circumvented by placing the observer unobtrusively in the situation for several days before observational data are actually "counted." This procedure allows subjects the time to habituate to the observer's presence. Lengthening the observational period also may serve the same purpose.

Asher, Renshaw, Gerachi, and Dor (1979) suggested that behavioral observation methodology has inherent limitations for some assessment purposes. For example, they noted that many relevant behaviors such as those that result in children being liked (e.g., altruistic behaviors) or disliked (e.g., aggression, cheating) are low-frequency events that increase in diversity as children grow older. They noted also that many of these behaviors occur outside the school classroom. Thus, in order to avoid missing salient behaviors, lengthy observation in multiple settings may be essential, though cumbersome and expensive. Finally, Jacobson (1985a, 1985b) noted that direct observation does not provide information about cognitive and affective events that may play important roles in a child's problems. Behavioral coding schemes have tended to focus on relatively detailed behaviors that may lack social validity. That is, the focus on discrete behaviors — readily captured through simple coding schemes — may be misleading, because certain single behaviors may be of limited importance in a child's day-to-day adjustment.

During the past several years the focus of observational studies has broadened from the assessment of behaviors in structured situations (e.g., the classroom) to encompass the world of the child on the playground, at home, and elsewhere. The recent proliferation of coding systems specifically designed for clinically relevant behaviors (e.g., hyperactivity and noncompliant behavior), social skills deficits, and social contexts (e.g., entry into new peer groups, interactions among family members) illustrates this point.

The aforementioned limitations to behavioral observation provide direction to the planning and implementation of observational techniques. Foster, Bell-Dolan, and Burge (1988) emphasized that clinicians must be careful to select meaningful behaviors to observe and that the nature of the selected behavior determines the method to be used for its assessment. Finally, they suggested that data from direct observation be carefully interpreted; too frequently these data are interpreted to represent response domains other than those assessed.

With these caveats in mind, behavioral observation remains an important component of cognitive-behavioral assessment when publicly observable behavior is the focus of concern and observation is feasible. In disorders of attention, social interaction, and anxiety, behavioral observation can provide crucial information for treatment. Specific issues regarding behavior observation of these difficulties will be covered in a later section of this chapter.

Behavior Rating Scales

In cognitive-behavioral outcome research the ratings or judgments of teachers have been used as primary indices of behavioral adjustment (e.g., Kendall & Wilcox, 1980). Teacher assessments of student behavior are also a primary source of referrals to special resources (Strain, Cooke, & Apolloni, 1976). These ratings often allow for the identification of low-frequency behaviors that may be missed in naturalistic observations, and they enable teachers to compare the target child's behavior with that of other children (McMahon, 1984). Fortunately, data are available to support the concurrent validity (e.g., Greenwood, Walker, & Hops, 1977) and the predictive validity (reviewed in Strain et al., 1976) of teacher ratings. Moreover, collection of such data is inexpensive and is a less time-and-energy consuming task than observational assessment.

Parent reports are also important in the assessment process. Parents are able to observe their children over a long period of time and in a wide variety of settings, thus providing a valuable source of information about child behavior problems (Achenbach & Edelbrock, 1978). Parent reports often are used in conjunction with teacher ratings and can provide a comprehensive assessment. Several teacher and parent rating scales that have been used in the cognitive-behavioral intervention process are reviewed below.

Child Behavior Checklist (CBCL)

The Child Behavior Checklist (Achenbach & Edelbrock, 1981, 1983) is one of the most widely used parent-report measures of child behavior. The checklist covers 113 problem behavior items to which the parent responds by indicating whether the behavior in question is "very or often true" (2), "somewhat or sometimes true" (1), or "not true" (0) with regard to his or her child "now or within the past 12 months." The items are intended to provide broad coverage of behavior problems that can be rated with minimal inference required. Additional "social competence" items are included to canvass the child's involvement and attainment in various activities (e.g., sports, hobbies, jobs and chores), social relations, and academic performance.

A Total Behavior Problems score, two "broad band" scale scores (internalizing and externalizing problem behavior), nine "narrow band" scale scores (including depressed, obsessive-compulsive, aggressive, and hyperactive), and three Social Competence scale scores are derived from the CBCL. These scores were based on factor analysis of parent ratings for a large sample of clinic children. Each score is standardized separately for children of each sex within three broad age groups (4–5, 6–11, and 12–16), based on norms derived from stratified age samples of normal children (Achenbach & Edelbrock, 1983). A computer scoring program is available from the authors, although the profile is easily scored by hand.

The psychometric soundness of the CBCL is particularly well established. Test-retest reliabilities for the 12 scales and for Internalizing, Externalizing, and Total Behavior Problem scores are generally quite high (.72 to .97) over brief time intervals (about 1 week). The short-term stability of the overall profile of scale scores appears to be quite high as well (Q correlation = .86). Over longer time intervals (9–27 months), stability decreases but remains significant for individual scores (.26-.79) and for the profile as a whole (Q correlation = .64) (Achenbach, 1978). Agreement between mothers and fathers also appears to be moderately high both for individual scale scores (.58-.87) and for the profile as a whole (Q correlation = .69) (Achenbach, 1978) and may be particularly pronounced for children viewed as problematic (Garrison & Earls, 1985).

The CBCL has consistently discriminated disturbed or clinic-referred children from normals in a number of comparisons (Achenbach, 1978; Achenbach, Conners, Quay, Verhulst, & Howell, 1989; Friedlander, Weiss, & Traylor, 1986). Moreover, ratings derived from the instrument appear to discriminate meaningfully within disturbed samples. For example, Cohen, Gotlieb, Kershner, and Wehrspann (1985) examined 163 6- to 11-year-old consecutive referrals to a child psychiatry outpatient department. Children with CBCL internalizing profile types were more adaptive on a number of measures of cognitive, personality, and social functioning than were children with externalizing profiles—a finding that is in keeping with a wider literature on Internalizers and Externalizers.

Teacher Report Form of the CBCL (TRF)

The availability of a teacher report version of the CBCL—comparable in format and factor structure, reliability, and validity—offers a distinct advantage to clinicians interested in obtaining multiple perspectives on children's behavior across settings. Like the CBCL, the TRF also contains 113 problem behavior items (rated on the same 0–2 scale), plus some additional items pertaining to social competence. The CBCL and TRF each contain 25 items that are specific to home and school situations, respectively, while 88 items are identical across the two versions.

The factor-derived scores also are comparable in meaning and composition. In addition to the Total Behavior Problems score and the two broad band scores for Internalizing and Externalizing behavior, the TRF yields eight narrow band scale scores (e.g., anxious, social withdrawal, aggressive, inattentive, unpopular). Each score is again standardized separately for children of each sex within two (rather than three) broad age groups (6–11 and 12–16) based on norms derived from stratified age groups of normal children (Achenbach & Edelbrock, 1986). Scoring is easily accomplished by hand, although a computer program is also available from the authors.

Research to date supports the psychometric soundness of the TRF. Test-retest reliabilities for the eight scales and for Internalizing, Externalizing, and Total Behavior Problem scores appear to be quite high (.76 to .96) over brief time intervals (about 1 week). Over longer time intervals, stability decreases but remains significant (.63–.88 over 2 months and .54–.82 over 4 months), with reliability appearing to be unsatisfactory (.25) only for the "Unpopular" scale score (Achenbach & Edelbrock, 1986).

Agreement between teachers and teacher aides appears to be moderately high (.42–.72) with the TRF (Achenbach & Edelbrock, 1986), and scores appear to correlate significantly with ratings made from direct observations of school behavior (Reed & Edelbrock, 1983). Finally, the moderate level of agreement obtained between parent ratings made with the CBCL and teacher ratings made with the TRF supports the construct validity of both instruments. For example, in their review of 12 pertinent studies, Achenbach, McConaughy, and Howell (1987) reported mean and median correlation coefficients of .35 and .36, respectively.

The TRF appears to discriminate disturbed or clinic-referred children from normals (Achenbach & Edelbrock, 1986). Moreover, ratings derived from the instrument appear to discriminate meaningfully within disturbed samples. For example, Edelbrock, Greenbaum, and Conover (1985) found that children diagnosed as attention deficit disordered scored significantly higher on the Inattention scale of the TRF than did a comparison group of clinically referred children with other diagnoses. Harris, King, Reifler, and Rosenberg (1984) successfully distinguished between two groups of 6- to 12-year-old boys, one group attending a special school for emotionally disturbed youngsters and the other group attending a school for the learning disabled.

Several other studies support the convergent and discriminant validity of the TRF. For example, Wolfe, Finch, Saylor, Blount, Pallmeyer, and Carek (1987) found that self-report measures of depression and anxiety were significantly correlated with Internalizing scores from the TRF but were unrelated to Externalizing scores. Similarly, Edelbrock et al. (1985) reported strong correspondence between the Hyperkinesis Index of the Revised Connors Teacher Rating Scale (TRS) and the three externalizing scales of the TRF (.58-.82). The total TRS score also correlated more strongly with the TRF Externalizing score (.89) than with the Internalizing score (.34).

Walker Problem Behavior Identification Checklist (WPBIC)

The WPBIC is a 50-item teacher rating scale designed to measure classroom behaviors that interfere with successful academic performance (Walker, 1983). Teachers check each item on a two-choice response format as either observed or not observed. Items are weighted and converted to a standard score with a mean of 50 and a standard deviation of 10. A score of 60 or above is considered to be an indication of possible disturbance. Factor analysis of the WPBIC has yielded five subscales: acting out, withdrawal, distractibility, disturbed peer relations, and immaturity. Walker (1983) reported a split-half reliability coefficient of .98. Noland and Gruber (1976) reported average test-retest correlations in the .60 range.

There is some evidence of positive correlation between WPBIC scale scores and observed behavior (Greenwood et al., 1977). Noland and Gruber (1976) reported a significant relationship between academic achievement and WPBIC scores, especially on the acting out, withdrawal, and immaturity factors. Annesley (1974) found that problem children identified by the WPBIC showed lower scores than nonproblem children on measures of reading achievement, locus of control, and self-concept regarding work habits. Copeland and Weissbrod (1978) reported correlations of .65, .58, and .48, respectively, between the Conners (1969, 1973) hyperactivity scale and the distractibility, acting out, and peer problems subscales of the WPBIC. However, no relationship was found between teacher ratings (WPBIC and Conners hyperactivity scale) and either latency or error scores on the Matching Familiar Figures Test (Kagan, 1966).

The WPBIC is a fairly global measure of disturbed behavior, and the two-choice format of the items may limit the sensitivity of the instrument for measuring varying degrees of behavioral improvement in studies of treatment outcome (e.g., see Garrigan & Bambrick, 1975, and Allen et al., 1976). However, the WPBIC may prove to be a useful screening device for the rapid identification of children with behavior problems.

Self-Control Rating Scale (SCRS)

The SCRS (Kendall & Wilcox, 1979) was developed for use by teachers and parents to assess the generalization of self-controlled behavior following therapeutic intervention and to investigate the laws or rules associated with self-control in children. The SCRS was developed according to a cognitive-behavioral conceptualization of self-control defined as having two components: a cognitive (legislative) and a behavioral (executive) component. The self-controlled child governs his or her own behavior to attain certain ends. This governing requires the cognitive skills to generate and evaluate behavioral alternatives and the behavioral capacity to inhibit acting on the discarded alternatives while engaging in the selected option (Kendall & Wilcox, 1979).

Each of the 33 SCRS items is rated on a seven-point scale. Ten of these items are descriptive of self control (e.g., "Does the child stick to what he or she is doing until he or she is finished with it?"). Thirteen items are indicative of impulsivity (e.g., "Does the child grab for the belongings of the others?"). Ten items are worded to denote both possibilities (e.g., "Does the child interrupt inappropriately in conversations with peers, or wait his or her turn to speak?"). Total SCRS scores are computed by adding the rating scores for each item. The higher the SCRS score, the greater the child's *lack* of self-control. Factor analysis identified one principal factor reflecting cognitive-behavioral self-control (Kendall & Wilcox, 1979). Internal consistency of the SCRS was quite high (alpha = .98), and test-retest reliability for a 3- to 4-week interval was .84 (Kendall & Wilcox, 1979).

The SCRS has demonstrated significant correlations (in the .2 to .4 range) with a variety of self-control indices for elementary school-age children, such as the latency and error scores from the MFF, the Q score from the Porteus Maze Test, and behavioral observations (Kendall & Wilcox, 1979). These correlations remained significant even when both mental age and chronological age were partialled out. Moreover, children referred for self-control training received SCRS scores that were significantly and markedly higher than the scores of nonreferred children who were matched on age, sex, and IQ.

Robin, Fischel, and Brown (1984), using 4- to 18-year-old lower-class subjects, demonstrated that parents can be used effectively as raters and that the SCRS discriminated psychologically distressed from nondistressed subjects. Reynolds and Stark (1986) found that the SCRS differentiated between nonreferred children and children referred by classroom teachers for lack of self-control and impulsive behavior. Furthermore, the authors reported high intercorrelations among the SCRC, the Teacher's Self-Control Rating Scale, and the Conners Teacher Rating Scale, ranging from .83 to .88 for homeroom teachers and .84 to .90 for other teachers. Internal consistency was high, with correlations of .97 for homeroom teachers and .96 for other teachers, and the interrater reliability obtained was .66. Significant correlations also have been reported between teachers' SCRS ratings and the actual frequency of behaviors observed in the classroom (Kendall, Zupan, & Braswell, 1981). Some additional data have been reported to suggest that the SCRS is sensitive to changes produced by cognitive-behavioral self-control training (Kendall & Braswell, 1982; Kendall & Wilcox, 1980; Kendall & Zupan, 1981) and that it yields score changes that parallel observed changes in classroom behavior.

Home and School Situations Questionnaires

Home and school situations questionnaires were designed to identify the specific *contexts* in which children elicit problem behavior rather than to rate actual behaviors per se (Barkley, 1981; Barkley & Edelbrock, 1987). The questionnaires provide a picture of a child's behavior across multiple situations at home and at school and frequently have been used to assess children who exhibit undercontrolled (e.g., conduct disorder and hyperactivity) behavior problems.

The Home Situations Questionnaire (HSQ) presents 16 common situations (e.g., Mealtimes, In Supermarkets, While with a Babysitter) in which parents may experience child management problems. Parents first are asked to indicate whether or not the child exhibits a behavior problem in the given situation and, if so, to rate the severity of the behavior on a 9-point scale. Two summary scores are produced: the number of problem situations and a mean severity score. The HSQ often yields valuable information that can be used to plan parent training programs (Barkley, 1988).

The School Situations Questionnaire (SSQ) presents 12 school situations in which children commonly engage in disruptive behavior (e.g., In the Hallways, On Field Trips, On the Bus). The questionnaire is presented to teachers in a format identical to the HSQ; again, the same two summary scores are derived.

Barkley, Fischer, Newby, and Breen (1988) reported test-retest reliability coefficients for the HSQ of .66 for the number of problem situations and .62 for the mean severity score. For the SSQ, correlations of .78 for the number of problem situations and .63 for the mean severity score were obtained. However, these findings were derived from a drug-trial design of attention deficit disorder children, and they may be lower estimates than would be found in a more conventional evaluation of reliability (Barkley et al., 1988).

Unlike conventional assessment measures, the HSQ and the SSQ highlight the role of situational variables in the development and maintenance of children's behavior problems. They offer a valuable and unique piece of information to the assessment process.

Health Resources Inventory (HRI)

In contrast to traditional emphasis on pathological behavior in teacher or parent rating scales, the HRI was developed to measure personal and social competencies in primary-grade school children (Gesten, 1976). The teacher scale consists of 54 five-point items borrowed from prior health scales or drawn from previous literature concerned with the nature of psychological health. With two samples of first- through third-grade children, varimax and oblique factor analyses indicated a stable five-factor structure: "good student," including items related to effective learning; "gutsy," reflecting adaptive assertiveness and ego strength; "peer sociability," reflecting effective interpersonal functioning; "rule following," reflecting the child's ability to function within the constraints of the school environment; and "frustration tolerance," measuring the child's ability to cope with failure and other social pressures. A summary score reflects "overall competence." This same factor structure was verified more recently (Weissberg et al., 1987) with a large sample of elementary school children.

Test-retest reliability for a 4- to 6-week interval was .87 for the entire scale, with coefficients ranging from .72 to .91 for individual factor scores. Intercorrelations among individual HRI factors were positive and significant (.28 to .53; median $r = .47$).

The HRI has gained recognition during the last several years and has proved sensitive enough to discriminate between a normal and disturbed sample (boys in special day treatment schools) as well as between levels of competence (high, middle, low) in a normal school sample (Gesten, 1976) and clinic-referred group of children (Cohen, Kershner, & Wehrspann, 1988). Moreover, total HRI scores have shown substantial negative correlations with behavioral symptoms (Clarfield, 1974; Kirschenbaum, 1979; Weissberg et al., 1987) as well as with peer sociometric ratings and observed behavior in the classroom (McKim & Cowen, 1987). An early intervention study with primary-grade inner-city children also indicated that the HRI may be sensitive to cognitive-behavioral therapeutic effects (Kirschenbaum, 1979).

Self-Report Measures

For many years behaviorally oriented therapists viewed self-report instruments with skepticism because of research that indicated that reports of subjective states did not coincide with observable behavior (Finch & Rogers, 1984). Despite this inconsistency, the use of self-report measures has increased dramatically over recent years, even among "strict" behaviorists (Kendall, 1990). Indeed, the view of the cognitive-behaviorist is that self-report data provide a complementary, not competitive, source of information about overall adjustment; an individual's own perception of reality can provide crucial data for the development of treatment goals (Finch & Rogers, 1984).

It must be emphasized that self-report measures, if used in isolation, can lead to erroneous problem formulation; therefore, whenever possible, self-report should be used in combination with other measures. Many self-report measures are designed to assess specific affective or cognitive states (e.g., depression, anxiety), and some of these will be reviewed in detail in a later section of this chapter. Below we describe several measures that assess features of cognitive style or affective state.

Attributions

Recent advances in understanding the nature of social cognition have witnessed the increasing development of attributional analyses of behavior. A rather large literature has developed regarding adult attributions (e.g., Metalsky & Abramson, 1982; Weiner et al., 1971). The attributional styles of children have not been examined so intensively. Nevertheless, attributional styles may play an important role in cognitive-behavioral therapy, as the explanations that children generate for their behavior and for the events they anticipate or observe may moderate the effects of treatment. For example, children who attribute their behavioral improvement to personal effort may be more likely to show generalization of improvement than children who attribute behavior change to luck, fate, or chance. Attributions also may be involved in the child's pathology, as in the depressed child's tendency to attribute positive events to external causes and negative events to internal causes (Asarnow & Bates, 1988; Leon, Kendall, & Garber, 1980) or the aggressive child's tendency to attribute aggressive motives to peers in social interaction (e.g., Dodge, Murphy, & Buchsbaum, 1984).

Locus of control is one of the most frequently researched attributional constructs. Rotter (1966) suggested that individuals can be distributed along a continuum defined by the degree to which they view environmental events as being under the control of their personal efforts. Persons with an *external* locus of control are said to attribute causality to forces outside their personal control, whereas persons with an *internal* locus of control view response outcomes as a consequence of their own behavior.

Nowicki-Strickland Internal-External Scale for Children   This scale, developed by Nowicki and Strickland (1973), is perhaps the most widely used locus of control measure for children and has been employed in over 700 studies (Strickland, 1989). It was designed to assess a generalized attributional tendency rather than a situation-specific response. The scale consists of 40 questions to which children respond "yes" or "no." A high score indicates an externally oriented locus of control. Nowicki and Duke (1974a, 1974b) also developed a cartoon type preschool/primary form of the scale as well as adult and elderly versions, thereby allowing for the collection of life-span data. Test-retest reliabilities for the Nowicki-Strickland locus of control measure for third-, seventh-, and tenth-graders ranged from .63 to .71 over a 6-week interval. Estimates of internal consistency were similar in magnitude, ranging from .63 to .81 (Nowicki & Strickland, 1973). Factor-analytic studies have identified distinct factors for emotionally disturbed, delinquent, and normal groups of children (Kendall, Finch, Little, Chirico, & Ollendick, 1978).

A complete review of the voluminous literature on children's locus of control is far beyond the scope of this chapter (see Strickland, 1989, for a review). It should be noted, however, that an individual's belief about how his or her behavior affects outcomes appears to be a powerful determinant of social behavior and academic achievement (e.g., see Lefcourt, 1976; Phares, 1976; Rotter, 1966). Moreover, a variety of social-cognitive intervention strategies have been shown to enhance perceptions of internal control (Searcy & Hawkins-Searcy, 1979), accompanied by improvements in behavior (e.g., McClure, Chinsky, & Larcen, 1978; Reid & Borkowski, 1987; Sarason & Ganzer, 1973).

Children's Attributional Styles Questionnaire (CASQ) The CASQ (Kaslow, Tannenbaum, & Seligman, 1981) is a 48-item self-report measure for children that is based on the revised learned helplessness model (Abramson, Seligman, & Teasdale, 1978). Each item describes either a positive or negative situation, and the child chooses the reason that best explains why this event occurred from a pair of possible causes (e.g., "You get an 'A' on a test": [(a)] "I studied hard"; [(b)] "The test was easy."). The six subscales, based on three attributional dimensions (i.e., internal-external, stable-unstable, specific-global), yield an overall summary score as well as a positive composite score and a negative composite score. Normative data reported by Seligman et al. (1984) and by Nolen-Hoeksema, Girgus, and Seligman (1986) indicate moderate to low intercorrelations among scores. A low difference score between the two composite scores suggests a depressive attributional style (Kaslow, Rehm, & Siegel, 1984).

The attributional styles measured by the CASQ have been found to be significantly associated with beliefs of self-worth, academic competence, social acceptance, athletic ability, and behavior (Asarnow & Bates, 1988). In addition, the CASQ appears to differentiate between nondepressed and depressed children (Kaslow, Rehm, Pollack, & Siegel, 1988; McCauley, Mitchell, Burke, & Moss, 1988; Saylor, Finch, Baskin, Furey, & Kelly, 1984). The CASQ also has demonstrated sensitivity to treatment effects (Benfield, Palmer, Pfefferbaum, & Stowe, 1988).

The Children's Perceived Self-Control Scale (CPSCS) Humphrey (1982) developed this self-report measure to assess both cognitive and behavioral components of self-control. The CPSCS is based on the Self-Control Rating Scale (Kendall & Wilcox, 1979), and the content areas correspond to a teacher's version of the scale (Teacher's Self-Controlling Rating Scale-TSCRS; Humphrey, 1982). The scale consists of 11 items to which the child responds "usually yes" or "usually no" to indicate whether the statement describes him or her. Normative data were collected on several hundred fourth- and fifth-grade children (Humphrey, 1982). Test-retest reliability for the total scale was .71 over a 2½- to 3-week period. No information concerning validity has been reported, and internal consistency reliability was found to be low (.61.) However, three separate factors were found to have adequate test-retest reliability: Interpersonal Self-Control ("If someone pushes me I fight them."); Personal Self-Control ("I make mistakes because I work too fast."); Self-Evaluation ("If the work is too hard I switch to something else.").

Although Humphrey (1982) did not find a correlation between children's reports of self-control on the CPSCS and classroom observations, Reynolds and Stark (1986) found low to moderate correlations between the CPSCS and parent/teacher ratings of self-control and the Matching Families Figures Test (MFFT) (Kagan, 1966), indicating that the CPSCS may hold potential importance for assessing self-control.

Other Measures In contrast to the Nowicki-Strickland and CASQ scales, various other measures have been devised to assess children's locus of control in specific contexts such as academic achievement situations (e.g., Crandall, Katkovsky, & Crandall, 1965). Parcel and Meyer (1978) developed a measure to assess children's sense of control in the context of personal health. Another instrument, the Multidimensional Measure of Children's Perceptions of Control (Connell, 1985), taps a child's understanding of his or her locus of control in three domains: cognitive (school), social (peer), and physical (sports). In addition to measuring knowledge of internal and external control, this instrument also assesses a child's perception of unknown control (e.g., "Many times I can't figure out why good things happen to me."). Many research studies have devised creative strategies to assess a representative sample of each child's attributional style (see Dweck, 1975; Dweck & Reppucci, 1973; Metalsky & Abramson, 1982). Although such assessments may yield information that is useful for devising cognitive-behavioral interventions, the psychometric properties of such makeshift tests need to be investigated. Additional research also is required to clarify the important role of attributional processes in behavior change and to identify important attributional dimensions in various child psychopathologies.

Specific Dimensions of Assessment

Problems in Social Relationships

Problems in interacting with other children are a common impetus for child referrals, and a concomitantly large literature has evolved regarding the assessment and treatment of child social skill deficits. Positive social interactions are believed to result from a complex combination of skills, including understanding social relationships (social cognition) and demonstrating socially accepted behaviors. We describe methods used to assess both of these general skill areas below.

Behavioral Observation of Peer Interaction

Social behaviors assessed through observational methods range from frequency counts of specific behaviors to elaborate systems that attempt to code the quality of complex interactions. For example, Allen, Hart, Buell, Harris, and Wolf (1964) simply recorded a socially isolated girl's proximity to adults and other children, as well as the frequency of her interaction with them. A much more elaborate coding system was devised by Wahler (1975), who employed 19 separate response categories to evaluate five general classes of behavior (autistic, work, play, compliance-opposition, and social behaviors).

For a time the most popular coding systems recorded the frequency of interaction as a measure of social competence (e.g., O'Connor, 1969, 1972; Greenwood, Walker, Todd, & Hops, 1979, 1981). An underlying assumption of this approach to observation was that children who exhibit lower rates of interaction miss out on crucial social interaction experiences (Asher, Markell, & Hymel, 1981). However, Gottman et al. (1976) noted that the total frequency of interaction may be an insensitive criterion for identifying socially isolated or rejected children and for assessing the effects of intervention efforts. Gottman (1977) developed a coding system designed to assess both the frequency and *quality* of peer interaction. In this system each child in the classroom is observed for a brief interval in a specified sequence. The sequence is repeated until all children have been observed for a substantial period of time. Fewer observational errors are associated with this method than with the more frequently employed contiguous procedure in which each child is observed for an extended period of time before proceeding to the next child, who is observed in a similar fashion. Gottman et al. (1976) found intercoder reliability ranging from .90 to .96 for observations of the frequency and quality of peer interaction.

Several researchers have been able to differentiate between sociometrically defined popular and unpopular children on the basis of observational assessment of the quality of social behavior in the classroom. Gottman et al. (1975) found that popular third-grade children were less frequently off task (i.e., daydreaming) and that they distributed and received more positive reinforcement than unpopular peers. Similarly, Dodge, Coie, and Brakke (1982) found that socially rejected children approached classmates more frequently than popular children, but their approaches occurred at socially inappropriate times. Gresham (1982) observed the classroom behaviors of third- and fourth-grade students and was able to predict a child's acceptance and friendship based on the initiation of interaction and the receipt of positive interaction.

The use of analogue situations to study the quality of peer interaction has enabled investigators to measure social behavior more accurately over the course of time and in more controlled settings (Coie & Kupersmidt, 1983; Dodge, 1983; Putallez, 1983). Moreover, the results of these studies provide additional support for the use of behavioral observation in the identification of specific patterns of social interaction that may play a role in the development and maintenance of a child's social competence and peer acceptance.

Among analogue measures, behavioral role-play tests have become a popular method for assessing children's social skills. Several advantages of role-play tests over other measures (i.e., direct observation, checklists, sociometric ratings) have been noted (Gresham & Elliott, 1984). Foremost, behavioral role-play tests measure actual behaviors and do not rely on others' ratings or perceptions of a skill. In addition, the laboratory setting can be more tightly controlled in order to measure children's responses to specific social situations. This procedure also allows for the identification of low-frequency social skills that tend to be missed through direct observation. Role-play tests also are less expensive than naturalistic observations.

Numerous role-play tests have been designed to assess children's verbal and nonverbal (e.g., eye contact, facial expressions) responses in various social situations (Bornstein, Bellack, & Hersen, 1977; Hughes et al., 1989; Ollendick, 1981; Reardon, Hersen, Bellack, & Foley, 1979; Williamson, Moody, Granberry, Lethermon, & Blouin, 1983). The Behavioral Assertiveness Test for Children (BAT) (Bornstein et al., 1977, 1980) has served as the prototype for the development of other role-play measures. Role-play tests are usually conducted in a laboratory setting, and the scenes are presented via videotape, narrator, or live model. A confederate generally is used to deliver a standard prompt to which the child then responds. Consider the following example (Bornstein et al., 1977):

> *Narrator:* "You're playing a game of kickball in school, and it's your turn to get up. But Bobbie decides he wants to get up first."
>
> *Prompt:* "I want to get up."

The issue has been raised as to whether the behaviors assessed through role-play measures are representative of the skills required for social competence in the natural environment (Jacobson, 1985). Bellack (1983) also questioned whether children can legitimately respond to an adult confederate as if the confederate were a peer. Further, he suggested that social skills may be more situationally determined (e.g., based on familiarity with the situation and the age and sex of peer) than role-play tests take into account.

Behaviors identified through role-play measures have been found to have low correlations with teacher reports and with sociometric ratings (Hughes et al., 1989; Kazdin, Matson, & Esveldt-Dawson, 1984; Van Hasselt, Hersen, & Bellack, 1981; Williamson et al., 1983).

Despite the intuitive appeal of role-play tests for the identification of skill deficits, the consistency with which this last finding has been documented calls into question their validity. Nevertheless, role-play measures may be useful in evaluating differences between children's knowledge of competent behavior and their performance or ability to apply their knowledge in an effective manner (Gresham & Elliott, 1984). In this way, role-play procedures provide an additional piece of useful information to the assessment process.

Social Cognition

Research concerned with the development of *social cognition,* or the nature of our understanding of the social world and the interpersonal relationships that define it, has focused on "what" children know (content) as well as on "how" they come to know it (process). However, Shantz (1983) noted that the cognitive processes involved in interpreting cues from other persons or situations are not yet well delineated for either adults or children. Several processes seem to be involved, including the matching of the other's affective state, the imitation of motor behavior or posture, and the making of inferences about another from available cues (Allport, 1961). Role taking (or perspective taking, as it is sometimes called) is a cognitive process – or group of processes – that has been proposed as a primary means by which one comes to know and understand others (Baldwin, 1906; Kohlberg, 1969; Mead, 1934).

Current thought on social cognition goes back to Piaget and Inhelder (1956), who suggested that as children develop, they emerge from a relative state of "egocentrism" in which they are unable to differentiate accurately their own internal emotional states, thoughts, and perceptions from those of other persons. In play, children engage in role taking, or the cognitive activity of assuming the position of others, and this activity helps them develop the ability to infer the perspective of others. Eventually children become able to overcome or move beyond egocentrism. More recently, information-processing models (e.g., Flavell, Botkin, Fry, Wright, & Jarvis, 1968) have attempted to account for the ability to infer and adopt the perspective of another by detailing the sequence of cognitive acts involved in learning to take another's role or perspective. In contrast, Selman and colleagues (e.g., Selman, 1980; Selman & Byrne, 1974) propose a structural model that attempts to describe the stage-by-stage development that occurs in perspective taking. Interested readers may wish to consult Shantz's (1983) excellent review for a detailed explication of such models.

A variety of tasks have been devised in an attempt to measure various aspects of role-taking ability. These tasks generally can be classified according to whether they require inference about another person's (a) thoughts or intentions (cognitive role taking), (b) feelings and internal emotional states (affective role taking), or (c) visual and sensory perceptions of objects in the environment (perceptual role taking) (Denham, 1986; Kurdek & Rogdon, 1975; Shantz, 1983; van Lieshout, Leckie, & Smits-van-Sonsbeek, 1976). However, correlations among measures of these different types of role taking are frequently low, nonsignificant, or inconsistent across studies (Ford, 1979; Kurdek, 1977; Kurdek & Rogdon, 1975; Piche, Michline, Rubin, & Johnson, 1975; Shantz, 1983; Zahn-Waxler, Radke-Yarrow, & Brady-Smith, 1977). These inconsistencies may be due to low internal consistency and reliability of the various tasks themselves as well as to variations in difficulty level, structure, and content across tasks (Kurdek, 1977; Rubin, 1978; Urberg & Docherty, 1976).

Some of the more thoroughly researched and/or clinically relevant measures of role-taking ability and social understanding will be reviewed here. Discussion of other aspects of social cognition and alternative approaches to assessment is beyond the scope of this chapter. These include the assessment of moral reasoning (Hann, Smith, & Block, 1968; Kurtines & Grief, 1974; Rest, 1983), the assessment of role taking as manifested in children's referential communication skills (Flavell et al., 1968; Glucksberg & Krauss, 1967; Glucksberg, Krauss, & Higgins, 1975), and the assessment of role taking through a variety of other methods, including guessing games (DeVries, 1970; Flavell et al., 1968; Selman, 1971), persuasion and preference tests (Flavell et al., 1968; Zahn-Waxler et al., 1977), analysis of communication patterns in videotaped play sessions (Garvey & Hogan, 1973), and analysis of children's comprehension of audiotaped or filmed interaction sequences (Chandler, Greenspan, & Barenboim, 1973; Deutsch, 1974; Flapan, 1968; Wood, 1978).

Role-Taking Task: Chandler Bystander Cartoons (Chandler, 1973)   Of the cognitive role-taking tasks in the literature, the most complete set of reliability data are available for this particular task (Chandler, Greenspan, & Barenboin, 1974; Enright & Lapsley, 1980; Kurdek, 1977, 1982; Rubin, 1978). Across various studies, interrater reliability ranges from .78 to .96; short-term (2–4 week) test-retest correlations are around .80. Kurdek (1977) reported a test-retest correlation of .68 after a slightly longer 5-week period.

Chandler's (1973) measure of *cognitive* role-taking ability requires a child to tell a series of stories based on cartoon sequences printed on a set of cards. The child is instructed to pay particular attention to what the main character is thinking and feeling in each story. After completing the initial version, the child is asked to retell the story from the point of view of a bystander who arrives in the middle of the action and is unaware of what happened at the story's beginning. The child receives an "egocentrism" score based on the degree of privileged information ascribed to the bystander (i.e., information that is available to the child from the previous part of the story but that is not known by the bystander).

Kurdek (1979) reported no sex differences in performance on this task, although role taking did increase with age. Rubin (1978) confirmed this age trend but concluded that the task is too difficult for preschoolers (see also Urberg & Docherty, 1976) and that it may be too easy for many children over age 10 or 11.

Correlations between IQ and role-taking performance on this task have typically fallen in the range of .2 to .4 across studies (e.g., Chandler, 1973; Rubin, 1978). Other studies demonstrated significant correlations between this task and other measures of cognitive perspective taking (Kurdek, 1977) and with teachers' ratings of children's self-control (Kendall, Zupan, & Braswell, 1981). In general, results are far from consistent. For example, Rubin (1978) found low or nonsignificant correlations with other measures and concluded that there was little convergent or discriminant validity for role-taking tasks.

Nevertheless, Chandler (1973) reported that his role-taking measure successfully discriminated normal control children from a group of chronic delinquent preadolescent boys. Urbain and Kendall (1981) also reported differences in role-taking performance between a group of impulsive-aggressive second- and third-graders and a group of nonimpulsive children. Similarly, Cohen, Kershner, and Wehrspann (1985) found that clinic-referred children with externalizing symptoms (particularly boys) provided more immature perspective-taking responses than children with internalizing symptoms. Based on a peer rating measure, LeMare and Rubin (1987) found that third-grade children who were identified by their peers as socially "Isolate" performed less well on the Chandler task than their "Average" and "Sociable" classmates. Leahy and Huard (1976) found that children with good role-taking skills had more positive ideal self-images and greater disparity between real and ideal self-image than children who performed less well on this role-taking task.

Several training studies employing the bystander cartoon measure also have been reported (Chandler, 1973; Chandler et al., 1974; Little, 1978; Urbain & Kendall, 1981; Kendall & Zupan, 1981). In general, it appears that the task is sensitive to treatment effects, and some studies have found that role-taking task improvement has been associated with improvements in behavior (Chandler, 1973; Kendall & Zupin, 1981). Unfortunately, the findings have been far from universal (Chandler et al., 1974; Little, 1978; Urbain & Kendall, 1981), perhaps due to differences in training procedures and to the length and intensity of the intervention programs employed across studies.

Borke's Interpersonal Awareness Measure   In contrast to the previously described measure of cognitive role taking, Borke's (1971, 1973) Interpersonal Awareness measure was developed to assess *affective* role-taking ability. In this procedure the examiner first makes sure that the child can discriminate among drawings of faces representing the basic emotions of happiness, fear, anger, and sadness. Then the child is told a series of stories in which the main character's experiences (e.g., eating a favorite snack, getting lost in the woods at night, being forced to go to bed at night) are likely to arouse a particular targeted emotion (e.g., pleasure, fear). The child's task is to select the picture of the face that best shows how the child in the story is feeling. This procedure is followed by the presentation of eight stories involving peer interaction in which the child is asked to identify the predictable feeling of a character in response to specific actions (e.g., sharing cars, pushing him or her off a bike, refusing to let him or her play).

Given that a child's response to each story is scored simply as correct or incorrect according to preestablished criteria, Rubin's (1978) report of 100% interrater reliability scoring agreement is not surprising. Interitem correlations and test-retest reliability data have not been reported in the published literature.

Performance on this task is within the response capabilities of children as young as three years (Borke, 1971, 1973; Urberg & Docherty, 1976). However, the degree to which functional and well-developed affective role-taking ability is present at this early age is questionable (Borke, 1972; Chandler & Greenspan, 1972). By 5 years of age most children have mastered the task.

With the exception of one study (vanLieshout et al., 1976), correlations of this task with other cognitive and affective role-taking measures have been low or nonsignificant (Kurdek & Rogdon, 1975; Rubin, 1978). However, performance on Borke's measure has been shown to be related to positive peer nominations in kindergarten (Spence, 1987) and to predict prosocial behavior in preschool children (Roopnarine, 1987). Murray and Aammer (1977) found a relationship between a measure of cooperative behavior and a modified version of Borke's task for a sample of 4- to 5-year-olds, but they failed to find improvement on these tasks following training in role taking. Similarly, Iannotti (1978) reported a lack of treatment effects on similar tasks following role-taking training procedures. Ridley and Vaughn (1982) found no differences on pre- and posttest measures of empathy following a problem-solving training program.

Borke's task appears useful as a general measure of developing abilities for affect identification in preschool children, but its relationship to behavioral indices of competence is unclear. The global nature of the social-cognitive skill being measured probably renders the instrument somewhat insensitive to the specific cognitive-behavioral deficits to which intervention programs often must be addressed.

Selman's Measure of Interpersonal Understanding   Selman (1980) and his colleagues developed a series of open-ended dilemmas to explore the development of children's interpersonal understanding. Each dilemma is geared toward a particular age group and is presented in audio-visual filmstrip format. For example, in one story a new girl in town asks a classmate to go with her to an ice-skating show on the following day. However, this classmate previously has made plans to play with her best friend. To complicate matters further, the best friend has already made it clear that she does not care for the new girl. A semistructured interview follows the presentation of each dilemma. In the case of the sample story outlined above, conceptions of friendship are explored and probed in detail (e.g., how do friendships develop, what makes a good friendship, what accounts for jealousy). Other dilemmas and their corresponding interviews are designed to examine conceptions of people (e.g., how do people get to be the way they are, how do people change) and conceptions of group relations (e.g., how do peer groups form, what makes a group cohesive). Each discrete interview response is scored by comparing it to examples of reasoning at five hypothetical stages of development in interpersonal understanding.

Exact agreement for stage scores has been reported to be around 70% (Cooney, 1977; Pellegrini, 1985), while interrater reliability has generally exceeded .85 (Pellegrini, 1985; Selman & Jaquette, 1978; Selman, Jaquette, & Lavin, 1977). Enright (1977) reported test-retest reliability of .92 over 2 weeks, although stability appears to decline over longer time intervals. For example, Cooney (1977) reported reliability of .61 for 2 months and .63 for 5 months, and Brion (1977) reported comparable reliability for a 6-month interval. Internal consistency reliability also appears to be relatively high, although it is variable across concept domains (Pellegrini, 1985, 1986; Selman & Jaquette, 1978).

In a broad sense, interpersonal understanding appears to relate to social adjustment. For example, Selman (1976) reported that clinic children showed highly significant and increasing deficits in interpersonal understanding relative to normals, even after controlling for differences in IQ. Longitudinal follow-ups suggested that the developmental lags of the disturbed children diminished gradually over the course of time and treatment (Gurucharri, Phelps, & Selman, 1984; Gurucharri & Selman, 1982).

Selman (1976) also reported that interpersonal understanding was related (inversely) to negative sociometric status, although it was not related to positive status. In another study, interpersonal understanding was associated with teacher ratings of behavioral competence and positive mental health, but it was not associated with ratings of behavior problems (Selman et al., 1977). In a factor-analytic study of diverse measures of cognitive functioning, Pellegrini, Masten, Garmezy, and Ferrarese (1987) found interpersonal understanding to be related to social problem-solving ability and to humor appreciation, comprehension, and production. Although strongly related to IQ, this broad factor (labeled "Social Comprehension") was a significant predictor of social competence as reflected by teacher and peer judgments in school.

Two attempts (Cooney, 1977; Enright, 1977) to enrich the interpersonal understanding of children in structured group situations met with mixed results, and, unfortunately, neither attempt employed a measure of behavioral impact. However, Selman and Demorest (1984) proposed an exciting prototype of intervention with socially maladaptive children. In this approach to "friendship therapy," an adult counselor works with youngsters in pairs, helping them to experience the process of making friends in practice as they play and in theory as they reflect upon their own experiences.

Despite its promise, Selman's interpersonal understanding measure has some basic limitations as an assessment device for general practice. First, its verbally laden, probing interviews may yield a measure of comprehension that exaggerates the level of understanding that children actually employ in real-life social interaction. Consequently, Selman, Schorin, Stone, and Phelps (1983) developed strategies for the naturalistic assessment of interpersonal understanding as it is reflected in ongoing peer-group behavior and conversation. The discrepancy between comprehension and performance may, itself, be of clinical significance.

Secondly, the Interpersonal Understanding interviews require a thorough working knowledge of Selman's (1980) structural model and the traditional skill of a clinical interviewer. Nevertheless, for clinicians who are able and willing to familiarize themselves with the model and with the assessment procedures, the detailed explication of a child's level of maturity in reasoning through interpersonal dilemmas promises considerable payoff in designing therapeutic interventions to remediate maladaptive social relations.

Interpersonal Problem Solving

In the area of human problem-solving processes, the direction of research has shifted from the measurement of cognitive abilities related to nonsocial problems through puzzle-type tasks, anagram problems, and various intellectual creativity tasks (e.g., Simon & Newell, 1971) to the assessment of interpersonal problem-solving skills. Jahoda (1953, 1958) was among the first writers to place explicit theoretical emphasis on the relation of effective interpersonal problem solving to social and emotional adjustment. D'Zurilla and Goldfried (1971) defined interpersonal problem solving as "a behavioral process . . . which (a) makes available a variety of potentially effective response alternatives for dealing with problematic situations and (b) increases the probability of selecting the most effective response from among these various alternatives" (p. 108).

The relationship between interpersonal problem solving, social-cognitive abilities, and positive social behavior has prompted interest, attention, and research efforts. Interpersonal problem solving might best be understood as the application of one's social understanding to conflict areas in social interaction. Response alternatives are likely to be generated in part through role-taking ability, and the more mature one's social understanding, the more likely it is that an effective response will be chosen from among the alternatives generated. On the other hand, while accurate understanding of the thoughts and feelings of other persons may facilitate problem solving, it certainly does not guarantee that the most adaptive solution will be chosen in a particular interpersonal problem. A child may require other types of information and may need to learn new behavioral skills before developing effective means for solving the problem.

Research in the area of interpersonal problem solving has attempted to delineate a variety of discrete yet interrelated interpersonal cognitive problem-solving skills that are hypothesized to be important components of social problem solving. At the same time an interpersonal problem-solving approach to intervention has gradually evolved. This approach is characterized by a primary emphasis on adaptive *thinking processes* as opposed to an emphasis on internal psychodynamics or on specific overt behaviors per se as major factors in psychological adjustment (Pellegrini & Urban, 1985; Spivack, Platt, & Shure, 1976). There have been numerous approaches to the assessment of interpersonal problem-solving ability (see Butler & Meichenbaum, 1981; D'Zurilla & Nezu, 1982). We will focus on the most widely researched measures.

Preschool Interpersonal Problem-Solving Test (PIPS)   The PIPS constitutes perhaps the most widely used measure of social problem solving. It was developed to measure a young child's ability to generate alternative solutions to interpersonal problems (Shure & Spivack, 1978; Spivack et al., 1976), an ability that is hypothesized to be an important component of interpersonal problem solving in early childhood.

The test consists of two sets of age-relevant interpersonal problems. The first set deals with a peer issue (conflict over a toy), and the second deals with an authority figure issue (avoiding maternal anger for misbehavior). To sustain interest in the task, new characters are introduced in varied situations depicting essentially the same type of problem. Active probing procedures encourage the child to generate the maximum number of alternative solutions. The child's score is the total number of alternatives generated to both types of problems. Spivack et al. (1976) also developed a similar test for older children, and numerous investigators have modified the content, presentation, and/or scoring procedures of the PIPS to explore alternative-solutions thinking ability in various samples (see Krasnor & Rubin, 1981).

It appears relatively easy to determine the number of relevant solutions with a very high degree of interrater reliability (Spivack & Shure, 1974). Alternative-solutions thinking also appears to be relatively stable. One week test-retest reliability was .72 for a sample of 4-year olds, while 3- to 5-month test-retest reliability was .59 for a different sample (Spivack et al., 1976). Correlations of .51 to .59 were found between the number of solutions generated in response to the peer and authority figure problems (Spivack et al., 1976).

Spivack et al. (1976) reported that performance on PIPS and intellectual ability, as measured by various IQ tests, are not highly related (Shure, Spivack, & Gordon, 1972; Shure, Spivack, & Jaeger, 1971). Where low but significant relationships were found, the predictive power of the PIPS was not attributed solely to its relationship to IQ or to sheer verbal productivity (Shure & Spivack, 1978).

A significant relationship between alternative-solutions thinking ability, as measured by the PIPS, and behavioral adjustment in a school-type setting has been found consistently, even with IQ and verbal fluency controlled. Spivack et al. (1976) reported, for example, that a sample of middle-class preschoolers provided significantly more solutions than did their lower-class counterparts, and their solutions were characterized by a greater range of diversity of approach. However, within both social classes, individual children rated by teachers as less well adjusted gave the fewest and least diverse solutions. Middle-class children who were deficient in alternative-solutions thinking ability were reported to be shy, inhibited, and withdrawn, whereas deficient lower-class children presented more disruptive behaviors. In subsequent studies the PIPS test has been shown to differentiate between normal reference groups and preschoolers rated by their teachers as either impulsive or excessively inhibited and withdrawn (e.g., Shure et al., 1971; Shure, Newman, & Silver, 1973; Shure, Spivack, & Powell, 1972).

Although Spivack et al. (1976) concluded that the ability to conceive of a wide range of solutions, rather than the specific content of solutions, is most predictive of well-adjusted behavior, it has been suggested that the quality of alternative solutions (i.e., type and effectiveness) may be an equally important predictor of children's behavioral adjustment (Fischler & Kendall, 1988; Guerra & Slaby, 1989). For example, Gouze (1987) assessed the relationship of attention and problem-solving ability to aggression in preschool boys. She found the content of the solutions given on the PIPS to be a better predictor of aggressive classroom behavior than the number of solutions that were generated.

There have been a few successful attempts to train alternative-solutions thinking in preschoolers. In two separate studies, teachers trained in the problem-solving approach facilitated significant improvements in both

PIPS test scores and in problem behaviors (Spivack & Shure, 1974; Shure & Spivack, 1975). Moreover, in the majority of cases, improvements of trained children were sustained for 1 year, and children who improved the most in PIPS performance also showed the most substantial behavioral improvement. In another study, mothers taught social problem-solving skills to their own children who had been identified by teachers as disruptive or inhibited in the preschool classroom (Shure & Spivack, 1978). Improvement on the PIPS was again related to behavioral improvement as judged by the teachers who were unaware of the study. Mothers with the best interpersonal problem-solving skills obtained the best training results.

However, the results of other studies have been equivocal. For example, Sharp (1981) and Rickel, Eshelman, and Loigman (1983) were unable to replicate the findings of Spivack and Shure (1974). Although children who received problem-solving training were better able than untreated children to generate alternative solutions to problems, no differences between the two groups were found on observational measures of classroom behavior or on teacher ratings of child adjustment.

Means–Ends Problem-Solving Test (MEPS)   Another widely used measure, the MEPS, was developed to assess a child's ability to plan in careful, sequential fashion the step-by-step procedures or "means" needed to reach an intended goal (Shure & Spivack, 1972). Means–ends thinking is hypothesized to be a higher-order and more sophisticated component of social problem solving than alternative-solutions thinking.

The MEPS procedure presents a child with a series of stories portraying hypothetical problems of an interpersonal nature. Separate stories have been developed for use with elementary school-age children and adolescents. Only the initial situation and the final outcome of the problem are presented. The child's task is to "fill in the middle of the story," indicating various means by which the problem solution might be reached. Story responses are scored for total number of overall means generated (as well as the specified steps within each mean), perception of potential obstacles to carrying out a particular mean, and accurate use of time sequences in the problem-solving process. Factor analysis of total MEPS scores across different subject samples has yielded one primary factor of means–ends thinking.

Platt and Spivack (1975) reported 91% exact agreement between two judges concerning the number of means, obstacles, and time references, as well as total score, for a sample of 30 latency-age children. In general, interrater reliability falls in the .85–.99 range (Pellegrini, 1985; Urbain & Kendall, 1981; Kendall & Zupan, 1981; Platt & Spivack, 1975). Depending on the sample, average interitem correlations range from .12 (university upper-class students) to .33 (psychiatric patients). Item-total correlations range between .32 (delinquent adolescents) and .48 (female student beauticians) (see Platt & Spivack, 1975).

Sex differences in performance on the MEPS have not been noted (Pellegrini, 1985). Although Shure and Spivack (1972) and Pellegrini (1985) failed to find significant social class differences in MEPS performance, Braswell, Kendall, and Urbain (1982) did find such differences. Correlations between MEPS test scores and IQ have been modest but generally significant (Shure & Spivack, 1972; Spivack et al., 1976). For example, Pellegrini (1985) reported that means, obstacles, and time references correlated with WISC-R Vocabulary scores in the .32 to .42 range, and these measures correlated with Block Design scores in the .29 to .34 range.

Nevertheless, means–ends thinking, as measured by the MEPS, has been found to differentiate between normal controls and (a) institutionalized delinquent adolescents (Platt, Spivack, Altman, Altman, & Peizer, 1974) and (b) emotionally disturbed adolescents (Platt et al., 1974; Shure & Spivack, 1972), even with the effect of IQ controlled. Urbain and Kendall (1981) found large differences between impulsive-aggressive second- and third-grade children and a group of nonimpulsive children on a modified version of the MEPS. Kettlewell and Kausch (1983) reported significant gains in the total problem-solving scores and in the number of alternative solutions on the MEPS for a group of aggressive children who participated in a cognitive-behavioral treatment program. Shure and Spivack (1972) noted that emotionally disturbed children not only generate fewer means than normals but also tend to limit their responses to pragmatic, impulsive, or physically aggressive means, while the means of normals tend to reflect greater planning and foresight. Larcen (reported in Allen, Chinsky, Larcen, Lochman, & Selinger, 1976) reported a negative relationship between MEPS scores and measures of emotionality, inability to delay, and social aggression in a group of latency-aged children placed in institutions for reasons of parental neglect. Pellegrini (1985) found scores on a modified version of the MEPS to be modestly and positively correlated with "positive" peer reputation and inversely correlated with both "isolated" and "disruptive" reputation and with academic achievement and teacher ratings of adaptive social behavior, even with intelligence controlled. Similarly, Fischler and Kendall (1988) found that children whose problem-solving responses were more consistently active across different MEPS stories were rated by their teachers as less inattentive and withdrawn in classroom activities.

Unfortunately, as with the PIPS, a considerable amount of variation exists in administration of the MEPS, in story content and in scoring procedures (e.g., Allen et al., 1976; Krasnor & Rubin, 1981; Pellegrini, 1985), and there is need for ecological validation (Butler & Meichenbaum, 1981; Krasnor & Rubin, 1981) and for development of alternate forms

(Kendall & Zupan, 1981). Nevertheless, this instrument might prove to be a valuable clinical assessment tool for elementary school-age children and adolescents.

Other Measures   Numerous other attempts have been made to measure interpersonal problem-solving ability in children (for a more comprehensive review, see Butler & Meichenbaum, 1981). For example, the Preschool Interpersonal Problem-Solving Test (Rubin, 1982) is an extension of the PIPS and was developed to assess both the quantity and quality of alternative solutions. The "Open Middle Test" (McKim, Weissberg, Cowen, Gesten, & Rapkin, 1982) constitutes yet another adaptation of the PIPS. In this measure, age-relevant peer problems are presented as cartoon stories. Separate scores are derived for the number of alternative solutions, irrelevant responses, and solution effectiveness. The Purdue Elementary Problem-Solving Inventory, designed to assess problem-solving abilities of disadvantaged elementary school children from various ethnic backgrounds, presents interpersonal problem scenarios via an audio-visual filmstrip and employs a multiple-choice response format (Feldhusen & Houtz, 1975; Feldhusen, Houtz, & Ringenbach, 1972). It has been shown to differentiate interpersonal problem-solving ability in elementary school children at various grade levels (White & Blackham, 1985).

A number of investigators have employed simulated real-life problem-solving situations to assess the translation of interpersonal cognitive problem-solving abilities into effective problem-solving behavior (e.g., Larcen, reported in Allen et al., 1976; McClure et al., 1978; Ridley & Vaughn, 1982). With further refinements, "in vivo" assessment of interpersonal problem-solving ability should prove to be particularly useful for directing clinical interventions. (See also Krasnor & Rubin, 1981, for a discussion of observational approaches to assessing behavioral problem-solving skills in naturalistic settings.)

Self-Report Measures

Coincident with the increased popularity of self-report measures, several paper-and-pencil measures have been developed to assist in the assessment of social skills.

The Matson Evaluation of Social Skills with Youngsters (MESSY)   This instrument was developed to assess a wide range of children's social skills (Matson, Rotatori, & Helsel, 1983) and is available in both child self-report (62 items) and teacher (64 items) versions. The items are rated on 5-point Likert-type scales and reflect the extent to which the child endorses the specific behavior (e.g., "I show my feelings"; "I pick on people to make them angry").

Satisfactory test-retest reliability coefficients were obtained at 2 weeks for the self-report (.50) and teacher report (.55), and two consistent factors emerged for both reports: Appropriate Social Skill and Inappropriate Assertiveness. In addition, although sex and age differences were found, the results were inconsistent and varied between teacher/child reports and each of the factors.

Endorsement of prosocial behaviors on the MESSY has been found to be negatively related to depression in children (Helsel & Matson, 1984). Significant but low correlations were reported between parent ratings on the CBCL and the child's self-report on the MESSY for groups of psychiatric inpatient children (Kazdin et al, 1984). In addition, ratings of parents and teachers accurately differentiated between nonreferred children and children referred for anxiety disorder, although the MESSY did not discriminate between the self-reports for these two groups (Strauss, Lease, Kazdin, Dulcan, & Last, 1989). Similarly, no relationships were observed between the child's report on the MESSY and role-play measures and direct observation of social interaction (Kazdin et al., 1984) or peer nominations (Matson, Esveldt-Dawson, & Kazdin, 1983). Although the MESSY holds promise as a self-report measure of children's social skills, additional validation is needed.

Children's Action Tendency Scale (CATS)   This self-report measure was developed to evaluate a child's level of assertiveness (Deluty, 1979). The scale consists of 13 conflict situations that are arranged in a paired-comparisons format (i.e., three sets of responses are provided for each item) in an attempt to control for social desirability. The scale assesses a child's tendency to endorse aggressive, assertive, or submissive responses.

Coefficients for the internal consistency of the aggressive, assertive, and submissive subscales were .77, .63, and .72, respectively. At 4 months, test-retest reliabilities for these subscales were .48, .60, and .57 (Deluty, 1979). Deluty (1984) also conducted naturalistic behavioral observations over an 8-month period in a variety of school situations. He obtained concurrent validity for several components of assertiveness. However, because normative data have not yet been established for clinical subgroups, it is difficult to generalize these findings to other populations (Williamson & McKenzie, 1988).

Children's Assertive Behavior Scale (CABS)   The CABS (Michelson & Wood, 1982) is a 27-item scale that measures the intensity of a child's nonassertive responses and the degree to which nonassertive responses lead toward passivity or aggression. Each item consists of five response choices that measure degrees of assertiveness, aggressiveness, and submissiveness. The child is asked to identify the option that best describes his or her behavior in a particular situation.

Normative data were obtained for two samples of elementary school children (see Michelson & Wood, 1982). Internal consistency was .78 and .80 for each of the groups, and the test-retest reliability coefficients obtained after 4 weeks were .66 and .86. In addition, the CABS was successful in discriminating between children who received assertiveness training and untreated control children (Michelson & Wood, 1980).

Children's Assertiveness Inventory (CAI)   The CAI was developed for children between 6 and 12 years of age (Ollendick, 1981, 1984). It contains 14 "yes"/"no" items that measure a child's assertive responses in both positive and negative situations (e.g., "When you do something good, do you tell someone your age about it?"; "When someone your age takes something that is yours, do you let them take it?").

Normative data were derived from three samples of normal children and from one sample of socially withdrawn children (Ollendick, 1984). Internal consistency ranged between .20 and .31; the low correlations seemingly were related to the heterogeneity of the items (Ollendick, 1984). Adequate test-retest reliability coefficients were obtained after 1 week (.76) and 3 months (.61) for two different samples. The CAI also was found to have positive correlations with sociometric peer ratings, role-play assertion, and direct observation. Negative correlations were obtained with teachers' assessments of social withdrawal (Ollendick, 1984). In addition, no differences were found in assertive behavior between girls and boys or for varying levels of socioeconomic status. However, the major weakness with the CAI is its inability to discriminate between assertion and aggression (Deluty, 1979).

The CATS, CABS, and the CAI would be useful in identifying a range of behaviors as part of broad-based screening or as part of a larger approach to assessment. Moderate correlations among the CATS, CABS, and CAI have been reported (Scanlon & Ollendick, 1986), but more precise understanding of the relationships among these three measures is needed. The relationship between these measures and teacher, peer, and parent ratings also warrants additional study. The use of a combination of these measures is recommended to tap more fully the dimension of assertive behavior (Scanlon & Ollendick, 1986).

Problems in Attention and Impulsivity

Numerous labels including "hyperkinesis," "minimal brain damage," "impulsivity," and "hyperactivity" have been used to describe children who demonstrate difficulty maintaining sustained attention, inhibiting impulsive responses, and regulating their activity level. The most recent psychiatric nomenclature for this disorder, "attention deficit-hyperactivity disorder" or

ADHD (American Psychiatric Association [APA], 1987), was chosen to reflect the most current understanding of this complex array of problems (Barkley, 1989). The multifaceted nature of ADHD warrants comprehensive multimethod assessment; some of the techniques relevant to cognitive-behavioral assessment will be reviewed below.

Behavioral checklists, described earlier in this chapter, are a frequent component of the assessment of ADHD and can provide valuable information about a child's functioning in a variety of circumstances. Indeed, Barkley (1989) described a "comprehensive" assessment of disorders in attention and impulsivity as one that uses several informants across multiple settings, employing a variety of assessment techniques that measure academic and social functioning, as well as the primary symptoms of ADHD.

Other parent and teacher checklists of ADHD symptoms have achieved widespread use, especially those developed by Conners (1973) and by Werry, Weiss, and Peters (Werry, 1968).

Attentional Focusing

Several observational schemes have been developed to assess behaviors thought to be incompatible with academic learning (e.g., Becker, Madsen, Arnold, & Thomas, 1967; Werry & Quay, 1969). In general, observational studies of classroom behaviors have revealed a rather consistent pattern of moderate positive correlations of task-oriented attentive behaviors with achievement. These studies have shown similar negative correlations for nonattentive and disruptive behaviors. Moreover, several studies have suggested that behavioral ratings of attention in first grade may predict later achievement better than early achievement test scores (Lahaderne, 1968; Meyers, Attwell, & Orpet, 1968).

One useful system for the naturalistic observation of attentional focusing was developed by Cobb (1972, 1973). In this procedure, students are best observed in structured academic settings where a range of activities is likely to occur in a given classroom period (e.g., group lessons and discussions, individual academic deskwork, and question-and-answer periods). A trained observer assumes an inconspicuous position from which the target child (or children) can be seen. Behavior is observed and recorded at regular intervals throughout the period (e.g., every 15 seconds). When multiple children are of concern, they are observed sequentially at regular intervals. The categories of behavior that are coded include: (1) attending, (2) talking to the teacher (positive), (3) interacting with peers (positive), (4) complying, (5) self-stimulation, (6) playing, (7) talking to the teacher (negative), (8) interacting with peers (negative), (9) not complying, and (10) not attending.

With a minimum amount of training (4 hours as reported in Cobb, 1972), observers can use the system with a high degree of interrater reliability. For example, Cobb (1972) reported 88% exact agreement across codes. Similarly, Soli and Devine (1976) achieved 86% exact agreement. Comparison of ratings collected on "even" days yielded a correlation of .56 across codes, although the behavioral categories that consistently contributed the highest percentage of variance in regression analyses had a mean stability coefficient of .71.

Cobb (1972) found that behavioral observations taken during arithmetic lessons correlated .63 to .69 with standardized arithmetic test scores, and combinations of behaviors were found to be better predictors of achievement than single behaviors. When cross-validated in a different academic setting, correlations remained robust, ranging from .50 to .58. However, the behavior-achievement relationship found among children of higher socioeconomic status could not be cross-validated among children of lower status. Devine and Tomlinson (1976) found the Cobb scheme to be sensitive enough to differentiate accurately among elementary school children assigned by teachers to one of four criterion groups based on the quality of their classroom adjustment.

Problem-Solving Style

In addition to differences in overt behavior, ADHD children seem to differ in their nonsocial problem-solving style. For example, when faced with a number of response alternatives on a task, especially when there is a great deal of uncertainty as to which response is correct, ADHD children tend to respond quickly. Their failure to evaluate thoroughly all possibilities leads to frequent mistakes. Children who respond in this way (not all of whom are diagnosed as ADHD) are said to have an "impulsive" conceptual tempo (Kagan, 1966). Other children are apt to delay responding until all the alternatives have been carefully considered, and these "reflective" children are less prone to mistakes (Kagan, 1966).

A number of tests have been developed to assess problem-solving style and its relationship to adjustment. Two of these tests appear to be useful additions to a cognitive-behavioral assessment battery.

Matching Familiar Figures Test (MFFT) The MFFT was developed by Kagan and his colleagues (Kagan, Rosman, Day, Albert, & Phillips, 1964) to assess conceptual tempo. It is a 12-item task in which the child is shown a single picture of a familiar object projected on a screen and an array of six similar, but not identical, variants. The child is instructed to select from among the variants the one picture that is identical to the standard stimulus (preschoolers choose among four variants). Two scores are derived: the average response latency per trial and the total number of response errors. Children whose scores are above the median error score and below the median latency score are identified as impulsive (i.e., fast *and* inaccurate).

Messer's (1976) review of reliability data on the MFF found test-retest correlations to range from .58 to .96 for latencies and from .34 to .80 for errors. Internal consistencies for latencies were .89 and only .58 to .62 for errors. Ault, Mitchell, and Hartmann (1976) further detailed the low reliability of the error scores (.23 to .43 over 3-week to 2½-year intervals) and added that, although they were statistically significant, the error scores were below acceptable standards for test-retest reliability. In an investigation of the short-term stability of three versions of the MFFT, Egeland and Weinberg (1976) reported that the MFFT was more successful at the consistent classifying of reflective subjects than of impulsive subjects. These authors concluded that while MFFT reliability data compared favorably with those of other measures of cognitive style and personality, they were not ideal.

Numerous studies have considered strategies for modifying the conceptual tempo of children who appear to be impulsive based on their performance on the MFFT. Early studies examined the effects of imposed delay (e.g., Kagan, Pearson, & Welch, 1966), while later studies evaluated modeling techniques (e.g., Hemry, 1973; Massari & Schack, 1972), self-instructional training (e.g., Finch, Wilkinson, Nelson, & Montgomery, 1975), and combinations of these procedures (e.g., Kendall & Finch, 1976, 1978; Meichenbaum & Goodman, 1971). Although the cumulative results remain ambiguous, it appears reasonable to conclude that an impulsive cognitive tempo can be modified and that the combined training approaches offer considerable promise (see Kendall & Braswell, 1985, for a more thorough review of cognitive impulsivity and self-instructional training).

Several commentaries have noted major criticisms of the MFFT. For example, Ault et al. (1976) pointed out statistical problems associated with analyses of the data derived from the administration of the MFFT, and questions have been raised about defining conceptual tempo on the basis of latency and error rates. A later version of the MFFT promises greater reliability. The MFF20 (Cairns & Cammock, 1978) contains 20 items and is appropriate for children between 7 and 11 years of age. Cairns and Cammock (1978) reported split-half correlations of .91 for latency scores and .89 for errors over a 2-week period. Test-retest correlations over a 5-week period were .85 for latency scores and .77 for error scores. Moreover, in contrast to the original measure, there do not appear to be floor and ceiling effects on the MFF20 or a decrease in the correlations between latency and errors for children over 10 years of age (Cairns & Cammock, 1984).

Conceptual tempo as measured by the MFFT has been positively related to reading difficulties (see Messer, 1976) and depression (Swartz, Friedman, Lindsay, and Narrol, 1982); however, the extent to which the MFFT is related to behavioral adjustment remains a matter of controversy (Block, 1987; Block, Block, & Harrington, 1974, 1975; Block, Gjerde, & Block, 1986; Kagan, 1987). Nonetheless, the MFFT has demonstrated some utility as an outcome measure for impulsivity training programs (see Kendall & Finch, 1979), and Egeland and Weinberg (1976) developed three 8-item alternate test forms that increase the usefulness of the MFFT in evaluating treatment efforts by allowing for repeated assessments.

Porteus Maze Test Porteus (1933) originated the Maze Test as an adjunct to early measures of intelligence; however, he quickly recognized its usefulness in the assessment of social adjustment. The test consists of a series of paper-and-pencil mazes of graded difficulty, with each maze slightly more difficult than the preceding one. Three separate series (i.e., Vineland Revision, Extension Series, and Supplement Series) were developed for repeated administration of the test (Porteus, 1955). Each set of mazes is said to measure aspects of planning ability, foresight, and impulsivity.

Two distinct scores are calculated. The quantitative Test Quotient (TQ) score is based on the highest level maze successfully completed and the number of trials required by the subject to solve each maze. The Qualitative (Q) score is based on the number of qualitative errors: lifting the pencil contrary to instructions, cutting across corners in the maze, and bumping into or crossing the sides of maze alleyways. However, the number of pencil lifts has emerged as a somewhat separate score in factor-analytic studies.

In their review of the Porteus Maze Test literature, Riddle and Roberts (1974) reported TQ test-retest and alternate form reliabilities varying from .43 to .97. They concluded that .50 is the magnitude of reliability to be expected. Interrater reliabilities for the Q score were found to range from .89 to .99, although test-retest reliabilities for the Q score were around .60.

In a recent study, Pellegrini et al. (1987) found that performance on the Porteus Maze Test and the MFFT defined a "cognitive efficiency" factor in a sample of 9- to 14-year-old children. Moreover, this factor was significantly correlated with indices of social competence and academic achievement. In another recent study (Kuehne, Kehle, & McMahon, 1987), the Porteus Maze Test accurately discriminated between attention deficit disordered children (ADD) and normal controls. In addition, the combination of children's scores on the Porteus Maze Test, the MFFT, the Conners Parent Questionnaire, and the Conners Teacher Questionnaire correctly classified 96.7% of the ADD children. Thus, information derived from this test may be useful in the identification of ADD children and in the planning of intervention strategies.

The Porteus mazes frequently have been used to evaluate the effects of cognitive-behavioral treatments for impulsive, hyperactive, and non-self-controlled children. Douglas, Parry, Marton, and Garson (1976), for example, analyzed TQ, Q, and pencil lift scores. The test appears to be a sensitive indicator of therapeutic change, reflecting children's planning, judgment, and attentional focusing.

Problems in Mood and Affect

Although childhood is often viewed as a carefree time, current research and clinical work suggest that children can experience significant distress. Recognizing and measuring these difficulties has been enhanced by the use of self-report measures that provide access to children's thoughts and feelings. Comprehensive assessment of anxiety and depression, the most common disturbances in mood and affect, includes the use of many of the methods described earlier in this chapter. In addition, the self-report measures described below prove especially helpful in understanding experiences that children often find difficult to articulate.

Anxiety

Childhood fears and anxieties are sufficiently common occurrences to be considered a "normal" part of development (Johnson & Melamed, 1979). However, these emotional states become the concern of clinicians when they are of a severity or duration that impinges negatively on the child or on those within his or her circle of familial or social interaction (Wells & Vitulano, 1984). Although parents and teachers may provide a behavioral account of a child's suspected fears and anxieties, the most direct information comes from self-report (Barrios & Hartmann, 1988). The child's description of subjective feelings of anxiety-producing or fearful situations is crucial in gaining a more complete picture of the presenting problem. Similarly, an understanding of a child's self-statements or internal dialogues about a given situation or problem-solving strategy is an equally important component of the cognitive-behavioral assessment process (Kendall & Ronan, 1990).

Anxiety and fear are assumed to comprise symptoms arising from three domains: subjective reports of distress and discomfort; physiological reactions, including sweating and increased heart rate, respiration rate, and muscular tension; and behavioral responses, including avoidance, escape, and/or tentative approach (Nietzel, Bernstein, & Russell, 1988). Ideally, comprehensive assessment involves measurement of each of these domains.

Unfortunately, physiological assessment of anxiety requires special, often expensive, equipment and is plagued by numerous technical problems that make accurate, unbiased measurement of physiological reactivity extremely difficult (Nietzel et al., 1988). A comprehensive review of the complex literature on physiological assessment is beyond the scope of the present chapter; interested readers are referred to Sturgis and Gramling (1988).

This leaves behavioral responses and subjective reports as the primary areas to be assessed. Behavioral responses such as avoidance and tentative approach are a direct focus of desensitization treatment and should be measured as precisely as possible prior to treatment (e.g., How long can the child tolerate exposure to the feared stimulus? How close can the child stand to the feared stimulus?).

Several self-report measures are available for measuring children's anxieties and fears (see Barrios & Hartmann, 1988). Two of the most frequently used self-report inventories are reviewed below.

The Revised Children's Manifest Anxiety Scale (RCMAS)   The RCMAS (Reynolds & Richmond, 1978), also referred to as the "What I Think and Feel" scale, is based on the Children's Manifest Anxiety Scale (CMAS) (Castaneda, McCandless, & Palermo, 1956) and provides a general index of a child's anxiety. The new version takes less time to administer and has been adjusted for a lower reading level, making it appropriate for children 6 to 18 years of age.

The measure consists of 37 items (28 items make up an anxiety scale, and 9 items make up a lie scale). The anxiety scale contains physiological, worry/oversensitivity, and concentration subscales, and a total anxiety score is obtained by summing the number of statements that the child indicates are true for him or her (e.g., "I worry about what is going to happen").

Test-retest reliability coefficients for the anxiety and lie subscales were reported to be .77-.88 and .65-.75, respectively, for 1-week and 5-week periods (Wisniewski, Mulick, Genshaft, & Coury, 1987), and .68 and .58, respectively, for a 9-month period (Reynolds, 1981). In addition, the RCMAS has been shown to correlate significantly with the state scale of the State-Trait Anxiety Inventory for Children (Spielberger, 1973). Normative data also are available for several other groups of children (Reynolds & Paget, 1981).

Fear Survey Schedule for Children-Revised (FSSC-R)   The FSSC-R (Ollendick, 1983) is a revision of the Fear Survey Schedule for Children that was developed by Scherer and Nakamura (1968). The original 80 items were retained, although the 5-point scale was changed to a 3-point scale ("none," "some," and "a lot") to enhance the ease with which younger children, mentally retarded children, and other impaired children could complete the measure. Normative data were collected on two samples of normal elementary school children and a clinical population of children with school phobia (Ollendick, 1983). Indices of internal consistency on each of the normal samples were extremely high (about .95). Test-retest reliability coefficients were .82 over a 1-week period and .55 over a 3-month period. In addition, total anxiety scores differentiated between the school-phobic and normal children.

The RCMAS and the FSSC-R appear to be reliable and valid measures of anxiety and fear. Although both measures could be used to screen children for treatment and to measure the effects of intervention, the RCMAS is a more general inventory of anxiety, as it does not pinpoint specific sources of anxiety. The FSSC-R is a more precise instrument in identifying specific fears.

Depression

Beginning in the early 1970s there was increasing recognition that children can and do experience depression, a notion that was inconsistent with psychoanalytic theories of ego development (Kazdin, 1989). Understanding of childhood depression has evolved through constructs such as "masked depression" and "depressive equivalents." Current theory posits that the syndrome of depression exists in children and encompasses an array of symptoms including loss of interest in activities, feelings of worthlessness, sleep disturbances, sadness, and changes in appetite.

As is the case for other disorders discussed in this chapter, assessment of depression typically begins with a broad overview of a child's functioning through interviews with the child and parent and the use of behavioral checklists. Structured diagnostic interviews, such as the K-SADS (Chambers et al., 1985) sample a broad range of symptoms. Likewise, behavioral checklists can provide valuable information about overall functioning.

Withdrawal from peers and age-appropriate activities is not uncommon among depressed children, and this can result in a disruption in the development of social relationships and social skills. Assessment of social competence using methods described earlier in this chapter can prove helpful and should be considered as a piece of the assessment mosaic.

Cognitive-behavioral formulations of depression also emphasize the role of negative cognitions, negative biases in memory, and attributional style in childhood depression—factors that have begun to receive empirical support (Haley, Fine, Marriage, Moretti, & Freeman, 1985; Kaslow et al., 1984; Meyer, Dyck, & Petrinack, 1989; Nolen-Hoeksema, Girgus, & Seligman, 1986; Whitman & Leitenberg, 1990). Consequently, the identification and delineation of these cognitive factors are paramount to a better understanding of childhood depression.

Unfortunately, the measurement of childhood depression is complicated by several methodological and conceptual problems. For example, Kazdin (1989) noted that developmental differences are not always considered in the assessment of depression. He speculated that the ability of children at various ages to report depressive feelings may demand different forms of measurement for different age groups (Kazdin, 1989). Moreover, children tend to report fewer symptoms of depression than parents and clinicians who are asked to describe these children (Kazdin, Colbus, & Rodgers, 1986). This makes it difficult to obtain consistent reports of childhood depression across informants. Although the number of assessment instruments is growing, many are very similar in format and content, and they often assess a wide range of depressive symptoms over various lengths of time (Kazdin & Petti, 1982). In addition, few of these instruments have undergone adequate tests of reliability and validity (Kazdin, 1987).

Despite these difficulties, several measures have been developed to assess childhood depression, with self-report instruments being the most widely researched. The most popular self-report measures of childhood depression are reviewed below. (See Kazdin, 1988 and Kendall et al., 1989, for a description of other measures.)

Children's Depression Inventory (CDI)   The CDI (Kovacs, 1980/81) is the most widely used measure of childhood depression. It is modeled on the Beck Depression Inventory (BDI) for adults (Kovacs & Beck, 1977). The BDI statements were modified for use with children, and several items were added to assess school-related areas and peer relations. The scale contains 27 items for which the child chooses one of three responses that best describes how she or he has felt over the past 2 weeks (e.g., "(S)he does not feel alone.", "(S)he feels alone many times.", "(S)he feels alone all the time."). The child's response indicates the intensity of the depressive symptom (i.e., normal to clinically depressed).

Reliability data were reported by Saylor, Finch, Spirito, and Bennett (1984). Test-retest reliability over 1 week was .38 for a group of psychiatric inpatients and .87 for a group of regular school children. Internal consistency also was acceptable.

Validational efforts have yielded equivocal results to date. For example, in one study (Saylor et al., 1984), although the CDI discriminated between clinic (hospitalized) children who had emotional and behavioral problems and normal elementary school children, it failed to distinguish between depressed and nondepressed hospitalized children. In addition, clinic children's self-report of depression on the CDI correlated with other self-report measures such as Piers and Harris's (1969) Self-Concept Scale and the CASQ (Seligman et al., 1984).

Similarly, in a recent treatment study comparing the effects of self-control therapy and behavioral problem-solving therapy, children who received treatment reported less depression on the CDI than children in the control group (Stark, Reynolds, & Kaslow, 1987). However, parent ratings of depression across groups failed to distinguish between children who received therapy and those who did not.

Although the CDI appears useful for identifying children with broad emotional problems (Gross & Wixted, 1988), these somewhat inconsistent findings suggest that additional research is necessary on the construct of childhood depression in general and on the CDI in particular.

Children's Depression Scale   The Children's Depression Scale (Tisher & Lang, 1983) is a 66-item self-report measure that yields two scores: a depressive score and a positive score. A unique feature of this measure is its administration format. Each item is printed on a separate card that is presented individually to the child. The child then places the card in 1 of 5 boxes ranging from "very wrong" to "very right." Although this measure also can be used to obtain parent perceptions of childhood depression (Tisher & Lang, 1983), more information is needed on its construct and predictive validity.

Child Depression Scale (CDS)   The CDS (Reynolds, 1989) was developed for use in regular schools. It can be administered individually or in a group to children between 8 and 13 years of age. The scale consists of 30 items — 29 items that represent clinically defined symptoms and 1 item that asks the child to mark the "smiley type face" that best shows how he or she feels. The severity of depression is rated on a 4-point scale.

High internal consistency ($\alpha = .89$) has been reported for the CDS (Bartell & Reynolds, 1986). In addition, this measure appears to be significantly correlated with the CDI ($r = .68$) and with teacher ratings of depression (Bartell & Reynolds, 1986).

Closing Comments

We offer three comments for consideration — a caution, a reflection, and a recommendation. The caution arises from an awareness of the nonobservable nature of some of the cognitive data that we suggest are essential in a comprehensive assessment. The nonobservable qualities of cognitions make them extremely difficult to assess and to study. Nevertheless, their opaque quality does not render them less essential to an understanding of the development of specific psychological disorders or to prescriptions for the treatment of such disorders.

The reflection is based on Meichenbaum's (1976) call for cognitive-behavioral assessments. The cognitive-behavioral assessment literature concerned with children has been somewhat "test" oriented. That is, there has been a tendency to use a variety of tests or tasks to "measure" cognition. Unfortunately, the functional analysis of cognition that Meichenbaum called for has not been adequately pursued. Perhaps there has not been sufficient time for such studies to be conducted, analyzed, and reported. Meichenbaum's (1976) call itself deserves renewed support, for our attention belongs on the child's actual cognitive activity in the social situations that prompt maladjustment. As a result, greater attention to the ecological validity of currently used measures will be necessary (Butler & Meichenbaum, 1981).

Finally, the recommendation is to study the specific cognitive events (i.e., self-statements) that are beneficial for children without behavior problems. More interesting, perhaps, would be the study of children who once displayed behavior problems but who are no longer seen as problematic. What are the "adjusting" children saying to themselves and doing interpersonally that differentiates them from their poorly adjusted peers? Again, ecologically valid assessments are essential.

References

Abikoff, H., Gittelman-Klein, R., & Klein, D. F. (1977). Validation of a classroom observation code for hyperactive children. *Journal of Consulting and Clinical Psychology, 45,* 772–783.

Abramson, L. Y., Seligman, M. E. P., & Teasdale, J. (1978). Learned helplessness in humans: Critique and reformulation. *Journal of Abnormal Psychology 87,* 49–74.

Achenbach, T. M. (1978). The child behavior profile: I. Boys aged 6–11. *Journal of Consulting and Clinical Psychology, 46,* 478–488.

Achenbach, T. M., Conners, C. K., Quay, H. C., Verhulst, F. C., & Howell, C. T. (1989). Replication of empirically derived syndromes as a basis for taxonomy of child/adolescent psychopathology. *Journal of Abnormal Child Psychology, 17,* 299–323.

Achenbach, T. M., & Edelbrock, C. S. (1978). The classification of child psychopathology: A review and analysis of empirical efforts. *Psychological Bulletin, 85,* 1275–1301.

Achenbach, T. M., & Edelbrock, C. S. (1981). Behavioral problems and competencies reported by parents of normal and disturbed children aged 4 through 16. *Monographs of the Society for Research in Child Development, 46 (1).*

Achenbach, T. M., & Edelbrock, C. S. (1983). *Manual for the Child Behavior Checklist and Revised Behavior Profile.* Burlington, VT: Department of Psychiatry, University of Vermont.

Achenbach, T. M., & Edelbrock, C. S. (1986). *Manual for the Teacher's Report Form and Teacher Version of the Child Behavior Profile.* Burlington, VT: Department of Psychiatry, University of Vermont.

Achenbach, T. M., McConaughy, S. H., & Howell, C. T. (1987). Child/adolescent behavioral and emotional problems: Implications of cross-informant for situational stability. *Psychological Bulletin, 101,* 213–232.

Achenbach, T. M., Verhulst, F. C., Baron, G. D., & Althaus, M. (1987). A comparison of syndromes derived from the child behavior checklist for American and Dutch boys aged 6–11 and 12–16. *Journal of Child Psychology and Psychiatry, 28,* 437–453.

Allen, G., Chinsky, J., Larcen, S., Lochman, J. E., & Selinger, H. (1976). *Community psychology and the schools: A behaviorally oriented multilevel preventive approach.* New York: Erlbaum.

Allen, K. E., Hart, B., Buell, J. S., Harris, F. R., & Wolf, M. M. (1964). Effects of social reinforcement on isolate behavior of a nursery school child. *Child Development, 35,* 511–518.

Allport, G. W. (1961). *Pattern and growth in personality.* New York: Holt, Rinehart & Winston.

American Psychiatric Association (APA). (1987). *Diagnostic and statistical manual of mental disorders* (3rd ed., rev.). Washington, DC: APA.

Annesley, F. (1974). A study of the relationship between normal and behaviour problem children on reading achievement, intelligence, self concept, and locus of control. *Slow-learning child – The Australian Journal on the Education of Backward Children, 21,* 185–196.

Asarnow, J. R., & Bates, S. (1988). Depression in child psychiatric inpatients: Cognitive and attributional patterns. *Journal of Abnormal Child Psychology, 16,* 601–615.

Asher, S. R., Markell, R. A., & Hymel, S. (1981). Identifying children at risk in peer relations: A critique of the rate-of-interaction approach to assessment. *Child Development, 52,* 1239–1245.

Asher, S. R., Renshaw, P. D., Gerachi, R. L., & Dor, A. K. (1979, March). Peer acceptance and social skill training: The selection of program content. In *Promoting social development.* Symposium conducted at the meeting of the Society for Research in Child Development, San Francisco.

Ault, R. L. (1973). Problem-solving strategies of reflective, impulsive, fast-accurate, and slow-accurate children. *Child Development, 44,* 259–266.

Ault, R. L., Mitchell, C., & Hartmann, D. P. (1976). Some methodological problems in reflection-impulsivity research. *Child Development, 47,* 227–231.

Baldwin, J. M. (1906). *Social and ethical interpretations of mental development.* New York: Macmillan.

Barkley, R. A. (1981). *Hyperactive children: A handbook for diagnosis and treatment.* New York: Guilford Press.

Barkley, R. A. (1988). Attention deficit disorder with hyperactivity. In E. J. Mash & L. G. Terdal (Eds.), *Behavioral assessment of childhood disorders* (2nd ed., pp. 69–104). New York: Guilford Press.

Barkley, R. A., & Edelbrock, C. (1987). Assessing situational variation in children's problem behaviors: The Home and School Situations Questionnaires. In R. J. Prinz (Ed.), *Advances in behavioral assessment of children and families* (Vol. 3, pp. 157–176). Greenwich, CT: JAI.

Barkley, R. A., Fischer, M., Newby, R. F., & Breen, M. J. (1988). Development of a multimethod clinical protocol for assessing stimulant drug response in children with attention deficit disorder. *Journal of Clinical Child Psychology, 17,* 14–24.

Barrios, B. A., & Hartmann, D. P. (1988). In E. J. Mash & L. G. Terdal (Eds.), *Behavioral assessment of childhood disorders* (2nd ed., pp. 196–262). New York: Guilford Press.

Bartell, N., & Reynolds, W. M. (1986). Depression and self-esteem in academically gifted and nongifted children: A comparison study. *Journal of School Psychology, 24,* 55–61.

Becker, W., Madsen, C., Arnold, C., & Thomas, D. (1967). The contingent use of teacher attention and praise in reducing classroom behavior problems. *Journal of Special Education, 1,* 287–307.

Bellack, A. S. (1983). Recurrent problems in the behavioral assessment of social skill. *Behaviour Research and Therapy, 21,* 29–41.

Bellack, A. S., & Herson, M. (Eds.). (1988). Behavioral assessment: A practical handbook. New York: Pergamon Press.

Benfield, C. Y., Palmer, D. J., Pfefferbaum, B., & Stowe, M. L. (1988). A comparison of depressed and nondepressed disturbed children on measures of attributional style, hopelessness, life stress, and temperament. *Journal of Abnormal Child Psychology, 16,* 397–410.

Block, J. (1987). Misgivings about the Matching Familiar Figures test: Premature or overdue? *Developmental Psychology, 23,* 740–741.

Block, J., Block, H. J., & Harrington, D. M. (1974). Matching Familiar Figures Test as a measure of reflection-impulsivity. *Developmental Psychology, 10,* 611–632.

Block, J., Block, J. H., & Harrington, D. M. (1975). Comment on the Kagan-Messer reply. *Developmental Psychology, 11,* 249–252.

Block, J., Gjerde, P. F., & Block, J. H. (1986). More misgivings about the Matching Familiar Figures test as a measure of reflection–impulsivity: Absence of construct validity in preadolescence. *Developmental Psychology, 22,* 820–831.

Borke, H. (1971). Interpersonal perception of young children: Egocentrism or empathy? *Developmental Psychology, 5,* 263–269.

Borke, H. (1972). Chandler and Greenspan's "Ersatz Eogcentrism": A rejoinder. *Developmental Psychology, 7,* 107–108.

Borke, H. (1973). The development of empathy in Chinese and American children between 3 and 6 years of age: A cross-culture study. *Developmental Psychology, 9,* 102–108.

Bornstein, M., Bellack, A. S., & Hersen, M. (1977). Social skills training for unassertive children: A multiple-baseline analysis. *Journal of Applied Behavior Analysis, 10,* 183–195.

Bornstein, M., Bellack, A. S., & Hersen, M. (1980). Social skills training for highly aggressive children. *Behavior Modification, 4,* 173–186.

Braswell, L., Kendall, P. C., & Urbain, E. S. (1982). A multistudy analysis of the role of socioeconomic status (SES) in cognitive-behavioral treatments with children. *Journal of Abnormal Child Psychology, 10,* 443–449.

Brion, S. (1977). *Helping, sharing and cooperation: An intervention study of middle childhood.* Unpublished doctoral dissertation, University of Utah.

Bugental, D. B., Collins, S., Collins, L., & Chaney, L. A. (1978). Attributional and behavioral changes following two behavior management interventions with hyperactive boys: A follow-up study. *Child Development, 49,* 247–250.

Bugental, D. B., Whalen, C. K., & Henker, B. (1977). Causal attributions of hyperactive children and motivational assumptions of two behavior-change approaches: Evidence for an interactionist position. *Child Development, 48,* 874–884.

Butler, L., & Meichenbaum, D. (1981). The assessment of interpersonal problem-solving skills. In P. C. Kendall & S. D. Hollon (Eds.), *Assessment strategies for cognitive-behavioral interventions.* New York: Academic Press.

Cairns, E., & Cammock, T. (1978). Development of a more reliable version of the Matching Familiar Figures test. *Developmental Psychology, 14,* 555–560.

Cairns, E., & Cammock, T. (1984). The development of reflection-impulsivity: Further data. *Personality and Individual Differences, 5,* 113–115.

Cameron, R. (1984). Problem-solving inefficiency and conceptual tempo: A task analysis of underlying factors. *Child Development, 55,* 2031–2041.

Castaneda, A., McCandless, B. R., & Palermo, D. S. (1956). The children's form of the manifest anxiety scale. *Child Development, 27,* 317–326.

Chandler, M. J. (1973). Egocentrism and antisocial behavior: The assessment and training of social perspective-taking skills. *Developmental Psychology, 9,* 326–332.

Chandler, M., & Greenspan, S. (1972). Erstz egocentrism: A reply to H. Borke. *Developmental Psychology, 7,* 104–106.

Chandler, M., Greenspan, S., & Barenboim, C. (1973). Judgments of intentionality in response to videotaped and verbally presented moral dilemmas: The medium is the message. *Child Development, 43,* 315–320.

Chandler, M., Greenspan, S., & Barenboim, C. (1974). Assessment and training of role-taking and referential communication skills in institutionalized emotionally disturbed children. *Developmental Psychology, 10,* 546–553.

Ciminero, A. R., Calhoun, K. S., & Adams, H. E. (Eds.). (1986). *Handbook of behavioral assessment* (2nd ed.), New York: Wiley.

Ciminero, A. R., Nelson, R. O., & Lipinski, D. P. (1977). Self-monitoring procedures. In A. R. Ciminero, K. S. Calhoun, & H. E. Adams (Eds.), *Handbook of behavioral assessment* (pp. 195–232). New York: Wiley.

Clarfield, S. P. (1974). The development of a teacher referral form for identifying early school maladaptation. *American Journal of Community Psychology, 2,* 199–210.

Cobb, J. A. (1972). Relationship of discrete classroom behaviors to fourth-grade academic achievement. *Journal of Educational Psychology, 63,* 74–80.

Cobb, J. A. (1973). Effects of academic survival skill training on low-achieving first grades. *Journal of Education Research, 67,* 108–113.

Cohen, N. J., Gotlieb, H., Kershner, J., & Wehrspann, W. (1985). Concurrent validity of the internalizing and externalizing profile patterns of the Achenbach Child Behavior Checklist. *Journal of Consulting and Clinical Psychology, 53,* 724–728.

Cohen, N. J., Kershner, J., & Wehrspann, W. (1985). Characteristics of social cognition in children with different symptom patterns. *Journal of Applied Developmental Psychology, 6,* 277–290.

Cohen, N. J., Kershner, J., & Wehrspann, W. (1988). Correlates of competence in a child psychiatric population. *Journal of Consulting and Clinical Psychology, 56,* 97–103.

Coie, J. D., & Kupersmidt, J. B. (1983). A behavioral analysis of emerging social status in boys' groups. *Child Development, 54,* 1400–1416.

Cone, J. D., & Hawkins, R. P. (Eds.). (1977). *Behavioral assessment: New directions in clinical psychology.* New York: Brunner/Mazel.

Connell, J. P. (1985). A new multidimensional measure of children's perceptions of control. *Child Development, 56,* 1018–1041.

Conners, C. K. (1969). A teacher rating scale for use in drug studies with children. *American Journal of Psychiatry, 126,* 884.

Conners, C. K. (1973). Rating scales for use in drug studies with children. *Psychopharmacology Bulletin* (Special Issue: Psychotherapy in Children), 24–84.

Cooney, E. W. (1977). Social-cognitive development: Applications to intervention and evaluation in the elementary grades. *The Counseling Psychologist, 6,* 6–9.

Copeland, A. P., & Weissbrod, C. S. (1978). Behavioral correlates of the hyperactivity factor of the Connors Teacher Questionnaire. *Journal of Abnormal Child Psychology, 5,* 339–343.

Crandall, V. C., Katkovsky, W., & Crandall, V. S. (1965). Children's beliefs in their control of reinforcements in intellectual-academic achievement situations. *Child Development, 36,* 91–109.

Davids, A. (1971). An objective instrument for assessing hyperkinesis in children. *Journal of Learning Disabilities, 4,* 499–501.

Deluty, R. H. (1979). Children's Action Tendency Scale: A self-report measure of aggressiveness, assertiveness, and submissiveness in children. *Journal of Consulting and Clinical Psychology, 47,* 1061–1071.

Deluty, R. H. (1984). Behavioral validation of the Children's Action Tendency Scale. *Journal of Behavioral Assessment, 6,* 115–130.

Denham, S. A. (1986). Social cognition, prosocial behavior, and emotion in preschoolers: Contextual validation. *Child Development, 57,* 194–201.

Denney, D. R. (1973). Reflection and impulsivity as determinants of conceptual strategy. *Child Development, 44,* 614–623.

Deutsch, F. (1974). Female preschoolers' perceptions of affective responses and interpersonal behavior in videotaped episodes. *Developmental Psychology, 10,* 733–740.

Devine, V. T., & Tomlinson, J. R. (1976). The workclock: An alternative to token economies in the management of classroom behaviors. *Psychology in the Schools, 13,* 163–170.

DeVries, R. (1970). The development of role-taking as reflected by behavior of bright, average, and retarded children in a social guessing game. *Child Development, 41,* 759–770.

Dodge, K. A. (1983). Behavioral antecedents of peer social status. *Child Development, 54,* 1386–1399.

Dodge, K. A., Coie, J. D., & Brakke, N. P. (1982). Behavior patterns of socially rejected and neglected preadolescents: The roles of social approach and aggression. *Journal of Abnormal Child Psychology, 10,* 389–410.

Dodge, K. A., Murphy, R. R., & Buchsbaum, K. (1984). The assessment of intention-cue detection skills in children: Implications for developmental psychopathology. *Child Development, 55,* 163–173.

Dodge, K. A., Pettit, G. S., McClaskey, C. L., & Brown, M. M. (1986). Social competence in children. *Monographs of the Society for Research in Child Development, 51,* (2, Serial No. 213).

Douglas, V. I. (1972). Stop, look, and listen: The problem of sustained attention and impulse control in hyperactive and normal children. *Canadian Journal of Behavioral Science, 4,* 259–282.

Douglas, V. I., Parry, P., Marton, P., & Garson, C. (1976). Assessment of a cognitive training program for hyperactive children. *Journal of Abnormal Child Psychology, 4,* 389–410.

Dweck, C. S. (1975). The role of expectations and attributions in the alleviation of learned helplessness. *Journal of Personality and Social Psychology, 31,* 674–685.

Dweck, C. S., & Reppucci, N. D. (1973). Learned helplessness and reinforcement responsibility in children. *Journal of Personality and Social Psychology, 25,* 109–116.

D'Zurilla, T., & Goldfried, M. (1971). Problem solving and behavior modification. *Journal of Abnormal Psychology, 78,* 107–126.

D'Zurilla, T. J., & Nezu, A. (1982). Social problem solving in adults. In P. C. Kendall (Ed.), *Advances in cognitive-behavioral research and therapy* (Vol. 1). New York: Academic Press.

Edelbrock, C. S., & Achenbach, T. M. (1984). Teacher version of the Child Behavior Profile: I. Boys aged 6–11. *Journal of Consulting and Clinical Psychology, 52,* 207–217.

Edelbrock, C. S., Greenbaum, R., & Conover, N. C. (1985). Reliability and concurrent relations between the Teacher Version of the Child Behavior Profile and the Conners Revised Teacher Rating Scale. *Journal of Abnormal Child Psychology, 13,* 295–304.

Egeland, B. P., Bielke, P., & Kendall, P. C. (1980). Achievement and adjustment correlates of the Matching Familiar Figures test. *Journal of School Psychology, 18,* 361–372.

Egeland, B., & Weinberg, R. A. (1976). The Matching Familiar Figures test: A look at its psychometric credibility. *Child Development, 47,* 483–491.

Enright, R. D. (1977). *Social cognitive development: A training model for intermediate school-age children.* St. Paul, MN: Pupil Personnel Division, Minnesota State Department of Education.

Enright, R. D., & Lapsley, D. K. (1980). Social role-taking: A review of the constructs, measures, and measurement properties. *Review of Educational Research, 50,* 647–674.

Feldhusen, J., & Houtz, J. (1975). Problem solving and the concrete-abstract dimension. *Gifted Child Quarterly, 19,* 122–129.

Feldhusen, J., Houtz, J., & Ringenbach, S. (1972). The Purdue Elementary Problem-Solving Inventory. *Psychological Reports, 31,* 891–901.

Finch, A. J, Jr., Kendall, P. C., Deardorff, P. A., Anderson, J., & Sitarz, A. M. (1975). Reflection-impulsivity, locus of control, and persistence behavior in emotionally disturbed children. *Journal of Consulting and Clinical Psychology, 43,* 748.

Finch, A. J., Jr., & Nelson, W. M., III. (1976). Reflection-impulsivity and behavior problems in emotionally disturbed boys. *Journal of Genetic Psychology, 128,* 271–274.

Finch, A. J., & Rogers, T. R. (1984). Self-report instruments. In T. H. Ollendick & M. Hersen (Eds.), *Child behavioral assessment: Principles and procedures* (pp. 106–123). New York: Pergamon Press.

Finch, A. J., Jr., Wilkinson, M. D., Nelson, W. M., III, & Montgomery, L. E. (1975). Modification of an impulsive cognitive tempo in emotionally disturbed boys. *Journal of Abnormal Child Psychology, 3,* 47–51.

Fischler, G. L., & Kendall, P. C. (1988). Social cognitive problem solving and childhood adjustment: Qualitative and topological analyses. *Cognitive Therapy and Research, 12,* 133–153.

Flapan, D. (1968). *Children's understanding of social interaction.* New York: Teachers College Press.

Flavell, J., Botkin, P., Fry, C., Wright, J., & Jarvis, P. (1968). *The development of role-taking and communication skills in children.* New York: Wiley.

Ford, M. E. (1979). The construct validity of egocentrism. *Psychological Bulletin, 86,* 1169–1188.

Foster, S. L., Bell-Dolan, D. J., & Burge, D. A. (1988). Behavioral observation. In A. S. Bellack & M. Hersen (Eds.), *Behavioral assessment: A practical handbook.* New York: Pergamon Press.

Foster, S. L., & Cone, J. D. (1986). Design and use of direct observation procedures. In A. R. Ciminero, K. S. Calhoun, & H. E. Adams (Eds.), *Handbook of behavioral assessment* (2nd ed., pp. 253–324). New York: Wiley.

Friedlander, S., Weiss, D. S., & Traylor, J. (1986). Assessing the influence of maternal depression on the validity of the Child Behavior Checklist. *Journal of Abnormal Child Psychology, 14,* 123–133.

Garrigan, J., & Bambrick, A. (1975). Short term family therapy with emotionally disturbed children. *Journal of Marriage and Family Counseling, 1,* 379–385.

Garrison, W. T., & Earls, F. (1985). The Child Behavior Checklist as a screening instrument for young children. *Journal of the American Academy of Child Psychiatry, 24,* 76–80.

Garvey, C., & Hogan, R. (1973). Social speech and social interaction: Egocentrism revisited. *Child Development, 44,* 562–568.

Gesten, E. L. (1976). A health resources inventory: The development of a measure of the personal and social competence of primary-grade children. *Journal of Consulting and Clinical Psychology, 44,* 775–786.

Glenwick, D. S., Barocas, R., & Burka, A. (1976). Some interpersonal correlates of cognitive impulsivity in fourth-graders. *Journal of School Psychology, 14,* 212–221.

Glucksberg, S., & Krauss, R. (1967). What do people say after they have learned how to talk: Studies of the development of referential communication. *Merrill-Palmer Quarterly, 13,* 309–316.

Glucksberg, S., Krauss, R., & Higgins, R. (1975). The developmental of referential communication skills. In F. D. Horowitz (Ed.), *Review of child development* (Vol. 4). Chicago: University of Chicago Press.

Gottman, J. M. (1977). Toward a definition of social isolation in children. *Child Development, 48,* 513–517.

Gottman, J., Gonso, J., & Rasmussen B. (1975). Social interaction, social competences, and friendship in children. *Child Development, 46,* 709–718.

Gottman, J. M., Gonso, J., & Shuler, P. (1976). Teaching social skills to isolated children. *Journal of Abnormal Child Psychology, 4,* 179–197.

Gouze, K. R. (1987). Attention and social problem solving as correlates of aggression in preschool males. *Journal of Abnormal Child Psychology, 15,* 181–197.

Greenwood, C. R., Walker, H. M., & Hops, H. (1977). Issues in social interaction/withdrawal assessment. *Exceptional Children, 43,* 490–499.

Greenwood, C. R., Walker, H. M., Todd, N. H., & Hops, H. (1979). Selecting a cost-effective screening device for the assessment of preschool social withdrawal. *Journal of Applied Behavioral Analysis, 12,* 639–652.

Greenwood, C. R., Walker, H. M., Todd, N. H., & Hops, H. (1981). Normative and descriptive analysis of preschool free play social interaction rates. *Journal of Pediatric Psychology, 6,* 343–367.

Gresham, F. M. (1982). Social interactions as predictors of children's likability and friendship patterns: A multiple regression analysis. *Journal of Behavioral Assessment, 4,* 39–54.

Gresham, F. M., & Elliott, S. N. (1984). Assessment and classification of children's social skills: A review of methods and issues. *School Psychology Review, 13,* 292–301.

Gross, A. M., & Wixted, J. T. (1988). Assessment of child behavior problems. In A. S. Bellack & M. Hersen (Eds.), *Behavioral assessment: A practical handbook* (3rd. ed., pp. 578–608). New York: Pergamon Press.

Guerra, N. G., & Slaby, R. G. (1989). Evaluative factors in social problem solving by aggressive boys. *Journal of Abnormal Child Psychology, 17,* 277–289.

Gurucharri, C., Phelps, E., & Selman, R. (1984). Development of interpersonal understanding: A longitudinal and comparative study of normal and disturbed youths. *Journal of Counseling and Clinical Psychology, 52,* 26–36.

Gurucharri, C., & Selman, R. L. (1982). The development of interpersonal understanding during childhood, preadolescence, and adolescence: A longitudinal follow-up study. *Child Development, 53,* 924–927.

Hann, N., Smith, M. B., & Block, J. (1968). Moral reasoning of young adults: Political-social behavior, family background, and personality correlates. *Journal of Personality and Social Psychology, 10,* 183–201.

Haley, G., Fine, S., Marriage, K., Moretti, M., & Freeman, R. (1985). Cognitive bias and depression in psychiatrically disturbed children and adolescents. *Journal of Consulting and Clinical Psychology, 53,* 535–537.

Harris, F. R., Johnston, M. K., Kelley, C. S., & Wolf, M. M. (1964). Effect of positive social reinforcement on regressed crawling of a nursery school child. *Journal of Educational Psychology, 55,* 35–41.

Harris, J. C., King, S. L., Reifler, J. P., & Rosenberg, L. A. (1984). Emotional and learning disorders in 6–12-year-old boys attending special schools. *Journal of the American Academy of Child Psychiatry, 23, 431*–437.

Hartup, W. W., Glazer, J. A., & Charlesworth, R. (1967). Peer reinforcement and sociometric status. *Child Development, 38,* 1017–1024.

Haynes, S. N. (1978). *Principles of behavioral assessment.* New York: Gardner Press.

Helsel, W. J., & Matson, J. L. (1984). The assessment of depression in children: The internal structure of the Child Depression Inventory (CDI). *Behaviour Research and Therapy, 22,* 289–298.

Hemry, F. P. (1973). Effect of reinforcement conditions on a discriminative learning task for impulsive vs. reflective children. *Child Development, 44,* 657–660.

Hughes, J. N., Boodoo, G., Alcala, J., Maggio, M., Moore, L., & Villapando, R. (1989). Validation of a role-play measure of children's social skills. *Journal of Abnormal Child Psychology, 17,* 633–646.

Humphrey, L. L. (1982). Children's and teachers' perspectives on children's self-control: The development of two rating scales. *Journal of Consulting and Clinical Psychology, 50,* 624–633.

Hymel, S., & Asher, S. R. (1977). *Assessment and training of isolated children's social skills.* Paper presented at the meeting of the Society of Research in Child Development, New Orleans. (ERIC Document Reproduction Service No. ED 136 930).

Iannotti, R. J. (1978). Effect of role-taking experiences on role-taking, altruism, empathy, and aggression. *Developmental Psychology, 14,* 119–124.

Jacob, R. G., O'Leary, K. D., & Rosenblad, C. (1978). Formal and informal classroom settings: Effects on hyperactivity. *Journal of Abnormal Child Psychology, 6,* 47–59.

Jacobson, N. S. (1985a). The role of observational measures in behavior therapy outcome research. *Behavioral Assessment, 7,* 297–308.

Jacobson, N. S. (1985b). Uses versus abuses of observational measures. *Behavioral Assessment, 7,* 323–330.

Jahoda, M. (1953). The meaning of psychological health. *Social Casework, 34,* 349–354.

Jahoda, M. (1958). *Current concepts of positive mental health.* New York: Basic Books.

Johnson, S. B., & Melamed, B. G. (1979). The assessment and treatment of children's fears. In B. B. Lahey & A. E. Kazdin (Eds.), *Advances in child clinical psychology* (Vol. 2, pp. 107–139). New York: Plenum Press.

Kagan, J. (1966). Reflection–impulsivity: The generality and dynamics of conceptual tempo. *Journal of Abnormal Psychology, 71,* 17–24.

Kagan, J. (1987). Misgivings about the Matching Familiar Figures Test: A brief reply to Block, Gjerde, and Block (1986). *Developmental Psychology, 23,* 738–739.

Kagan, J., Pearson, L., & Welch, L. (1966). Modifiability of an impulsive tempo. *Journal of Educational Psychology, 57,* 359–365.

Kagan, J., Rosman, B. L., Day, D., Albert, J., & Phillips, W. (1964). Information processing in the child: Significance of analytic and reflective attitudes. *Psychological Monographs, 78* (1, whole No. 578).

Kaslow, N. J., Rehm, L. P., Pollack, S. L., & Siegel, A. W. (1988). Attributional style and self-control behavior in depressed and nondepressed children and their parents. *Journal of Abnormal Child Psychology, 16,* 163–175.

Kaslow, N. J., Rehm, L. P., Siegel, A. W. (1984). Social-cognitive and cognitive correlates of depression in children. *Journal of Abnormal Child Psychology, 12,* 605–620.

Kaslow, N., Tannenbaum, R., & Seligman, M. E. P. (1981). *Kastan: A Children's Attributional Style Questionnaire.* Unpublished manuscript, University of Pennsylvania.

Kazdin, A. E. (1977). Artifact, bias, and complexity of assessment: The ABCs of reliability. *Journal of Applied Behavior Analysis, 10,* 141–150.

Kazdin, A. E. (1987). Assessment of childhood depression: Current issues and strategies. *Behavioral Assessment, 9,* 291–319.

Kazdin, A. E. (1988). Childhood depression. In E. J. Mash & L. G. Terdal (Eds.), *Behavioral assessment of childhood disorders* (2nd ed., pp. 157–195). New York: Guilford Press.

Kazdin, A. E. (1989). Developmental differences in depression. In B. B. Lahey & A. E. Kazdin (Eds.), *Advances in clinical child psychology* (Vol. 12, pp. 193–219). New York: Plenum Press.

Kazdin, A. E., Colbus, D., & Rodgers, A. (1986). Assessment of depression and diagnosis of depressive disorder among psychiatrically disturbed children. *Journal of Abnormal Child Psychology, 14,* 499–515.

Kazdin, A. E., Matson, J. L., Esveldt-Dawson, K. (1984). The relationship of role-play assessment of children's social skills to multiple measures of social competence. *Behaviour Research and Therapy, 22,* 129–139.

Kazdin, A. E., & Petti, T. A. (1982). Self-report and interview measures of childhood and adolescent depression. *Journal of Child Psychology and Psychiatry, 23,* 437–457.

Keller, M., & Wood, P. (1989). Development of friendship reasoning: A study of interindividual differences in intraindividual change. *Developmental Psychology, 25,* 820–826.

Kendall, P. C. (1981). Assessment and cognitive-behavioral interventions: Purposes, proposals, and problems. In P. C. Kendall & S. D. Hollon (Eds.), *Assessment strategies for cognitive-behavioral interventions* (pp. 1–13). New York: Academic Press.

Kendall, P. C. (1990). Behavioral assessment and methodology. In C. M. Franks, G. T. Wilson, P. C. Kendall, & J. P. Foreyt (Eds.), *Review of behavior therapy,* (Vol. 12). New York: Guilford Press.

Kendall, P. C., & Braswell, L. (1982). Cognitive-behavioral self-control therapy for children: A components analysis. *Journal of Consulting and Clinical Psychology, 50,* 672–689.

Kendall, P. C., & Braswell, L. (1985). *Cognitive-behavioral therapy for impulsive children.* New York: Guilford Press.

Kendall, P. C., Cantwell, D. P., & Kazden, A. E. (1989). Depression in children and adolescents: Assessment issues and recommendations. *Cognitive Therapy and Research, 13,* 109–146.

Kendall, P. C., & Finch, A. J., Jr. (1976). A cognitive-behavioral treatment for impulse control: A case study. *Journal of Consulting and Clinical Psychology, 44,* 852–857.

Kendall, P. C., & Finch, A. J., Jr. (1978). A cognitive-behavioral treatment for impulsivity: A group comparison study. *Journal of Consulting and Clinical Psychology, 46,* 110–118.

Kendall, P. C., & Finch, A. J. (1979). Developing nonimpulsive behavior in children: Cognitive-behavioral strategies for self-control. In P. C. Kendall & S. D. Hollon (Eds.), *Cognitive-behavioral interventions: Theory, research, and problems.* New York: Academic Press.

Kendall, P. C., Finch, A. J., Little, V. L., Chirico, B. M., & Ollendick, T. H. (1978). Variations in a construct: Quantitative and qualitative differences in children's locus of control. *Journal of Consulting and Clinical Psychology, 46,* 590–592.

Kendall, P. C., & Hollon, S. D. (Eds.). (1979). *Cognitive-behavioral interventions: Theory, research, and procedures.* New York: Academic Press.

Kendall, P. C., & Korgeski, G. P. (1979). Assessment and cognitive-behavioral interventions. *Cognitive Therapy and Research, 3,* 1–21.

Kendall, P. C., Pellegrini, D. S., & Urbain, E. S. (1979). Approaches to assessment for cognitive-behavioral interventions with children. In P. C. Kendall & S. D. Hollon (Eds.), *Assessment strategies and cognitive-behavioral interventions.* New York: Academic Press.

Kendall, P. C., & Ronan, K. R. (1990). Assessment of children's anxieties, fears, and phobias: Cognitive-behavioral models and methods. In C. R. Reynolds & R. W. Kamphaus (Eds.), *Handbook of psychological and educational assessment of children* (pp. 223–244). New York: Guilford Press.

Kendall, P. C., & Wilcox, L. E. (1979). Self-control in children: Development of a rating scale. *Journal of Consulting and Clinical Psychology, 47,* 1020–1030.

Kendall, P. C., & Wilcox, L. E. (1980). Cognitive behavioral treatment for impulsivity: Concrete versus conceptual training with non–self-controlled problem children. *Journal of Consulting and Clinical Psychology, 48,* 80–91.

Kendall, P. C., & Zupan, B. A. (1981). Individual versus group application of cognitive-behavioral self-control procedures with children. *Behavior Therapy, 12,* 344–359.

Kendall, P. C., Zupan, B. A., & Braswell, L. (1981). Self-control in children: Further analyses of the Self-Control Rating Scale. *Behavior Therapy, 12,* 667–681.

Kent, R. N., O'Leary, D. K., Diament, C., & Dietz, A. (1974). Expectation biases in observational evaluation of therapeutic change. *Journal of Consulting and Clinical Psychology, 42,* 774–780.

Kettlewell, P. W., & Kausch, D. F. (1983). The generalization of the effects of a cognitive-behavioral treatment program for aggressive children. *Journal of Abnormal Child Psychology, 11,* 101–114.

Kirby, F. D., & Toler, H. C. (1970). Modification of preschool isolate behavior: A case study. *Journal of Applied Behavioral Analysis, 3,* 309–314.

Kirschenbaum, D. S. (1979). Social competence intervention and evaluation in the inner city: Cincinnati's social skills development program. *Journal of Consulting and Clinical Psychology, 47,* 778–780.

Kohlberg, L. (1969). Stage and sequence: The cognitive-developmental approach to socialization. In D. A. Goslin (Ed.), *Handbook of socialization theory and research*. New York: Rand-McNally.

Kovacs, M. (1980/81). Rating scales to assess depression in school-aged children. *Acta Paedopsychiatric, 46,* 305–315.

Kovacs, M., & Beck, A. T. (1977). An empirical-clinical approach toward a definition of childhood depression. In J. G. Schulterbrandt & A. Raskin (Eds.), *Depression in childhood: Diagnosis, treatment and conceptual models* (pp. 1-25). New York: Raven Press.

Krasnor, L. R., & Rubin, K. H. (1981). The assessment of social problem-solving skills in young children. In T. V. Merluzzi, C. R. Glass, & M. Genest (Eds.), *Cognitive assessment* (pp. 452–476). New York: Guilford Press.

Kuehne, C., Kehle, T. J., & McMahon, W. (1987). Differences between children with attention deficit disorder, children with specific learning disabilities, and normal children. *Journal of School Psychology, 25,* 161–166.

Kurdek, L. A. (1977). Structural components and intellectual correlates of cognitive perspective taking in first through fourth grade children. *Child Development, 48,* 1503–1511.

Kurdek, L. A. (1979). Generality of decentering in first through fourth grade children. *Journal of Genetic Psychology, 134,* 89–97.

Kurdek, L. A. (1982). Long-term predictive validity of children's social-cognitive assessments. *Merrill-Palmer Quarterly, 28,* 511–521.

Kurdek, L. A., & Rodgon, M. M. (1975). Perceptual, cognitive, and affective perspective taking in kindergarten through sixth-grade children. *Developmental Psychology, 11,* 643–650.

Kurtines, W., & Grief, E. G. (1974). The development of moral thought: Review and evaluation of Kohlberg's approach. *Psychological Bulletin, 81,* 453–470.

Lahaderne, H. M. (1968). Attitudinal and intellectual correlates of attention: A study of four sixth-grade classrooms. *Journal of Educational Psychology, 58,* 320–324.

Laufer, M. W., & Denhoff, E. (1957). Hyperkinetic behavior syndrome in children. *Journal of Pediatrics, 50,* 463–474.

Leahy, R., & Huard, C. (1976). Role taking and self-image disparity in children. *Developmental Psychology, 12,* 504–508.

Lefcourt, H. M. (1976). *Locus of control: Current trends in theory and research.* Hillsdale, NJ: Erlbaum Press.

LeMare, L. J., & Rubin, K. H. (1987). Perspective taking and peer interaction: Structural and developmental analyses. *Child Development, 58,* 306–315.

Leon, G. R., Kendall, P. C., & Garber, J. (1980). Depression in children: Parent, child, and teacher perspectives. *Journal of Abnormal Child Psychology, 53,* 647–656.

Little, V. L. (1978). *The relationship of role-taking ability to self-control in institutionalized juvenile offenders.* Unpublished doctoral dissertation, Virginia Commonwealth University, Richmond.

Lorion, R. P., Cowen, E. L., & Caldwell, R. A. (1975). Normative and parametric analyses of school maladjustment. *American Journal of Community Psychology, 3,* 291–301.

Marshall, H. R., & McCandless, B. R. (1957). A study in prediction of social behavior of preschool children. *Child Development, 28,* 149–159.

Mash, E. J., & Terdal, L. G. (1988). Behavioral assessment of child and family disturbance. In E. J. Mash & L. G. Terdal (Eds.), *Behavioral assessment of childhood disorders* (2nd ed., pp. 3-65). New York: Guilford Press.

Massari, D. J., & Schack, M. L. (1972). Discrimination learning by reflective and impulsive children in a function of reinforcement schedule. *Developmental Psychology, 6,* 183.

Matson, J. E., Esveldt-Dawson, K., & Kazdin, A. E. (1983). Validation of methods for assessing social skills in children. *Journal of Clinical Child Psychology, 12,* 174-180.

Matson, J. L, Rotatori, A. F., & Helsel, W. J. (1983). Development of a rating scale to measure social skills in children: The Matson Evaluation of Social Skills with Youngsters (MESSY). *Behaviour Research and Therapy, 21,* 335-340.

McCauley, E., Mitchell, J. R., Burke, P., & Moss, S. (1988). Cognitive attributes of depression in children and adolescents. *Journal of Consulting and Clinical Psychology, 56,* 903-908.

McClure, L., Chinsky, J., & Larcen, S. (1978). Enhancing social problem-solving performance in an elementary school setting. *Journal of Educational Psychology, 70,* 504-513.

McFall, R. M. (1986). Theory and method in assessment: The vital link. *Behavioral Assessment, 8,* 3-10.

McKim, B. J., & Cowen, E. L. (1987). Multiperspective assessment of young children's school adjustment. *School Psychology Review, 16,* 370-381.

McKim, B. J., Weissberg, R. P., Cowen, E. L., Gesten, E. L., & Rapkin, B. D. (1982). A comparison of the problem-solving ability and adjustment of suburban and urban third-grade children. *American Journal of Community Psychology, 10,* 155-169.

McMahon, R. J. (1984). Behavioral checklists and rating scales. In T. H. Ollendick & M. Hersen (Eds.), *Child behavioral assessment: Principles and procedures* (pp. 80-105). New York: Pergamon Press.

Mead, G. (1934). *Mind, self, and society.* Chicago: University of Chicago Press.

Meichenbaum, D., & Goodman, J. (1971). Training impulsive children to talk to themselves: A means of developing self-control. *Journal of Abnormal Psychology, 77,* 115-126.

Mercatoris, M., & Craighead, W. E. (1974). The effects of non-participant observation on teacher and pupil classroom behavior. *Journal of Educational Psychology, 66,* 512-519.

Messer, S. B. (1976). Reflection–impulsivity: A review. *Psychological Bulletin, 83,* 1026-1052.

Metalsky, G., & Abramson, L. (1982). Attributional style: Toward a framework for conceptualization and assessment. In P. C. Kendall & S. D. Hollon (Eds.), *Assessment strategies for cognitive-behavioral interventions.* New York: Academic Press.

Meyer, N. E., Dyck, D. G., & Petrinack, R. J. (1989). Cognitive appraisal and attributional correlates of depressive symptoms in children. *Journal of Abnormal Child Psychology, 17,* 325-335.

Meyers, C. E., Attwell, A. A., & Orpet, R. E. (1968). Prediction of fifth grade achievement from kindergarten test and rating data. *Educational and Psychological Measurement, 28,* 457-463.

Michelson, L., & Wood, R. (1980). Behavioral assessment and training of children's social skills. In M. Hersen, R. M. Eisler, & P. M. Miller (Eds.), *Progress in behavior modification* (Vol. 9, pp. 242-292). New York: Academic Press.

Michelson, L., & Wood, R. (1982). Development and psychometric properties of the Children's Assertive Behavior Scale. *Journal of Behavioral Assessment, 4,* 3–13.

Milich, R., Loney, J., & Landau, S. (1982). Independent dimensions of hyperactivity and aggression: A validation with playroom observation data. *Journal of Abnormal Psychology, 91,* 183–198.

Murray, J. P., & Aammer, I. M. (1977). *Kindness in the kindergarten: A multidimensional program for facilitating altruism.* Paper presented at the meeting of the Society for Research in Child Development, New Orleans.

Nay, W. R. (1979). *Multimethod clinical assessment.* New York: Gardner Press.

Nietzel, M. T., Bernstein, D. A., & Russell, R. L. (1988). Assessment of anxiety and fear. In A. S. Bellack & M. Hersen (Eds.), *Behavioral assessment: A practical handbook.* New York: Pergamon Press.

Nelson, R. O., & Hayes, S. C. (1979). Some current dimensions of behavioral assessment. *Behavioral Assessment, 1,* 1–16.

Noland, M. & Gruber, J. (1976). Academic achievement, personality, and behavior in emotionally disturbed children. *American Corrective Therapy Journal, 30,* 182–186.

Nolen-Hoeksema, S., Girgus, J. S., & Seligman, M. E. P. (1986). Learned helplessness in children: A longitudinal study of depression, achievement, and exploratory style. *Journal of Personality and Social Psychology, 51,* 435–452.

Nowicki, S., & Duke, M. P. (1974a). A locus of control scale for college as well as noncollege adults. *Journal of Personality Assessment, 38,* 136–137.

Nowicki, S., & Duke, M. P. (1974b). A preschool and primary locus of control scale. *Developmental Psychology, 10,* 874–880.

Nowicki, S., Jr., & Strickland, B. R. (1973). A locus of control scale for children. *Journal of Consulting and Clinical Psychology, 40,* 148–154.

O'Connor, R. D. (1969). Modification of social withdrawal through symbolic modeling. *Journal of Applied Behavior Analysis, 2,* 15–22.

O'Connor, R. D. (1972). Relative efficacy of modeling, shaping, and the combined procedures for modification of social withdrawal. *Journal of Abnormal Psychology, 79,* 327–334.

Ollendick, T. H. (1981). Assessment of social interaction skills in school children. *Behavioral Counseling Quarterly, 1,* 227–243.

Ollendick, T. H. (1983). Reliability and validity of the Revised Fear Survey Schedule for Children. *Behaviour Research and Therapy, 21,* 685–692.

Ollendick, T. H. (1984). Development and validation of the Children's Assertiveness Inventory. *Child and Family Behavior Therapy, 5,* 1–15.

Ollendick, T. H., & Cerny, J. A. (1981). *Clinical behavior therapy with children.* New York: Plenum Press.

Ollendick, T. H., & Herson, M. (Eds.). (1984). Child behavioral assessment: Principles and procedures. New York: Pergamon Press.

Parcel, G. S., & Meyer, M. P. (1978). Development of an instrument to measure children's health locus of control. *Health Education Monographs, 6,* 149–159.

Patterson, G. R. (1982). *Coercive family process.* Eugene, OR: Castalia.

Patterson, G. R. (1986). Performance models for antisocial boys. *American Psychologist, 41,* 432–444.

Patterson, G. R., Ray, R. S., Shaw, D. A., & Cobb, J. A. (1969). *Manual for coding family interaction.* Document No. 01234, 6th revision. (Available from ASIS National Auxiliary Publications Service, c/o CCM Information Service, Inc., 909 Third Ave., New York, NY 10022.)

Pellegrini, D. S. (1985). Social cognition and competence in middle childhood. *Child Development, 56,* 253–264.

Pellegrini, D. S. (1986). Variability in children's level of reasoning about friendship. *Journal of Applied Developmental Psychology, 7,* 341–354.

Pellegrini, D. S., Masten, A. S., Garmezy, N., & Ferrarese, M. J. (1987). Correlates of social and academic competence in middle childhood. *Journal of Child Psychology and Psychiatry, 28,* 699–714.

Pellegrini, D. S., & Urbain, E. S. (1985). An evaluation of interpersonal cognitive problem solving training with children. *Journal of Child Psychology and Psychiatry, 26,* 17–41.

Perry, M. A. (1990). The interview in developmental assessment. In J. H. Johnson & J. Goldman (Eds.), *Developmental assessment in clinical child psychology.* New York: Pergamon Press.

Phares, E. J. (1976). *Locus of control and personality.* Lawrencetown, NJ: General Learning Press.

Piaget, J., & Inhelder, B. (1956). *The child's conception of space.* London: Routledge and Kegan Paul.

Piche, G., Michlin, M., Rubin, D., & Johnson, F. (1975). Relationships between fourth graders' performance on selected role-taking tasks and referential communication accuracy. *Child Development, 46,* 965–969.

Piers, E. V., & Harris, D. B. (1969). *The Piers-Harris Children's Self-Concept Scale.* Nashville, TN: Counselor Recordings and Tests.

Platt, J. J., & Spivack, G. (1975). *Manual for the Means–Ends-Problem-Solving Procedure.* Philadelphia: Department of Mental Health Services, Hahnemann Community Health/Mental Retardation Center.

Platt, J., Spivak, G., Altman, N., Altman, D., & Peizer, S. B. (1974). Adolescent problem-solving thinking. *Journal of Consulting and Clinical Psychology, 42,* 787–793.

Porteus, S. D. (1933). *The maze test and mental differences.* Vineland, NJ: Smith.

Porteus, S. D. (1955). *The maze test: Recent advances.* Palo Alto, CA: Pacific Books.

Putallaz, M. (1983). Predicting children's sociometric status from their behavior. *Child Development, 54,* 1417–1426.

Reardon, R. C., Hersen, M., Bellack, A. S., & Foley, J. M. (1979). Measuring social skills in grade school boys. *Journal of Behavioral Assessment, 1,* 87–105.

Reed, M. L., & Edelbrock, C. (1983). Reliability and validity of the Direct Observation Form of the Child Behavior Checklist. *Journal of Abnormal Child Psychology, 11,* 521–530.

Reid, J. B. (1970). Reliability assessment of observation data: A possible methodological problem. *Child Development, 41,* 1143–1150.

Reid, J. B., Baldwin, D. V., Patterson, G. R., & Dishion, T. J. (1988). Observations in the assessment of childhood disorders. In M. Rutter, A. H. Tuma, & I. S. Lann (Eds.), *Assessment and diagnosis in child psychopathology* (pp. 156–195). New York: Guilford Press.

Reid, M. K., & Borkowski, J. G. (1987). Causal attributions of hyperactive children: Implications for teaching strategies and self-control. *Journal of Educational Psychology, 79,* 296–307.

Rest, J. R. (1983). Morality. In J. H. Flavell & E. M. Markman (Eds.), P. H.

Mussen (Series Ed.), *Handbook of child psychology* (Vol. 3, 4th ed., pp. 556–629). New York: Wiley.

Reynolds, C. R. (1981). Long-term stability of scores on the Revised Children's Manifest Anxiety Scale. *Perceptual and Motor Skills, 53,* 702.

Reynolds, W. M. (1989). *Reynolds Child Depression Scale.* Odessa, FL: Psychological Assessment Resources.

Reynolds, C. R., & Paget, K. D. (1981). Factor analysis of the Revised Children's Manifest Anxiety Scale for blacks, whites, males, and females with a national normative sample. *Journal of Consulting and Clinical Psychology, 49,* 352–359.

Reynolds, C. R., & Richmond, B. O. (1978). What I think and feel: A revised measure of children's manifest anxiety. *Journal of Abnormal Child Psychology, 6,* 271–280.

Reynolds, W. M., & Stark, K. D. (1986). Self-control in children: A multimethod examination of treatment outcome measures. *Journal of Abnormal Child Psychology, 14,* 13–23.

Rickel, A. U., Eshelman, A. K., & Loigman, G. A. (1983). Social problem solving training: A follow-up study of cognitive and behavioral effects. *Journal of Abnormal Child Psychology, 11,* 15–28.

Riddle, M., & Roberts, A. H. (1974). *The Porteus mazes: A critical evaluation.* Unpublished manuscript, Department of Psychiatry, University of Minnesota: Report Number PR-74-3.

Riddle, M., & Roberts, A. H. (1977). Delinquency, delay of gratification, recidivism, and the Porteus Maze tests. *Psychological Bulletin, 84,* 417–425.

Ridley, C. A., & Vaughn, S. R. (1982). Interpersonal problem solving: An intervention program for preschool children. *Journal of Applied Developmental Psychology, 3,* 177–190.

Roberts, R. R., & Renzaglia, G. A. (1965). The influence of tape-recording on counseling. *Journal of Counseling Psychology, 12,* 10–16.

Robin, A. L., Fischel, J. E., & Brown, K. E. (1984). The measurement of self-control in children: Validation of the Self-Control Rating Scale. *Journal of Pediatric Psychology, 9,* 165–175.

Roopnarine, J. L. (1987). Social interaction in the peer group: Relationship to perceptions of parenting and to children's interpersonal awareness and problem-solving ability. *Journal of Applied Developmental Psychology, 8,* 351–362.

Ross, A. D. (1980). *Psychological disorders of children: A behavioral approach to theory, research, and therapy* (2nd ed.). New York: McGraw-Hill.

Rotter, J. B. (1966). Generalized expectancies for internal versus external control of reinforcement. *Psychological Monographs, 30* (whole No. 1).

Rubin, K. H. (1978). Role taking in childhood: Some methodological considerations. *Child Development, 49,* 428–433.

Rubin, K. H. (1982). Nonsocial play in preschoolers: Necessarily evil? *Child Development, 53,* 651–657.

Rutter, M. (1988). Depressive disorders. In M. Rutter, A. H. Tuma, & I. S. Lann (Eds.), *Assessment and diagnosis in child psychopathology.* New York: Plenum Press.

Sarason, I. G., & Ganzer, V. J. (1973). Modeling and group discussion in the rehabilitation of juvenile delinquents. *Journal of Counseling Psychology, 20,* 442–449.

Saylor, C. F., Finch, A. J., Jr., Baskin, C. H., Furey, W., & Kelly, M. M. (1984). Construct validity for measures of childhood depression: Application of multitrait-multimethod methodology. *Journal of Consulting and Clinical Psychology, 52,* 977–985.

Saylor, C. F., Finch, A. J., Jr., Spirito, A., & Bennett, B. (1984). The Children's Depression Inventory: A systematic evaluation of psychometric properties. *Journal of Consulting and Clinical Psychology, 52,* 955–967.

Scanlon, E. M., & Ollendick, T. H. (1986). Children's assertive behavior: The reliability and validity of three self-report measures. *Child and Family Behavior Therapy, 7,* 9–21.

Scherer, M. W., & Nakamura, C. Y. (1968). A fear survey schedule for children (FSS-FC): A factor analytic comparison with manifest anxiety (CMAS). *Behaviour Research and Therapy, 6,* 173–182.

Schwartz, M., Friedman, R., Lindsay, P., & Narrol, H. (1982). The relationship between conceptual tempo and depression in children. *Journal of Consulting and Clinical Psychology, 50,* 488–490.

Searcy, J. D., & Hawkins-Searcy, J. (1979). Locus of control research and its implications for child personality. In A. J. Finch and P. C. Kendall (Eds.), *Clinical treatment and research in child psychopathology.* New York: Spectrum.

Seligman, M. E. P., & Peterson, C. (1986). A learned helplessness perspective on childhood depression: Theory and research. In M. Rutter, C. E. Izard, & P. B. Read (Eds.), *Depression in young people* (pp. 223–249). New York: Guilford Press.

Seligman, M. E. P., Peterson, C., Kaslow, N. J., Tannenbaum, R. L., Alloy, L. B., & Abramson, L. Y. (1984). Attributional style and depressive symptoms among children. *Journal of Abnormal Psychology, 93,* 235–238.

Selman, R. L. (1971). The relation of role taking to the development of moral judgment in children. *Child Development, 42,* 79–91.

Selman, R. L. (1976). A structural approach to the study of developing interpersonal relationship concepts. In A. Pick (Ed.), *Tenth annual Minnesota symposia on child psychology.* Minneapolis: University of Minnesota Press.

Selman, R. L. (1980). *The growth of interpersonal understanding: Developmental and clinical analyses.* New York: Academic Press.

Selman, R. L., & Byrne, D. F. (1974). A structural-developmental analysis of levels of role taking in middle childhood. *Child Development, 45,* 803–806.

Selman, R. L., & Demorest, A. P. (1984). Observing troubled children's interpersonal negotiation strategies: Implications of and for a developmental model. *Child Development, 55,* 288–304.

Selman, R. L., & Jaquette, D. (1978). Stability and oscillation in interpersonal awareness: A clinical-developmental analysis. In C. B. Keasy (Ed.), *The twenty-fifth Nebraska symposium on motivation.* Lincoln: University of Nebraska Press.

Selman, R. L., Jaquette, D., & Lavin, R. (1977). Interpersonal awareness in children: Toward an integration of developmental and clinical child psychology. *American Journal of Orthopsychiatry, 47,* 264–274.

Selman, R. L., Schorin, M. Z., Stone, C. R., & Phelps, E. (1983). A naturalistic study of children's social understanding. *Developmental Psychology, 19,* 82–102.

Shantz, C. U. (1983). Social cognition. In J. H. Flavell & E. M. Markman (Eds.), P. H. Mussen (Series Ed.), *Handbook of child psychology* (Vol. 3, 4th ed., pp. 495–555). New York: Wiley.

Sharp, K. C. (1981). Impact of interpersonal problem-solving training on preschoolers' social competency. *Journal of Applied Developmental Psychology, 2*, 129–143.

Shure, M. B., Newman, S., & Silver, S. (1973). *Problem-solving thinking among adjusted, impulsive and inhibited Head Start children.* Paper presented at the meeting of the Eastern Psychological Association, Washington, DC.

Shure, M. B., & Spivack, G. (1972). Means–ends thinking, adjustment, and social class among elementary-school–aged children. *Journal of Consulting and Clinical Psychology, 38*, 348–353.

Shure, M. B., & Spivack G. (1975). *Interpersonal cognitive problem-solving intervention: The second (kindergarten) year.* Paper presented at the meeting of the American Psychological Association, Chicago.

Shure, M. B., & Spivack, G. (1978). *Problem-solving techniques in childrearing.* San Francisco: Jossey-Bass.

Shure, M. B., Spivack, G., & Gordon, R. (1972). Problem-solving thinking: A preventive mental health program for preschool children. *Reading World, 111*, 259–273.

Shure, M. B., Spivack, G., & Jaeger, M. A. (1971). Problem-solving thinking and adjustment among disadvantaged preschool children. *Child Development, 42*, 1791–1893.

Shure, M. B., Spivack, G., & Powell, L. (1972). *A problem-solving intervention program for disadvantaged preschool children.* Paper presented at the meeting of the Eastern Psychological Association, Boston.

Simon, H. A., & Newell, A. (1971). Human problem-solving: The state of the theory in 1970. *American Psychologist, 26*, 145–159.

Soli, S. D., & Devine, V. T. (1976). Behavioral correlates of achievements: A look at high and low achievers. *Journal of Educational Psychology, 68*, 335–341.

Spence, S. H. (1987). The relationship between social-cognitive skills and peer sociometric status. *British Journal of Developmental Psychology, 5*, 347–356.

Spielberger, C. D. (1973). *Manual for the State-Trait Anxiety Inventory for Children.* Palo Alto, CA: Consulting Psychologists Press.

Spivack, G., Platt, J., & Shure, M. B. (1976). *The problem-solving approach to adjustment.* San Francisco: Jossey-Bass.

Spivack, G., & Shure, M. B. (1974). *Social adjustment of young children.* San Francisco: Jossey-Bass.

Spring, C., Blunden, D., Greenberg, L. M., & Yellin, A. M. (1977). Validity and norms of a hyperactivity rating scale. *Journal of Special Education, 11*, 314–321.

Stark, K. D., Reynolds, W. M., & Kaslow, N. J. (1987). A comparison of the relative efficacy of self-control therapy and a behavioral problem-solving therapy for depression in children. *Journal of Abnormal Child Psychology, 15*, 91–113.

Strain, P., Cooke, T., & Apolloni, T. (1976). *Teaching exceptional children: Assessing and modifying social behavior.* New York: Academic Press.

Strauss, C. C., Lease, C. A., Kazdin, A. E., Dulcan, M. K., & Last, C. G. (1989). Multimethod assessment of the social competence of children with anxiety disorders. *Journal of Clinical Child Psychology, 18*, 184–189.

Strickland, B. R. (1989). Internal-external control expectancies. *American Psychologist, 44*, 1–12.

Sturgis, E. T., & Gramling, S. Psychophysiological assessment. In A. S. Bellack &

M. Hersen (Eds.), *Behavioral assessment: A practical handbook*. New York: Pergamon Press.

Tallmadge, J., & Barkley, R. A. (1983). The interactions of hyperactive and normal boys with their mothers and fathers. *Journal of Abnormal Child Psychology, 11*, 565–579.

Taplin, P. S., & Reid, J. B. (1973). Effects of instructional set and experimenter influence on observer reliability. *Child Development, 44*, 547–554.

Tisher, M., & Lang, M. (1983). The Children's Depression Scale: Review and further developments. In D. P. Cantwell & G. A. Carlson (Eds.), *Childhood depression* (pp. 181–203). New York: Spectrum.

Ullmann, R. K., Sleator, E. K., & Sprague, R. L. (1984). A new rating scale for diagnosis and monitoring of ADD children. *Psychopharmacology Bulletin, 20*, 160–164.

Urbain, E., & Kendall, P. C. (1980). A review of social-cognitive problem solving interventions with children. *Psychological Bulletin, 88*, 109–143.

Urbain, E. S., & Kendall, P. C. (1981). *Interpersonal problem-solving, social perspective-taking, and behavioral contingencies: A comparison of group approaches with impulsive-aggressive children*. Unpublished manuscript, University of Minnesota.

Urberg, K., & Docherty, E. (1976). Development of role-taking skills in young children. *Developmental Psychology, 12*, 198–203.

van Hasselt, V. B., Hersen, M., & Bellack, A. S. (1981). The validity of role play tests for assessing social skills in children. *Behavior Therapy, 12*, 202–216.

van Lieshout, C., Leckie, G., & Smits-Van-Sonsbeek, B. (1976). Social perspective-taking training: Empathy and role-taking ability of preschool children. In K. F. Riegal & J. A. Meacham (Eds.), *The developing individual in a changing world*. Chicago: Aldine.

Wahler, R. G. (1975). Some structural aspects of deviant child behavior. *Journal of Applied Behavioral Analysis, 8*, 27–42.

Walker, H. M. (1983). *Walker Problem Behavior Identification Checklist (WPBIC-Revised)*. Los Angeles: Western Psychological Services.

Weiner, B., Frieze, I., Kukla, A., Reed, L., Rest, S., Rosenbaum, R. M. (1971). *Perceiving the causes of success and failure*. Morristown, NJ: General Learning Press.

Weissberg, R. P., Cowen, E. L., Lotyczewski, B. S., Boike, M. F., Orara, N. A., Stalonas, P., Sterling, S., & Gesten, E. L. (1987). Teacher ratings of children's problem and competence behaviors: Normative and parametric characteristics. *American Journal of Community Psychology, 15*, 387–401.

Wells, K. C., & Vitulano, L. A. (1984). Anxiety disorders in childhood. In S. Turner (Ed.), *Behavioral theories and treatment of anxiety* (pp. 413–433). New York: Plenum Press.

Werry, J. S. (1968). Studies on the hyperactive child, IV. An empirical analysis of the minimal brain dysfunction syndromes. *Archives of General Psychiatry, 19*, 9–16.

Werry, J. S., & Quay, H. C. (1969). Observing the classroom behavior of elementary school children. *Exceptional Children, 35*, 461–470.

White, P. E., & Blackham, G. J. (1985). Interpersonal problem-solving ability and sociometric status in elementary school children. *Journal of School Psychology, 23*, 255–260.

Whitman, P. B., & Leitenberg, H. (1990). Negatively biased recall in children with self-reported symptoms of depression. *Journal of Abnormal Child Psychology, 18,* 15–27.

Williamson, D. A., & McKenzie, S. J. (1988). Children's Action Tendency Scale. In M. Hersen & A. S. Bellack (Eds.), *Dictionary of behavioral assessment techniques* (pp. 102–104). New York: Pergamon Press.

Williamson, D. A., Moody, S. C., Granberry, S. W., Lethermon, V. R., & Blouin, D. C. (1983). Criterion-related validity of a role-play social skills test for children. *Behavior Therapy, 14,* 466–481.

Wisniewski, J. J., Mulick, J. A., Genshaft, J. L., & Coury, D. L. (1987). Test-retest reliability of the Revised Children's Manifest Anxiety Scale. *Perceptual and Motor Skills, 65,* 67–70.

Wolfe, V. V., Finch, A. J., Saylor, C. F., Blount, R. L., Pallmeyer, T. P., & Carek, D. J. (1987). Negative affectivity in children: A multitrait-multimethod investigation. *Journal of Consulting and Clinical Psychology, 55,* 245–250.

Wood, M. E. (1978). Children's developing understanding of other people's motives for behavior. *Developmental Psychology, 14,* 561–562.

Zahn-Waxler, C., Radke-Yarrow, M., & Brady-Smith, J. (1977). Perspective-taking and prosocial behavior. *Developmental Psychology, 13,* 87–88.

Zentall, S. S. (1984). Context effects in the behavioral ratings of hyperactivity. *Journal of Abnormal Child Psychology, 12,* 345–352.

CHAPTER FIVE

Childhood Aggression

Cognitive-Behavioral Therapy Strategies and Interventions

A. J FINCH, JR.   W. M. NELSON III

JON H. MOSS

During the past decade, violence has become an increasingly severe problem in the United States. Violence is now a "social problem" as well as a major mental health issue. Aggressiveness, conduct disorders, and antisocial behavior represent the most frequent referral problems to outpatient clinics and account for 30% to 50% of these referrals (Finch, Saylor, & Nelson, 1987; Herbert, 1978; Robins, 1981). Such percentages are likely to be misleading, because many aggressive youth come into contact with the legal system rather than with the mental health system. In fact, juveniles account for 39% of all arrests for homicide, rape, robbery, aggravated assault, burglary, larceny, motor vehicle theft, and arson. The rate of violent juvenile crime increased by 233% between 1960 and 1979. Thus, not only is the incidence of juvenile crime growing, but the aggressive and violent nature of such crime is increasing as well (Emysey, 1982; Stumphauzer, 1981). Problems with aggression adversely affect a child or adolescent's adaptive functioning in the family, in school, at work, and with peers. Apart from the personal problems associated with such behaviors, there are significant repercussions for the victims of aggression. Aggressive youths typically strain the tolerance limits of those who must deal with them. This strain is most clearly seen in the "get tough" attitude that has been increasingly promoted over the past decade. In this country there has been a shift from a system that advocated rehabilitation to a system that promotes punishment and severe confinement (Goldstein & Glick, 1987).

Numerous theoretical explanations have been proposed for pathological behaviors and have included multiple biological, sociological, and psychological factors to explain aggressive behaviors (see Herbert, 1978; Reid, 1978). In observing violence and aggression in America, Neubauer (1987) aptly stated:

> *On one hand we appreciate and document the long, complex, multi-faceted etiology of the phenomenon while on the other hand we are led by our values, beliefs, and professional training to seek resolution of the problem by locating it with the individual and searching for means of effective individual intervention. (p. 6)*

Thus, violence and aggression have been addressed by both clinical and legal interventions. In regard to clinical interventions, a variety of treatment approaches have been proposed and used, although relatively few have been empirically evaluated. In general, however, a growing body of research attests to the fact that cognitive-behavioral approaches hold notable promise for dealing with aggressive, violent youth (Feindler & Ecton, 1986; Keith, 1984; Wilson, 1984).

This chapter describes the application of a self-control training approach to the treatment of aggressive disorders in children and defines self-control as individual governing of behavior to attain specific goals. The chapter focuses primarily on therapeutic strategies that target cognitive skills necessary to inhibit impulsive acting out and to generate and evaluate more adaptive behavioral alternatives. Children who have developed adequate self-control are better able to deal with complex interpersonal and societal demands and do not seem to be at the mercy of environmental provocations. In addition, the development of self-control leads to more durable improvements in behavioral change. The learning of self-control skills is particularly important for the maturing youngster who must deal with an array of developmental tasks. According to Kendall and Williams (1982), self-control deficits can involve:

1. Behavioral skills deficits such as problems in self-observation, self-reinforcement, and self-evaluation
2. Cognitive deficits such as poor discrimination, distorted attribution, and deficient problem-solving ability
3. Performance deficits such as the inability to exhibit self-management skills because of moderate emotional arousal such as anger, anxiety, or depression

Although a significant amount of research has been conducted to examine various aspects and elaborations of self-control training, we will outline treatment procedures that stem primarily from the basic format of Raymond Novaco (1975, 1976b, 1976c, 1976d, 1978) who pioneered a self-control approach based on Donald Meichenbaum's stress inoculation model (Meichenbaum, 1975). In this chapter the Novaco approach is integrated with the problem-solving methods of George Spivack and his colleagues (Spivack, Platt, & Shure, 1976; Spivack & Shure, 1974). We will outline an approach that appears to be best suited for an age range of 8 to 15 years, and we suggest that traditional behavioral modification procedures are probably more appropriate for younger children (e.g., time out, token economies, etc.). The clinician may find that in dealing with older adolescents, adult strategies are more useful.

The procedures outlined in this chapter are meant to be viewed as a *flexible* set of guidelines that can be modified to fit the specific needs of individual clients. These procedures were developed by working with children in both inpatient and outpatient settings and were modified by the extensive research that examines the effects of such techniques with children and adolescents. The reader is advised to refer to the more comprehensive reviews of cognitive-behavioral modification (e.g., Feindler & Ecton, 1986; Goldstein & Glick, 1987; Mahoney & Arnkoff, 1977; Meichenbaum, 1985).

Novaco (1978) stated that anger is the "most talked-about but least studied of human emotions" (p. 130), and this is probably a "function of behavioristic traditions that favored the study of aggressive behavior over that of anger" (pp. 135–136). In the strict behavioral tradition, overt aggressive behavior was the only legitimate focus of therapy. Aggression was considered to be the result of a pattern of learned responses to external factors and to be maintained by consequences such as social reinforcement, relief from aversive stimulation, and the acquisition of concrete rewards (Varley, 1984). Although the cognitive-behavioral approach places increased emphasis on the interrelationship among feelings, thoughts, and behavior, "anger and its cognitive correlates remain neglected phenomena, when compared to the extent of study that has been given to other emotions such as anxiety, depression and pain" (Novaco, 1978, p. 136).

Novaco (1979) viewed anger as a reaction to stress. Individuals who experience difficulty with anger tend to lack the necessary psychological resources for coping with stress and are, therefore, prone to reacting negatively whenever placed in a provocation situation. Novaco hypothesized that in order to cope with anger, an individual needs to learn how to effectively manage psychological stress. Thus, anger-management procedures focus on the concept that an individual's reaction to emotional arousal is determined in large part by the distorted and inadequate cognitive structuring of the situation. Modification of an individual's cognitions concerning anger-provoking situations results in the modification of the resultant behavior.

There has been considerable support in the literature as to the influence of cognitive factors on the occurrence of aggressive behavior (Berkowitz, 1974; Bandura, 1973; Dodge, 1985; Feshbach, 1970). In addition, the theoretical work of Beck (1976) and Ellis (1973, 1977) emphasized the influence of cognitions on emotions. The reader is referred to Mahoney and Arnkoff (1977) and Meichenbaum (1977) for a historical perspective and to Goldstein and Glick (1987) for a more recent review of the varieties of cognitive and self-control therapies.

As previously indicated, Novaco developed a treatment procedure that involves cognitive regulation and skill-acquisition training. The treatment model was based upon Meichenbaum's cognitive model of self-control, which is referred to as *stress inoculation training* (Meichenbaum & Cameron, 1972; Meichenbaum, 1975). The stress inoculation procedures focus on developing the client's ability to adapt to stressful events in a manner that reduces the environmental/psychological stress and allows the individual to achieve some personal goal. The client is exposed to manageable doses of stress that are arousing but not overwhelming. As the amount of stress is slowly increased, the client learns to cope with stressful events that have a high probability of occurrence.

Meichenbaum (1975) proposed a three-stage process to account for behavior change in therapy. Therapeutic change was believed to be a function of sequential, mediating processes. In the first stage the child becomes aware of maladaptive intra/interpersonal behaviors, cognitions, and emotions. This process of "self-observation" leads to Stage Two, in which these self-observations serve as a stimulus for emitting a series of incompatible thoughts and behaviors. Stage Three involves the manner in which the child appraises behavior change, and this appraisal determines the duration of the treatment effects and the degree to which generalization takes place. Meichenbaum believed that altering the internal dialogue results in behavior change because (a) self-instructions play a direct role in changing behavior, (b) self-instructions and images affect behavior through influencing the direction of attention, and (c) self-instructions influence a child's interpretation and experience of his or her physiological state. By use of stress inoculation training, the child can obtain a sense of accomplishment and resourcefulness. Stress inoculation has been successfully applied to anxiety (Meichenbaum & Cameron, 1972; Meichenbaum, 1975; Spirito, Finch, Smith, & Cooley, 1981), pain (Nelson, 1981; Turk, 1975; Turk, Meichenbaum, & Genest, 1983), and anger (Feindler & Ecton, 1986; Lochman, Burch, Curry, & Lampron, 1984; Novaco, 1975, 1977; Schrader, Long, Panzer, Gillet, & Kornblath, 1977).

Currently, two of the authors (Finch and Nelson) are applying the stress inoculation model in the treatment of anger-control problems with children. The procedures outlined in this chapter are under constant review and revision, and the reader is reminded that the procedures serve only as flexible guidelines for treatment. The actual therapeutic interventions or steps in treatment are not meant to be rigidly imposed by the clinician. In addition, it should be remembered that cognitive-behavioral procedures attempt to alter a child's maladaptive cognitions and thus change the inherent affect and problematic overt behaviors. Although therapeutic intervention takes place at the cognitive level, the effectiveness of the cognitive procedures is anchored in demonstrations that the child's overt behavior is improved.

Assessment of Anger

Although there have been attempts to define anger and aggression, there is no well-validated conception of anger arousal that enables us to determine specifically the parameters of anger disorders. Contributing to the problem of assessment of these disorders is the fact that anger cannot be construed as simply a negative emotion. In certain situations the expression of anger may have very adaptive functions. Because of this, the determination of whether or not a person's anger constitutes a problem must be based upon how his or her behavior affects interpersonal relationships, school performance, health, family functioning, and so forth.

In terms of diagnostic systems, the DSM-III-R (1987) defines several categories that reflect aggressive behaviors in children. The diagnosis of conduct disorder includes persistent patterns of negativistic, hostile, and defiant behavior that violate the basic rights of others or of major age-appropriate societal norms; the diagnosis of oppositional defiant disorder is based on these same behaviors without reference to others' rights or societal standards. Other diagnoses that involve some degree or form of aggressive acting out include attention-deficit hyperactivity disorder, intermittent explosive disorder, antisocial personality disorder, and even major depressive disorder.

In terms of childhood and adolescent psychopathology, a broad band disorder of internalizing versus externalizing has been obtained repeatedly by factor analysis (Quay, 1986). The locus of conflict occurs between youth and their environment and is expressed in a variety of acting-out ways. Children who exhibit externalized aggressive behaviors may benefit from self-control intervention procedures, regardless of their specific diagnosis.

As with all treatment, the importance of an accurate assessment of the problem(s) cannot be overemphasized. Whether assessment takes the form of a traditional psychological evaluation, of behavioral observation, of some combination of the two, or of some novel approach, it is essential to develop an accurate understanding of the problem if treatment is to be effective. In cognitive-behavioral approaches such as stress inoculation training for anger management, assessment must include not only the observable behaviors of the child but also private cognitions. Meichenbaum (1985) distinguished three types of cognitions: (a) cognitive events, (b) cognitive processes, and (c) cognitive structures. *Cognitive events* refer to more easily accessible and concise thoughts, self-statements, private speech, and images. Meichenbaum referred to these as "internal dialogue," and Beck (1976) called them "automatic thoughts." Such events include attributions, expectancies, self-evaluations, and/or task-relevant or -irrelevant self-statements and images. *Cognitive processes* are less accessible and refer to the way individuals process information emotionally or unconsciously (e.g., long- and short-term memory processes, inferential and retrieval processes). Our awareness of such cognitive processes and our ability to control them reflect metacognition. Because such processes are normally out of conscious awareness, they are somewhat more difficult to utilize in treatment. Finally, *cognitive structures* are the more fundamental abstractions, beliefs, and memories that individuals hold and that influence the way behavior is organized. Such structures also have been called *schemata,* and they reflect the mental organization of experience. Because cognitive events are more readily accessible than cognitive processes or cognitive structuring, most stress inoculation procedures with children and adolescents focus on this level. The more highly developed cognitive capabilities of adults allow them to benefit from intervention techniques aimed at all three levels of cognition.

Given the fact that much of cognitive-behavioral therapy is based on private experiences, self-report is an important method by which information is obtained, and the therapist must be sensitive to what the individual shares. It is not necessary for the therapist to accept everything that is reported at face value, but it is necessary to view these reports as information that is as important as that obtained from other sources. Private speech is not necessarily more valuable than observable behaviors, but it can provide important information.

Obviously, one of the problems encountered by the cognitive-behavioral therapist who attempts to enter the private world of a client is that the individual must be willing and able to share private speech. With children this can be a major problem, because their verbal expressive abilities are not as well developed as those of adults. The child may have considerable difficulty expressing feelings, emotions, and/or thoughts and, in addition, may not choose to share this private information with the therapist. These problems present the therapist with an opportunity to demonstrate flexibility and creativity in employing and developing procedures to facilitate the acquisition of this information.

It is difficult to ascertain which angry and aggressive youngster can benefit most from cognitive-behavioral anger management interventions. However, various assessment methods will be outlined for screening children and adolescents for such therapeutic interventions and for guiding the development of such interventions.

The Cognitive-Behavioral Interview with the Child and Adolescent

The clinical interview is one of the main strategies employed in assessment within a cognitive-behavioral framework. The usual rules of interviewing apply to the cognitive-behavioral assessment, and these include the placing the child at ease and attempting to obtain information in a nonthreatening manner. Regardless of theoretical orientation, care must be taken to ensure that the interviewer does not fall into the role of inquisitor, and this is particularly important when interviewing a youngster who has been referred because of behavioral problems. By the time the child meets the therapist, he or she has usually been lectured, scolded, and made to feel guilty by many adults. Frequently the child has been told that the therapist is going to find out what is wrong and that the therapist will make the child stop doing all those "bad things." Anyone who has interviewed children referred for problem behaviors has encountered clients who seemed to believe that execution is not only a possibility but also a probability. Also, it should be noted that the age and verbal ability of the child determine the usefulness of the clinical interview.

Within the format of the clinical interview, there are a number of specific techniques that seem particularly suited for obtaining the type of information employed in cognitive-behavior therapy. In some cases, having the child "run a movie" provides a great deal of information and insight into the nature of the problem. In this relatively simple procedure the child is made comfortable and asked to close his or her eyes. Next, the youngster is asked to visualize the last time there was a problem with anger management. The therapist helps to focus the child's images by asking appropriate directing questions in a nonthreatening manner. The focus of the inquiry may be on internal speech, physiological sensations, and other potentially important information such as the physical appearance of the other person(s) involved. This procedure helps the therapist gain an understanding of the problem from the child's perspective and provides information and details that will be useful in developing treatment scenes and hierarchies.

At times, children may feel uncomfortable with "running a movie," and, in fact, most youngsters are initially reluctant to engage in this activity.

However, it is usually possible to make the child feel more comfortable about engaging in this exercise by providing reassurance that it can be helpful and that many other children are hesitant initially. When the youngster is particularly reluctant, it is useful to begin with nonthreatening scenes. However, it is generally unnecessary to do more than reassure the child and to provide encouragement to "give it a try."

Children below the age of 10 are frequently unable to maintain their focus during the task of running a movie; therefore, with young children it is necessary to obtain information and details through other procedures. An alternative to running a movie is a drawing task variation of the movie. In this procedure the youngster describes a scene and watches as the therapist makes a quick stick-figure sketch. Again, the therapist can ask focusing questions, and most younger children find this task entertaining and are willing and eager to provide the requested information. Simple figures are desirable in this drawing task because of the speed with which they can be produced. In a "cartoon format," distinctions can be made between covert and overt speech through the use of bubbles for thinking and of continuous lines for talking (see Figure 5-1). Most children are familiar with this distinction from comic strips and books. In addition to its usefulness in securing the desired information, this procedure serves to defuse a youngster's fear of discussing emotionally charged situations. Furthermore, it helps the child look at behavioral problems while maintaining perspective and a sense of humor.

Self-Report Measures

In addition to interview procedures the therapist can employ various self-report measures. For a number of years we have been working on the standardization and development of a self-report scale designed to assess children's anger responses on six of the seven parameters of anger outlined by Novaco (Children's Inventory of Anger—Finch, Saylor, & Nelson, 1983, 1987). This instrument consists of 71 items that are rated by the child on a 4-point anger scale, ranging from "I don't care. That situation doesn't even bother me. I don't know why that would make anyone mad (angry)" to "I can't stand that! I'm furious! I feel like really hurting or killing that person or destroying that thing!" The items cover situations that might occur at school, at home, in interactions with peers, and in other situations that could be viewed as anger provoking. The items are written on a fourth-grade reading level, but the situations described appear to be appropriate for children in grades two through eight. An example of this assessment tool can be seen in Table 5-1.

FIGURE 5-1 • *Example of Stick Figures Using Overt and Covert Speech*

Another self-report scale that seems to hold promise is the Children's Hostility Inventory (Kazdin, Rodgers, Colbus, & Siegel, 1987), which contains 38 items designed to be completed by parents and evaluates aggression and hostility in children. Preliminary results with this scale suggest that it is potentially useful with children from 6 to 12 years of age.

A more extensive list of paper-and-pencil measures that may be helpful for the clinician working with specific populations can be found in Feindler and Ecton (1986).

Interviews and Ratings by Others

Additional information about the nature of the child's anger management must be obtained from the significant others who have observed the problem. In addition to providing the therapist with useful information about the child's behavior, the precipitating events, and the subsequent consequences, the interview with family members and other relevant individuals (e.g., teachers, counselors, peers) can set the stage for ensuring their cooperation in later stages of treatment. The time involved in obtaining such information is well spent, because children and adolescents referred for acting out are often defensive and may minimize their problems. In

TABLE 5-1 • *Children's Inventory of Anger*

1 2 3 4 (46) Your sister breaks your favorite toy after you have asked her not to play with it.

1 2 3 4 (47) Your parents won't give you a "yes" or "no" answer but say "we'll see" when you want to plan on doing something.

1 2 3 4 (48) Your parents make you eat something you hate (e.g., spinach) in order to "clean your plate."

1 2 3 4 (49) You tell your mom that you don't have any homework but she makes you study anyway.

1 2 3 4 (50) The bus driver takes your name for acting up on the bus, but everybody else was acting up too.

1 2 3 4 (51) You have to go to bed at 9:30 even in the summertime and your friends get to stay up until 10:30 or 11:00.

1 2 3 4 (52) Your mom says that you have to do your homework as soon as you get home before you can go out to play.

1 2 3 4 (53) You get lost at the shopping center and when you finally find your parents your dad is mad and screams at you.

1 2 3 4 (54) At lunch, you select a piece of pie and the kid behind you knocks it out of your hand.

1 2 3 4 (55) At school, two bigger kids come and take your basketball and play "keep away" from you.

1 2 3 4 (56) You didn't notice that someone put gum on your seat on the bus and you sit on it.

1 2 3 4 (57) You run to catch the bus to go home but just as you get there, it drives away.

1 2 3 4 (58) You want to go to sleep, but your brother keeps making noise.

1 2 3 4 (59) Every Sunday, the minister talks 20 minutes overtime.

1 2 3 4 (60) You accidentally bump into a stranger on the bus and he threatens to beat you up if you get near him again.

addition, children may not always be able to provide the information that the clinician needs in order to appreciate the problem and to begin an effective intervention plan. It is important for the clinician to gather information about the following issues:

1. The informant's view of the child's complaint, symptoms, and stressors
2. The informant's view of the child's current environment (home, school, peers)
3. The informant's view of the child's development and history and the informant's expectations about the future

To ensure a thorough assessment, it is also helpful to augment interviews with more global behavioral checklists. Currently the most frequently used rating scales that include an acting-out dimension are the Child Behavior Checklist (Achenbach & Edelbrock, 1983) and the Revised Behavior Problem Checklist (Quay & Peterson, 1983).

In certain settings (i.e., schools, residential settings) it may be possible to obtain sociogram data that identify the child or children who are viewed by their peers as most often getting into trouble, having the fewest friends, being the meanest, fighting most frequently, and so forth. These data serve a dual purpose in that they not only aid in identification of "problem" children but also provide the clinician with outcome data to determine the effectiveness of the program. We have found it helpful to use the Peer Nomination Inventory of Anger (Finch et al., 1987), which contains items that are indicative of anger problems as well as items that identify more positive qualities (see Table 5-2).

We have found it almost impossible to obtain any type of reliable behavioral counts within a psychiatric hospital setting. We have been amazed at the impressive data generated at other facilities and have even voiced doubts about our own ability to do "good" behavioral interventions without actual counts of behavior. An example of the difficulty encountered in this area may serve to demonstrate why we no longer employ behavior counts or time samples (Nelson, Fleming, & Hart, 1982).

An 11-year-old boy hospitalized for numerous tics was referred for a behavioral program to address his touching behavior. This youngster frequently touched the nursing staff and teachers on the breast and in the genital areas. This boy's behavior obviously had a markedly adverse effect on his relationships with the staff, because none of them felt comfortable working with him. After considerable discussion and work with the staff, an intervention program was developed. Staff were to record the number of times he touched or attempted to touch during various periods. After several days of baseline, treatment began and seemed to be progressing well. However, one day the therapist was late in returning to the unit to collect the counts. When he arrived, he found not only the data for the completed period but also data for the period that was just *beginning*. In other words, the data were completely fake! After sitting down with the staff involved, it became evident that they were following through on the program reason-

TABLE 5-2 • *Peer Nomination Inventory of Anger*

Directions: Below you will find statements that describe students' behavior. Answer each statement by giving the name of the student in your class that the statement best describes.

1. Gets angry easily.

2. Spends most of the time being angry.

3. Spends the least amount of time being angry.

4. Student would least like to work with because of anger.

5. Student would most like to work with because does not get angry.

6. Student most likely to be unable to complete work due to anger.

7. Student who cusses the most.

8. Student who slams the door the most.

9. Student who spends the most time in the Quiet Room.

10. Student most likely to start fighting over nothing.

11. Student most likely to get others angry.

12. Student who teases others the most.

13. Student least likely to respect the belongings and property of others.

14. Student most likely to respect the belongings and property of others.

15. The most cooperative student.

16. The least cooperative student.

17. The easiest student to get along with.

18. Does not forget things that anger him/her.

19. The easiest student to work with.

20. The most difficult student to work with.

21. Student most infuriated by any form of discipline.

22. Has to have everything his or her own way.

23. When angry, refuses to speak to anyone.

24. Fights back if another student has been asking for it.

25. Argues with the teacher.

26. Boasts of own toughness.

27. Fights with smaller children.

28. Never speaks up even when there is cause to be angry.

Continued

TABLE 5-2 • *Continued*

29. Is interested in school work.

30. Tries to get other children into trouble.

31. Does things just to attract attention.

32. Never fights back, even if someone hits or pushes first.

33. Is popular with classmates.

34. Never sticks up for self when picked on by other children.

35. Threatens to hurt other children when angry.

36. Finds fault with instructions given by adults.

37. Seems unconcerned when misbehaving.

38. Cries easily.

39. When angry will do things like slamming the door or banging the desk.

40. Acts in a "dare-devil," fearless manner.

ably well but were not counting behaviors. Following several similar attempts at counting target behaviors, we have accepted the fact that most psychiatric nurses and nursing aides are not going to count accurately for an extended period of time, even when they have requested and helped design aspects of the programs.

For these reasons we use individually tailored behavioral rating scales (Finch, Deardorff, & Montgomery, 1974) and checklists (Kolko, Dorsett, & Milan, 1981). These tailored measures are designed to reflect the particular behavior problem manifested by each individual child. Most of the descriptors employed are obtained from the people who work most closely with the child—such as parents, teachers, or staff in inpatient settings. It is important that the language used in these scales is generated by the people who will be responsible for recording the ratings. Usually ratings are from 1 to 5, although other ranges have been employed. The 5-point range of scores makes it possible to detect changes in the individual's behaviors but minimizes the need for fine discriminations. Each value is anchored to a set of actual behavioral descriptors, which makes the rating process easier. Simplicity and clarity of descriptors are exceedingly important when accurate information is sought with this type of measure (see Table 5-3). We have found individually tailored behavior rating scales to be very useful in obtaining accurate information about the child's progress in treatment. Furthermore, we have encountered far fewer problems in obtaining accurate and genuine data than when we attempted to obtain behavior counts

TABLE 5-3 • *Individually Tailored Behavior Rating Scale for Gary's Aggressive Behaviors*

5. Gary hit, kicked, or fought with another youngster or staff member more than twice during the day.

4. Gary hit, kicked, or fought with another youngster or staff member one or two times during the day.

3. Gary argued extensively with other children or staff and was generally antagonistic. No reference to physical fighting.

2. There was some arguing and bickering but not an excessive amount. No reference to physical fighting.

1. Gary was generally pleasant without reference being made to fighting or arguing. No reference to physical fighting.

and time samples. On numerous reliability checks obtained in a variety of ways, the rating scales have been acceptable.

Role-Play Techniques

Behavior therapists have traditionally viewed direct observation of problem behavior as the sine qua non of assessment. Such methods, however, create significant difficulty when aggression is the problem behavior. Expressions of anger, whether verbal or physical, are likely to be markedly influenced if children or adolescents are aware that they are being observed. In addition, such assessment methods are time-consuming and costly. Therefore, role-play or analogue assessment may provide suitable alternatives. In a controlled situation, observations of behavior are made in staged conflict or anger-eliciting situations. It is helpful to have semistructured scripts and confederates to role play these emotionally charged conflict situations. Efforts should be made to approximate real-life situations as much as possible. In dealing with severely acting-out individuals, it is important to build in a "stop-the-action" signal to use when the intensity of anger increases. We have found that a preestablished signal of raising one's hand can be used by any participant who judges that "things are getting out of hand." At such times, all participants must stop the interaction and sit down in prearranged places. After participants "cool off," processing the event can provide valuable clinical information. The cognitive-behavioral clinician attends to and questions the client about cognitive events, self-talk, and images. In addition, it is important to ascertain the physiological and behavioral cues that the client noticed as the anger intensified. Videotaping of role-played conflicts is highly recommended. These tapes can be reviewed with the client by stopping them at "critical points." This review provides additional assessment data and can also educate the client about the cognitive, physiological, and behavioral components of anger. Although such assessment methods are influenced by demand characteristics, the data obtained are clinically rich in nature.

General Issues in Assessment

Novaco (1978) outlined seven parameters that should be examined to determine the adaptive or maladaptive function of anger reactions to provocation events. These parameters are (a) frequency, (b) intensity, (c) duration, (d) mode of expression, (e) effect on performance, (f) effect on relationships, and (g) effect on health. With adults and older children, information on these parameters can be obtained through a clinical interview and through a self-reporting rating scale (Novaco Anger Scale — Novaco, 1975; Children's Inventory of Anger — Finch et al., 1987). In order to determine the specific situations and the specific individuals that are typically involved in the child's maladaptive behavior, we suggest a "situation × person × mode of expression" analysis of the child's anger problem. Together, the child and clinician conduct this analysis to determine if the child has a predictable set of social contacts that result in anger. For example, a child named Chris reacted violently whenever someone said the word "piss." Analysis of this behavior revealed the fact that two of his classmates always taunted him on the school playground by screaming, "Chris, Piss." Treatment focused on preparing the child for this consistent provocation event and helping him learn how to cope with the actions of these two boys. Once Chris was able to modify his reaction to this specific provocation, he no longer reacted violently to the trigger word.

Assessment of anger should focus not only on events in the child's life (external factors) but also on how these events are interpreted (internal processes) and how the child reacts during and after the occurrence of these events (behavioral reactions). Most important are the external events that arouse the child's anger with greatest frequency. Novaco (1978) stated that external events are "provocative because they are at variance with expectations" (p. 164); therefore, the child's interpretation of the "aversive" event must be determined. According to Novaco (1976b), three forms of cognitive thought seem to influence anger arousal — appraisals, expectations, and private speech. *Appraisal* refers to the meaning assigned to the aversive event and includes the child's view of his or her ability to cope effectively with the situation. *Expectations* are the child's subjective probabilities for future events. Novaco (1976c) stated that anger can be influenced by a person's expectations in several ways:

> *(a) [H]igh expectations for desirable consequences they do not obtain can make the undesired event more aversive, (b) high expectations that someone else will behave aversively can reduce one's inclination to behave antagonistically, and (c) low expectations that one can effectively manage a conflict situation can lead to anger and aggression as a desperate attempt to achieve control. (p. 8)*

Private speech of the child reflects appraisals and expectations and has a direct influence on arousal and action. Antagonistic self-statements, excessive ruminations about aversive experiences, and negative self-statements all serve to inflame and prolong one's anger. The content of the child's private speech will provide information about the child's cognitive structuring of provocation situations, and it enables the clinician to obtain an understanding of the child's ability to cognitively restructure behavior.

In addition to cognitive components, somatic process also must be evaluated. Factors such as tension, temperament, and empathy all influence how a child reacts to a frustrating or provoking event. If a child is uptight or extremely agitated, the ability to cope with problematic situations in an appropriate fashion is drastically decreased. Therefore, it is necessary to determine to what extent a child is able to counteract the effect of tension by relaxing or taking slow, deep breaths.

After assessment the three steps of stress inoculation for anger management can begin. Actually, we believe that assessment is just as important as the later stages of treatment, and we consider assessment as the first of four phases in stress inoculation. The reader is referred to texts by Feindler and Ecton (1986) and Meichenbaum (1985) that provide more extensive explanations of stress inoculation procedures.

Cognitive-Behavioral Techniques

The anger-management procedure outlined in this chapter attempts to intervene at the cognitive, somatic, and behavioral levels. This procedure is designed to assist the child in developing adaptive coping skills to deal with provocations and frustrations. It is meant to be a flexible program that can be changed or adjusted to fit a particular child or a particular set of problem events. Because of this, numerous behavioral techniques may be employed at any given time. Such techniques include self-monitoring, problem solving, didactic training, modeling (filmed or in vivo), social and material reinforcement, relaxation training, and self-instructional training. The stress inoculation approach presented here places particular emphasis on self-instructional training and relaxation procedures. In addition, we have integrated problem-solving procedures into our basic anger-control program. The basic stress inoculation approach (emphasizing verbal self-instructions and relaxation procedures) will be described, and this approach will be illustrated with a case study. The conceptual integration of the stress inoculation model and the problem-solving procedures will then be presented and will be followed by a suggested outline for structuring group therapy sessions.

The Stress Inoculation Approach: Verbal Self-Instructions and Relaxation Procedures

Verbal self-instructions can assist in developing an internal set of controls that permit the child to prepare for a possible anger-provoking event and to deal effectively with that event. Most children who experience anger problems are extremely impulsive, and, therefore, the latency between the onset of the anger-provoking event and the expression of anger is quite short. By imposing a set of verbal instructions, the child is forced to slow down and to decide what action should be taken. The verbalizations employed by the child should be directly related to the specific presenting problems. These verbalizations are modeled by the therapist and then rehearsed by the child. The modeling and rehearsal sessions follow a defined sequence outlined by Meichenbaum and Goodman (1971):

1. The trainer models the task and talks out loud while the child observes (overt, cognitive modeling).
2. The child performs the task, instructing himself or herself aloud, with assistance from the trainer (overt, external guidance).
3. The child performs the task aloud with no assistance (overt, self-guidance).
4. The trainer models the same statements but now whispers them (faded overt, modeling).
5. The child performs the task whispering to himself or herself (faded overt, self-guidance).
6. The trainer performs the task using silent verbalizations (covert, guidance modeling).
7. The child now performs the task using silent verbalizations (covert, self-guidance).

These self-statements involve dissecting a provocation experience into a sequence of stages: (a) preparing for a provocation ("Hell, here comes

John. He's mad at me because of what happened in class. This could be tough, but I know how to deal with it."), (b) impact and confrontation ("Keep cool. There is no need to get mad. Don't take it personally."), (c) coping with arousal ("I'm tightening up. He's getting to me. OK, relax. Take a deep breath. Cool it."), and (d) subsequent reflection ("Hey, I handled that one pretty well. I made it without getting angry. – or – Well, I blew this one, didn't settle anything, but I'm not going to let it bother me.").

Incorporated into the stress inoculation training are systematic relaxation procedures that have been found to be very effective in dealing with stress and anxiety. Novaco (1976c) recommended the Jacobsen (1938) procedure of alternative tensing and relaxing muscles, because angry people "are inclined to tense their muscles and this procedure tells them to do what they are already doing, thus minimizing resistance to relaxation induction" (p. 17). However, these techniques appear to be somewhat difficult to use with children (especially young children). Meichenbaum (1973) offered alternative procedures for inducing relaxation with younger clients, and Koeppen (1974) developed a useful set of procedures for teaching children to relax. Her procedure involves relaxation instructions that use fantasy in such a way that the child automatically attends to the appropriate muscle groups. For example, the child imagines that an elephant is getting ready to step on his or her stomach. The child tenses stomach muscles and then is told to imagine that the elephant moves away. Koeppen's procedure focuses on seven muscle groups (hands and arms, arms and shoulders, shoulder and neck, jaw, face and nose, stomach, and legs and feet).

If it is impossible to conduct a complete relaxation procedure, the child should be instructed in deep breathing exercises, and emphasis should be placed on the importance of breathing control to achieve relaxation. With such therapeutic strategies in mind, the following outlines the three fundamental phases of a stress inoculation approach in dealing with anger problems: Cognitive Preparation, Skill Acquisition, and Application Training.

Phase 1: Cognitive Preparation (Education Phase)

The first phase of stress inoculation training is a discussion and explanation of the functions of anger and how individuals usually react to anger-provoking situations. This discussion introduces a similar language system between the child and therapist and provides the rationale of treatment. During this phase the child's anger problem is assessed, and both the therapist and child attempt to understand how and why the child reacts to a particular situation in a particular way. While exploring a child's reaction to provocation, the therapist can offer alternative solutions or behaviors the child might have used. During this phase the therapist's task is to form an alliance with the child and to show the child that there are other ways to deal with anger. It is important for the child to learn that the expression of anger is appropriate in certain situations and that the therapy will focus on situations in which an angry response is inappropriate and on how to express anger appropriately and effectively.

Phase 2: Skill Acquisition (Rehearsal Phase)

The second phase of the training program is designed to provide the child with specific techniques, both cognitive and behavioral, to use during the coping process. During this phase, interventions are attempted at cognitive, affective, and behavioral levels, and relaxation techniques, anger-reducing self-statements, assertion skills, and problem-solving techniques are introduced.

On the cognitive level the child is taught to view the provocation events in a different manner and to modify the importance of these events. This is done by alteration of the appraisal of the aversive events and by teaching the child "not to take things personally." Because most children have limited ability in cognitive restructuring of events, the use of positive self-verbalizations is employed in the systematic manner described previously, which involves overt, cognitive modeling; overt, external guidance; overt, self-guidance; faded overt, modeling; faded overt, self-guidance; covert, guidance modeling; and covert, self-guidance.

Intervention at the affective level involves relaxation training. In addition, the child is encouraged to develop a sense of humor as an alternative to anger. Behavioral goals are determined in order to promote communication of feelings, assertive behavior, and problem-solving behavior as alternatives to direct expression of anger. The goal is to help the child recognize the arousal of anger, to decide whether or not expression of anger is appropriate, and then to either communicate feelings (anger) in a non-hostile, more adaptive manner or to engage in some form of problem-solving action that may include direct expression of feelings. (Specific problem-solving strategies will be discussed later in this chapter in the context of group interventions.)

Phase 3: Application Training (Practice, Practice, and More Practice)

Once the child has become proficient in the skills taught during Phase 2, the opportunity is provided to test these skills in controlled situations. The child needs to know that it is possible to effectively handle anger-provoking situations and needs to "practice" these new skills. The practice can be conducted in numerous ways. If the clinician is dealing with a single client, imaginal anger-provoking situations can be used. In addition, the therapist and child can engage in structured role playing to test these new skills. Both imaginal and role-play strategies should employ a hierarchy of anger situations that the child is likely to encounter in real life. Coping skills are first applied to the mildest anger situations and then progress to more potent anger-arousing situations. Another application training technique is the use of "barbs"—a technique based on the original suggestions of Kaufmann and Wagner (1972). A "barb" is a provocation statement that is applied in situations other than the training/therapy setting. The rationale and procedure are explained to the client, who is then warned that "I'm going to barb you" (e.g., "Don't look at me like that! You're grounded tomorrow."). The person delivering the barbs (e.g., parent, teacher, staff member) records the client's responses for review and discussion during the following therapy session. Gradually the barbs are designed to more directly approximate the actual problem provocation, and the warning is dropped. To maximize generalization, this procedure should be utilized on an intermittent basis by a variety of individuals.

If the therapist is working on developing anger control with a group of children, the entire group can be used to test and practice the new skills. Each child can be given the opportunity to use the skills as the other group members attempt to arouse anger. If a group procedure is used, hierarchies of situations should be established for each child, and the situations should be presented systematically from mildest to strongest. This procedure provides social reinforcement for success and also helps each child develop the new-found skill further by teaching and helping others. The group procedure begins with the therapist standing next to the child, giving encouragement and necessary coaching. When the child demonstrates the ability to handle the situation, the therapist moves away, remaining available for additional coaching. After the child demonstrates coping skills in the provoking situation, the procedure is repeated with another child in the group.

Helpful Hints

The following points are offered as a foundation for the anger-management approach, which will be presented in detail.

1. The most important aspect of this program is flexibility. The following outline is not meant to be adhered to religiously. In order for any

cognitive-behavioral program to be successful, the therapist must fit the program to the specific needs of the individual child.

2. The setting is important. Both the therapist and the child should be comfortable. Distractions should be kept to a minimum. Many of the procedures can be carried out in a multitude of settings. In fact, to enhance generalization it may be best to shift a number of the "rehearsal" sessions to nonclinic settings (e.g., outdoors, in the classroom, at home, etc.).

3. Humor is important. The interjection of humor appears to permit the child to more effectively apply what has been learned, and humor in itself is an inhibitor that tends to "short-circuit" the maladaptive anger response.

4. The use of both social and material reinforcements for successively better performance is effective. The use of reinforcement should be built into the program to enhance performance. Also, the therapist may consider the use of a response-cost procedure in the training package.

5. Every effort should be made to establish a solid relationship between the therapist and child. If such a relationship has not been established prior to training, the child may feel that the procedures and self-statements are "stupid" or "useless" and may not react favorably.

6. The therapist should be animated and responsive to the child. The selection of self-statements and the use of age-appropriate, child-appropriate language should be carefully monitored. One does not use a white, middle-class language and value system when dealing with a black, ghetto-raised child.

7. Emphasis should be placed on the development of coping skills. The child must learn that mistakes will be made and that sometimes he or she will become angry and upset. Emphasis should be placed on coping with mistakes.

8. Promoting generalization is an important consideration. To enhance generalization it may be helpful to vary "trainers" and the training setting. We have found it useful to produce some sort of objective "cue" that the child can use to trigger the coping skills. This can be accomplished by incorporating teachers and parents into the training sessions and by having them supply the cues for control. This cue is generally a word that is agreed on by the therapist and the child. For example, the word *focus* was employed with one girl and served as her cue to emit relaxing self-statements to relax.

9. Generalization may also be aided by group training that allows the child to train other children and to practice new skills under varying levels of stress. Group treatment may also foster behavior change via group discussion and pressure.

Session-by-Session Guidelines

Session 1

The first session follows the collection of pretreatment anger data. In general, the assessment process moves from the general to the more specific. First, the client and parents are interviewed, and a general measure of psychopathology is obtained (e.g., Child Behavior Checklist—Achenbach & Edelbrock, 1983). Next, individually tailored self-monitoring forms may be developed, or specialized instruments might be completed (e.g., Children's Inventory of Anger—Finch et al., 1987). Although a diagnosis may or may not be helpful, efforts should be made to operationally define the problematic behaviors and to determine the specific measures of treatment outcome.

In the first session the development of rapport continues to be an important focus. In addition, a discussion of anger is initiated. The degree to which the nature and function of anger are explored depends upon the age and sophistication of the child. For immature children a simple, concrete approach is most effective. As age and maturity increase, information about external events, internal variables, and behavioral factors can increase. In any event, the discussion should be keyed to the child's problem and should use the language system of the child.

Throughout the training sessions it is critical for the clinician to use the verbal style of the child—the phrases and terms that the child provides. This helps establish the clinician's relationship with the child and guards against "talking down" to the child. To be effective the therapist must be a "ham," using gestures and tone of voice to "hook" the child into treatment. It is important to personalize the conceptualization of anger management; however, the child needs to know that there is nothing "weird, crazy, or sick" about losing control of anger and that other children have the same or similar "problems."

The first session is considered to be a part of the Cognitive Preparation (assessment/educational) phase of stress inoculation training. It should be remembered that assessment is an ongoing process, that it is not completed in a single session, and that it occurs throughout treatment. Depending on the cognitive maturity of the child, the material presented in this session may be continued in Session 2 and Session 3.

Session Activities
During this educational phase it is important to:

1. Reach an understanding with the child regarding:

   a. The degree to which anger leads to trouble for the child

      b. The greatest concern or problem that anger poses for the child

      c. How control of anger would make life different

2. Define anger, stressing the positive and negative functions of anger (see Novaco, 1976a, p. 4). Talk about anger as a *feeling* or *emotion* and talk about aggression as a *behavioral* result of anger.

3. Point out that when anger becomes a problem, it is due to increases in one or more of the following:

      a. Frequency—how often the child experiences anger

      b. Intensity—how strongly the child experiences anger

      c. Duration—how long the child's angry feelings last

      d. Aggressive consequences—what happens as a result of the child's experience of anger

4. Conduct a "situation × person × mode of expression" analysis of the anger problem. Have the child identify the particular settings in which anger is experienced, the particular people involved with the experience of anger, and the behaviors that are emitted as a result of the angry feelings. Self-report measures often help in this analysis.

5. Discuss the *determinants* of anger arousal. Have the child imagine a particular situation and use this to discuss:

      a. *External factors* (frustrations, annoyances, irritations, verbal and physical abuse, etc.)

      • What is it about the situation that provokes the child's anger?

      • Are there any general situations which trigger anger?

      • Was the expression of anger appropriate in the particular situation?

      b. *Internal factors—cognitive and affective* (*Cognitive* factors involve our thoughts and the things we say to ourselves. How we view the situation (appraisal), our expectations about the way things should be (expectations), and what we say to ourselves that influences our appraisals and expectations (self-statements) help to prolong or shorten our anger.)

      • What expectations trigger the child's anger?

      • How does the child see this situation, and why does that produce anger?

      (*Affective* factors refer to how we feel (uptight, tense, wound up, or relaxed). How we feel has a great influence on how we react to situations. If we are tense or in a bad mood, we will react differently than if we are relaxed and feel good.)

      • How does the child handle anger when in a "good" mood versus when in a "bad" mood?

c. *Behavioral factors*
- What does the child usually do when confronted or provoked? How does the child feel after crying, throwing a rock, getting into a fight, and the like? What effect does this behavior have on others?

In order to help the child understand the factors that influence anger, the clinician uses examples developed from the child's responses or created from experiences with other children. Emphasis is placed on the use of self-statements, and these statements are demonstrated to the child. This is a good time for the clinician to "run through" an anger-provoking situation, using self-statements to show how anger-provoking situations can be perceived, how one can feel during a provocation, and how one "chooses" to respond.

Homework
Depending on the age of the child, the clinician assigns some form of "homework." Older children may be asked to maintain a diary of anger experiences. The adolescent is instructed to record the frequency of angry outbursts, the intensity of these outbursts, the circumstances surrounding the provocation, and a rating of how they handled the provocation. Parents and/or teachers may be asked to help younger children in this data collection. All clients are encouraged to "listen" to their "private speech" in order to identify positive and negative self-statements. Sometimes keeping a diary is disruptive; some children do not have the necessary skills, and many parents are unwilling to help when they themselves are angry at the child. The diary is primarily important when it increases the child's awareness of problematic situations and provides the therapist with further assessment data. It is not essential and should be discontinued if it becomes disruptive.

Session 2

The initial part of the second session is devoted to a short review of the first session's activities, for it is important to be sure that the child understands the treatment rationale. Next the therapist reviews the homework assignments. This review gives the therapist an opportunity to assist the child in record keeping and permits a more refined view of the circumstances that relate to anger expression.

Based on the initial assessment data and the child's anger diary, an anger-situation hierarchy is established. Although Novaco (1976c) suggested that seven situations should be produced, the actual number depends on the particular problems presented by the child. The development of the hierarchy should be a joint effort of the clinician and the child, and it is important to determine the accuracy and the relative potency of each situation.

Once the hierarchy has been established, the child is told that each situation can be broken down into several stages: *preparing for provocation, impact and confrontation, coping with arousal,* and *reflecting on the provocation.* The child is shown that positive self-statements can help in coping with anger in each stage.

1. *Preparing for Provocation* — "This stage occurs whenever you know that you will soon be faced with something that will make you angry. When you can anticipate, you can figure out how to cope with the situation in advance. This does not always work, because sometimes you get angry without warning, but you may be able to say things to yourself to help keep your cool." When the client can generate private talk independently, it is likely to be more meaningful. For example, the child might say:

   • "Keep cool. Remember, don't get angry."
   • "Don't take what he says personally. Stick to the issues."
   • "If I fight, I will get into trouble. So keep calm."
   • "What is it I have to do to keep from getting mad?"
   • "He will try to get me mad, but I know how to deal with him."
   • "If I don't get mad, my parents will be proud of me."
   • "I'm cool, and he will not make me lose it."

2. *Impact and Confrontation* — "These are the messages that you say to yourself when you can recognize that you are in a situation that might make you mad."

   • "Don't get bent out of shape."
   • "I'm not going to let him get to me."
   • "He's pretty stupid-looking acting like that."
   • "Stay calm. Relax."
   • "What she says isn't going to get to me. Everything is under control."

3. *Coping with Arousal* — "As the situation gets worse, you may become more tense and upset. If you find yourself losing control, it is time to really try to keep cool. Sometimes it is very hard to stay calm, but keep trying."

- "Time to take a deep breath."
- "Take it easy. Don't get pushy."
- "Let him make a fool out of himself. I'm not."
- "I'm not going to get pushed around, but I'm not going bananas either."

4. *Reflecting on the Provocation* — "This is when you take time to think about what got you so upset in the first place. After the situation has passed, you can think of either how well you handled it or what went wrong."

Unresolved:
- "Quit thinking about what happened. I am only getting more upset."
- "With more practice, I'll get better."
- "Relax. Think about the good things that happened."

Resolved:
- "Fantastic. I kept my cool."
- "It worked."
- "That wasn't too hard."
- "I finally made it through that situation without getting angry."

At this point, relaxation procedures are introduced. The child is informed that it is impossible to be angry and relaxed at the same time and that being tense and upset may interfere with the ability to cope with provocation. The child is told that it is possible to manage anger more successfully by learning how to control breathing and how to relax muscles. The clinician can either use relaxation procedures mentioned previously or instruct the child in deep-breathing exercises. When the child is relaxed, the therapist introduces the first anger hierarchy scene by saying: "Just continue relaxing like that. Now, I want you to imagine the following scene. (*Present the scene.*) See it as clearly as you can. If you feel the least bit angry, signal me by raising the index finger of your right hand." If the child does not signal anger for 15 seconds, the clinician instructs the child to "think about something else and continue to relax. You are doing great." If anger is signalled, the clinician says: "You are getting angry. Imagine yourself handling the situation. You are composed, relaxed, settling down." The therapist continues with this scene for 30 seconds, and then instructs the child to think about something else for 30 seconds.

The therapist encourages the child to practice relaxing at home, to continue "listening" to the internal dialogue, and to tune in to the anger-eliciting private speech.

Session 3

A brief review of Sessions 1 and 2 precedes the beginning of the Skill Acquisition (rehearsal) phase of training. The therapist makes sure that the child understands the use of self-instructions and recognizes relaxation as a method of anger control. In reviewing earlier sessions and homework assignments, emphasis is placed on the maladaptive self-statements that lead to anger and on the adaptive self-statements and relaxation techniques that serve to counter the anger. At this point the child is given a written list of specific statements that can be used in the cognitive modeling procedures. In addition, the therapist helps the child determine the situations ("triggers") in which anger is justified, because it is important for the child to learn to recognize when it is appropriate and inappropriate to be angry and to learn to express anger in a more adaptive fashion.

The initial process in the skill-acquisition phase involves *cognitive modeling* by the therapist. In this session the therapist models the task while talking aloud. The therapist displays the types of skills (self-statements) relevant to successful completion of the task—preparation for provocation, impact and confrontation, coping with stress, self-reinforcement, or self-evaluative coping skills (reflecting on the provocation). The therapist selects one of the anger hierarchy scenes and role plays "coping" with the provocation. The following therapist script is an example of a cognitive modeling procedure.

"OK, now I'm going to show you how you can use what we learned about how to deal with your anger. I am going to pretend that I am on the playground at school, and I see John coming over to me. I know that John likes to call me names and that every time he calls me a certain name (trigger), I go nuts (maladaptive response), ending up in the office being yelled at (consequence). I want you to listen closely to me, and if you can tell me some of the things I said after I'm done, then you'll get a reward (token reinforcement)."

(*Preparing for the provocation*) "Oh, here comes John (trigger) . . . That turkey is going to give me a hard time. . . . I just know that he is going to call me "Chris . . . Piss" and laugh at me (anger-arousing private speech). All he wants to do is to get me in trouble. Well, I'm not going to get mad. . . . I know how to deal with him. . . . Time to relax . . . take some deep breaths . . . calm down . . . ignore him. . . . Remember . . . don't get mad" (anger-reducing self-statements).

(*Impact and confrontation*) "Stay calm . . . continue to relax . . . those are just words, and words can't hurt. . . . I know if I say anything to him, I'll end up fighting. . . . I'm not going to let him get to me. Look at him, he's funny looking . . . other people are laughing at him, not at me . . . there's nothing he can say to get me mad . . . it's not worth fighting . . ." (anger-reducing self-statements).

(*Coping with arousal*) "He's getting to me . . . I can feel myself getting tense . . . if he keeps this up I may hit him (anger-arousing self-statement). . . . OK, take another deep breath, try to relax. . . . Here comes the teacher—she will stop him. I do not have to do anything . . . keep calm. . . . Boy, he really wants me to fight, but I'm not going to. . . . My friends will not think that I'm a chicken. . . . If I fight, they will think that I am stupid" (self-reinforcement).

(*Reflecting on the provocation—conflict resolved, successful coping*) "Hot-damn, I did it! . . . I did not get mad. . . . I knew I could do it. . . . Look at John—the teacher is really mad at him. . . . Everybody is laughing. . . . I am glad that they are not laughing at me. . . . That wasn't as hard as I thought" (self-reinforcement).

(*Reflecting on the provocation—unresolved conflict, expression of anger*) "Well, I blew that one. . . . I must have been really stupid to let him get to me. . . . I almost made it without getting mad. . . . With some more practice, I will get better. . . . I need to relax more. . . . Next time I will try it. . . ."

The therapist reviews the coping sequence, provides a reward for each adaptive self-statement recalled by the child, and points out statements that were forgotten. Learning these anger-reducing self-statements occurs via shaping, and considerable modeling or coaching by the therapist is needed in the initial stages. At this point the child practices the relaxation techniques. When a state of relaxation is reached, the therapist introduces the next hierarchy scene and instructs the child to imagine coping with the anger experience on a cognitive level. Finally, the therapist reviews the day's session, asks the child what he or she specifically learned, and reminds the child to practice the new skills at home.

Session 4

The therapist and client review the previous sessions and homework assignments. Specific attention focuses on the child's progress in the situations that were practiced in Session 3. The therapist consults the child to determine whether the hierarchy needs to be altered.

This session is devoted to overt, external guidance. The child role plays one of the anger hierarchy scenes, talking aloud, while the therapist instructs and prompts. The child can role play the anger-provoking scene used in Session 3 or move to another scene. As the child attempts to cope with anger, the therapist encourages the child to remain relaxed and helps fill in the missing gaps in the self-statements. It may be helpful for the therapist to offer possible solutions (alternative ways of reacting) to the provocation, especially if the child is unable to think of adaptive behaviors. It is helpful to remind the child of the stages (preparation, impact, coping, and reflection/self-reinforcement) and to provide a "script" for the child to follow in case there are any difficulties in generating adaptive self-statements. At the end of the session, the therapist praises the child for doing a good job.

Session 5

In this session the child performs the task while talking aloud (overt, self-guidance). The therapist provides minimal prompting and guidance, because the goal of this session is for the child to begin assuming responsibility for generating the self-statements. The selection of the particular hierarchical scene depends on the child's current needs and progress. If the child experiences difficulty in imagining the scene, the therapist can play the role of the person who provokes the anger, taking care to guard against producing too much stress.

After the child has become proficient at generating self-statements, the therapist introduces a problem-solving or assertion-training approach for coping with the conflict. To ensure learning it is important to progress slowly. The child probably needs to learn adaptive ways to communicate feelings, assertive skills to facilitate explicit requests for change in another person's behavior, and task orientation to remain focused on the desired outcomes of a particular anger situation. Specifics of problem-solving procedures are discussed in the following section entitled "The Stress Inoculation Approach Within a Problem-Solving Framework."

Session 6

In this session the therapist models the self-statements by whispering them while performing the task (faded, overt modeling), and the child engages in the same faded, overt self-guidance. Continued modeling may not be necessary at this point; however, it should be used if the child experiences difficulties. The therapist follows the procedure used in Session 5 and continues discussion of alternative coping behaviors.

Session 7

This is the final rehearsal training session, and the procedure is identical to the previous two sessions, except that the child uses *covert self-instructions*. The child imagines one of the hierarchy scenes (by this time the scenes should be increasing in severity of anger arousal) and visualizes coping *cognitively* with anger and successfully dealing with the situation. Upon completion the therapist inquires about the self-statements that were used and asks about their effectiveness in dealing with anger. It is important to praise and reinforce a job well done. The therapist checks on the effectiveness of homework assignments and on how milder anger provocation situations were handled outside of treatment. Feedback is provided about adaptive and maladaptive strategies that were employed.

Session 8 and Beyond

This portion of training is the Application Phase of stress inoculation. To this point, therapy has focused on helping clients change their view of stress and develop coping skills. Now, to maximize generalization, clients are encouraged to practice their newly learned skills. Because the application sessions cannot be conducted in the child's environment, the therapist uses the remaining hierarchical scenes to further solidify coping skills. These sessions can involve either role playing the provocation scene with just the therapist and child or can include another person(s) in the scene (e.g., family, teachers).

The Application Phase is ideal for group involvement. In a group setting the therapist can use the circle game, in which one child is placed in the middle of a circle while group members try to provoke anger (with the ground rules of no physical hitting or spitting). In this procedure the therapist stands next to the child to prompt or to aid in maintaining control or one group member can be asked to help the child in the circle. By assisting others, children can strengthen their new cognitive coping skills. However, a note of caution is needed for any approach that "stresses/provokes" the child in a therapeutically controlled situation. The therapist must maintain control and must not allow the procedure to deteriorate into grossly inappropriate expressions of anger. A useful ground rule is that the child in the middle can stop the game by some specified signal, such as raising a hand or saying "Stop."

Whatever method is employed, the therapist moves in a paced mastery fashion, keeping the role playing short and gradually increasing intensity and stress as the scenes change. At the end of each role play, the child is asked to describe the effect of using self-statements, with particular emphasis on self-efficacy development. Generalization of coping skills seems to occur most readily when the child feels that the new self-statements and behaviors can be produced (efficacy expectations) and that these self-statements and behaviors lead to the desired outcome (outcome expectations—Bandura, 1986). Rewards are provided liberally for actual and attempted appropriate responses to anger provocation.

Case Presentation

Gary: The Angry Young Man

This case study involves a 15-year-old boy who was treated with stress inoculation while he was a psychiatric inpatient. Gary was involved in the total treatment program of the hospital—group therapy, music therapy, occupational therapy, art therapy, and recreational therapy. Therefore, although treatment outcome related to anger management is believed to be due to the stress inoculation therapy program, this cannot be established conclusively.

Gary was referred for inpatient treatment by a protective services worker from a rural county. At the time of the referral, Gary was in residence at a children's home. Referral was instigated because of poor peer relations, excessive aggression and hostility, and sexual abuse of younger children. Gary was large for his age, weighing approximately 180 pounds, and he was very strong. Because of his size, strength, and aggressiveness, the children's home did not think that he could continue to be managed in their setting. In addition, his recently manifested sexual acting out was very frightening for the group home staff, because they were legally responsible for the welfare of the younger children who were victimized by Gary.

When Gary was 7½ months of age, he was removed from his mother by protective services because of child abuse and neglect. Subsequently, he lived in numerous foster homes and had constant problems wherever he went. By the time he was referred for this inpatient hospitalization, Gary had already been hospitalized in two psychiatric facilities and had resided in three residential placements for children. He had been involved in individual and/or group therapy off and on from the age of 7.

A psychiatric evaluation indicated an alert, well-oriented, and cooperative adolescent who was physically well developed. No bizarre behaviors or verbalizations were noted. Gary's behavior seemed somewhat immature, and he seemed rather unsure of himself, but there were no indications of impairment of reality contact. Depression was noted to be at a rather marked level, and Gary was assessed to be of at least Low Average intellectual ability with limited insight. Furthermore, there were suggestions of sexual identity confusion and of failure to establish adequate object relations.

A psychological evaluation indicated a boy of Low Average intellectual functioning who exhibited perceptual-motor problems. Furthermore, psychological tests indicated marked depression and profound feelings of low self-esteem. In addition, the test data documented Gary's inordinate need for attention and affection from others. Fears of rejection were extensive, and major defenses at that time were denial, repression, and withdrawal from personal contacts.

The evaluation team felt that Gary was in need of residential treatment, and he was given a DSM-III-R diagnosis of Dysthymic Disorder. His problems were identified as poor peer relations (mainly fighting and aggression), immature behaviors, sexual confusion, and school difficulties.

Approximately 1 week before his admission to the hospital, Gary was assigned for individual therapy to one of the authors (Finch), who was responsible for designing and coordinating his overall treatment program. Gary was admitted to the adolescent unit without incident and seemed relatively pleased to be at the hospital. In fact, for the first week and a half, Gary was the "model" patient; he interacted appropriately with staff and peers and failed to exhibit any behavior that would warrant his hospital admission. Gradually, however, his aggressive behaviors appeared, and by the end of the first month, everyone was well aware of why Gary was in the hospital.

There seemed to be a rather consistent pattern to Gary's aggressive behavior. Someone would call him a name or say something that he disliked, and he would immediately "fly off the handle" and exhibit very aggressive behaviors such as striking out or throwing objects at the other individual. He became increasingly enraged and frequently had to be restrained by the staff. He began to spend an inordinately large portion of the day either being restrained or being placed in the "quiet room" (a seclusion room used to help control a patient during major outbursts).

For the first couple of weeks of therapy, the main emphasis was on establishing a therapeutic alliance with Gary, who interacted freely and was a very likable youngster in a one-to-one situation. He characteristically attributed his difficulties to others and frequently stated that if other people would leave him alone, he would not have any problems. Gary was extremely sensitive to rejection from others and tended to interpret everything in an overly personalized manner. He felt that the slightest affront was evidence of his worthlessness and that he needed to prove himself by striking back in an aggressive manner. By the end of 3 weeks, the therapist felt that he had a good relationship with Gary, whom he had seen on a twice-a-week basis. The major impression gained in the initial interactions with this boy was that of a youngster with marked feelings of depression that were just below the surface. It was decided that Gary could benefit from the clinical research program that the authors were developing for the management of anger in youngsters.

The remaining portion of this case study will focus on the stress inoculation training for anger management that was instituted approximately 6 weeks after Gary's hospitalization. The primary reason for the delay in the initiation of this program was twofold. First, because Gary seemed to experience a "honeymoon period" after he was first admitted to the hospital, the program was not warranted earlier. Second, after he began exhibiting the behaviors that had necessitated his hospitalization, and before beginning formal treatment, baseline data were collected on his aggressive acting-out behaviors. In order to obtain this information, certain assessments were done. First, an individually tailored behavior rating scale was developed along the lines outlined earlier (see Table 5-3 for a copy of this rating scale). Also, the Children's Inventory of Anger (Finch et al., 1987) was administered. On this scale most of Gary's responses were 3s and 4s, resulting in an overall anger inventory score of 249. This score is considerably above what would be expected based on normative data. Further assessment included extensive interview material obtained from Gary and from the staff. The following verbatim transcript was the part of the initial interview that focused on Gary's anger-management problems.

Dr. Finch: Do you know why you are here this morning?

Gary: Yeah, 'cause I get in a lot of fights in school, and I get in a lot of fights on the unit. Other kids call me names.

Dr. Finch: You just get in a lot of fights and have trouble getting along with some of the other kids?

Gary: Yeah.

Dr. Finch: . . . when some of the kids are calling you names, what kind of names do they call you?

Gary: Call me fat slob, pig . . .

Dr. Finch: They get on to you about your weight a little bit.

Gary: Unhuh.

Dr. Finch: Then what happens?

Gary: I get uptight. I get mad and want to fight.

Dr. Finch: Do you punch them out? Do you really fight with them?

Gary: I just feel like it, but I really don't do it.

Dr. Finch: What do you do?

Gary: I tell them if they don't stop calling me names, I will hit them and then I tell them that they know I'm pretty strong so stop testing me.

Dr. Finch: Does that work?

Gary: Yes—they stop.

Dr. Finch: Do you have to get pretty loud with them sometimes?

Gary: Yeah.

Dr. Finch: That's what I heard—that you scream a lot at them and that kind of stuff?

Gary: Yeah.

Dr. Finch: Is there anybody in particular who you have a really hard time with?

Gary: Yeah, Tommy. (*patient*)

Dr. Finch: Tommy—Does he call you names?

Gary: Yeah, he calls me a fat slob.

Dr. Finch: It gets you pretty angry. I was wondering, when he's calling you names, what kind of things you're thinking about? What do you say to yourself? Can you hear yourself talk sometimes?

Gary: Yeah. I say to myself, "How dare him to say something like that. He won't get away with it. I don't like it. I say if you don't stop, I will hit him."

Dr. Finch: Do you get concerned about what the other kids are thinking about?

Gary: Yeah. If I don't hit him, the guys on the unit will get me.

Dr. Finch: They'll think that you're chicken?

Gary: Unhuh.

Dr. Finch: And pick on you a little bit. It's kind of like if somebody starts picking on you, the other guys will pick on you if you don't stand up and defend yourself.

Gary: Yeah.

Dr. Finch: Any other kind of thing that gets you really upset and mad?

Gary: Nothing else really.

Dr. Finch: I heard something the other day about you and Jane (female patient).

Gary: Yeah.

Dr. Finch: What was that all about?

Gary: She was saying that she would rather go with somebody else besides me, and she likes somebody else better than me. I threatened to hit her.

Dr. Finch: Is that when you threw the water on her?

Gary: Unhuh.

Dr. Finch: What kind of things were you thinking to yourself then?

Gary: I didn't like the way she was talking to me.

Dr. Finch: You didn't like being told those kind of things?

Gary: Yeah.

Dr. Finch: So who ended up getting in trouble?

Gary: I did.

Dr. Finch: So you threw the water, and instead of it doing any good, *you* are the one who got in trouble.

Gary: Unhuh.

Dr. Finch: OK . . . I wonder if you were saying anything else to yourself other than, "I don't like her talking to me that way."

Gary: Nothing else really.

Dr. Finch: Sometimes guys get upset when girls like somebody else 'cause they kind of think they must not be any good or something like that 'cause the girls don't like them. Does anything like that go through your head?

Gary: Sometimes.

During this portion of the interview the therapist learned that Gary saw his anger problems as related to being called names and being teased about his weight. He reported that he attempted to cope with his anger by telling the other children to stop, and frequently he raised his voice. Fighting was denied, and even though the therapist knew that this report was basically a denial or avoidance of responsibility, Gary was not confronted about this. Rather, during this phase the therapist accepted what Gary was willing to give, with the expectation that he would become more open as the sessions progressed. It is easy to fall into the trap of confronting a child with inaccurate reports or statements when, in most cases, it is not necessary. Later Gary learned to freely admit and discuss his fighting.

During this first portion of the interview, the therapist learned that one individual (Tommy) gave Gary the most trouble and that Gary said various things to himself that tended to exacerbate his anger. Furthermore, Gary was afraid of being teased or picked on even more by the other children if he did not stand up for himself.

In the final portion of this interview, the therapist moved into another area that was exacerbating Gary's anger—the relationship with his girl-friend. This portion is included as an example of how a therapist can begin to point out that an individual's anger problems cause trouble. It was important for Gary to realize what his anger-management problems were actually costing him, because he was more likely to work toward change when this connection was appreciated.

Later in this session, Gary was asked to "run a movie" to learn more about his interactions with Tommy. Gary was able to do this after some initial hesitation, and additional information was gained that proved useful in the later portions of treatment.

Dr. Finch: I want us to think about the last time Tommy came running up to see you, and you saw Tommy coming and got mad at him. And sometimes it helps to kind of think about this if you close your eyes and pretend you are watching a movie and think about the . . . you think that is kind of funny?

Gary: (Nod, laugh)

Dr. Finch: (Laugh) OK, well it helps to think about these things sometimes. Pretend you are watching a movie, and just remember the last time he came up and tell me what is going on when he was walking down the hall and what happened and what kind of things happened to you. Just run the whole scene through your head. OK? Think you can do that?

Gary: Unhuh, I guess.

Dr. Finch: All right, you're still not real comfortable with that. I can tell. OK, well let's try it. Go ahead and close your eyes, and tell me what you are seeing.

Gary: Well, I see Tommy coming down the hall.

Dr. Finch: What does he look like?

Gary: He looks like he is in a bad mood. Looks like he needs somebody to pick on. I see that I'm the only one out in the hall. I figure I had better be ready to get picked on.

Dr. Finch: So you are trying to get yourself ready for this.

Gary: Yeah.

Dr. Finch: OK, what happens?

Gary: He starts coming down the hall, and he starts hollering at me and calling me names.

Dr. Finch: What's he saying?

Gary: He's saying, "You fat slob! You look ugly!" So I start calling him names back.

Dr. Finch: What are you feeling?

Gary: I'm feeling that he don't like me—that he hates me.

Dr. Finch: How about your body? How is it feeling?

Gary: My body is feeling tight.

Dr. Finch: Where can you feel it?

Gary: In my arms—I want to hit him.

Dr. Finch: Can you feel it anywhere else?

Gary: No, not really.

Dr. Finch: Mainly, in your arms you feel it.

Gary: Yeah. I'm starting to breathe fast.

Dr. Finch: Can you kind of feel your heart pounding away?

Gary: Unhuh.

Dr. Finch: OK, go ahead and run the movie. You are feeling your heart pounding and you're breathing fast, your arms are getting all tense. What else happens? Here he comes down the hall calling you names. "You fat pig!"

Gary: I told him that if he didn't shut up I was going to hit him. I told him that my body was getting tight. And if he didn't stay away from me I was going to hit him.

Dr. Finch: What did he do?

Gary: He stopped calling me names, and then we sat down and talked about what went wrong.

Dr. Finch: Let's try to think about one when something happened in which you really got in trouble—when you didn't handle it quite that good. OK?

Gary: Like what?

Dr. Finch: All right, let's just set another scene, one where something went wrong, where you weren't able to handle it. Either that or you tried to handle it, and he just continued to call you names, and you got upset and got in a fight and that kind of stuff.

Gary: OK, I hit him.

Dr. Finch: So you hit him . . .

Gary: . . . While he was talking.

Dr. Finch: What happened?

Gary: He went and told the staff, and the staff told me to sit in the hall, and I refused to, and he came out in the hall and started laughing at me. So I went charging at him. The staff grabbed me and took me to the quiet room. I stayed in there for a while until I cooled off.

Dr. Finch: OK, so he came at you, was calling you some names, and you hit him, and he went and told the staff. You were still feeling all tense and upset. He came out, and the staff wanted you to sit down. In the hall?

Gary: Unhuh. I refused to.

Dr. Finch: I guess you were mad, huh? And weren't ready to cool down then, huh?

Gary: Right.

Dr. Finch: What kind of things were you saying to yourself?

Gary: I was saying that I wasn't going to sit in the hall, 'cause I wanted to get a chance to fight with him. I wanted to show him *how much* of a fat slob that I was.

Dr. Finch: Unhuh, that you just weren't ready to cool down, that he had gotten you stirred up, and you were going to teach him a lesson.

Gary: Yeah.

Dr. Finch: All right, so you ended up getting put in the quiet room, huh?

Gary: Yeah.

Dr. Finch: What happened to Tommy?

Gary: I guess he had to sit out in the hall until he cooled off. When I came out of the quiet room, he was already back on the unit.

Dr. Finch: So you got in more trouble than he did.

Gary: Unhuh.

Dr. Finch: OK, how did that make you feel when you're the one who gets in more trouble . . . it doesn't seem like it works out real good for you to get all upset and angry. You can open your eyes. You got all upset and angry, and you're the one that got all in trouble. Although he started it, you got in the most trouble, didn't you?

Gary: Unhuh. Staff didn't give me a chance to say my side. They just listened to what he had to say.

Dr. Finch: You think that might have something to do with the fact that you lost your cool and he kept his a little bit better?

Gary: Unhuh.

Dr. Finch: I think sometimes Tommy sets you up in those positions, doesn't he? Because he can pull your trigger pretty quick.

Gary: Unhuh.

Dr. Finch: And *you* end up getting in trouble because of it. Let's see. So we have talked about a couple of things—that you were saying things to yourself that made you more and more angry. "Here comes Tommy; looks like he's in a bad mood." You were getting ready for trouble then, weren't you? When you saw him coming.

Gary: Unhuh.

Dr. Finch: Then you started getting tight and tense and getting upset, and the more you got yourself upset, the more he called you names, and the madder you got, it seems like.

Gary: Unhuh.

Dr. Finch: Then you just got really tense and hit at him. You just lost your cool. That happens sometimes with this anger and it gets you into trouble.

During the beginning of Session 2, the therapist discussed the forthcoming anger-control program with Gary. In addition, the anger model was explained and discussed (Education Phase), and the therapist made a specific effort to ensure that Gary's own language was used in the treatment explanation. The therapist introduced the importance of self-statements and spent considerable time discussing the things that Gary said to himself in provoking situations. Gary was told that his self-statements were crucial in learning to handle his anger more effectively. Other material was discussed in terms of its particular relevance to Gary in a situation × person × mode of expression analysis of his anger-management problems.

The later portion of Session 2 and most of sessions 3, 4, and 5 were spent teaching Gary relaxation techniques. During Session 6 the material originally discussed in Session 1 was reviewed. Gary and the therapist worked together to establish a hierarchy of anger-evoking stimuli and to develop a number of anger-reducing self-statements. By agreement it was decided to focus most of the scenes on Gary's interactions with Tommy, because Gary felt that this was the most important problem area for him at this time. During the later portion of this session, the therapist instructed Gary to use the relaxation technique he had learned, while the therapist introduced a provoking scene. Also, the therapist told Gary that he would model some of the coping self-statements while Gary visualized himself coping with the situation. The following dialogue took place.

Dr. Finch: You feeling all relaxed now, Gary?

Gary: Yeah.

Dr. Finch: Got things pretty good?

Gary: Yeah.

Dr. Finch: Your arms feeling relaxed?

Gary: Unhuh.

Dr. Finch: Not tense, now you're relaxed all over. All your muscles are relaxed?

Gary: Unhuh.

Dr. Finch: OK. Now, I'm going to introduce the scene again. One of the scenes will have Tommy coming in, and I'm going to ask you if you start feeling anxious. I want you to raise your index finger when you feel anxious or angry, OK?

Gary: (Nod)

Dr. Finch: All right. You are standing out in the hall. It's the break between school periods, and you see Tommy walking down the hall. He's coming down, and he's looking like he is in a bad mood, and he's walking toward you, and he starts calling you names. "Hey, you big fat pig. You fat pig, what are you doing out here?" Does that make you feel kind of anxious there? If it does, I want you to raise your finger.

Gary: (Raises arm)

Dr. Finch: OK, you can just raise your finger on this. So that makes you feel a little bit anxious, and you start feeling angry. Now, what I want to do is run through and provide you with some statements, and I want you to keep a movie running through, and I'm going to run the scene back through for you, and I'm going to have you coping with the scene . . . some of the things you can do. You know this stuff we've talked about. All right, you see Tommy coming down the hall, and so you are going to start to prepare. You know there is going to be trouble. You can tell by the look on his face that he's looking for trouble. So you can tell there is going to be trouble so . . . here is the type thing you can say. "I'm not going to let him get at me. If I blow it *I'll* get into trouble. *I'm* going to keep my cool." All right, here he comes. "I can handle this. I'm going to keep my cool." All right, here he comes, getting close. He comes on down. All right, here come the names. "I can tell he is going to call me a name." Tommy says, "You fat pig." "Why can't he keep his fucking mouth closed. I don't want to hear this! I don't have to listen to this! Whoops . . . stay cool, stay relaxed. I got to keep relaxed. Keep cool. All right, don't get mad. *I'm* in control. *I* can handle this. He is not going to make me lose my cool. I don't want to end up in that quiet room. Just keep relaxed. Just keep cool. All right. I feel myself getting a little bit tense. I need to cope with this. All right, what can I do? All right, let's relax. Ah, he is calling me a fat pig, but you know he is kind of skinny . . . a little skinny scarecrow-looking character. I'm not going to get pushed around, but I'm not going to get into trouble either. I'm not going to lose my cool. I'm not going to go bananas about this whole situation. He's not going to get me mad. I'm not going to let it work this time. *I'm* going to be in control. Take another deep breath and relax. Keep coping with this. I can handle it. All, all right, he's gone. I've handled this really good. I did a good job. That wasn't so bad. I was able to do this OK. That worked out pretty good. I kept my cool, and now I'm not in trouble. I'll get to go back out and play on the courtyard now and won't have to stay in that quiet room. I can bear it. It only lasts a few minutes, the trouble."

Now, I want you to imagine the same scene that I just went through. I'm going to present it, but this time you are going to have a little bit of trouble handling it. You are going to get mad and blow it. He comes down and you get mad, get in a fight, and end up getting put in the quiet room having to settle down. "Well, I really blew it that time. Oh, my god! Well, that's all right. It's over. Done with. I'll put it behind me. Take a deep breath to help me relax. I messed up this time, but I can do it next time. I'll be able to handle it. I'll just have to practice a little more. I'll have to practice my relaxation. I'll have to keep my cool. I let him get me that time but he won't do it again. I can handle it. I'll just shake it off and forget about it. It's over with. It's done with now." You can open your eyes now. Could you keep all that pretty well visualized — what I was talking about?

Gary: Yeah.

Dr. Finch: OK, that's the type of thing I want you to do. When you see him coming, start preparing. Get yourself all prepared for what's going to happen like we've talked about. When you see there is going to be a trouble situation, you can anticipate it. What you are doing is kind of like solving a problem or a puzzle or something. You have to kind of set up the steps, and if you see there is going to be a problem, you get ready for it. Then when the problem comes, you are ready. You start dealing with it. You start coping with it as soon as you see it. You can get yourself relaxed so you won't get upset, 'cause you can't be relaxed and mad at the same time very well. Then you can handle it. You talk to yourself. You say the good things to yourself so that you are not going to end up getting in trouble. And then when you've done a good job, you deserve to praise yourself, don't you?

Gary: Yeah.

Dr. Finch: "I did a good job, I handled that all right" — and if you don't do a good job it's not the end of the world, huh? You will get another chance. There are plenty of chances with Tommy, right?

Gary: Yeah.

Dr. Finch: Lot of practice, huh?

Session 7 began with a discussion of what had been done up to this point. Considerable time was spent reviewing a copy of the self-statements and the importance of keeping things in perspective. The remaining portion of the session was spent with Gary's being relaxed while the therapist again modeled the self-statements. Finally, the session ended with Gary's attempting to employ some of the self-statements with the assistance of the therapist's prompting (overt, external guidance in the Skills Acquisition Phase). This interaction follows.

Dr. Finch: You all relaxed now?

Gary: Yeah.

Dr. Finch: All right. This time I'm going to run the scene through, and I want you to make the statements to yourself. The things we've been talking about. I'll help you as we go through. All right, you're standing out in the hall. It's break between school, and you're standing out there minding your own business, and here comes Tommy walking down the hall. Can you see that?

Gary: Yeah.

Dr. Finch: What do you say?

Gary: I better get ready for it. I'm not going to let him get to me.

Dr. Finch: Here comes Tommy. Not going to let him get to you this time. Looks like he is in a bad mood. What do you say?

Gary: I say he's getting ready to call me names.

Dr. Finch: OK, here come the names. "You fat pig." What are you going to say?

Gary: He's calling me a fat pig, but he looks like a little skinny scarecrow himself.

Dr. Finch: What are you going to do?

Gary: I'm just going to keep my cool.

Dr. Finch: Stay calm. Stay relaxed. Keep your cool, right?

Gary: Let him call me names if he wants to.

Dr. Finch: They are just words, aren't they?

Gary: Yeah.

Dr. Finch: What do you know about words?

Gary: That they can't hurt you.

Dr. Finch: Just words. "I'm not going to get put in the quiet room." All right, he is calling you names! Uh oh, you feel yourself starting to get tense. What do you say?

Gary: Tommy, stay back from me, or I'm going to hit you.

Dr. Finch: Now, take a deep breath. "I'm getting angry. I need to relax. I don't want to blow my cool. Just keep cool. Relax." Can you handle it?

Gary: Yeah.

Dr. Finch: All right. "I'm not going to be pushed around, but I can handle it. I'll stay cool." Can you say some of those statements — coping statements?

Gary: I don't know what they are. I've forgotten them all.

Dr. Finch: OK. "I'm not going to get pushed around, but I'm not going to go bananas" — are you?

Gary: Nope.

Dr. Finch: What happens when you go bananas? This is when you get put in the quiet room.

Gary: I'm just going to keep my cool and walk away from him.

Dr. Finch: "Handle it as best I can."

Gary: Unhuh.

Dr. Finch: Now, you've done it. He went on when he saw he wasn't getting you angry. What do you say to yourself?

Gary: I handled that very well.

Dr. Finch: (Laugh) . . . you did a good job, did you?

Gary: Right.

Dr. Finch: All right, fantastic! What if you really blow it and get put in the quiet room? What then, is that the end of the world?

Gary: No, there is always another chance.

Dr. Finch: What's going to happen the next time?

Gary: I'm going to learn not to take it so seriously.

Dr. Finch: Just keep it cool. Not take it seriously. That's good. Handle it good.

Session 8 consisted primarily of practice (Application Training Phase) and having Gary engage in self-reinforcing statements without the therapist's assistance (overt, self-guidance in the Skills Acquisition Phase). Again, maintaining a task-oriented approach to provocation was emphasized. Session 9 reviewed much of the previously covered material and continued the practice of this material. In addition, the self-statements were moved from an overt level to a whispering phase, and the session ended with practice of covert self-statements (faded overt, self-guidance and covert, self-guidance).

During the first portion of Session 10, previously covered material was reviewed. During the second portion of Session 10, Gary did a great deal of role playing, which allowed him to practice using the skills which he was developing. During Session 11 a co-therapist was introduced into the therapy situation to aid in role playing. The co-therapist pretended to be a child on the unit who exhibited a number of provoking behaviors. Thus, Gary practiced his newly acquired skills in a more lifelike situation (Application Training Phase).

Session 12 reviewed all of the previous material and provided an opportunity to practice in areas that seemed to need particular attention. These 12 sessions were spread over approximately 3 weeks, and each lasted approximately 1 hour and 15 minutes.

Results of Intervention

As previously mentioned, it is almost impossible to obtain behavior counts and time sampling in a hospital setting. Consequently, an individually tailored behavior rating scale was employed to ascertain the effectiveness of the intervention procedures (see Table 5-3). As the rated information came directly from the unit chart, it was a nonobtrusive measure. During the 2-week baseline period before treatment began, Gary received ratings of 4s and 5s for aggressive behavior. During the 3 weeks of treatment, the ratings declined gradually, and this decline continued after treatment. Finally, Gary's aggressive behavior was rated at the level of 1s and 2s, ratings that were considered to be well within the normal limits of behaviors on the units.

Gary's time in the quiet room was used as an additional measure of treatment effectiveness. Because quiet room time was charted for each child on the unit, this information was naturally available and useful. At the beginning of treatment, Gary was spending approximately 45 minutes a day in the quiet room — usually for fighting and aggressive behavior. This time declined gradually, and toward the end of his stay in the hospital, Gary was only occasionally in the quiet room. Actually, by the end of treatment, Gary's time in the quiet room was usually at his own request when he was feeling somewhat overwhelmed; this was interpreted as an increased capacity for self-control. In addition, Gary was readministered the Children's Inventory of Anger and obtained a score of 152 — considerably lower than his pretreatment score of 249.

Discussion

The results of this case study support the use of stress inoculation for anger management. However, as previously noted, this youngster participated in the total hospital treatment program, and the effects of other treatment modalities cannot be separated out. Gary was discharged to the care of a new set of foster parents. The therapist met with Gary once after his discharge and maintained telephone contact with the foster family. Because of the distance between the foster home and the hospital (90 miles), there was no plan for continued contact. After approximately 2 years, Gary continued to do well with no major problems of anger management.

The Stress Inoculation Approach Within a Problem-Solving Framework

Problem-Solving Techniques

The preceding section outlined the cognitive-behavioral approach of stress inoculation in the treatment of anger disorders in children. Problem solving is another treatment modality that has been utilized in the Skills Acquisition phase of stress inoculation (Goldfried & D'Zurilla, 1969; Heppner, Neal, & Larsen, 1984; Spivack et al., 1976).

In examining the skills that must be learned in order to cope with an increasingly complex world, it is clear that a child is continually confronted with situations that demand more and more sophisticated emotional, cognitive, and behavioral capabilities. From the point of view of the child's own adaptation and the effect on society, anger and aggressive acting out have crucial implications. Although it is beyond the scope of this chapter to discuss the ever-changing physical and cognitive capabilities that are characteristic of child development, it is important to keep in mind the fact that children's expression of anger changes with age. For example, 2- or 3-year-old children have temper tantrums and are more likely to use purely physical means of aggression (e.g., push, hit, kick) than older children. Nursery children are more physically and verbally aggressive towards others and are more likely to seize objects from other children (Feshbach, 1970). Elementary school children insult, tease, and call each other names more than younger children do. In response to an insult, preschoolers are more likely to respond by hitting, while school-age children respond with another insult (Hartup, 1974). All of these behaviors can be viewed as developmentally influenced attempts to deal with frustration.

Anger arousal and aggressive behavior are viewed as adaptive or maladaptive responses to problem situations encountered by the child, and angry and/or aggressive responses are viewed as attempts to solve the distressing problem. The therapeutic strategies that are designed to address the maladaptive expression of anger are based on the supposition that anger is an emotional response to a problem and a signal that problem-solving strategies need to be cognitively processed and behaviorally implemented. The "problem" can involve a variety of factors such as difficulties of an interpersonal nature (e.g., wanting something someone else has, being verbally or physically assaulted, feeling unjustly treated) or frustrations with environmental obstacles (e.g., having difficulty with school work, being unable to fix a bicycle).

From a cognitive-behavioral point of view, it is not the stimulus itself that provokes a child's response but rather the child's cognitive processing of the event. Thus, when a child is called a "fat slob" or "pig," this stimulus can be perceived in a number of ways. For example, it might be perceived as a friendly joke or as a threat to self-esteem. Certainly, aggressive children seem to have significantly lower self-esteem (e.g., Deluty, 1981) and to believe that interpersonal threats and provocations exist even when they do not (Lochman, 1984). The child who perceives the stimulus as a threat that must be dealt with may respond by becoming physiologically more aroused and may begin to cognitively process a response to the perceived threat. Angry children often report that their heart and respiration rates increase, their muscles tighten up (especially stomach, hands, and arms), and their faces flush. As they cognitively process responses to the external stimulus, children often report that their attention becomes more narrowly focused on the threatening problem, and they disregard other cues and thoughts. Aggressive children seem to have ineffective linguistic control skills, especially at the level of covert mediation (Camp, 1977). As a child becomes older, competence in verbal communication is essential to the control of anger during provocative interchanges. Developmental studies of aggression demonstrate that verbal aggressiveness increases as children grow older, emphasizing the need for competence in verbal communication skills and anger-management strategies.

As a function of deficits in private speech, aggressive children may react to perceived threat in problem situations in an impulsive, reflexive fashion (White, 1965). These children spend little, if any, time cognitively processing behavioral alternatives, and in terms of their consequential thinking (Spivack & Shure, 1974), they rarely anticipate any but the most immediate consequences. Behaviorally these cognitive deficits can be seen when a child is asked to think of alternatives to an aggressive interchange. Usually the response is either a self-esteem–saving remark (e.g., "it wasn't my fault" or "I didn't do anything") or a "blank stare" as if an aggressive reaction was the only possible course of action in the situation.

Behavioral reactions to the problem situation follow physiological and cognitive reactions. Thus, in response to an anger-arousing situation, the child can *choose* (based on a cognitive mediation strategy) to react directly (e.g., to retaliate verbally or physically) or indirectly (e.g., to exclude another from a group, club, or team), to withdraw passively, to accept the threat and try to ignore it (e.g., to become immobile), or to assertively attempt to cope with the threat (e.g., to use humor or other effective communication skills). A child is seen as having a problem if he or she relies exclusively on behaviors other than assertive responses. Aggressive behavior in any situation is determined not only by the current environmental situation but also by the child's past learning history, by the present physiological state (e.g., increased heart rate, tightening of muscles), and by ongoing cognitive events (e.g., appraisal, expectations, private speech). Thus, the child's experience of anger is determined by an intricate interaction among external events, internal processes, and behavioral reactions.

The problem-solving treatment strategies for anger control focus on altering the child's cognitive processing capabilities. More specifically, the focus of this treatment approach is based on a series of interpersonal cognitive problem-solving skills that have been identified as being relevant for successful coping in various social situations (Spivack et al., 1976; Spivack & Shure, 1974). These skills include sensitivity to identifying problems, ability to spontaneously link cause and effect (causal thinking), capacity to think through possible consequences of actions (consequential thinking), ability to generate solutions (alternative thinking), ability to conceptualize step-by-step means for attaining specific goals (means–ends thinking), and ability to view situations from the standpoint of other involved children (perspective taking). In dealing with children it is important to recognize that these skills develop at different ages. A child's capacity to problem solve adaptively in anger-arousing situations seems to depend on whether the child has actually learned the cognitive skills or whether the situation itself arouses emotions that preclude using previously learned skills.

Although specific problem-solving approaches to anger control have not been evaluated extensively, existing strategies rely heavily on general psychological literature describing the angry/aggressive child, on the work that has been done in the cognitive regulation of anger in adults by Novaco (1975, 1979), and on the problem-solving techniques developed by Spivack, Shure, and their associates at the Hahnemann Medical College and Hospital in Philadelphia (Spivack et al., 1976; Spivack & Shure, 1974). The Hahnemann group developed two manuals that outline their problem-solving program—*Interpersonal Problem-Solving Group Therapy Manual* (Platt, Spivack, & Swift, 1975) and *Workbook for Training in Interpersonal Problem Solving Thinking* (Platt & Spivack, 1976). Feindler and Ecton (1986) also developed a treatment manual entitled *The Art of Self-Control: A Group Anger Control Program.* Although there are many overlapping components between the problem-solving approach of Spivack and Shure and the approach outlined in stress inoculation strategies, the latter emphasize deep-muscle relaxation and specific anger-reducing self-statements to teach children to control their anger reactions. In problem solving the focus is on the specific cognitive problem-solving skills that seem to be deficient in angry/aggressive children.

The following discussion summarizes session-by-session problem-solving procedures that can be incorporated into a stress inoculation framework and can be used with groups. This section builds upon the material and procedures outlined in the first part of this chapter. The basic phases that were described in the stress inoculation section (Cognitive Preparation, Skill Acquisition, and Application Training) are employed, but the specific therapeutic activities differ.

Pregroup Assessment

Referral for treatment of anger-control problems necessitates the assessment process described earlier. Following an individual assessment the recommendation of group therapy depends on the availability and/or feasibility of group treatment. It is necessary to consider a variety of factors such as whether or not to create a homogenous or heterogenous group—a group composed of children who present an array of problem behaviors or a group composed of children whose problems are clearly defined as difficulties with anger control. We have found a homogenous group composition to be more effective in treating children for anger-management problems. Distractibility and immaturity are also important variables that should be carefully assessed before recommending group treatment. Although these behaviors are often related to aggressive acting out, they contraindicate group treatment when they are excessive (Lochman, Nelson, & Sims, 1981). Techniques for anger-control groups presented in this chapter are more effective for acting-out children than for children who are referred because of high rates of distractibility or immaturity. Thus, stress inoculation and problem-solving therapeutic techniques focus specifically on the control of anger arousal and aggressive behavior. In addition, because many of the stress inoculation strategies involve some form of modeling, they are not effective for the highly distractible child who has an exceptionally difficult time focusing on salient behaviors that are being modeled by the therapist or other group participants.

Group size is another factor that needs to be carefully considered in forming treatment groups for aggressive children. In our work with emotionally disturbed adolescents (where one therapist per group is typically utilized), anger-control groups were increasingly difficult to manage if more than four clients were included. With less severely disturbed adolescents, it is likely that larger groups could be managed by a single therapist. The age of the child is also relevant to group size. In our work with elementary school children who were referred for aggressive behavior, no more than five children could be adequately managed with one therapist. We also found that including a "better adjusted" peer was extremely facilitative in the amount of progress made by the group. Such a group member often contributed to the group process by exhibiting more "appropriate" self-controlled behavior and serving as a positive model in the various exercises and role-playing situations.

Cognitive Preparation Phase

Session 1

The goals of this session are both administrative (i.e., to introduce group members to each other, to set up regularly scheduled meeting times, to establish group rules, etc.) and educational in nature (to introduce members to the cognitive-behavior scheme for understanding their angry feelings and aggressive behavior). The data previously gathered in the individual assessments are discussed within the group, emphasizing that one's aggressive *behavior* is a choice that is made in various situations and that it can be adaptive or maladaptive. Emphasis is also placed on the fact that the assessment data reveal that group members respond differently to various "problem" situations. Some become angry and act aggressively in certain situations while others respond to the same problem situation in a nonaggressive manner. This discussion is designed not only to promote self-awareness but also to stimulate interest and curiosity about why and how others react differently in the same situation. (The answer to be forthcoming in later sessions is that many of these "differences" depend upon cognitive factors and problem-solving capabilities.) For younger children (elementary school age) who are more concrete in their reasoning, various activities are arranged to promote self-awareness by noting physical, behavioral, emotional, and attitudinal differences and similarities between group members. It is useful to include activities such as taking pictures of each group member with an instant camera or doing body tracings on large pieces of paper and to follow these activities with group discussions.

Session 2

The goal of this session is to continue to explore the physiological, cognitive, and behavioral components of the child's reaction to various situations such as cooperating with, being controlled by, and being distracted by peers. Activities can include acting as pairs of robots or building domino towers while being verbally distracted by peers. A 10-minute modeling videotape developed by Nelson, Lochman, and Sims (1978) is also shown to the group members. This tape depicts a young boy being reprimanded by his mother for not doing his homework and then telling an off-screen narrator how he feels physically (e.g., tight muscles, clenched teeth). He then describes his negative self-statements (e.g., "I want to get back at my mother and teacher for making me miss a television show") and the positive self-statements that he could use to decrease his anger arousal (e.g., "If I stick to the homework rules, I can watch T.V. sooner."). This "awareness training" tape was designed to educate and structure the child's conceptualization of "anger problems"; the implicit message is that the experience of anger is a summation of a physiological state of arousal and the cognitive labeling of this state.

Session 3

Group members are asked to recall the tape viewed in the previous session, and the content of the tape is discussed in detail. If necessary, the tape is presented again. Group members are encouraged to actively display and exaggerate their physiological reactions to various problem situations that were identified in the pregroup assessment period. They are also instructed to "think out loud" as they encounter a problem situation, and the therapist highlights the adaptive and nonadaptive cognitions that are generated. Finally, there is a discussion of the behavioral responses that proceed from the physiological and cognitive experience of anger.

In these three sessions the child is "educated" or prepared for the introduction of the specific anger-control skills that are to be presented in the Skill Acquisition Phase. By becoming increasingly aware of the components of anger and his or her idiosyncratic cognitive-behavioral responses in various problem situations, the child's anger takes on a different meaning. Anger is now redefined so that the child can experience a sense of control and can develop the ability to master his or her emotional state, cognitions, and behavior.

Skill Acquisition Phase

Session 4

The goal of this session is to introduce the specific problem-solving/anger-control strategies that the child will actually use to deal with problem situations. The following problem-solving outline is taught.

Steps	*Self-Statements*
1. Problem Identification	What's the problem?
2. Goal Selection	What is it I want to do?
3. Generation of Statements	What can I do?
4. Consideration of Consequences	What might happen?
5. Decision Making	What's my decision?
6. Implementation	Let's try it!
7. Evaluation	Did it work?

The first step in the problem-solving process is to identify problem situations as they arise and to determine which aspects of the situation create a problem and lead to anger arousal ("What's the problem?"). Activities include identifying problems in brief stories and in role-played situations. Exercises entitled "Learning the Facts" presented in Platt and Spivack's workbook (1976) are particularly useful in this regard.

Sessions 5 and 6

The goal of these sessions is to teach effective strategies to inhibit the impulsive aggressive reaction that characterizes the behavior of most children who have been identified as having anger problems. Major strategies are the cognitive anger-reducing self-statements and appraisals that have been more thoroughly discussed in the previous section on stress inoculation techniques of verbal self-instruction and relaxation. Problem situations are carefully selected from the individual assessment data (goal selection). As these situations are listed on a blackboard, the group members are asked "What goes through your mind?" Role playing these scenes is a natural way to learn to "talk out loud," and it is important for the therapist to provide prompting and assistance at "critical points." The idea is to demonstrate to group members that their thoughts and images have a direct influence not only on how they feel (increasing anger or not) but also on how they behave (aggressively or not). The therapist should highlight the naturally occurring coping self-statements that might be employed to increase the child's sense of control and ability to cope with the situation.

Sessions 7 and 8

Once a problem situation can be readily identified and after the initial impulse to strike out aggressively has been inhibited, the problem-solving regimen points to the need for generating various possible alternative solutions (generation of alternatives). The goal of this session is based on "brainstorming" techniques (Osborne, 1963), which emphasize the process of temporarily withholding judgments about the quality of possible solutions in order to produce good solutions. Group members are asked to generate as many solutions as possible to problem situations in which they characteristically react in an aggressive fashion; these solutions are listed on a blackboard. For younger children, activities include presenting various cartoon sequences of interpersonal problems (e.g., one child has a bicycle that another wants to ride) and asking group members to come up with various solutions (e.g., wait until he's done riding it, ask him to take turns, fight him). Coupled with generating alternatives is the ability to effectively evaluate these alternatives to find the best solution (consideration of consequences). The focus is on developing "consequential thinking" by "thinking through" or role playing the proposed solutions in order to identify both positive and negative consequences before making a decision about the relative value of the alternatives. Group participants can view a series of videotapes (Lefton, 1979; Hart, 1981) depicting a child or adolescent in various anger-provoking situations. At the end of each scene, group members are prompted to generate alternative solutions to the problem posed within the scene. For younger children who require a more concrete presentation, several alternative solutions can be presented with pictures prefaced by covert inhibiting speech illustrated in cartoon form. The solutions are role played, and group members vote for the most appropriate solutions (consideration of consequences and decision making). Positive participation in these exercises is often rewarded with token chips that can be exchanged for a variety of reinforcers at the end of the session. This strategy reinforces the child for engaging in the behaviors that cognitive researchers and theorists believe are likely to produce cognitive and behavioral change.

Another treatment technique that appears to hold therapeutic promise is that of goal setting (e.g., Lochman et al., 1984). It is also important for children to establish weekly goals for controlling their aggressive behavior/ outbursts. Goal setting can be done individually or in group sessions. It is suggested, however, that the more "public" the goal, the greater the social pressure to achieve that goal. Thus, by publically stating and making a goal and then reporting back to the group, the child is more likely to succeed.

Effective adjunct treatment components also include external monitoring of goals (i.e., by a classroom teacher) and the reinforcement of appropriate behavior and inhibition of anger responses in applied classroom settings (Forman, 1980). Thus, it is necessary to involve significant others (e.g., parents and teachers) in treatment planning to ensure that the newly learned cognitive-behavioral strategies are actually applied by the child in day-to-day functioning. This addresses the issue of the distinction between the acquisition of and the actual performance of learned behaviors (Bandura, 1986).

Sessions 9, 10, 11, and Beyond

The goal of these sessions is to integrate coping and problem-solving skills into a more solid cognitive-behavioral response to problem situations. Group members are encouraged to "test out" and to practice their newly learned skills in a hierarchical fashion (implementation). While such "dry run" practice can take many forms, the most useful approach involves role playing recent problems that the child has encountered. To allow the therapist to highlight this process and to emphasize the most potent coping techniques, a videotape of these "dry run" situations is recommended. The therapist can then review the tape and point out the various steps taught in the Skill Acquisition Phase—problem identification, goal selection, self-statements, generation of alternative solutions to the problem, consideration of consequences, decision making, implementation of the "best alternative," and evaluation. Such review and coaching permits the therapist to highlight the important components in real-life situations that group members present. Also useful at this stage of training is the "Circles Game" (Goodwin & Mahoney, 1975), which emphasizes the benefit of ignoring the verbal provocation of others and maintaining your "cool" by engaging in anger-reducing self-statements. In this game, masking tape is placed on the floor to form a circle approximately 6 feet in diameter. Within this larger circle a 3-foot circle is made. Each child takes a turn in the middle, and the group members attempt to make the target child angry using any means other than physical touch or spitting. This verbal taunting game enables the child to try out newly learned skills when confronted with a variety of verbal threats. Upon successful completion of "being in the middle" of the Circles Game, a great deal of praise and reinforcement is given to the child for having "stayed cool" in such a stressful situation. It is important to discuss and explore the implications of how this kind of self-control can be utilized in real-life situations.

We have been very encouraged by our results in dealing with highly aggressive children and adolescents both in individual and group contexts. We encourage other clinical researchers to join us in the process of systemically evaluating anger-control programs. The resulting modifications and further refinements can optimize the therapeutic benefits of helping children learn effective skills for the control of maladaptive angry reactions and aggressive behavior.

References

Achenbach, T., & Edelbrock, C. (1983). *Manual for the Child Behavior Checklist and Revised Behavior Profile.* Burlington: University of Vermont, Department of Psychiatry.

American Psychiatric Association. (1987). *Diagnostic and statistical manual* (3rd ed. rev.). Washington, DC: APA.

Bandura, A. (1973). *Aggression: A social learning analysis.* Englewood Cliffs, NJ: Prentice-Hall.

Bandura, A. (1986). *Social foundations of thought and action: A social cognitive theory.* Englewood Cliffs, NJ: Prentice-Hall.

Beck, A. (1976). *Cognitive therapy and the emotional disorders.* Madison, CT: International Universities Press.

Berkowitz, L. (1974). Some determinants of impulsive aggression: Role of mediated associations with reinforcements for aggression. *Psychological Review, 81,* 165-176.

Camp, B. (1977). Verbal mediation in young aggressive boys. *Journal of Abnormal Psychology, 86,* 145-153.

Cromwell, D. H., Evans, I. M., & O'Donnell, C. R. (1987). *Childhood aggression and violence: Source of influence, prevention and control.* New York: Plenum Press.

Deluty, R. H. (1981). Adaptiveness of aggressive, assertive, and submissive behavior for children. *Journal of Clinical Child Psychology, 10,* 155-158.

Dodge, K. A. (1985). Attributional bias in aggressive children. In P. C. Kendall (Ed.), *Advances in cognitive-behavioral research and therapy* (pp. 73-110). New York: Academic Press.

D'Zurilla, T. J., & Goldfried, M. R. (1971). Problem-solving and behavior modification. *Journal of Abnormal Psychology, 78,* 107-126.

Ellis, A. (1973). *Humanistic psychology: The rational-emotive approach.* New York: Julian Press.

Ellis, A. (1977). *How to live with and without anger.* New York: Reader's Digest Press.

Emysey, L. T. (1982). Behavior approaches to juvenile delinquency: Future perspectives. *American delinquency: Its meaning and construction.* Homewood, IL: Dorsey Press.

Feindler, E. L., & Ecton, R. B. (1986). *Adolescent anger control: Cognitive-behavioral techniques.* New York: Pergamon Press.

Feshbach, S. (1970). Aggression. In P. H. Mussen (Ed.), *Carmichael's manual of child psychology* (Vol. 2, 3rd ed.) (pp. 159-259). New York: Wiley.

Finch, A. J, Jr., Deardorff, P. A., & Montgomery, L. E. (1974). Individually tailored behavioral rating scales: A possible alternative. *Journal of Abnormal Child Psychology, 2,* 209-216.

Finch, A. J, Jr., Saylor, C., & Nelson, W. M., III (1983). *The Children's Inventory of Anger: A self-report measure.* Paper presented at the annual meeting of the American Psychological Association, Anaheim, California.

Finch, A. J, Jr., Saylor, C., & Nelson, W. M., III (1987). Assessment of anger in children. In R. J. Prinz (Ed.), *Advances in behavioral assessment of children and families,* (Vol. 3) (pp. 235–265). Greenwich, CT: JAI Press.

Forman, S. G. (1980). A comparison of cognitive training and response cost procedures in modifying aggressive behavior of elementary school children. *Behavior Therapy, 11,* 594–600.

Gilbert, G. M. (1957). A survey of "referral problems" in metropolitan child guidance centers. *Journal of Clinical Psychology, 13,* 37–42.

Goldfried, M., & D'Zurilla, T. (1969). A behavior-analytic model for assessment of competence. In C. Spielberger (Ed.), *Current topics in clinical and community psychology.* New York: Academic Press.

Goldstein, A. P., & Glick, B. (1987). *Aggression replacement training.* Champaign, IL: Research Press.

Goodwin, S. E., & Mahoney, M. J. (1975). Modification of aggression through modeling: An experimental probe. *Journal of Behavior Therapy and Experimental Psychiatry, 6,* 200–202.

Hart, K. (1981). *A cognitive/problem-solving treatment of anger.* Unpublished master's thesis, Xavier University, Cincinnati, OH.

Hartrup, W. (1974). Aggression in childhood: Developmental perspectives. *American Psychologist, 29,* 336–341.

Heppner, P., Neal, G., & Larsen, L. (1984). Problem-solving training as prevention with college students. *Personnel and Guidance Journal, 62,* 514–519.

Herbert, M. (1978). Conduct disorders of childhood and adolescence: A behavioral approach to assessment and treatment. Chichester, England: Wiley.

Jacobsen, E. (1938). *Progressive relaxation.* Chicago: University of Chicago Press.

Kaufmann, L., & Wagner, B. (1972). Barb: A systematic treatment technology for temper control disorders. *Behavior Therapy, 3,* 84–90.

Kazdin, A., Rodgers, A., Colbus, D., & Siegel, T. (1987). Children's Hostility Inventory: Measurement of aggression and hostility in psychiatric inpatient children. *Journal of Clinical Child Psychology, 16,* 320–328.

Keith, C. R. (1984). *The aggressive adolescent: Clinical perspectives.* New York: Free Press.

Kendall, P. C., & Williams, C. L. (1982). Assessing the cognitive and behavioral components of children's self-management. In P. Karoly & F. Kanfer (Eds.), *Self management and behavior change; From theory to practice.* New York: Pergamon Press.

Koeppen, A. S. (1974). Relaxation training for children. *Elementary School Guidance and Counseling,* October, 14–21.

Kolko, D. J., Dorsett, P. G., & Milan, M. A. (1981). A total assessment approach to the evaluation of social skills training: The effectiveness of an anger control program for adolescent psychiatric patients. *Behavioral Assessment, 3,* 383–402.

Lefton, W. (1979). *The effects of modeling and the coaching and rehearsal of modeled coping statements on aggression.* Unpublished master's thesis, Xavier University, Cincinnati, OH.

Lochman, J. E. (1984). Psychological characteristics and assessment of aggressive adolescents. In C. R. Keith (Ed.), *The aggressive adolescent: Clinical perspectives.* New York: Academic Press.

Lochman, J. E., Burch, P. R., Curry, J. F., & Lampron, L. B. (1984). Treatment and generalization effects of cognitive-behavioral and goal setting interventions with aggressive boys. *Journal of Consulting and Clinical Psychology, 52*, 915–916.

Lochman, J. E., Nelson, W. M., III, & Sims, J. P. (1981). A cognitive-behavioral program for use with aggressive children. *Journal of Clinical Child Psychology, 10*, 146–148.

Mahoney, M., & Arnkoff, D. (1977). Cognitive and self-control therapies. In S. L. Garfield & A. E. Bergin (Eds.), *Handbook of psychotherapy and behavior change* (2nd ed.). New York: Wiley.

Meichenbaum, D. (1973). *Therapist manual for cognitive behavior modification.* Unpublished manuscript, University of Waterloo, Ontario, Canada.

Meichenbaum, D. (1975). A self-instructional approach to stress management: A proposal for stress inoculation training. In C. Spielberger & I. Sarasen (Eds.), *Stress and anxiety* (Vol. 1). New York: Wiley.

Meichenbaum, D. (1977). *Cognitive behavior modification: An integrative approach.* New York: Plenum Press.

Meichenbaum, D. (1985). *Stress inoculation training.* New York: Pergamon Press.

Meichenbaum, D., & Cameron, R. (1972). *Stress inoculation: A skills training approach to anxiety management.* Unpublished manuscript, University of Waterloo, Ontario, Canada.

Meichenbaum D., & Goodman, J. (1971). Training impulsive children to talk to themselves: A means of developing self-control. *Journal of Abnormal Psychology, 77*, 115–126.

Meichenbaum, D., & Jaremko, M. (1983). *Stress reduction and prevention.* New York: Plenum Press.

Nelson, W. M., III. (1981). A cognitive-behavioral treatment for disproportionate dental anxiety and pain: A case study. *Journal of Clinical Child Psychology, 10*, 79–82.

Nelson, W. M., III, Fleming, C., & Hart, K. (1982). *Cognitive behavioral treatment studies in the applied setting: Can they be done?* Paper presented at the annual meeting of the Southeastern Psychological Association, New Orleans, LA.

Nelson, W. M., III, Lochman, J. E., & Sims, J. P. (1978). *Components of anger: Awareness training for children and adolescents* [Videotape]. University of Texas Health Science Center, Dallas.

Neubauer, D. (1987). Childhood aggression and violence. In D. H. Cromwell, I. M. Evans, & C. R. O'Donnell (Eds.), *Childhood aggression and violence: Source of influence, prevention and control.* New York: Plenum Press.

Novaco, R. W. (1975). *Anger control: The development and evaluation of an experimental treatment.* Lexington, MA: Heath, Lexington Books.

Novaco, R. W. (1976a). *Anger and coping with provocation: An instructional manual.* University of California, Irvine.

Novaco, R. W. (1976b). The functions and regulations of the arousal of anger. *American Journal of Psychiatry, 133*, 1124–1128.

Novaco, R. W. (1976c). *Therapist manual for stress inoculation training: Clinical intervention for anger problems.* University of California, Irvine.

Novaco, R. W. (1976d). Treatment of chronic anger through cognitive and relaxation control. *Journal of Consulting and Clinical Psychology, 44*, 681.

Novaco, R. W. (1977a). Stress inoculation: A cognitive therapy for anger and its application to a case of depression. *Journal of Consulting and Clinical Psychology, 45*, 600–608.

Novaco, R. W. (1977b). A stress inoculation approach to anger management in the training of law enforcement officers. *American Journal of Community Psychology, 5,* 327–346.

Novaco, R. W. (1978). Anger and coping with stress. In J. P. Foreyt & D. P. Rathjen (Eds.), *Cognitive behavior therapy: Research and application.* New York: Plenum Press.

Novaco, R. (1979). The cognitive regulation of anger and stress. In P. C. Kendall & S. D. Hollon (Eds.), *Cognitive-behavioral interventions: Theory, research, and procedures* (pp. 241–285). New York: Academic Press.

Osborne, A. F. (1963). *Applied imagination: Principles and procedures of creative problem-solving* (3rd ed.). New York: Scribner's.

Platt, J. J., & Spivack, G. (1976). *Workbook for training in interpersonal problem-solving thinking.* Philadelphia: Hahnemann Medical College and Hospital, Department of Mental Health Sciences.

Platt, J. J., Spivack, G., & Swift, M. S. (1975). *Interpersonal problem-solving group therapy.* Philadelphia: Hahnemann Medical College and Hospital, Department of Mental Health Sciences.

Quay, H. C. (1986). Classification. In H. C. Quay & J. S. Werry (Eds.), *Psychopathological disorders of childhood.* New York: Wiley.

Quay, H. C., & Peterson, D. (1983). *Interim manual of the Revised Behavior Problem Checklist.* Coral Gables, FL: University of Miami Press.

Reid, W. H. (1978). *The psychopath: A comprehensive study of antisocial disorders and behaviors.* New York: Brunner/Mazel.

Robins, L. N. (1981). Epidemiological approaches to natural history research: Antisocial disorders in children. *Journal of the American Academy of Child and Psychiatry, 20,* 566–580.

Schrader, C., Long, J., Panzer, C., Gillet, D., & Kornblath, R. (1977, December). *An anger control package for adolescent drug abusers.* Paper presented at the annual meeting of the Association for Advancement of Behavior Therapy, Atlanta, GA.

Spirito, A., Finch, A. J., Smith, T., & Cooley, W. (1981). Stress inoculation for anger and anxiety control: A case study with an emotionally disturbed boy. *Journal of Clinical Child Psychology, 10,* 67–70.

Spivack, G., Platt, J. J., & Shure, M. B. (1976). *The problem-solving approach to adjustment.* San Francisco: Jossey-Bass.

Spivack, G., & Shure, M. B. (1974). *Social adjustment of young children: A cognitive approach to solving real-life problems.* San Francisco: Jossey-Bass.

Stumphauzer, J. (1981). Behavioral approaches to juvenile delinquency: Future perspectives. In L. Mechelson, M. Hersen, & S. Turner (Eds.), *Future perspectives in behavior therapy.* New York: Plenum Press.

Turk, D. (1975). *Cognitive control of pain: A skills training approach for the treatment of pain.* Unpublished manuscript, University of Waterloo, Ontario, Canada.

Turk, D., Meichenbaum, D., & Genest, M. (1983). *Pain and behavioral medicine: A cognitive-behavioral perspective.* New York: Guilford Press.

Varley, W. H. (1984). Behavior modification approaches to the aggressive adolescent. In C. Keith (Ed.), *The aggressive adolescent: Clinical perspectives.* New York: Free Press.

Wasik, B. (1984). *Teaching parents effective problem-solving: A handbook for professionals.* Unpublished manuscript. University of North Carolina, Chapel Hill.

White, S. H. (1965). Evidence for a hierarchical arrangement of learning processes. In L. P. Lyssett & C. C. Spiker (Eds.), *Advances in child development and behavior* (Vol. 2). New York: Academic Press.

Wilson, R. (1984). A review of self-control treatment for aggressive behavior. *Behavioral Disorders, 9,* 131–140.

CHAPTER SIX

Social Skills Training with Physically Aggressive Children

JAMES POLYSON   WILLIAM KIMBALL

Helping children learn more effective and socially appropriate ways of interacting with others has become an important research topic in clinical psychology and related fields. From its initial focus on socially withdrawn children in school settings (see Conger & Keane, 1981), social skills training has been used more recently with various clinical populations. In fact, there has been an explosion of enhanced awareness and research in this area. The rapid developments in social skills training are evident in the fact that entire issues of journals have been devoted to this topic, and there have been numerous presentations discussing the effectiveness of social skills training for a variety of subpopulations (e.g., aggressive children, clinically hospitalized youth, depressed youngsters, children with mental retardation or learning disabilities). Included in the social skills training literature are a number of outcome studies with physically aggressive children and adolescents in psychiatric and correctional facilities (Amish, Gesten, Smith, & Clark, 1988; Baum, Clark, McCarthy, & Sandler, 1986; Bornstein, Bellack, & Hersen, 1980; Elder, Edelstein, & Narick, 1979; Ollendick & Hersen, 1979; Olson & Roberts, 1987; Schneider & Byrne, 1987). These studies show that social skills training can be effective in reducing delinquent or aggressive behaviors while increasing socially effective behaviors. The interest in social skills training has cut across disciplines and has attracted many professionals who work with children.

This chapter presents an overview of the literature on social skills training along with a sample social skills training program for use with physically aggressive children and adolescents. Although a wide variety of problematic behaviors has been addressed using social skills training as the primary intervention technique, this chapter will present such a program for "acting-out" youngsters. This approach was selected primarily because of the high rate of referrals for "externalization of conflict" problems (e.g., aggression and conduct difficulties) (Gardner & Cole, 1987). The first section of this chapter will highlight some key issues in the definition and assessment of social skills and in the implementation of social skills training. The training program in the second section of the chapter provides general guidelines and suggestions derived, in part, from work with child clients at Children's Neurological Services, Richmond, Virginia, and at the Community Mental Health Center of Mercy Hospital, Watertown, New York.

Literature Review and Key Issues

Definition

As used originally by Combs and Slaby (1977) and Rinn and Markle (1979), social skills are broadly defined to include a wide variety of situation-specific skills—both verbal and nonverbal. In general, social skills help the individual maximize desirable outcomes and avoid undesirable outcomes in interpersonal relations without infringing on the rights of others. Published reports of social skills training have addressed such basic skills as conversing, maintaining eye contact, greeting, smiling, grooming, complimenting, and maintaining proper voice tone and volume. In the past few years the focus has shifted somewhat to include social problem solving in a more general sense and to emphasize the role of cognition in the problem-solving process.

The basic goal of social skills training is to help the child avoid interpersonal rejection and to gain acceptance by significant adults and peers. Inadequate social skills are a major cause of unpopularity and rejection among children in nonclinical populations (e.g., Gottman, Gonso, & Rasmussen, 1975) and are strongly implicated in the etiology of emotional disturbance (for a review, see Hartup, 1989).

Social skills deficits are also exhibited by children whose primary presenting problems involve physical aggressiveness (Camp, Zimet, van Doornick, & Dahlem, 1977; Freedman, Rosenthal, Donahoe, Schlundt, & McFall, 1978; Krehbiel & Milich, 1986; Ollendick & Cerny, 1981; Wool & Clements, 1975). According to a study by LaGreca (1981), it appears that these children (primarily boys) are rejected by peers and adults on the basis of their aggressive behavior, which may be highly noxious and potentially dangerous. In therapy, if the aggressive behavior involves impulsivity or rage reactions to stressful situations, cognitive behavioral interventions, such as those presented in chapters 5 and 7 of this book, may be indicated. Many of these children will also need to learn a broader repertoire of positive interaction skills. Social skills training can be used in conjunction with other cognitive-behavioral interventions to help the physically aggressive child replace the "tough guy" role with a more effective interpersonal style. Research indicates that aggressive or delinquent boys often show deficits in overt social behaviors such as basic conversational skills (e.g., Wool & Clements, 1975) as well as deficits in covert mediational problem solving (e.g., Camp et al., 1977). A cognitive-behavioral model of social skills training may be indicated if both types of problems need to be addressed in therapy.

In social skills training with aggressive children, the definition of therapy goals and target skills is not an easy task. Peer popularity is a relevant but insufficient criterion (see Foster, Bell-Dolan, & Berger, 1986). The clinician must take into consideration the points of view of the child, the peer group, the teachers, the parents, and the society at large. The client needs to be an active participant in the ongoing process of defining therapy goals and target skills. Difficult decisions may be required. For example, reference groups such as parents and peers may apply unfair, even contradictory, role expectations. Healthy differences in viewpoint may arise, and the therapist may need to take a directive stance in the selection of some target skills. Some children, for example, may be reluctant to alter the aggressive behaviors that led to their referral or incarceration because these behaviors have been reinforced (even admired) by certain peers. It is the task of the therapist to help the child look beyond immediate peer approval in order to prepare for the more adaptive and prevalent social environment.

Etiology of Social Skills Deficits

According to the cognitive-behavioral model, social skills deficits are due to a combination of environmental and cognitive factors. Environmental variables include the reinforcement history, the current sources of reinforcement, the models present in the environment, and the current environmental stimuli or situational variables. Cognitive variables include the child's attention to particular environmental stimuli, the child's belief system, the child's problem-solving style, and the child's developmental competencies. A basic understanding of these factors is necessary in order to plan strategies that will increase generalization (i.e., reinforcement of newly acquired social skills by the natural environment). Certain emotional factors that can influence social skills will also be discussed briefly.

Reinforcement Variables

The child's reinforcement history and current sources of reinforcement may hinder the acquisition and performance of social skills. If social skills are inadequate, adults may have failed to reinforce (or to reinforce as strongly and consistently as required) the performance of appropriate social behaviors (Kazdin, Matson, & Esveldt-Dawson, 1980). Also, in many instances, inappropriate behavior such as whining or screaming may receive negative attention. The reinforcement of aggressive behavior may occur in a coercive family network (Dodge, 1983; Patterson, 1976), or peers may reward socially unacceptable behaviors that imply that the child is "tough" (Cairns, Cairns, Neckerman, Gest, & Gariepy, 1988). It is helpful to determine which roles and behaviors have been reinforced by the peer group. In addition, peers may have reinforced aggressive behavior by acquiescing or by submitting to the aggressive acts, either because of fear of ensuing aggression or because of a desire for negative attention from the aggressor. In summary, it is important to determine which behaviors are being reinforced in the child's environment and by whom. If being tough is the child's only "claim to fame," the clinician may have to convince the child that more satisfying reinforcers are available for performance of more adaptive social skills.

Stimulus Variables

The child may have learned that reinforcement for certain social behaviors is available in particular situations or with certain individuals. It is likely that aggression is partly a function of the stimulus variables present in a given situation. In other words, the therapist must determine the social cues that elicit effective social skills (Morrison & Bellack, 1981).

Modeling and Rehearsal

Lack of appropriate models and/or the presence of inappropriate models may also contribute to the development of poor social skills. Peers, adults, and famous personalities frequently provide models for the child, and it is important to determine which models the child has selected to imitate. Also, the child may have observed appropriate skills but may still have difficulties if he or she has been deprived of opportunities to practice those skills in relevant situations.

Cognitive Variables

Research with both children and adults suggests that cognitive and social perception factors play a crucial role in the development of relationship skills (Hartup, 1989; Rathjen, Rathjen, & Hinker, 1978). Cognitive variables, such as the child's beliefs and interpretations of situations, may be at least as important as environmental contingencies (Dubow, Huesmann, & Eron, 1987). Much of the clinical research in social skills training has included a cognitive-behavioral component. Relevant factors include the child's selective attention and retention, the child's belief system and self-statements, and the child's developmental competencies.

Selective Attention and Retention Particularly with impulsive children who have limited attention spans or with withdrawn children who display limited interests, attention to appropriate models may be very poor.

The child's choice of models is a crucial determinant of social skills. Some children may have selectively attended to and retained the lessons presented by aggressive models including those in the media (for a more comprehensive review of the effects of television on children, see Liebert & Sprafkin, 1988). In social skills training a major role of the therapist is that of an adaptive model. Also, video resources can be used to increase a child's attention to models who respond effectively to social conflict (Harwood & Weissberg, 1987).

An important study by Dodge and Newman (1981) found that selective attention is a key factor in the inadequate decision-making process used by aggressive boys who paid less attention to important social cues than did nonaggressive boys. They also selectively recalled negative information about others, which contributed to their aggressive reactions in interpersonal situations. In social skills training it may be essential that the child learn to attend to relevant cues and to recall nonselectively.

Belief Systems/Self-Statements   Research with physically aggressive children demonstrates that their belief systems and the ways in which they interpret events play a major role in their aggressive acting out (DiGiuseppe, 1983; Dodge, 1981; Forman, 1980; Lochman & Curry, 1986). Forman (1980) found that aggressive children respond with significantly more irrational thoughts and more critical evaluations of others than do nonaggressive children. Physically aggressive boys also exhibit a greater tendency to attribute hostile intentions to others in unwarranted circumstances (Dodge & Newman, 1981; Nasby, Hayden, & DePaulo, 1980).

The physically aggressive child's rigid and egocentric, dysfunctional belief system may center on the notion that the only way to win respect is to be the "boss" or the tough guy. Threatening others may be viewed as the only way to achieve interpersonal goals. In addition, a common irrational belief is that it is intolerable to be criticized or told what to do. Other maladaptive self-statements may include cognitions such as "Nobody can call me names!", "If things don't go right (my way), I'll fix them!", or "No one is tougher than me!" Various ideas reflecting a "dog-eat-dog" world view or schema may also be present.

Another type of belief system relates to the values that children place on peer relationships (Evers-Pasquale & Sherman, 1975). These investigators found that children who placed a high value on peer relationships profited more from social skills training. This finding supports the importance of cognitive factors related to the stimulus value of the child's peer group. Also, it suggests the importance of peer involvement as an important element of social skills training—to promote generalization.

Developmental Competencies   According to Shantz (1975), role-taking ability, moral reasoning, and interpersonal problem-solving skills are determinants of a child's success in dealing with interpersonal conflict. Reviews by Michelson, Foster, and Ritchey (1981) and Hops (1983) discuss the relationship between these variables and social skills deficits. Unfortunately, as noted by Conger and Keane (1981), developmental issues that pertain to social skills training have not been adequately researched. Nevertheless, it is important for the therapist to consider the child's developmental level in assessing social skills and in planning treatment.

Emotional Variables

Emotional states seem to have at least an indirect impact on social skills problems. Experimental research (e.g., Cialdini, Kenrick, & Baumann, 1981) found that negative mood states such as anxiety and depression can impair children's performance of prosocial behavior (i.e., sharing). These authors suggest that under conditions of negative affect, a child is less able to enjoy the cognitive self-reinforcement that is necessary for long-term maintenance of prosocial skills. For some children, emotional factors seem to have a substantial impact on the possibility of aggressive peer relations; for example, children of divorce show increased rates of aggressive acting out (Hetherington & Martin, 1986). In other cases the causal link between emotional problems and social skills deficits is not so clear.

The findings of Spence and Spence (1981) suggest that social skills training does not produce a lasting amelioration of a child's emotional problems, although improvements in self-esteem have been noted (e.g., Lochman & Curry, 1986). In social skills training with physically aggressive children, the therapist should evaluate the client's emotional needs as well as the maladaptive social skills. It is important to remember that many aggressive children have themselves been the victims of violence (e.g., Combs & Slaby, 1977). Also, many of these children have suffered repeated peer rejections and prolonged social isolation (Krehbiel & Milich, 1986; Polyson, 1981; Shaver & Rubenstein, 1980).

Assessment and Identification of Socially Unskilled Behavior

Assessing a child's need for social skills training is not an easy task. In the research literature the most frequent approaches have been sociometric measures and their behavioral correlates. Additional approaches include analogue and naturalistic observations, cognitive-behavioral measures, rating scales, and the child's self-report/ratings.

Sociometric Measures

The most frequently used method for identifying socially unskilled children has been the sociometric or peer nomination rating, in which children are asked to name the peers they would or would not like to play with or the peers who are their best friends. The child's score is then computed according to the number of nominations received. The ratings have typically employed positive nominations, although negative nomination ratings have also been used (Dunnington, 1957; Moore & Updegraff, 1964). One disadvantage of sociometric measures is that it is impractical to administer them on a frequent basis, and there is often a lack of stability in the norm group (e.g., patient "turnover"). More importantly, recent data have cast doubts on the validity of sociometry as a way of measuring the need for social skills training (Foster et al., 1986). Sociometric ratings are not direct measures of interpersonal competence, nor do they indicate which behaviors the child is performing to lose or gain social acceptance. In some situations, children may gain popularity through antisocial behaviors. Another important consideration for the practicing clinician is the ethical/legal issue, which has become a prominent concern to many school personnel, particularly since comments are being made by children rather than by professionals. In summary, sociometric ratings may provide important information, but other measures are needed in planning effective social skills training, especially in the clinical setting.

Naturalistic Observations

Observational measures take a variety of forms. For example, O'Conner (1972) observed the frequency of peer interactions in a group of nursery school children and defined as socially withdrawn those children who interacted in less than 15% of the observations. However, research by Gottman (1977) demonstrated that it is important to assess qualitative aspects of peer interactions as well as frequency of interactions. With aggressive children it is extremely useful to observe peer and family interactions that might reward unskilled behaviors or punish attempts at more appropriate behaviors. These observations can be integrated with treatment on an ongoing basis if family members or peers are invited into the training sessions or if a group treatment approach is employed (Anderson, Rush, Ayllon, & Kandel, 1987; Duncan, Beck, & Granum, 1988). The problem with naturalistic direct observations — and the reason for the infrequency of their use — is the need for experienced observers (e.g., trained staff may be required several hours a day). Also, rater reactivity can be problematic in that the presence of a rater can markedly affect the behavior being observed and result in information that is not representative of the child's typical performance.

Analogue Measures

In addition to or instead of naturalistic observations, the therapist may use analogue measures in the form of role playing. The therapist and the client can role play standard or predetermined scenes, or they can enact scenes that relate to real situations or issues that have been problematic for the child. The Behavioral Assertiveness Test for Children (BAT-C) was an initial standardized role-play instrument (Bornstein, Bellack, & Hersen, 1977). This battery consists of nine interpersonal situations in which children are likely to have social skill problems. Ollendick and Hersen (1984) developed a 12-item version of the BAT-C. For example:

Narrator: You're part of a small group in science class. Your group is trying to come up with an idea for a project to present to the class. You start to give your idea when Amy begins to tell hers also.

Prompt: Hey, listen to my idea.

The most extensively researched standardized analogue measure is the Social Skills Test for Children (SST-C) developed by Williamson, Moody, Granberry, Letherms, and Biougin (1983). This instrument yields 30 social skills scores and covers a variety of interpersonal scenes including giving and accepting both help and praise as well as assertiveness. While role playing provides valuable information concerning the child's strengths and weaknesses, several research articles have reported a low correlation between analogue and naturalistic measures (Beck, Forehand, Neeper, & Baskin, 1982; Kazdin et al., 1980; Rinn & Markle, 1979). It appears that in comparison with naturalistic observations, role-play assessment may yield a somewhat more favorable estimate of the child's social skills in a given situation (e.g., Beck et al., 1982) and may have limited generalizability to the natural environment. Therefore, analogue measures should be used in conjunction with other assessment procedures. In spite of their limitations, role plays are informative, they are fun, and, as a treatment technique, they provide an integrative, ongoing method of social skills assessment.

Rating Scales

The Matson Evaluation of Social Skills with Youngsters (MESSY; Matson, Heinze, Halsel, Kapperman, & Rotatori, 1986) is a widely researched self-rating and teacher/parent-rating instrument. The MESSY includes 62 items for the self-report version and 64 items for the teacher/parent report. In addition to instruments specifically designed to assess social skills, a variety of standardized rating scales have been used as corollary measures in social skills training. These include the Revised Problem Behavior Checklist (Quay & Peterson, 1983), the Child Behavior Checklist (Achenbach & Edelbrock, 1983), and the Walker Problem Behavior Identification Checklist (Walker, 1970). Completed by teachers or parents, these instruments may provide qualitative indications of the child's interpersonal strengths and weaknesses. However, these scales are useful primarily for determining a child's social skills level on global dimensions such as "acting out" or "withdrawal." To determine a child's specific social skills deficits and to assess progress in treatment, a brief, individually tailored rating scale may be more useful. The need for individualized assessment is further indicated by the fact that treatment is more effective when it is individualized (Schneider & Byrne, 1987) and by the fact that a relatively small number of discrete social skills have been the focus of empirical research (MacDonald & Cohen, 1981).

Cognitive Measures

Recent literature strongly suggests that in addition to overt interpersonal skills training, social skills training should include a cognitive emphasis (e.g., Harwood & Weissberg, 1987; Gresham, 1986; LeCroy, 1987). Methods and issues regarding cognitive assessment are addressed in Chapter 4 of the present book.

Conclusion

There are a number of assessment procedures available for use in social skills training, and each has certain limitations with respect to reliability, social validity, and clinical utility. At present the best approach is probably a combination of the various methods (Kolko, Dorsett, & Milan, 1981). One very important factor in social skills assessment is a sound therapy relationship in which the child can openly relate thoughts, feelings, and interpersonal experiences either in discussions or role plays.

In defining the target behaviors for social skills training, it is important to evaluate the absence of socially effective behavior, as well as the presence of inappropriate or noxious behavior (see Dubow et al., 1987; Krehbiel & Milich, 1986; Olson & Roberts, 1987; Bierman, Miller, & Stabb, 1987). Ultimately, as Gresham (1986) has argued, the basic criterion for selecting target skills is social significance or social validity—that is, the extent to which a given behavior will be acknowledged and reinforced by the child's social environment. Therefore, generalization is a primary concern during assessment, as well as during treatment.

Treatment Approaches

In their review of the social skills training literature, Beck and Forehand (1979) outlined four basic treatment approaches: contingent reinforcement; peer mediation; modeling; and treatment packages. The training format outlined in this chapter incorporates each of these approaches in order to give the reader an overview of possible options in utilizing social skills training as an intervention procedure. Although the training format addresses specific issues of importance in working with aggressive, acting-out youngsters, similar procedures have been employed with other problem behaviors.

Contingent Reinforcement

A number of studies have used contingent praise and other reinforcers to increase appropriate peer interactions and/or to reduce aggressive behaviors (Anderson et al., 1987; Dubow et al., 1987; Pinkston, Reese, LeBlanc, & Baer, 1973). In social skills training with physically aggressive children, an important issue is whether to focus on the reduction of inappropriate aggressive behavior through time-out procedures, coaching, and so forth or on the training and contingent reinforcement of incompatible prosocial behavior. Studies that have shown a decrease in aggression by focusing solely on incompatible prosocial behaviors have generally used classroom rather than clinical populations (e.g., Ladd, 1981). More recent research has demonstrated greater effectiveness when both therapeutic objectives are pursued (e.g., Bierman et al., 1987; Dubow et al., 1987; Olson & Roberts, 1987), and the need for a bilateral approach is indicated by the threat posed by a child's physical aggression along with the social skills deficits exhibited by many of these children.

Reinforcement by the therapist will facilitate skills acquisition; however, treatment efficacy will depend, ultimately, on the reinforcement of behavioral changes by peers, teachers, family, and others. The therapist must address the question of how to encourage more favorable responses to these children who often must overcome a "bad reputation." This can be facilitated by individualized treatment planning (Schneider & Byrne, 1987) and through the use of peer-mediated approaches or activity groups (e.g., Duncan et al., 1988).

Peer-Mediated Approaches

Several studies have explored the use of socially competent peers as change agents for socially unskilled children. One approach consists of enlisting socially competent peers or adults to collaborate in role plays with the less competent child. In two studies (Strain, Shores, & Timm, 1977; Weinrott, Corson, & Wilchesky, 1979), this peer-mediated approach was judged to be effective. The use of peer mediation within a therapy group has also been used successfully (e.g., Duncan et al., 1988; LaGreca & Santogrossi, 1980). Activity groups may be particularly useful for enhancing generalization if the social skills training is integrated into naturalistic, enjoyable activities such as basketball (Anderson et al., 1987) or board games (LeCroy, 1987).

Modeling

O'Connor (1972) developed a narrative film depicting young children as they gradually entered into positive social interaction with other children. Socially isolated children who viewed the film increased their social interaction levels, and similar results have been obtained by other researchers (Gottman, 1977; Harwood & Weissberg, 1987; Keller & Carlson, 1974). It is clear that symbolic modeling can be a valuable technique for improving children's social skills. The use of live modeling can also be effective with physically aggressive adolescents (Goldstein, Sherman, Gershaw, Sprafkin, & Glick, 1978).

Treatment Packages

A treatment package is any combination of approaches such as coaching, modeling, role playing, rehearsal, feedback, guided practice, and reinforcement. For example, Bornstein et al. (1977) employed coaching, rehearsal, modeling, and feedback to increase children's assertive behaviors. In another study (Ollendick & Hersen, 1979), a social skills treatment package helped incarcerated juvenile delinquents adjust to the programs offered in the institution. Treatment packages show great promise; however, the therapist should not assume that the use of a treatment package will automatically ensure generalization (Baum et al., 1986).

Summary

Social skills training can help a child acquire a more adaptive behavioral repertoire for use in interpersonal relations. Additional research is needed to determine which approach or combination of approaches is most effective and which variables promote generalization of treatment. The reader will find elements of each approach in the manual that follows.

The Training Manual

Outline of Training

The following outline of social skills training offers general guidelines that can be altered according to the child's individual needs. The manual is designed for children and adolescents approximately 8–15 years old. For younger children, gamelike techniques such as puppets or story telling may be more effective (Combs & Slaby, 1977; Kelly, 1981). The techniques in this manual can be used with an individual child or can be adapted for small groups.

The length of the training sessions should not exceed the attention span and stamina of the child. Sessions of excessive length will likely become boring or tedious and thus lose impact. For example, in a 50-minute therapy session, 20 minutes might be spent on social skills training. Videotape feedback makes the sessions more exciting, for many children enjoy "hamming it up" in front of a camera. The videotapes can also provide valuable feedback as the therapist and client review the session.

The *assessment phase* begins the social skills training program, and during this phase the various deficits and excesses in the child's behavior are ascertained. In the second phase of the program, the *initial treatment phase,* modeling and role playing are emphasized in analogue situations. During the third phase of the program, the *initial generalization phase,* significant peers, parents, teachers, or other therapists are introduced into the sessions as generalization agents. It is desirable for children to practice with as many models as possible from their natural environment. During the final phase of the program, the *second generalization phase,* efforts are made to reinforce appropriate social skills in the child's natural environment. This may involve consultations with parents, teachers, siblings, mental health paraprofessionals, and others.

With some children, reinforcement or response-cost procedures will stimulate motivation to participate in the social skills training program. In a response-cost system the child is given a set number of tokens as each session begins, and chips are lost for behaviors such as leaving a session early or refusing to comply with instructions. At the end of each session, the remaining chips can be exchanged for small tangible rewards. We always provide a minimum number of tokens for "showing up." (For the resistant child, attendance is a successive approximation toward participation, and should be rewarded.)

An alternative approach is to provide rewards for cooperative behavior during specific time intervals or to reward the child with a game period following the skills training. Actually, with many children, tangible rewards will not be necessary. Also, as the therapist becomes more skilled and more creative, the training procedures themselves will become more enjoyable.

The following is a session-by-session outline of the basic training procedures. The order in which the skills are taught is flexible. In this example we start with a fundamental interpersonal skill — voice tone — and then move to cognitive factors related to the child's aggressive outbursts. The final sessions involve the training of adaptive prosocial behaviors such as complimenting others and expressing thanks, and they include the use of peer mediation to enhance generalization.

Session 1

Initially, the primary goal is to establish a solid relationship. The therapist might begin by discussing the child's likes and dislikes. In doing so, potential reinforcers can be identified for later use in treatment. In language that the child understands, the therapist discusses the rationale for social skills training. Without good rapport and an understandable, meaningful rationale, the likelihood of success is low. Potential gains should be emphasized but not exaggerated. The child needs to understand that in certain situations, certain behaviors lead to fighting, to making peers mad, and to losing friends. In the same situations, other behaviors can lead to making friends. We discourage the idea that social skills training will lead to "popularity." Instead, we emphasize improved outcomes in specific situations, along with the self-esteem that accompanies improved social efficacy (e.g., Lochman & Curry, 1986). The following is an example of what might be said to the child:

> Lots of kids do things that "turn off" other kids. They either make the other kids angry, get in fights, or lose their temper. We've talked about how that sometimes happens to you. You do real well some of the time, but every once in a while you either say the wrong thing, lose your temper, or turn somebody off—either a friend, a teacher, or parent. You're going to be learning some ways to be more likable and to have more fun with kids your age. These aren't easy things to learn, so you will have to try hard and to practice what you learn. So, in here we're going to act things out in little plays to learn ways of keeping your parents, your teachers, and your principal off your back and to help you make more friends and to avoid hassles.

After a discussion of the rationale and the reinforcement system (if used), training begins with an initial target behavior, probably selected from the initial assessment. For aggressive children a distinct and observable social skill such as voice tone may be a good starting point. The therapist enlists the child's help in drawing up a hierarchy of scenes in which hostile and pleasant voice tones can be contrasted. Whether this is done in a formal or informal fashion, the development of a hierarchy is considered important for "pacing" the sessions and for not trying to accomplish everything at once. Difficulties may be encountered if a hierarchy is not formally developed. For example, the most problematic situation may be tackled first, and this is where the child will face the biggest challenge in learning/exhibiting more adaptive responses. Obviously, such a process can promote failure. A typical hierarchy begins with relatively neutral scenes and proceeds to more dramatic scenes in future sessions. Having the child play the part of the "receiver" and the "giver" of the hostile voice tone (i.e., role reversals) will help the child understand the importance of voice tone in social interactions. With certain children it may be necessary to discuss, demonstrate, and "try on" sarcastic or whiny voice tones, as well as hostile and pleasant tones.

The scenes that follow provide examples that may be useful in understanding the importance of voice tone. Model a hostile versus a pleasant voice or a loud versus calm voice, and ask the child to describe the emotional impact of the various voice tones. Enact and discuss favorable and negative outcomes for each scene.

1. You are walking down the street and see a classmate from school. You say, "Hey, what's happening?"

   a. The classmate says, "Nothing much!"
   b. The classmate says, "None of your business!"

2. You are at home watching television, and your mom says, "Come to dinner!"

   a. You say, "OK, Mom, right away."
   b. You say, "Aw, Mom, this show isn't over yet!"

3. In school, the teacher says, "Sit in your chair!"

   a. You say, "I was just throwing something in the trash!"
   b. You say, "Sorry, I forgot the rules."

4. You're playing a game with Danny, and you say, "Hey, let's play something else!"

   a. Danny says, "That's a good idea."
   b. Danny says, "What's wrong with the one we're playing now?"

Instruct the child to make up scenes that illustrate the impact of voice tone. Ham it up, and have a good time. Praise and fun are important elements of social skills training with children and adolescents.

End the session by informing the child that he or she will learn more things about voice tone in the next session, and encourage the child to notice hostile and pleasant voice tones used by other people.

Session 2

Begin by reviewing the prior session and asking if the child has noticed voice tones that others use. Talk about how different voice tones affect other people. Start the session with slightly more threatening and emotionally difficult situations, but leave the most difficult situations for later sessions. Again, have the child play each part in the role play while trying out different voice tones. Remember to role play varying outcomes.

1. During a basketball game, tell Johnny he stepped out of bounds.
2. Tell your mother that you don't want peas for dinner.
3. Susan asks to borrow your game, and you say, "No, I want to play with it now."
4. Ask your brother or sister to quiet down because you want to watch T.V.

Begin with the above scenes, and try to involve the child in longer dialogues. Enact situations in which one child's hostile voice tone leads to a hostile response by the other child, setting up a cycle of aggression. In preparation for the next session, encourage the child to remember conflict situations as they occur during the week and to bring them in for practice situations in the next session. At the end of the session, briefly review the different voice tones and emphasize the value of speaking in a calm, even voice to avoid or minimize conflict. Praise the child's participation.

Session 3

Begin this session by reviewing the prior two sessions and by discussing the child's progress. Depending on the degree of progress, continue up the hierarchy to more difficult situations. Discuss how a hostile voice tone can lead to fighting and to losing friends, while a calm, firm voice tone ("not losing your cool") can help in getting along with others. Ask the child to recall real-life situations in which voice tones influenced the outcome.

At the appropriate time, tell the child, "You've done really well so far, and now we're going to see how well you can do on some even tougher situations. I really want to see if you can keep your voice low and firm. Remember, it's important to keep your voice calm even if the other person starts to talk louder."

Note: With the examples presented below, try to extend the situation into a dialogue. Challenge the child to maintain a nonbelligerent voice tone (unless, of course, the child has not shown adequate progress in prior sessions).

The following scenes may be role played.

1. You are standing out on the playground, and another child bumps into you. You say, "Hey, what's going on!"
2. The teacher counts your points wrong on a test. You say, "Count them over, I think I have enough for a 'B'."
3. Jeffrey spills some milk, and you're accused of it. You say, "I didn't do it."
4. Carol peeked in "hide and seek," and you say "I'm not gonna play if you cheat."

Ask the child to develop situations from recent experiences. As always, use role reversal, and emphasize how different voice tones affect the recipient. Praise successive approximations. Again, ask the child to remember instances in the coming week in which voice tones are used well or poorly.

Session 4

Assuming that the child has made progress, this session will serve as a review and an extension of the prior session. At the end of the session, the child's progress can be assessed through retesting on the baseline assessment tasks.

Practice with the situations below. As in the last session, try to engage the child in role-play dialogues in which it is difficult to maintain an appropriate voice tone. This time, ask the child to generate optional responses.

1. David tells you that he will give back your ball tomorrow morning, but you want it back now. You say, "I want it back now."
2. Jason tells you that you better "shut the hell up," because he is trying to tell you something. You say, "I had something to tell Barbara."
3. You step on your cousin's toe by mistake, and he yells, "You damn bastard."
4. Cindy makes fun of your haircut, and you say, "I don't like you bugging me about my hair."

Have the child reenact events of the past week. If it appears that adequate progress is being made, suggest some situations in which the new social skill might be attempted. If a reinforcement system is employed, offer a bonus prize for "real-world" applications.

Session 5

After several sessions of good progress, it may be time to introduce another skill. For instance, aggressive children sometimes make poor use of physical distance. When they become angry, aggressive children may move close to the target of their aggression and may place their hands on or near the other's chest. Being very close to the other child, clenching one's fists, or placing one's arms in an offensive stance may accelerate the cycle of aggression. A skillful alternative might be to move back a few steps from the other child, with arms hanging at the side and with open palms. (Modeling is helpful when introducing these social skills.)

Therapist: You were great on voice tone! Now it's time to try some more ways to keep cool and to avoid fights. Today we're going to work on how you position your body. Let's try these exercises.

Exercise 1 (Physical Distance)   "Let's have a little talk about sports (or whatever the child is interested in) and see if you notice anything unusual."

Model A. During the conversation, therapist is very close.

Model B. During the conversation, therapist is a few steps away.

Model C. During the conversation, therapist is very far away.

Discuss physical distance and the feelings associated with different positions.

Exercise 2 (Physical Distance and Arm Placement)

Model A. Child asks therapist to return a borrowed toy. Therapist says "no" and moves very close with arms in an offensive position near the child's chest, with fists clenched.

Model B. Repeat Model A with more appropriate physical distance and hands at side with palms open. Alter voice tone to match the nonprovocative body language.

Discuss the feelings elicited by physical distance and arm placement, and model different options in a variety of situations. Use role reversal to help the child see how the model scene feels from the different perspectives. Emphasize how nonverbal cues can escalate a conflict. Praise improvement, however small.

Session 6
Continue the skills addressed in the previous session, and use increasingly difficult situations. These might be actual problem situations that the child has faced. Review the idea of maintaining proper voice tone, maintaining proper physical distance, and keeping arms down with palms open.

The scenes that follow provide possibilities for integrating previously learned skills. Use role reversals. As always, one of the best motivational tools is to ham it up and have fun.

1. Greg fouls you intentionally while trying to steal the basketball. You say, "Don't do that again."
2. Todd calls you an S.O.B., and you say, "I don't appreciate you calling me names." (The clinician may wish to discuss the fact that names are not "sticks and stones" and cannot hurt the client, introducing a cognitive element of the training.)

3. Your sister screams at you to get out of her room when her friends are visiting.
4. Andrea asks for her Batman cars back. You say, "I want to keep them longer."

Help the child generate scenes. Discuss favorable and negative outcomes, and generate possible follow-up responses in either case. The goal is to stimulate consequential thinking in the child by highlighting the connection between certain behaviors and their consequences. If the child is catching on, you may wish to reassess progress by repeating the baseline scenes. If sufficient progress has been made, it might be a good time to bring a significant peer, a parent, or a teacher into a session to be involved in the role plays. It is beneficial for the child to practice with many people from the "real" environment. This promotes generalization and also gives the child a chance to try out these new roles with someone else while you are there to provide guidance and support. This initial generalization phase can be fun for everyone involved.

Session 7

The next few sessions emphasize a rational-emotive approach (Ellis, 1973) to develop more socially appropriate responses in conflict situations. In addition to building on the prior lessons, these sessions focus on eliminating inappropriate behaviors and cognitions and replacing them with more socially effective ones. (Some of the material is similar to the stress inoculation procedures discussed in Chapter 5.) For instance, many aggressive children have beliefs such as "Being tough is how to be cool!," "No one can tell me I'm not right!," "I must get even with anybody that crosses me," "I cannot tolerate being treated unfairly!," and "If you don't like my behavior, the hell with you!" Many physically aggressive children are impulsive and fail to "stop and think" before acting (see Dodge & Newman, 1981). It is important to assess the specific thoughts and behaviors that cause interpersonal difficulties for the child. The following exercises provide some rough guidelines.

Introduction for the Child "Now we'd like to move on to some other ways to help you stay out of trouble and to make friends. We're going to see how the thoughts that go through your mind can make you real mad or can keep you calm. What goes on upstairs—in your head—that's what makes you feel the way you do. Here's what I mean (give examples)."

In order to help the child understand self-statements, use examples that have led to aggressive episodes in the child's life. Review anger-provoking situations using various self-statements to show how conflict situations can be perceived in different ways. Tell the child that you will be "thinking out loud." The goal of these exercises is to demonstrate that situations don't produce anger—thoughts do.

Exercise 1 (Being Called Names)   "Listen to these two examples. In both cases the child has been called names like 'Stupid' or 'Baby.' Guess which child would be more likely to get in a fight." (If the child guesses correctly, provide social and/or tangible reinforcement.)

> *Model A* (thinking out loud with exaggerated anger). "It's horrible to be called a name! I'm going to get that guy. Nobody can do that to me and get away with it!"
>
> *Model B* (calmly thinking out loud). "Being called a name is not the end of the world. He doesn't know what he's talking about. I'm not going to bother with him. I'll go on with my business."

Discuss this example with the child.

Exercise 2 (Being Criticized)   "The teacher says that you have to stay in from recess to complete your math assignment."

> *Model A* (thinking out loud with exaggerated anger). "I just have to go to recess! Nobody can do that to me! I'm going to tell her where she can go."
>
> *Model B* (calmly thinking out loud). "Well, that's a bummer! I guess I have to do it or I'll be in trouble. I'll just relax and get the work done. Missing one recess is bad, but it isn't terrible."

Discuss which child would be more likely to be involved in an argument with the teacher and what the consequences of that argument would be.

Exercise 3 (Everything Must Be Fair)   "A hit is unfairly called 'foul' in a baseball game."

> *Model A* (thinking out loud with exaggerated anger). "How can anyone do that to me! It's not fair! I absolutely hate it when somebody's unfair to me! He'd better be fair, or else!"
>
> *Model B* (calmly thinking out loud). "It was in. Oh, well, what a pain. But I'm not gonna get bent out of shape about it. I'll hit the next one."

Again, discuss which child might be more likely to get in trouble. Further, discuss the importance of making appropriate self-statements. Have the child describe thoughts that create problems in specific situations. Discuss how other people are not to blame for loss of temper, and emphasize that one's own thoughts determine how the situation turns out. Ask the child to consider which types of self-statements will lead to anger and which ones will not. Provide appropriate examples such as "Keep cool," "Don't let it bug you," and "Don't get bent out of shape." Always begin by thinking out loud. Tell the child that later practice will focus on whispering the self-statements and eventually on saying the self-statements silently. These concepts may be quite difficult for some children to master and may require much practice. Be sure to praise successive approximations.

Session 8

Begin the session by reviewing the meaning and importance of self-statements. (The therapist needs to be familiar with the stress inoculation steps in Chapter 5: preparing for confrontation, impact and confrontation, coping with arousal, and reflecting on the provocation.) Practice the appropriate self-statements in a variety of situations, beginning with less difficult situations. Continue to examine any aggressive beliefs or irrational attitudes. Use some of the role plays from prior sessions, and note how voice tone, physical posture, and rational self-talk all go together. The following scenes may be used.

1. You are falsely accused of hitting a child.
2. Your brother (or friend) walks in the room and switches the T.V. dial without asking.
3. A friend asks you to dinner but your dad says "no."
4. A kid you didn't like anyway says your favorite NFL team sucks.

Model several alternative responses, and let the child select the best one. If the child is unable to integrate the previously learned skills, a review may be necessary. Challenge the child, but don't push him or her too hard. The rate of progress will determine when new skills are added.

Sessions 9 and 10

Review the prior session and the steps involved in the stress inoculation package. By being gradually more confrontive in the role plays, make it increasingly difficult for the child to stay cool. Do not take small improvements for granted—reinforce them! Review the child's aggressive belief system, and discuss more adaptive ways of achieving goals. Discuss alternative ways of gaining social status. Tell the client that you and many other people respect a person who can walk away from trouble. Make sure that the alternatives to aggression have meaning for the child; otherwise the training will be unproductive.

During these sessions, problem-solving options can be generated in a brainstorming activity. The options may also be provided by the therapist in a structured format. The "Keep Cool Rules" (Cox & Gunn, 1977) that are listed below provide a good example of a structured format.

1. Make a polite request for behavior change.
2. State the request more firmly, without anger.
3. Give a reason to the other person for your request.
4. Ask the other person for the reason for noncompliance.
5. Ignore the behavior.
6. Move to another location.
7. Threaten to inform an authority figure about the problem.
8. Go find the authority figure and follow through with #7.

These options are presented as a hierarchy of possibilities for responding to interpersonal conflict. When faced with conflict, the child can try Step 1 and can gradually move down the hierarchy. Integrate these guidelines with rational self-statements and nonverbal social skills, and practice them in role plays. Gradually have the child whisper the self-statements as a successive approximation toward covert problem solving.

Sessions 11 and 12

Keep in mind that it is essential to individualize the treatment to meet the child's needs and to promote generalization. At this point it is important to assess what the child has learned from the prior sessions and to identify situations that continue to pose problems. It is equally important to assess progress in the natural environment by observing the child, by interviewing significant others, and by collecting data whenever possible. With the client's permission, invite others to participate in the role plays.

During Sessions 11 and 12, continue to practice appropriate self-statements and social skills in increasingly difficult situations. Engage the child in dialogues that test his or her progress. Review the steps involved in the Keep Cool Rules. Have the child practice saying the self-statements silently. Individualize the practice situations and emphasize alternative behaviors and self-statements. If the child is doing well, move on to the next skill. If not, continue practicing. Remember that in previous conflict situations the child has relied on aggressiveness as a source of self-esteem and that switching to other sources is quite a risk. Praise heartily, and let the child know how highly you regard anyone who has the "guts" to try new ways of solving problems.

Sessions 13 and 14

During these two sessions, training can be extended to include prosocial skills that are relevant in nonconflict situations. The child can learn ways of giving and receiving compliments, how to share and take turns, and how to offer inclusion to others in activities. If children can engage in positive interactions with others, there will be less need to rely on negative attention-seeking behavior. Some children may need to discuss the irrational belief that being a "nice guy" means being a "sissy." During these two sessions, practice various skills that enable the child to reinforce others for behavior that is pleasing to him or her.

Giving and Receiving Compliments, Praise, Expressing Thanks Have the child play the giver and receiver of compliments in the following situations. Model alternative responses, including appropriate silence.

1. You have been cleaning up your room. Your mother comes in and says, "That's a very good job you've done." You say: _____
2. You are in school, and the teacher compliments you on your work. The teacher says, "That's a good job. You worked really hard." You say: _____
3. You've had a nice talk with some of your classmates at lunch. You say: _____
4. Your mother cooks your favorite dinner. You say: _____

Role play situations in which the child can compliment himself or herself for doing a good job. Have the child talk about how it feels to receive compliments or to be thanked. Encourage the child to increase the number of prosocial statements expressed to self and to others.

Sharing Encourage the child to practice sharing. Discuss possible situations in which this would be feasible, as well as the possible favorable effects on the child's peer relations. Role play some of those situations. By definition, sharing is giving up something of value. Emphasize that it is usually a *temporary* sacrifice. Improvements should be praised heavily.

Offering an Invitation Aggressive children may feel uncomfortable about asking others to join in an activity. For example, a teenage boy may feel anxious about asking a girl to join him in a game of checkers. If the child is progressing well, this may be an opportune time to bring significant peers and/or adults into the sessions. Let the client extend the invitation after practicing it in role plays.

Generalization Training

As emphasized throughout the text, effective social skills training cannot be conducted independently from the child's natural environment. Generalization is a primary goal of treatment (Stokes & Baer, 1977). Strategies to facilitate the maintenance and generalization of the newly acquired social skills include bringing the child's peers into the sessions, encouraging others to reinforce the child's improvements in the natural environment, and training parents and teachers to be more effective models and sources of problem-solving options.

Summary

The training program outlined in this chapter provides general guidelines for social skills training from a cognitive-behavioral pespective. Effective social skills training is always designed to fit the individual needs and interests of the child. The assessment process must be comprehensive in order to obtain pertinent data regarding the characteristics of children identified for treatment and in order to determine the precise nature of their social skills deficits. In addition, the assessment process must be continuous in order to provide timely feedback for clients and to assist the therapist in determining the next steps in the social skills training program. A solid therapeutic relationship is essential for a successful outcome in social skills training with children. Finally, as we have emphasized often, generalization and maintenance of change require the inclusion of individuals who are important in the real world of the child. Although much more work needs to be done in the therapeutic utilization of social skills training, the strategies described in this chapter and elsewhere (e.g., Matson & Ollendick, 1988) can be useful in helping children learn more effective and socially appropriate ways of interacting with others.

References

Achenbach, T. M., & Edelbrock, C. (1983). *Manual for the Child Behavior Checklist and Revised Child Behavior Profile.* Burlington, VT: Queen City Printers.

Amish, P. L., Gesten, E. L., Smith, J. K., & Clark, H. B. (1988). Social problem-solving training for severely emotionally and behaviorally disturbed children. *Behavioral Disorders, 13,* 175–186.

Anderson, C. G., Rush, D., Ayllon, T., & Kandel, H. (1987). Training and generalization of social skills with problem children. *Journal of Child and Adolescent Psychotherapy, 4,* 294–298.

Baum, J., Clark, H., McCarthy, W., & Sandler, J. (1986). An analysis of the acquisition and generalization of social skills in troubled youths: Combining social skills training, cognitive self-talk, and relaxation training. *Child and Family Behavior Therapy, 8,* 1–27.

Beck, S., & Forehand, R. (1979). *Social skills training for children: A review and methodological analysis of behavior modification studies.* Unpublished manuscript, University of Georgia, Athens.

Beck, S., Forehand, R., Neeper, R., & Baskin, C. H. (1982). A comparison of two analogue strategies for assessing children's social skills. *Journal of Consulting and Clinical Psychology, 50*(4), 596–597.

Bierman, K. L., Miller, C. L., & Stabb, S. D. (1987). Improving the social behavior and peer acceptance of rejected boys: Effects of social skills training with instructions and prohibitions. *Journal of Consulting and Clinical Psychology, 55,* 194–200.

Bornstein, M., Bellack, A., & Hersen, M. (1977). Social skills training for unassertive children: A multiple-baseline analysis. *Journal of Applied Behavior Analysis, 10,* 183–195.

Bornstein, M. R., Bellack, A. S., & Hersen, M. (1980). Social skills training for highly aggressive children. *Behavior Modification, 4,* 173–186.

Cairns, R. B., Cairns, B. D., Neckerman, H. J., Gest, S., & Gariepy, J. L. (1988). Social networks and aggressive behavior: Peer support or peer rejection? *Developmental Psychology, 24,* 815–823.

Camp, B., Zimet, S., van Doornick, W., & Dahlem, N. (1977). Verbal abilities in young aggressive boys. *Journal of Educational Psychology, 69,* 129–135.

Cialdini, R. B., Kenrick, D. T., & Baumann, D. J. (1981). Effects of mood on prosocial behavior in children and adults. In N. Eisenberg-Berg (Ed.), *The development of prosocial behavior.* New York: Academic Press.

Combs, M., & Slaby, D. (1977). Social skills training with children. In B. Lahey & A. Kazdin (Eds.), *Advances in clinical child psychology* (Vol. 1). New York: Plenum Press.

Conger, J. C., & Keane, S. P. (1981). Social skills intervention in the treatment of isolated and withdrawn children. *Psychological Bulletin, 90,* 478–495.

Cox, R., & Gunn, W. (1977). *Interpersonal skill development with the schools: The Keep-Cool Rules and other strategies.* Paper presented at the Seventh Annual Symposium of the Houston Behavior Therapy Association, Houston, Texas.

DiGiuseppe, R. (1983). Rational-emotive therapy and conduct disorders. In A. Ellis & M. Bernard (Eds.), *Rational-emotive approaches to problems of childhood* (pp. 111–137). New York: Plenum Press.

Dodge, K. A. (1981, May). *Social competence and aggressive behavior in children.* Paper presented at the meeting of the Midwestern Psychological Association, Detroit, Michigan.

Dodge, K. A. (1983). Behavioral antecedents of peer social status. *Child Development, 54,* 1386–1399.

Dodge, K. A., & Newman, J. P. (1981). Biased decision-making processes in aggressive boys. *Journal of Abnormal Psychology, 90,* 375–379.

Dubow, E. F., Huesmann, L., & Eron, L. (1987). Mitigating aggression and promoting prosocial behavior in aggressive elementary schoolboys. *Behaviour Research and Therapy, 25,* 527–531.

Duncan, K., Beck., D., & Granum, R. (1988). Project Explore: An activity-based counseling group. *School Counselor, 35,* 215–219.

Dunnington, M. J. (1975). Behavioral differences of sociometric status groups in nursery school. *Child Development, 28,* 103–111.

Elder, J., Edelstein, B., & Narick, M. (1979). Adolescent psychiatric patients: Modifying aggressive behavior with social skills training. *Behavior Modification, 3,* 161–178.

Ellis, A. (1973). *Humanistic psychotherapy: The rational-emotive approach.* New York: Julian Press.

Evers-Pasquale, W., & Sherman, M. (1975). The reward value of peers. *Journal of Abnormal Child Psychology, 3,* 179–189.

Forman, S. G. (1980). Self-statements of aggressive and nonaggressive children. *Child Behavior Therapy, 2,* 49–57.

Foster, S. L., Bell-Dolan, D., & Berger, E. S. (1986). Methodological issues in the use of sociometrics for selecting children for social skills research and training. *Advances in Behavioral Assessment of Children and Families, 2,* 227–248.

Freedman, B., Rosenthal, L., Donahoe, C., Schlundt, D., & McFall, R. (1978). A social-behavioral analysis of skills deficits in delinquent and nondelinquent adolescent boys. *Journal of Consulting and Clinical Psychology, 46,* 1448–1462.

Gardner, W. I., & Cole, C. L. (1987). Conduct problems. In C. Fione & J. Matons (Eds.), *Handbook of assessment in childhood psychopathology: Applied issues in differential diagnosis and treatment evaluation.* New York: Plenum Press.

Goldstein, A. P., Sherman, M., Gershaw, N. J., Sprafkin, R. P., & Glick, B. (1978). Training aggressive adolescents in prosocial behavior. *Journal of Youth and Adolescence, 7,* 73–92.

Gottman, J. (1977). The effects of a modeling film on social isolation in preschool children: A methodological investigation. *Journal of Abnormal Child Psychology, 5,* 69–77.

Gottman, J., Gonso, J., & Rasmussen, B. (1975). Social interaction, social competence and friendship in children. *Child Development, 46,* 709–718.

Gresham, F. M. (1986). Conceptual and definitional issues in the assessment of children's social skills: Implications for classification and training. *Journal of Clinical Child Psychology, 15,* 3–15.

Hartup, W. W. (1989). Social relationships and their developmental significance. *American Psychologist, 44,* 120–126.

Harwood, R. L., & Weissberg, R. P. (1987). The potential of video in the promotion of social competence in children and adolescents. *Journal of Early Adolescence, 7,* 345–363.

Hetherington, E. & Martin, B. (1986). Family factors and psychopathology in children. In H. C. Quay and J. Werry (Eds.), *Psychopathological Disorders of Childhood.* New York: Wiley & Sons.

Hops, H. (1983). Children's social competence and skill: Current research practices and future directions. *Behavior Therapy, 14,* 3–18.

Kazdin, A., Matson, J., & Esveldt-Dawson, K. (1980). Training interpersonal skills among mentally retarded and socially dysfunctional children. *Behavior Therapy and Research, 18,* 419–427.

Keller, M., & Carlson, P. (1974). The use of symbolic modeling to promote social skills in preschool children with low levels of social responsiveness. *Child Development, 45,* 912–919.

Kolko, D. J., Dorsett, P. G., & Milan, M. A. (1981). A total-assessment approach to the evaluation of social skills training: The effectiveness of an anger control program for adolescent psychiatric patients. *Behavioral Assessment, 3,* 383–402.

Krehbiel, G. G., & Milich, R. (1986). Issues in the assessment and treatment of socially rejected children. *Advances in Behavioral Assessment of Children and Families, 2,* 249–270.

Ladd, G. W. (1981). Effectiveness of a social learning method for enhancing social interaction and peer acceptance. *Child Development, 52,* 171–178.

LaGreca, A. M. (1981). Peer acceptance: The correspondence between children's sociometric scores and teachers' ratings of peer interactions. *Journal of Abnormal Child Psychology, 9,* 167–178.

LaGreca, A. M., & Santogrossi, D. A. (1980). Social skills training with elementary school students: A behavioral group approach. *Journal of Consulting and Clinical Psychology, 48,* 220–227.

LeCroy, C. W. (1987). Teaching children social skills: A game format. *Social Work, 32,* 440–442.

Liebert, R. M., & Sprafkin, J. (1988). *The early window: Effects of television on children and youth.* New York: Pergamon Press.

Lochman, J. E., & Curry, J. F. (1986). Effects of social problem-solving training and self-instruction training with aggressive boys. *Journal of Clinical Child Psychology, 15,* 159–164.

MacDonald, M. L., & Cohen, J. (1981). Trees in the forest: Some components of social skills. *Journal of Clinical Psychology, 37,* 342–347.

Matson, J. L., Heinze, A., Halsel, W. J., Kapperman, G., & Rotatori, A. (1986). Assessing social behaviors in the visually-handicapped. The Matson Evaluation of Social Skills with Youngsters (MESSY). *Journal of Clinical Child Psychology, 15,* 78–87.

Matson, J. L., & Ollendick, T. H. (1988). *Enhancing children's social skills: Assessment and training.* New York: Pergamon Press.

Meichenbaum, D. (1977). *Cognitive-behavior modification.* New York: Plenum Press.

Michelson, L., Foster, S. L., & Ritchey, W. L. (1981). Social skills assessment of children. In B. B. Lahey & A. E. Kazdin (Eds.), *Advances in clinical child psychology.* New York: Plenum Press.

Moore, S. G., & Updegraff, R. (1964). Sociometric status of preschool children related to age, sex, nurturance giving and dependency. *Child Development, 35,* 519–524.

Morrison, R. L., & Bellack, A. S. (1981). The role of social perception in social skill. *Behavior Therapy, 12,* 69–79.

Nasby, W., Hayden, B., & DePaulo, B. (1980). Attributional bias among aggressive boys to interpret unambiguous social stimuli as displays of hostility. *Journal of Abnormal Psychology, 89,* 459–468.

O'Connor, R. (1972). Relative efficacy of modeling, shaping and the combined procedures for modification of social withdrawal. *Journal of Abnormal Psychology, 79,* 327–334.

Ollendick, T. H., & Cerny, J. A. (1981). *Clinical behavior therapy with children.* New York: Plenum Press.

Ollendick, T. H., & Hersen, M. (1979). Social skills training for juvenile delinquents. *Behaviour Research and Therapy, 17,* 547–554.

Olson, R. L., & Roberts, M. W. (1987). Alternative treatments for sibling aggression. *Behavior Therapy, 18,* 243–250.

Patterson, G. R. (1976). The aggressive child: Victim and architect of a coercive system. In E. J. Mash, L. A. Hammerlynk, & L. C. Handy (Eds.), *Behavior modification and families.* New York: Brunner/Mazel.

Pinkston, E., Reese, N., LeBlanc, J., & Baer, D. (1973). Independent control of a preschool child's aggression and peer interaction by contingent teacher attention. *Journal of Applied Behavior Analysis, 6,* 115–124.

Polyson, J. A. (1981, June). *The plight of the socially unskilled child.* Paper presented at the annual meeting of the Indiana Child and Adolescent Services Conference, Nashville, IN.

Quay, H. C., & Peterson, D. R. (1983). *Interim Manual of the Revised Behavior Problem Checklist*. Coral Gables, FL: University of Miami Press.

Rathjen, D., Rathjen, E., & Hinker, A. (1978). A cognitive analysis of social performance. In J. Forety & D. Rathjen (Eds.), *Cognitive behavior therapy: Research and applications*. New York: Plenum Press.

Rinn, R., & Markle, A. (1979). Modification of skill deficits in children. In A. Bellack & M. Hersen (Eds.), *Research and practice in social skills training*. New York: Plenum Press.

Schneider, B. H., & Byrne, B. M. (1987). Individualizing social skills training for behavior-disordered children. *Journal of Consulting and Clinical Psychology, 55,* 444–445.

Shantz, C. (1975). The development of social cognition. In E. M. Hetherington (Ed.), *Review of child development research* (Vol. 5). Chicago: University of Chicago Press.

Shaver, P., & Rubenstein, C. (1980). Childhood attachment experience and adult loneliness. In L. Wheeler (Ed.), *Review of personality and social psychology* (Vol. 1). Beverly Hills, CA: Sage.

Spence, A. J., & Spence, S. H. (1981). Cognitive changes associated with social skills training. *Behaviour Research and Therapy, 18,* 265–272.

Stokes, T., & Baer, O. (1977). An implicit technology of generalization. *Journal of Applied Behavior Analysis, 10,* 349–368.

Strain, P., Shores, R., & Timm, M. (1977). Effects of peer social interaction on the behavior of withdrawn preschool children. *Journal of Applied Behavior Analysis, 10,* 289–298.

Walker, H. (1970). *Problem Behavior Identification Checklist*. Los Angeles: Western Psychological Services.

Weinrott, M., Corson, J., & Wilchesky, M. (1979). Teacher-mediated treatment of social withdrawal. *Behavior Therapy, 10,* 281–294.

Williamson, D. A., Moody, S. C., Granberry, S. W., Letherms, V., & Biougin, D. C. (1983). Criterion-related validity of a role-play social skills test for children. *Behavior Therapy, 14,* 466–481.

Wool, R., & Clements, C. B. (1975). Adolescent verbal behavior: An investigation of noncontent styles as related to race and delinquency status. *Journal of Abnormal Child Psychology, 3,* 245–254.

CHAPTER SEVEN

Cognitive Self-Instruction for Impulse Control in Children

A. J FINCH, JR.   ANTHONY SPIRITO

PAMELA S. IMM   EDITH S. OTT

This chapter is designed to serve as a guide for clinicians who are interested in using self-instructional procedures to modify impulsive responding in children. The procedures outlined are drawn from Donald Meichenbaum's work and from our own clinical and research activity. We recognize that these procedures will not work with all children, and, in fact, we have found a number of children for whom they have been ineffective. Although we have not been able to determine how to predict which children will benefit from these procedures, we have not had a single incident in which a child became more impulsive as a result of our training. Thus, the techniques we describe appear to be worth trying without concern for risk.

The guidelines presented in this chapter are not to be followed rigidly. Flexibility of approach and individuality of training are emphasized. We have learned that when one is working with children, cognitive training (as well as any form of treatment) must be conducted in a relaxed, natural manner that is comfortable and even fun for the child. Otherwise, the best laid plans and procedures are sabotaged by boredom, lack of interest, or statements to the effect that "This is dumb!" Therefore, it is recommended that each therapist who attempts to employ these procedures should adapt them to suit his or her own style and to fit the age and maturity of the youngster involved.

This chapter is divided into two parts. First we will review the development and process of our interest in impulsive responding and the research generated by that interest. We intend to present this material in the informal manner that has characterized our collaborative efforts for almost 20 years (rather than in the more formal, scientific style that has characterized its appearance in the clinical literature). Because this chapter is not designed to provide a comprehensive review of literature in the area of impulsive responding, the work of other clinical researchers is not emphasized. This exclusion is not intended to minimize the significance of their contribution. See Kendall and Finch (1979a), Kendall and Braswell (1985), and Whalen, Henker, and Hinshaw (1985) for more detailed reviews.

The second part of this chapter presents the actual training procedures, which give a session-by-session description of general procedures and provide suggestions for training materials. In addition, we include helpful hints for the actual implementation, planning, and execution of verbal self-instructions with impulsive children. Again, we do not provide a rigid script but rather a set of flexible guidelines to be tailored to meet the needs of the individual child.

Background Review

In the early 1970s while one of the authors (Finch) worked with a group of brain-damaged children at the Devereux Foundation, a token economy program was established for the home and living unit. After gathering considerable behavioral observations of baseline and treatment, he felt reasonably comfortable with the results of the program. However, at a staff meeting a teacher complained that the children were still being "careless" in their classroom work. Annoyed by this minor staff insurrection, the young clinician decided to make some further behavioral observations in the classroom. Much to his surprise, he immediately observed what the teacher called "carelessness." Children were responding quickly without considering all of the stimuli that were present and, consequently, were making numerous mistakes in their work. These mistakes seemed to be more a function of their response style than of their ability to comprehend the material. For example, a youngster might begin working on math problems without paying attention to the sign of the operation to be performed. Although the child had the ability to solve the problem, incorrect solutions appeared to be the result of carelessness.

A colleague suggested that this type of carelessness seemed similar to the impulsivity described by Jerome Kagan at Harvard. Kagan was interested in response styles or cognitive styles of children and had developed a test called Matching Familiar Figures (MFF) to assess these styles. In this test, children are asked to look at a standard stimulus and at six variants. The task is simply to choose the variant that is like the standard. By dividing children according to response latencies and number of errors, Kagan operationalized impulsivity. We began to speculate about the similarity between this cognitive impulsivity that Kagan was investigating and the carelessness or behavioral impulsivity that we were observing in the classroom. In order to investigate the similarities of these two concepts, we designed the initial study in our research program.

Ollendick and Finch (1973) compared MFF performance of a group of brain-damaged children (a group traditionally described as clinically impulsive) and a group of normal children matched on mental age. Our interest was to investigate the possibility of a relationship between performance on this brief instrument and the type of impulsive behavior that we were seeing in a clinical population. As hypothesized, we found that the brain-damaged group responded more quickly in their choices and made more mistakes or, as Kagan would say, were more "impulsive."

Our research efforts then moved to the Virginia Treatment Center for Children, where we began to work with emotionally disturbed children and decided to continue this line of investigation because many of the children we saw were indeed impulsive. Montgomery (1974) compared the responses of emotionally disturbed and normal children. He found that although there was no difference in the length of time they took to respond (i.e., their latency), the emotionally disturbed children made significantly more errors.

Although we were encouraged by these results, we were concerned that our initial hypothesis (that emotionally disturbed children would respond more impulsively than normal children) might have been formulated somewhat impulsively. Many emotionally disturbed children *are* impulsive and might be expected to respond in a like manner on the MFF, but many of these children are also inhibited and withdrawn. Therefore, in the next study we compared emotionally disturbed children who were inhibited with emotionally disturbed children who were behaviorally impulsive. Montgomery and Finch (1975) obtained locus of conflict ratings of a group of emotionally disturbed children. In addition, each youngster was individually administered the MFF. The cognitively impulsive children were more likely to be rated by their teachers as externalizing their symptoms than were the reflective children. In addition, the reflective children (those who respond slowly and accurately) were more likely to be rated as internalizing their symptoms. We were very encouraged by these results and interpreted them as further supporting a relationship between the cognitive impulsivity measured by the MFF and the behavioral impulsivity that we saw in our clinical population.

In order to further explore our hypotheses, we decided to examine the relationship between performance on the MFF and the behavioral ratings from parents of children admitted to the hospital (Finch & Nelson, 1976). Results indicated a difference between impulsive and reflective children as rated by their parents. For instance, we found that emotionally disturbed boys who were impulsive on their MFF performance were more likely than reflective boys to talk of others blaming them unfairly, to threaten injury to themselves, to hit and bully other children, and to be excessively rough in play. In contrast, the reflective children (as measured by the MFF) were more likely to be reluctant to talk to adults outside of the family. Continuing along these lines, Finch, Kendall, Deardorff, Anderson, and Sitarz (1975) investigated the relationship between persistence on a task and performance on the MFF. As anticipated, we found that children who were impulsive in their MFF performance were more likely to give up easily and to be less persistent on a task.

The final study (Finch, Pezzuti, Montgomery, & Kemp, 1974) that supported the relationship between behavior and impulsivity was designed to investigate the relationship between performance on the MFF and academic achievement. We compared achievement scores of impulsive and reflective children and found, in terms of achievement level, no difference between these two groups of emotionally disturbed children. Both were achieving approximately one year below grade expectancy. However, we found that when placed at the Treatment Center, the impulsive children were approximately two grade levels behind reflective children. That is, the impulsive children had been retained for approximately two grades, whereas the reflective children generally had not been retained. Although both groups were actually achieving at about the same grade level, the impulsive children were achieving at a level above their grade placement. We interpreted these results to mean that the behavioral differences between these groups accounted for their grade placements. It is possible that teachers viewed the impulsive children as more immature and more likely to benefit from retention. Also, the impulsive children may have had more difficulty demonstrating that they had met the learning objectives required for promotion.

We have reviewed our research to highlight the relationship between the performance of children on the Matching Familiar Figures test and their actual clinical behaviors. We present this review because a number of our research hypotheses and research strategies developed as a result of looking at children who differ on their performance on the MFF.

However, some researchers have questioned the construct validity of the MFF (Bentler & McClain, 1976; Block, Block, & Harrington, 1974; Messer, 1976). The controversy appears to be centered around the conceptualization and operationalization of the construct of reflection–impulsivity. In addition, there is some concern about the inherent assumption that a child's performance in one test situation can be generalized to another test situation or to aspects of the child's behavior in natural settings. Also, there are data to suggest that the MFF as a measure of reflection is less valid with preschoolers than with school-age children (Kagan & Messer, 1975). Although the debate about the construct validity of reflection–impulsivity is not resolved, there is evidence to suggest a relationship between cognitive and behavioral impulsivity (Egeland, Bielke, & Kendall, 1980). As a result, the MFF continues to be used as a dependent measure of cognitive impulsivity.

Continuing our research program, we examined the possible differences between impulsive and reflective children and the implications for treatment. Because it was theorized that a positive relationship exists between a youngster's fear of failure and cognitive tempo and between fear of failure and anxiety, we investigated the relationship between impulsivity and anxiety.

In his doctoral dissertation, Montgomery (1974) compared impulsive and reflective emotionally disturbed and normal children on their responses to the State-Trait Anxiety Inventory for Children (Spielberger, 1973). He found no relationship between impulsivity and anxiety and no differences among the groups in response to a statement about fear of failure. Consequently, there did not appear to be a relationship between self-reported anxiety and fear of failure. In addition, it was found that the high level of anxiety experienced by emotionally disturbed children did not have an adverse effect upon their performance (Stein, Finch, Hooke, Montgomery, & Nelson, 1975).

Our next area of investigation was prompted by clinical observations of impulsive and reflective children as they worked on the MFF. We noted that reflective children frequently talked to themselves as they attempted to select the correct response. On the other hand, impulsive children rarely verbalized, and when they did, their verbalizations generally consisted of irrelevant remarks. As a result, we decided to examine the possible differences between the thought processes of impulsive and reflective children. Jerome Bruner (Bruner, Oliver, & Greenfield, 1966) proposed that during the course of the development of thinking, a child moves through three stages: (a) thinking primarily through action (reactive), (b) thinking primarily in pictures (ionic), and (c) thinking symbolically or with words (representational). We hypothesized that the thought process of impulsive children is more immature than the thought process of reflective children. In order to test this hypothesis, we conducted two studies (Finch & Montgomery, 1973; Stein et al., 1975). In general, these studies supported the hypothesis that impulsive children think primarily with pictures (ionic stage) and reflective children think primarily with words (representational stage).

We then attempted to determine if there is a relationship between an impulsive cognitive style and locus of control. Observation and clinical judgment suggested to us that a relationship exists between MFF performance and a child's belief in his or her ability to influence good and bad life occurrences. In our first study (Finch, Nelson, Montgomery, & Stein, 1974) a small sample was used, and although there was a difference between impulsive cognitive style and locus of control, it failed to reach significance. In a larger study (Finch et al., 1975), it was found that impulsive children were more external in their locus of control, whereas reflective children were more internal in their locus of control.

Finally, we looked at the relationship between impulsive behavior and need for achievement. Again, we reasoned that there was a difference between impulsive and reflective children on motivational variables, and we found that children with a high need for achievement took longer to respond on the tasks and were more reflective (Finch, Crandell, & Deardorff, 1976).

In the above-mentioned studies we learned that impulsive children are not more anxious than reflective children, that impulsive children tend to employ pictures rather than words when they think, that impulsive children do not perceive event outcomes as being under their control, and that impulsive children possibly have a lower need for achievement than reflective children. Having demonstrated these differences, we then shifted our endeavors to a more practical application of this information. As clinicians we wanted to find ways to use this new information in our work with child-clients.

We soon discovered that related research in this area fit nicely with our own research findings. Meichenbaum and Goodman (1971) had taught impulsive children to talk to themselves while problem solving. Their training approach made impulsive children more reflective in their responding. From our point of view, which was developed and guided by our empirical findings, it seemed logical that self-instructional training taught impulsive children to think more symbolically, to see the relationship between their behavior and event outcomes, and consequently to develop a more reflective cognitive style. We decided to conduct a study with hospitalized emotionally disturbed impulsive children to test these hypotheses. Finch, Wilkinson, Nelson, and Montgomery (1975) compared three groups of youngsters. One group received training in verbal self-instructions, a second group only received training to delay before responding, and a third group was a test-retest control group. Results indicated that the children who were trained to employ verbal self-instructions were less impulsive in their responding, while children who were trained simply to delay took longer before responding but made as many mistakes as previously. The control group did not change. We were encouraged by the results of this initial treatment study but were somewhat humbled by the fact that although we had taught these children to respond more carefully, their performance was still more impulsive than that of normal children. That is, although their responding was slower and more careful, they would still be categorized as impulsive children.

We next decided to focus on the motivational aspects suggested by Finch et al. (1976) to explore the most efficient way to improve motivation in impulsive children. Nelson, Finch, and Hooke (1975) suggested that the reflection–impulsivity dimension might involve a motivation-for-success component as well as a fear-of-failure component. They reasoned that the behavior repertoire of the impulsive child might include the necessary components to respond in a more reflective manner but that the impulsive child might not have sufficient motivation to employ these components. In order to test this hypothesis, Nelson et al. (1975) compared a group of impulsive and reflective youngsters under reinforcement versus response-cost contingencies. Results of this study proved quite interesting, and we were pleasantly surprised by the findings. It was apparent that impulsive children responded better under conditions of response-cost, while reflective children responded better under conditions of reinforcement. That is, the impulsive children responded better when they were given rewards (tokens that could be later traded in on valued items) at the beginning of the session and had one taken away for each mistake made on the various tasks. Interestingly, there are apparently similar findings in studies with adult sociopaths. The exact nature of this relationship needs to be further investigated, but it opened some interesting possibilities for our study of impulsivity in children.

Taking this additional bit of information — that is, that impulsive children respond better to conditions of response-cost than they do to conditions of reinforcement — we decided to add a response-cost component to our treatment package for impulsive youngsters. Fortunately, at about this time a very impulsive boy was referred to our outpatient clinic, and he provided us with the opportunity to refine our procedures in a treatment case. (We believe that the case study format or single-subject experimental design lends itself to the development and refinement of new procedures. By focusing on an individual case, the therapist is able to examine and explore the problems that are actually encountered in the implementation of treatment. However, the case study should be seen as a vehicle to reach a goal rather than as the actual goal itself. Acknowledging our bias as clinical researchers, we propose that true treatment effectiveness needs to be demonstrated through carefully controlled comparison studies between matched groups.) Kendall and Finch (1976) instituted a multiple-baseline design in order to evaluate a combined response-cost and self-instruction procedure with this impulsive youngster. Observed behaviors improved, and report card and teacher comments indicated that the improvement actually generalized to the classroom situation. It should be noted that this youngster came to our attention again three years following the initial treatment. He was again manifesting behavioral problems and having difficulty in school, but his difficulty was not of an impulsive nature. In fact, he was readministered the MFF, and his responses were still categorized as reflective.

Major difficulties seemed to center around the increasing turmoil in the family, and it seems unlikely that symptom substitution can account for the difficulties that this boy was experiencing.

After these encouraging case study results, Kendall and Finch (1978) designed a group comparison study to evaluate the combined package of response-cost and verbal self-instructions on the impulsive behavior of emotionally disturbed youngsters. Again, the findings were encouraging, as there was evidence of generalization to the classroom. No change was observed in the hospital living units of the patients, however. This may have been due, at least in part, to the nature of the training tasks that were employed, because the materials were psychoeducational in nature. (Training tasks will be discussed in a later section.) The impulsive behavior on the living units generally involved aggressive and anger problems and eventually resulted in our moving into the area of investigating anger control with youngsters.

Furguson (1978) replicated the Kendall and Finch (1978) study and obtained mixed results. Again, there were indications of improvement in classroom behavior, but there was a failure of generalization to the living units. In addition, generalization to the classroom was demonstrated by teachers' ratings but not by the actual frequency counts of behaviors. The significance and meaning of this finding present some interesting possibilities. Further investigation might determine whether the categories of observed behaviors were somewhat insensitive to change or whether cognitive self-instructions resulted in more qualitative than quantitative changes in behavior.

Abikoff and Ramsey (1979) questioned the finding of Kendall and Finch (1978) on a statistical basis. They suggested that because the treatment and control groups were matched on the basis of MFF performance and not on the basis of behavioral ratings, an analysis of covariance would have been more appropriate for the behavioral ratings. When they conducted this analysis, Abikoff and Ramsey (1979) failed to find significant generalizations to the classroom. In responding to this criticism, Kendall and Finch (1979b) suggested that the question of generalization is certainly open to debate and that there is a need for data that look more closely at the type of generalization that might be expected.

Addressing this question, Kendall and Wilcox (1979) introduced a teacher rating scale designed to measure behaviors that might be expected to generalize in self-instructional training. In a treatment study conducted by these researchers (Kendall & Wilcox, 1980), the potential usefulness of this scale was demonstrated. Employing the teacher rating scale and a hyperactivity rating scale, they found significant generalization effects when a self-instructional training group was compared to a control group. Generalization of the effects of self-instructional training is a serious issue in the relevant clinical literature. An early assumption about cognitive-behavioral approaches was that they would lead to greater generalization than traditional behavior modification. Kendall and Braswell (1985) noted that early arguments for self-instructional training included the expectation that the child would acquire skills in one situation that could be transferred to other situations. Because children were taught to stop and think on their own, generalization would be increased. However, as noted by many investigators, including Whalen et al. (1985), this anticipated generalization has not always been found. Kendall and Braswell (1985) offered a number of suggestions for increasing the likelihood that skills learned in cognitive-behavioral training will transfer to other situations.

Nelson (1976) designed a study to evaluate the individual components in our treatment program. Fifty second- and third-grade children who were identified as impulsive were assigned to one of five groups: (a) response-cost plus verbal self-instructions, (b) response-cost, (c) verbal self-instructions, (d) a test-retest control group, and (e) a response-cost contingency group that was administered the MFF under response-cost contingencies during the second testing and under standard conditions otherwise. Each group was tested before and after training and given follow-up testing at 2½ weeks and at 6½ weeks after the posttesting. Results indicated that at posttesting, latency scores increased significantly in all treatment groups. However, only the verbal self-instructions training, the response-cost plus verbal self-instructions, and the response-cost contingency groups significantly decreased their error rates. At 2½ week follow-up testing, the performance of the response-cost plus verbal self-instructions training group (Group a) and the verbal self-instructions training group (Group c) was significantly more reflective when compared to the control group (Group d) in terms of both latencies and errors. The response-cost contingency group (Group e) differed from the control group only in terms of latencies. At 6-week follow-up, increased latencies and decreased errors on the MFF were maintained for the response-cost plus verbal self-instructions training and the verbal self-instructions groups, while the response-cost contingency group maintained only increased latencies.

The results of Nelson's (1976) study suggest that the verbal self-instructions portion of the treatment package produced the most enduring decrease in impulsiveness and that the gains obtained from the response-cost training were more short-lived. However, it should be noted that although significance was not reached, the greatest gains were made by the group receiving training in both verbal self-instructions and response-cost.

A study by Parrish and Erickson (1981) was designed to test the relative effectiveness of two cognitive strategies — visual scanning and verbal self-instructions. Parrish assigned 24 third-grade boys and girls to one of four groups: (a) scanning strategy instructions, (b) self-verbalization instructions, (c) scanning strategy plus self-verbalization instructions, and (d) attention control. Each child attended six 30-minute training sessions in which the particular training condition was applied, and each child was tested before, immediately after, and 5 weeks after training. At post-testing, both immediately after training and 5 weeks later, children in all of the cognitive treatment groups made fewer errors than children in the control group. In addition, at 5-week follow-up testing, children who received self-verbalization training or the combined treatment package responded less rapidly than the no-treatment control group. Children who received only scanning instructions did not respond less rapidly than the control group.

In summary, our interest in impulsive behavior grew out of our observations of children within clinical settings. Our research in the area began with laboratory studies investigating the nature of impulsivity. These early research efforts led to laboratory studies of treatment of impulsive children. Finally, we have conducted clinical treatment studies that have supported the utility of cognitive self-instructions for the treatment of impulsive children.

Training Materials

In our various research and clinical efforts, we have used a wide variety of training materials. Mazes are consistently enjoyed (by children as well as by trainers), and children seem to find them very interesting and challenging. In addition, mazes lend themselves to many choice points, many verbalizations, and many potential mistakes. We have used some of the Porteus Maze material and mazes we have found in various children's publications and educational material. In addition, we have attempted to design mazes that children enjoy and find motivating, such as a maze that depicts a tank attempting to travel across a mine field. Other mazes consist of treasure hunts, spy activities, and various obstacle courses. The challenge is to provide a task that will hold the attention and interest of a distractible, impulsive youngster long enough for us to be able to go through the tedious and sometimes boring process of self-instructions.

We have found that dot-to-dot drawings are also useful and interesting for children who are involved in learning to become less impulsive. When using this type of material, we frequently vary the letters and numbers in an alternating fashion so that the child must stop and think before progressing to the next dot. We have also used psychoeducational materials that present a series of plates containing four pictures, three of which are conceptually similar. The youngster's task is to find the one that does not belong with the others. In working on this problem the child verbalizes cognitions such as "What is it I have to do? — find the three that go together and the one that doesn't fit. This is a horse, this is a cow, this is a dog, and this is a shovel. Therefore these three are *animals,* so they go together. The answer is the shovel, because it doesn't go with the others." The therapist encourages reflective deliberation, regardless of the material being used.

We have also used a psychoeducational task in which figures, beads, or other geometric figures are presented in a sequential pattern that requires the youngster to choose the next in the series from an array of alternatives. Again, in impulsivity training the emphasis is on providing the youngster with a number of alternative responses and helping him or her engage in the verbal self-instructions/mediations that consider and evaluate the possibilities before choosing the one that is correct.

An additional training task consists of incomplete line drawings superimposed on square configurations of evenly spaced dots. The youngster is asked to use a pencil to complete the drawing so that it will be the same on both sides. This task is very similar to the mazes in that the youngster is presented with alternatives and must choose the one that will best reach the eventual goal of completing the figure. Also, we have used some of the items from the Leiter International Performance Scale and other test material that lends itself to the use of verbal self-instructions. Recently Kendall (1989) developed a book of potential training materials that are useful in working with impulsive youngsters.

Other resources we have used with good success are the Palkes, Stewart, and Kahana (1968) training aids. These aids consist of 5-by-7–inch visual reminder cards upon which instructions and self-directed commands are printed. Each card also contains ink line drawings that emphasize the nature of the desired response. We find these to be exceedingly useful with youngsters, for in addition to providing cues for appropriate verbalizations, they also provide a certain degree of comic relief. The trainer can comment on the need for a boy to pretend that he has big ears, that his eyes are wide open, and that he needs to use them as he's coming to a stop sign. For those who are interested in teaching children to engage in verbal self-instructions, we strongly suggest the Palkes article.

More interpersonally focused materials have been employed in some studies, such as those by Camp, Blom, Herbert, and van Doornick (1977), and it may be that if the interpersonal training materials were varied to fit the problem of the youngster, more powerful generalization could be obtained. This is open to future investigation.

It must be emphasized that the primary importance of training materials is to encourage the youngster to engage in verbal self-instructions. Although the training materials are necessary and should be carefully selected according to the age and interests of the child, the clinician must focus primary attention on the cognitive processes of the child.

Verbal Self-Instructions

Verbal self-instructions are actually step-by-step verbalizations about defining the problem (What is it I am to do?), approaching the problem (I'm to find my way out of this mine field without bumping into a mine; I'll do fine if I go carefully and slowly), focusing attention (I need to look ahead and choose my path carefully), making coping statements (Uh oh, that's not right; let me erase that; I need to go more slowly), and developing statements of self-reinforcement (Hey, I'm doing a neat job. I took my time and did that one right). These self-statements must be closely geared to match the needs of the child and designed to follow a specific sequence. Initially the therapist models the task performance and talks out loud to himself or herself while the youngster observes (cognitive modeling). Next the child performs the task using verbal self-instructions and talking aloud (overt self-guidance). The therapist then models the task while whispering the self-instructions (faded, overt modeling), and this step is followed by having the child perform the task while whispering the verbal self-instructions (faded, overt self-guidance). Next the therapist performs the task after telling the child that although the self-talk will continue, it will take place "inside" and will not be heard. At this point it is advisable for the therapist to occasionally whisper one or two important words. Finally the youngster performs the task while employing the verbal self-instructions in a covert manner (covert self-guidance). In this phase of training we frequently check to make sure that the child is talking to himself or herself, and we continue to provide encouragement to do so.

Clinical observation suggests that conceptual rather than concrete self-instructions are more effective, and this assumption is supported by at least one study. Kendall and Wilcox (1980) examined different types of instructional training and the training outcome with a group of subjects who were referred by teachers because of an apparent lack of self-control. Instructional training included concrete labeling or conceptual labeling. Children in the concrete-labeling group received instructions relevant to a specific task, while those in the conceptual group received instructions relevant to the task but broad enough to possibly generalize to other behaviors and situations. The authors reported that at posttest and 1-month follow-up, teacher ratings improved for self-control and hyperactivity, with stronger treatment effects for the conceptual-labeling group.

We cannot overemphasize the importance of creating an easy-going, lighthearted situation in which the youngster can have some fun and the therapist can "ham it up." Learning verbal self-instructions is not inherently fun for most impulsive children. Therefore, the therapist needs to make an effort to ensure that the youngster's work is worthwhile and is reinforced. At times we have become nearly desperate in our attempts to encourage youngsters to engage in the training, and we have used a wide variety of procedures to motivate them to participate. Used most frequently (and developed as a result of our research) is a response-cost component, which will be discussed in more detail later. Another procedure is telling the youngster such things as, "Yes, we know it's not fun, but it's kind of like taking medicine—it's good for you, and it makes you feel better." This is generally said in a joking manner, and frequently the therapist will vary voice tone and inflection to mimic an "old crone" or maybe even a "witch doctor" or some other humorous character.

Response-Cost Component

As mentioned earlier, the motivational aspects of the child's willingness to engage in verbal self-instruction are extremely important. Many youngsters feel that verbal self-instructions are difficult, a waste of time, and unnecessary. Therefore, in addition to our assurances and explanations about the importance of self-instructions, we have found it necessary to include a response-cost component. The child is given a group of chips or paper money and told that an array of reinforcements is available at the end of the session. Youngsters are told that they will lose the "tokens" for failure to engage in the self-instructions. It is explained that the response-cost is contingent upon the youngster's failure to exhibit verbal instructions rather than on actually getting the correct answer. The sequence might go as follows: "All right now, these are your chips. You have 12 chips that you can keep, and at the end of the session you can trade them in for one of the items you see here (the therapist points to a card or reinforcement menu with a wide array of small edibles and trinkets taped on it). However, each time that you don't do the verbal self-instructions, you're going to lose one of your chips. Therefore, the more you work at doing the verbal self-instructions, the more chips you will have left at the end of the session to trade for these items. OK, do you understand that?" At this point the therapist encourages the youngster to repeat the conditions that are in effect for the session to ensure that these contingencies are understood. We have found that a youngster typically will not lose more than two or three chips during a training session. In addition, we have rarely found it to be a major problem when a chip is removed. Of course, some youngsters complain, but most accept it as being the consequence of their behavior. After a chip is forfeited, the rules are explained again, and we generally try to use more conceptual labeling in our explanations. That is, we say, "You are not using the verbal self-instructions; you weren't talking to yourself," or "You weren't thinking aloud. That's why you lost one of your chips." In the few instances that became problematic, training was stopped briefly, and the rules were explained again to the youngster to ensure understanding and to restore a more calm and receptive state.

Training Setting

Training should be conducted in a quiet setting that is relatively free from distraction. For instance, care should be taken to limit interruptions from telephones, colleagues, and other children. As much as possible the room should be barren of material that might distract the child. At times we have found it necessary for particularly distractible youngsters to come to the training room for a couple of initial sessions to participate in structured tasks. This serves the purpose of habituating the child to the new environment. When working with very difficult children, we have used rooms that do not have windows. Although this is sometimes depressing for the therapist or trainer, it is of considerable help with many of the distractible, impulsive youngsters with whom we work.

Training Sessions

Generally we use 8 to 10 training sessions in working with impulsive youngsters in a clinical setting. We have used a minimum number of 6 sessions, and we have conducted as many as 20 sessions. In our experimental work with these procedures, we set a definite predetermined number of sessions for each individual. Although this ensures experimental rigor, it limits the flexibility available to the clinician who is more interested in tailoring the program to an individual youngster. Those instances that have required us to extend the usual number of sessions involved particularly difficult children for whom a wide variety of procedures were needed to obtain maximum cooperation and effort.

The following is a breakdown of session-by-session procedures. Again, the reader should remember that these are only guidelines and are not firm, inflexible procedures. We are, of course, more rigid and standardized in our research efforts than in our clinical work. When our main goal is to reduce impulsive behaviors, we tend to be very flexible, and the format of the sessions is altered according to the needs of the particular child.

Session 1

During Session 1 the youngster is introduced to the idea of verbal self-instructions. The therapist tells the youngster that some children have problems because they respond so quickly that they do not consider all of the possibilities available to them. The youngster is then engaged in conversation and is encouraged to see how this description fits some of the behaviors that have resulted in the referral for treatment. Next the young-ster is given a brief description of the type of procedures that will be used and is asked if there are any questions about these procedures. Most youngsters are very hesitant to ask questions, and the therapist may wish to address the questions that are not asked. For example, many children are embarrassed when they initially engage in self-instructions. The therapist can say, "You know, a lot of boys and girls are a little hesitant to do this when they first start, because it makes them feel kind of funny or embar-rassed. But it's really the way we all kind of think anyway, and there is nothing to be embarrassed about. No one will be able to hear you but me, and I really like to hear children talk to themselves." Some children may be concerned about appearing "crazy" if they talk to themselves (especially in an inpatient setting). We usually respond to this concern by explaining that all of us talk to ourselves in one way or another and that the people who are seen as being crazy are not talking to themselves but to someone who is not there. The therapist must attend to these issues and to idiosyncratic ques-tions, which demand honest, straightforward, reasonable explanations to the child.

After these reassurances the therapist introduces the first task and reminds the child that the task will be performed aloud so that the child can learn how to do it. The first sequence might go something like this (in a "Which One Doesn't Fit?" task):

> *Let's see now; what am I supposed to do? I am supposed to find out which of these things doesn't go with the others. All right, I see there are four pictures here, so I need to look at each one of these very, very carefully. All right, the first one is a clock. The second one is a clock, too. Here's another clock, too. Ah, but this one is a cup and saucer. These three go together because they're clocks. OK, I got this one. It's the cup and saucer that doesn't belong. All right, I did good because I stopped, thought about what it was I was supposed to do, took my time doing it, and thought about everything carefully.*

After using verbal self-instructions in solving the problem task, the therapist instructs the child to do the same thing. When a response-cost component is used, we generally introduce it very early in the session before presenting the training task, and we take care to explain the purpose and procedure to the child. The following instructions can be used.

> *All right, what I'm going to do is give you these 10 chips, which you can trade in at the end of the session for one of the rewards that I've shown you. Remember, each time that you don't engage in the verbal self-instructions, I will take one of the chips away from you. You will*

lose a chip for not talking to yourself. OK, do you have any questions?

The therapist then presents the training material and asks the youngster to complete the task, using verbal self-instructions. At this point in training the child often needs the therapist's help to exercise appropriate self-talk (overt, external guidance). Many youngsters are still hesitant to engage in the verbal self-instructions, and they need to be encouraged. There is no hard and fast rule about achievement of an acceptable level of verbal self-instruction, but we generally take a successive approximation approach. As long as the youngster puts forth effort and tries to develop self-talk skills, no chips are forfeited. Most children learn to exhibit an acceptable level of verbal self-instruction after only two or three tasks modeled by the therapist. As they learn, we continue to work in the same manner—that is, we provide the verbal self-instructions for each task and then have the youngster do the same. Overlearning takes place because the youngster works on several tasks beyond an acceptable performance level. By this time the youngster is probably beginning to tire. Session 1 is terminated after approximately 20 to 30 minutes. Again, the sessions are designed to be brief, interesting, and relaxed.

Session 2

The therapist begins Session 2 by asking the child to recall the first session and to give a brief explanation of what took place. If this explanation is acceptable, the therapist introduces a new task utilizing new materials. If necessary, the therapist may reiterate the rules and objectives. As a review, the therapist models appropriate self-talk, and the youngster engages in the verbal self-instructions while performing a training task. At this point the child may need assistance in engaging in this more reflective self-talk (overt, external guidance); however, after two or three training tasks have been completed without difficulty, the therapist introduces the next section (faded, overt modeling). This may be done in the following manner.

OK, now I'm going to continue to talk to myself and kind of think out loud, but what I'm going to do is kind of whisper to myself so you won't be able to hear me as well as you could before. I'm going to continue to stop, think, and consider all the alternatives that I have, but I'm going to be doing it in a whispering manner. Now watch me.

After the therapist whispers while solving a task, the youngster is instructed to do the same. By this point, most youngsters understand the concept of verbal self-instructions and find it easy to make the transition to whispering. However, we have encountered several instances in which a youngster continued to talk out loud and had to be encouraged to talk more softly. We generally do not take chips from the youngster for failure to whisper but simply continue to encourage "softer and softer" self-verbalizations. If this becomes an issue, it is helpful to employ a cassette recorder with a voice-operated light that flashes when the youngster's voice reaches a certain level. In this way, feedback can easily be provided to a youngster who is not whispering.

During the second session the main goal is to ensure that the youngster is whispering appropriate verbal self-instructions. Because some children reach this goal quickly, the therapist may introduce covert speech at this point. For this introduction the following sequence may be used.

All right, I'm going to be solving the problems just like we've been doing, and I'm going to be talking to myself. But you know what? This time, you're not going to be able to hear me. I'm going to be talking way back in my throat, and it's not going to be a whisper because you're not even going to be able to hear it at all. I'm going to be talking to myself. OK?

At this point, children often laugh and think this is a funny idea. On the other hand, some children do not quite understand what the therapist means; therefore, further explanation may be needed. When it is clear that the child understands the procedure, the therapist solves a task while using covert verbal self-instructions. The child observes. We believe that it is helpful to let one or two key words "slip" in a very faint whisper (just loudly enough for the youngster to hear), such as, "Take my time. Think before I do it." This emphasizes that the therapist is actually talking covertly while working on the task.

Session 3

The therapist begins Session 3 by asking the youngster to describe the previous session. By this point, most children have become involved and can explain what is going on without any difficulty. The therapist reintroduces the task, sets the rules again, and, regardless of the youngster's progress in the previous session, begins with the initial phase of talking out loud (cognitive modeling). This serves as a check on the child's ability to perform the task and also provides continuity between the sessions. Usually only one or two tasks are required before moving on to a review of the whispering phase. Depending upon the child's progress in the previous session, the covert speech training is followed by training in covert self-guidance. As emphasized throughout, the therapist must organize and conduct the session to meet the needs and progress of the child.

Session 4

By now the youngster usually knows what to expect during the session, and the therapist can move rapidly through the steps before introducing the next stage. Reinforcement and praise need to be given freely, and the youngster is encouraged to verbalize self-reinforcement. This is an important issue for each session, but it needs to be emphasized during these latter phases as the child progresses toward independence.

Sessions 5, 6, 7, and 8

During the final sessions the structure of training continues as before. At the end of each session, a new phase is included to concretize the newly learned cognitive strategies. In this additional phase the child's task is to become the teacher of verbal self-instructions. The most efficacious way of doing this in the therapy situation is simply to reverse roles. The therapist becomes the student, and the child conducts the session. The following role-reversal format might be followed.

> *All right, this is what we're going to do now. I'm going to let you be the therapist/doctor/me, and I'm going to be you. Now, we're going to pretend that I'm just coming in, and your job is to teach me all about this talking-to-yourself stuff and explain why we do it. OK?*

Most youngsters enjoy this activity, particularly when, in role playing the child, we intentionally "go too far," make an error, and lose some tokens. However, a few children have been reluctant to participate in role reversal and have needed encouragement.

In a variation of the role-reversal procedures, Nelson and Evans (1984) obtained modest results in their attempt to have a "trained" youngster instruct another impulsive child. Although work such as this is exploratory, it should be noted that the severity of both the impulsivity and the interpersonal deficits of many inpatient children might prohibit such an approach. The pairing or "yoking" of two impulsive children must be done carefully, and, at the very minimum, there must be an interpersonal attraction between the two youngsters who work together. In addition, we have been concerned that a youngster who has just completed the training might imitate the more impulsive behavior of the newly introduced child. However, Nelson and Behler (1990) conducted a single-subject experiment to examine the effect of self-instructional peer teaching with two 10-year-old hospitalized boys. Multiple dependent measures were employed to ascertain changes in both the "child-teacher" and the "child-pupil" — for example, direct behavior observations of on- and off-task classroom behavior, teacher-assessment measures of self-control and hyperactivity, cognitive impulsivity assessment, and self-reported behavioral and self-concept measures. On most of these measures, beneficial effects were noted for the child-teacher after the traditional individualized self-instructional training, and further improvements were evident after he taught the self-instructional procedures to the other child. Some improvements were also apparent for the child-pupil, and these improvements were maintained at a 2-week follow-up. There was significant variability among the multiple dependent measures, as they tapped into a wide range of improvements that could be expected from self-instructional training. Overall, this single-subject inquiry suggests cautious optimism in utilizing such an approach with more disturbed children.

Similarly, Kendall and Zupan (1981) examined the relative effectiveness of cognitive-behavioral treatment in an individual versus a group setting and compared these treatment groups with a control group. They found that children who were trained in a group setting demonstrated significant improvement. However, caution should be used to ensure that appropriate behaviors are being modeled and that an increase in the number of children being trained does not reduce the probability of successful treatment.

Concluding Remarks

The preceding session-by-session guide must be individually tailored for each boy or girl whose impulsive cognitive style creates difficulties at home, at school, and in interpersonal situations. Each therapist who works with impulsive children will need to devise self-instructional techniques that work best for him or her.

We have used a number of procedures in attempts to ensure that these reflective cognitive strategies are actively utilized by the child in situations outside the therapy sessions. These procedures include providing multiple therapists to do the training, conducting training in several environments, varying the type of material used in the training sessions, and using various imagined/play techniques (e.g., in the last session the child imagines that the therapist is actually the teacher who is assigning a task in the classroom). Training gains may also be enhanced by having the teacher help the youngster modify these self-instructions to actual classroom material.

We have also included parents in the training sessions and have encouraged them to continue these procedures at home. To facilitate home instruction we have provided a number of games such as the parlor game of "Twenty Questions." Parents are instructed to introduce the game in a natural situation (e.g., riding in the car) as an activity for a relatively quiet period. The parent asks the child to guess "the item that I am thinking about" and tells the child that "yes" or "no" responses will be given to the guesses. Most impulsive children will immediately attempt to guess the correct response, and this haphazard method will not be successful. After the child gives up, or after a certain number of questions have been asked (usually 20), the parent says, "OK, now it's your turn to think about something, and I'll see if I can guess what it is. Remember, only answer questions with 'yes' or 'no'." The parent then proceeds to ask questions. The sequence may be:

All right, what I'm supposed to do is to figure out what it is that you're thinking about. All right, is it an animal? (Child says "no"). OK, it's not an animal; therefore, that eliminates a lot of things around here. Let's see, is it something that you eat? (Child says "yes"), and so on.

By employing these constraint-seeking questions the parent models a more reflective approach and can volunteer to teach this approach to the child. Thus, a different environment provides the opportunity for the youngster to practice the skills that have been learned in the training sessions. We have observed that many parents work hard to develop unique and innovative ways to use verbal self-instructions and that children enjoy the additional attention that the games and tasks provide. Also, teachers can be encouraged to use such games with targeted children or with the entire class.

Final Thoughts

In addition to providing guidelines for the use of self-instructional techniques with children, this chapter has outlined relevant research in the area of cognitive training with children. In recent years, many researchers and clinicians have provided useful strategies to guide those who use cognitive techniques as a treatment method. Although the effectiveness of self-instructional techniques has been demonstrated for certain behaviors, current research continues to seek the situations and contexts that are most appropriate for these techniques. After their review of studies using self-instruction techniques with children, Kendall & Braswell (1985) concluded that cognitive training works best in combination with behavioral contingencies.

In addition, they highlighted the need for the cognitive training to be an interactive process between the therapist and the child — a process in which the therapist teaches self-instructional techniques, models the appropriate behaviors, and provides opportunity for practice.

Outcome studies that use self-instructional techniques to modify impulsive behavior show a diverse pattern of findings, and, therefore, we have purposely highlighted studies demonstrating both favorable and less-than-favorable outcomes. Although the inconsistent findings may be somewhat disappointing, short-term gains have been shown in numerous studies. Specific treatment variables continue to interest researchers and clinicians in their work for maintenance and generalization of treatment gains.

In her comprehensive review of self-instructional techniques, Copeland (1982; Copeland & Hammell, 1980) outlined major subject variables to consider in the use of cognitive intervention. In concluding our remarks we will address three of these variables (age, cognitive level, and child involvement).

Copeland reported that elementary school children are more likely to benefit from self-instructional training than preschoolers. Pressley (1979) suggested that preschoolers need training in concrete strategies, and conceptual training was found to be superior to concrete training in a group of 8–12-year-old non–self-controlled children (Kendall & Wilcox, 1980).

Although Kendall (1977) emphasized that success in training requires attention to the child's level of cognitive development, Cohen, Meyers, Schlesser, & Rodick (1982) demonstrated that the cognitive level of the child interacts with different types of training. The authors reported that the concrete operational children who received a "directed discovery" approach were best able to generalize these skills to other situations.

Involvement and participation in training have been shown to predict treatment gains. Braswell, Kendall, Braith, Carey, and Vye (1985) postulated that the child's level of involvement in the self-instruction training would affect the treatment outcome. They examined the child's suggestions for the therapy sessions, and, as expected, improvement on teacher ratings was greatest for children who were perceived to be the most involved by offering the most suggestions. Also, it appears that generalization of treatment effects is enhanced when cognitively prepared children are actively involved in their training (Kendall & Braswell, 1985).

Although Abikoff and Gittleman (1985) found no added benefits of cognitive training as an adjunct to treatment with stimulants, there are some indications that the effects of self-instructional training and stimulant medications are additive. In a case study, Pelham, Schredler, Bologna, and Contrearas (1980) reported increased treatment effectiveness in a design which combined medication with a behavioral program that included self-instruction. Likewise, Hinshaw, Whalen, and Henker (1984) reported that combining cognitive-behavioral interventions with methylphenidate significantly improved the behavior of attention deficit disordered boys. For clinicians and researchers this is an area that hold promise and interest, as the combination of biological and psychological treatments is receiving increased attention in the research community. In fact, this currently seems to be the treatment of choice for many children who have attention deficit disorders (DuPaul & Barkley, 1990).

References

Abikoff, H., & Gittleman, R. (1985). Hyperactive children treated with stimulants: Is cognitive training a useful adjunct? *Archives of General Psychiatry, 42,* 953–961.

Abikoff, H., & Ramsey, P. P. (1979). A critical comment on Kendall and Finch's cognitive behavioral group comparison study. *Journal of Consulting and Clinical Psychology, 47,* 1104–1106.

Bentler, P. M., & McClain, J. A. (1976). A multitrait-multimethod analysis of reflection–impulsivity. *Child Development, 47,* 218–226.

Block, J., Block, J., & Harrington, D. (1974). Some misgivings about the Matching Familiar Figures test as a measure of reflection–impulsivity. *Developmental Psychology, 10,* 611–632.

Braswell, L., Kendall, P. C., Braith, J., Carey, M., & Vye, C. (1984). "Involvement" in cognitive-behavioral therapy with children: Process and its relationship to outcome. *Cognitive Therapy and Research, 9*(6), 611–630.

Bruner, J. S., Oliver, R. R., & Greenfield, P. M. (1966). *Studies in cognitive growth.* New York: Wiley.

Camp, B. W., Blom, G., Herbert, R., & van Doornick, W. (1977). "Think Aloud": A program for developing self-control in young aggressive boys. *Journal of Abnormal Psychology, 5,* 157–168.

Cohen, R., Meyers, A., Schlesser, R., & Rodick, J. D. (1982). *Generalization of self-instructions: Effects of cognitive level and training procedures.* Unpublished manuscript, Memphis State University.

Copeland, A. P. (1982). Individual differences factors in children's self-management: Toward individualized treatments. In P. Karoly & F. H. Kanfer (Eds.), *Self-management and behavior change: From theory to practice.* New York: Pergamon Press.

Copeland, A. P., & Hammel, R. (1980). Subject variables in cognitive self-instruction training. *Cognitive Therapy and Research, 5,* 405–420.

DuPaul, G. P., & Barkley, R. A. (1990). Medication therapy. In R. A. Barkley (Ed.), *Attention deficit hyperactivity disorder: A handbook for diagnosis and treatment.* New York: Guilford.

Egeland, B., Bielke, P., & Kendall, P. (1980). Achievement and adjustment correlates of the Matching Familiar Figures test. *Journal of School Psychology, 18,* 361–372.

Finch, A. J, Jr., Crandell, C., & Deardorff, P. A. (1976). Reflection–impulsivity and need for achievement in emotionally disturbed children. *Journal of Genetic Psychology, 129,* 329–331.

Finch, A. J, Jr., Kendall, P. C., Deardorff, P. A., Anderson, J., & Sitarz, A. M. (1975). Reflection–impulsivity, locus of control and persistence behavior in emotionally disturbed children. *Journal of Consulting and Clinical Psychology, 43,* 748.

Finch, A. J, Jr., & Montgomery, L. E. (1973). Reflection–impulsivity and information seeking in emotionally disturbed children. *Journal of Abnormal Child Psychology, 1,* 358–362.

Finch, A. J, Jr., & Nelson, W. M., III. (1976). Reflection–impulsivity and behavior problems in emotionally disturbed boys. *Journal of Genetic Psychology, 128,* 271–274.

Finch, A. J, Jr., Nelson, W. M., III, Montgomery, L. E., & Stein, A. B. (1974). Reflection–impulsivity and locus of control in emotionally disturbed children. *Journal of Genetic Psychology, 125,* 273–275.

Finch, A. J, Jr., Pezzuti, K. A., Montgomery, L. E., & Kemp, S. R. (1974). Reflection–impulsivity and academic attainment in emotionally disturbed children. *Journal of Abnormal Child Psychology, 2,* 71–74.

Finch, A. J, Jr., Wilkinson, M. D., Nelson, W. M., III, & Montgomery, L. E. (1975). Modification of an impulsive cognitive tempo in emotionally disturbed boys. *Journal of Abnormal Child Psychology, 3,* 47–51.

Furguson, K. *Modification of impulsive responding.* Unpublished master's thesis, Virginia Commonwealth University, Richmond.

Hinshaw, S. P., Whalen, C. K., & Henker, B., (1984). Cognitive-behavioral and pharmacologic interventions for hyperactive boys: Comparative and combined effects. *Journal of Consulting and Clinical Psychology, 52,* 739–749.

Kagan, J., & Messer, S. B. (1975). A reply to "some misgivings about the Matching Familiar Figures Test as a measure of impulsivity, *11,* 244–248.

Kendall, P. C. (1989). *Stop and think workbook.* Unpublished manuscript, Temple University, Philadelphia.

Kendall, P. C., & Braswell, L. (1985). *Cognitive-behavioral therapy for impulsive children.* New York: Guilford.

Kendall, P. C., & Finch, A. J, Jr. (1976). A cognitive-behavioral treatment for impulse control: A case study. *Journal of Consulting and Clinical Psychology, 44,* 852–857.

Kendall, P. C., & Finch, A. J, Jr. (1978). A cognitive-behavioral treatment for impulsivity: A group comparison study. *Journal of Consulting and Clinical Psychology, 46,* 110–118.

Kendall, P. C., & Finch, A. J, Jr. (1979a). Developing nonimpulsive behavior in children: Cognitive-behavioral strategies for self-control. In P. C. Kendall & S. D. Hollon (Eds.), *Cognitive-behavioral interventions: Theory, research, and procedures.* New York: Academic Press.

Kendall, P. C., & Finch, A. J, Jr. (1979b). Reanalysis: A reply. *Journal of Consulting and Clinical Psychology, 47,* 1107–1108.

Kendall, P. C., & Wilcox, L. E. (1979). Self-control in children: Development of a rating scale. *Journal of Consulting and Clinical Psychology, 47,* 1020–1029.

Kendall, P. C., & Wilcox, L. E. (1980). Cognitive-behavioral treatment for impulsivity: Concrete versus conceptual training in non-self-controlled problem children. *Journal of Consulting and Clinical Psychology, 48,* 80–91.

Kendall, P. C., & Zupan, B. A. (1981). Individual versus group application of cognitive-behavioral strategies for developing self-control in children. *Behavior Therapy, 12,* 344–359.

Meichenbaum, D. H., & Goodman, J. (1971). Training impulsive children to talk to themselves: A means of developing self-control. *Journal of Abnormal Psychology, 77,* 115–126.

Messer, S. B. (1976). Reflection–impulsivity: A review. *Psychological Bulletin, 83,* 1026–1052.

Montgomery, L. E. (1974). Reflection–impulsivity in emotionally disturbed and normal children. Unpublished doctoral dissertation, University of Southern Mississippi, Hattiesburg.

Montgomery, L. E., & Finch, A. J, Jr. (1975). Reflection–impulsivity and locus of control in emotionally disturbed children. *Journal of Genetic Psychology, 126,* 89–91.

Nelson, W. M., III. (1976). Cognitive-behavioral strategies in modifying an impulsive cognitive style. Unpublished doctoral dissertation, Virginia Commonwealth University, Richmond.

Nelson, W. M., III, & Behler, J. (1990). Cognitive impulsivity training: The effects of peer teaching. *Journal of Behavior Therapy and Experimental Psychiatry, 20,* 303–309.

Nelson, W. M., III, & Evans, H. (1984). Cognitive-behavioral impulsivity training: The effects of peer teaching on "teachers" and "pupils." Unpublished manuscript, Xavier University, Cincinnati, OH.

Nelson, W. M., Finch, A. J, Jr., & Hooke, J. F. (1975). Effects of reinforcement and response-cost on cognitive style in emotionally disturbed boys. *Journal of Abnormal Psychology, 84,* 425–428.

Ollendick, T. H., & Finch, A. J, Jr. (1973). Reflection–impulsivity in brain-damaged and normal children. *Perceptual and Motor Skills, 36,* 654.

Palkes, H., Stewart, M., & Kahana, B. (1968). Porteus Maze performance of hyperactive boys after training in self-directed verbal commands. *Child Development, 39,* 817–826.

Parrish, J. M., & Erickson, M. T. (1981). A comparison of cognitive strategies in modifying the cognitive style of impulsive third-grade children. *Cognitive Therapy and Research, 5,* 71–84.

Pelham, W. E., Schnedler, R. W., Bologna, N. C., & Contreras, J. A. (1980). Behavioral and stimulant treatment of hyperactive children: A therapy study with methylphenidate probes in a within-subject design. *Journal of Applied Behavior Analysis, 13,* 221–236.

Pressley, M. (1979). Increasing children's self-control through cognitive interventions. *Review of Educational Research, 49,* 319–370.

Spielberger, C. D. (1973). Preliminary manual for the State-Trait Anxiety Inventory for Children. Palo Alto, CA: Consulting Psychologist Press.

Stein, A. B., Finch, A. J, Jr., Hooke, J. F., Montgomery, L. E., & Nelson, W. M., III. (1975). Cognitive tempo and the mode of representation in emotionally disturbed and normal children. *Journal of Psychology, 90,* 197–201.

Whalen, C. K., Henker, B., & Hinshaw, S. P. (1985). Cognitive-behavioral therapies for hyperactive children: Premises, problems, and prospects. *Journal of Abnormal Child Psychology, 13,* 391–410.

CHAPTER EIGHT

Coping Skills for Anxiety Control in Children

NANCY GRACE ANTHONY SPIRITO

A. J FINCH, JR. EDITH S. OTT

The last two decades have witnessed the growth of cognitive-behavioral theory and research in clinical psychology. The abundance of research in this area has resulted in numerous publications and in the birth of a journal, *Cognitive Therapy and Research*. For the most part the published research has been devoted to cognitive-behavioral intervention techniques with a wide variety of subject populations — from test-anxious college students to persons with chronic pain. Although the professional reader can easily grasp the general flavor of the cognitive-behavioral techniques, the subtleties of the treatment process are for the most part ignored. Consequently, the clinician who is interested in using a cognitive-behavioral approach in the treatment of a specific client is often left grasping at straws. It is necessary to leaf through books and articles in the attempt to discern the basic treatment strategy and to adapt techniques for test-anxious college students to the more perplexing and diffuse presenting problems of a "real client," adult or child.

This chapter is designed for the practicing clinician who is interested in developing a cognitive-behavioral treatment program for a child/adolescent client whose presenting problem is anxiety. It does not offer a set of inflexible principles that must be followed in order to achieve therapeutic results. Rather, the chapter presents guidelines that can be modified according to the needs of the individual child or adolescent and the presenting problem.

These guidelines are based on cognitive-behavioral methods that incorporate a "coping" component. Coping techniques typically involve active involvement of clients in the identification of anxiety and in the implementation of anxiety-reducing methods. The goals of coping techniques are to teach skills that will eventually enable the client to cope independently with distressing events and to apply these skills to a wide range of anxiety-provoking situations beyond the initial target problem. Two methods that have been developed to facilitate the individual as a "coper" include anxiety management training (Suinn & Richardson, 1971; Suinn, 1986) and stress inoculation (Meichenbaum, 1975, 1977, 1985). These were selected for discussion because of their applicability to anxiety problems and because they have been used in the treatment of childhood and/or adolescent anxiety disorders. Stress inoculation will be emphasized because it is one of the most effective techniques for work with children.

The following sections will provide (a) a general review of the research that discusses coping methods for the treatment of anxiety, (b) descriptions of anxiety management training and stress inoculation as well as guidelines for their implementation, and (c) a sample videotape script for a test-anxious child.

Coping Approaches to Anxiety Management

Behavior therapists have become increasingly interested in teaching their clients active coping skills to provide them with resources to cope independently with anxiety-provoking situations. A major reason for teaching coping skills is a desire to increase the generalizability of training effects (Meichenbaum, 1977). Traditional behavioral procedures for anxiety disorders tend to focus on a situation-specific response to discrete stimuli, whereas the client who acquires coping skills can apply these skills to many anxiety-provoking situations. An additional reason for the increased attention to coping techniques for the treatment of anxiety is the notion that coping can be used as prevention. Barrios and Shigetomi (1979) noted that people tend to learn to cope with anxiety in a haphazard manner. Preferably, coping skills are taught to individuals in an organized fashion and can limit the development of debilitating anxiety.

In pursuit of these goals a number of studies have attempted to apply coping skills techniques in order to control anxiety. The majority of these studies have been conducted with various kinds of adult anxieties. For example, Jerremalm, Jansson, and Ost (1986) and Jaremko and colleagues (Jaremko, 1980, 1983; Jaremko, Hadfield, & Walker, 1980) used stress inoculation with socially anxious adults who were experiencing a wide range of social interaction problems including dating and speech anxiety. Also, anxiety management training has been used to treat anxiety-state disorders (Jannoun, Oppenheimer, & Gelder, 1982), to reduce general anxiety among college students (Daley, Bloom, Deffenbacher, & Stewart, 1983), and to lessen specific anxieties such as evaluation anxiety (Deffenbacher, Michaels, Daley, & Michaels, 1980). Other coping methods have also been used for the treatment of anxiety related to sports (Mace & Carroll, 1985), to writing (Salovey & Haar, 1983), to chronic anxiety (Long, 1985), and to professional stress-related problems, such as those involved in nursing and in military training (Novaco, Cook, & Sarason, 1983; West, Horan, & Games, 1984).

Relative to research conducted with adults, few studies have been published involving coping procedures used to manage anxiety among children and adolescents (Ramirez, Kratochwill, & Morris, 1987). Kendall, Howard, and Epps (1988) suggested that in the literature related to this youthful population, the effectiveness of coping procedures has been most frequently documented for control of test anxiety, anxiety associated with medical and dental procedures, and general fears, particularly children's nighttime fears.

Test and Evaluation Anxiety

Stevens and colleagues (Stevens, 1979; Stevens & Phil, 1983) pointed out that students who fail scholastically, regardless of remediation, are more anxious, less confident, and utilize fewer coping statements. In addition, Zatz and Chassin (1983) identified the self-statements made by test-anxious children. These include debilitating self-comments such as "I'm doing poorly; everyone usually does better than me; I don't do well on tests like this." Furthermore, these children make fewer positive, adaptive statements such as "I am doing this the best I can." These self-statements can inhibit the child from responding adaptively and thus can lead to confirmation regarding the inability to perform well on tests (Ollendick & Francis, 1988). In light of these findings, several researchers examined the efficacy of modifying self-talk among test-anxious children. Stevens and Phil (1983) assessed the effectiveness of coping skills training among seventh-graders who, compared to a control group of average students, were at risk for school failure. Two coping programs were utilized. Both involved role playing, modeling, and rehearsal. In addition, the structured program emphasized self-instruction techniques and also used problem solving (D'Zurilla & Goldfried, 1971). In contrast, students in the unstructured program were encouraged to develop their own coping strategies. Results indicated that both coping groups improved with respect to performance on the Coding and Mazes subtests of the WISC-R, teacher evaluation of coping abilities, and the number and quality of the strategies that they were able to generate. Although no significant differences between coping and control groups were found in posttraining performance under stressful testing conditions, there was a trend for the coping groups — particularly for the at-risk students — to show improved performance under stressful conditions. In addition, although there were no significant differences between the coping and control groups with respect to improved grades, there was a tendency toward improved mathematics grades for the at-risk students who received training.

Leal, Baxter, Martin, and Marx (1981) evaluated the relative effectiveness of systematic desensitization and cognitive treatment with test-anxious tenth graders. The adolescents were screened to ensure that test anxiety was not simply an artifact of generalized anxiety. Treatment was administered in six 1-hour weekly group sessions. The cognitive modification procedure was based on techniques used by Holroyd (1976) and Meichenbaum (1972) and involved an explanation that anxiety resulted from self-talk occurring before and during the exams. Subjects were taught to become aware of these self-statements, to label emotional arousal, and to replace negative self-talk with more positive statements. The systematic desensitization was also conducted in a group format and followed procedures outlined by Holroyd (1976). Results demonstrated that subjects who received cognitive modification treatment reported significantly lower levels of anxiety as compared to those who received systematic desensitization. No clinically significant conclusions were drawn with respect to differences in actual performance on the Raven's Standard Progressive Matrices because of variability in the performance scores among the cognitive modification group.

Fox and Houston (1981) investigated the effectiveness of cognitive self-statements for reducing anxiety among fourth-grade students during a simulated evaluative situation (reciting memorized material). Children were divided into low- and high-trait anxiety groups on the basis of their responses to the State-Trait Anxiety Scale for Children (Spielberger, 1973). The treatment conditions involved either (a) teaching subjects self-instruction that focused on the "reappraisal" of the aversive aspects of the situation (e.g., "Even if I don't do this correctly, nothing terrible will happen") or (b) a more "minimal treatment" that involved self-instruction focused on practical aspects such as "It won't be long before I am finished." These treatment conditions were compared to a no-treatment control group. Contrary to expectations, teaching subjects to focus on negative aspects of the stressful situation and to reappraise these aspects actually increased anxiety in some children. Specifically, children in the reappraisal group exhibited more anxious behavior during recitations of poems than children in either the minimal treatment or the control groups. In addition, both treatment groups tended to hurry through their poems, whereas the control group took more time. Furthermore, high trait-anxiety subjects who had been taught to reappraise the stressful situation experienced more anxiety when anticipating the poem recital than their cohorts who had been given minimal training or no training at all.

The examination of possible explanations for these negative results suggests an important practical feature to consider when teaching children to use self-statements. The authors indicated that the self-statements taught to the reappraisal group involved focusing on the negative features of the experience ("Doing this poem in front of others won't be so unpleasant"), rather than using straightforward positive statements ("I can do well on this poem"). Fox and Houston (1981) suggested that statements emphasizing negative features may sensitize children and may have a detrimental effect, in contrast to self-instructions that have a positive message. In addition, the authors pointed out that reappraisal involved more cumbersome statements, which may have compounded the difficulty of the task (i.e., remembering to use the lengthy self-statements and being able to recite the poem).

Medical and Dental Procedures

A number of researchers have evaluated the effectiveness of coping skills for children who undergo medical and dental procedures. Certainly, anxious reactions to invasive procedures do not constitute an "anxiety disorder" (Kendall et al., 1988); however, coping skills methods appear to help prevent or reduce debilitating anxiety and to facilitate behavior management of children experiencing such procedures. (Also, see Chapter 11). Similar to the demonstration that maladaptive self-talk occurs more frequently among test-anxious children, a greater frequency of negative self-statements has also been found in highly anxious children undergoing invasive procedures (Prins, 1985). Thus, in part, anxiety regarding medical/dental procedures is likely mediated by cognitive events (e.g., self-talk, images, attitudes). This notion has provided the impetus for the development of a number of "coping packages" that include a "self-talk component."

In addition, because children in a medical setting often experience a number of different stressors, the remedial, traditional interventions (i.e., systematic desensitization) for each specific fear would be inefficient. Consequently, several coping packages have been developed for children undergoing medical and dental procedures.

Siegel and Peterson (1980) examined the effectiveness of a coping skills package and sensory information for reducing anxiety among preschool dental patients who had never been to a dentist. Children were assigned to one of three conditions: coping skills training; sensory information; or an attention control condition. Coping skills consisted of teaching deep breathing and relaxation paired with the cue words "calm and nice." Relaxing imagery was also employed. In addition, the children were taught to use calming self-talk (i.e., "I will be all right in just a little while"). Children in the sensory information condition were given descriptions of sensations, sights, and sounds that they would experience. For example, subjects were exposed to an audiotaped drill sound. Self-report, behavioral indices, and physiological arousal were measured.

Behaviorally, children receiving either the coping skills or the sensory information were found to be less anxious and more cooperative than the control group. Following the dental procedure, children in both experimental groups had lower pulse rates compared to the controls. Children in the coping skills group, however, also showed lower pulse rates immediately before dental treatment began than children in either the sensory information or the control groups. Gains were maintained by both treatment groups during a second dental appointment approximately a week later (Siegel & Peterson, 1981).

Coping techniques have also been shown to enhance the efficacy of standard treatments used to prepare presurgical patients. Peterson and Shigetomi (1981) demonstrated that in the preparation of young surgery patients (ages 2½–10½ years), anxiety decreased when a combination of three coping techniques was added to the more widely used modeling film and preoperative information. Children who received a package of cue-controlled muscle relaxation (Russell & Sipich, 1974), distracting mental imagery (Lazarus & Abramovitz, 1962), and comforting self-talk (Meichenbaum & Goodman, 1971) displayed less distress than children who received only information or children who received information and viewed the film. The patient group that received the coping package plus the modeling appeared to fare the best. The authors speculated that providing these children with methods to inhibit anxiety as well as with a model of adaptive behavior may have facilitated their ability to cope with invasive procedures. A noteworthy addition to this study is the role of parent participation. Parents helped teach the coping procedures to their children. This was particularly salient for the younger children who otherwise may not have been able to use the methods on their own. Peterson and Shigetomi (1981) suggested that, aside from facilitating the use of coping skills, increased interaction between parent and child in the coping skills group may have contributed to improved results. In addition, they noted that parental involvement in the training program may have reduced parents' anxiety and, consequently, may have affected the children's level of stress. The investigators suggested that further studies be conducted in order to understand the influence of these separate factors and that it may be beneficial to include the parent as a coach when teaching young children coping skills for anxiety.

Campbell, Clark, and Kirkpatrick (1986) sought to reduce anxiety in school-age children (6–17 years old) who were preparing to undergo cardiac catheterization. Treatment consisted of providing children and their parents with a package of stress management skills that included: (a) progressive muscle relaxation and deep breathing (assisted by biofeedback via electromyographic readings); (b) guided imagery, in which the child visualized a tranquil place to enhance relaxation; (c) self-hypnosis; and (d) cognitive reframing, which incorporated the use of self-talk to facilitate coping. Treatment results showed that, compared to children in a control group, children in the treatment condition demonstrated less "upset" behavior during stressful periods of the hospitalization. In addition, the experimental group appeared to manage the stressors more efficiently than the control group. For example, despite nonsignificant differences between the two groups in levels of expressed fear, the experimental group was able to cooperate more fully than the control group.

Rose, Firestone, Heick, and Faught (1983) utilized anxiety management training to reduce stress among adolescent diabetic patients in order to improve their diabetic control. Based on research indicating that juvenile diabetics are likely to have poor diabetic control during emotionally stressful periods, these investigators hypothesized that reduction of stress through Anxiety Management Training (AMT) might lead to an improvement in metabolic control. Treatment consisted of 7 hours of anxiety management training over a 2-week period. Results indicated that all participants displayed clinically valuable decreases in their daily mean urine glucose levels. The authors hypothesized that stress and anxiety may have direct metabolic effects; thus, reduction of anxiety and stress may affect physiological mechanisms influencing diabetic control. Surprisingly, participants' subjective appraisal of anxiety was unaffected by AMT. However, the authors questioned the ability of these youngsters to report anxiety accurately, given that there were instances in which they denied feeling upset, while behaviorally demonstrating anxiety.

A coping package was utilized to reduce distress among patients experiencing one of the most traumatic medical procedures administered to children — bone marrow aspiration. Jay, Katz, Elliott, and Siegel (1987) compared the effectiveness of a cognitive-behavioral intervention in reducing patients' distress to the administration of Valium and to minimal treatment attention. Children between the ages of 3½ to 13 years of age were randomly assigned to one of the three groups. The cognitive-behavior therapy intervention consisted of a package including filmed modeling that portrayed a young patient using positive coping self-statements (i.e., "I know I can do it"), breathing exercises, positive incentive, imagery/distraction, and behavioral rehearsal. The imagery/distraction consisted of having the patient develop a fantasy of being involved with a superhero. For example, a patient might imagine being on a mission that involved a painful procedure. The goal of this technique was to change the meaning of the pain. The behavioral rehearsal for younger children involved using the actual equipment to give a doll a bone marrow aspiration. Older children gave a bone marrow demonstration that involved step-by-step instructions for the administration of the procedure. The Valium condition consisted of administering this drug 30 minutes prior to the procedure, and dosage was based on 5 milligrams for an average 5-year-old. In the minimal treatment-attention control group, children watched cartoons for 30 minutes prior to bone marrow aspiration. Results indicated that, compared to those in the minimal treatment-attention control condition, children using the behavioral coping package showed fewer behaviors associated with distress, had lower pulse scores, and self-reported less experience of pain. When subjects in the Valium group were compared to subjects in the control group, they did not differ with respect to behavioral measures of distress, pulse rates, or self-reported pain scores. However, the Valium group did exhibit lower diastolic blood pressure than the attention control group. More recently, McGrath (1990) presented a comprehensive review of treatment strategies for use with children experiencing various types of pain.

General Fears and Phobias

Graziano and colleagues (Graziano & Mooney, 1980, 1982; Graziano, Mooney, Huber, & Ignasiak, 1979) demonstrated the usefulness of verbal controlling responses for children's severe, debilitating nighttime fears. In the first two studies (Graziano et al., 1979; Graziano & Mooney, 1980), children ages 6 to 13 years were instructed in coping statements (adapted from Kanfer, Karoly, & Newman, 1975): "I am brave; I can take care of myself when I am alone; I can take care of myself when I am in the dark." In addition, they were taught to use muscle relaxation and relaxing imagery, and they were reinforced for practicing coping skills and for "being brave." The overall results (Graziano & Mooney, 1982) indicated that there was a substantial reduction in nighttime fears in 39 of 40 children. Furthermore, 34 of the children were followed 2½ to 3 years later, and it was found that 31 children had maintained their significant improvements (Graziano & Mooney, 1982).

Giebenhain and O'Dell (1984) extended coping training for children's fear of the dark to include a parent training manual that included instructions in teaching desensitization, reinforcement, and coping self-statements. The effectiveness of the parent training manual is important in that it demonstrates that children's fear of the dark may be reduced or eliminated cost-effectively. Giebenhain and O'Dell (1984) noted that the intervention took only a few minutes of parent time each evening and required only that the therapist maintain phone contact with the parents. For data collection purposes a minimal number of home visits was required. Evaluation of this intervention strategy was evident in that positive effects in reducing children's fear of the dark were maintained 1 year later.

Bornstein and Knapp (1981) used a coping procedure that involved self-control desensitization to treat a 12-year-old experiencing separation anxiety, fear of developing illness, and fear of automobile travel. Self-control desensitization involved instructing the youngster to relax and to imagine the anxiety-provoking scene. However, rather than terminate the scene once anxiety was experienced, as in traditional systematic desensitization, the child was instructed to use relaxation skills to cope actively with the anxiety. Subsequent to completion of the three separate hierarchies (for separation anxiety, fear of illness, and fear of traveling in cars), real-life exposure to anxiety-provoking situations was encouraged. Results demonstrated marked improvements, as indicated by a near absence of fear-related verbalizations and by considerable improvement in school attendance, peer interaction, and involvement in age-appropriate activities. One-year follow-up indicated maintenance of treatment gains.

Kendall, Kane, Howard, and Siqueland (1989) developed a structured 16-session treatment program for anxious children and young adolescents. This program incorporates four major components: a) recognizing anxious feelings and somatic reactions to anxiety; b) clarifying cognitions in anxiety-provoking situations (i.e., unrealistic or dysfunctional expectations or beliefs); c) developing a strategy to cope with the problematic situation (i.e., changing anxiety-intensifying self-talk into coping self-talk as well as generating coping actions that might be helpful); and d) evaluating the success of the coping plan and self-reinforcement as appropriate. The training program is divided into two phases. The first eight sessions are devoted to training, and the second eight sessions focus on practice. In addition, a session between the therapist and parent(s) (or other significant person in the child's life) is scheduled between the third and fourth treatment sessions. This cognitive-behavioral treatment package was successfully employed with four children (ages 9–13) diagnosed as Overanxious Disorder. All showed improvement on clinician ratings, parent report, and self-report. Such therapeutic gains were maintained at 3–6 month follow-ups (Kane & Kendall, in press).

In general, although these studies provide convergent support for the effectiveness of coping skills in the treatment of child and adolescent anxieties, researchers have emphasized the need for further study. Investigation should focus on "teasing" apart the effective treatment components of coping skills, on the efficacy of coping skills in a naturalistic environment, and on the degree of generalizability.

Coping Skills Guidelines

For the practicing clinician the following sections provide guidelines for the implementation of two coping skills techniques—anxiety management training and stress inoculation. Guidelines are also provided for training parents to reduce their children's fear of the dark. The two coping strategies were selected because of their demonstrated effectiveness with child and/or adolescent populations (Jason & Burrows, 1983; Rose et al., 1983; Siegel & Peterson, 1980). In addition, these two types of coping methods may be differentially effective with certain kinds of anxiety responses. Deffenbacher (1988) suggested that in treatment selection a match might be made between treatment and the most salient aspects of the client's anxiety response. For example, Anxiety Management Training may be best suited for the client whose anxiety reaction is manifested by intense emotional-physiological arousal and whose dysfunctional thoughts are not as prominent. Stress inoculation training, which includes both a cognitive and a relaxation component, may be more effective for anxiety problems involving physiological reactiveness and/or maladaptive cognitions. In addition, because stress inoculation targets a broader range of anxiety responses, it might also be preferred for prevention programs (Deffenbacher, 1988).

Equivocal results have been found in research examining individual response patterns and the effects of different treatment methods (Ost, Jerremalm, & Johansson, 1981, 1984; Ost, Johansson, & Jerremalm, 1982). However, determining the best treatment for the individual client should not be difficult if the therapist maintains close communication with the child and adjusts treatment in response to feedback. Giebenhain and O'Dell's (1984) parent training package demonstrates that parents can be utilized effectively as trainers in reducing children's anxiety. The practicing clinician may find it advantageous to train parents as "coaches" for several reasons: (a) it appears to be cost-effective, (b) it may increase the likelihood that young children will practice their coping skills on a daily basis, and (c) it may facilitate the use of coping skills in the natural environment.

Anxiety Management Training

Suinn and Richardson (1971) developed Anxiety Management Training (AMT), which is a coping skills model that utilizes relaxation as an active coping component. The procedure is based on the view that clients can identify early signs of anxiety and can independently utilize techniques designed to reduce anxiety. From this perspective it is unimportant for the client to be able to identify specific stressors; rather, the focus is on identification of symptoms (physical or cognitive) that indicate the presence of anxiety (Suinn & Deffenbacher, 1988). With training, clients can become aware of these anxiety response cues and can use them to signal use of relaxation coping skills.

Suinn (1986) and Suinn and Deffenbacher (1988) provide explicit details of the procedures used in AMT, and the reader is encouraged to become familiar with these sources. However, the basic components of AMT, outlined by Suinn & Deffenbacher (1988), are described below.

Typically, treatment is conducted in five or more 1-hour weekly sessions. Homework is done during the interim weeks, and anxiety is monitored on an ongoing basis throughout the weeks.

Session 1

The first session begins with a brief rationale describing AMT as a method used to train clients in the early identification of anxiety and in the elimination of anxiety through relaxation. For example, the discussion may include an explanation of how relaxation is taught, of the importance of perceiving early signs of stress, of the expected duration of training, and of the fact that weekly homework will be assigned. In addition, the trainer may explain that anxiety-arousing scenes will be induced during the session and that the client will learn to "turn on" relaxation skills to relax away the stress. These skills are then applied to "real-life" situations that arouse anxiety (i.e., taking a test). Following the overview of the rationale and procedure, a relaxation scene is constructed and relaxation training is provided. The relaxation scene is one that the client has actually experienced, and the client should provide as many sensory details as possible to facilitate later recall. Relaxation training usually follows the procedures proposed by Jacobsen (1938); however, these techniques can be somewhat cumbersome when young clients are involved. Consequently, a number of modifications have been proposed for teaching children to use relaxation procedures. One particularly applicable procedure was described by Koeppen (1974), who includes fantasy in her relaxation instructions so that the appropriate muscle groups are used automatically without prior tensing.

Having completed the relaxation exercise, the client extends the relaxed state by vividly imagining the relaxation scene. After termination of this imagery the therapist conducts a "relaxation review," instructing the client to attend to the feelings of relaxation of the different body parts (without muscle tension). Finally, the relaxation scene is again induced. During the next week's homework, the client practices progressive muscle relaxation only, on a daily basis, monitoring on a 1 to 100 scale the level of tension experienced prior to and following relaxation. With children and adolescents, particular attention needs to be paid to their motivational levels and cognitive capabilities when asking them to self-monitor (see Chapter 3).

Session 2

The second session begins with the construction of a moderately intense anxiety scene that the client has experienced. This level of intensity should approximate 60 on a 1–100 rating scale. Again, the scene should be described vividly, including thoughts and physiological reactions that occurred in the situation. It is important to note that scenes involving inappropriate solutions, such as escape, are not acceptable because of the possibility that repeatedly imagining such behaviors may reinforce them. After construction of the anxiety scene, the therapist instructs the client to attend to and let each muscle group relax. Slow and deep breathing is used to increase the level of relaxation.

Anxiety arousal is induced after the client has signaled a state of relaxation. The therapist instructs the client to visualize the anxiety scene and then describes details of the scene. When anxiety is experienced, the client signals the therapist, who terminates exposure to the scene after about 10 to 15 seconds. Immediately afterwards, relaxation is reintroduced, and a brief review of relaxation of muscle groups is conducted along with deep breathing. The alternation between anxiety and relaxation scenes continues throughout the remainder of the session. The relaxation scene is enhanced by reviewing relaxation of the muscle groups. Homework involves practicing progressive muscle relaxation in places other than at home.

Session 3

The third session introduces self-initiated relaxation in which the client induces a relaxed state without the therapist's assistance. This takes the form of attending to and relaxing each muscle group. When relaxed, the client signals the therapist, and the anxiety scene is "turned on." When the client signals that anxiety is being experienced, the therapist begins training the client to attend to this experience so that it is possible to identify the early symptoms of anxiety. For example, the therapist may say, "Pay attention to how you experience anxiety; perhaps it is in body signs such as your neck muscles tensing, or your heart rate, or in some of your thoughts" (Suinn, 1986). The therapist then instructs the client to induce relaxation and briefly reviews muscle relaxation. Anxiety images are induced throughout the session, and the client is assisted in attending to symptoms and then "relaxing away" the anxiety that is experienced. Homework involves continued relaxation practice, and the client is instructed to attempt to use the relaxation procedure in response to minimal stressors in a variety of situations.

Session 4

The fourth session introduces a more intense anxiety scene that approximates 90 on a 1–100 rating scale. More moderate-level anxiety scenes are used intermittently. In addition, the client is now required to take on more responsibility for inducing relaxation after exposure to anxiety. This is accomplished by having the client decide how long anxiety exposure will last and when to begin relaxation. Homework involves attention to early warnings of anxiety and induction of a relaxed state when anxiety is perceived.

Session 5

Session 5 involves turning over most of the responsibility to the client and fading out the influence of the therapist. How quickly this can be done depends on how the previous sessions have progressed. The client begins by initiating relaxation. After the therapist instructs the client to visualize the anxiety scene, the client signals when anxiety is experienced and independently attends to anxiety symptoms. Subsequently, the client induces relaxation while continuing to visualize the anxiety scene. This sequence is repeated throughout the session. Homework is a repetition of the homework in Session 4.

Further sessions are modeled after Session 5, and new anxiety scenes may be utilized to promote the client's self-control. During these sessions the client also can be encouraged to test out coping skills in anxiety-provoking situations. This allows the client to gain a sense of confidence that progress has been made in combating anxiety.

Stress Inoculation Training

Stress Inoculation Training (SIT) (Meichenbaum & Cameron, 1972; Meichenbaum, 1977, 1985) involves a structured self-statement modification package that allows for the management of small amounts of stress and "which provides inoculation against greater intensities of threat" (Meichenbaum, 1977). Stress inoculation is based on a cognitive model of self-control postulated by Meichenbaum (1975). According to this cognitive model, altering the internal dialogue of the child accounts for behavior change, regardless of the particular therapy orientation. Changing an internal dialogue leads to behavior change because (a) self-instruction plays a direct role in changing behavior, (b) self-instruction and images affect behavior through influencing attentional direction, and (c) self-instructions influence a child's interpretation and experience of the physiological state.

The treatment occurs in three phases: (a) conceptualization, (b) skills acquisition and rehearsal, and (c) application and follow-through. A discussion of these phases follows.

Conceptualization

The first phase of stress inoculation training is used to establish a relationship with the child and to provide an explanation about the nature of the response to stressful stimuli. Meichenbaum and Deffenbacher (1988) suggested that the relationship should be a collaborative one in which the child is "the expert on his/her anxiety," and the therapist works with the child to understand the nature of the anxiety. The anxiety should be discussed in a face valid manner and in such a way that it is plausible and leads naturally to an acceptance of the specific coping techniques that follow. Thus, for example, it is not important to present and defend Schacter's theory of emotion (1966) but to describe a conceptual framework for anxiety that is appropriate to the child's level of cognitive development.

Skill, Acquisition and Rehearsal

Phase 2 of the stress inoculation program is designed to provide the client with the specific techniques — both direct behaviors and cognitive methods — to use during the coping process. The child is taught that early symptoms of anxiety serve as cues to employ coping methods. Specific techniques include self-monitoring, problem solving, didactic training, modeling, reinforcement, relaxation training, and self-instruction. The two key components involved in stress inoculation training are relaxation training and self-instruction. The former has been discussed in the section on anxiety management training, and a script for its use is included in the chapter appendix. The following are guidelines for self-instruction training.

Verbal Self-Instructions   Verbal self-instructions follow a step-by-step sequence and consist of verbalizations that are related to the specific presenting problems of the child, are modeled by the therapist, and then are rehearsed by the child. The modeling and rehearsal sessions follow the sequence defined below (Meichenbaum & Goodman, 1971).

1. The therapist models the task and talks out loud while the child observes.
2. The child performs the task, instructing himself or herself out loud with assistance from the therapist.
3. The child performs the task aloud with no assistance.
4. The child performs the task whispering to himself or herself.
5. The child performs the task using covert (silent) verbalizations.

The verbalizations modeled by the therapist and rehearsed by the child are generally of four types: (a) problem definition ("What is it that I should do in this situation?"); (b) focusing of attention ("I have to concentrate and do what I'm supposed to do."); (c) coping statements ("I'm starting to feel nervous; I've got to take a deep breath and relax"); and (d) self-reinforcement ("Great! I did it. That was good").

Application and Follow-Through

Once the child has become proficient in the skills taught in the previous phase, the skills are practiced in increasingly more stressful situations. In addition, the child is exposed to stressful situations other than the actual anxiety-provoking situation so that there is opportunity to practice and to apply coping skills to a variety of problems. Another important component of this phase is relapse prevention, which highlights the importance of helping children prepare for "backsliding" so that failures can be interpreted as learning experiences rather than as catastrophes and as evidence of personal inadequacy (Marlatt & Gordon, 1984). It is emphasized that the goal is not to eliminate anxiety but to increase adaptive responding in anxiety-provoking situations (Meichenbaum & Deffenbacher, 1988).

Outline of Training

This outline of stress inoculation training is meant to serve as a guideline that can be altered according to the needs of the individual child. For the purpose of illustration, a stress inoculation procedure for a child with test anxiety will be described. The procedure fits the previously discussed three-phase conceptualization, with sessions 1 and 2 devoted to education, sessions 3 through 7 used for rehearsal, and sessions 8 and 9 focused on application training. The sessions are designed to last between ½ hour and 1 hour, depending on the individual child.

Before instituting a stress inoculation procedure for anxiety, the therapist must first conceptualize the role of self-statements in the origin of the form of anxiety in question. For example, in Richardson's (1975) manual for treating test anxiety in college students, he proposed that the thinking processes of test-anxious students may be categorized as follows:

1. Worrying about one's performance, including comparing oneself to other students.
2. Considering, at length, all the alternative answers.
3. Becoming overly concerned with the physiological reactions associated with anxiety.
4. Ruminating over the possible consequences of a poor performance on the test.
5. Feeling inadequate—subjecting oneself to self-criticism, calling oneself worthless, etc.

Baseline   The baseline assessment stage precedes actual training, and the assessment measures depend upon the nature of the individual child's presenting problems. For example, in the case of a test-anxious child, assessment measures might include: the Test Anxiety Scale for Children (Sarason, Davidson, Lighthall, Waite, & Ruebush, 1960), an individually tailored rating scale describing the anxiety-related behaviors manifested in the classroom during the test (see the example in Finch, Deardorff, & Montgomery, 1974), completion of the State-Trait Anxiety Inventory for Children (Speilberger, 1973) while taking a test or while imagining feelings when taking a test, or physiological measures while the child is taking the test. The measures employed should be amenable to pre- and posttesting and, consequently, sensitive to intraindividual change.

Session 1   The first session follows the collection of baseline data. Besides establishing a working relationship with the child, this session focuses on two areas. First, it is important to discuss the child's likes and dislikes in order to delineate potential reinforcers for use later in treatment. Second, the therapist initiates a discussion with the child about the nature of anxiety. A simplistic, concrete approach to education is most effective; therefore, in most cases the discussion of anxiety is limited to the context of the child's presenting problem. As discussed above, the critical factor is plausibility. A foundation must be established so that the training to follow "makes sense" to the child. According to Meichenbaum (1977), "what transpires between client and therapist prior to the implementation of specific treatment procedures plays an important role in understanding the change process" (p. 151). This is particularly important with children, because, unfortunately, most child psychotherapy is somewhat nebulous, and the child often loses sight of the purpose of therapy.

In discussing the basis of anxiety with the child, it is often helpful to explain that other children have this problem, too. However, for the purposes of treatment, it is important to personalize and to individualize the conceptualization. Thus, the child discusses and explores in detail the thoughts and feelings experienced during test-taking situations. During this process the therapist can pull for the relevant self-statements of the individual child. Several procedures have been developed to elicit self-talk from young clients. One effective means of discovering these self-statements is to have the child "run a movie through your head" of reactions during the most recent anxiety-provoking situation.

In addition, the "Think Aloud" procedure (Meichenbaum, 1977) is useful in eliciting self-statements. This involves having the child do a task and "think out loud" at the same time. Initially the therapist may need to model a task while thinking aloud. For example, if the child has anxiety regarding performance on mathematics tests, the therapist may work on a moderately difficult arithmetic problem and think out loud, "I must be stupid not to figure this out; I know this is the wrong answer." Once the child feels comfortable engaging in this exercise, it can be useful in uncovering negative self-statements the child is using. Fox, Houston, and Pittner

(1983) found that fourth-grade children had little trouble using this procedure and, in fact, did not even require practice. Some children may be taught to think out loud with a tape recorder to facilitate pre- and posttreatment comparisons.

A story-telling technique (Elkin, 1983) may also be helpful in revealing maladaptive self-talk. This technique involves the use of ambiguous pictures that are relevant to the anxiety-laden situation (i.e., test taking). The child is asked to make up a story about the picture and to include thoughts, feelings, and potential solutions to the problem situation. Elkin (1983) suggested prompting, if necessary. Prompts might include "What's going on in this picture? How will the little boy get out of the situation? What do you think he is thinking?".

The particular phrasing, vocabulary, and content of the presentation should be tailored to the individual child. The first session might proceed as follows:

> *Lots of people, both kids and grown-ups, are a little bit afraid of taking tests, especially math tests. So we're going to be teaching you and some other kids how to be less scared when you take math tests.*
>
> *(If the child says, "I'm not afraid, so I don't have to do this," then the therapist says, "Oh, then this will probably be easy for you. If you can follow directions and do well, when we're done you can choose a reward from our reward box." Show possible rewards.)*
>
> *(If there is no resistance, say, "If you can try this and do well, we have some rewards over here, and you can choose one when we're done.")*
>
> *Let me tell you a few things about being afraid. When people are afraid of math tests, or other things, they say certain things to themselves. For example, if you were afraid of math tests, when it came time to take a math test you might say: "I have to do good on this math test. But it's a hard test, and I'll probably make some mistakes, and that's awful. I should be able to do this test, but I can't. I'm such a dummy. And if I do bad on this test, my friends will laugh at me and think I'm stupid. My teacher will think I'm dumb, too, and not like me anymore. And my mother and father won't talk to me anymore and they will yell at me."*
>
> *So you see, when people are afraid, they say lots of scared things to themselves. And you know what happens when you say these things to yourself? You get even more scared and do even worse on the test. (Emphasis here—"ham it up").*
>
> *(Try to elicit child's statement if possible—for example, "Why don't you try running a movie through your head of the last time you got scared taking a test.")*

In the preceding example it is obvious that the conceptualization focuses entirely on self-statements. However, depending on the individual child, physiological arousal descriptions may be more important. Inclusion of physiological arousal descriptions might be phrased as follows:

> *Sometimes when people are afraid of tests, their bodies also do funny things. For some kids, their stomach starts to feel all funny and tense, or their neck starts to feel stiff. Or maybe your heart starts to pound real fast, or you start to breathe faster, or your palms start to sweat.*

Once again, the task of the therapist is to elicit the particular physiological reactions that the child experiences and to emphasize and elaborate these. When the session ends, the child is rewarded for participation.

Session 2   The initial part of the second session is devoted to a short review of the activities in Session 1, and the child is asked to bring up any questions about the rationale. Next the child is taught a number of adaptive self-statements designed to reduce anxiety. This lesson might be phrased as follows:

> *Now, do you know what? People who are not afraid say different things like:*
>
> > *"This is a hard test, but it's not terrible to fail."*
> > *"If I do bad I can always try again."*
> > *"And besides, I'm not the first kid to do bad on a test."*
> > *"And even if my friends laugh at me, it won't kill me, and it doesn't mean they don't like me."*
> > *"My teachers won't think I'm dumb. They're giving the test to find out where I'm worst in math so they can help me do better."*
>
> *So you see, these people help themselves not to be afraid because they say brave things to themselves, and they don't get very scared.*
> *Now, here's what we're going to do. We're going to teach you how to say the right things to yourself so that you won't be afraid when you take your test.*

Additional comments regarding the importance of relaxation procedures might also be incorporated in this session. If an extensive set of relaxation procedures is to be employed, then the therapist should introduce relaxation techniques during this session. At times, more limited relaxation procedures might also be used. An example of such a procedure is:

Now, I'd like to show you some other things you can do when you take tests. When you start to feel your stomach get tense, or your hands sweat, you could say:

"Relax, don't feel nervous."
"Don't worry; worrying won't help me at all."
"I'm getting scared, time to take a deep breath."

At this point the therapist reviews the self-statements and asks the child to repeat them. At the end of the session, the therapist gives the child the homework assignment of listening to self-statements outside the sessions. The child is rewarded based on participation or for each self-statement remembered by the child.

Session 3 A brief review of the previous sessions is needed before actually beginning the rehearsal phase of training. This review centers on the maladaptive statements that lead to anxiety and on the adaptive self-statements and relaxation techniques that counter the anxiety. The therapist also determines if the child has noted self-statements in the interval between sessions. The first form of rehearsal involves cognitive modeling, as the therapist models the task while talking aloud. In this stage it is important that the therapist display the types of skills, noted previously, that are relevant to successful completion of the task: (a) problem definition ("What is it I have to do?"); (b) focusing attention and response guidance ("Now I've got to concentrate on the test and try to answer this first question."); (c) self-reinforcement ("I got that one right. I'm doing fine so far"); and (d) self-evaluative coping skills and error-correcting options ("It's not awful to make a mistake. I can always try it again").

The following therapist dialogue is an example of the type of cognitive modeling procedure that might be used for a test-anxious child.

OK, now, I'm going to show you how you can use what I taught you to help you do better on tests. I'm going to pretend I'm taking a test. I want you to listen to what I say, and if you can tell me some of the things I said after I'm done, then you'll get a reward.

(Have a short test ready to be used during this phase.)

The first thing I have to do is read the directions carefully. Now, I'll read the whole test quickly before I start. That way I'll know how to divide up my time so I'll get to all the questions (read test). OK, I'm ready to go now. Now I have to concentrate on the test and forget everything else.

What does this first question ask? I understand it, but this problem is really hard. This is awful. What am I gonna do? Wait, it's not awful to make a mistake. I'm in control; I don't have to get scared. I'll just relax and concentrate on the problem. Wait, there it is. I can do this one (write answer to problem).

Good, I talked myself into the right answer that time. It's working; I can control how I feel.

Wow. This second one is hard, too, but if I do bad on this test, I can always try again and try to do better next time. I know, I'll skip this one and come back to it later.

Now I'll try the third problem. I've got to remember to think positively. Slow down a little—don't rush and get all panicked (take five seconds to concentrate and read problem). OK, I've read it twice, and I can do this one (compute answer). Did it. Great. That wasn't bad. Better check it before I go on to the next one.

Oh no! It's wrong. My friends will laugh at me for missing this one. Wait. Stop and think. It's not awful to make a mistake. Relax, take a couple of slow, deep breaths.

OK, it's just a simple mistake. (Correct problem). There, it's right now.

Better move on, time's almost up.

You get the idea about how saying things to yourself can help you get through tests. Do you have any questions? OK, now can you tell me some of the things I said that helped me get through the test?

Reward all of the child's appropriate verbalizations and any new adaptive self-statements. Point out statements that the child did not remember, and ask the child to say them aloud again. A reading of the above script points out the use of performance-relevant statements—that is, problem definition, focusing attention and response guidance, self-reinforcement, and self-evaluative coping skills and error-correcting options.

Session 4   This session is devoted to overt, external guidance. That is, the child performs the task while talking aloud, and the therapist instructs and prompts. In this session the child is asked to complete a few problems as the trainer did in the cognitive modeling session. The tasks (e.g., math problems) should include several questions that are somewhat difficult but can be solved, in addition to several problems that are more difficult for the child. The test should be hard enough to make the child somewhat anxious but not so difficult as to frustrate the child completely. In addition, the tougher problems may lead the child to make an error, and thus may provide an opportunity for the utilization of error-correcting self-statements.

In this session the therapist plays the role of a teacher administering the test, and the child is asked to pretend that this is a real test and to recite aloud all coping statements. Some children have difficulty imitating this process, and for them the therapist must continue to model the procedure. The therapist should lead and prompt the child when difficulty is encountered and should also reward the child for all correct verbalizations. Many children neglect the use of self-reinforcing statements, and the therapist should be sure to emphasize such statements. At the end of the session, the therapist answers any questions, praises the child for a good job, and reminds the child that more rewards are available next time.

Session 5   In this session the child performs the task while talking aloud (overt self-guidance). Ideally the child should be able to repeat the self-statements alone; however, it may be necessary to provide occasional prompts. If at all possible, prompting should be kept at a minimum, because the goal of this session is for the child to begin to assume responsibility for making self-statements. Therefore, it is usually preferable to review the self-statements briefly at the beginning of the session and to point out the self-statements that were neglected when the child performed the task.

For a test-anxious child the procedure is often augmented by having the child begin repeating the self-statements in the hallway. The self-statements are rehearsed while approaching the training room, while waiting outside the door, while entering the room, while approaching the seat, and then as the child actually sits down. Reinforcements can be used, if necessary, to improve the child's performance and to help maintain attention. If the child does not do very well, it may be necessary to model the procedure again and to provide rewards for closer and closer approximations of the desired goal.

Session 6   This session is identical to Session 5 with the exception that during this session the child whispers the instructions while performing the task (faded, overt self-guidance). Once again, the child starts making self-statements in the hallway and continues while moving toward the classroom and sitting down. The remainder of this session focuses on the same procedures used in Session 5.

Session 7   This is the final rehearsal training session. Procedures are those used in sessions 5 and 6 with the exception that the child uses covert self-instructions—that is, the task is performed silently. Before beginning the child is informed that this is the last training session and that he or she is now ready to "do it" by talking silently to himself or herself. The child is informed that the therapist will inquire about the self-statements at the end of the session. At the conclusion of the session, the therapist rewards the child and asks about the self-statements and how effective they were for the task.

Session 8   Sessions 8 and 9 are devoted to application training. These sessions are designed to give the child an opportunity to use the new coping techniques in a stressful situation. In most cases the application training should be conducted in situations similar, but not identical, to the actual stress-inducing circumstances that have prompted treatment.

In the training of test-anxious children, the application sessions can be conducted in the child's actual classroom, with the therapist posing as a teacher. Ideally, the child's own teacher conducts the session. The child is asked to complete a test that is sufficiently difficult to raise his or her anxiety level. If the child seems to be handling the stress adequately, additional stress may be applied by having the teacher (trainer) stand close to the child and make provoking statements such as "That's wrong" or "You can't get that one?" The suitability of applying additional stress must be assessed by the therapist and gauged according to the individual child. The procedure and the dialogue for Session 8 might be as follows:

> *Today is the second-to-last session, but it's going to be a little differ-ent. I'm going to have you take a practice math test. It won't be exactly the same as a real math test, but it will be good practice. I want you to talk to yourself in the brave way you've learned how to do. OK, let's go to the classroom and try it.*
>
> *(If there's any reluctance, say, "Well, it's only practice and doesn't count for anything. And, if you do it OK, you'll get a reward. After we start, if you decide you don't want to do it, that's OK. No one will force you.")*
>
> *(As you leave the room and head to the classroom, go over the whole coping routine, prompting the child in proper statements. When the child is seated, emphasize: "This is what you will do when you take real tests." The teacher/trainer then administers the test.)*

When the test is completed, the therapist asks the child to talk about what it was like to use the self-statements in an actual test situation. Also, the therapist determines which statements were utilized and points out any that were neglected. If the child does well, the therapist provides profuse rewards.

Session 9   This session is essentially the same as Session 8. Variations can include having the child's teacher administer the test, taking the test in the child's classroom, and so forth. In addition, the therapist might use other procedures to increase the stressfulness of the situation, such as employing very difficult test materials or conducting the session in a classroom with many distracting stimuli.

An important component of this phase is to help the child prepare for relapse. The therapist emphasizes that failures are learning experiences and helps the child identify high-risk situations in which relapses are likely to occur. The therapist can tell the child that "slipping back to old habits is expected."

Helpful Hints

Ideally, stress inoculation for anxious children follows the outline described above. In the clinic, however, many "snags" are often encountered in an ideal treatment package. The following recommendations may assist the reader in implementing the stress inoculation program and/or in increasing the efficacy, duration, and generalization of the treatment effects.

1. Flexibility in implementing the stress inoculation procedure is most important in work with children (Meichenbaum, 1977). Consequently, the therapist must be keenly aware of individual differences. Flexibility determines the rate of treatment. Some children require many trials of overt self-instructions, while others move much more quickly. Indeed, some children become embarrassed by repeating the self-statements aloud; others become angry, because they see the training as demeaning. Self-pacing must be carefully considered for each child.

Flexibility also applies to the exact words, style, and content of the presentation used in the training. For example, Meichenbaum (1977, p. 90) notes that "children readily comply with the instruction to 'think out loud' while doing a task, whereas the instruction to 'talk out loud to yourself' elicits negative connotations (viz., that is something that crazy people do)." The latter problem seems to occur much more frequently with psychiatrically hospitalized children.

The need for flexibility applies not only to the individual child but also to the particular presenting problem. For example, in working with test-anxious children, it is advantageous to build a set of self-statements related to study skills techniques. These self-statements might include:

"Read the directions carefully. Then I'll understand what to do."

"Read the whole test first. Then I'll know how much time to spend on each question."

"Read each problem twice, so I'll be sure I know what they want."

"Skip any questions I don't know the answers to, and come back to them later."

2. In general, the operant component of the stress inoculation procedure is devised so that material (usually edibles) and social reinforcements are contingent on successively better approximations of the self-statements. As training proceeds, these reinforcers should be faded out rapidly and/or given only at the close of a session. Other more potent reinforcers, such as backgammon games between child and therapist, may be used in the training program. In the place of reinforcement, a response-cost procedure may also be considered in the training package. Indeed, for children with self-control problems, response-cost procedures have proven more effective than direct reinforcement (Nelson, Finch, & Hooke, 1975).

3. Reinforcement is only one way to increase a child's incentive to comply with the training package. Kendall (1977) pointed out three additional methods for attaining and maintaining a child's interest in the training: (a) a favorable relationship between the therapist and child; (b) age-appropriate, interesting training tasks; and (c) a favorable scheduling of sessions, that is, during class time as opposed to free time.

4. The attractiveness of the training package may be enhanced through the use of a videotape model. For example, in the cognitive modeling stage the trainer might utilize a videotape of someone using the coping self-statements to reduce anxiety. Watching someone else practice the coping skills can be quite enjoyable and can be used to "hook" the child on the idea of a stress inoculation program. The playback of a videotape recording of the child using the coping self-statements is likely to enhance the child's interest and to provide important feedback. Also, children who are initially resistant to engaging in the training program might be more amenable to treatment if they view a videotape model whom they respect, such as their therapist, a teacher, or a peer. A sample videotape script for a test-anxious child can be reviewed in Appendix A at the end of this chapter. If at all possible, the actor should mimic the anxious behaviors that the particular child displays and then cope with the anxiety effectively.

5. In the cognitive modeling stage, whether in vivo or on videotape, it is important to include maladaptive self-statements and errors that are corrected with adaptive self-statements and solutions. Dealing successfully with anxiety and errors is the key to the program, because, as Meichenbaum (1977) has pointed out, the child is being taught coping, rather than mastery, skills. Thus, the trainer should put appropriate emphasis on coping with errors.

6. Training may also be enhanced by conducting the sessions within the medium of the child's play (Meichenbaum, 1977). This suggestion is not necessarily applicable to a test-anxious child but can be used with a shy child whose anxiety is manifested in interpersonal situations. It is also important to have a therapist who is animated and responsive to the child.

7. With children it is important to provide a large number of self-statements, from which they can select those that they enjoy and believe are

most salient. Of course, self-generated statements are of even more value, but children are not usually adept at this task. It appears that the number of self-statements is less important than having several salient statements that can be called readily to one's attention. Indeed, in our experience and in Meichenbaum's (1977) opinion, children often gravitate to a specific combination of self-statements during the course of the rehearsal stage.

8. The child's "cognitive capacity" (Kendall, 1977) also must be considered when implementing a stress inoculation program. When the child has limited intellectual abilities, Kendall (1977) suggests initial training in some of the component skills of self-instruction. For example, remembering the self-instructions is a prerequisite to behavior change, so rote memorizing should precede the training package. Training in the actual use of self-instructions (i.e., when and where to stop and think before responding) may be needed with a child of lower intelligence. Also, the modeling component may need to be lengthened and emphasized with less intelligent children, because such children process information at a slower rate (Bandura, 1977). In regard to the role of intelligence, some interesting findings were reported by Ridberg, Parke, and Hetherington (1971) in their work with impulsive children. They found that combining verbal and nonverbal cues worked best with low-IQ subjects but that with high-IQ children the combined cues did little to add to the efficacy of training (probably by interfering with mediational processes). It also seems likely that low-IQ children may require a greater number of sessions of shorter duration.

9. The rehearsal and application phases of the stress inoculation package are particularly important. Simple rote repetition of the self-statements probably does not lead to a great deal of self-control. "Instead, affective modeling and practice in synthesizing and internalizing the meaning of one's self-statements are needed" (Meichenbaum, 1977, p. 89). The important component is the actual trying out of the self-statements in real situations.

10. Stress inoculation training conducted in group sessions may also prove useful. Group treatment has the advantage of saving therapist hours. In addition, group treatment may help foster behavior change via group discussion and pressure. However, group treatment may prove difficult, because it is rare to find a group of children who are anxious about the same "thing" in the same way. Thus, if the situation presents itself, it is advisable to conduct group training early in the process, because the group can be dissolved and individual sessions begun if the therapist deems it necessary. From his experience in conducting group sessions in self-instructional training, Drummond (1974) made the following recommendations:

a. Training should be done early in the school day to avoid the fatigue factor and also to allow the children the chance to try out their new skills in the classroom.

b. Limiting the group to three, rather than five, children makes the session more manageable.

c. Supplemental equipment, such as videotapes and the children's prerecorded self-statements, is helpful.

d. Children younger than those in third and fourth grades are better candidates for the training.

11. An advantage of the stress inoculation approach is that "booster" programs can be built into the treatment package if the effects of training seem to diminish over time. That is, if the child begins to show signs of anxiety in the actual threat situations, brief rehearsal sessions may be appropriate and also sufficient to bring the anxiety under control again rather quickly.

12. When more extensive relaxation procedures are taught, it is important for the child to employ the coping statements while relaxing. The type of relaxation procedure employed in training depends on factors such as the child's imaging ability. One important consideration is the type of situation the child is being trained to manage. For example, if the child is being trained to cope with test anxiety, extensive relaxation procedures may hinder academic performance by slowing down the actual test-taking process. The type of relaxation procedure will also have an effect on the length of the sessions used in the training program.

13. Because the objective of stress inoculation training is to bring the child's behavior in line with self-statements, Meichenbaum (1977) suggested supplementing self-instructional training with "correspondence training." In such training the therapist tries to establish correspondence between what the child says and what the child does. Correspondence training might include having the child state the goals for a training session (e.g., not to exhibit any anxious behaviors — hands sweating, feet shaking — while taking the practice test) and then providing feedback as to how well the child met the stated goals.

14. Promoting generalization is an important consideration in stress inoculation training. Several approaches can be employed to increase generalization. First, the training materials, training setting, and trainers may be varied. Second, Kendall (1977) suggested that using the child's own self-produced coping statements is an efficient strategy to produce generalized behavior change. Third, Kendall (1977) also proposed that conceptual labeling may promote greater generalization better than concrete labeling. That is, the therapist can model self-instructions that have meaning to the specific training task (concrete) as well as to related tasks in general (conceptual). Although empirical research is lacking in this area, it may be that initial concrete labeling that fades into conceptual labeling is the most efficient means of producing generalization (Kendall, 1977). An additional

strategy that can enhance generalization as well as efficacy is to teach the child's family and friends the basic ideas of the training package so that they can assist and support the child. A final means of consolidating the child's coping strategies is to have the child train another child with a similar problem in the stress inoculation procedure (Meichenbaum, 1977). This follows the basic principle that the best way to learn something is to teach it (e.g., Nelson & Behler, 1990).

Appendix A: Videotape Script

Introduction: "OK, let me show you what I mean by talking to yourself. I'm going to show you a movie on this T.V., and the movie will show someone getting ready to take a test. He starts out a little bit afraid but then says brave things to himself and takes the test without being afraid. Watch and listen to what he says. When it's done, if you can tell me some of the things he said, then you'll get a reward."

Actor: OK, today I'm gonna take the math test. The first thing I have to do is relax. Worrying won't help me at all. Here comes the teacher now.

Teacher: Hi. Today we're going to give you a math test so we can find out where you are in math and get ready for your return to school in the fall.

Actor: You're just trying to find out what parts of math I'm not so good in so you can help me do better, right?

Teacher: That's right. We just want you to do the best you can. OK?

Actor: And if I do bad, I can always try again, right?

Teacher: Right. Here's the test and a pencil. We'll give you 5 minutes to finish it. When time's up, I'll come and get the paper from you. OK, work as fast as you can and good luck.

(Teacher goes off camera and "child" talks to himself.)

Actor: OK, the first thing I have to do is read the directions carefully. (Reads directions). OK, I understand the directions, so now I have to read the whole test before I start. That way, I'll know how to divide up my time so I'll get to all the questions. (Reads test). OK, I'm ready to go now. Now, I have to concentrate on the test and forget everything else.

Gosh, this first problem is hard. This is awful. What am I gonna do? Wait, it's not awful to make a mistake. No, I'll just relax and concentrate on the problem. Wait, there it is. I can do this one. (Writes answer to problem).

Good, I talked myself into the right answer this time.

Wow. This second one is hard, too, but if I do bad on this test I can always try again and try to do better next time. I know, I'll skip this one and come back to it later.

Now I'll try the third problem. I've got to remember to think positively. (Takes 5 seconds to concentrate and read problem). OK, I've read it twice and I can do this one. (Computes answer). Did it. Great. That wasn't bad. Better check it through before I go on to the next one. Oh no, it's wrong! My friends will laugh at me for missing this one. Wait. Stop and think. It's not awful to make a mistake. And even if my friends laugh at me, it doesn't mean they don't like me. Concentrate again. OK, it's just a simple mistake. There, it's right now.

Better move on. Time's almost up.

(He leans over and works on test, whispering to himself. Then the teacher comes back on camera.)

Teacher: OK, time's up. How was it?

Actor: Boy, that was a hard test, but it's not terrible to fail. Besides, I'm not the first or last kid to ever do bad on a test.

Teacher: It was a hard test, wasn't it? But I was watching you while you took the test and you didn't look scared like you usually do.

Actor: That's because I was saying brave things to myself, and that way I don't get scared. Besides, I know you'll still like me even if I don't do good on this test.

Teacher: That's right. I bet saying brave things to yourself helped you do better on the test, too.

Actor: I hope so.

References

Bandura, A. (1977). *Social learning theory.* Englewood Cliffs, NJ: Prentice-Hall.

Barrios, B. A., & Shigetomi, C. C. (1979). Coping-skills training for the management of anxiety: A critical review. *Behavior Therapy, 10,* 491–522.

Bornstein, P., & Knapp, M. (1981). Self-control desensitization with a multi-phobic boy: A multiple baseline design. *Journal of Behavior Therapy and Experimental Psychiatry, 12,* 281–285.

Campbell, L., Clark, M., & Kirkpatrick, S. (1986). Stress management training for parents and their children undergoing cardiac catheterization. *American Journal of Orthopsychiatry, 56,* 234–243.

Daley, P. C., Bloom, L. J., Deffenbacher, J. L., & Stewart, R. (1983). Treatment effectiveness of anxiety management training in small and large group formats. *Journal of Counseling Psychology, 30,* 104–107.

Deffenbacher, J. (1988). Some recommendations and directions. *The Counseling Psychologist, 16,* 91–95.

Deffenbacher, J. L., Michaels, A. C., Daley, P. C., & Michaels, T. (1980). A comparison of homogeneous and heterogeneous anxiety management training. *Journal of Counseling Psychology, 27,* 630–634.

Drummond, D. (1974). *Self-instructional training: An approach to disruptive classroom behavior.* Unpublished doctoral dissertation, University of Oregon.

D'Zurrilla, R. J., & Goldfried, M. R. (1971). Problem solving and behavior modification. *Journal of Abnormal Psychology, 78,* 107–126.

Elkin, A. (1983). Working with children in groups. In A. Ellis & M. E. Bernard (Eds.), *Rational-emotive approaches to the problems of childhood.* New York: Plenum Press.

Finch, A. J, Jr., Deardorff, P. A., & Montgomery, L. E. (1974). Individually tailored behavioral rating scales: A possible alternative. *Journal of Abnormal Child Psychology, 3,* 209–214.

Fox, J., & Houston, K. (1981). Efficacy of self-instructional training for reducing children's anxiety in an evaluative situation. *Behaviour Research and Therapy, 19,* 509–515.

Fox, J., Houston, K., & Pittner, M. S. (1983). Trait anxiety and children's cognitive behaviors in an evaluative situation. *Cognitive Therapy and Research, 1,* 149–154.

Giebenhain, J., & O'Dell, S. (1984). Evaluation of a parent-training manual for reducing children's fear of the dark. *Journal of Applied Behavior Analysis, 17,* 121–125.

Graziano, A., & Mooney, K. (1980). Family self-control instruction for children's nighttime fear reduction. *Journal of Consulting and Clinical Psychology, 48,* 206–213.

Graziano, A., & Mooney, K. (1982). Behavioral treatment of children's "night-fears": Maintenance of improvement at 2- to 3-year follow-up. *Journal of Consulting and Clinical Psychology, 50,* 598–599.

Graziano, A., Mooney, K., Huber, C., & Ignasiak, D. (1979). Self-control instruction for children's fear reduction. *Journal of Behavior Therapy and Experimental Psychiatry, 10,* 221–227.

Holroyd, K. A. (1976). Cognition and desensitization in the group treatment of test anxiety. *Journal of Consulting and Clinical Psychology, 44,* 991–1001.

Jacobsen, R. (1938). *Progressive relaxation.* Chicago: University of Chicago Press.

Jannoun, L., Oppenheimer, C., & Gelder, M. (1982). A self-help treatment program for anxiety state patients. *Behavior Therapy, 13,* 103–111.

Jaremko, M. (1980). The use of stress inoculation training in the reduction of public speaking anxiety. *Journal of Clinical Psychology, 36,* 735–738.

Jaremko, M. (1983). Stress inoculation training for social anxiety, with emphasis on dating anxiety. In D. Meichenbaum & M. Jaremko (Eds.), *Stress reduction and prevention.* New York: Plenum Press.

Jaremko, M., Hadfield, R., & Walker, W. (1980). Contribution of an educational phase to stress inoculation of speech anxiety. *Perceptual and Motor Skills, 50,* 495–501.

Jason, L., & Burrows, B. (1983). Transition training for high school seniors. *Cognitive Therapy and Research, 7,* 79–92.

Jay, S., Katz, E., Elliott, C. H., & Siegel, S. E. (1987). Cognitive-behavioral and pharmacological interventions for children's distress during painful medical procedures. *Journal of Consulting and Clinical Psychology, 55,* 860–865.

Jerremalm, A., Jansson, L., & Ost, L. (1986). Cognitive and physiological reactivity and the effects of different behavioral methods in the treatment of social phobia. *Behaviour Research and Therapy, 24,* 171–180.

Kane, M. T., & Kendall, P. C. (in press). Anxiety disorders in children: A multiple-baseline evaluation of a cognitive-behavioral treatment. *Behavior Therapy.*

Kanfer, F., Karoly, P., & Newman, A. (1975). Reduction of children's fear of the dark by competence-related and situational threat-related verbal cues. *Journal of Consulting and Clinical Psychology, 43,* 251–258.

Kendall, P. C. (1977). On the efficacious use of verbal self-instructional procedures with children. *Cognitive Therapy and Research, 1*(4), 331–341.

Kendall, P., Howard, B., & Epps, J. (1988). The anxious child: Cognitive-behavioral treatment strategies. *Behavior Modification, 12,* 281–310.

Kendall, P. C., Kane, M. T., Howard, B. L., & Siqueland, L. (1989). Cognitive-behavioral therapy for anxious children: Treatment manual. Unpublished manuscript, Temple University.

Koeppen, A. S. (1974). Relaxation training for children. *Elementary School Guidance and Counseling,* October, 14–21.

Lazarus, A., & Abramovitz, A. (1962). The use of "emotive imagery" in the treatment of children's phobias. *Journal of Mental Science, 108,* 191–195.

Leal, L., Baxter, E., Martin, J., & Marx, R. (1981). Cognitive modification and systematic desensitization with test anxious high school students. *Journal of Counseling Psychology, 28,* 525–528.

Long, B. (1985). Stress-management interventions: A 15-month follow-up of aerobic conditioning and stress inoculation training. *Cognitive Therapy and Research, 9,* 471–478.

Mace, R., & Carroll, C. (1985). The control of anxiety in sport: Stress inoculation training prior to abseiling. *International Journal of Sports Psychology, 16,* 165–175.

Marlatt, A., & Gordon, J. (1984). *Relapse prevention: A self-control strategy for the maintenance of behavior change.* New York: Guilford Press.

McGrath, P. A. (1990). *Pain in children: Nature, assessment and treatment.* New York: Guilford Press.

Meichenbaum, D. (1972). Cognitive modification of test-anxious college students. *Journal of Consulting and Clinical Psychology, 39,* 370–380.

Meichenbaum, D. (1975). Toward a cognitive theory of self-control. In G. Schwartz & D. Shapiro (Eds.), *Consciousness and self-regulation: Advances in research.* New York: Plenum Press.

Meichenbaum, D. (1977). *Cognitive-behavior modification: An integrative approach.* New York: Plenum Press.

Meichenbaum, D. (1985). *Stress inoculation training.* New York: Pergamon Press.

Meichenbaum, D., & Cameron, R. (1972). *Stress inoculation: A skills training approach to anxiety management.* Unpublished manuscript, University of Waterloo, Ontario, Canada.

Meichenbaum, D., & Deffenbacher, J. (1988). Stress inoculation training. *The Counseling Psychologist, 16,* 69–90.

Meichenbaum, D., & Goodman, J. (1971). Training impulsive children to talk to themselves: A means of developing self-control. *Journal of Abnormal Psychology, 77,* 115–126.

Nelson, W. M., III, Finch, A. J, Jr., & Hooke, J. F. (1975). Effects of reinforcement and response-cost on cognitive style in emotionally disturbed boys. *Journal of Abnormal Psychology, 84,* 426–428.

Nelson, W. M., & Behler, J. J. (1990). Cognitive impulsivity training: The effects of peer teaching. *Journal of Behavior Therapy and Experimental Psychiatry, 20,* 303–309.

Novaco, R., Cook, T., & Sarason, I. (1983). Military recruit training: An arena for stress-coping skills. In D. Meichenbaum & M. Jaremko (Eds.), *Stress reduction and prevention.* New York: Plenum Press.

Ollendick, T., & Francis, G. (1988). Behavioral assessment and treatment of child phobias. *Behavior Modification, 12,* 165–192.

Ost, L. G., Jerremalm, A., & Johansson, J. (1981). Individual response patterns and the effects of different behavioral methods in the treatment of social phobia. *Behaviour Research and Therapy, 19,* 1–16.

Ost, L. G., Jerremalm, A., & Johansson, J. (1984). Individual response patterns and the effects of different behavioral methods in the treatment of agoraphobia. *Behaviour Research and Therapy, 20,* 697–707.

Ost, L. G., Johansson, J., & Jerremalm, A. (1982). Individual response patterns and the effects of different behavioral methods in the treatment of social phobia. *Behaviour Research and Therapy, 20,* 445–460.

Peterson, L., & Shigetomi, C. (1981). The use of coping techniques in minimizing anxiety in hospitalized children. *Behavior Therapy, 12,* 1–14.

Prins, P. (1985). Self-speech and self-regulation of high- and low-anxious children in the dental situation: An interview study. *Behaviour Research and Therapy, 23,* 641–650.

Ramirez, S., Kratochwill, T., & Morris, R. (1987). Child anxiety disorders. In L. Michelson & L. M. Ascher (Eds.), *Anxiety and stress disorders* (pp. 149–175). New York: Guilford Press.

Richardson, F. (1975). *Coping with test anxiety: A guide.* Unpublished manual, University of Texas at Austin, Department of Educational Psychology.

Ridberg, E., Parke, R., & Hetherington, E. (1971). Modifications of impulsive and reflective cognitive styles through observation of film-mediated models. *Developmental Psychology, 5,* 369–377.

Rose, M., Firestone, P., Heick, H., & Faught, A. (1983). The effects of anxiety management training on the control of juvenile diabetes mellitus. *Journal of Behavioral Medicine, 6,* 381–395.

Russell, R. K., & Sipich, J. F. (1974). Cue-controlled relaxation in the treatment of test anxiety. *Journal of Behavior Therapy and Experimental Psychiatry, 4,* 47–49.

Salovey, P., & Haar, M. (1983, April). *Treating writing anxiety: Cognitive restructuring and writing process training.* Paper presented at the annual meeting of the American Educational Research Association, Montreal.

Sarason, S. B., Davidson, K. S., Lighthall, F. F., Waite, R. R., & Ruebush, B. R. (1960). *Anxiety in elementary school children.* New York: Wiley.

Schachter, S. (1966). The interaction of cognitive and physiological determinants of emotion. In C. Spielberger (Ed.), *Anxiety and behavior.* New York: Academic Press.

Siegel, L. J., & Peterson, L. (1980). Stress reduction in young dental patients through coping skills and sensory information. *Journal of Consulting and Clinical Psychology, 48,* 785–787.

Siegel, L. J., & Peterson, L. (1981). Maintenance effects of coping skills and sensory information on young children's responses to repeated dental procedures. *Behavior Therapy, 12,* 530–535.

Spielberger, C. D. (1973). *State-Trait Anxiety Inventory for Children: Preliminary manual.* Palo Alto, CA: Consulting Psychologist Press.

Stevens, R. (1979). *The failure disabled student: Three studies of the adolescent at-risk for school failure and a suggested remedial model.* Unpublished doctoral dissertation, McGill University, Montreal.

Stevens, R., & Phil, R. (1983). Learning to cope with school: A study of the effects of a coping skill training program with test-vulnerable 7th grade students. *Cognitive Therapy and Research, 7,* 155–158.

Suinn, R. M. (1986). *Manual: Anxiety management training (AMT).* Fort Collins, CO: Rocky Mountain Behavioral Science Institute.

Suinn, R., & Deffenbacher, J. (1988). Anxiety management training. *The Counseling Psychologist, 16,* 31–49.

Suinn, R., & Richardson, F. (1971). Anxiety management training: A non-specific behavior therapy program for anxiety control. *Behavior Therapy, 2,* 498–510.

West, D., Horan, J., & Games, P. (1984). Component analysis of occupational stress inoculation applied to registered nurses in an acute care hospital setting. *Journal of Counseling Psychology, 31,* 209–218.

Zatz, S., & Chassin, L. (1983). Cognitions of test-anxious children. *Journal of Consulting and Clinical Psychology, 51,* 526–534.

CHAPTER NINE

Child and Adolescent Depression

Cognitive-Behavioral Strategies and Interventions

MICHAEL P. CAREY

In comparison to the literature on adult depression, progress in the investigation of child and adolescent depression has been slow. Nonetheless, in the last 15 years there has been a noticeable increase in the interest in and the study of child and adolescent depression. Clinicians and researchers have agreed that children and adolescents experience symptoms of depression such as sadness or dysphoric mood. However, only in recent years have mental health providers recognized that young people and adolescents can and do experience groups of symptoms that make up depressive syndromes and/or disorders (Clarizio, 1989). This increased knowledge and the acceptance of the study of depression within childhood and adolescence have been sparked by a number of developments in the mental health field that merit discussion, as they provide a foundation for examining cognitive-behavioral treatment approaches.

The development and application of relevant assessment and diagnostic criteria have contributed to the increase in the study of child and adolescent depression. Most of the assessment instruments have been self- and parent-report inventories; during the past several years clinician rating scales and semistructured diagnostic interviews have been developed (Witt, Cavell, Heffer, Carey, & Martens, 1988). By quantifying the number, duration, and/or severity of depressive symptoms, semistructured diagnostic interviews such as the Schedule for Affective Disorders and Schizophrenia for School-age Children (K-SADS—Chambers, Puig-Antich, & Tabrizi, 1978) and Interview Schedule for Children (ISC—Kovacs, 1982) have aided in the accurate diagnosis of childhood and adolescent depression. It has been proposed that child and adolescent depression can be diagnosed using the same criteria as those employed with adults (Puig-Antich & Gittleman, 1982). This position has gained popularity and partially explains why separate criteria have not been developed for diagnosing depression with children and adolescents. Unfortunately, this position ignores the salience and relevance of developmental factors in the expression of depression (Cicchetti & Schneider-Rosen, 1986). Nevertheless, the influence of the *DSM-III-R* (1987), which views child and adult depression as the same disorder, has been so pervasive that there has been limited examination of possible differences. The *DSM-III-R* criteria are presented in Table 9-1. In general, the major depressive symptoms observed in children are dysphoric mood or irritability, self-deprecation, aggression, diminished socialization, changes in school performance as well as attitude toward school, somatic complaints, loss of energy, and changes in weight and/or appetite.

In spite of the lack of consideration of developmental factors, there has been a realization that depression is a prevalent disorder within children and adolescents. Studies of childhood depression in the general population indicate a prevalence rate between 2% and 3%, whereas in child and adolescent psychiatric patients the rate is estimated to be between 7% and 27% (Finch, Casat, & Carey, 1990). Moreover, new data from the Lewinsohn, Hops, Roberts, and Seeley (1989) epidemiological study of adolescent depression suggest that the incidence and life-time prevalence of major and minor depression is higher than originally estimated. Lewinsohn and his

TABLE 9-1 • *DSM-III-R Criteria for Major Depressive Disorder*

1. Depressed mood
2. Loss of interest or pleasure
3. Significant weight loss or weight gain or failure to make expected weight gains in children
4. Insomnia or hypersomnia
5. Psychomotor agitation or retardation
6. Fatigue or loss of energy
7. Feelings of worthlessness or excessive/inappropriate guilt
8. Diminished concentration
9. Recurrent thoughts of death, suicidal ideation, suicide attempt, or specific plan for committing suicide

Five or more of these symptoms must be present for a diagnosis of major depressive disorder.

colleagues interviewed a random sample of approximately 1,200 adolescents with the K-SADS-E semistructured diagnostic interview and found a prevalence rate of 2.7%, a 12-month incidence rate of 5.3%, and a life-time prevalence rate of 20.2%. These findings point to the need for the development of effective interventions for depression in children and adolescents.

The need for effective interventions is emphasized further by the realization that childhood depression is not a transient disorder (Kovacs, Fienberg, Crouse-Novak, Paulauskas, & Finkelstein, 1984). Kovacs et al. used a longitudinal design employing a semistructured interview, and on the basis of their findings, they persuasively declared that children with an early age of onset had a more extended and treatment-resistant illness. Their findings refuted the assertion by Lefkowitz and Burton (1978) that depression within childhood is a transient phenomenon and provided strong evidence of the stability of depressive disorders within childhood. This study also demonstrated the utility of employing standardized diagnostic interviews.

Although suicide is not tantamount to depression, the rise of adolescent suicide within the past two decades also has served as a catalyst for the study of child and adolescent depression. Recent studies have suggested that the rate of suicide within adolescence has doubled within the past 10 years (Hawton, 1986). As a result of the steady increase, suicide is currently ranked as the third leading cause of death within adolescence. Moreover, several studies have indicated that depression is an important risk factor for suicide and suicidal ideation (Blumenthal & Hirschfeld, 1984; McGuire, 1983).

In summary, the expansion of literature addressing depression in children and adolescents has been reflected by an increase in the number of published studies appearing in scholarly journals such as the *Journal of Consulting and Clinical Psychology, Journal of Abnormal Child Psychology, Journal of the American Academy of Child and Adolescent Psychiatry, American Journal of Psychiatry,* and *Journal of Clinical Child Psychology.* The findings from the literature on depression have suggested that childhood depression can be reliably assessed and diagnosed. Moreover, depressive disorders within childhood and adolescence are disorders that are not transient in nature and that are associated with an increased risk of suicide behavior.

The purpose of this chapter is to acquaint the reader with cognitive-behavioral intervention strategies for the treatment of child and adolescent depression. Because a cognitive-behavioral perspective emphasizes the necessary relationship between assessment and treatment, the initial section of this chapter focuses on the process and content of assessment. This initial section is followed by an overview of the basic principles and treatment components of the most widely cited cognitive-behavioral treatment approaches to depression. The remainder of the chapter reviews the literature supporting the use of cognitive-behavioral interventions with depressed children and adolescents.

Assessment of Childhood and Adolescent Depression

Within a cognitive-behavioral framework, assessment is a continuous process in which the therapist repeatedly evaluates and adjusts the course and speed of treatment. The formal assessment phase provides the therapist with information regarding the frequency, duration, and scope of the problem as well as with an evaluation of the impact on adaptive functioning (e.g., school performance, peer relationships, family relations, work habits). Thus, the diagnostic criteria of the *DSM-III-R* can be employed as a guide at this stage of treatment. The assessment process also may provide the therapist with information regarding hindrances to the therapeutic process, and the assessment findings can guide the cognitive-behavioral therapist in the development of a treatment plan and the selection of target behaviors and treatment techniques.

Typically, the initial phase of assessment will include one or more interviews with the client and parents. The interview is followed by gathering information from other sources (e.g., teacher, peers, siblings) and methods (e.g., rating scales, behavioral observations, psychological testing). Open-ended clinical interviews can be conducted with the client and parents separately or together, depending on the type of information solicited and the preference of the therapist. Three major issues need to be addressed: (a) the parents' and child's particular views of the complaints, symptoms, and stressors; (b) the parents' and child's particular views of the current environment (home, school, peers) and current daily functioning (sleeping, eating, digestion and elimination habits, as well as the sexual interests of adolescents); and (c) the parents' and child's particular views of development, history, and projections about the future. Thus, during the clinical interviews, information is obtained regarding the client's presenting problems, social history, school and occupational history, family psychiatric history, previous treatment, physical health, and family environment. An open-ended interview increases the likelihood of gathering such descriptions of everyday life and of identifying antecedents and consequences surrounding the problem behaviors.

The information obtained may be supplemented by information from ratings scales for depression and associated problems (see Table 9-2 and Table 9-3). A review of specific rating scales and structured diagnostic

TABLE 9-2 • *Selected Assessment Devices for Child and Adolescent Depression*

Assessment Instrument	Reference
Self-Report	
Children's Depression Inventory	Kovacs (1982)
Beck Depression Inventory	Beck & Beamesderfer (1974)
Reynolds Adolescent Depression Scale	Reynolds (1987)
Reynolds Child Depression Scale (RCDS)	Reynolds (1989)
Clinician Ratings	
Children's Depression Rating Scale—Revised	Poznanski, Freeman, & Mokros (1984)
Hamilton Depression Rating Scale	Hamilton (1960)
Belleview Index of Depression—Revised	Kazdin, French, Unis, & Esveldt-Dawson (1983)
Diagnostic Interviews	
Child Assessment Schedule—Child Form	Hodges (1985)
Interview Schedule for Children	Kovacs (1982)
Schedule for Affective Disorders and Schizophrenia for School-Age Children	Chambers, Puig-Antich, & Tabrizi (1978)

interviews is beyond the scope of this chapter; therefore, the reader is referred to one of several excellent review chapters on the assessment of depression (e.g., Edelbrock & Costello, 1984; Finch et al., 1990; Witt et al., 1988). The use of rating scales has several advantages, such as making it possible to gather a considerable amount of information in a time-efficient fashion. Moreover, assuming that standardized assessment devices are used, the therapist is able to compare the client's relative standing to normal youths with the same demographic characteristics (e.g., gender, race, age, and socioeconomic status). Also, cut-off scores for depression are provided. However, the clinician should remember that the diagnosis of depression is not dependent on a cut-off score or on a single assessment instrument.

Two other approaches in assessment have received limited attention, although they seem to hold considerable promise—direct observation strategies and biological markers. While direct observation procedures have been described in more detail elsewhere (Frame & Matson, 1987), they

TABLE 9-3 • *Assessment Devices of Related Constructs*

Assessment Instrument	*Reference*
Hopelessness Scale for Children	Kazdin, Rodgers, & Colbus (1986)
Revised Children's Manifest Anxiety Scale	Reynolds & Richmond (1985)
Adolescent Activity Checklist	Carey, Kelley, Buss, & Scott (1986)
Life Events Checklist	Johnson & McCutcheon (1980)
Differential Emotions Scale	Blumberg & Izard (1986)
Family Environment Scale	Moos & Moos (1986)
Suicide Ideation Questionnaire	Reynolds (1988)
Child Behavior Checklist Child, Teacher, & Youth Forms	Achenbach & Edelbrock (1983, 1986, 1987)

basically involve developing an operational definition of the target behaviors, rating these behaviors in the child's natural environment, and establishing the reliability of such ratings. There are three specific classes of behaviors that seem particularly relevant when dealing with depressed children (Williams, Barlow, & Agras, 1972): (a) social activities (e.g., talking with others, playing games, duration of participating in group activities, interacting with others); (b) solitary behavior (e.g., playing alone, reading, studying, listening to music or watching T.V. alone, staying in one's room); and (c) affect-related expression (e.g., smiling, frowning, arguing, complaining). As with other direct observation procedures, these strategies are limited because of their complexity and costliness.

In regard to biological markers, the dexamethasone suppression test (DST — Carroll, 1982) has received the most interest. This test is based on the premise that when an individual is depressed, cortisol levels are not suppressed following the administration of dexamethasone, a synthetic cortisol. In addition to the fact that DST is not always a precise measure, it appears that it may not be specific to depression (Arana, Baldessarini, & Ornsteen, 1985). Furthermore, less is known about this procedure with children and adolescents than with depressed adults (Casat, Arana, & Powell, 1989).

Muscle tension, which has been found in very depressed adults (Whatmore & Kohli, 1968), may ultimately offer biological assessment information regarding depressed children; however, the usefulness of this physiological phenomenon remains hypothetical. Although biological markers may eventually be useful adjuncts to other assessment techniques, they do not have a current role in evaluating childhood depression.

In summary, a comprehensive assessment of depression incorporates information from multiple sources and culminates in the development of an initial diagnosis and treatment plan. At this point in the assessment process, there should be a clear delineation of specific target behaviors and a specific plan for measuring the outcome of treatment.

Cognitive-Behavioral Intervention Models of Depression

The most prominent cognitive-behavioral models of depression include Ellis's Rational Emotive Therapy (Bernard & Joyce, 1984), Beck's Cognitive Therapy (Beck, Rush, Shaw, & Emery, 1977), Rehm's Self-Control theory (Fuchs & Rehm, 1977), Lewinsohn's conceptualization of depression (Clarke, Lewinsohn, & Hops, 1990; Lewinsohn & Hoberman, 1982; Lewinsohn, Clarke, & Rohde, 1989), and the reformulated Learned Helplessness Model (Abramson, Seligman, & Teasdale, 1978). Each of these models was developed originally for adults and has been extended to treatment of children and adolescents with or without modifications. Although the reformulated learned helplessness model is considered to be a cognitive-behavioral model of depression, no specific treatment approach is based on this theory; therefore, this model will not be discussed. The remaining four models are presented and discussed in the context of their relevance to the treatment of child and adolescent depression. The reader is reminded that a variety of other modalities are useful in working with depressed youngsters. Professionals who are interested in a more indepth discussion of assessment and treatment procedures are referred to recent publications by Matson (1989), Finch et al. (1990), and Finch, Lipovsky and Casat (1989).

Ellis's Model

Basic Principles
Ellis's Rational Emotive Therapy (RET) was perhaps the first cognitive-behavioral intervention employed with children and adolescents (Clarizio, 1989). The approach is similar to RET as practiced with adults except that it takes into account the child's cognitive and linguistic development (Ellis & Bernard, 1983). Other cognitive-behavioral techniques such as problem solving, social skills training, and stress inoculation training are often incorporated into RET with children and adolescents.

The basic principle of RET is that an individual's emotional discomfort is caused by faulty or irrational thinking. Ellis generated 11 irrational beliefs that he proposed as central to the development and maintenance of emotional disturbance. Waters (1982) extended Ellis's work to the treatment of depression in children and adolescents and generated 10 irrational beliefs according to developmental level. The irrational beliefs associated with children include:

1. It's awful if others don't like me.
2. I'm bad if I make a mistake.
3. Everything should go my way; I should always get what I want.
4. Things should come easy to me.
5. The world should be fair, and bad people must be punished.
6. I shouldn't show my feelings.
7. Adults should be perfect.
8. There's only one right answer.
9. I must win.
10. I shouldn't have to wait for anything. (p. 572)

Similarly, Waters (1981) identified irrational beliefs that characterize adolescents:

1. It would be awful if peers didn't like me. It would be awful to be a social loser.
2. I shouldn't make mistakes, especially social mistakes.
3. It's my parents' fault I'm so miserable.
4. I can't help it—that's just the way I am, and I guess I'll always be that way.
5. The world should be fair and just.
6. It's awful when things do not go my way.
7. It's better to avoid challenges than to risk failure.
8. I must conform to my peers.
9. I can't stand to be criticized.
10. Others should always be responsible. (p. 6)

According to RET, these irrational beliefs play an important role in the development of low self-esteem and in the subsequent formation of depression (Bernard & Joyce, 1984). Ellis explicated an elaborate theory of emotional disturbance that is commonly referred to as the *ABC-DE* theory. In RET the therapist begins by asking the child or adolescent to describe the problem and by noting that the response will be either a description of the emotional and behavioral consequences (*C*) (e.g., "I'm feeling sad or down," "I don't want to do anything except stay in my room") or the activating event (*A*) (e.g., "Nobody likes me at school," "My parents are getting a divorce"). RET assumes that the activating event (*A*) precipitates the emotional and behavioral consequence (*C*), but that the irrational belief (*B*) is the causal agent of *C*.

The *D* and *E* in Ellis's model are the agents which provide the curative features of RET. The *D* represents disputation, the RET intervention. According to Ellis's theory the youngster's irrational beliefs can be disputed via cognitive, emotional, and/or behavioral means. The net outcome of the therapist's disputation of the client's irrational beliefs is what Ellis referred to as the effect (*E*). The effect is the adoption of a new and more rational and adaptive cognitive philosophy or style by the client.

Treatment Components

Rational Emotive Therapy is a confrontational and active therapy. Unlike traditional psychotherapy, an educational/didactic model is employed. Thus, in RET the therapist often serves as a teacher who emphasizes that emotional distress is self-inflicted by retaining irrational and unrealistic beliefs about one's self. Therefore, RET teaches children and adolescents to be more rational and realistic. Although the primary focus is on the client's irrational beliefs, treatment also addresses emotional and behavioral aspects of the youth's depression.

In the initial sessions of RET, the therapist attempts to establish a good working relationship with the client in order to maximize the ability to dispute the youth's irrational beliefs. Bernard and Joyce (1984) noted that in order to facilitate self-disclosure the therapist may need to proceed at a slower pace with younger clients. Wagner and Glicken (1966) suggested several features that are helpful for establishing rapport with a child or adolescent client: (a) use of simple language that is consistent with the client's developmental and cognitive abilities; (b) liberal use of humor; (c) accentuation of the self-defeating features of the client's behavior; (d) frequent use of concrete examples; (e) treating the child with respect; (f) use of "ice breaker" statements when asking the child or adolescent a question; (g) willingness to acknowledge that others, including parents, are not infallible; and (h) emphasis on the importance of homework and practice in order to achieve treatment gains.

Once rapport is established with the child, the therapist begins to educate the client as to the goals of RET. With younger children the rationale is simplified and may not involve teaching the ABCs of RET. However, older children are provided with a more detailed explanation of the ABCs and goals of RET. Much of the time in the early sessions of therapy focuses on identifying the client's irrational beliefs and teaching the components of the ABCs. In working with younger clients the liberal use of charts and diagrams assists the didactic process.

The early sessions also involve teaching the child or adolescent several cognitive techniques such as substituting rational self-statements for irrational beliefs. Assuming that the client is able to discriminate facts, opinions, and inferences from thoughts and beliefs, the use of empirical analysis or hypothesis testing also may be useful. As with other cognitive-behavioral interventions, practice and homework assignments are essential in learning and internalizing skills presented by the RET clinician.

The middle sessions continue to build on the successes of earlier ones. A great deal of time is spent discussing homework and dealing with resistance to homework completion. At this stage the therapist may decide to include the child's parents in the sessions. Family participation can be very beneficial, for parents can be taught to notice their child's irrational beliefs and then to assist their child to think in a more rational, realistic fashion. Parents who are taught to be "therapists" can help not only their child but also themselves, as there is evidence that the parents of children who experience emotional problems are more likely to be experiencing difficulties also.

As the client approaches the later phase of treatment, the content of the sessions shifts from discussing and planning homework assignments to discussing ways of enhancing treatment generalization. A key component to the maintenance of treatment gains is the therapist's emphasis on the importance of continuing to practice rational thinking in a variety of settings and situations. Again, it is likely that generalization efforts will be enhanced if parents are taught to be therapists and to work actively with their child beyond the formal therapy sessions. Finally, arrangements should be made for the incorporation of "booster" sessions on an as needed basis.

Beck's Model

Basic Principles

Beck's therapy and treatment of depression provide the most widely cited cognitive-behavioral model of depression (Beck et al., 1979). The approach has been rigorously evaluated with adult depressed patients and found to be an effective psychosocial intervention. During the last decade, researchers and clinicians have examined the utility of cognitive therapy in treating childhood and adolescent depression (Emory, Bedrosian, & Garber, 1983).

Beck's theory assumes that "cognitions do not cause depression or any other psychopathological disorder but are an intrinsic part of the disorder" (Beck & Weishaar, 1989, p. 23). The theory postulates that cognitions and cognitive processes often become distorted when an individual is faced with physical or psychological distress. For instance, when faced with an emotionally provoking event, an individual may selectively attend and/or recall the event in a distorted fashion. Rather than the 11 faulty beliefs used in RET, the focus is on a more general group of faulty modes of thinking.

A central concept of Beck's cognitive theory of depression is the notion of the "cognitive triad," which includes a negative view of the self, world, and the future. The negative view of the self implies that the depressed individual perceives himself or herself as defective, inadequate, and worthless. This depressogenic theme also colors the depressed individual's perception of the world. The distorted view of the world is often manifested through the use of disparaging comments concerning the excessive demands placed on the individual by the environment. Also, the depressed individual's depressogenic theme is manifested through the tendency to misperceive situations and infer impending doom. The negative view of the future further reinforces the expectations for failure and leads to the perception that he or she is a burden on the family and society. Thus, the depressed individual sees no way out of the abyss and subsequently feels hopeless. These feelings further reinforce the individual's feelings of worthlessness and minimize mastery experiences.

Another important component of Beck's theory is the concept of cognitive distortion. Beck hypothesized that during times of psychological distress, distorted cognitive processes are evident through examination of the individual's "systematic errors in reasoning." Beck has identified six cognitive distortions: (a) arbitrary inferences, (b) selective abstraction, (c) overgeneralization, (d) magnification or minimization, (e) personalization, and (f) dichotomous thinking. Arbitrary inference involves jumping to conclusions on the basis of inadequate information (e.g., the adolescent who has problems with a math homework assignment might conclude, "I'll never be able to learn math in this class"). In selective abstraction, the child or adolescent attends only to the negative aspects of experiences (e.g., the adolescent who believes that "because my dad and I had a fight, the whole day is ruined" not because this is true, but because other pleasurable events during the day have been screened out). Overgeneralization is observed in children who make sweeping judgments on the basis of single instances (e.g., "I can't ever do anything right!"). Magnification involves "making mountains out of molehills" (e.g., the child who thinks he or she is basically a "bad" person for having gotten angry and "talked back" to the mother), and minimization involves seeing a molehill where a mountain exists. In personalization the youngster assumes responsibility for things that have little to do with him or her (e.g., children who feel responsible for their parents' divorce). Finally, dichotomous thinking refers to reasoning in extremes or seeing things as being "black or white" (e.g., the adolescent who believes that "if I can't get 100 on this test, it's not worth even trying").

These systematic cognitive errors help to maintain problematic behaviors and reinforce a self-fulfilling prophecy of worthlessness and inadequacy. As a result the individual is depressed.

Treatment Components

Beck's treatment package incorporates both behavioral and cognitive intervention techniques and, as practiced with children and adolescents, shares a resemblance to RET. The goal of therapy is to modify the individual's faulty cognitions and perceptions via a collaborative relationship with the therapist. In essence, the therapeutic techniques employed in cognitive therapy allow the client and therapist to challenge depressogenic schema and systematic cognitive errors.

In general, the skills and techniques involved in Beck's cognitive-behavioral therapy for childhood and adolescent depression limit its applicability to those individuals who possess at least concrete operational meta-cognitive development (Schleser, Meyers, & Cohen, 1981). Thus, children with preoperational thought processes are unlikely to benefit from this approach to treatment. Children and adolescents in the formal operations period of development will probably derive the most benefit from the cognitive strategies involved in the therapy, although this needs to be empirically examined in much greater detail.

DiGiuseppe (1989) discussed several modifications needed to accommodate the child's cognitive and linguistic development. For instance, he proposed that the therapist should make use of concrete examples when challenging distorted cognitions. Additionally, it is also helpful to use visual aids and to allow the child to learn by doing (DiGiuseppe, 1989).

As with any therapeutic endeavor the therapist's first task is to develop a working relationship with the youngster. Once the relationship is established, the therapist serves as a collaborator in the process of examining the child's thoughts, behavior, and emotions. Usually the cognitive processes are assessed by (a) helping the child become increasingly aware of times when he or she feels sad, down in the dumps, unhappy, and so forth; (b) teaching the child to self-monitor the situation or precipitating event as well as thoughts and feelings about the event; and (c) determining the degree to which the child believes the dysfunctional thoughts.

After evaluating the faulty cognitive processes, the therapist and the child begin work on the skills acquisition phase of treatment in which the therapist teaches the child how to solve problems in interpersonal and/or emotional situations (DiGiuseppe, 1989). Problem-solving skills enable the child or adolescent to appreciate the relationship between thoughts, feelings, and behavior. It is then possible to teach strategies that assist in gaining control over thoughts, in changing behavior patterns, and in modifying emotions.

The final phase of treatment requires the client to practice the skills in role-play situations during the sessions and through homework assignments between sessions. During this phase of therapy the therapist and client collaborate on setting the session's agenda and review progress and setbacks prior to negotiating the next homework assignment.

Rehm's Model

Basic Principles

Rehm's self-control theory of depression (Fuchs & Rehm, 1977) is a modification of Kanfer's (1970) self-control theory. Rehm's model postulates that depression occurs as a result of deficits in one or more of the three hypothesized regulatory components of self-control: self-monitoring, self-evaluation, and self-reinforcement. Rehm proposed that an individual's depression is reflected by each of the following factors: (a) negative self-evaluations, (b) inadequate rates of self-reinforcement, and (c) high rates of self-induced punishment.

According to Kaslow and Rehm (1983), the depressed client has two problems with respect to self-monitoring. First, a depressed individual tends to selectively attend to negative events and to ignore positive events. Second, the depressed client tends to focus on the immediate rather than on long-term consequences of behavior.

Similarly, two deficits have been identified in the depressed person's self-evaluation. Kaslow and Rehm (1983) noted that a depressed individual sets unrealistic goals and makes inaccurate attributions concerning successes and failures. Thus, the client's distorted attribution process reinforces feelings of inadequacy and pessimism.

The third component of Rehm's self-control theory of depression involves deficits in self-reinforcement. Specifically, Rehm's theory proposes that these deficits are evident through the depressed individual's tendency to be overly self-critical and self-punitive. Also, depressed children and adolescents provide themselves with inadequate self-reinforcement.

Treatment Components

Kaslow and Rehm (1985) provided an overview of the treatment of childhood depression via self-control therapy. As outlined by these authors, self-control therapy is a didactic treatment program that stresses the importance of homework assignments between sessions. Ideally the treatment is conducted in a group, but it can be adapted to an individual therapy format. Following an initial assessment to identify the client's strengths and weaknesses, the therapy is completed in 10 highly structured sessions. The goals of therapy include remedying the deficits in self-monitoring, self-evaluation, self-attribution, and self-reinforcement.

During the initial session the client is acquainted with the self-control model of depression and is shown the relationship between depressed mood and negative self-statements. In a didactic format the child learns that during depressive episodes individuals tend to selectively filter out positive self-statements and to augment negative self-statements. The initial therapy session concludes with the request that the child self-monitor daily mood and participation in pleasant and unpleasant activities.

The second session involves a discussion of the previous week's homework and teaches the client how to graph daily ratings of mood and activity. The graph provides a visual aid that is useful in teaching and illustrating the relationship between mood and behavior. The child is encouraged to increase participation in pleasant or pleasurable activities and to continue to monitor daily mood.

Session 3 focuses on discrimination training, which teaches the child to differentiate the immediate and long-term consequences of behavior. The child continues to self-monitor behavior and mood between sessions and is instructed to identify a positive delayed effect of behavior on a daily basis.

Attribution training is introduced in Session 4. The child is taught to make more realistic and rational self-statements concerning successes and failures. Sessions 5 and 6 address the depressed client's tendency to set unrealistic goals. The client is taught to reduce goals into subgoals and to operationally define individual goals that are actually attainable.

The seventh and eighth sessions focus on the issue of self-reinforcement. The child learns the meaning of this concept and is taught how to self-reinforce with self-praise and with tangible reinforcers—both overtly and covertly. Self-reinforcement is then incorporated into the client's self-monitoring homework exercises. The final two sessions focus on review and practice.

Lewinsohn's Model

Basic Principles

One of the more widely cited theories of depression is Lewinsohn's cognitive-behavioral formulation (Clarke, et al., 1990; Lewinsohn & Hoberman, 1982). Lewinsohn's original theory of depression focused on the relationship between reinforcement and punishment rates and the onset and maintenance of depression. Specifically, Lewinsohn and associates proposed that depression is the outcome of experiencing a low rate of response-contingent reinforcement from the environment and/or experiencing a high rate of aversive or punishing events. As a result the individual develops overt signs of depression—such as social withdrawal and passivity—in addition to the cognitive and motivational characteristics of depression.

Lewinsohn's theory has subsequently been revised and applied to depressed adolescents (Lewinsohn et al., 1989). The revised theory postulates a circular model that involves seven interrelated components. The model assumes that individuals have predisposing "vulnerabilities" (e.g., history of depression, poor social skills, oversensitivity to aversive events) and "immunities" (high social skills, high frequency of engagement in pleasant activities) that either increase or decrease the likelihood of the development of depression.

According to the circular model, the onset of depression is preceded by an "Antecedent"—that is, an evoking event sets into action a chain of events that is either buffered or augmented by the individual's personal vulnerabilities and/or immunities. The depression-evoking event subsequently leads to a disruption in the individual's behavior pattern and/or an immediate emotional response. The individual experiences either a reduction in the rate of positive reinforcement and/or an elevation in the rate of aversive experiences. This, in turn, is followed by heightened self-focus, self-awareness, and self-criticism and results in an increased sense of dysphoria. The sequence culminates in the behavioral, cognitive, emotional, somatic, and interpersonal manifestations of depression. Moreover, the manifestations of the individual's depression reinforce the negative expectations and lead to an increased predisposition to develop recurrent episodes of depression.

Treatment Components

Clarke et al. (1990) developed a detailed treatment program that is a simplified modification of the Adult Coping with Depression Course (Lewinsohn, Antonuccio, Steinmetz, & Teri, 1984) and includes a section on conflict resolution. This structured, multicomponent intervention program targets areas that are often problematic for depressed adolescents: anxiety and discomfort, dysfunctional and irrational thoughts, social skills, low rate of engagement in pleasant activities, and conflict resolution.

The treatment program is designed as a formal class, and the adolescent client attends sixteen 2-hour sessions over a span of 8 weeks. Also, an abbreviated class for the parents involves nine 2-hour sessions that review the skills being taught to the adolescent and teach problem solving and communication skills. The authors have developed detailed treatment manuals for both the adolescent and parent Coping with Depression Courses (Clarke, et al., 1990).

Except for the initial visit, the sessions are highly structured. Generally, each session includes setting an agenda, reviewing the previous week's homework assignments, and discussing new skills associated with role-play and/or practice exercises. Each session concludes with the assignment of homework and a preview of the next session's agenda. Typically, a skill is introduced and taught during the course of several sessions, and skill review during later sessions is tailored to the adolescent's homework assignments.

In the initial session of the adolescent program, the therapist presents a social learning perspective on the onset and maintenance of depression and then sets the ground rules (e.g., equal time, confidentiality). The adolescent is told that depression results from "problems in living" (Lewinsohn et al., 1989) and that it is possible to overcome one's depression by learning new skills. Specifically, the youth is advised that overcoming depression involves examining the relation between thoughts, behavior, and feelings. Additionally, the client receives instruction in basic communication skills such as starting a conversation and joining and exiting a group.

Sessions 2 and 3 provide further social skills instruction, and during these sessions the adolescent discusses and identifies enjoyable activities. The youth's baseline activity level is assessed, and the client and therapist determine a reasonable goal with regard to increasing activity. Prior to the completion of the second session, a behavioral contract is negotiated and evaluated, and during the third session, progressive relaxation is introduced.

Sessions 4 and 5 continue the assessment and monitoring of participation in pleasurable activities. In addition, the client receives further instruction in the use of several progressive relaxation techniques, and an effort is made to develop practical applications of these techniques. During Session 5 the cognitive skills training model is introduced.

Sessions 6 through 10 include practice of relaxation techniques and a focus on cognitive skills training. The cognitive skills training involves the identification of frequently experienced negative and positive cognitions. The client is taught to create "positive counter-thoughts" and is instructed in finding alternate ways to cope with depression-evoking events. Self-monitoring of daily mood, engagement in pleasant activities, and practice of the relaxation techniques are reviewed and discussed. In Session 6, social skills are reviewed, and additional social skills training is provided during sessions 7 and 8. Instruction in communication skills dominates sessions 9 and 10. Active listening skills are taught, and the client learns to state feelings while minimizing accusatory statements. The communication skills training content focuses primarily on parent-adolescent conflicts.

Sessions 11 through 14 provide the client with an opportunity to learn and practice problem-solving skills. The adolescent is taught the five steps of problem solving—defining the problem, brainstorming, choosing a solution, reaching an agreement/contract, and reevaluating the agreement/contract. The client is encouraged to practice problem-solving skills via role plays. As in previous sessions, self-monitoring of mood, engagement in pleasant activities, and practice of the relaxation techniques are reviewed as part of the homework assignments during Sessions 11 and 12.

Sessions 15 and 16 focus on setting short- and long-term goals. There is emphasis on refining the client's ability to detect a relapse and to formulate plans to overcome depression-evoking events. These two sessions also include a review of the youth's homework assignments and address issues related to termination.

Summary

There are common characteristics among the cognitive-behavioral treatment models of depression that have been presented. Each model stresses the importance of practicing behavioral and cognitive skills within therapy sessions and the necessity of completing homework assignments. In addition, each model integrates procedures that have traditionally been considered behavioral treatment techniques (e.g., self-monitoring) and cognitive techniques (e.g., cognitive restructuring). However, the approaches emphasize different key components in treatment (e.g., cognitions, behavior, and emotions). In spite of their similarities, each model places more or less emphasis on specific techniques (e.g., relaxation, activity scheduling, etc.). This review provides the basis for the following section, which examines the available evidence supporting the use of cognitive-behavioral interventions in the treatment of childhood and adolescent depression.

Efficacy of Cognitive-Behavioral Intervention Strategies

The utility of cognitive-behavioral interventions for adult depression is well established (see Freeman, Simon, Beutler, & Arkowitz, 1989). In contrast, only a few treatment-outcome studies have been conducted to examine the effectiveness of cognitive-behavioral interventions for childhood and adolescent depression. The available outcome studies have been based on one of the four theoretical models of depression discussed in the previous section of this chapter, and each of these models has been adapted and extended for the treatment of depressed children and adolescents. This section presents an overview of the status of the treatment-outcome literature with respect to the efficacy of cognitive-behavioral therapies for depressed children and adolescents.

Currently the evidence for the efficacy of Rational Emotive Therapy rests on a small number of case studies (Bernard & Joyce, 1984; Ellis & Bernard, 1983). Only one treatment-outcome study has been conducted with children utilizing Ellis's cognitive restructuring technique as one of the treatment conditions (Butler, Miezitis, Freidman, & Cole, 1980).

Butler et al. (1980) compared the efficacy of two treatments—a role-play treatment condition and a cognitive restructuring condition—to attention-placebo and classroom-control conditions. The study was conducted with a group of 56 fifth- and sixth-grade children who were selected on the basis of cut-off scores on a battery of self-rating measures, including measures of self-esteem, depression, locus of control, and a self-appraisal questionnaire. Each of the two active treatment conditions consisted of ten 1-hour sessions.

The role-play condition involved identifying situations that the child found problematic, such as dealing with rejection, failure, guilt, and loneliness. The sessions involved a number of components, including a warm-up period, a brief review of role play, the identification of a problem area, enacting the problem, a practice time, the identification of a second problem, a summary of the session highlights, and the assignment of homework. The purpose of the sessions was to increase the child's ability to take others' perspectives, to instruct the child in social and problem-solving skills, and to increase the child's sensitivity to the feelings and thoughts of others.

The second active treatment condition, cognitive restructuring, was modeled after Beck's and Ellis's treatment approaches to depression. The objectives of this condition were to teach each child to identify irrational beliefs and to develop more positive and logical self-statements. The treatment also sought to teach the children the relationship between thoughts and feelings.

The findings indicated that, compared to the control groups, both active treatment conditions produced treatment gains. The role-play condition was the superior treatment; however, it was only marginally better than the cognitive restructuring condition. The marginal superiority of the role-play condition might be an artifact of the insufficient duration of the cognitive restructuring treatment. Also, the demands of the cognitive-restructuring condition may have been beyond the level of cognitive development of these children.

Among the many limitations of this study was the use of self-report measures for selecting depressed subjects. Apparently none of these children had been referred for treatment, and a structured interview was not conducted. Consequently the degree of clinical depression is unknown. In addition to the use of a nonreferred sample, the sketchy description of the treatment procedures employed and the lack of follow-up data limit the usefulness of its findings. Nonetheless, this was the first treatment-outcome investigation to demonstrate the effectiveness of psychosocial interventions for childhood depression. Moreover, this study provided initial encouragement for the use of cognitive-behavioral interventions with depressed children.

Following this initial investigation of the effectiveness of cognitive-behavioral interventions (Butler et al., 1980), other treatment-outcome studies appeared in the literature. Rehm's Self-Control Therapy was evaluated in a well-controlled comparative treatment-outcome study with children (Stark, Reynolds, & Kaslow, 1987). Similarly, a study with adolescents examined the effectiveness of a cognitive-behavioral intervention that incorporated several aspects of Beck's and Lewinsohn's treatment approaches (Reynolds & Coats, 1986).

Stark et al. (1987) examined the efficacy of a behavior therapy condition as compared to a self-control therapy condition and a wait-list control group. The 29 subjects ranged in age from 9 to 12 years and were randomly assigned to one of the three conditions and assessed at pretreatment, posttreatment, and 8 weeks after the completion of treatment. Prior to the beginning of treatment the authors developed treatment manuals for each of the active treatment conditions. Each treatment condition consisted of twelve 50-minute sessions conducted over a 5-week period.

Subjects were selected on the basis of a three-stage screening process. In the initial phase the Children's Depression Inventory (CDI—Kovacs, 1981) was administered to 372 children enrolled in grades four through six. Children who obtained scores of 16 or more were readministered the CDI, and those children who received a score of 13 or more were assigned to one of three conditions (i.e., self-control, behavior therapy, wait-list control). A semistructured clinical interview (i.e., Children's Depression Rating Scale—Poznanski, Freeman, & Mokros, 1984) and measures of anxiety and self-esteem were given to the subjects, and parents completed the Child Behavior Checklist (Achenbach & Edelbrock, 1983).

The behavior therapy condition was based on Lewinsohn's original model of depression. Subjects were taught a behavioral rationale for the etiology and treatment of depression, stressing the importance of the relationship between mood and the engagement in pleasant or unpleasant events. During the first four sessions, subjects self-monitored their engagement in pleasant/unpleasant activities and their associated thoughts and mood. In the fifth session, subjects received instruction and modeling of problem-solving skills. They were also taught methods designed to increase their engagement in pleasant activities and to decrease engagement in unpleasant activities. The sixth session focused on teaching the subjects to better understand the effects of their actions on the behavior of others. The remaining six sessions focused on the refinement of problem-solving skills and increasing engagement in pleasant activities. Subjects also received tangible and social rewards for completing homework assignments.

The self-control condition was modeled on Rehm's treatment for adult depression. Treatment was designed to teach adaptive skills for monitoring behavior, evaluating performance, and providing self-reinforcement. The format included didactic sessions in addition to in-session and homework assignments, and cartoon characters were used to present and to illustrate the concepts being taught. During the first four sessions, subjects were taught to self-monitor their behavior, their self-statements, and their mood using a 0–10-point scale and were intermittently reinforced for completing homework assignments. The fifth session focused on teaching subjects to monitor the delayed consequences of their actions. The sixth and seventh sessions provided training in ways to achieve a more adaptive attributional style; sessions eight and nine focused on self-evaluation skills. The three remaining sessions instructed the subjects to self-reinforce more frequently and to decrease self-punishment.

The results indicated that children in both active groups improved in comparison to the wait-list control group on self- and clinician-ratings of depression. No differences were noted between the behavior therapy and the self-control therapy groups. Gains were maintained at 8 weeks after the termination of treatment, providing support for the use of cognitive-behavioral therapy for childhood depression.

Stark et al. (1987) conducted a well-designed study that can provide direction for clinicians who work with depressed children. Although they went to great lengths to ensure that the interventions were implemented with integrity, their use of an analogue sample unfortunately makes it difficult to generalize the findings to clinical patients.

Reynolds and Coats (1986) compared the treatment efficacy of a cognitive-behavioral therapy program to a relaxation training therapy program and a wait-list control group with 30 nonreferred adolescents from grades 9–12 (mean age of 15.65 years). Subjects were randomly assigned to one of the three conditions and were assessed at pretreatment, posttreatment, and 5 weeks after the completion of treatment. Treatment manuals were developed for both of the active conditions prior to the beginning of this study. Each treatment condition consisted of ten 50-minute sessions conducted over a 5-week period.

Selection of subjects was based on a three-stage screening process using the Reynolds Adolescent Depression Scale (RADS), Beck Depression Inventory (BDI), and the Belleview Index of Depression (BID). The procedure was similar to the procedure used in subject selection by Stark et al. (1987). Adolescents who obtained BDI scores greater than or equal to 10 and RADS scores of 72 or greater were readministered the BDI and RADS as well as the BID. Those who received a BDI score of 12 or more, a RADS score of 72 or greater, and a BID score of 20 or greater on the second occasion were assigned to one of three conditions (i.e., cognitive-behavioral, relaxation training, wait-list control). The subjects also were administered anxiety and self-concept measures.

The cognitive-behavioral condition was modeled after Rehm's Self-Control treatment model and incorporated some of Beck's cognitive techniques and Lewinsohn's behavioral components. Session by session, content was similar to the self-control intervention protocol used in the Stark et al. (1987) study.

The relaxation training condition was modeled after Jacobsen's progressive muscle relaxation-training script. Subjects were presented with a rationale that stressed the relationship between stressful events, depression, and the development of muscle tension, and the treatment was designed to teach subjects how to induce a state of passive muscle relaxation. Subjects were expected to practice the relaxation skills between sessions.

The results of the study indicated that, compared to the wait-list control group, both active treatments produced significant treatment gains in depressive symptomatology. No differences were observed between the two active treatments. Not surprisingly, only the relaxation training produced significant decreases in anxiety. Although the results of this study were encouraging, the use of an analogue population limits the ability to generalize findings to clinical populations.

A fourth outcome study was recently completed by Lewinsohn, Clarke, Hops, Andrews, and Williams (1989). The objective of the study was to evaluate which of two cognitive-behavioral interventions was more effective in the treatment of adolescent depression. The study involved 59 high school students aged 14 to 18 who were randomly assigned to one of three conditions (i.e., Coping with Depression Course — adolescent only, Coping with Depression Course — adolescent and parent, wait-list control group).

Unlike the previously reviewed studies, all subjects met *DSM-III* or Research Diagnostic Criteria for major or minor depression. The diagnosis was determined via semistructured diagnostic interview (i.e., K-SADS). In addition to the interview, the subjects also completed the BDI as well as several abbreviated measures. Parents of the subjects completed the Child Behavior Checklist. Subjects in the three conditions were assessed at pretreatment, posttreatment, and at 2-years posttreatment.

Treatment manuals were developed for each of the active treatment conditions prior to the beginning of the study. Each treatment condition consisted of fourteen 2-hour sessions in a group format. In addition, parents in the adolescent-plus-parent treatment condition received seven 2-hour group sessions.

The Coping with Depression Course for Adolescents is designed to be taught as a class and includes extensive reading materials that require good reading skills (i.e., seventh-grade reading level). The treatment protocol was previously presented in detail in the discussion of Lewinsohn's model earlier in this chapter, and the reader is referred to that section for a detailed description of the course as it is used for adolescents individually and with their parents.

The results of this study indicated that subjects in the two active treatment groups improved significantly when compared to subjects in the wait-list control group. Although there were few significant differences between the two treatment conditions, the authors reported strong trends favoring the adolescent-plus-parent treatment condition. A particularly encouraging finding was the maintenance of treatment gains at 2-year follow-up.

In summary, the Lewinsohn et al. (1989) study is the first to be conducted with a referred sample of depressed adolescents. The strengths of this study are noteworthy. They include the use of a structured diagnostic interview to aid in diagnosis, an adequate sample size, a well-specified treatment protocol, the suitable handling of developmental issues, and the incorporation of long-term follow-up (i.e., 2 years). However, there are some weaknesses in this investigation. For instance, the sample selected for inclusion was restricted to middle and late adolescence; therefore, the findings cannot be generalized to younger clients. Particularly problematic is the fact that adolescents were excluded from treatment if their reading comprehensive skills were below a seventh-grade level. Although this limits the application of treatment to higher-functioning adolescents, the Lewinsohn study has made a significant contribution to the literature on the treatment of adolescent depression.

Summary and Conclusions

Over the past 15 years, child and adolescent depression has been recognized as a serious psychiatric condition that requires timely and effective intervention. Much progress has been made with respect to the assessment, diagnosis, and understanding of depression with this young population (Finch et al., 1990; Moretti, Fine, Haley, & Marriage, 1985), and these developments have allowed researchers and clinicians to begin objective evaluation of the efficacy of psychosocial and pharmacological interventions (Moran & Lambert, 1983; Tramontana & Sherrets, 1983).Unfortunately, very few controlled studies have examined the effectiveness of psychosocial interventions for depression (Matson & Carey, 1988). The most extensively researched intervention strategies have been the cognitive-behavioral interventions, and the initial findings of studies examining the efficacy of these interventions with nonreferred samples of depressed children and adolescents have been encouraging. Furthermore, the findings of the Lewinsohn et al. (1989) study suggest that their cognitive-behavioral therapy approach is an effective intervention for clinically depressed adolescents. These and other research findings must stand the test of further study and replication.

Clearly, future research needs to address the treatment efficacy of alternative psychosocial interventions and to examine whether the combination of psychopharmacologic and psychosocial interventions is more effective than either intervention strategy alone. In addition, research is needed to examine the influence of development on the expression and treatment of depressive disorders within childhood and adolescence.

This chapter has provided the reader with an overview of the four most commonly cited and most extensively studied cognitive-behavioral models and intervention programs for the treatment of childhood and adolescent depression. Each of these cognitive-behavioral approaches uses a variety of strategies that can guide the practitioner in developing, implementing, and evaluating treatment for children and adolescents who are depressed.

References

Abramson, L., Seligman, M., & Teasdale, J. (1978). Learned helplessness in humans: Critique and reformulation. *Journal of Abnormal Psychology, 87,* 49–74.

Achenbach, T. M., & Edelbrock, C. S. (1983). *Manual for the Child Behavior Checklist and Revised Child Behavior Profile.* Burlington, VT: University of Vermont, Department of Child Psychiatry.

Achenbach, T. M., & Edelbrock, C. S. (1986). *Manual for the teacher's report form and teacher version of the Child Behavior Profile.* Burlington, VT: University of Vermont, Department of Child Psychiatry.

Achenbach, T. M., & Edelbrock, C. S. (1987). *Manual for the youth self report form and self report version of the Child Behavior Profile.* Burlington, VT: University of Vermont, Department of Child Psychiatry.

American Psychiatric Association. (1987). *Diagnostic and statistical manual of mental disorders* (3rd ed., rev.). Washington, DC: APA.

Arana, G., Baldessarini, R., & Ornsteen, M. (1985). The dexamethasone suppression test for diagnosis and prognosis in psychiatry: Commentary and review. *Archives of General Psychiatry, 42,* 1193–1204.

Beck, A., & Beamesderfer, A. (1974). Assessment of depression: The depression inventory. In P. Pichot (Ed.), *Psychological measurements in psychopharmacology, modern problems in pharmacopsychiatry* (Vol. 7) (pp. 151–169). Switzerland: Karger.

Beck, A. T., Rush, A. J., Shaw, B. F., & Emery, G. (1979). *Cognitive therapy of depression.* New York: Guilford Press.

Beck, A. T., & Weishaar, M. (1989). Cognitive therapy. In A. Freeman, K. M. Simon, L. E. Beutler, and H. Arkowitz (Eds.), *Comprehensive handbook of cognitive therapy* (pp. 21–36). New York: Plenum Press.

Bernard, M., & Joyce, M. (1984). *Rational Emotive Therapy with children.* New York: Wiley.

Blumberg, S. H., & Izard, C. E. (1986). Discriminating patterns of emotions in ten and eleven year old children's anxiety and depression. *Journal of Personality and Social Psychology, 51,* 852–857.

Blumenthal, S., & Hirschfeld, R. (1984). *Suicide among adolescents and young adults.* Washington, DC: National Institute of Mental Health.

Butler, L., Miezitis, S., Freidman, R., & Cole, E. (1980). The effect of two school-based intervention programs on depressive symptoms in preadolescents. *American Educational Research Journal, 17,* 111–119.

Carey, M. P., Kelley, M. L., Buss, R. R., & Scott, O. (1986). Relationship of activity to depression in adolescents: Development of the Adolescent Activity Checklist. *Journal of Consulting and Clinical Psychology, 56,* 320–322.

Carroll, B. J. (1982). The dexamethasone suppression test for melancholia. *British Journal of Psychiatry, 140,* 292–304.

Casat, C., Arana, G., & Powell, K. (1989). The DST in children and adolescents with major depressive disorder. *American Journal of Psychiatry, 46,* 503–507.

Chambers, W. J., Puig-Antich, J., & Tabrizi, M. A. (1978). *The ongoing development of the Kiddie-SADS (Schedule of Affective Disorders and Schizophrenia for School-age Children).* Paper presented at the meeting of the American Academy of Child Psychiatry, San Diego, CA.

Cicchetti, D., & Schneider-Rosen, K. (1986). An organizational approach to childhood depression. In M. Rutter, C. Izard, & P. Read (Eds.), *Depression in young people.* (pp. 71–134). New York: Guilford Press.

Clarizio, H. F. (1989). *Assessment and treatment of depression in children and adolescents.* Brandon, CT: Clinical Psychology Pub.

Clarke, G., Lewinsohn, P. M., & Hops, (1990). *Leader's manual for adolescent groups: Adolescent coping with depression course.* Eugene, OR: Castalia.

DiGiuseppe, R. (1989). Cognitive therapy with children. In A. Freeman, K. M. Simon, L. E. Beutler, and H. Arkowitz (Eds.), *Comprehensive handbook of cognitive therapy* (pp. 515–533). New York: Plenum Press.

Edelbrock, C., & Costello, A. J. (1984). Structured psychiatric interviews for children and adolescents. In G. Goldstein & M. Hersen (Eds.), *Handbook of psychological assessment.* New York: Pergamon Press.

Ellis, A., & Bernard, M. (1983). *Rational-emotive approaches to the problems of childhood.* New York: Plenum Press.

Emery, S., Bedrosian, R., & Garber, J. (1983). Cognitive therapy with depressed children and adolescents. In D. Cantwell & G. Carlson (Eds.), *Affective disorders in childhood and adolescence: An update* (pp. 445–472). New York: Spectrum Press.

Finch, A. J, Casat, C. D., & Carey, M. P. (1990). Depression in children and adolescence. In S. B. Morgan & T. M. Okumabua (Eds.), *Child and adolescent disorders: Developmental and health psychology perspectives* (pp. 135–172). Hillsdale, NJ: Erlbaum.

Finch, A. J, Lipovsky, J., & Casat, C. (1989). Anxiety and depression in children and adolescents: Negative affectivity or separate constructs. In P. C. Kendall and D. Watson (Eds.), *Anxiety and depression: Distinctive and overlapping features.* San Diego, CA: Academic Press.

Frame, C. L., & Matson, J. L. (1987). *Handbook of assessment in childhood psychopathology: Applied issues in differential diagnosis and treatment evaluation.* New York: Plenum Press.

Freeman, A., Simon, K. M., Beutler, L. E., & Arkowitz, H. (1989). *Comprehensive handbook of cognitive therapy.* New York: Plenum Press.

Fuchs, C. Z., & Rehm, L. (1977). A self control behavior therapy for depression. *Journal of Consulting and Clinical Psychology, 45,* 206–215.

Hamilton, M. (1960). A rating scale for depression. *Journal of Neurology, Neurosurgery, and Psychiatry, 23,* 56–62.

Hawton, K. (1986). *Suicide and attempted suicide among children and adolescents.* Beverly Hills, CA: Sage.

Hodges, K. K. (1985). *Manual for the Child Assessment Schedule.* Unpublished manuscript, University of Missouri, Columbia.

Johnson, J. H., & McCutcheon, S. (1980). Assessing life stress in older children and adolescents: Preliminary findings with the Life Events Checklist. In I. G. Sarason & C. D. Spielberger (Eds.), *Stress and anxiety* (Vol 7). Washington, DC: Hemisphere.

Kanfer, F. H. (1970). Self-regulation: Research, issues and speculations. In C. Neuringer & J. L. Michael (Eds.), *Behavior modification in clinical psychology.* New York: Appleton-Century-Crofts.

Kaslow, N., & Rehm, L. (1983). Childhood depression. In R. J. Morris & T. R. Kratochwill (Eds.), *The practice of child therapy.* New York: Pergamon Press.

Kaslow, N., & Rehm, L. (1985). Conceptualization, assessment and treatment of depression in children. In P. Bornstein and A. E. Kazdin (Eds.), *Handbook of clinical behavior therapy.* New York: Pergamon Press.

Kazdin, A. E., French, N., Unis, A., Esveldt-Dawson, K. (1983). Assessment of childhood depression: Correspondence of child and parent ratings. *Journal of the American Academy of Child Psychiatry, 22,* 157–164.

Kazdin, A. E., Rodgers, A., & Colbus, D. (1986). The Hopelessness Scale for Children: Psychometric characteristics and concurrent validity. *Journal of Consulting and Clinical Psychology, 54,* 241–245.

Kovacs, M. (1981). Rating scales to assess depression in school-aged children. *Acta Paedopsychiatrica, 46,* 305–331.

Kovacs, M. (1982). *The longitudinal study of child and adolescent psychopathology: I. The semi-structured psychiatric Interview Schedule for Children (ISC).* Unpublished manuscript, University of Pittsburgh.

Kovacs, M. (1982). *The Children's Depression Inventory: A self-rated depression scale for school-aged youngsters.* Unpublished manuscript, University of Pittsburgh.

Kovacs, M., Feinberg, T., Crouse-Novak, M., Paulauskas, S., & Finkelstein, R. (1984). Depressive disorders in childhood: I. A longitudinal prospective study of characteristics and recovery. *Archives of General Psychiatry, 41,* 229–237.

Lefkowitz, M. M., & Burton, N. (1978). Childhood depression: A critique of the concept. *Psychological Bulletin, 85,* 716–726.

Lewinsohn, P. M., Antonuccio, D. O., Steinmetz, J., & Teri, L. (1984). *The Coping with Depression Course: A psychoeducational intervention for unipolar depression.* Eugene, OR: Castalia Press.

Lewinsohn, P. M., Clarke, G., Hops, H., Andrews, J., & Williams, J. (1989). *Cognitive-behavioral treatment for depressed adolescents.* Manuscript submitted for publication.

Lewinsohn, P. M., Clarke, G., & Rohde, P. (November, 1989). *The Adolescent Coping with Depression Course.* Workshop presented at the 23rd annual meeting of the Association for the Advancement of Behavior Therapy, Washington, DC.

Lewinsohn, P. M., & Hoberman, H. M. (1982). Behavioral and cognitive approaches. In E. S. Paykel (Ed.), *Handbook of affective disorders* (pp. 338–345). New York: Guilford Press.

Lewinsohn, P. M., Hops, H., Roberts, R., & Seeley, J. (November, 1989). *Prevalence and incidence of adolescent depression in a community sample.* Paper presented at the 23rd annual meeting of the Association for the Advancement of Behavior Therapy, Washington, DC.

Matson, J. L. (1989). *Treating depression in children and adolescents.* New York: Pergamon Press.

Matson, J., & Carey, M. P. (1988). Psychosocial interventions for child and adolescent depression. In J. L. Matson (Ed.), *Treating child and adolescent psychopathology: A handbook.* New York: Pergamon Press.

McGuire, D. (1983). Teenage suicide: A search for sense. *International Journal of Offender Therapy and Comparative Criminology, 27,* 211–217.

Moos, R., & Moos, B. (1986). *Family Environment Scale: Manual.* Palo Alto, CA: Consulting Psychologists Press.

Moran, P. W., & Lambert, M. (1983). A review of current assessment tools for monitoring changes in depression. In M. E. Lambert (Ed.), *The assessment of psychotherapy outcome* (pp. 263–303). New York: Guilford Press.

Moretti, M. M., Fine, M. B., Haley, M. A., & Marriage, M. B. (1985). Child and adolescent depression: Child-report versus parent-report information. *Journal of Abnormal Child Psychology, 24,* 298–302.

Poznanski, E. O., Freeman, L. N., & Mokros, H. B. (1984). Children's Depression Rating Scale — Revised. *Psychopharmacology Bulletin, 21,* 979–989.

Puig-Antich, J., & Gittelman, R. (1982). Depression in childhood and adolescence. In E. S. Paykel (Ed.), *Handbook of affective disorders.* New York: Guilford Press.

Reynolds, C. R., & Richmond, B. O. (1985). Revised Children's Manifest Anxiety Scale (RCMAS). Los Angeles: Western Psychological Services.

Reynolds, W. M. (1987). *Assessment of depression in adolescents: Manual for the Reynolds Adolescent Depression Scale (RADS).* Odessa, FL: Psychological Assessment Resources.

Reynolds, W. M. (1988). *Manual for the Reynolds Suicide Ideation Questionnaire (SIQ).* Odessa, FL: Psychological Assessment Resources.

Reynolds, W. M. (1989). *Assessment of depression in children: Manual for the Reynolds Children's Depression Scale (RCDS).* Odessa, FL: Psychological Assessment Resources.

Reynolds, W. M., & Coats, K. I. (1986). A comparison of cognitive-behavioral therapy and relaxation training for the treatment of depression. *Journal of Consulting and Clinical Psychology, 54,* 653–660.

Schleser, R., Meyers, A., & Cohen, R. (1981). Generalizations of self-instructions: Effects of general versus specific content, active rehearsal, and cognitive level. *Child Development, 52,* 335–340.

Stark, K., Reynolds, W. M., & Kaslow, N. (1987). A comparison of the relative efficacy of self-control therapy and a behavioral problem-solving therapy for depression in children. *Journal of Abnormal Child Psychology, 15,* 91–113.

Tramontana, M. G., & Sherrets, S. D. (1983). Assessing outcome in disorders of childhood and adolescence. In M. Lambert (Ed.), *The assessment of psychotherapy outcome* (pp. 406–449). New York: Guilford Press.

Wagner, E. E., & Glicken, M. (1966). Counseling children: Two accounts. *Rational Living, 1,* 26–30.

Waters, V. (1981). The living school. *RETwork, 1,* 1.

Waters, V. (1982). Therapies for children: Rational Emotive Therapy. In C. R. Reynolds and T. B. Gutkin (Eds.), *Handbook of school psychology.* New York: Wiley.

Whatmore, G. B., & Kohli, D. (1968). Dysponesis: A neurophysiologic factor in functional disorders. *Behavioral Science, 13,* 102–104.

Williams, J. G., Barlow, D. H., & Agras, W. S. (1972). Behavioral measurement of severe depression. *Archives of General Psychiatry, 27,* 330–333.

Witt, J. C., Cavell, T. A., Heffer, R. W., Carey, M. P., & Martens, B. K. (1988). Child self-report: Interviewing techniques and rating scales. In E. S. Shapiro and T. R. Kratochwill (Eds.), *Behavioral assessment in the schools: Conceptual foundations and practical applications* (pp. 385–453). New York: Guilford Press.

CHAPTER TEN

Cognitive-Behavioral Intervention for Adolescent Drug Abuse

W. ROBERT NAY   GEORGE R. ROSS

In recent years the problem of drug abuse by children, adolescents, and young adults has received a great deal of media attention. Although the "drug problem" gained prominence when university students of the middle to late 1960s expressed their political beliefs in terms of dress, lifestyle, and demeanor, it soon became apparent that abuse of marijuana and a variety of so-called harder drugs had begun to appear in the nation's high schools and, more alarmingly, in the elementary school setting. Since 1971 the National Institute of Drug Abuse (N.I.D.A.) has conducted a sophisticated, confidential, cross-sectional survey of defined demographic strata in order to document the dimensions of the problem. One of the surveys (N.I.D.A., 1979) is not comforting to clinicians who are alarmed by the use of chemicals as a means of facing everyday life problems. Since 1971 dramatic increases in the use of all of the commonly abused drugs have been shown for youth, young adults, and even the older population. Most recently (1987), it was found that 89% of tenth graders have used alcohol, 35% have used marijuana, and 10% have used cocaine. To add to the growing concern about the health effects of marijuana, there is increasing concern about alcohol abuse (e.g., see Manatt, 1979; Johnston, O'Malley, & Bachman, 1985).

For the clinician who works with children, questions surrounding the assessment and treatment of substance abuse have been addressed systematically in the past decade. Although much information has been collected regarding methods for detoxifying or providing a drug maintenance program for the abuser of opiate derivatives, the traditional models for adult drug treatment have not been well suited to the youth whose use of a spectrum of drugs is influenced by a powerful peer culture. Among intervention methods the "institutional" model has been a notable failure in treating youths who are involved with illicit drugs and who may be on a path to ultimate and potentially lethal involvement with harder drugs. This model may involve placing the child in a secure facility for some set (nonbehavior-dependent) time period, weaning the child from using one drug by using an alternative substance, and providing exposure to general group therapies. This model fails to deal with the specific aspects of the child's life situation that instigate drug use, to assess and/or work with the family system, and to provide a positive peer environment in the community to offset the negative influence of drug-using friends when the child returns home. Thus, removing a youth from the community and into a non-normalized, medical setting is one way to terminate drug use, but this approach may lack the necessary ingredients to foster generalization and maintenance of change to the community environment where the youth must ultimately function (e.g., Kanfer & Goldstein, 1980). It is our belief that any successful intervention for the child/adolescent drug problem must assume a thorough and comprehensive approach to assessment (e.g., see Lazarus, 1976; Nay, 1979). Assessment and intervention must adopt an ecological approach and must occur at levels ranging from the intrapersonal to the social system within which the individual functions. However, it is clear from our own work that a major thrust of intervention must be focused toward changing the client's attributions and beliefs about self and the use of drugs. Merely terminating a child's access to drugs will be just as unsuccessful as using physical restraints to control aggressive behavior or as locking the refrigerator door to control obesity. As soon as the environmental restraints are removed, the individual may be expected to resume the habitual behavior pattern.

Drug Abuse Myths

Before turning to issues of assessment and treatment, it is important to dispel a few of the myths that we have found to be attendant to the issue of child/adolescent drug abuse. Each of these myths will be stated and briefly discussed.

Myth: The main problem is one of physical addiction, and an extensive program of detoxification is necessary in order to intervene. We have found that with the major drugs of abuse for youth, physical addiction to any single drug is rare (and let's remember that only certain drugs will promote physical addiction). The goal of the typical young person is to "get high." Most clients have abused a kaleidoscope of substances ranging from marijuana and alcohol to prescription drugs. Although not physically addicted to any single drug, they have developed a very intense behavioral and belief system that supports drug use, and a variety of harmful effects may be observed in the life situation—for example, arrests, deteriorization of school performance, disruption of family relationships, depression, and withdrawal. The prominence of this behavioral/belief system suggests that a cognitive approach that focuses upon these psychological dimensions is necessary for effective treatment. It is also worth noting that the young person habitually interacts with people who are selling and using harder drugs and that it becomes increasingly difficult to get high as tolerance develops. The youth may begin experimenting with ever harder drugs, and opiates and narcotic analgesics may be explored along with dangerous prescription drugs. Thus, physical dependence is possible if the pattern of psychological dependence is not interrupted early.

Myth: Whenever a youth uses drugs there are deep personality or psychological problems or necessary difficulties in the family system. As we will suggest in our conceptualization, given the myriad of possible combinations of person and life factors that may combine to influence a child's use of chemicals, a thorough assessment must be performed. A variety of events may compel a reasonably well-adjusted youth from a functional family to initiate drug use. We do not believe that any monolithic model to explain drug abuse will be supported empirically. In fact, due to the complexity of variables within an overall ecological framework, the issues for the researcher become monumental.

Myth: There is a need for more powerful, new treatment techniques. Perhaps. But we argue that many sound intervention methods have already been employed to treat drug abuse. We believe that what is lacking is a sound conceptualization of the variables that instigate and maintain drug use. Efficacious assessment tools and intervention schemes emerge only from a sound conceptual framework. In an attempt to remedy an apparent deficiency in the field, this chapter emphasizes conceptualization over the usual compendium of treatment methods. We hope that our efforts will provide the practitioner with a conceptual model for better understanding the phenomenon of adolescent substance abuse and, more importantly, with a sound framework for intervention.

Recognition of the Problem

Ries, Batran, and Schuckit (1980) aptly summarize a serious dilemma facing today's practitioner:

> *Patients who abuse drugs and those who seek treatment for depression or other functional complaints are frequently a diagnostic dilemma.*

> . . . Abuse of drugs is associated with a wide variety of psycho-
> pathologies. . . . suicidal depressions . . . high levels of anxiety, and
> a variety of psychotic behaviors, which at any time can be identical to
> the cross sectional symptomatology of schizophrenia. These drug
> induced states can last from hours to days or even months. (p. 18)

The diagnostic dilemma is compounded further by a basic lack of education and experience on the part of most practitioners in dealing with child/adolescent drug abuse. Family and pediatric practitioners too often assume the role of child advocate after observing elevated states of anger, embitterment, and resentment on the parents' part. It is concluded that the parents are the primary "cause" of the problem and that they are in need of individual and marriage counseling. Thus, assessment may completely overlook the possibility of an underlying drug problem.

The diagnostic process may also be compounded by the practitioner's lax and sometimes condoning attitude toward drugs, stemming from little information about the widespread usage and potential ill effects of many drugs, especially marijuana, on teenagers (see Barbour, 1981; Voth, 1980; Latner, O'Brien & Voth, 1980). Also, many young practitioners themselves have experimented with marijuana, cocaine, or other drugs and may have a permissive attitude toward "occasional" or "recreational" drug use. Obviously these beliefs may influence the assessment to bias therapeutic objectives away from a focus on drug use. Given that all youth begin problem drug use by "experimenting," we see this phenomenon as worthy of attention of all professionals who work with young people.

With the aforementioned dilemma in mind, a review of the following checklist of symptoms and behaviors should prove useful to the practitioner in recognizing possible substance abuse. One or two of these characteristics may appear in any youth as a part of normal development through the teen years, but consistent and extreme examples should not be overlooked, especially if a pattern emerges. A major thrust of the assessment is to note *change* in any of the following dimensions over time.

- School—Does the child bring home lower grades and seem to have developed a negative attitude toward school? Does he or she skip classes? Has he or she been suspended or expelled? Heavy drug users usually drop out of school.
- Dishonesty—Has the child concealed drug use and either denied or minimized it when discovered? Has the child been caught stealing from parents or shoplifting? Does the child lie about friends and activities? The child may resort to cheating at school and forging school excuses.

- Personality changes—Immaturity and withdrawal from family relationships are common. Has the child changed friends, started using foul language, or begun lying about activities? Seclusiveness and avoidance of adults are common. Taste in music may change. Irritability and fits of anger or rage with little or no provocation are common. There is a loss of motivation, lowering of ambition, loss of drive toward goals, and no quest for excellence. The child becomes very selfish.
- Family relationships—Does the child avoid being seen with parents or siblings and avoid family outings? Are household responsibilities and chores neglected? The child may be argumentative or passive, the two extremes. Does the child accuse parents of "hassling" or not trusting? Is the child very manipulative, striving to create conflict between parents?
- Sexual behavior—Promiscuity is common, with consequences of venereal disease or pregnancy.
- Law breaking—Traffic violations (often an early sign of drug use), vandalism, shoplifting, or breaking and entering may occur.
- Physical appearance—Personal grooming and hygiene may deteriorate. Speech and actions may be detectably slowed. Note any change in gait and/or posture. Clothing and hair style may change. Younger teenagers may have decreased physical development of sexual characteristics. In girls, menstruation may become infrequent and decreased. The youngster may exhibit a lack of vitality with a need for excessive sleep at unusual times. Eating habits may be altered, and weight loss may occur. Bloodshot eyes, dilated pupils, volubility, excessive or inappropriate laughter along with slowed speech and decreased coordination may indicate marijuana use. The youth may attempt to conceal bloodshot eyes with eye drops.
- Medical conditions—Infections of the skin and respiratory tract are common. A chronic cough without apparent infection may occur. Extreme fatigue and lassitude are common. The youngster may complain of frequent colds or chest pain.
- Behavioral characteristics—Is the youth extremely willful, demanding to take care of himself or herself? There may be a "Jekyll and Hyde" personality: sweet one moment and enraged the next. Conduct will be unpredictable. An extremely neat child may suddenly begin to prefer a messy room. The youngster may not be able to communicate in complete sentences and may forget thoughts in mid-sentence.
- Other—The youth may openly admit to sexual activity or involvement with drugs. Paraphernalia such as rolling papers, pipes, roach clips, and actual traces of drugs may be found hidden behind stereo speakers, inside record albums, and so forth.

From Conceptualization to Assessment

In order to make sense of the foregoing signs and symptoms and to provide the theoretical structure upon which any reasonable assessment scheme must be built, we offer a conceptualization for the major sources of influence that instigate and maintain drug-taking behavior as well as for the attitude/belief system that surrounds drug use. This conceptualization assumes that the behavior of taking an illicit drug is controlled by a complex set of variables that occur at the level of the individual, the family, the subculture, and the very society in which we all function. Although this conceptual scheme is not meant to be exhaustive and may be elaborated or modified by others, it is a beginning point that reflects our combined clinical experience in working with hundreds of adolescent substance abusers and their families.

The reader is referred to Figure 10-1, which depicts a series of factors (A, B, C, D, E) that culminate in experimentation with and oftentimes

---

FIGURE 10-1 • A Conceptual Model of Adolescent Substance Abuse

---

Environmental Factors (A)
1. Breakdown of family influence
2. Cultural approval of chemicals to alter mood
3. Focus on painless/immediate gratification in media
4. Ready availability of substances

Attitudes/Beliefs (B)
1. Importance of immediate/external/stimulation
2. Importance of accepting/conformity to peers
3. Values that emphasize self-gratification
4. Belief in magical attainment of goals

Feeling States (C)
1. Boredom, feeling understimulated
2. Anxiety, apprehension
3. Dissatisfaction, lack of empathy
4. Impatience

Motives (D)
1. Seeking stimulation
2. Self/peer acceptance
3. Avoidance of unpleasantness or responsibility
4. Relief from uncomfortable thoughts/feelings

Behavior: Substance Use (E)
1. Violates morals/laws
2. Impairs cognitive/behavioral functioning
3. Instigates psychological defenses (e.g., denial, rationalization, projection)

---

habitual use of legal and illegal drugs. The reader should pay special attention to factor D, which describes a series of motives (preaddiction/ addiction) that in our opinion serve as necessary instigators for drug taking. The satisfaction of any of these motives could be achieved via behavior other than the taking of a drug; however, we have found that one of these four motives is always a part of an individual client's phenomenology of involvement in drugs. For each of these motives, the reader will note certain premotivational beliefs and feelings (B, C) in the context of the individual's environment (A).

One category of motive, "Seeking Stimulation" (D_1) has to do with the high level of stimulation that young people have become accustomed to within our society. From the barrage of cartoons on Saturday morning to the sugar "highs" promulgated by the breakfast foods, candy, and soft drink industries to the dazzling, multimedia electronic games and loud, pulsing rock music of an afternoon or evening out, it is clear that our youth are exposed to vastly greater amounts of stimulation across all sensory channels than virtually any past generation. In addition, the impact of rapid and expected change in our society goes far toward producing a young person who seeks high levels of external stimulation on a regular basis, frequently complaining of boredom or "nothing to do." This notion is supported further by examining the multimillion dollar recording and leisure time industries. It follows that the taking of drugs that provide euphoria and distort reality while producing a high is a logical alternative means of self-stimulation. The taking of a drug in this context is part of a well-learned pattern of behavior and reinforcement in which a lack of high-level stimulation is discomforting to the individual. "Self/Peer Acceptance" (D_2) is construed as the active attempts of peers to encourage and to reinforce drug use via the known impact of peer modeling and reinforcement. So-called peer "pressure" is the most frequent reason for drug use offered by clients. This is not surprising given the increasing numbers of youth who use illicit drugs. The ready availability of substances (A_4) as well as communications media (A_3) that continually reinforce the use of marijuana or alcohol as necessary ingredients of the social occasion do much to enhance the power of peer acceptance in this regard. For each of these two motives (D_1, D_2), cognitive and affective components are described (B_1, C_1, B_2, C_2).

Another category of motivation for taking a drug is removing the client from unpleasant situations of responsibility (D_3) or providing relief from uncomfortable feelings or thoughts (D_4)—a negative reinforcement paradigm. The premotivational beliefs shown at B_3 and B_4 are often irrational and dysfunctional and elicit feelings of anger, sadness, or frustration as affective possibilities. The internal dialogues that accompany these premotivational beliefs must be identified and replaced if the client is to terminate drug use.

At point E in Figure 10-1, the actual use of a given substance is one alternative for dealing with the four motives listed at D. Such behavior is obviously influenced by communications media that model or recommend drug taking to deal with most events in life (A_3), a culture that approves of certain legal drugs for purposes of seeking stimulation and/or relief from uncomfortable feelings (A_2) (e.g., alcohol, prescription tranquilizers, non-prescription "mood lifters"), and the skyrocketing availability provided by the multibillion dollar illicit drug importation industry (A_4). All of these factors exist within the community and may influence a given youth's decision to use a particular substance.

Behavioral consequences are attendant to the act of drug use. Implicit in such use is the violation of numerous well-learned, ethical, value-related, and legal standards (E_1). A youth who uses illicit drugs is engaging in an illegal activity and may begin a behavior pattern that involves concealment (from parents, teachers, and others), lying to manage this concealment, and a variety of activities that may be necessary to support drug use (e.g., stealing, dealing drugs to others). Once the youth initiates a pattern of violating laws and standards, the relationship with parents and others may be changed. Certain feelings and behaviors must be concealed from those who may be in an excellent position to help. In addition, a demanding and unforgiving peer group, composed of individuals who also are engaging in dishonest activity, may further support and maintain this pattern of deceptive and standard-dissonant behavior.

As our model suggests, the youth may have learned to deal with unpleasant thoughts and feelings by engaging in behavior that provides emotional relief. If the resulting behavior is drug use, it may now be necessary to mobilize a variety of psychological defenses (E_3) that involve irrational and dysfunctional thinking (e.g., denial, rationalization, projection). These psychological defenses support the continued taking of drugs as a further means of avoiding this internal conflict and are maintained by negative reinforcement processes. Thus, a self-maintaining self-system emerges when points E-B-C-D-E, (etc.) become a repeated pattern for the individual. As this self-system is played and reinforced repeatedly, it becomes well learned and very difficult to interrupt via standard therapeutic methods. Thus, the youth who is found to be using drugs may not be motivated to be honest with the interested mental health professional, for the described self-system is functional and well entrenched. We find that the client is most likely to deny drug use, or, if it is undeniably observed, will cast blame and responsibility elsewhere — on parents, teachers, coaches, and others — as a further means of rationalizing current behavior and providing relief from uncomfortable thoughts and feelings. Furthermore, repeated drug use may culminate in the development of an underlying self-defeating motive — that the only way to resolve the four major motives (D) is to get high. As noted later, an intervention more powerful than simple confrontation is necessary to interrupt this self-system.

Finally, an examination of Figure 10-1 illuminates a variety of personal behavioral domains (E_2) that are disrupted or may deteriorate with continued drug use. A vast and growing literature tells us of the ways in which drugs may impair the youth's thought processes, may interfere with the ability to function at school or in the job situation, and may provoke inappropriate emotional responses to life stress. This reminds us that the youth who has been using drugs for any period of time may be unable to self-evaluate thoughts and feelings rationally and systematically. Indeed, we find that, typically, it is necessary for a period of 45 to 60 days to elapse before the youth who has been involved extensively in drug use (particularly with hallucinogens and stimulants) is able to make use of the therapeutic process.

It is obvious, then, that the youth who is currently or recently on drugs is a very poor candidate for traditional psychotherapy. As we will note, the first stage of intervention must be to place the individual in a chemically free environment. This point is missed by many well-meaning psychologists, psychiatrists, and other counselors who insist on doing individual psychotherapy with clients who are currently using drugs. In our experience, most clients report that they were sent to a therapist by parents, the school, or other well-meaning persons and were high during one or more of the therapy sessions. This says a lot about the ability of many professionals to detect drug use, and it suggests that traditional psychotherapy may not be in the client's best interests.

In summary, we have examined the elements of the internal dialogue (some of which may be influenced by drug taking itself) as well as behaviors and external influences that motivate the individual to use drugs. We will now discuss the cognitive-behavioral interventions that may be employed to alter the client's irrational beliefs surrounding self and drugs, to increase the ability to solve life problems in a rational manner, and to undermine the self-system that maintains drug use as depicted in Figure 10-1.

Intervention Targets and Cognitive Treatment Alternatives

Although the goals of this chapter preclude a thorough analysis of efforts aimed at broader societal/community levels within the ecological system that surrounds individual drug use, it is important to remember that the process of psychological dependency/addiction is maintained by a system of social reinforcement and negative self-reinforcement and is supported by a variety of basic dysfunctional and irrational beliefs. This fact makes a cognitive-behavioral approach (e.g., Ellis, McInerney, DiGiuseppe, & Yeager, 1988) a natural choice for assessment and treatment of substance abuse. For example, targets such as the basic beliefs and resulting thoughts (Figure 10-1) surrounding the client's pattern of feelings and motives are essential in the assessment and treatment process. Unfortunately, there is not an extensive published literature addressing the utility of cognitive-behavioral interventions in dealing with the adolescent drug abuse problem. It is our hope the ideas presented here will stimulate further practical application and research. Prior to discussing a series of stages of intervention with accompanying cognitive behavioral and other treatment techniques, we will first review important general issues of intervention.

Voth (1980) and Stanton (1979) proposed certain necessary conditions for successful treatment of drug problems regardless of the specific treatment modality employed. These conditions provide an ideal backdrop for the material that is to follow.

1. The substance abuser must be placed in an environment that takes over complete responsibility for the abuser to ensure that access to drugs is removed for a minimum of 3 months.
2. The environment must provide physical security for the client — i.e., meet basic needs of adequate food, clothing, shelter, medical need, and be free of physical abuse or threat.
3. Counselors working with the abuser need to exemplify behaviors of warmth and empathy and to provide effective discipline.
4. Positive, constructive peer influence should be readily available.
5. Counselors working with the abuser should exemplify a lifestyle that is free of drugs, including alcohol.
6. Therapeutic goals should involve treatment of the entire family.
7. It is desirable to have open and honest discussion of basic cultural values — e.g., honesty, family relationships, school, vocations, friendships, leisure time, and sharing.
8. The treatment program should be well structured, with rules, regulations, and expectations clearly defined, explicitly stated, and consistently enforced.

We believe that prior to an effective cognitive-behavioral intervention aimed at altering important basic constructs and dysfunctional styles of thinking, the deterioration of cognitive, affective, and behavioral functioning that has occurred as a result of drug use must be halted and reversed as much as possible. Given the clouded sensorium and disorganized thought processes that are often presented to the clinician by the youth who has been involved extensively in drugs, interventions that require active attending, clear thinking and decision making — or the implementation of an organized self-instructional scheme — are likely to fail if the client is approached at this stage. Because we believe that cognitive intervention with the substance abuser requires some necessary preconditions to therapy, we have formulated a series of stages that must be addressed within the intervention process. The length of time required for a particular client to traverse each stage depends upon the particular drugs abused, the duration of drug use, and the strength of the learned self-system involving irrational thoughts, denial, psychological defenses and drug taking already depicted in Figure 10-1 (the sequence from A to E, etc.). The time required also depends upon a variety of external events that may serve as motivators (e.g., being court-ordered to treatment, the enforcement of criminal charges dependent upon the child's successful completion of treatment, pressure and support from parents, etc.).

A description of each stage of the rehabilitation process will be followed by suggested cognitive-behavioral and other treatments that we have found to be effective. It is not our intention to discuss the basic premise or methods of cognitive-behavioral procedures that are well known and described in detail elsewhere and in this book. Rather, we provide more extensive examples of how the intervention may be applied to adolescent drug abuse in a novel way. The reader who is sophisticated in cognitive-behavioral interventions will discover quickly that our suggestions and recommendations are not exhaustive. They are, however, methods that have been effective for us, and we offer them with the hope of stimulating the cognitive processes of our peers who work with drug problems on a daily basis. Following this review of stages and methods, we will then provide a brief example of an intervention program that illustrates a comprehensive integration of the methods and issues discussed. The reader will discover that successful intervention for adolescent drug abuse will not be performed easily in the individual consulting room and that a programmatic structure is required to carry out important steps suggested by each of the intervention stages.

The first and most crucial stage of intervention is *awareness*. It is here that the client, often at the intense prodding or direction of others, seeks initial treatment and begins the process of examining past behavior and current objectives. The client's perceptions, interpretations, feelings, intentions, and behaviors must become unraveled within the confines of a drug-free environment. This environment is difficult to achieve at the outset, when the client may have access to drug-using friends and "stashes" (drugs that have been hidden at home or elsewhere). The client placed in treatment while also being exposed to punitive sanctions from peers who themselves are threatened when drugs are declined is in an intolerable situation. Because the client's former belief system and behavioral repertoire surrounding drug use are much better established and have more habit strength than the new behaviors welcomed by the therapist, it is obvious that the likely outcome of this difficult situation is a therapeutic failure. We recommend removing the child from the community (e.g., school, job, etc.), as well as from the home. For the child who has lived at home, we find that family communications have often broken down and that the family relationship has deteriorated as parents have been unsuccessful in the various methods with which they have attempted to solve the problem. Thus, prior to a reunion with their child, it is crucial that the parents receive training in how to deal with the youth. During this time of removal the parents may be assisted in examining their past methods for handling the child's drug problem. We frequently observe signs of parental guilt and self-doubt (e.g., assuming that they are at "fault" and questioning their competence as parents) that must be faced and processed. Thus, we recommend that parents participate in an active training program that permits them to examine issues such as thoughts and feelings about the child and the child's use of drugs, their own use of chemicals (e.g., alcohol, prescription drugs), their methods of communication, and their expectations and style of discipline. Also, further down the road, sessions of family therapy intervention can be most helpful in rebuilding patterns of communication while undermining dysfunctional and destructive coalitions within the family system. We often find that at least one of the parents serves the role of "enabler" or "rescuer," providing a pattern of justification and support for the child's behavior (see Nay, 1984). An example of a parenting program that involves exposure to a cognitive-behavioral conceptualization, training in communications skills and assertiveness, a review of roles and models of discipline, and delivery of other important information will be provided in the application example that follows this section.

During the awareness stage the youth should be placed in an environment that requires confrontation of dishonesty and of the psychological processes of denial and rationalization that defend a good deal of submerged information. We believe this is best accomplished by trained peer counselors who have themselves previously been involved in drugs, as they can easily identify and recognize the various tactics the youth will employ to avoid honest self-exploration. Although the professional clinician may also be able to accomplish this process, we think that the peer counselor trained in basic relationship and therapeutic communication skills is in an excellent position to "relate" via personal past experiences and successful drug-free solutions to life problems. Also, given the role similarity, the peer counselor is less likely to be rejected by the client as a source of information. Peers can serve also as effective models of rational and direct expressions of thought, feelings, and behavior as the youth begins to experience some of the emotions (about past actions) that have been defended or pushed down via drug use. To many therapists, this may seem a harsh process. We may wish to believe everything that the client says or to employ exclusively the nondirective skills that foster "opening up." It is important to remember that the self-system depicted in Figure 10-1 has become strengthened to the point that the youth may have difficulty separating objective fact from a well-rehearsed, personal version of the "truth" and may have pushed down feelings for so long that simple directives such as "share your feelings" or "tell us how you are feeling" may be met with a blank, unknowing look. Only by encouraging the client to openly discuss the past actions that may have caused hurt to others or to self and to begin to attach those actions to feelings do we provide a motivational base for the client to move to the next stage of commitment. When the client begins to rediscover the feelings of guilt and anxiety that ordinarily occur as internal standards are violated, there is a source of motivation for learning to deal with those uncomfortable feelings and to avoid using drugs to manage life in the future. If the youth fails to experience and to express those uncomfortable but socially necessary feelings, the clinician is apt to continue to see various signs of defensiveness (e.g., angry lashing out at the therapist or the treatment program, withdrawing by refusing to participate or to discuss problems or concerns, actively deceiving the therapist in accounts of past or current motives). Thus, the client needs to look more objectively at past events, behaviors, and outcomes and to contact feelings that should have been experienced and dealt with as past events originally occurred.

In terms of methods, the relationship techniques of asking open-ended questions, reflecting feelings that are unstated but apparent via the client's nonverbal behavior, confronting the client's use of denial, rationalization, projection of blame, and other defensive tactics, and providing (via peer modeling) exposure to peers as they discuss past behavior combine to provide an atmosphere in which the client may begin to open up. At this stage we can expect that the youth will become emotionally vulnerable. Feelings of inferiority, resentment, guilt, frustration, and loneliness have been suppressed by the intoxicating influence of the substances being used. As the youth becomes free of the artificial and superficial effects of chemicals, honest (factual) examination of actual feelings and behaviors is encouraged. It is now possible to make a commitment to do what is necessary to change the present life situation.

The second stage in the intervention process involves *commitment* to setting well-defined, attainable objectives and to the achievement of those objectives within the process of change. We believe that it is important that this commitment be made in some public sense, perhaps by using an oral or written behavioral contract. This commitment is typically achieved as the client begins to experience discomfort surrounding thoughts and feelings that have previously been denied or diminished with drugs. In order to deal with these feelings and to ensure that in the future they will be managed in healthy, appropriate ways, the client makes a commitment to change, particularly when exposed to other youth who serve as powerful, positive models of substance-free living. We have emphasized repeatedly the importance of positive support and modeling provided by the peer counselors and other peers within the group therapy situation. For this reason we believe that the two initial stages of intervention are best traversed in the context of a program that includes peers at later levels of progress in their own attitudinal and behavioral change.

In the private consulting office, the awareness and commitment stages of the change process may have been already addressed by the client who is motivated to seek treatment for problems. For the client who is psychologically dependent upon drugs, the *active instigation* of motivation and commitment to change is a necessary precondition for cognitive-behavioral — or any form of — intervention. It is our experience that the Alcoholics Anonymous model (1980), or some version of it, provides an excellent structure for this process of commitment, provided that it is presented in a language and manner suitable to the age and developmental level of the client.

A third stage of intervention involves the *identification of dysfunctional thoughts and cognitive structures.* It is important to identify the irrational and dysfunctional statements and attributions that are observed during the stages of awareness and commitment. Careful consideration of the client's descriptions of self and relationships permits a review of internal dialogue as the youth becomes more honest and open. Typically this internal dialogue is filled with denial, blaming of others, and faulty and illogical attributions about drug use, as well as with incomplete and illogical rationalizations defending past events — such as overdosing, being arrested, violent confrontations with parents and others, or being placed in a psychiatric facility (see Ellis & Bernard, 1984). As shown in Figure 10-1, a variety of irrational thoughts may occur at the "premotivational" level and may continue to support drug use. This irrational thinking may focus on uncomfortable thoughts surrounding fear of rejection by peers (B_2), coupled with a desire to maintain a "cool," sophisticated posture. The focus may be related also to discomforting life events such as failures in school or job, relationship difficulties with parents or friends, or unpleasant responsibilities (B_3). Figure 10-1 also shows a variety of well-developed psychological defenses (E_3) that are implicitly irrational in that they remove the youth from dealing with objective reality in a valid fashion (e.g., "It's my parents' fault that I am here," "My friends will think I'm a [expletive] if I'm straight," "My old man is always hassling me," "My teachers aren't fair," etc.). If such irrational thinking is not altered, the interventions will not be successful.

Stage 3 implies that a commitment has been made, and it is now possible to begin the process of systematically challenging the dysfunctional and irrational statements. We have found a number of useful techniques. From the first day of treatment, the client is instructed in the use of — and asked to write — a daily *Moral Inventory*. The Moral Inventory (M.I.), borrowed from the first step of the Alcoholics Anonymous program, requires the client to review himself or herself honestly and to examine his or her thoughts, feelings, actions, intentions, and goals. The M.I. should be supervised by a peer counselor or by a more advanced client who can give the youth feedback and support for initial efforts. The M.I. must be used carefully with those youths whose first language is not English or who cannot write. In this case it is suggested that the M.I. be "told" to another peer who then writes the information for the client. In this way the process can be employed with youth of varying educational/ethnic backgrounds. We recommend that the M.I. be used throughout treatment as an excellent means for the client to keep track of progress (or lack of it). The cognitively oriented therapist will find the M.I. to be an excellent vehicle for obtaining clues to the client's internal dialogue. The M.I. is often filled with rich evidence of psychological defenses and style of thinking. An example of a M.I. is found in Figure 10-2.

Next the client is provided with a brief, clear explanation of what is meant by "thoughts," "feelings," and "behavior." Most of our clients show a very poor understanding of internal events and lack a useful vocabulary for describing what happens "inside." Thus, providing a vocabulary and a conceptual understanding of such internal events is a necessary precondition for use of the specific cognitive techniques to follow. An effective teaching method is the didactic technique that we call "the awareness wheel." The hub of the wheel represents the situation encountered by the client; the spokes are made up of the sensations, thoughts, feelings, actions, and intentions experienced by the client in relation to the situation. Drawn on poster board, the awareness wheel provides an excellent vehicle for identifying these components and for discovering their interrelationships. The client should be aware of the basic tenets of the cognitive-behavioral model (e.g., Ellis, 1962; Ellis et al., 1988; Meichenbaum, 1977) *before* formal cognitive intervention is begun and should be shown how situations themselves do not cause feelings. We find that most of our clients are quickly able to grasp the basic principle that feelings are caused by the way one chooses to think when faced with a situation. We believe that the A, B, C model of Ellis should ideally be expanded to include the A–E format developed by this chapter's second author (Ross, 1979). Within this model, each of the alphabetic letters stands for the following:

A = Situation or event

B = Those thoughts the individual chooses to have about that event

C = The individual's feelings, caused by thinking those thoughts (B)

D = Thoughts that may be cued or elicited by those feelings at C; thoughts about one's feelings and what individuals should do about them (e.g., "Boy, I'm really becoming afraid"; "I feel so bad"; "Therefore, I'll run away.")

E = Actions or behaviors

FIGURE 10-2   •   *An Example Moral Inventory (M.I.) Written by a 14-Year-Old Client*

Challenges
1. I need to work on not getting down because of where I am at my age.
2. I am going to work on making the rest of my program simple and positive.
3. I need to work on not holding myself back.

---

1. Today I went through a lot of disappointment because I turned 14 and I'm sitting in a drug rehab. I feel really angry because I can't spend my 14th birthday going to a movie or at Disney World or any place other than the building. I can make a change because I do have a program at this young age and I'll have a lot longer to have the good feelings than someone who's 17 on up. I need to look at the positive side of things because I think that 14 years old is a hell of a lot better than 21 because I've got a lot more years of fun ahead of me.

Good Point
I feel good about my first *straight* birthday in 3½ years, because I'm 14.
2. I stepped outside of myself today when I was doing chores and looked at my whole program from day one up until now. I have made my program difficult up until lately but I saw where a little bit of work and a lot of honesty can make things really simple. I made a commitment about a month ago to make things simple, and I have stayed consistent with it, and now all I need is to make my changes positive, like getting excited about it. The one thing I think can make things really positive is giving out to people because it's a joy to my heart when I help someone change. I need to take more of a sense of humor to my challenge because it's a big load or burden when I get too serious.

Good Point
I feel good about my whole attitude towards things tonight and what I'm getting out of my challenges.
3. Tonight I didn't want to wrestle, joke around and laugh and a bunch of other stuff because I thought since I was 14 I had to be Mr. Mature and set a good example. I do this a lot everywhere I go because I'm afraid people will think I'm being boppy. I am making a change because I start to feel like I did in my past when I worry so much about other people and I know I don't want to feel that way so I just act the way I feel. I feel really good right now so I'm not going to worry about my foster brothers and let it show. I'm going to be strong with this because I've seen plenty of people use it as an excuse to screw around in group without worrying about hurting themselves.

Good Point
I feel good about being able to honestly say that I love myself from all my heart.

Goals
I am going to take this positive attitude of mine into Homes Rap and show all those people that I know what being straight is about.
I am going to make this weekend so positive that my Dad and I will never forget it.

FIGURE 10-2 • *Continued*

I am not going to go to bed without telling myself 10 positive things about
  being straight.
I am going to tell my newcomer how good I feel and get him positive.
I am going to show and tell my appreciation to my foster mom about tonight.
I am going to tell about my *birthday* in group.

Blessings
I'm thankful for being able to get straight and live a normal life at 14.
I'm thankful for the courage to make changes I need to be straight.
I'm thankful for my care towards my family relationship.
Please bless John and give him good health and please bring him to the
  program. I know he needs it and I love him very much. Please bless
  Grandpa—he needs your care and strength. Please help Staff with the ability
  to share their awareness more than ever to their group. I'm special. I love
  me—Edward W. Amen.

Within this model we teach clients that with repetition in specific situations, one's thoughts at B and D become so well learned that feelings and behaviors may become automatic when a particular life situation occurs. Thus, when feelings and behaviors are automatic (the A, C, E components or "ACE"), we speak of the development of an attitude. We have found that in a few 2-hour sessions, clients as young as 11 or 12 years of age are able to learn the difference between the various components of the awareness wheel and to understand each of the points and the interrelationships in the A, B, C, D, E configuration. Following initial training, we repeatedly reinforce the model by challenging client statements such as "My father *made me* angry." (*Counselor:* "No, who makes you angry? Your thoughts—change your thoughts and you'll change your feelings.") This constant reemphasis on the importance of speaking clearly about one's thoughts and feelings helps the client to internalize what has been learned. We find that as intervention proceeds, we begin to observe client statements such as "I made myself angry over . . ."; "When my father said X, I thought Y . . . I really felt angry." This transition in the client's language is a most important clue to the success of the intervention and should be observed carefully as a sign of progress. In addition, clues to the clarity and rationality of the client's thinking are provided for assessment by keeping track of the client's M.I.s.

Next it is important to provide the client with a basic framework for evaluating whether or not a particular thought is rational or irrational, given that irrational thinking leads to uncomfortable or unpleasant feelings or dysfunctional actions. We employ the "Five Criteria" originally developed by Maultsby (1975, 1980, 1984). These criteria have been neatly drawn on posterboards and placed in conspicuous locations in our treatment facility so that the clients receive frequent visual reminders of criteria for evaluating their thoughts. It is hoped that the client will internalize these criteria and, when uncomfortable feelings are detected, will evaluate the rationality of thoughts, using this information to challenge and change those that are irrational. The Five Criteria are listed below. To be rational, a thought must:

1. Be based on objective reality
2. Protect my life
3. Be goal producing (short term and long term)
4. Make me feel and act the way I need to
5. Keep me out of trouble with others.

The client is now able to identify and label thoughts and to evaluate whether or not they are rational. At this point it is important to provide a systematic means by which irrational thoughts can be replaced by new, appropriate thoughts so that more desirable feelings and more effective actions can take place. Whether it is a provocative situation involving parents or teachers, handling an invitation from a drug-using peer to go along with the group, or dealing with negative thoughts of self, it is critical that the client is provided with mechanisms to alter those thoughts in the natural environment. We employ the Rational Self-Analysis (RSA— Maultsby, 1975), which has been used successfully with various clients, including alcoholics. The written RSA requires the client to describe self-actions in and the characteristics of a problem situation and, working backwards, to describe the way he or she felt and the thoughts that preceded those feelings. Then the RSA instructs the client to consider carefully the alternative thoughts that would lead to desired feelings and actions when confronted with that situation again. These are written down. This technique brings to life the conceptualization already presented to the client and provides a practical means of problem solving those situations in which unfortunate actions or uncomfortable feelings are experienced.

Formal training in the RSA should occur after the client has passed through the first two stages of the rehabilitation process and is cognitively able and willing to receive this material. The RSA can be taught individually or in a group situation; however, individual homework—to write RSAs as difficult life situations are encountered—is necessary for mastery and should be reviewed carefully to provide feedback to the client. Thus, each client should be asked to write a set number of RSAs, and individual progress should be monitored carefully. An example of the RSA is found in Figure 10-3.

We have successfully employed this technique with youth as young as 11 years old. Continual social reinforcement for progress in employing

FIGURE 10-3 • *An Example Rational Self-Analysis (RSA) Written by a 17-Year-Old Client*

Situation (A)	Disagreeing with Mom and sister
Old Feelings (C)	Angry, resentful, pity, frustration
Desired Feelings (C$_1$)	Happy, caring, closeness
Old Behavior (E)	Rolled my eyes, leaned up against refrigerator
Desired Behavior (E$_1$)	Paid attention to them and talked

Old Thoughts (B)
1. I feel angry.
2. Here we go again—everyone against me.
3. I'm not going to apologize.
4. She had no right to say that.
5. No matter what happens it's always her and Jane against me.
6. She is full of it.
7. I hate her sometimes.
8. I don't think that was fair at all.
9. All of a sudden she doesn't feel good about me.
10. I don't want to give up on staff.
11. That's what they want.
12. She is just jealous.
13. They don't care.
14. They are always bitching at me.
15. I'm sick of it.
16. Just like the past.
17. Everytime I feel good some dumb problem comes up.
18. Don't they want me to have any friends?
19. I hate when they gang up on me.
20. Maybe it's just me.
21. We just don't get along.
22. Maybe I'd be happier at a foster home.
23. It's not my fault I'm never home.
24. She says I need it, but then she bitches about it.
25. Some Mother's Day.
26. Just today I was talking about how I appreciate my mom.
27. I haven't spent much time with her lately.
28. It's not all me.
29. This ruins everything.

New Thoughts (B$_1$)
1. I control how I feel so I'm not going to feel angry over this situation.
2. No one is against me—they are offering me help.
3. I am going to apply my program and admit up to my wrongs and make amends.
4. My mom can say anything she wants to.
5. I'm going to be honest. No one is against me.
6. My mom has a lot of awareness and I'm going to listen to her.
7. I love my mom.
8. No one says what is fair and what isn't. I'm going to accept what she said.

Continued

FIGURE 10-3 • Continued

9. She didn't say she didn't feel good about me—she is giving me constructive criticism.
10. I want to be on staff and I'm going to.
11. My family wants what is in my best interest.
12. I'm not going to judge other people.
13. My mom and my sister do care about me—they just don't agree with what I said.
14. They are offering me help.
15. I'm glad they care enough to reach out to me.
16. This isn't like the past because we are all straight.
17. I will have challenges everyday—I can keep growing.
18. My family wants what is best for me.
19. I'm glad they are taking the time to reach out to me.
20. I'm going to be honest with myself.
21. I do have a very strong and close relationship with my family.
22. I'm happy with my family.
23. I'm going to take advantage of the time I am home.
24. I'm going to listen to what my mom has to say.
25. I have had a really good day so far—I'm going to keep on having one.
26. I do appreciate my mom and I'm going to show her by listening.
27. I'm going to sit and talk with my mom when we are together.
28. We are going to talk about this together.
29. I'm glad this happened because I have learned from it.

the RSA is most important. Verbal modeling of the RSA on a frequent basis in both individual and group therapy situations is also beneficial. For example:

Counselor: Let's turn the situation around. How did you wish to act in the situation?

Client: (Describes desired actions.)

Counselor: How did you wish to feel?

Client: (Describes desired feelings.)

Counselor: What thoughts would you need to have to feel and thus act in that way?

Client: (Is helped to develop new, rational thought, using the Five Criteria as a guide.)

We have found that the RSA technique, coupled with specific instruction in the definition of and a conceptualization for anger, is an effective means of dealing with the frequent angry outbursts these clients have shown prior to treatment. Clients whose thinking is filled with subvocal cursing, negative blaming, and other categories of aggressive self-talk should be singled out for special training in anger management. The focus here should be upon being aware of thoughts and feelings *early on* in a provocative situation so that cognitive intervention (changing the thoughts) can take place prior to the building up of intense angry feelings. In addition, learning how to evaluate *in advance* those situations that may be difficult — and to work at changing those situations — is important. Finally, the RSA is an excellent means of changing the thoughts and feelings that may lead to verbal or physical aggression in the situation. We find temper management to be a common problem for our clients, and specific attention should be paid to anger-control training as a part of an overall cognitive-behavioral approach to drug problems. More is said about anger management in Chapter 5.

Next attention must be given to those repetitive *styles of thinking* that are revealed over time by the client's choice of language. A number of styles of thought have been identified by a variety of writers (e.g., Beck, 1976; Ellis et al., 1988), and these are no doubt well known to the reader of this text; however, it is worth noting some specific styles that we find to be particularly pronounced with this adolescent population.

- *Absolutes* — viewing the world in absolutes. Examples: She is *always* mean to me. He *never* does anything right. I *always* fail.
- *Should and Ought* — demanding that the world, others, or yourself should or must be different. Examples: There *should* be fairness in the world. I *should* not foul up. My teacher *should* not talk to me like that. My mom *should* not treat me like she does.
- *Awfulizing* — viewing life's experiences as being awful or terrible. Examples: It will be just *awful* if I don't make cheerleader. It would really be *terrible* if my friends didn't talk to me.
- *Trying-Versus-Doing* — saying you tried to accomplish something but never doing any of the necessary things to make it happen. Examples: I really *tried* to do better. I really *tried* to stop smoking so much.
- *Can't* — saying you cannot do something when you really have chosen not to do something, because you are afraid to or simply did not *want to*. Examples: I *can't* do that modern math. I *can't* go with you (I do not choose to go with you). I *can't* go through this with you one more time. I *can't* get off coke!
- *Yes, But* — saying you want to change or to do something about a problem but then making excuses not to do the necessary things to change. Examples: I really wanted to go to the dance, *but* I could not get a ride. I hear what you said, *but* . . .
- *Abuse of Generalities* — viewing the world in abstract, undefined terms. Examples: I just want to be *free*. *Independence*, that is what I want. I don't want to be *hassled*.

Employing one of these styles of thinking often insulates the client from taking personal responsibility in actively solving problems. Each of these styles is implicitly irrational and dooms the habitual user to uncomfortable or unpleasant feelings that must then be dealt with either via psychological defense mechanisms or by the use of drugs (within the negative reinforcement paradigm shown in Figure 10-1). Thus, these styles must be identified, challenged, and altered. As each thinking style is observed in the therapy situation, the client should be made aware of it and should develop a plan for change as part of the specific goals for using the Five Criteria and the RSAs.

In addition, most of these clients have developed a well-organized self-language surrounding the denial that there is a problem and the denial of any personal responsibility for life difficulties. This denial, as well as rationalizing and projecting of internal feelings upon others (parents, teachers, "society"), will be noted by the clinician during the first two stages of the rehabilitation process. Such psychological defenses m٢ ،t be confronted actively through further probing and challenging of the client's statements, as well as by taking real-life information that the therapist possesses and presenting it to the client in a reality therapy fashion. In this way the client is literally forced to integrate this objectively valid information into a new and developing view of his or her past. This confrontation process is not easy and can be best accomplished by trained peer counselors who have a real understanding of their own internal states when exposed to similar situations involving the law, school, parents, or others. When peers model a more adaptive and rational way of thinking about life situations, clients not only begin to listen actively, but also the psychological boundaries surrounding the system of denial begin to crumble. This process is supported best by a group of peers who provide positive social reinforcement for honest self-examination. In contrast, in the client's past, peers provided social reinforcement for lying, dishonesty, and self-deception.

Finally, as the client's self-dialogue becomes more apparent and as various styles of thinking are identified, the therapist begins to obtain a better impression of the basic constructs that a particular client employs to view himself or herself and the world. Most of our clients have developed rather limited and narrow constructs (in terms of range of convenience, see Kelly, 1955) for evaluating themselves, other people in their lives, and the world around them. While the term "poor self-concept" is one that is certainly abused by mental health professionals, we find it applicable in most cases with this particular category of client. The pattern of dishonesty and the self-system depicted in Figure 10-1 involve the pushing down of situation-appropriate feelings and supplanting them with psychological defense mechanisms designed to maintain distance from significant others (e.g., parents, siblings, teachers). Youths begin to see themselves very negatively. Much of the anger and aggressive acting out that we often observe is a projection of an internal dialogue filled with self-doubt and self-blame. These youths have frequently met (understandable) social punishment and, finally, rejection by their parents, the school, and society as represented by police and the courts. They learn that other drug-using "friends" are not reliable. This chapter could be filled with accounts we have received from young people whose so-called friends abandoned them when they were in the process of overdosing, in jeopardy with the law, or without money to purchase drugs. The sexual promiscuity and the shallowness of past social relationships may also strengthen negative beliefs about self-worth and ability. Perhaps due to the effects of drugs, most of these clients are doing poorly in school or have dropped out, again reinforcing a self-image filled with failure and disappointment. Thus, if intervention is to be successful, it is important to challenge and to change these negative and dysfunctional beliefs about self and to confront the negative, blame-projecting attitudes employed to understand authority figures and the "straight" culture.

We contend that the only way to address these beliefs is to work at the level of the client's self-talk — talk that results from the interaction of a basic construct/belief and the situations that the youth faces. As irrational statements about self and others are confronted and as alternatives are suggested by peers, therapists, or by the client's use of the RSA, we find that these basic dysfunctional belief systems (as evidenced by the client's talk and actions) change over a period of 6 to 8 months of intervention. In addition, it is also useful to provide desirable and reinforcing positive roles that the client can play, along the lines of the role construct approach of Kelly (1955). As privileges are earned via appropriate behavior, the client also might be encouraged to take on important (role) responsibilities within the treatment facility (e.g., answer the telephones, help with certain housekeeping duties, or assume supervision for new clients). The process of systematically achieving and receiving public recognition for accomplishments from peers, parents, staff, and others helps alter internal dialogue so that it begins to include success experiences and positive outcomes. The youth must learn that it is possible *functionally* to alter those outcomes; when this occurs, the seeds of self-confidence and self-security have been sown.

We recommend that the treatment program be constructed so that the client progresses through a series of phases, stages, or levels of accomplishment based upon behavior. Graduation to later stages in the program carries a good deal of social reinforcement. Being placed in the position of "peer counselor in training" or being selected to serve as a peer counselor is a positive and attainable goal that the client can work to achieve. We recommend intervention that permits the client to remain *in the community*, with increasingly liberal access to community resources as progress is shown, so that at all times the client is in a position to receive natural positive consequences for appropriate actions. This also sets aside the issue of generalization from a self-contained treatment program to the real world (Nay, 1980; Kanfer & Goldstein, 1980). An important stage of this process is the client's return to school or job where there is exposure to other substance-using youth who will provide active encouragement for drug use. Having access to "support" peers who also have been through drug treatment and who can serve as positive resources further strengthens the client's beginning efforts at self-mediation and self-control.

A fourth stage of intervention is that of *dissonance*, which occurs as the youth returns to the community and is exposed to a previous lifestyle and the active encouragement to resume drug use. It is during this stage that the client is required to apply newly learned cognitive strategies. These coping strategies can permit the client to manage dissonance, or the pull between former thinking habits and newly learned functional thinking habits that compete for control of emotional and behavioral responses. It is almost as if the client were a rider on a horse that was previously taught to go to the right and is now being requested to travel straight ahead. As functional thinking directs the horse forward, much resistance is exerted from the horse (past irrational dysfunctional thinking). Resistence, dedication, and practice are required to overcome dissonance. The client must be continually reinforced for practicing new behavior and continuously exposed to peers who share and understand the dilemma. It is imperative that the therapist encourage open communication with the client to discuss those thoughts and feelings that occur as reexposure to the natural environment fosters this expected dissonance. If the youth believes that it is improper to discuss negative thoughts (which might disappoint the therapist), the stage is set for a therapeutic failure. It is important to remember that the well-learned styles of thinking, feeling, and behavior that were brought into treatment are still high in habit strength. With reexposure to old cues (e.g., old settings, "druggie" peers, etc.), a reversal of therapeutic gain can easily occur. For this reason it is also most important that the youth be restricted from interacting with past drug-using friends. Using modeling and behavioral rehearsal, the youth can be given behavioral strategies for dealing with those former friends (e.g., "It is not in my best interest to be with you," avoiding druggie hangouts, etc.). Rational Emotive Imagery (Maultsby, 1980, 1984) permits the client to rehearse and plan for future provocation.

A final and continuing stage of intervention is that of *follow-up*. Almost any program that provides incarceration or intensive supervision of the client can restrict a client's access to drugs and thus be successful initially. The real challenge is to foster enduring change. We believe that the foregoing intervention stages will succeed not only in terminating drug use but also in disrupting those external and self-mediated systems of reinforcement that have supported this behavior in the past. Ideally, at this point the client has identified and altered the basic self-beliefs that provided the psychological climate for drug use and has modified the system of irrational thoughts and styles of thinking that defended drug-related actions. This process has taken place within the context of careful supervision by peers (e.g., in the schools) who can continue to provide support and by parents and other family members who have learned more adaptive communication skills. The client now must employ those tools to make wise decisions. We believe that continued and close supervision, involving initial daily contact with the treatment program, should be systematically "faded out" only as the client continues to show progress in self-control. Continued use of the M.I. and daily RSAs are effective means of linking the treatment to the natural setting and of monitoring progress; these can be performed at any time in any environment. Follow-up must be deliberate and should involve continued contacts with peer counselors and with treatment staff for at least 1 year following completion of formal intervention.

A brief description of the intervention program mentioned in our discussions will serve as an example of how the conceptual and treatment issues that we have described can be incorporated into a comprehensive program.

An Application: The L.I.F.E. Program

The methods and issues subsumed in the five stages of intervention that we have described are incorporated in an ongoing drug rehabilitation program in Sarasota County, Florida. In a 6-month to 1-year day treatment program, Life Is For Everyone (L.I.F.E.) serves the full socioeconomic spectrum, from 12 to 22 years of age.

The L.I.F.E. program was designed to deal with the problem of drug rehabilitation and incorporates a number of features that we have found to foster comprehensive and lasting behavior change as the youth returns to the community. First, the program makes use of the power of peer influence by creating and providing a positive peer group. The client learns that there are alternative ways of relating socially to one's peers—ways that don't involve the use of drugs. This is accomplished through group "raps" or therapy sessions as well as by the assigning of an "oldcomer" (positive role model) to each of the "newcomers." It is through the child's oldcomer that he or she has a further opportunity to question past beliefs and behavior with respect to drugs. Significant friendship relationships are established— relationships that can continue as the youth is returned to job or school during later phases of the program. As increased numbers of young people complete our program, there are more positive peer resources available in the local junior and senior high schools. These positive contacts offset the negative pressures exerted by past drug-using friends. Thus, there is a change in the peer environment itself.

In addition to providing a positive peer group in the program and in school, another important treatment component is the requirement that the client's parents and siblings participate actively in the program. A series of educational sessions, raps, and workshops provides instruction in the "basics" of the program as well as training in communication skills, assertiveness techniques, and child management skills for parents. Workshop offerings in areas such as couples communication and human sexuality are provided to those parents who are experiencing marital problems that must be addressed before meaningful family change can occur. Siblings attend a special rap, and if it is found that they are also abusing drugs, they are referred for intake and for possible program placement. Thus, our focus is upon change in the family system itself.

Most of our clients have developed a variety of illogical and irrational thoughts as well as ineffective problem-solving styles, particularly surrounding their drug use. Therefore, another component of our program is the training in cognitive-behavioral change procedures that teach the client to identify ineffective and irrational styles of thinking and to substitute more appropriate and functional thoughts and beliefs for problem solving. We believe that it is impossible to change a client's *behavior* pattern with respect to drugs without changing the *attitudes* and *beliefs* that underlie the behaviors. The interrelationships between thoughts, feelings, and behavior are stressed, and the client is taught to evaluate effectively his or her feelings in a situation by examining the underlying thoughts which lead to those feelings. The awareness procedure, the Five Criteria, and the RSA technique are employed. In this way the youth is given powerful tools that will be useful across a variety of problem life situations in the future. In addition, *all* parents receive workshop training in the techniques of cognitive behavior change. Our goal is to help clients and their families evaluate the situation, evaluate their thoughts and feelings, decide on a course of action, and implement that solution within a problem-solving strategy.

The program is composed of five phases that the child completes sequentially as progress is shown. During the first phase the child lives away from home in a "foster" placement (the family of an oldcomer in the program). While in this phase the child is asked to be truthful and to acknowledge the exact nature of the problem. When the child is able to look honestly at his or her past and to define goals and objectives, the second phase of the program returns the youth to the natural family. At this point the emphasis is on improving one's family relationships. The youth is encouraged to be open, honest, and direct in interacting with parents and siblings. The reader will recall that within their rap sessions, parents also have been learning skills to facilitate this communication process more effectively. During a third program phase the child returns to school or to the job situation and is encouraged to work on academic or job-related tasks. During the fourth program phase the child is encouraged to make effective use of leisure time while continuing to work on all of the previous areas. Finally, the child who has advanced to the fifth phase of the program is given the privilege of standing at the side of the group during group raps and open meetings as a sign of that child's status as an oldcomer/overseer of newcomers within the program. The "fifth-phaser" is asked now to "give back" to the program, and this giving process (the leading of raps, helping on intakes, taking newcomers home to live) provides a rich opportunity to learn about himself or herself and to take responsibility for emphasizing the basic steps of the program. A final special phase of the program is called the "Seventh Step." Entry into the Seventh Step Society is a sign that the formal program (five phases) has been completed and that staff and peers feel good about the client's ability to manage the demands of daily living, using both the program and common sense as a means of solving problems. Thus, we expect the Seventh Stepper to begin to function in a more autonomous fashion. Through required monthly family interviews and weekly Seven Step Raps (part of the follow-up process), we actively encourage the family to continue to be a part of our program family. This active monitoring and follow-up during the seventh step ensures that maintenance of program gains will be achieved and that change is, in fact, durable. Also, it is from the group of Seven Steppers that youth are carefully selected for staff training and development. Thus, existing program staff are selected from those who have successfully completed the program and have demonstrated leadership ability. This combination of nonprofessional and professional staff provides an excellent blend of talents, incorporating both the experiential and the conceptual/theoretical components of our program.

An ongoing program evaluation (see Hoogerman, Huntley, Griffith, Petermann, & Koch, 1984) revealed that of 314 clients, 63% of females and 49% of males remained substance free for at least 1 year. Much more work remains, especially in the area of programmatic evaluation. Clearly, the problem of adolescent drug abuse and its impact on society is most serious. However, the existing and potential therapeutic technology for treatment is promising. A final note should be made about therapist survival skills when working with substance-abusing adolescents. Use common sense and take care of yourself. Working with such a population is very demanding, and striving to do it effectively is likely to be quite time- and energy-consuming.

References

Alcoholics Anonymous. (1980). *Alcoholics Anonymous.* New York: Alcoholics Anonymous World Services.

Barbour, J. (1981). *Marijuana and your child.* New York: Associated Press.

Beck, A. (1976). *Cognitive therapy and emotional disorders.* New York: International University Press.

Ellis, A. (1962). *Reason and emotion in psychotherapy.* New York: Stuart.

Ellis, A., & Bernard, M. (Eds.). (1984). *Rational emotive approaches to the problems of childhood.* New York: Plenum Press.

Ellis, A., McInerney, J. B., DiGiuseppe, R., & Yeager, R. (1988). *Rational-Emotive Therapy with alcoholics and substance abusers.* New York: Pergamon Press.

Hoogerman, D., Huntley, D., Griffith, B., Petermann, H., & Koch, C. (1984). Effective early intervention for adolescents harmfully involved in alcohol and drugs. *Journal of Florida Medical Association, 71,* 227–232.

Johnston, L. D., O'Malley, P. M., & Bachman, J. G. (1985). Use of licit and illicit drugs by America's high school students, 1975–1984. (NIDA Research Monograph No. ADM 85-1384). Washington, DC: U.S. Government Printing Office.

Kanfer, F. H., & Goldstein, A. (Eds.). (1980). *Maximizing treatment gains.* New York: Academic Press.

Kelly, G. (1955). *The psychology of personal constructs* (Vol. 1 & Vol. 2). New York: Norton.

Latner, I., O'Brien, J., & Voth, H. (1980). Answering questions about marijuana use. *Patient Care, 10,* 112–148.

Lazarus, A. (1976). *Multimodal behavior therapy.* New York: Springer.

Manatt, M. (1979). *Parents, peers and pot.* Rockville, MD: National Institute on Drug Abuse.

Maultsby, M. (1975). *Help yourself to happiness.* New York: Institute for Rational Living.

Maultsby, M. (1980). *The handbook of rational self-counseling.* Lexington, KY: Rational Self-Help Books.

Maultsby, M. (1984). *Rational Behavior Therapy.* Englewood Cliffs, NJ: Prentice-Hall.

Meichenbaum, D. (1977). *Cognitive-behavior modification: An integrated approach.* New York: Plenum Press.

National Institute on Drug Abuse, Training and Resource Development (Ed.). (1979). *Drugs in perspective.* Rockville, MD: N.I.D.A.

Nay, W. R. (1979). *Multimethod clinical assessment.* New York: Gardner Press.

Nay, W. R. (1980). Parents as reinforcers: Increasing generalization of parent training. In F. H. Kanfer & A. Goldstein (Eds.), *Maximizing treatment gains.* New York: Academic Press.

Nay, W. R. (1984). Family therapy with the substance abusing adolescent. In P. Keller & L. Ritt (Eds.), *Innovations in clinical practice: A source book,* (Vol. 3). Sarasota, FL: Professional Resources Exchange.

Ries, R., Batran, J., & Schuckit, M. (1980). Recognizing the drug abuser with psychiatric complaints. *Behavioral Medicine, 3,* 18–21.

Ross, G. (1979, August). *Cognitive therapy and Alcoholics Anonymous: An integrated approach for the treatment and prevention of teenage substance abuse.* Paper presented to the National Drug Abuse Conference, New Orleans.

Stanton, M. (1979). Drugs and the family: A review of the literature. *Marriage and Family Review, 2*(1), 1–10.

Voth, H. (1980). *How to get your child off marijuana.* Los Angeles: Patient Care Publications.

CHAPTER ELEVEN

Children and Coping with Pain

A Cognitive-Behavioral Management Approach

W. M. NELSON, III

What Is Pain?

Until the advent of seventeenth-century empiricism and scientific investigations of the physical world, conceptions of pain were based primarily upon the teaching and writings of ancient Greek philosophers. For over 2,000 years, pain was thought to originate from an imbalance among the four vital body fluids—blood, black bile, yellow bile, and phlegm. During the Middle Ages in Europe (about A.D. 500–1500), the notion of pain—and of any abnormal behavior—was usually characterized by superstition and ritual. It was believed (and still is, by certain religious groups) that pain and illnesses were caused by sins—the more severe the pain, the greater the sin that had been committed. Only in the seventeenth century did ideas about pain begin to shift, and pain began to be viewed in more morality-free contexts. Rene Descartes's (1596–1650) writings formed the foundation upon which Johannes Muller (1838) and Von Frey (1894) built the *specificity theory,* which maintains that pain is communicated to the brain via independent connections or pathways just like any of the other sensations (touch, sight, hearing, etc.). Thus, it was postulated that there are special pain receptors in the periphery of the body that respond to certain stimuli preferentially by sending impulses to the brain, which then produces the specific "pain" reaction. Pain, therefore, was seen as being a direct result of the amount of tissue damage and could ultimately be adequately understood by identifying and specifying the parameters of the noxious physical stimuli. Although specialized nerve fibers (A-delta and C fibers) associated with pain have been identified in the outer layers of the skin, these do not seem to respond exclusively to pain as the specificity theory predicts. Another way of conceptualizing the experience of pain crystallized late in the nineteenth century and became known as the *pattern theory* (see Sinclair, 1955; Crue & Carregal, 1975). According to this theory the experience of pain was not simply a matter of having a pain receptor respond directly to a particular stimulus. Rather, it was the timing or patterning of impulses both in the pain receptors themselves and in the neighboring fibers that resulted in the phenomenal experience of pain. Still, both of these theories — specificity and pattern — are unidimensional models of pain and explain the experience of pain as a result of stimulation of specific fibers whether these are localized, more general, or patterned (see Figure 11-1).

The most significant theoretical shift in conceptualizing pain was postulated by Melzack and Wall (1965) and Melzak (1973). In their *gate control theory,* pain is viewed as a very complex phenomenon that is the

FIGURE 11-1 • *Unidimensional Model of Pain (Specificity and Pattern Theories)*

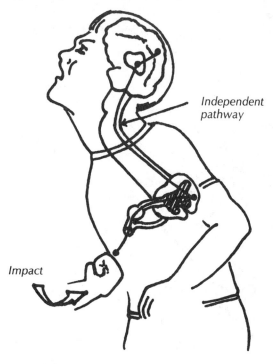

Independent pathway

Impact

result of the interplay of three systems — sensory-discriminative, motivational-affective, and cognitive-evaluative (see Figure 11-2). The sensory-discriminative component refers to the actual sensory information arising from the noxious stimulation. The way in which individuals verbally convey such sensory data is reflected in words like "wrenching," "shooting," "stinging," and "itching" (Melzack & Torgerson, 1971). The motivational-affective element refers to subjective feelings while experiencing pain. Linguistically, reports that the pain is "frightening," "killing," "blinding," "aching," and "tender" reflect this dimension. The cognitive-evaluative system determines the meaning of the sensory experience. Here, the individual cognitively compares the noxious sensations to past experiences and evaluates the various response alternatives in responding to such stimuli. Such cognitive processes (which involve private speech and images) result in verbal evaluations of the pain such as "horrible," "unbearable," "troublesome," and "annoying." Although the psychological and anatomical basis

FIGURE 11-2 • *Multidimensional Model of Pain*
(Gate Control Theory)

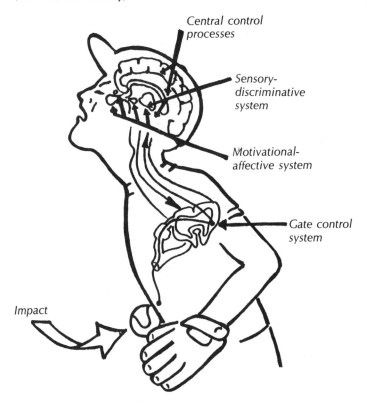

for the gate control theory has been scrutinized and subsequently questioned (e.g., Iggo, 1972; Kerr, 1975; Nathan, 1976), its multidimensionality and overall inclusiveness have been applauded (e.g., Hilgard & Hilgard, 1975; Tursky, 1976).

Melzack and Wall's (1965) gate control theory is revolutionary in that pain is no longer viewed as a direct function of sensory input (specificity theory) or even as a "summation" of varying patterns of nerve impulses arising from the injured site (pattern theory). Rather, the experience of pain is the result of an active integration of many different kinds of signals that arise in different areas of the nervous system and that involve both physiologic and psychologic mechanisms. Thus, the neural input arising from the "painful" area in the periphery of the body and traveling to the spinal cord and up to the brain is only one factor in this complex experience that is responsible for the overt behavioral responses that characterize pain. It is speculated that these nocioceptive impulses are carried in the smaller, phylogenetically older "C" and "A-delta" nerve fiber system. Other signals originate in the brain, travel downward, and, in effect, modulate the experience of pain. These other signals are primarily cognitive and affective in nature. They include one's comparison of incoming sensations to past experiences, one's present attentiveness and expectation, one's perception of the causes and consequences of these sensations, one's current level of anxiety and physiological state, one's cultural background, and other psychological/cognitive factors. These presumably nonpainful impulses are thought to be carried in a phylogenetically newer, larger, faster fiber system. Thus, the gate control model clearly makes pain a complex psychobiological phenomenon. The concept of pain as multidimensional receives additional support from the growing body of literature that points to psychosocial stressors as essential components in understanding the etiology of disease and pain processes (e.g., Cassel, 1976; Friedman & Glasgow, 1974; Mason, Buescher, Belfer, Artenstein, & Mougey, 1979; Syme, 1975). In fact, interpretations given to these psychosocial stressors and to the actual physical insult itself are significant factors in the subjective experience of pain (e.g., Lazarus, 1966; Mason, 1971; Roskies & Lazarus, 1980).

In addition, the multifaceted nature of pain becomes obvious when one examines the inadequacies of pain treatments derived solely from the unidimensional specificity or pattern theories. If pain is solely a function of the stimulation of pain receptors or even of particular patterns of nerve impulses, it theoretically could be completely eradicated by cutting or blocking the so-called "pain pathways" to the brain or by removal of parts of the brain where "pain signals" register (e.g., thalamus). Such treatments have included the use of many types of potentially addictive pharmacological agents (e.g., narcotics), anesthetic nerve blocks (e.g., Novocaine) that require injection directly into the nerve root, and numerous surgical procedures (e.g., ranging from severing peripheral nerves to prefrontal loboto-mies) designed to slice these pathways anywhere from the skin to the brain. Not only do such procedures often have deleterious effects and numerous side effects (Melzack, 1973), but also they prove to be impotent in that the original pain frequently is not adequately or permanently ameliorated (Clark & Hunt, 1971; Liebeskind & Paul, 1977; Toomey, Ghia, Mao, & Gregg, 1977; Weisenberg, 1975). The narrowness of the unidimensional sensory-physiological theories was highlighted by Melzack and Casey (1968):

> *The surgical and pharmacological attacks on pain might well profit by redirecting thinking toward the neglected and almost forgotten contri-bution of motivational and cognitive processes. Pain can be treated not only by trying to cut down sensory input by anesthetic blocks, surgical intervention and the like, but also by influencing the motiva-tional-affective and cognitive factors as well. (p. 435)*

It is important to note that the actual distinction between organic and psychogenic pain is blurred at best. As such, children's pain has been classified into three generic categories — disease-related pain, recurrent pain syndromes, and medical procedural pain (Elliott & Jay, 1987). The most common types of disease-related pain are associated with renal infections, Chrone's disease, vertebral disease and intraspinal tumor, hemophilia, sickle-cell anemia, and cancer (the second leading cause of death in 1- to 14-year-olds [O'Malley, Koocher, Foster, & Slavin, 1979]). Recurrent pain syndromes include headaches (as many as 18% of children from 10 to 12 years old suffer frequent headaches [Tomasi, 1979]) and abdominal pain (most commonly encountered pain complaint in children between 6 and 15 years of age, affecting 10–15% of children [Apley, 1975; Astrada, Lic-amele, Walsh, & Kessler, 1981]). Pain associated with various medical procedures also affects a significant proportion of children; these pro-cedures include bone marrow aspiration and lumbar puncture, burn de-bridement, chemotherapy, surgery, and orthodontia. In examining the liter-ature on pain, however, it becomes obvious that most theorizing and research has been conducted either as downward extensions of data gener-ated from work with adults or as upward extensions of work done with animals which have undergone various laboratory pain inductions. In either case, relatively little has been done dealing specifically with children. Clearly, there is little empirical basis for the longstanding belief that youn-ger children experience less severe pain than adults because of immature development of their nervous systems.

The remainder of this chapter will discuss the assessment of pain in children and review noncognitive-behavioral treatment approaches that assist children in managing the fear, anxiety, and pain associated with disease-related and recurrent pain syndromes and with various diagnostic and medical procedures. The focus will then turn to a description of specific cognitive-behavioral interventions that can be employed to assuage the pain and suffering of children. The primary purpose of this chapter is to examine the theoretical basis and concomitant procedural guidelines of cognitive-behavioral management of pain. However, the reader should be cognizant of the paucity of child-related research in this area. Although cognitive-behavioral approaches have gained wide acceptance in the area of clinical psychology, much work needs to be done directly with children in regard to pain assessment and management. The existing literature is a valuable source for many intervention strategies that hold significant promise for use with adult populations (see Bradley & Kay, 1985; Turk, Meichenbaum, & Genest, 1983), but the usefulness of these procedures with children remains an empirical question (see McGrath, 1989, for a review of pain in child populations). The challenge of assisting children in coping not only with disease-related and recurrent pain syndromes but also with the pain resulting from various medical and surgical procedures is considerable. It should also be noted that with such pain there is concomitant psychological stress, and this is compounded by the changing cognitive and emotional responses that occur naturally as a result of the child's physical, cognitive, and psychosocial development (Bush, 1987). Therefore, it is hoped that this chapter will not only provide a general working framework of cognitive-behavioral strategies for clinicians who deal with children experiencing pain but also will highlight the need for further examination of this model by child researchers.

Assessment of Pain in Children: A Brief Overview

During the last eight years there has been a dramatic increase in research on the utility of different techniques for measuring pain in children. Currently there are a variety of methods available for assessing acute, recurrent, and chronic pain in children. Such research has filled a major gap in the endeavors to assist children in pain, because without being able to objectively assess the quality and magnitude of pain, it would not be possible to identify a child's personal experience of pain. It would also be difficult to determine the consequences of pain or to evaluate the effectiveness of intervention efforts. A complete discussion of assessment measures is beyond the scope of this chapter; however, such reviews can be found elsewhere (see Beyer & Byers, 1985; Keefe & Williams, 1989; Lavigne, Schulein, & Hahn, 1986; Jay, 1984; McGrath, 1987, 1989).

Methodological problems abound in trying to assess something as complex and subjective as "pain." Basically, however, to understand pain in children, health professionals generally attempt to assess three related variables: (a) behavioral response, (b) physiological indicators, and (c) psychological signs. Behavioral responses include general observations of crying patterns, facial expressions, and specific motor activity as well as objectively detailed behavior assessment rating scales (e.g., Procedural Behavioral Rating Scale–Revised; Katz, Kellerman, & Siegel, 1980) used with pediatric oncology patients. A possible fruitful extension of rating children's behavioral responses involves sampling pain behavior in standardized situations. Such performance testing has become more widely utilized with adult patients. For example, Keefe and Block (1982) videotaped behavior samples of patients with low back pain engaging in activities likely to increase pain and found that behaviors were reliable indexes of pain. Such assessment procedures go beyond the use of traditional pain diaries designed to record gross categories of behavior (e.g., time spent out of bed, medication intake). How those assessment techniques can be extended to use with children remains to be seen. Physiological indicators of pain include measures of respiration and heart rate, cortisol levels, palmar sweat, and endorphin levels; however, the experience of pain cannot be unequivocally inferred from signs of autonomic arousal as completely as it can be ruled out in the absence of such signs.

Psychological measures are essential in evaluating children's pain, not only because of the deficits in the behavioral and physiological methods but also because the experience of pain is so subjective. Although psychological methods have included projective techniques (e.g., pain inferred from children's color selections, drawings, and cartoon interpretations), more direct methods are more frequently employed (e.g., interviews, self-report measures, interval rating scales, and visual analogue scales). Obviously, such techniques require that the child has the necessary verbal skills to communicate directly about the experience of pain. An example of a structured interview is the Children's Comprehensive Pain Questionnaire (McGrath, 1989), which was designed to assess multiple dimensions of children's chronic or recurring pain. It provides thorough quantitative information about sensory dimensions of pain, emotional variables, and situational factors. More precise attempts to quantify pain include category rating scales, graded thermometers, facial scales, and visual analogue scales. It should be noted that simple verbal descriptions of pain have major limitations. For instance, children age 9–12 years were found to describe pain in very general terms along sensory, affective, and intensity dimensions. Also, verbal descriptions of pain differed according to gender and according to whether or not the child was hospitalized (Savedra, Gibbons, Tesler, Ward, & Wegner, 1982). It is not clear whether verbal reports are influenced markedly by personality differences, by the specific form of the injury or pain, by the age of the child, or by other factors. Regardless of their limitations, the subjective assessment strategies hold a great deal of potential for future development, and traditionally they have been considered as the most reliable indicators or most valid evidence of pain.

In summary, a multifactored approach to pain assessment in children is necessary because of the multidimensional nature of the pain experience. Currently there is no one pain measure that can provide all the information needed for a thorough assessment. The practicing clinician is encouraged to become familiar with the various assessment strategies and to use them according to the particular child and his or her developmental level, the type of pain encountered, and the specific situation in which the child is being seen. In the meantime, it is hoped that our knowledge about the assessment of the pain phenomenon with children will continue to progress rapidly.

Intervention Techniques: Other Management Strategies

Techniques for managing pediatric pain can be organized broadly into pharmacological and psychological approaches. Basic procedures for inducing and maintaining general anesthesia and for administrating analgesics are beyond the scope of this chapter and can be found elsewhere (e.g., Bush, 1987). Therefore, before turning to cognitive-behavioral approaches to the management of pain in children, other psychological approaches will be reviewed.

Probably one of the most frequently used intervention strategies designed to lessen the stress and pain experienced by children is "psychological preparation," which provides the child with factual information about a painful diagnostic or medical procedure. This approach seems to hold particular promise when behavioral regulation and anxiety reduction are major goals. Although there are procedural differences in imparting information to the child, such strategies are similar in three respects: (a) they attempt to correct the child's misinformation, (b) they help the child cope with the painful experience by making it possible to anticipate medical procedures and to understand their purpose, and (c) they enhance the child's coping process through anticipation of the expected sensations.

A variety of booklets and storybooks are designed specifically for children to facilitate their understanding of hospitalization and of various special and surgical procedures (e.g., Green, 1963; Rey & Rey, 1966; Simpson, 1973; Stein, 1974; Wolinsky, 1971). Also, toys are utilized in play programs to demonstrate medical procedures before they are performed (e.g., Adams, 1976; Azarnoff & Flagel, 1974). Nevertheless, these supportive-educational or bibliotherapeutic approaches frequently are not sufficient to enhance behavioral adjustment or to alleviate the anxiety and fears that are usually associated with painful medical procedures. Such approaches assume that by being given "facts" about an upcoming diagnostic or medical procedure (e.g., onset, duration, intensity, sensations, and other details), the child will automatically begin to organize thoughts, feelings, and actions about the event or, as Janis (1958) stated, to engage in the "work of worrying." Unfortunately, there is little child research to ascertain the critical components of patient preparation and how different types of procedural information might interact with the various personality characteristics and the ages of children. Cognitive-behavioral methods seem to be more useful than techniques that simply expose children to information about what is going to happen to them, because the child's coping strategies themselves are the target of change. A direct training method involving information on how and when to act and the prior rehearsal of coping behavior was suggested by Leventhal and his colleagues (Leventhal, Singer, & Jones, 1965; Leventhal & Watts, 1966). Thus, it may be that the positive effects of bibliotherapy can be increased by the clinician who takes the time to assess how exposure to such material influences the child's cognitive understanding of the particular medical procedure. The child might ask: "What are the facts? What am I up against? How much will it hurt? How much pain will I feel? How can I cope with it? How do my thoughts influence my ability to cope?"

Puppet therapy (Cassell, 1965; Cassell & Paul, 1967) and play therapy (Dimock, 1960) also have been used to prepare children for a variety of medical procedures. The underlying assumption is that such strategies enhance a cathartic release, which lessens psychic tension and enhances the child's mastery of overwhelming experiences. In fact, it has been argued that with traditional individual psychotherapy for pediatric pain patients (particularly when a psychogenic component has been diagnosed), employing empathy may actually exacerbate pain by positively reinforcing such complaints (Varni, 1984). Although this type of intervention is based on the traditional psychoanalytic model with its well-known shortcomings, in actual practice such techniques can be fruitfully adopted by cognitive-behavioral clinicians. From the cognitive-behavioral model, however, these therapeutic processes are not about the "working out" of conflicts between the id, ego, and superego or about the cathartic "releasing" of tension. Instead, they involve a carefully planned treatment regimen in which irrational thinking and imaginings are first translated into concrete self-statements that the child is taught to recognize and to use as signals to engage in more adaptive coping private speech, imagery, and overt coping behavior.

Modeling, whether filmed or live, is another means of preparing children psychologically for stress that results from medical procedures (e.g., Adelson & Goldfried, 1970; Melamed, Hawes, Heiby, & Glick, 1975; Melamed & Siegel, 1975; Vernon & Bailey, 1974). It is assumed that by observing a model who participates in the feared or anxiety-arousing procedures without experiencing negative consequences, the child's maladaptive response patterns will be vicariously extinguished. Evidence in the coping-versus-mastery distinction suggests that the therapeutic effectiveness of treatment is enhanced when a coping model is employed (Debus, 1970; Kazdin, 1974a, 1974b; Meichenbaum, 1971; Wolpin & Raines, 1966). According to a cognitive model, it is not as important for the fear and anxiety to be "extinguished" or eradicated as it is for the child to learn to function/ cope in spite of and while experiencing the anxiety and pain that often accompany various diagnostic and medical procedures. The cognitive model suggests that prior to therapy the child's reaction to physical and/or psychological stressors led to the intensification of anxiety and maladaptive behaviors. According to this model, the child experiences the same feelings and sensations following therapy but now uses these as cues to engage in coping strategies, in spite of anxiety and the fact that medical procedures often do result in unavoidable pain.

Intervention Techniques: Cognitive-Behavioral Strategies

Before attempting to implement treatment procedures developed from the cognitive-behavioral model of human behavior, it is essential for the practicing clinician or other helping agent to have a thorough understanding not only of the theories of pain that have been briefly discussed but also of the theory that underlies cognitive-behavior modification (see Bandura, 1977, 1986; Mahoney, 1974; Meichenbaum, 1977; Turk et al., 1983). It is important to note that cognitive approaches are not proposed as replacements for the more traditional medical treatments for pain and stress experienced by children. Rather, they are offered as potentially useful adjuncts for the clinician who is helping the child cope with both the physical and psychological stressors that must inevitably be faced during childhood. The therapist's conceptualization of the experience of pain structures his or her thinking about the role of the child's cognitions in this physiological/ psychological experience. This conceptualization does not merely influence but also directly determines the questions asked of a child, the tests employed during the assessment phase of treatment, the understanding of the problem, and the treatment techniques that are implemented.

The following outline describes the cognitive-behaviorist's view of the coping process associated with the experience of pain. Regardless of the etiology of the child's experience of pain (e.g., previous "traumatic" medical experiences, preconceived notions about an upcoming surgery procedure), from a cognitive-behavioral framework the crucial task is to determine how the child's *present* behavior is self-defeating. Even though the child may be behaving "because" of previous events, his or her difficulties are connected with actions in the current situation. The child's emotional and behavioral response is aroused not only by actual stimuli but also by accompanying verbal and/or conceptual mediators. Thus, the child's cognitions and images play a determining role in the present problem and/or perception of pain. The basic assumption underlying the cognitive-behavioral assessment procedure is that the child's thoughts and images play a crucial role in the emotional upset, experience of pain, and maladaptive behavior. Self-talk prior to, accompanying, and following the presentation of any noxious stimulation becomes the target of analysis.

During the assessment phase of therapy, the concern of the cognitive-behavioral clinician is to determine the style and incidence of the child's cognitions and their relationship to maladaptive behavior and subjective reports of pain. To do this, the clinician must determine not only the content of a child's cognitions but also the thoughts and images that could lead to more adaptive behavior and to less frequent and intense reports of pain. The child's cognitions are viewed not as *reflections* of the capacity to cope with noxious stimulations but as *integral components* in his or her repertoire of coping skills. The capacity to handle pain-producing stimuli differs because of the frequency and intensity with which children produce anxiety- and pain-engendering self-statements and the images that interfere with their overt adaptive behavior. In a real sense, then, a child's thoughts, images, and self-statements can be used directly in teaching him or her to prepare for and/or to confront physical stressors.

Assessment: Cognitive-Behavioral Procedures

Assessment techniques are essential in developing effective, individually tailored treatment regimens for children who must undergo hospitalization, endure some type of painful medical procedure, and/or experience disease-related pain or recurrent pain syndromes. From a cognitive-behavioral learning model, assessment requires investigation of how three sets of factors—cognitive, behavioral, and environmental—interact reciprocally. This analysis of "reciprocal determinism" (Bandura, 1977, 1986) reflects the growing awareness that psychological functioning involves an intricate interplay among these influences. The particular factor or combination of factors targeted in therapy depends upon the therapist's own theoretical orientation. The pros and cons of employing self-reported cognitive processes as valid subject matter within the field of psychology have been scrutinized elsewhere (e.g., Lieberman, 1979; Nisbett & Wilson, 1977; Smith & Miller, 1978).

The major assumption in the therapy of behavior change proposed by cognitive behaviorists, however, is that the individual's cognitions and images play a determining role in present maladaptive functioning. Thus, emotional arousal and aberrant behavior are mediated by the interpretation of external and internal stimulation. This premise has developed from the popular notion that people talk to themselves and that overt speech, at least in children, can effectively regulate behavior (Luria, 1961; Vygotsky, 1962). More specifically in regard to pain, the gate control theory (Melzack & Wall, 1965) also highlights the contributing effects of psychologic mechanisms in the experience of pain. It should be noted that it is incumbent upon clinicians and researchers who "think" that cognitions are important in the experience of pain and in pain behavior to demonstrate scientifically that mental events do increase predictive power when children are asked to make public their cognitive processes by verbalization and/or other techniques.

With this caution in mind, how does the cognitive-behavioral clinician attempt to discern the style and incidence of a child's internal dialogue with its thoughts, self-statements, and images? Among the assessment procedures and techniques reviewed in an earlier chapter (Chapter 4), several seem to hold particular promise for children who have to cope with pain: imagery, behavioral exposure, and TAT-like approaches. The following assessment procedures are not the ones reviewed earlier in this chapter but rather are techniques that might be helpful for cognitive-behaviorally oriented clinicians in their attempt to gather data for the development of a specific treatment program. Also, it is important to use a variety of assessment procedures when gathering data regarding two aspects of pain—pain threshold (the point at which pain is perceived) and pain tolerance (the extent to which a person can endure pain). Further, the clinician must remember that a detailed assessment is very important in dealing with children experiencing various types of pain, and the assessment should include a detailed history of the pain, its role in the child's life, and the child's relationship with the family and/or caretaker.

Imagery

Trying to elicit information about a child's thoughts, feelings, and images in a strictly verbal didactic fashion is not always successful, probably because many children are not verbally adept. Instead, the clinician and child can play a "game" in which, with eyes closed, the child is instructed to "run a movie through your head"—a movie that tells about the most recent or intense incident of pain and other physical stressors. This technique is particularly useful for the child who must again undergo a painful medical/ surgical procedure that has already been experienced. Under the guidance of the therapist, the child is slowly and sequentially led through a specific, concrete experience that requires preparation for, confrontation of, and evaluation of performance in dealing with painful stimulation. At each of these stages the therapist guides the child with open-ended questions (to avoid "putting words into the child's mouth") to report on the sequence of thoughts, images, feelings, and behaviors.

The therapist must be particularly sensitive to the self-statements, thoughts, feelings, or images that reflect a child's "catastrophizing" of the painful sensations (e.g., "I'm going to die," "I can't stand it") and the feelings of losing control (e.g., "No matter what I do I know I'm going to cry and scream," "I can't handle it"). These processes seem to occur frequently in children whose inability to tolerate noxious stimulation becomes very problematic.

A variation of this imagery assessment procedure involves guiding the child to report on the "worst" things that could happen as a result of confronting the feared physical stressor. Using this catastrophizing technique, the clinican may discover a gap between reality and the child's fantasy as well as further clues to the child's maladaptive ideations and behaviors (see Singer, 1974, and Krueger, 1987 for a more thorough discussion of imagery techniques).

Behavioral Exposure

A particularly useful assessment tool for clinicians is a technique that probes the child's cognitions and images during a "dry run" exposure to physical stressors. Whenever possible, it is extremely helpful to expose the child to situations involving the noxious stimuli—possibly even to the aversive stimuli itself. In a controlled situation the therapist is able to ascertain the particular aspects of the environment that trigger specific coping or noncoping cognitions and ideations. At what point does the child become anxious? How much does the child think it will "hurt"? When does the child experience loss of control? Are there any coping self-statements or images? If so, when, and at what point do they occur in confronting the noxious stimuli?

A variation of the in vivo exposure involves videotaping the child undergoing behavior exposure. The therapist can then review the tape with the child and can reconstruct the thoughts and feelings that were experienced, as well as the maladaptive and adaptive behavior that was observed (e.g., Meyers & Nelson, 1986). A similar interview can be conducted after a role-playing session of the anxiety-arousing, pain-producing situation.

TAT-Like Approaches

Assessing or "tapping into" a child's internal dialogue can also be accomplished by employing a variety of TAT-like pictures that depict the painful stimuli or situations. This projective procedure capitalizes on the child's tendency to interpret situations in conformity with past experiences and present difficulties. The pictures used for this purpose are not the actual TAT pictures but rather a set of pictures or slides that depict the fear/pain-producing diagnostic or medical procedures. Using this medium the therapist can elicit in an open-ended fashion the child's perception of what is happening in the picture and what the child in the picture is thinking, feeling, and doing to cope with the situation. The therapist should structure the testing procedure so as to "pull" from the child's internal dialogue, and this information can then be evaluated in relation to the child's overt behavior. In order to gain useful information for developing an appropriate treatment strategy, it is not necessary to adhere to the rather rigid testing instructions recommended in the TAT manual. Instead, the emphasis is on determining the irrational, self-defeating aspects of the child's thinking style, self-statements, and images. Nelson and Cholera (1986) employed this assessment procedure with adolescents who were about to undergo various types of dental procedures. They found that when disruptive "in-chair" behavior increased, so did the percentage of coping self-statements, presumably reflecting attempts to deal with the threatening situation. Also, they found that as self-reported levels of anxiety increased, the percentage of coping self-statements decreased.

A similar projective procedure is employed when the therapist presents the child with a videotape or movie of another child (model) who is in the process of preparing for, confronting, and handling painful stimuli. The assessment strategy involves stopping the tape/movie at "critical points" and asking the child what the model is thinking, feeling, and doing in that situation. Although such projective devices have not been validated, they can provide a provocative source of hypotheses and speculation regarding the nature of the child's self-defeating behavior. More importantly, these techniques can yield crucial information for structuring the actual treatment regimen.

It should be noted that all of these assessment techniques rely on self-report and think-aloud methods (see Genest & Turk, 1981, for a more detailed analysis of these methods of cognitive assessment). These techniques may present particular difficulties for the child clinician in that the child's changing level of cognitive development undoubtedly has a significant effect upon the ability to reflect on his or her own thinking style. For research purposes, unstructured assessment techniques may often provide idiosyncratic data that are difficult to quantify. In addition, open-ended types of assessment/interviewing may often lead to situations in which children report on irrelevant cognitive events. These problems can be alleviated by using age-appropriate rating scales that ask children to rate private cognitions on various objective scales. Test items can be developed to provide information not only about the intensity of pain (e.g., "How much do you think that would hurt?") but also about the frequency of particular self-statements (e.g., "I thought I was going to die," "I knew I was going to cry"). Five-point rating scales ranging from 1 ("Never") to 5 ("Very often") are frequently useful in this regard. This method of cognitive assessment is still in its infancy in regard to children, and much more experimental work needs to be conducted in this area (see Merluzzi, Glass, & Genest, 1981, for cognitive assessment strategies that have been developed principally for adults and McGrath, 1989, for child assessment strategies).

Treatment: Stress Inoculation and the Management of Pain

The original stress inoculation training regimen was developed by Meichenbaum (1977) and has been employed for a variety of problems experienced by adults (e.g., social anxiety, test anxiety, alcoholism, social incompetence, anger, phobias). Although others (Langer, Janis, & Wolfer, 1975; Levendusky & Pankratz, 1975) have developed multidimensional treatments that incorporate affective, cognitive, and behavioral components in the management of pain, Meichenbaum (1977) and Turk (1975) were the first to apply the stress inoculation model to experimentally induced pain in adults. Cognitive-behavior therapeutic regimens offer efficacious preventive and remedial approaches to pain (Turk & Genest, 1979; Turk et al., 1983), and they hold promise for use with children (Nelson, 1981).

Operationally, stress inoculation training involves three phases: (a) education, (b) skills training, and (c) application training. These stages are outlined below, with an emphasis on utilizing this model with children who will encounter and must cope with pain.

Educational Phase

The first phase is designed to provide the child with a plausible conceptual set for understanding the nature of stressful/painful reactions. The exact content of the educational component varies greatly with the type of diagnostic and/or medical problem as well as with the age and cognitive capabilities of the child. The basic components of the cognitive preparation include teaching the child to:

1. Recognize his or her own idiosyncratic stress/pain reactions, which include cognitive, physiological, and behavioral determinants.
2. Perceive quickly the cognitive-affective-behavioral links early in the pain-producing response chain.
3. Discriminate the specific environmental stimuli that trigger the painful response pattern.

In addition, but perhaps most crucial in dealing with children, there is the clinician's ability to reinforce the notion that the child has or can learn to have control over overt and covert behaviors and to elicit the child's cooperation and trust in the therapist and in the coping strategies that will be learned.

In practice there is no sharp distinction between assessment procedures and the educational phase of stress inoculation training. In the assessment of any problem, the clinician not only analyzes the nature of the child's deficit but also directly or indirectly influences the child's view of the problem. In the stress inoculation model, children receive a strong message that they can control their thoughts and that they are not helpless victims solely at the mercy of aversive stressors.

Although adults can be given rather elaborate explanations of their emotional/painful reactions based on Schachter's (1966) theory of emotion or Melzack and Wall's theory of pain (1965), such explanations are often too complicated for children. The therapist must rely on clinical ability to gain the child's cooperation and trust, for only within a solid therapeutic relationship can the clinician effectively introduce the child to specific coping strategies. Thus, through skillful persuasion the therapist convinces the child that it is possible to learn to cope with anxiety-engendering aversive stimuli by following the "game plan" that has been developed as a result of the assessment procedures (and which will be taught to the child in the rehearsal phase). The thrust of this educational phase is not to convince the child that medical procedures will not hurt or be painful (this is an irrational/unrealistic belief in many cases) but that in spite of the reality, it is possible to learn to cope more effectively with aversive stimuli and to alter their impact.

Skills Acquisition Training Phase

The skills acquisition phase involves training in the specific coping skills and strategies that the child will use to deal with the actual stress and pain. Although the manner in which the coping techniques are taught can vary greatly, the most productive way of doing this with children is to model the specific self-statements and coping techniques for the child, who then approximates the therapist's verbalizations until the procedures are mastered. Throughout, the basic idea is to conduct this training in a systematic fashion in order to reinforce the child's notion that it is possible to cope with stressfully painful feelings. After the specific feared/painful procedures are identified, the child is taught to cope more effectively with these stimuli in a four-step procedure originally outlined by Turk (1975).

1. *Prepare for the painful stressor* by remembering and thinking to yourself that you can cope with the pain and anxiety that you will experience (e.g., "What is it I have to do?" "I can handle it").
2. *Confront and handle anxiety and/or pain* by employing self-statements that reduce such feelings (e.g., "One step at a time; I can do it," "Keep my mind on what I have to do," "I'm in control").
3. *Cope with feelings of being overwhelmed by anxiety and pain* by employing the specific strategies outlined below.
4. *Give self-reinforcement for coping* by saying to yourself ("Hey, I did it!" "I can handle it!").

The specific techniques that the child is taught to employ at critical times during the diagnostic or medical procedure involve both behavioral and cognitive coping strategies. Behavioral strategies include techniques that range from those that enhance the child's control over the medical procedure (e.g., having the child raise a finger to momentarily stop the procedure) to techniques such as relaxation and deep breathing. Lazarus and Rachman (1957) employed relaxation in systematically desensitizing children who were afraid of hospitals and ambulances, and Koeppen (1974) developed relaxation procedures that emphasize playful imagery techniques to help children achieve deep muscle relaxation. In addition, Nelson (1981) found that deep breathing was one of the most effective coping strategies for a dental-phobic girl. Varni (1984) reviewed applications of relaxation training for children with various types of pain. The usefulness of various "adjuncts" with relaxation training have been suggested. For example, it may be beneficial to combine relaxation training, the use of a "comfort object" (e.g., a teddy bear), gentle touching, and soothing talk (McGrath & Vair, 1984).

A variety of cognitive coping methods is useful in enhancing pain tolerance in adults. Although there is little research examining the usefulness of these methods with children, the techniques are presented as possibilities for the child clinician to explore in assisting children to cope with painful sensations. These methods include a number of imagery and non-imagery techniques such as:

1. *Imaginative transformation of pain* (e.g., Blitz & Dinnerstein, 1968) — acknowledging the sensations of pain but minimizing these sensations

by viewing them as being trivial and thus tolerable. For instance, in receiving an injection the child imagines that his or her arm is made of wax, jello, or rubber or that the injection feels like a "mosquito bite."

2. *Imaginative transformation of context* (e.g., Wolff & Horland, 1967) — acknowledging the sensations of pain but imagining that the situation in which the pain is occurring is different. For example, a boy imagines that he is Superman being exposed to "kryptonite" while having a tooth extracted, or that he is playing in the Super Bowl with an injury, or that he is James Bond (Agent 007) trying to escape from the "bad guys" after being wounded.

3. *Attention diversion via self-generated distraction* (e.g., Kanfer & Goldfoot, 1966) — focusing attention on completely unrelated external or internal processes to the exclusion of the painful sensations. For example, the child counts ceiling or floor tiles, counts backwards from 100 by threes, sings the words of a favorite song, or pretends to be watching a favorite T.V. show and describes it out loud. As a rule, the more vivid the image or distraction, the less other events are attended to and the less pain will be experienced.

McCaffery (1979) summarized points that are useful for the therapist to keep in mind when using imagery procedures. Although these recommendations are typically made for adults, they can be beneficial for children.

1. Assess the extent to which the child already uses his or her imagination. Good candidates for imagery are able to concentrate and to follow directions, and they are willing to respond to suggestions of images.

2. Explain imagery to the child in his or her own words and language. Emphasize the fact that imagery can affect how one feels and can be helpful as a coping device when experiencing pain.

3. Emphasize the child's involvement in the imagery process and that it is possible to remain in control by deciding whether or not imagery should be used at any given moment.

4. Utilize images the child has actually experienced to enhance vividness.

5. Encourage the child to use all five senses in imagining.

6. Teach the child to use one image at a time.

7. Guide the child by using permissive directions and suggestions as you direct the imagery.

8. Use relaxing, soothing, and positive descriptions in helping the child use imagery as a coping technique.

9. Be sensitive to and help the child identify and discuss concerns about the effectiveness of using imagery as a coping technique. Again, emphasize that the child is in control of the use and type of imagery and that employing such techniques does not mean giving up control.

The adult's fear of not being in control or being in a so-called "trance-like" state is usually not problematic for children, who are able to use imagery in a playful fashion.
10. Have the child practice imagery in other settings and situations.
11. Teach the child techniques for ceasing or ending imagery.

These coping strategies are incorporated into a self-instructional regimen that is developed by the therapist and the child together. Operationally, the therapist and the child rehearse a variety of more adaptive self-statements to utilize at each phase of the coping process. Of course, this coping process will vary according to the noxious medical procedure that the child will undergo.

Application Training Phase

In the last phase the child rehearses or "tests out" the recently learned coping skills by employing them in situations that are usually hierarchically arranged according to level of stress. This "dry-run" training may take various forms such as imaginal, role-play, or in vivo practice; it plays an integral part in enhancing the child's tolerance for pain. Although rehearsal can be conducted in the therapist's office, practice in the actual real-life environment should enhance generalization of treatment effects. Stressors that have been utilized in a graded fashion with adults include stress-inducing films, cold pressure tests, fatigue, and the like.

It should be noted again that the methods discussed in the skills training phase have not been experimentally validated as procedures to enhance pain tolerance *in children;* however, these strategies are presented as potentially useful techniques to use with this population. Further research needs to examine the effectiveness of these and other procedures with both clinical and pathological pain in children.

Case Study*

The client was an 11-year-old black female whose mother brought her to a community-based health care facility dental service. After 10 minutes in the office, the initial visit had to be cancelled by the dentist because of the child's disruptive behavior; she screamed, cried, and attempted to leave the dental chair. The child was then referred to the author. She was of low-average to average intelligence (Peabody Picture Vocabulary Test IQ = 89), and dental phobia was her only presenting problem. The girl's mother

*This case was originally published by the author and appeared in the *Journal of Clinical Child Psychology,* 1981, *10,* 79–82.

reported that academic performance and social adjustment were satisfactory. The Family Attitudes Toward Dentistry Questionnaire indicated that there were no inordinate fears in any other family members. The client's phobia appeared to be based on an incident four years earlier when she had four back teeth extracted. Although the mother reported that this experience was somewhat painful for her daughter, the client reported that she had "about died" from the incident. The child actually believed that this event almost killed her. Thus, it was not the event itself, but her *distorted perception* of that event that made the situation traumatic.

Assessment/Educational Phase

To evaluate the client's perception of this recent dental office incident, an imagery assessment technique was employed. While the girl closed her eyes and visualized her recent unsuccessful dental visit, the therapist guided her imagery and probed for thoughts, images, feelings, and behaviors at various critical periods (waiting in the dentist's office during the day of the appointment, entering the dental office, anticipating anesthetic injection and drilling, and so forth). This assessment technique revealed that the youngster conjured up images of her "teeth being pulled" and "holes being drilled into her teeth" and that she engaged in an inordinate amount of irrational private speech such as "the dentist is trying to hurt me," "I know I'm going to cry," and "I almost died the last time I went to the dentist." From a cognitive-behavioral viewpoint, this child's unrealistic perception of her *present* situation seriously interfered with her ability to cope with the dental visit. Current cognitive factors significantly determined how she misperceived related past events, which external events were most salient to her in the dental office, how these events were interpreted, and, thus, how she behaved during this visit.

The assessment period was combined with the educational phase of the stress inoculation training. The therapist told the child that her thoughts and self-statements resulted in her excessive fears and her behavior in the dentist's office. She agreed that this was the case after she was asked to consider how another girl her age would feel/behave if the girl engaged in more coping private speech (e.g., "I can handle this," "The shot isn't any big deal"). The goal, then, was to "work out a plan" that the patient could employ during her upcoming rescheduled dental visit.

Skills Acquisition Training Phase

The child was trained in coping techniques in a structured sequence. First the therapist modeled the appropriate coping self-statements by demonstrating more adaptive self-talk at each specific stage of the dental visit (cognitive modeling). Next the client verbalized the same self-statements under the direction of the therapist (external guidance). Finally the child role played various scenes while verbalizing these statements and strategies to herself (covert self-instruction). On the cognitive and behavioral levels, anxiety-reducing self-statements were specifically designed to assist the client in guiding her overt behavior by emitting more appropriate self-verbalizations to reduce the amount of verbally mediated subjective anxiety. Also, these self-statements were tailored to increase her sense of mastery over her castastrophizing ruminations. The self-statements were designed to help her: (a) prepare for the feared dental visit (e.g., "Worrying won't help anything," "The dentist is really my friend"), (b) confront and deal effectively with stress and/or pain (e.g., "Remember what the dentist says, and it will be over a lot quicker," "You're in control,"), and (c) cope with feelings of being overwhelmed by stress and/or pain at critical moments (e.g., "Just cool it and relax," "Take a slow, deep breath and relax your muscles," "Distract yourself by counting to 20 quickly"). The child was also taught to reinforce her newly learned coping techniques with positive self-statements (e.g., "I did it!" "It was nothing!" "Seeing the dentist was a snap!").

As another coping technique, the child learned to regulate and pace her breathing by taking slow, deep breaths when she became aware of her rapid, shallow breathing in the dental chair. Finally, for those critical times when she began to feel overwhelmed by pain, the client was taught a distraction/tolerance-increasing technique in which she covertly counted to 20 and vividly imagined the numbers in her mind. This technique was developed specifically for her, because she took pride in her mathematical ability in school. All of these coping strategies were "tested out" and rehearsed by having the client role play her upcoming dental visit.

It is important to note that the three major phases of the cognitive-behavioral management program are not independent or separate stages. Rather, they should be implemented in a flexible fashion, especially with children (Meichenbaum, 1977). Movement through these three treatment phases depends on the individual child and on the type of medical procedure that is anticipated.

The client underwent dental treatment after the second pain-management session, and behavioral ratings by the dentist and by an observer demonstrated an almost complete amelioration of her disruptive in-chair behavior. Improvement was maintained with two "booster sessions" over a 22-week period. During this time, three more dental visits were scheduled, and all of the dental treatments were completed. Although the child's self-reported levels of anxiety fluctuated during this time, her in-chair behavior was in the acceptable range according to the dentist.

From a clinical point of view, it is also interesting to note the marked changes in the Draw-A-Person (DAP) figures that the client completed prior to her second, third, fourth, and fifth dental visits, which were scheduled over a five-month period (see Figure 11-3). Extreme fright— bordering on fragmentation—and marked oral concerns were clearly evident in the first DAP drawing obtained just prior to the child's second dental visit. Questioning about this drawing revealed intense levels of anxiety, nervousness, and strong doubts about being able to keep herself together during the immediately upcoming dental procedure. However, questioning at the time of the drawing revealed that the "person" reportedly had a plan that she would "try" to use when undergoing dental treatment (referring to the cognitive-behavioral plan that she and the author had worked out in the two previous therapy sessions). The second drawing obtained immediately prior to the third dental visit reflected a much more integrated "12-year-old girl who was going to the dentist." The client stated that this girl would be "real nervous" but that the figure felt much more "under control," especially because she could "take deep breaths and count to 20 if it got bad." She noted that this girl was much more confident that "everything was going to be all right." The third drawing, obtained just prior to the fourth visit, was a "strong man" who was "scared about going to the dentist" but knew "it was going to be OK." The last drawing, which was obtained prior to the fifth dental visit, depicted a "10-year-old girl" who was "happy" because "she is able to relax, count to 20, take a deep breath, and tell herself that this will be over in a minute." The girl in this figure reportedly felt "comfortable and relaxed" and that "she is big enough now and can handle the situation." These statements, obtained via a projective format, indicated that the client had internalized the coping private speech and the coping strategies that had been developed 5 months earlier in two therapy sessions and in two booster sessions, the last of which was conducted approximately a month before the final dental appointment.

This demonstration of a cognitive-behavioral approach with an 11-year-old girl suffers from all of the drawbacks that plague single-case studies. Although there is very little cognitive-behavioral research in the area of pain management, this case indicates that cognitive-behavioral approaches hold promise for prevention and remediation of stressful situations that involve the experience of pain. The procedures that have proven useful with adult populations for the prevention of distress, the increase of pain tolerance, and the modification of pain behavior warrant more extensive consideration by both child clinicians and researchers. Although there is a need to demonstrate the usefulness of a complex, multifaceted pain-management regimen for children, we are not completely "groping in the dark" for direction in this regard, because such regimens seem to hold much promise with adults (see Turk & Genest, 1979; Turk et al., 1983). However, the clinician must exercise caution in generalizing and implementing such procedures directly with children. This is especially true in light of the ever-changing physical and cognitive capabilities that characterize child develop-

FIGURE 11-3 • *"Draw-A-Person" Drawings Obtained Prior to Second, Third, Fourth, and Fifth Dental Visits*

Second visit

Third visit

Fourth visit

Fifth visit

ment. All too often, treatment techniques are employed prematurely without really understanding the psychological and physiological processes. Even more distressing are premature claims of effective treatment strategies without adequate outcome studies or essential follow-up data. The intention of this chapter is to encourage clinicians to appreciate the multiple variables involved in understanding children's pain and to develop an interest in implementing and evaluating cognitive-behavioral procedures that can be useful in preparing for and managing pain.

References

Adams, M. S. (1976). A hospital play program: Helping children with serious illness. *American Journal of Orthopsychiatry, 46,* 416–424.

Adelson, R., & Goldfried, M. R. (1970). Modeling and the fearful child patient. *Journal of Dentistry for Children, 37,* 476–489.

Apley, J. (1975). *The child with abdominal pains.* Oxford, England: Blackwell Scientific Press.

Astrada, C., Licamele, W., Walsh, T., & Kessler, E. (1981). Recurrent abdominal pain in children and associated *DSM-III* diagnoses. *American Journal of Psychiatry, 138,* 687–688.

Azarnoff, P., & Flagel, S. (1974). *A pediatric play program.* Springfield, IL: Thomas.

Bandura, A. (1977). *Social learning theory.* Englewood Cliffs, NJ: Prentice-Hall.

Bandura, A. (1986). *Social foundations of thought and action: A social cognitive therapy.* Englewood Cliffs, NJ: Prentice-Hall.

Beyer, J., & Byers, M. L. (1985). Knowledge of pediatric pain: The state of the art. *Children's Health Care: Journal of the Association for the Care of Children's Health, 13,* 150–159.

Blizt, B., & Dinnerstein, A. (1968). Effects of different types of instruction on pain parameters. *Journal of Abnormal Psychology, 73,* 276–280.

Bradley, L. A., & Kay, R. (1985). The role of cognition in behavioral medicine. In P. C. Kendall (Ed.), *Advances in cognitive-behavioral research and therapy.* New York: Academic Press.

Bush, J. P. (1987). Pain in children: A review of the literature from a developmental perspective. *Psychology and Health, 1,* 215–236.

Cassel, J. (1976). The contribution of the social environment to host resistance. *American Journal of Epidemiology, 104,* 107–123.

Cassell, S. (1965). Effects of brief puppet therapy upon emotional responses of children undergoing cardiac catheterization. *Journal of Consulting Psychology, 29,* 1–8.

Cassell, S., & Paul, M. (1967). The role of puppet therapy on the emotional response of children hospitalized for cardiac catheterization. *Journal of Pediatrics, 71,* 233.

Clark, W., & Hunt, H. (1971). Pain. In J. A. Downey & R. C. Darling (Eds.), *Physiological basis of rehabilitative medicine.* Philadelphia: Saunders.

Crue, B. L., & Carregal, E. (1975). Pain begins in the dorsal horn—with a proposed classification of the primary senses. In B. L. Crue (Ed.), *Pain: Research and treatment.* New York: Academic Press.

368   *Part Two* • *Treatment Applications for Cognitive-Behavioral Procedures*

Debus, R. (1970). Effects of brief observation of model behavior on conceptual tempo in impulsive children. *Developmental Psychology, 2,* 202–214.

Dimock, H. G. (1960). *The child in hospital: A study of his social and emotional well being.* Philadelphia: Davis.

Elliott, E. H., & Jay, S. M. (1987). Chronic pain in children. *Behavior Research and Therapy, 25,* 263–271.

Friedman, S. B., & Glasgow, L. (1974). Psychological factors and resistance to infectious disease. In P. M. Insel & R. H. Moos (Eds.), *Health and the social environment.* Toronto: Heath.

Genest, M., & Turk, D. (1981). Think-aloud approaches to cognitive assessment. In T. Merluzzi, C. Glass, & M. Genest (Eds.), *Cognitive assessment.* New York: Guilford Press.

Green, C. (1963). *Doctors and nurses: What they do.* New York: Harper & Row.

Hilgard, E. K., & Hilgard, J. K. (1975). *Hypnosis in the relief of pain.* Los Altos, CA: Kaufman.

Iggo, A. (1972). Critical remarks on the gate control theory. In R. Janzen, W. Keidel, A. Herz, C. Steichele, J. Payne, & R. Burt (Eds.), *Pain: Basic principles, pharmacology, and therapy.* Stuttgart, Germany: Thieme.

Janis, I. (1958). *Psychological stress.* New York: Wiley.

Jay, S. M. (1984). Pain in children: An overview of psychological assessment and intervention. In A. Zeiner, D. Bendell, & C. Walker (Eds.), *Health psychology: Treatment and research issues.* New York: Plenum Press.

Kanfer, F., & Goldfoot, D. (1966). Self-control and tolerance of noxious stimulation. *Psychological Reports, 18,* 79–85.

Katz, E. R., Kellerman, J., & Siegel, S. E. (1980). Behavioral distress in children with cancer undergoing medical procedures: Developmental considerations. *Journal of Consulting and Clinical Psychology, 48,* 356–365.

Kazdin, A. (1974a). Covert modeling, model similarity, and reduction of avoidance behavior. *Behavior Therapy, 5,* 325–340.

Kazdin, A. (1974b). The effect of model identity and fear relevant similarity on covert modeling. *Behavior Therapy, 5,* 624–636.

Keefe, F. J., & Block, A. R. (1982). Development of an observation method for assessing pain behavior in chronic low back patients. *Behavior Therapy, 13,* 363–375.

Kerr, F. W. (1975). Pain: A central inhibitory balance theory. *Mayo Clinic Proceedings, 50,* 685–690.

Koeppen, A. S. (1974). Relaxation training for children. *Elementary School Guidance and Counseling, October,* 14–21.

Krueger, L. C. (1987). Pediatric pain and imagery. *Journal of Child and Adolescent Psychotherapy, 4,* 32–41.

Langer, E., Janis, I. L., & Wolfer, J. (1975). Reduction of psychological stress in surgical patients. *Journal of Experimental Social Psychology, 1,* 155–166.

Lavigne, J. V., Schulein, M. J., & Hahn, Y. S. (1986). Psychological aspects of painful medical conditions in children. I. Developmental aspects and assessment. *Pain, 27,* 133–146.

Lazarus, R. J. (1966). *Psychological stress and the coping process.* New York: McGraw-Hill.

Lazarus, A., & Rachman, S. (1957). The use of systematic desensitization in psychotherapy. *South African Medical Journal, 31,* 934–937.

Levendusky, P., & Pankratz, L. (1975). Self-control techniques as an alternative to pain medication. *Journal of Abnormal Psychology, 84,* 165–168.

Leventhal, H., Singer, R. E., & Jones, S. (1965). Effects of fear and specificity of recommendations. *Journal of Personality and Social Psychology, 2,* 20–29.

Leventhal, H., & Watts, J. C. (1966). Sources of resistance to fear arousing communications on smoking and lung cancer. *Journal of Personality, 34,* 155–175.

Lieberman, D. A. (1979). Behaviorism and the mind: A (limited) call for a return to introspection. *American Psychologist, 39,* 319–333.

Liebeskind, J., & Paul, L. (1977). Psychological and physiological mechanisms of pain. *Annual Review of Psychology, 28,* 41–60.

Luria, A. (1961). *The role of speech in the regulation of normal and abnormal behaviors.* New York: Liveright.

Mahoney, M. (1974). *Cognition and behavior modification.* Cambridge, MA: Ballinger.

Mason, J. W. (1971). A re-revaluation of the concept of "non-specificity" in stress theory. *Journal of Psychiatric Research, 8,* 323–333.

Mason, J. W., Buescher, E. L., Belfer, M. L., Artenstein, M. S., & Mougey, E. H. (1979). A prospective study of corticosteroid and catecholamine levels in relation to viral respiratory illness. *Journal of Human Stress, 5,* 18–27.

McCaffery, M. (1979). *Nursing management of the patient with pain* (2nd ed.). Philadelphia: Lippincott.

McGrath, P. (1987). An assessment of children's pain: A review of behavioral, psychological and direct seeking techniques. *Pain, 31,* 147–176.

McGrath, P. A. (1989). *Pain in children: Nature, assessment and treatment.* New York: Guilford Press.

McGrath, P., & Vair, C. (1984). Psychological aspects of pain management of the burned child. *Children's Health Care, 13,* 15–19.

Meichenbaum, D. (1971). Examination of model characteristics in reducing avoidance behavior. *Journal of Personality and Social Psychology, 17,* 298–307.

Meichenbaum, D. (1977). *Cognitive-behavior modification: An integrative approach.* New York: Plenum Press.

Melamed, B. G., Hawes, R. R., Heiby, E., & Glick, J. (1975). Use of filmed modeling to reduce uncooperative behavior in children during dental treatment. *Journal of Dental Research, 54,* 797–801.

Melamed, B. G., & Siegel, L. J. (1975). Reduction of anxiety in children facing hospitalization and surgery by use of filmed modeling. *Journal of Consulting and Clinical Psychology, 43,* 511–521.

Melzack, R. (1973). *The puzzle of pain.* Harmondsworth, England: Penguin.

Melzack, R., & Casey, K. (1968). Sensory, motivational, and central control determinants of pain: A new conceptual model. In D. Kenshalo (Ed.), *The skin senses.* Springfield, IL: Thomas.

Melzack, R., & Torgerson, W. S. (1971). On the language of pain. *Anesthesiology, 34,* 50–59.

Melzack, R., & Wall, P. (1965). Pain mechanisms: A new theory. *Science, 150,* 971–979.

Merluzzi, T. V., Glass, C. R., & Genest, M. (1981). *Cognitive assessment.* New York: Guilford Press.

Meyers, J. E., & Nelson, W. M., III. (1986). Cognitive strategies and expectations as components of social competence in young adolescents, *Adolescence, XXI,* 291–303.

Muller, J. (1838). *Handbuch der Physiologic des Menschen.* Cobblenz.

Nathan, P. W. (1976). The gate control theory of pain: A critical review. *Brain, 99,* 123–158.

Nelson, W. M., III. (1981). A cognitive-behavioral treatment for disproportionate dental anxiety and pain: A case study. *Journal of Clinical Child Psychology, 10,* 79–82.

Nelson, W. M., III, & Cholera, S. (1986). Projective-cognitive assessment of thoughts and feelings and their relationship to adaptive behavior in a dental situation. *Adolescence, XXI,* 855–862.

Nisbett, R. E., & Wilson, T. D. (1977). Telling more than we know: Verbal reports on mental processes. *Psychological Review, 84,* 232–259.

O'Malley, J., Koocher, G., Foster, D., & Slavin, L. (1979). Pediatric sequelae of surviving childhood cancer. *American Journal of Orthopsychiatry, 49,* 606–616.

Rey, M., & Rey, H. (1966). *Curious George goes to the hospital.* Boston: Houghton Mifflin.

Roskies, E., & Lazarus, R. S. (1980). Coping theory and the teaching of coping skills. In P. O. Davidson & S. M. Davidson (Eds.), *Behavioral medicine: Changing health life styles.* New York: Brunner/Mazel.

Savedra, M., Gibbons, P., Tesler, M., Ward, J., & Wegner, C. (1982). How do children describe pain? A tentative assessment. *Pain, 14,* 95–104.

Schachter, S. (1966). The interaction of cognitive and physiological determinants of emotional state. In C. Spielberger (Ed.), *Anxiety and behavior.* New York: Academic Press.

Simpson, J. (1973). *Come inside the hospital.* London: Studio Vista.

Sinclair, D. C. (1955). Cutaneous sensation and the doctrine of specific energy. *Brain, 78,* 584.

Singer, J. (1974). *Imagery and daydream methods in psychotherapy.* New York: Academic Press.

Smith, E. R., & Miller, F. D. (1978). Limits on perception of cognitive processes: A reply to Nisbett and Wilson. *Psychological Review, 15,* 35–48.

Stein, S. B. (1974). *A hospital stay.* New York: Walker.

Syme, S. L. (1975). Social and psychological risk factors in coronary heart disease. *Modern Concepts of Cardiovascular Diseases, 14,* 17–21.

Tomasi, L. (1979). Headaches in children. *Pediatrics, 5,* 13–19.

Toomey, T. C., Ghia, J. N., Mao, W., & Gregg, J. M. (1977). Acupuncture and chronic pain mechanisms: The moderating effects of affect, personality, and stress on response to treatment. *Pain, 3,* 137–145.

Turk, D. (1975). Cognitive control of pain: A skills training approach. Unpublished manuscript, University of Waterloo, Ontario.

Turk, D., & Genest, M. (1979). Regulation of pain: The application of cognitive and behavioral techniques for prevention and remediation. In P. Kendall & S. Hollen (Eds.), *Cognitive-behavioral interventions: Theory, research, and procedures.* New York: Academic Press.

Turk, D. C., Meichenbaum, D., & Genest, M. (1983). *Pain and behavioral medicine: A cognitive-behavioral perspective.* New York: Guilford Press.

Tursky, B. (1976). Laboratory approaches to the study of pain. In D. I. Mostofsky (Ed.), *Behavioral control and modification of physiological activity.* Englewood Cliffs, NJ: Prentice-Hall.

Varni, J. (1984). Pediatric pain: A biobehavioral perspective. *The Behavior Therapist, 7,* 23–25.

Vernon, D. T., & Bailey, W. C. (1974). The use of motion pictures in the psychological preparation of children for induction of anesthesia. *Anesthesiology, 40*, 68–72.

Von Frey, M. (1894). Bertrage zur Physiologie des Schmerzsinns. *Ber Sachs. Gesamte, Wiss, Math-Phys. Clone, 46*, 1985.

Vygotsky, L. (1962). *Thought and language.* New York: Wiley.

Weisenberg, M. (Ed.). (1975). *Pain: Clinical and experimental perspectives.* St. Louis, MO: Mosby.

Wolff, J., & Horland, A. (1967). Effect of suggestion upon experimental pain: A validation study. *Journal of Abnormal Psychology, 72*, 402–407.

Wolinsky, F. G. (1971). Materials to prepare children for hospital experiences. *Exceptional Children, 37*, 527–531.

Wolpin, M., & Raines, J. (1966). Visual imagery, expected roles and extinction as possible factors in reducing fear and avoidance behavior. *Behavior Research and Therapy, 4*, 25–37.

CHAPTER TWELVE

A Conceptualization of Psychotherapy with Children and Adolescents

P. M. POLITANO

This chapter will explore some of the more philosophical considerations for conducting psychotherapy with young people (children and adolescents) from a cognitive-behavioral framework. The exploration will begin with a brief historical review of the status of childhood and adolescence and then will focus more specifically on the differences between adults and young people that necessitate other perspectives on psychotherapy and treatment. Next, the "goals" and "givens" of psychotherapy with children and adolescents will be presented. A final section will provide a conceptual framework for the overall process of conducting psychotherapy with this younger population from a cognitive-behavioral perspective.

Historical Perspective

The emergence of childhood and later adolescence as distinct developmental periods is related to four factors that made their appearance during the mid- to late-nineteenth century. First, at a pragmatic level, there was an increase in the survival rate of infants and small children. Also, a middle-class society emerged and was accompanied by an increase in leisure time and in the financial means to enjoy this leisure (Tilker, 1975). Finally, during the mid-nineteenth century there was the development of a scientific interest in developmental phenomena across a broad spectrum of issues—ranging from geological to human (Bremner, 1971; McGraw, 1987).

An examination of the death rate of children shows that in 1750 the odds of a child reaching age 5 were still 3 to 1 against survival (Kessen, 1965). Shorter (1975) suggested that parent–child relationships were more functional than nurturing during this time because of the uncertainty of the survival of offspring. For parents during this period the possibility of death may have limited their investment in their children's early emotional, physical, social, or financial well-being. Consequently the lives of these children, precarious to begin with because of natural factors, may have been made even more precarious by parental attitudes that bordered on indifference. In addition to illness, disease, and neglect, other hazards existed, such as the practice of infanticide, separation of children from their families, abandonment, harsh handling by caretakers, and child labor (de Mause, 1974).

Through the sixteenth century, infanticide was practiced openly, with only sporadic punishment of offenders (Minde & Minde, 1986). Although legal prohibitions increased, the practice continued, but less openly. Children were "accidentally" killed or smothered "inadvertently" while sleeping with parents or wet nurses. Smothering became such a problem that in the late 1700s, both Austria and Prussia passed laws forbidding children up to age 5 (Austria) and age 2 (Prussia) from sleeping with parents (Langer, 1973, 1974). In addition to the standard means of eliminating children, wet nurses were hired specifically because of their reputations for dispatching children; wet nurses often were referred to as "killing nurses" or "she-butchers" (Beckman, 1977). As recently as the late 1800s it was not uncommon to find dead babies simply discarded on the streets of London (Langer, 1973, 1974).

The practice of separating children from their families was widespread in both the privileged and less privileged classes. In Paris during the year 1780 an estimated 21,000 babies were born. Of these, 17,000 were sent to stay full-time with professional wet nurses, 2,000 to 3,000 were placed in day-nursery homes by well-to-do parents, about 700 were nursed in their biological home by wet nurses, and only about 700 were nursed and cared for by their biological mothers (Kessen, 1965).

In addition to farming out children for care and nursing, many children were abandoned. In 1741 a home for infants was opened in London by Thomas Coram, a former ship's captain. By 1753 Coram's home was admitting 116 infants a day (Caulfield, 1931). In Dublin from 1775 to 1800, 10,272 infants were admitted to foundling homes, and only 45 survived (Kessen, 1965).

Children were also raised in ways that seem harsh by today's standards. Swaddling children was a common practice. A French physician of the seventeenth century cautioned that not swaddling would result in the child's failing to acquire appropriate adult posture and that the child would continue to walk on all fours like an animal (Still, 1931). Erickson (1983) described how in Elizabethan England, children were viewed as diminutive adults from the time they could walk and talk. They were dressed in miniature attire that duplicated the attire of adults, without consideration for comfort, freedom of movement, or developmental differences between children and adults.

In raising children, strict discipline was the general rule across all classes. This was a response to the religious proclamation that a willful child was a sinful child and was the product of the devil's handwork (Beckman, 1977; Erickson, 1983). Some of the "willfulness" of children was handled through medication. A physician, testifying before an English committee in 1871, reported a high incidence of the use of opium-based preparations for more than 3,000 children as a means of keeping them tranquil and quiet (Langer, 1973, 1974).

In addition to harsh childrearing practices in the home, schools in the nineteenth century were marked by opposing opinions. One position advocated the use of punishment as an inducement to learning. Another school of thought, headed by Horace Mann, insisted that the teacher's task was to make learning attractive so that the student would be a "grateful cooperator, instead of a toiling slave" (p. 512, Mann, cited in Cremin, 1969). This difference in opinion is illustrated by the abolition of corporal punishment in Poland in 1783 and the upholding of the use of caning in British schools by the British House of Commons in 1776 (Boonin, 1979; Tanner, 1978).

In the late 1800s the emergence of a well-to-do middle class coincided with a decrease in the use of children as laborers. These changes led to a general improvement in the status of children, for parents acquired both the time and the financial freedom to interact with their offspring. The increase in leisure time was accompanied by an awakening of scientific interest in a wide variety of phenomena, including human development. Even so, the nature of children was still debated, and improvements were not universal across classes. For example, the 1870 census indicated that one in six children still employed as a laborer; this decreased only to one in eight children by 1900 (Bremner, 1971).

This harsh perception of children can be traced into twentieth-century thinking. For approximately 300 years the question of the nature of the child has varied in adult thought, as evidenced by Jean-Jacques Rousseau's *Emile* (1762), in which he espoused the worth and dignity of the child, the Rev. John Abbott's *Mother at Home* (1833), in which he emphasized the tyrannical nature of young children (Segal & Yahraes, 1979), and the regular beating of the young Louis XIII (1601–1643) for such offenses as refusing to eat or not showing affection to his parents (Hunt, 1970). Furthermore, a survey conducted in England indicated that 75% of British children age 7 or younger reported being hit or threatened with being hit with anything from wooden spoons to canes or belts (Newson & Newson, 1976), the U.S. Supreme Court refused to deal with corporal punishment in schools (*Ingraham* v. *Wright,* 1977), and there is still a high incidence of physical and sexual abuse of children and adolescents in today's society (Emery, 1989).

However, regardless of the grim statistics, the lot of children has improved. In 1874 the first American branch of the Society for the Prevention of Cruelty to Children was formed in New York City (Bremner, 1971). That this organization was an offshoot of the Society for the Prevention of Cruelty to Animals gives some indication of the status of children. In 1896 at the University of Pennsylvania, Lightner Witmer opened the first psychological clinic for children with educational problems (Levine & Levine, 1970). Attention to emotional difficulties soon followed attention to educational problems. Levitt (1971) reported that in 1909 a clinic opened on the ground floor of the juvenile detention center in Chicago and was staffed with one psychiatrist, one psychologist, and a secretary. In 1909 this was the sum total of services available for children in the United States.

Thus, the notion of childhood as a recognized and protected state is relatively new. Even newer is the recognition of adolescence as a distinct developmental period, dating essentially from the post–World War II era (Garbarino, 1985). Another fairly recent phenomenon is the acknowledgment that children may require psychological treatment and that society can benefit from providing this treatment for children. The impetus for treatment facilities for children stems from the notion that troubled or sick children grow to be troubled or sick adults (the continuity hypothesis) and that treatment of troubled or sick children will reduce the incidence of troubled or sick adults (the intervention hypothesis) (Levitt, 1971).

Despite a lack of conclusive evidence to support the continuity or the intervention hypotheses (Levitt, 1971), the number of treatment facilities for children and adolescents has increased considerably since 1909.

Differences: Young People and Adults

Without any clearly identifiable guiding theory of its own, treatment of young people relied for its conception on existing treatment paradigms (Harrison, 1985). Those existing paradigms were based on treatment of adults, and, to some extent, the history of the treatment of young people has been one of trying to separate and to differentiate the needs of the young from the needs of adults. Clinicians continue to seek clarification of how those differences do or should impact theories of treatment, treatment models, and treatment techniques.

Because of the relatively short history of the treatment of young people, many of the general therapeutic approaches for children and adolescents still represent a downward extension of adult models, with a few exceptions—for example, Axline's play therapy (1969) and Moustakas's relationship therapy (1959). Even with a theory as heavily developmentally oriented as psychoanalytic theory, the treatment techniques were developed primarily within the confines of adult practice (Harrison, 1985; Freud, 1965).

The downward extension of models and theories from adults to younger people presumes a degree of applicability of the tenets of the model or theory to a wide variety of ages and developmental stages. Many of the objections that can be raised to the downward extension of pathological symptomatology from adults to young people can be raised to the downward extension of models or theories of treatment as well (see Gelfand & Peterson, 1985 and May, 1979). When one enters the special treatment world of the child or adolescent, one learns quickly that this is not the same arena inhabited by adults in treatment. In a somewhat "fuzzy," surrealistic way, the "rules" that govern adult treatment seem to fit — but only partially. It is as if everything is slightly askew, and those techniques/models/theories that fit adults do not fit as neatly for children and adolescents. This sense of asynchrony comes from the variety and profoundness of the differences between adults and young people. These differences center around four primary areas: expectations, maturation, cognitions, and emotions.

Expectations

It is rare that a child or adolescent self-refers for treatment (Bird & Kastenbaum, 1988; Harrison, 1985). Most referrals come from the adult world through parents, teachers, family physicians, ministers, and others who do not employ a standard set of symptoms or criteria to determine that a deviation from normal development has occurred. Rather, the referral process involves the application of somewhat idiosyncratic adult expectations of what child or adolescent behavior should be like. In some cases, both the accuracy of the adult's expectations of normal child or adolescent behavior and the motivations for the referral can be called into question (Bird & Kastenbaum, 1988).

However, regardless of the adult's perception of the problem, young people generally perceive that any changes that need to be made should be made in the environment rather than in themselves (Bates, Chassin, & Young, 1978; Bird & Kastenbaum, 1988; Harrison, 1985). This perception is influenced in part by a limited capacity for self-reflection, by a limited capacity for self-observation, by a limited vocabulary for expressing needs, concerns and emotions, and by an increased degree of self-focus that distorts the perception of the child's centrality in ongoing events (Bates et al., 1978; Bird & Kastenbaum, 1988; Cooper & Wanerman, 1977; Harrison, 1985).

The child or adolescent, unlike the self-referring adult, is not bound by expectations of the therapeutic situation—that is, to begin, continue, and complete treatment for the express purpose of gains in psychological comfort at some future point in time. The limited ability of the child to anticipate future improvement is a function of a limited ability to time-bind, of a strong self-focus, and of decreased autonomy—that is, the notion that one has control over one's fate and has the power to exercise that control.

Maturation

Children and adolescents are rapidly developing organisms. Rigidity and flexibility of psychological structures fluctuate over the developmental process, suggesting times of greater or lesser availability to treatment intervention (e.g., compare the fluidity of the 4-year-old's perception of reality as observed through rule behavior and the rigidity of the 6-year-old's perception of reality as evidenced by the omnipotent observer watching every move made within a rule-guided environment) (Damon, 1977; Halpern, 1953).

In addition to fluctuations in rigidity and flexibility, the security of the child's or adolescent's frame of reference—or cognitive structure—is developmentally less firm than that of an adult (Halpern, 1953; Harrison, 1985). Consequently, there is limited ability to construct and interpret reality or to perceive a solid place in the flow of ongoing events. Also, the security or insecurity of the young person's frame of reference results in pseudopathological behaviors as part of the normal maturational process. For example, disobedience is as high as 50% among normal 4-year-olds (Achenbach & Edelbrock, 1981), and lying is as high as 53% in normal 6-year-old males and as high as 48% in normal females of the same age (MacFarlane, Allen, & Honzik, 1954). These pseudopathological behaviors represent normal developmental fluctuations that may be perceived as abnormal at the time of appearance but that, if dealt with as part of a normal parenting process, will decrease in frequency as a result of ongoing maturation. Effort must be taken, then, to ensure that any intervention is appropriate for a legitimate problem as opposed to a normal developmental pattern.

Maturational fluctuations across psychological and behavioral systems must first be placed within the context of a rapidly changing physiological system that exerts its own demands and stress, and then the actual interaction of all systems must be considered simultaneously. Levitt (1971) suggested that failure to consider the rapid changes taking place in young people may lead to a false perception of the "cure rate," thus leading to premature dismissal from treatment. That is, a problem may be treated at one level (symptomatic), with the apparent eradication of the problem, only to have other symptoms appear later—a phenomenon that has been referred to as "symptom substitution." The appearance of symptoms at a later point in time might suggest that the underlying dimensions of the problem were not addressed initially. Or, as Wolpe (1969) pointed out, symptom substitution may occur when a particular overt behavior is eliminated but the underlying autonomic/emotional response remains. Indeed, the eradication of a set of symptoms may not even be in response to a particular treatment. Instead, symptom removal may represent a spontaneous remission or functionally different problems with different symptoms in response to maturational/developmental pressures (Levitt, 1971). It should be noted, however, that behaviorists challenge the issue of symptom substitution as basically an untestable tenet, because therapists who subscribe to this concept have specified neither the nature of the substitute symptom nor the circumstances under which it occurs (Bandura, 1969).

Cognitions

Adults can usually separate fact from fiction, generate hypotheses and test their accuracy in explaining events, reason both forwards and backwards to reach a conclusion, think about hypothetical situations, engage in abstraction, track several lines of thought simultaneously, operate according to a set of rules, and divide the flow of events accurately into past, present, and future (time-binding). In treatment, these adult capabilities may lead to such rewarding events as recognition of conflicts and concerns, changes in perceptions of self, world, and future, and changes in behavior—all traditionally attributed to a process called "insight."

Most young people do not demonstrate these abilities because such cognitive abilities are acquired sequentially through the developmental process (Elkind, 1974; Piaget, 1932, 1962; Piaget & Inhelder, 1969). The developmental changes in cognitive ability parallel and underpin developmental changes in perceptions of justice and authority (Damon, 1977, 1980), morality (Kohlberg & Kramer, 1969; Piaget, 1932), emotions (Lewis, 1977), and perceptions of self and others (Elkind, 1974). In the therapeutic endeavor with adults, regression to more elemental levels of cognitive representation is possible. With young people it is difficult, if not impossible, to create or provide sophisticated cognitive abilities that do not exist and for which the young person is not developmentally ready.

Therapeutically this developmental acquisition of cognitive abilities suggests that understanding and awareness play a less central role in change for young people than they do for adults. Even the adolescent who has developed many "adult" cognitive abilities has limited real-life experience; therefore, the cognitive abilities that appear mature are only functionally and structurally similar to adult process. The form of these cognitive processes may be quite different. In addition to limited life experience, adolescence is characterized by weak introspective abilities (Selman, 1980) and idiopathic adolescent perspectives, which are observed in cognitive conceit, the personalized fable, and the looking-glass self (Cooley, 1964; Elkind, 1974).

Emotions

Cognitive development influences emotional development. This is not to say that cognitive development leads to or causes emotional development; rather, cognitive development is necessary for the understanding and the communication of emotions to others through memory, recall, and language. Additionally, cognitions maintain emotions across time and situations through memory and recall of the emotional ambiance of past situations and experiences (Byrne & Clore, 1970; Napoli, Kilbride, & Tebbs, 1985; Staats, 1968; Santostefano, 1980) and through the maintenance of the "logic" of present behaviors based on past emotional experiences.

The close tie between cognitive development and emotional understanding and expression in young people suggests that the limitations of the cognitive structure have an impact on patterns of dealing with the emotional world. For example, young people may be less adept than adults at separating emotions from fantasy, less able than adults to keep feelings internalized, and less able than adults to recognize emotions and to attach or generate language in accurately describing them. In addition, young people may be less able than adults to recall emotions/feelings in the abstract apart from the experience that generated them and less able than adults to be introspective and to analyze their feelings and emotions (Bird & Kastenbaum, 1988; Cooper & Wanerman, 1977; Halpern, 1953; Harrison, 1985).

In summary, then, there are profound differences between young people and adults across the dimensions of expectations, maturational rates, cognitive abilities, and emotional sophistication. Differences between adults and young people that are of significance to psychotherapy center around "insight"-related behaviors (e.g., introspection and role taking, self-evaluation and self-direction) and linkage of emotions to cognitive restructuring of past or current situations and events.

Goals and Givens

More traditional psychotherapies (e.g., psychodynamic, humanistic) attempt to reduce symptoms that interfere with the normal sequence of development and adaptation or that impact negatively on self-esteem

(Achenbach, 1974; Freud, 1965). From this perspective the goal of therapy with young people is to restore the normal developmental progression according to the age of the child or adolescent (Freud, 1965). Depending on the therapist's theoretical orientation, the mechanisms of restoration may be varied and may involve working directly with the young person alone, working with the young person and the family, et cetera.

Although the cognitive-behavioral perspective does not argue with these goals per se, it emphasizes the interplay of environmental events, cognitions, affect, and behavior. Additionally, from a cognitive-behavioral view, emphasis is placed on self-efficacy—the idea that individuals have the capability to control, influence, and shape events that relate to them (Bandura, 1989). Therefore, within the process of resuming normal developmental progression, an additional goal from a cognitive-behavioral perspective is to teach, model, and develop skills that increase the child's or adolescent's perception of being able to direct events in a positive, adaptive direction. These, then, are the overall goals of therapy with young people.

The givens are as straightforward as the goals. They provide the grounding for any therapeutic orientation. These givens include patience, respect for the unique nature of the child or adolescent, concern for the youngster's safety both in and out of the therapy situation, creation of a therapeutic environment in which the child or adolescent is free to express himself or herself appropriately, adherence to the advocation of individual responsibility for behavior, acceptance of the narrative as the young person's own perception of events, and consideration for second-order effects of treatment (Graziano & Fink, 1973).

The last two givens requires some elaboration. With regard to an individual's perception of events, adults who seek psychotherapeutic help do so because they are aware that their perceptions and experiences do not fit objective reality or do not "work" in creating intrapsychic or interpersonal satisfaction. Children may or may not be aware of the mismatch between their perceptions and objective reality. They may or may not be able to articulate dissatisfaction about themselves or about their relationships with others. The therapist will probably find it easy to see the inconsistencies in the individual's perceptions of self, others, and reality. From the therapist's vantage point as an observer, the difficulties can be recognized, appreciated, and operationalized. The therapist's acceptance and serious consideration of the child's perception are givens in the therapeutic endeavor.

The process of working with distorted or maladaptive perceptions distinguishes therapeutic approaches. A client-centered approach emphasizes the creation of a therapeutic environment in which it is possible for the "natural" tendency toward health to grow and develop. A more traditional psychodynamic approach depends on the transference of ambivalent feelings to the therapist in order to work through the conflict. From the more traditional behavioral model, the role of the therapist is to teach more adaptive behaviors and to facilitate environmental restructuring so that these behaviors are reinforced and incorporated into general, enduring patterns. The cognitive-behaviorist emphasizes "cognitive" or "internal" processes (beliefs, attitudes, self-statements) that maintain and direct behavior and intervenes at this level (in addition to a behavioral level) to promote more adaptive behavior.

Young people's cognitions and perceptions — what they believe to be true — are functions of the sophistication of their developmental capabilities which, in turn, influence the understanding of their emotions. Given that a mature adult can distort external reality to the extent that treatment is required, consider the potential for distortion when the level of cognitive sophistication is less mature. The less developed cognitive and emotional capacity of young people may distance them from the full impact of understanding their situation and act as an insulator against stress. The child's evaluation of a problem situation does not control intervention decisions of the adults who appreciate the need for treatment or who are reacting to the strain of dealing with a difficult child or adolescent.

Second-order effects apply to those pressures that impact on treatment but that are external to the treatment process (Graziano & Fink, 1973). Examples, as applied to young people, are the cost of treatment to parents, the disruption in parental schedules to provide transportation to and from treatment, efforts of parents to find out what is going on in treatment, attempts to assign blame for the problem, and so forth. These external pressures on the young person (e.g., second-order effects) can detract from the treatment process and can create additional problems.

Conceptual Framework for Therapy

Having outlined the historical origins of childhood and adolescence and having looked briefly at differences between children and adults, we will now sit back, relax, and see if we can bring some focus to the process of therapy with children and adolescents through the use of imagination and an analogy. Picture, if you will, a house with several rooms — living room, den, kitchen, bedrooms, and bathrooms. Now imagine furniture in the rooms — furniture that you would normally expect such as couches, chairs, tables, lamps, bookcases, a toaster on the counter in the kitchen, and a picture on the wall. Now imagine the interior of that house if the furniture were awry. The couch is tipped over. The toaster is in the bedroom rather than in the kitchen. Books are on the floor instead of in the bookshelves. The picture is on the chair. The lamp is in a closet. Now equate the interior of that house with the interior of a person's mind—the psychological experiences that store the self-perceptions and the self-concept, maintained by attitudes, beliefs, and self-statements. The furniture and other parts of the house represent the internalization of the cognitive understanding of actual experiences over the individual's lifetime. The degree of distortion in the internal perceptions of those experiences equates with the extent to which the furniture is awry. The fusion of objective reality and the cognitive reconstructions of that reality represent a major component of the individual's perception of the environment. Interpretation and integration of the objective reality vary according to level of maturation and development. Every "house" has something awry: dust where it should not be, a magazine lying on the floor instead of in the magazine rack, or dishes that have not been put away. A few things out of place give us what we commonly refer to as our unique characteristics—our individual idiosyncrasies—and make us interesting characters. At some point, however, the degree of chaos in the arrangement of our internal furniture (i.e., cognitive distortions) will make us begin to look "peculiar" or outright "bizarre" to those around us.

When we begin to look peculiar or bizarre, we, or those around us, seek some intervention—somebody to come in and help us figure out just where things should go and what the optimal arrangement of furniture and knick-knacks should be. With the help of that person, we begin to rearrange our house. In this metaphor the therapist is the one who assists in putting the house in order, and the form of that assistance depends on the therapist's theoretical and experiential orientation. Depending on orientation the therapist may help us send some of our furniture off to the Salvation Army and replace it with new furniture (a behavioral strategy). Or the therapist may move furniture around and try to give us a new perspective (a cognitive-behavioral strategy). Or the therapist may try to put new covers on the existing furniture (a psychodynamic approach). Or the therapist may simply describe the arrangement and wait for us to make the changes (a client-centered approach). Regardless of the therapist's orientation, we may find ourselves resisting some of the suggestions of our interior design consultant. The disarray may be profound, the path from the bedroom to the living room may be cluttered, and the route may be almost impossible to negotiate, but at least we *know* that route. We have lived with it for years. So we may resist simply because the living arrangement is familiar—even when it is not functional.

As we progress in therapy, we may straighten up a good deal of the confusion and then say, in effect, "Enough—let me get used to this for now, and then I will come back and work on the rest." Indeed, we may come back later (a failure in maintenance?), or we may do some straightening on our own (generalization?), or we may not need to come back later, or things may just get all jumbled up again and out of place (functionally new problem?). Our receptivity to outside help is a variable process, and we may move in and out of treatment as there are changes in our perceptions of need, our level of stress, and our perceptions of gain.

The foregoing analogy gives a descriptive picture of the process of treatment from different theoretical perspectives, and the analogy applies to both adults and young people, regardless of developmental and cognitive differences.

How does intervention take place? Figure 12-1 explains the intervention process with young people. The therapist brings unique factors to the intervention process—his or her personality, training, skills, and theoretical orientation(s). While appreciating what might be termed "therapist variables," the cognitive-behavioral therapist emphasizes the importance of objective information and observable behavior in the process of designing and implementing treatment strategies. Therefore, with children and adolescents the cognitive-behavioral therapist is interested in obtaining as much information as possible about the child-client (Step 1). This information may include records (medical, school, etc.), reports by others (teachers, parents, etc.), the child's self-reports, test data, clinical interviews, and other data. In Step 2 the therapist determines the system(s) that will be addressed by the intervention, and in Step 3 the therapist selects the technique(s) that address the indicated system(s) and that fall within the expertise of the therapist.

How does the therapist select the system to be addressed by the intervention? Recall an earlier statement in which it was suggested that emotions may be clarified, communicated, and understood within the context of a cognitive system. When this view is applied to the analogy of treatment presented earlier, it is apparent that the arrangement of the furniture (emotions) in the house (e.g., where and how items are placed throughout the house, or, more succinctly, how the furniture got where it is in the first place) is aided and abetted by cognitions held by the person. No matter how rational or irrational those cognitions may be, they support the emotional arrangement. That is, we select (cognitive process) patterns of responses to environmental cues that, among other functions, serve to maintain a behavioral consistency with existing emotional states. Cognitions, then, can be seen as directing emotions that in turn can be seen as deriving from cognitions—essentially, an interactive system (Bandura, 1989; Flavell, 1985; Hofer, 1981; Piaget & Inhelder, 1969).

Does this view hypothesize that cognitions predate emotions or that emotions predate cognitions? The question is not readily answered by the research in developmental psychology, despite some spirited debate (see Lazarus, 1982 and Zajonc, 1984). Cognitive behaviorists suggest that emotion is shaped by cognition and is understood within the context of the cognitive system (Beck, 1976; Ellis, 1962). This position negates the possi-

FIGURE 12-1 • *Primary Stages in the Process of Psychotherapy with Children and Adolescents*

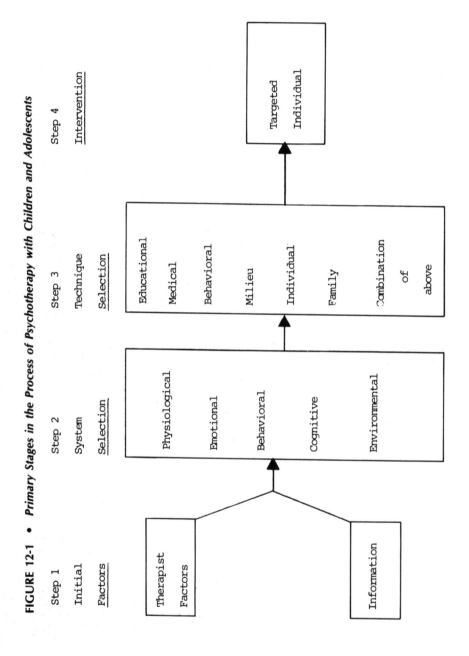

Step 1	Step 2	Step 3	Step 4
Initial	System	Technique	Intervention
Factors	Selection	Selection	

Therapist Factors

Information

Physiological
Emotional
Behavioral
Cognitive
Environmental

Educational
Medical
Behavioral
Milieu
Individual
Family
Combination
of
above

Targeted Individual

bility of an emotion in the absence of cognition. The accuracy of this position relates in part to how one defines cognition and how one distinguishes between cognitions, physiological response states, and emotions. For example, does the reflexive startle response to a loud clap of thunder evoke an emotional reaction prior to a cognitive awareness of the event itself? The physiological reaction that takes place may predate the cognition of the particulars of the event, and the physiological reaction may be similar to the "fear" reaction that follows. But does the physiological reaction, despite its similarity to the fear reaction, constitute an emotion prior to the cognitive recognition of the fear? The cognitive-behaviorist suggests that it does not.

However interesting this "chicken and egg" question may be from the standpoint of research, for the purposes of psychotherapy the question may be moot. By the time a child is referred for treatment, the sequence of the occurrence of the two systems is likely so complex that they probably will not be separated—even though they may be therapeutically approached *as if* they were separate systems (Greenberg & Safran, 1989; Santostefano, 1980). This means that the emotional arrangement of the furniture cannot be changed without clarifying the cognitions that maintain the arrangement. Likewise, the cognitions cannot be changed unless supporting behaviors are changed—again, an interactive system. That is, one cannot substantively change feelings without changing the thoughts and behaviors that relate to and maintain the feelings. An attempt to change feelings without changing one's way of thinking and behaving produces a situation in which what one says and does is not consistent with those feelings. The resulting pattern of conflicts and inconsistencies is likely to undermine a sense of self-efficacy. Cognitions and emotions go hand in hand.

Of these two systems, the emotional system has traditionally been viewed as more basic from a therapeutic standpoint. Whether or not this is a semantic effect matters little. Individuals do not come to therapy saying, "I think bad"; they come saying, "I feel bad." (Children, of course, rarely come on their own and rarely say either.) Given the individual's perspective of a "bad feeling," traditional psychotherapy has aimed at making them "feel better." The expectation is that a change in the internal state will make one "feel" better. (Again, children rarely have such expectations, but their parents or other adults may.) This general expectation is consistent with cognitive-behavioral therapy, in which the goal is also to make individuals feel better. Although in the more traditional psychotherapies the process of feeling better is somewhat nebulous, in cognitive-behavioral therapy the goal is obtained by changing the internal cognitions that maintain maladaptive behaviors. Both cognitions and maladaptive behaviors are linked to emotions.

As "psychologically tender," the emotional system has been viewed traditionally as more sensitive to direct intervention than the cognitive system. That is, a direct and early assault on the emotional system will likely activate defensive patterns and postures more quickly than will a direct and early assault on the cognitive system. From this viewpoint the more robust cognitive system is less threatening in rearranging the furniture.

Because of the integration of the cognitive and emotional systems, the cognitive system provides a relatively "safe" road to the emotional system. The suggested direction of therapy would be to work through the cognitive system, which is more objectively and behaviorally tied to the emotional system with its greater degree of "perceived" sensitivity to intrusion.

To reiterate an important point, the utility of the cognitive system as a vehicle to access emotional systems is a function of the sophistication of the cognitive system with which one is dealing. In turn, the sophistication of the cognitive system is a function of the developmental age of the child or adolescent and the neurodevelopmental integrity of that individual. This suggests that the link or interactive component of emotions, cognitions, and behavior will vary by age. In younger children, emotions may be close to the surface and less controlled, while in older children and adolescents, emotions may be more protected and less accessible (Cooper & Wanerman, 1977; Halpern, 1953; Harrison, 1985). Likewise, attribution of cause for difficulties may vary by age. Younger children may perceive the source of their difficulties as more external, while older children and adolescents are more likely to attribute the difficulty to an internal cause (Roberts, Beidleman, & Wurtele, 1981).

The Process of Change

How does one promote change in young people? That is, how does the therapist use the immature cognitive system to produce changes in the emotional system? The remainder of this chapter addresses that question and proposes the use of three processes to produce cognitive amplification. Those processes are elaboration, exploration, and pattern development.

Elaboration and Exploration

The asking of questions is a standard technique in psychotherapy. If questions that begin with "Why" or "How" are not asked at the right time, they can limit client responses. "Why" questions are geared toward finding perceived answers or causes with the eventual goal of problem solving. "Why" questions probe for personal explanations for behaviors through queries such as "Why did that happen?" or "Why did you do that at that point?". By contrast, "How" questions are geared to move more directly to the emotional system and are seen as the hallmark of the traditional therapies. The idea is that if people know how they felt when something happened, then a "cure" is just around the corner. However, if asked prematurely, such questions may elicit a somewhat disappointing response for the therapist who expects to quickly reach the core of the emotional system. For the child or adolescent the event may be too remote to recall or recapture—or too recent to have sorted-out feelings. In addition, the child or adolescent may not have the words or the cognitive constructs to describe the feelings. All too often the therapist may provide the child or adolescent with a menu of feelings, and the child may make selections according to what is believed to be "proper" and/or expected. At other times the child or adolescent may blurt out feelings in very clear, precise, and sometimes colorful language. Having "uncovered" the feeling, the therapist then waits for a change in behavior, with none forthcoming. When the child's expression of the emotion does not produce the "expected" progress and improvement, it is logical to ask what is missing. The absent change ingredient usually is the exclusion of the linked systems—particularly, the cognitive and behavioral systems. Voicing an emotion does not lead automatically to a change in behavior. Yet parents and teachers often judge success by the child's behaviors ("He smiles more, now—he seems happier" or "She and her sister don't fight as often").

Both "Why" and "How" questions can be important when asked at the right time. When used prematurely, they tend to lead toward dead-end attempts to intervene and to produce change, and they may frustrate both the client and the therapist. For children and adolescents these questions are more helpful when the events of interest have been explored and elaborated.

Elaboration and exploration are accomplished by asking "When," "What," and "Where" questions. These questions maintain a therapeutic focus on the cognitive system. Additionally, they serve to intensify and to vivify the cognitive recollection of an event so that it becomes more immediate and less time-framed in the past. Responses to these questions make the event and the specifics of the event more intense and available. Elaboration and exploration are also useful techniques for probing the child's "therapeutic" vocabulary. If the vocabulary is adequate or if terms are accurately matched with behaviors and feelings ("I hit him because I was angry!"), then there is a greater likelihood that later "How" and "Why" questions will be productive. At the very least, elaboration and exploration offer an opportunity to teach an accurate, descriptive vocabulary.

Pattern Development

It was stated earlier that "insight," an important component of psychotherapy with adults, is relatively weaker in adolescents and is usually missing in younger children. With this younger population, insight is replaced by pattern development.

Pattern development is a therapeutic process in which the therapist helps the child or adolescent link experiences that are similar and that contribute to maladaptive patterns of behavior. The linkage is made within the cognitive system so that the child or adolescent can recognize the pattern of experiences over time and can appreciate the consequences attendant to those experiences. The linkage can be made directly by the therapist. It may be acceptable initially (and periodically) to try to "tease" the linkage from the youngster in an effort to promote independent understanding of the relationship between cognition, feeling, and consquence. However, waiting for such insightful responses can turn into a long process that depends on the child's developmental growth. Consequently, teasing should be used sparingly.

Amplification

The interactive relationship of elaboration, exploration, and pattern development leads to amplification of events as illustrated by Figure 12-2. Elaboration and exploration will lead eventually to the vivification and elevation of an event to a more immediate cognitive time-frame. Ideally, over time, there is amplification of the various aspects associated with the event (Byrne & Clore, 1970). In essence, elaboration and exploration elevate the clarity of the cognitive components of an event, and the integration of the cognitive and the emotional systems elevates the emotional ambience of the situation along with an increase in cognitive clarity. It is probable that the emotional system does not elevate at a one-to-one ratio with the cognitive system, because young people often adopt defensive postures. Several cognitive events with similar emotional attachments may have to be elevated to produce emotional elevation. However, having achieved elevation of both systems, "How" and "Why" questions are likely to be more potent ("How did you get yourself into this situation?" "What is the pattern we have found that has led to this?" "Why do you think others do not like you given what we have been talking about?"). Of importance to the therapist and the client is that the cognitive configuration of the furniture (emotions) becomes heightened in awareness and subject to evaluation. It is now possible to assess the accuracy of the cognitions (beliefs, thoughts, self-statements) that are maintaining the emotions (furniture).

At the same time, through pattern development, connections are made between similar elaborated and expanded events. This connecting process may result in behavior change aimed at increasing patterns of positive consequences and avoiding patterns of negative consequences. Obviously, pattern development is enhanced by elaboration and exploration, and elaboration and exploration are enhanced by pattern development; all three contribute to amplification.

FIGURE 12-2 • *Relationship of Elaboration, Exploration, Pattern Development and Amplification*

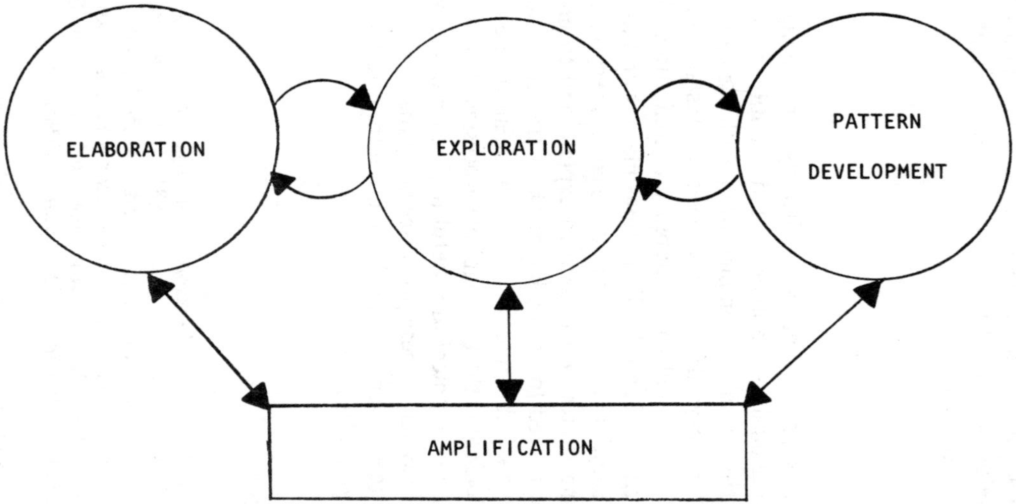

Within this process the child or adolescent may perceive the "why" of maladaptive behavior patterns with an adult-appearing "insight." More likely, changes will be more gradual in nature. In any case the process can lead to an understanding of how and why the world has become topsy-turvy. Within this understanding are the elements necessary for resuming normal development and for learning the cognitive strategies and processes that provide self-control.

Summary

This chapter suggests that psychotherapy with young people is markedly different from adult psychotherapy and that it is necessary to use therapeutic interventions that are commensurate with the capabilities of the young client. The primary differences between youths and adults are cognitive in nature and are related to developmental limitations that vary across the growth spectrum. Cognitive limitations place restrictions on the sophistication of the emotional system in that the cognitive system assists in maintaining emotional states and is used to explain and to understand emotions. Insight, considered to be the hallmark of traditional adult therapy, is not available in a reliable manner as a component of the therapy process with children. Consequently, the cognitive processes of elaboration, exploration, and pattern development are useful tools to produce amplification within the cognitive system. These processes bring that system to the forefront for review and reconstruction as a foundation for effective psychotherapy with children and adolescents.

References

Achenbach, T. M. (1974). *Developmental psychopathology.* New York: Wiley.
Achenbach, T. M., & Edelbrock, C. S. (1981). Behavioral problems and competence reported by parents of normal and disturbed children aged 4 through 16. *Monographs of the Society for Research in Child Development, 46.*
Axline, V. M. (1969). *Play therapy.* New York: Ballantine Books.
Bandura, A. (1969). *Principles of behavior modification.* New York: Holt, Rinehart & Winston.
Bandura, A. (1989). Human agency in social cognitive theory. *American Psychologist, 44,* 1175–1184.
Bates, J., Chassin, L., & Young, R. D. (1978). *Some suggestions for interviewing families and children.* Unpublished manuscript, Indiana University.
Beck, A. T. (1976). Cognitive therapy and the emotional disorders. New York: International Universities Press.
Beckman, D. (1977). *The mechanical baby: A popular history of the theory and practice of child raising.* Westport, CT: Hill.
Bird, H. R., & Kastenbaum, C. J. (1988). A semistructured approach to clinical

assessment. In C. J. Kastenbaum & D. T. Williams (Eds.), *Handbook of clinical assessment of children and adolescents* (Vol. 1, pp. 19–30). New York: New York University Press.

Boonin, T. (1979). The benighted status of U.S. school corporal punishment practice. *Phi Delta Kappan, 60,* 395.

Bremner, R. H. (1971). *Children and youth in America: A documentary history* (Vol. 2). Cambridge, MA: Harvard University Press.

Byrne, D., & Clore, G. L. (1970). A reinforcement model of evaluative responses. *Personality: An International Journal, 1,* 103–128.

Caulfield, E. (1931). *The infant welfare movement in the 18th century.* New York: Hoeber.

Cooley, C. H. (1964). *Human nature and the social order.* New York: Schocken.

Cooper, S., & Wanerman, L. (1977). Children in treatment: A primer for beginning psychotherapists. New York: Brunner/Mazel.

Cremin, L. A. (1969). *Horace Mann: Lectures on education.* New York: Arno Press.

Damon, W. (1977). *The social world of the child.* San Francisco: Jossey-Bass.

Damon, W. (1980). Patterns of change in children's social reasoning: A two-year longitudinal study. *Child Development, 51,* 1010–1017.

de Mause, L. (1974). *The history of childhood.* New York: Psychohistory Press.

Elkind, D. (1974). *Children and adolescents: Interpretive essays on Jean Piaget* (2nd ed.). London: Oxford University Press.

Ellis, A. (1962). *Reason and emotion in psychotherapy.* New York: Stuart.

Emory, R. E. (1989). Family violence. *American Psychologist, 44,* 321–328.

Erickson, C. (1983). *The first Elizabeth.* New York: Summit Books.

Flavell, J. H. (1985). *Cognitive development* (2nd ed.). Englewood, NJ: Prentice-Hall.

Freud, A. (1965). *Normality and pathology in childhood: Assessments of development.* New York: International Universities Press.

Garbarino, J. (1985). *Adolescent development: An ecological perspective.* Columbus, OH: Merrill.

Gelfand, D. M., & Peterson, L. (1985). *Child development and psychopathology.* Beverly Hills, CA: Sage.

Graziano, A. M., & Fink, M. (1973). Second order effects in mental health treatment. *Journal of Consulting and Clinical Psychology, 40,* 356–364.

Greenberg, L. S., & Safran, J. D. (1989). Emotion in psychotherapy. *American Psychologist, 44,* 19–29.

Halpern, F. (1953). *A clinical approach to children's Rorschachs.* New York: Grune & Stratton.

Harrison, S. I. (1985). Child psychiatry: Psychiatric treatment. In H. I. Kaplan & B. J. Sadock (Eds.), *Comprehensive textbook of psychiatry* (Vol. 4, pp. 1766–1785). London: Williams & Wilkins.

Hofer, M. A. (1981). *The roots of human behavior: An introduction to the psychobiology of early development.* San Francisco: Freeman.

Hunt, D. (1970). *Parents and children in history: The psychology of family life.* New York: Basic Books.

Ingraham v. *Wright,* 430 U.S. 651 (1977).

Kessen, W. (1965). *The child.* New York: Wiley.

Kohlberg, L., & Kramer, R. B. (1969). Continuities and discontinuities in childhood and adult moral development. *Human Development, 12,* 93–120.

Langer, W. (1973/74). Infanticide: A historical survey. *History of Childhood Quarterly, 1,* 354–365.

Lazarus, R. S. (1982). Thoughts on the relations between emotions and cognition. *American Psychologist, 37,* 1019–1024.

Levine, M., & Levine, A. (1970). *A social history of helping services.* New York: Appleton.

Levitt, E. E. (1971). Research on psychotherapy with children. In A. E. Bergin & S. L. Garfield (Eds.), *Handbook of psychotherapy and behavior change: An empirical analysis* (pp. 474–494). New York: Wiley.

Lewis, M. (1977). Language, cognition development, and personality. *Journal of the American Academy of Child Psychiatry, 16,* 646–661.

MacFarlane, J. W., Allen, L., & Honzik, M. P. (1954). *A developmental study of the behavior problems of normal children between 21 months and 14 years.* Berkeley, CA: University of California Press.

May, J. G. (1979). Nosology and diagnosis. In J. D. Noshpitz (Ed.), *Basic handbook of child psychiatry* (Vol. 2, pp. 144–156). New York: Basic Books.

McGraw, K. O. (1987). *Developmental psychology.* New York: Harcourt Brace Jovanovich.

Minde, K., & Minde, R. (1986). *Infant psychiatry: An introductory textbook.* Beverly Hills, CA: Sage.

Moustakas, C. E. (1959). *Psychotherapy with children.* New York: Ballantine Books.

Napoli, V., Kilbride, J. M., & Tebbs, D. E. (1985). *Adjustment and growth in a changing world* (2nd ed.). New York: West.

Newson, J., & Newson, E. (1976). *Seven years old in the home environment.* London: Allen & Unwin.

Piaget, J. (1932). *The moral development of the child.* New York: Harcourt Brace Jovanovich.

Piaget, J. (1962). *Play, dreams, and imitation.* New York: Norton.

Piaget, J., & Inhelder, B. (1969). *The psychology of the child.* New York: Basic Books.

Roberts, M. C., Beidleman, W. B., & Wurtele, S. K. (1981). Children's perceptions of medical and psychological disorders in their peers. *Journal of Clinical Child Psychology, 10,* 76–78.

Santostefano, S. (1980). Cognition in personality and the treatment process: A psychoanalytic view. In A. J. Solnit, R. S. Eissler, A. Freud, M. Kris, & P. B. Neubauer (Eds.), *The psychoanalytic study of the child* (Vol. 35, pp. 41–66). New Haven, CT: Yale University Press.

Segal, J., & Yahraes, H. (1979). *A child's journey: Forces that shape the lives of our young.* New York: McGraw-Hill.

Selman, R. L. (1980). *The growth of interpersonal understanding: Developmental and clinical analysis.* New York: Academic Press.

Shorter, E. (1975). *The making of the modern family.* New York: Basic Books.

Staats, A. W. (1968). Social behaviorism and human motivation: Principles of the attitude-reinforcer-discrimination system. In A. G. Greenwald, T. C. Brock, & T. M. Ostrom (Eds.), *Psychological foundations of attitudes* (pp. 33–66). New York: Academic Press.

Still, G. F. (1931). *The history of paediatrics.* Oxford, England: Oxford University Press.

Tanner, L. N. (1978). *Classroom discipline for effective teaching and learning.* New York: Holt, Rinehart & Winston.

Tilker, H. A. (1975). *Developmental psychology today.* New York: Random House.

Zajonc, R. B. (1984). On the primacy of affect. *American Psychologist, 39,* 117–123.

Author Index

Aammer, I. M., 110
Abikoff, H., 8, 240, 253
Abrammovitz, A., 262
Abramowitz, A., 10
Abramson, L., 102, 103, 104, 295
Achenbach, T. M., 26, 95, 96, 97, 158, 169, 213, 294, 307, 377, 380
Adams, M. S., 352
Adelson, R., 353
Agras, W. S., 294
Ainslie, G., 15
Albert, J., 121
Alcala, J., 106, 107
Allen, G., 47, 98, 116, 117
Allen, K. E., 105
Allen, L., 377
Allen, M. K., 13
Alloy, L. B., 103
Allport, G. W., 107
Altman, D., 116
Altman, N., 116
Amish, P. L., 206
Anderson, C. G., 212, 215, 216
Anderson, J., 236, 238
Andrews, J., 303, 304, 309, 310
Annesley, F., 98
Antonuccio, D. O., 303
Apley, J., 348
Apolloni, T., 95
Appelbaum, M. I., 31
Arana, G., 294
Arkowitz, H., 305
Arnkoff, D., 150, 151
Arnold, C., 120
Artenstein, M. S., 347
Asarnow, J. R., 15, 18, 102, 103
Asher, S. R., 48, 94, 105
Astrada, C., 348

Attwell, A. A., 120
Ault, R. L., 122
Axline, V. M., 375
Ayllon, T., 212, 215, 216
Azarnoff, P., 352
Azrin, N., 56

Baars, B. J., 2
Bachman, J. G., 315
Baer, D., 215
Baer, O., 227
Bailey, W. C., 353
Baldessarini, R., 294
Baldwin, D. V., 93
Baldwin, J. M., 107
Bambrick, A., 98
Bandura, A., 2, 3, 4, 7, 9, 11, 13, 14, 17, 27, 28, 29, 31, 50, 52, 68, 69, 74, 75, 76, 151, 177, 200, 281, 353, 354, 378, 380, 383
Barbour, J., 318
Barden, R. C., 74
Barenboim, C., 33, 40, 108, 109
Barkley, R. A., 100, 120, 254
Barling, J., 18
Barlow, D. H., 294
Barrios, B. A., 124, 258
Bartell, N., 128
Baskin, C. H., 103, 213
Bass, S., 33, 40
Bateman, D. F., 77, 78
Bates, J., 376
Bates, S., 102, 103
Batran, J., 317
Baum, J., 206, 216
Baumann, D. J., 211
Baxter, E., 260
Beach, D. R., 49
Beamesderfer, A., 293
Beck, A. T., 2, 5, 127, 151,

153, 293, 295, 298–301, 306, 307, 308, 335, 383
Beck, D., 212, 215
Beck, S., 213, 214
Becker, W., 120
Beckman, D., 373, 374
Bedrosian, R., 298
Behler, J., 10, 251, 283
Beidleman, W. B., 386
Belfer, M. L., 347
Bellack, A. S., 90, 106, 107, 206, 209, 213, 216
Bell-Dolan, D., 95, 208, 212
Belmont, T. M., 27
Benfield, C. Y., 103
Bennett, B., 127
Bentler, P. M., 236
Berger, E. S., 208, 212
Berkowitz, L., 151
Berman, J. S., 15, 16
Bernard, M., 295, 296, 297, 305, 328
Berndt, T., 31, 32, 44
Bernstein, D. A., 124
Beutler, L. E., 305
Beyer, J., 349
Bielke, P., 237
Bierman, K. L., 214, 215
Biougin, D. C., 213
Bird, H. R., 376, 379
Blackham, G. J., 117
Blitz, B., 360
Block, A. R., 350
Block, J., 108, 122, 236
Block, J. H., 122, 236
Blom, G., 12, 50, 243
Bloom, L. J., 259
Blouin, D. C., 106, 107
Blount, R. L., 97
Blumberg, S. H., 294
Blumenthal, S., 291
Boike, M. F., 101
Bologna, N. C., 253
Bolstad, O. D., 9, 14

Boodoo, G., 106, 107
Boonin, T., 374
Borke, H., 110
Borkowski, J. G., 103
Bornstein, M., 106, 206, 213, 216
Bornstein, P., 50, 57, 265
Botkin, P., 107, 108
Bowers, D. S., 79
Boyes, M., 34
Bradley, L. A., 349
Brady-Smith, J., 34, 36, 108
Braith, J., 253
Brakke, N. P., 105
Braswell, L., 3, 5, 10, 50, 51, 99, 100, 109, 116, 122, 234, 241, 252, 253
Breen, M. J., 100
Bremner, R. H., 372, 374, 375
Brion, S., 111
Broden, M., 72, 78
Brown, K. E., 99
Brown, M., 41, 93
Brownell, K. D., 68
Bruner, J. S., 237
Buchsbaum, K., 102
Buckley, N., 36
Buell, J. S., 105
Buescher, E. L., 347
Bugental, D., 50
Bunzl, M., 45
Burch, P. R., 151, 199
Burge, D. A., 95
Burka, A., 36
Burke, P., 103
Burrows, B., 266
Burton, N., 291
Bush, J. P., 349, 351
Buss, A. H., 14
Buss, R. R., 294
Butler, L., 113, 116, 117, 129, 305, 306
Byers, M. L., 349
Byrne, B. M., 206, 214, 215
Byrne, D., 107, 379, 388

Cairns, B. D., 209
Cairns, E., 122
Cairns, R. B., 209
Caldwell, B., 36, 38, 47
Callahan, J. W., 15, 18
Cameron, R., 6, 151, 269
Cammock, T., 122
Camp, B., 12, 48, 49, 50, 193, 207, 208, 243
Campbell, L., 263
Candes, B., 57

Cannizzo, S. R., 49
Cantwell, D. P., 127
Carbonell, J., 5
Carek, D. J., 97
Carey, M. P., 253, 289, 290, 293, 294, 295, 310
Carlson, P., 216
Carnirike, C. L., 15
Carregal, E., 345
Carroll, B. J., 294
Carroll, C., 259
Casat, C. D., 290, 293, 294, 295, 310
Casey, P., 348
Cassel, J., 347
Cassell, S., 352
Castaneda, A., 125
Catania, C. A., 69
Caulfield, E., 373
Cautela, J. R., 4, 8, 9
Cavell, T. A., 289, 293
Cerny, J. A., 207
Chambers, W. J., 290, 293
Chandler, M., 29, 33, 34, 36, 38, 40, 108, 109, 110
Charlesworth, R., 93
Chassin, L., 259, 376
Chinsky, J., 47, 49, 98, 103, 116, 117
Chirico, B. M., 103
Cholera, S., 54, 357
Cialdini, R. B., 211
Cicchetti, D., 290
Clarfield, S. P., 101
Clarizio, H. F., 289, 295
Clark, H., 206, 216
Clark, M., 263
Clark, W., 348
Clarke, G., 295, 302, 303, 304, 309, 310
Clement, P. W., 79
Clements, C. B., 207, 208
Clore, G. L., 379, 388
Coates, B., 31, 32
Coats, K. I., 307, 308
Cobb, J. A., 93, 120, 121
Coder, R., 45
Cohen, J., 214
Cohen, N. J., 96, 101, 109
Cohen, R., 253, 300
Coie, J. D., 105, 106
Colbus, D., 126, 156, 294
Colby, S., 38
Cole, C. L., 207
Cole, E., 305, 306
Collins, W., 31, 32, 33
Combs, M., 207, 211, 217
Cone, J. D., 93, 94

Conger, J. C., 206, 211
Connell, J. P., 104
Conners, C. K., 96, 98, 120
Conover, N. C., 97, 98
Contrearas, J. A., 253
Cook, T., 95, 259
Cooley, C. H., 379
Cooley, W., 151
Cooney, E. W., 38, 111, 112
Cooper, M., 38, 47
Cooper, S., 376, 379, 386
Copeland, A. P., 98, 253
Corson, J., 215
Costello, A. J., 293
Coury, D. L., 125
Cowan, P. A., 35
Cowen, E. L., 15, 48, 101, 117
Cox, R., 226
Craighead, W. E., 3, 7, 18, 94
Crandall, V. C., 104
Crandall, V. S., 104
Crandell, C., 238, 239
Cremin, L. A., 374
Crouse-Novak, M., 291
Crue, B. L., 345
Csikszentmihalyi, M., 34
Curry, J. F., 10, 151, 199, 210, 211, 218

Dahlem, N., 207, 208
Daley, P. C., 259
Damon, W., 29, 30, 42, 43, 44, 377, 378
Davidson, E., 15
Davidson, K. S., 272
Davison, G. C., 10
Day, D., 121
deApodace, R., 48
Deardorff, P. A., 160, 236, 238, 239, 272
Debus, R., 353
Deffenbacher, J., 259, 266, 267, 270, 271
Deluty, R. H., 118, 119, 193
de Mause, L., 373
Demorest, A. P., 112
Denham, S. A., 108
Denney, D., 32
DePaulo, B., 210
Descartes, R., 344
Deutsch, F., 36, 108
Devine, V. T., 121
DeVries, R., 108
Diament, C., 93
Dietz, A., 93

DiGiuseppe, R., 210, 300, 323, 329, 335
Dimock, H. G., 352
Dinnerstein, A., 360
Dishion, T. J., 93
Ditrichs, R., 75
Dobson, K. S., 17
Docherty, E., 108, 110
Dodge, K. A., 93, 102, 105, 106, 151, 209, 210, 223
Donahoe, C., 207
Dor, A. K., 94
Dorsett, P. G., 160, 214
Douglas, V., 13, 50, 123
Drabman, R. S., 55, 72, 74, 78
Drummond, D., 281
Dubey, D. R., 67, 74, 75, 76
Dubow, E. F., 209, 214, 215
Duerfeldt, P. H., 13, 76
Duke, M. P., 102
Duncan, K., 212, 215
Dunnington, M. J., 212
DuPaul, G. P., 254
Dweck, C. S., 10, 28, 29, 34, 104
Dyck, D. G., 126
D'Zurilla, T., 112, 113, 192, 259

Earls, F., 96
Ecton, R. B., 149, 150, 151, 156, 163, 195
Edelbrock, C. S., 26, 95, 96, 97, 98, 100, 158, 169, 213, 293, 294, 307, 377
Edelson, J. L., 81
Edelstein, B., 206
Egeland, B., 122, 123, 237
Eisenberg-Berg, N., 36
Elarado, P., 36, 38, 47
Elder, J., 206
Elkin, A., 273
Elkind, D., 378, 379
Elliott, C. H., 263, 348
Elliott, S. N., 106, 107
Ellis, A., 2, 5, 17, 151, 295–298, 305, 306, 323, 328, 329, 335, 383
Emery, G., 5, 295, 298
Emery, R. E., 375
Emery, S., 298
Emler, N., 41
Emysey, L. T., 148
Enright, R., 38, 108, 111, 112
Epps, J., 259, 261
Erickson, C., 373, 374

Erickson, M. T., 241
Erikson, E., 27, 28
Eron, L., 209, 214, 215
Eshelman, A. K., 115
Esveldt-Dawson, K., 15, 107, 118, 209, 213, 293
Evans, H. L., 69, 74, 76, 250
Evers-Pasquale, W., 210

Fantuzzo, J. W., 79
Faught, A., 263, 266
Feinberg, T., 291
Feindler, E. L., 149, 150, 151, 156, 163
Feldhusen, J., 117
Feldman, K., 41
Feldman, S. E., 75
Felixbrod, J. J., 75
Ferrarese, M. J., 111, 123
Feshbach, S., 151, 193
Fiendler, E. L., 195
Finch, A. J., Jr., 10, 11, 14, 18, 50, 97, 101, 103, 122, 123, 127, 148, 151, 155, 158, 160, 162, 169, 180–191, 234, 235, 236, 237, 238, 239, 240, 272, 280, 290, 293, 295, 310
Fine, M. B., 310
Fine, S., 18, 126
Fink, M., 380, 381
Finkelstein, R., 291
Firestone, P., 263, 266
Fischel, J. E., 99
Fischer, M., 100
Fischler, G. L., 114, 116
Fitch, D., 36
Flagel, S., 352
Flapan, D., 108
Flavell, J. H., 46, 49, 107, 108, 383
Fleming, C., 158
Fodor, E., 41
Foley, J. M., 106
Ford, M. E., 41, 108
Forehand, R., 213, 214
Fores de Apodaca, R., 15
Forman, S. G., 16, 200, 210
Foster, D., 348
Foster, S. L., 5, 93, 95, 208, 211, 212
Fowler, J. W., 33
Fox, J., 260, 261, 272
Frame, C. L., 293
Francis, G., 259
Freedman, B., 207
Freeman, A., 305

Freeman, L. N., 293, 307
Freeman, R., 18, 126
French, N., 15, 293
Freud, A., 376, 380
Freud, S., 25, 27, 28
Friedlander, S., 96
Friedling, C., 16, 50
Friedman, R., 122, 305, 306
Friedman, S. B., 347
Frieze, I., 102
Fry, C., 107, 108
Fuchs, C. Z., 295, 301
Furey, W., 103
Furguson, K., 240
Furman, W., 74

Gaelick, L., 9
Games, P., 259
Ganzer, V. J., 103
Garbarino, J., 375
Garber, A., 102
Garber, J., 298
Gardner, W., 32
Gardner, W. I., 207
Gariepy, J. L., 209
Garmezy, N., 111, 123
Garrigan, J., 98
Garrison, W. T., 96
Garson, C., 13, 50, 123
Garvey, C., 108
Gelder, M., 259
Gelfand, D. M., 376
Genest, M., 52, 54, 151, 349, 353, 357, 358, 365
Genshaft, J. L., 125
Gerachi, R. L., 94
Gershaw, N. J., 216
Gerson, R., 29, 30, 42, 43, 44
Gerst, M. S., 11
Gest, S., 209
Gesten, E. L., 15, 48, 100, 101, 117, 206
Geuvremont, D., 5
Gewirtz, J. L., 3
Ghia, J. N., 348
Gibbons, P., 350
Giebenhain, J., 258, 264, 265, 266
Gillet, D., 151
Gilligan, C., 43
Girgus, J. S., 103, 126
Gittleman, R., 253, 290
Gjerde, P. F., 122
Glasgow, L., 347
Glass, C. R., 52, 358
Glazer, J. A., 93
Glenwick, D., 36

Glick, B., 148, 150, 151, 216
Glick, J., 353
Glicken, M., 297
Glucksberg, S., 108
Glynn, E. L., 9, 14, 77, 78
Goldfoot, D., 361
Goldfried, M., 112, 192, 259, 353
Goldstein, A. P., 148, 150, 151, 216, 316, 338
Gollins, E. S., 36
Gonso, J., 36, 93, 105, 207
Goodman, J., 6, 9, 10, 11, 12, 14, 49, 50, 122, 164, 238, 262, 270
Goodwin, S. E., 200
Gordon, J., 271
Gordon, R., 114
Gotlieb, H., 96
Gottman, J., 36, 74, 78, 93, 105, 207, 212, 216
Gouze, K. R., 114
Gramling, S., 124
Granberry, S. W., 106, 107, 213
Granum, R., 212, 215
Graziano, A., 264, 380, 381
Green, C., 351
Greenbaum, R., 97, 98
Greenberg, L. S., 385
Greenfield, P. M., 237
Greenspan, S., 33, 40, 108, 109, 110
Greenwood, C. R., 95, 98, 105
Gregg, J. M., 348
Greif, E., 39
Gresham, F. M., 105, 106, 107, 214
Grief, E. G., 108
Griffith, B., 341
Gross, A. M., 67, 68, 74, 127
Gruber, J., 98
Grusec, J. E., 76
Guerra, N. G., 114
Gunn, W., 226
Gurucharri, C., 111

Haaga, D. A., 10
Haar, M., 259
Hadfield, R., 259
Hahn, Y. S., 349
Haley, G., 18, 126
Haley, M. A., 310
Hall, R. V., 72, 78
Hallahan, D. P., 77, 78
Halpern, F., 377, 379, 386

Halsel, W. J., 213
Hamilton, M., 293
Hamilton, S. B., 36
Hammell, R., 253
Hann, N., 108
Harrington, D., 122, 236
Harris, D. B., 127
Harris, F. R., 93, 105
Harris, J. C., 97
Harris, K. R., 28
Harris, S., 41
Harrison, S. I., 375, 376, 377, 379, 386
Hart, B., 105
Hart, K., 158, 199
Hartmann, D. P., 122, 124
Hartup, W., 31, 32, 93, 193, 207, 209
Harwood, R. L., 210, 214, 216
Hawes, R. R., 353
Hawkins, R. P., 94
Hawkins-Searcy, J., 103
Hawton, K., 291
Hayden, B., 210
Hayes, S. C., 70, 94
Haynes, S. N., 94
Heffer, R. W., 289, 293
Heiby, E., 353
Heick, H., 263, 266
Heingartner, A., 41
Heinze, A., 213
Helsel, W. J., 117, 118
Hemry, F. P., 122
Henker, B., 9, 50, 234, 241, 253
Heppner, P., 192
Herbert, F., 12, 50
Herbert, M., 148, 149
Herbert, R., 243
Hersen, M., 90, 106, 107, 206, 213, 216
Hess, V., 31, 32
Hetherington, E., 211, 281
Higgins, R., 108
Hildebrandt, D. E., 75
Hilgard, E. K., 347
Hilgard, J. K., 347
Hinker, A., 209
Hinshaw, S. P., 9, 234, 241, 253
Hirschfeld, R., 291
Hoberman, H. M., 295, 302
Hodges, K. K., 293
Hofer, M. A., 383
Hoffman, M. L., 35
Hogan, R., 108
Hohman, B., 57

Hollon, S. D., 6, 16, 17
Holroyd, K. A., 260
Holstein, C., 40
Homme, L. E., 4, 8
Honzik, M. P., 377
Hoogerman, D., 341
Hooke, J. F., 237, 239, 280
Hops, H., 95, 98, 105, 211, 290, 295, 302, 303, 304, 309, 310
Horan, J., 259
Horland, A., 361
Houston, K., 260, 261, 272
Houts, A. C., 68
Houtz, J., 117
Howard, B., 259, 261, 265
Howell, C. T., 96, 97
Huard, C., 109
Huber, C., 264
Huesmann, L., 209, 214, 215
Hughes, J. N., 106, 107
Humphrey, L. L., 103, 104
Hunt, D., 374
Hunt, H., 348
Huntley, D., 341
Hymel, S., 105

Iannotti, R., 36, 110
Iggo, A., 347
Ignasiak, D., 264
Inhelder, B., 107, 378, 383
Ironsmith, M., 74, 78
Izard, C. E., 294

Jacobsen, E., 165
Jacobsen, R., 267
Jacobson, N. S., 94, 106
Jaeger, M., 15, 114
Jahoda, M., 112
Janis, I., 352, 358
Jannoun, L., 259
Jansson, L., 258
Jaquette, D., 111
Jaremko, M., 258, 259
Jarvis, P., 107, 108
Jason, L., 266
Jay, S., 263, 348, 349
Jeffery, R. W., 11
Jennings, K., 36
Jerremalm, A., 258, 266
Johansson, J., 266
Johnson, D., 36, 37
Johnson, F., 34, 108
Johnson, J. H., 294
Johnson, S. B., 124
Johnson, S. M., 9, 14
Johnston, L. D., 315

Johnston, M. K., 93
Jones, R. T., 67, 69, 74, 77, 79
Jones, S., 352
Joyce, M., 295, 296, 297, 305
Jurkovic, G., 41

Kagan, J., 14, 98, 104, 121, 122, 234, 235, 237
Kahana, B., 243
Kandel, H., 212, 215, 216
Kane, M. T., 265
Kanfer, F. H., 4, 8, 9, 13, 68, 69, 76, 264, 301, 316, 338, 361
Kapperman, G., 213
Karoly, P., 7, 68, 70, 71, 74, 264
Kaslow, N. J., 16, 18, 103, 126, 127, 301, 307, 308
Kastenbaum, C. J., 376, 379
Katkovsky, W., 104
Katz, E., 263, 350
Kaufman, K. F., 73, 76, 78
Kaufmann, L., 167
Kausch, D. F., 116
Kay, R., 349
Kazdin, A. E., 3, 5, 8, 15, 26, 67, 70, 74, 75, 77, 79, 94, 107, 118, 126, 127, 156, 209, 213, 293, 294, 353
Keane, S. P., 206, 211
Keefe, F. J., 349, 350
Keeley, S. M., 5
Keeney, T. J., 49
Kehle, T. J., 123
Keith, C. R., 149
Keller, M., 30, 34, 216
Kellerman, J., 350
Kelley, C. S., 93
Kelley, M. L., 294
Kelly, G., 2, 3, 336, 337
Kelly, M. M., 103
Kemp, S. R., 236
Kendall, P. C., 3, 5, 6, 10, 11, 15, 16, 17, 18, 50, 51, 95, 98, 99, 100, 101, 102, 103, 109, 114, 115, 116, 117, 122–123, 124, 127, 149, 234, 236, 237, 238, 239, 240, 241, 243, 244, 251, 252, 253, 259, 261, 265, 280, 281, 282
Keniston, A. H., 32
Kennedy, C. B., 31
Kenrick, D. T., 211

Kent, R. N., 93
Kerr, F. W., 347
Kershner, J., 96, 101, 109
Kessen, W., 373
Kessler, S., 348
Kettlewell, P. W., 116
Keyser, V., 18
Kilbride, J. M., 379
King, S. L., 97
Kirkpatrick, S., 263
Kirschenbaum, D., 74, 101
Knapp, M., 265
Koch, C., 341
Koeppen, A. S., 165, 267, 360
Kohlberg, L., 27, 39, 40, 41, 42, 44, 107, 378
Kohli, D., 294
Kolko, D. J., 160, 214
Koocher, G., 348
Kornblath, R., 151
Kovacs, M., 127, 290, 291, 293, 307
Kramer, R. B., 378
Krasnor, L. R., 113, 116, 117
Kratochwill, T., 259
Krauss, R., 108
Krehbiel, G. G., 207, 211, 214
Krueger, L. C., 356
Kuehne, C., 123
Kuhn, D., 40
Kukla, A., 102
Kunzelman, H. D., 71
Kupers, C. J., 13, 76
Kupersmidt, J. B., 106
Kurdek, L., 34, 35, 36, 41, 108, 109, 110
Kurtines, W., 39, 108

Labbee, P., 75
Ladd, G. W., 215
LaGreca, A. M., 207, 215
Lahaderne, H. M., 120
Lambert, M., 310
Lampron, L. B., 151, 199
Landrum, T. J., 77, 78
Lang, M., 128
Langer, E., 358, 373, 374
Lapsley, D. K., 108
Larcen, S., 47, 98, 103, 116, 117
Larsen, L., 192
Larson, R., 34
Latner, I., 318
Lavigne, J. V., 349
Lavin, R., 111

Lazarus, A., 10, 262, 316, 360
Lazarus, R., 347
Lazarus, R. S., 347, 383
Leahy, R., 109
Leal, L., 260
LeBlanc, J., 215
Leckie, G., 108, 110
LeCroy, C. W., 214
Ledwidge, B., 5, 15, 16
Lefcourt, H. M., 103
Lefkowitz, M. M., 291
Lefton, W., 199
Leitenberg, H., 126
LeMare, L. J., 36, 109
Leon, G. R., 102
Lepper, M. R., 75, 78
Lesswing, N. J., 3
Lethermon, V. R., 106, 107
Letherms, V., 213
Levendusky, P., 358
Leventhal, H., 352
Levine, A., 375
Levine, M., 15, 375
Levitt, E. E., 375, 377, 378
Lewin, K., 28
Lewinsohn, P. M., 290, 295, 302–305, 307, 308, 309, 310
Lewis, M., 378
Licamele, W., 348
Lieberman, D. A., 355
Lieberman, M., 29, 44
Liebert, R. M., 13, 68, 76, 210
Liebeskind, J., 348
Lighthall, F. F., 272
Lindauer, B. K., 33
Lindsay, P., 122
Lipovsky, J., 295
Little, V. L., 103, 109
Lloyd, J. W., 77, 78
Lochman, J. E., 10, 47, 98, 116, 117, 151, 193, 196, 197, 199, 210, 211, 218
Loigman, G. A., 115
Long, B., 259
Long, J., 151
Lotyczewski, B. S., 101
Lumry, A., 17
Luria, A. R., 6, 11, 12, 49, 355

MacDonald, M. L., 214
Mace, R., 259
MacFarlane, J. W., 377
MacPherson, E., 57
MacQuiddy, S. L., 36

Madsen, C., 120
Maggio, M., 106, 107
Mahoney, M. J., 2, 3, 4, 6, 7, 8, 13, 67, 68, 70, 71, 150, 151, 200, 353
Maioni, T., 36
Maise, S. J., 36
Manatt, M., 315
Mann, H., 374
Mao, W., 348
Markell, R. A., 105
Markle, A., 207, 213
Marlatt, A., 271
Marriage, K., 18, 126
Marriage, M., 310
Marshall, H. R., 93
Marston, A. R., 13
Martens, B. K., 289, 293
Martin, B., 211
Martin, J., 260
Marton, P., 13, 50, 123
Marx, R., 260
Mash, E. J., 94
Mason, J. W., 347
Massari, D. J., 122
Masten, A. S., 111, 123
Masters, J., 74, 82
Matson, J. L., 107, 117, 118, 209, 213, 228, 293, 295, 310
Maultsby, M., 331, 332, 338
May, J. G., 376
McCaffery, M., 361
McCall, R. B., 31
McCandless, B. R., 93, 125
McCarthy, W., 206, 216
McCauley, E., 103
McClain, J. A., 236
McClaskey, C. L., 93
McClure, L., 103, 117
McConaughy, S. H., 97
McCutcheon, S., 294
McFall, R. M., 74, 78, 93, 207
McGrath, P. A., 264, 349, 350, 358, 360
McGraw, K. O., 372
McGuire, D., 291
McInerney, J. B., 323, 329, 335
McKenzie, S. J., 118
McKim, B. J., 15, 101, 117
McMahon, R. J., 76, 95
McMahon, W., 123
McMullen, L., 38
Mead, G., 107
Mead, H., 34, 35

Meichenbaum, D., 2, 4, 5, 6, 7, 8, 9, 10, 11, 12, 14, 17, 18, 49, 50, 52, 53, 54, 55, 113, 116, 117, 122, 128, 129, 150, 151, 153, 163, 164, 165, 238, 258, 260, 262, 269, 270, 271, 272, 279, 280, 281, 282, 283, 329, 349, 353, 358, 364, 365
Melamed, B. G., 124, 353
Melzack, R., 345, 346, 347, 348, 355, 359
Menlove, F. L., 76
Mercatoris, M., 94
Merluzzi, T. V., 52, 358
Messer, S. B., 14, 121, 122, 236, 237
Metalsky, G., 102, 104
Meyer, M. P., 104
Meyer, N. E., 126
Meyers, A., 3, 7, 18, 253, 300
Meyers, C. E., 120
Meyers, J. E., 356
Michaels, A. C., 259
Michaels, T., 259
Michelson, L., 118, 119, 211
Michlin, R., 34
Michline, M., 108
Miezitis, S., 305, 306
Milan, M. A., 160, 214
Milich, R., 207, 211, 214
Miller, C. L., 214, 215
Miller, F. D., 355
Miller, R. C., 15, 16
Minde, K., 373
Minde, R., 373
Minzer, P., 79n
Mischel, H., 28, 30, 39
Mischel, W., 27, 28, 30, 39, 49, 76
Mitchell, C., 122
Mitchell, J. R., 103
Mitts, B., 72, 78
Mokros, H. B., 293, 307
Montgomery, L. E., 14, 122, 160, 235, 236, 237, 238, 272
Moody, S. C., 106, 107, 213
Mooney, K., 264
Moore, L., 106, 107
Moore, S. G., 212
Moos, B., 294
Moos, R., 294
Moran, P. W., 310
Moretti, M., 126, 310
Morgan, J. R., 11

Morris, R., 259
Morrison, R. L., 209
Moss, S., 103
Mougey, E. H., 347
Moustakas, C. E., 375
Mozetti, M. M., 18
Mulich, J. A., 125
Muller, J., 344
Murphy, R. R., 102
Murray, J. P., 110
Mussen, P., 41

Nakamura, C. Y., 125
Nannis, E. D., 35
Napoli, V., 379
Narick, M., 206
Narrol, H., 122
Nasby, W., 210
Nathan, P. W., 347
Nay, W. R., 94, 316, 326, 338
Neal, G., 36, 192
Neckerman, H. J., 209
Neeper, R., 213
Neilson, W. M., III, 148
Nelson, R., 70
Nelson, R. E., 67
Nelson, R. O., 94
Nelson, W. M., III, 10, 11, 54, 122, 151, 155, 158, 162, 169, 180, 196, 197, 235, 237, 238, 239, 241, 250, 251, 280, 283, 356, 357, 358, 360
Ness, S., 36
Neubauer, D., 149
Newby, R. F., 100
Newell, A., 112
Newman, A., 264
Newman, J. P., 210, 223
Newman, S., 114
Newson, E., 374
Newson, J., 374
Nezu, A., 15, 113
Nietzel, M. T., 124
Nisbett, R. E., 355
Noland, M., 98
Nolen-Hoeksema, S., 103, 126
Novaco, R. W., 150, 151, 155, 162, 163, 165, 170, 171, 195, 259
Nowicki, S., Jr., 102
Nummedal, S., 33, 40

O'Brien, J., 318
O'Connor, R., 105, 212, 216

O'Dell, S., 258, 264, 265, 266
O'Leary, K. D., 16, 55, 73, 74, 75, 76, 78, 93
O'Leary, L., 55
O'Leary, S. G., 50, 55, 67, 74, 75, 76
Olejnik, A., 36, 41
Oliver, R. R., 237
Ollendick, T. H., 90, 103, 106, 119, 125, 206, 207, 216, 228, 235, 259
Olson, R. L., 206, 214, 215
O'Malley, J., 348
O'Malley, P. M., 315
Oppenheimer, C., 259
Orara, N. A., 101
Ornsteen, M., 294
Orpet, R. E., 120
Osborne, A. F., 199
Ost, L., 258, 266

Padawer, W., 68
Paget, K. D., 125
Palermo, D. S., 4, 125
Palkes, H., 243
Pallmeyer, T. P., 97
Palmer, D. J., 103
Pankratz, L., 358
Panzer, C., 151
Parcel, G. S., 104
Paris, S. G., 33
Parke, R., 55, 281
Parrish, J. M., 241
Parry, P., 13, 50, 123
Patterson, C., 49, 75, 78
Patterson, G. R., 93, 209
Paul, L., 348
Paul, M., 352
Paulauskas, S., 291
Pearl, R., 10
Pearson, L., 122
Peizer, S. B., 116
Pelham, W. E., 253
Pellegrini, D. S., 111, 113, 115, 116, 123
Perloff, B., 14, 74
Perry, D., 56
Perry, M. A., 92
Petermann, H., 341
Peterson, C., 29, 38, 103
Peterson, D., 158
Peterson, D. R., 213
Peterson, L., 10, 16, 33, 50, 262, 266, 376
Petrinack, R. J., 126
Petti, T. A., 127
Pettit, G. S., 93

Pezzuti, K. A., 236
Pfefferbaum, B., 103
Phares, E. J., 103
Phelps, E., 41, 111, 112
Phil, R., 259
Phillips, W., 121
Piaget, J., 25, 27, 30, 35, 39, 40, 107, 378, 383
Piche, G., 34, 108
Piers, E. V., 127
Pinkston, E., 215
Pittner, M. S., 272
Platt, J., 10, 36, 45, 46, 47, 113, 114, 115, 116, 150, 192, 194, 195, 198
Plomin, R., 14
Pollack, S. L., 103
Polyson, J. A., 211
Porteus, S. D., 123
Powell, K., 294
Powell, L., 114
Powers, M., 56
Poznanski, E. O., 293, 307
Prentice, N., 41
Pressley, M., 253
Prins, P., 261
Puig-Antich, J., 290, 293
Putallez, M., 106

Quay, H. C., 96, 120, 152, 158, 213
Quevillon, R., 50, 57

Rachlin, H., 68, 69
Rachman, S., 360
Radke-Yarrow, M., 34, 36, 108
Raines, J., 353
Rains, M., 48
Ramirez, S., 259
Ramsey, P. P., 240
Rapkin, B. D., 15, 117
Rasmussen, B., 36, 93, 105, 207
Rathjen, D., 209
Rathjen, E., 209
Ravenette, A. T., 53
Ray, R. S., 93
Reardon, R. C., 106
Reed, M. L., 97, 102
Reese, N., 215
Rehm, L., 103, 126, 295, 301–302, 307, 308
Reid, J. B., 93, 94
Reid, M. K., 103
Reid, W. H., 149
Reifler, J. P., 97
Renshaw, P. D., 48, 94

Renzaglia, G. A., 94
Reppucci, N. D., 104
Resnick, J. S., 31
Rest, J., 40, 108
Rest, S., 102
Rey, H., 351
Rey, M., 351
Reynolds, C. R., 125, 294
Reynolds, W. M., 16, 99, 104, 127, 128, 293, 294, 307, 308
Richardson, F., 258, 266, 271
Richmond, B. O., 125, 294
Rickel, A. U., 115
Ridberg, E., 281
Riddle, M., 123
Ridley, C. A., 110, 117
Ries, R., 317
Rimm, O., 82
Ringenbach, S., 117
Rinn, R., 207, 213
Ritchey, R. L., 211
Roberts, R., 94, 290
Roberts, R. C., 386
Roberts, R. H., 123
Roberts, R. W., 206, 214, 215
Robin, A. L., 99
Robins, L. N., 148
Rodgers, A., 126, 156, 294
Rodick, J. D., 253
Rogdon, M., 34, 35, 108, 110
Rogers, T. R., 101
Rogoff, B., 32
Rohde, P., 295
Romanczyk, R. G., 73, 76
Ronan, K. R., 124
Rondal, J. A., 49
Roopnarine, J. L., 110
Rose, M., 263, 266
Rosen, C., 37, 48, 56
Rosenbaum, R. M., 102
Rosenbaum, R. S., 72, 74, 78
Rosenberg, L. A., 97
Rosenthal, L., 207
Rosenthal, T., 27, 28, 31, 40
Roskies, E., 347
Rosman, B. L., 121
Ross, A. D., 90
Ross, G., 329
Rotatori, A., 117, 213
Rothenberg, B., 36
Rotter, J. B., 102, 103
Rubenstein, C., 211
Rubin, D., 34, 108

Rubin, K., 34, 35, 36, 41, 108, 109, 110, 113, 116, 117
Rubinstein, E. A., 32
Ruebush, B. R., 272
Rush, A. J., 5, 295, 298
Rush, D., 212, 215, 216
Rushton, J., 36, 41
Russell, R., 124, 262
Rutherford, E., 41

Safran, J. D., 385
Sagotsky, G., 75, 78
Salovey, P., 259
Sandler, J., 206, 216
Santogrossi, D. A., 73, 76, 215
Santostefano, S., 379, 385
Santrock, J., 31, 32
Sarason, I., 103, 259
Sarason, S. B., 272
Savedra, M., 350
Saylor, C., 97, 103, 127, 148, 155, 158, 162, 169, 180
Scanlon, E. M., 119
Schachter, S., 270, 359
Schack, M. L., 122
Scherer, M. W., 125
Schleser, R., 253, 300
Schlundt, D., 207
Schneider, B. H., 206, 214, 215
Schneider, F., 36, 41
Schneider-Rosen, K., 290
Schorin, M. Z., 41, 112
Schrader, C., 151
Schredler, R. W., 253
Schuckit, M., 317
Schulein, M. J., 349
Schwartz, M., 122
Schwartz, S., 41
Scott, O., 294
Searcy, J. D., 103
Seeley, J., 290
Segal, J., 374
Seligman, M. E. P., 18, 103, 126, 295
Selinger, H., 47, 98, 116, 117
Selman, R., 27, 29, 35, 36, 41, 44, 45, 52, 56, 107, 108, 111, 112, 379
Shantz, C., 34, 36, 47, 107, 108, 210
Shapiro, D., 16
Shapiro, D. A., 16
Sharp, K. C., 115

Sharp, M. T., 36
Shaver, P., 211
Shaw, B. F., 5, 17, 295, 298
Shaw, D. A., 93
Shaw, K. C., 10
Shemberg, K. M., 5
Sherman, M., 210, 216
Sherrets, S. D., 310
Shigetomi, C., 10, 16, 258, 262
Shirk, S. R., 37
Shores, R., 215
Shorter, E., 373
Shuler, P., 93, 105
Shure, M., 10, 15, 36, 45, 46, 47, 48, 50, 56, 113, 114, 115, 116, 150, 192, 194, 195
Siegel, A. W., 103, 126
Siegel, L., 36, 50, 262, 266, 353
Siegel, S. E., 263, 350
Siegel, T., 156
Silver, S., 114
Simon, H. A., 112
Simon, K. M., 305
Simpson, J., 351
Sims, J. P., 196, 197
Sinclair, D. C., 345
Singer, J., 356
Singer, R. E., 352
Sipich, J. F., 262
Siqueland, L., 265
Sitarz, A. M., 236, 238
Skevington, S., 29, 38
Slaby, D., 207, 211, 217
Slaby, R. G., 114
Slavin, L., 348
Smith, E. R., 355
Smith, J. K., 206
Smith, M. B., 108
Smith, T., 151
Smits-van-Sonsbeek, B., 108, 110
Snipelisky, B., 18
Snyder, J. J., 50
Soli, S. D., 121
Sollod, R., 25
Sorensen, D. A., 79
Spence, A. J., 211
Spence, S. H., 36, 110, 211
Spielberger, C. D., 125, 237, 260, 272
Spirito, A., 127, 151
Spitalnik, R., 55, 74, 78
Spivack, G., 10, 15, 36, 45,

46, 47, 48, 50, 56, 113, 114, 115, 116, 150, 192, 194, 195, 198
Sprafkin, J., 210
Sprafkin, R. P., 216
Staats, A. W., 379
Stabb, S. D., 214, 215
Stalonas, P., 101
Stanley, S., 45
Stanton, M., 324
Stark, K., 16, 99, 104, 127, 307, 308
Stein, A. B., 237, 238, 351
Steinmetz, J., 303
Sterling, S., 101
Stevens, R., 259
Stewart, M., 243
Stewart, R., 259
Still, G. F., 373
Stokes, T., 227
Stone, C. R., 41, 112
Stowe, M. L., 103
Strain, P., 95, 215
Strickland, B. R., 102, 103
Stuart, R. B., 69
Stumphauzer, J., 148
Sturgis, E. T., 124
Suinn, R., 258, 266, 267, 268
Suwalsky, J. T., 36
Swift, M. S., 195
Syme, S. L., 347

Tabrizi, M. A., 290, 293
Tannenbaum, R., 18, 103
Tanner, L. N., 374
Taplin, P. S., 94
Teasdale, J., 103, 295
Tebbs, D. E., 379
Terdal, L. G., 94
Teri, L., 303
Tesler, M., 350
Thomas, D., 77, 78, 120
Thoresen, C. E., 8, 13, 67, 68, 70, 71
Tiedmann, G. L., 76
Tilker, H. A., 372
Timm, M., 215
Tisher, M., 128
Todd, N. H., 105
Tolman, E. C., 2
Tomasi, L., 348
Tomlinson, J. R., 121
Toomey, T. C., 348
Torgerson, W. S., 346
Torney, D., 75
Toro, P. A., 15
Tramontana, M. G., 310

Traylor, J., 96
Turiel, E., 44
Turk, D., 6, 54, 151, 349, 353, 357, 358, 360, 365
Turkewitz, H., 74, 78
Tursky, B., 347

Unis, A., 15, 293
Updegraff, R., 212
Urbain, E. S., 16, 109, 113, 115, 116
Urberg, K., 108, 110

Vair, C., 360
van Doornick, W., 12–13, 50, 207, 208, 243
Van Hasselt, V. B., 107
van Lieshout, C., 108, 110
Varley, W. H., 150
Varni, J., 50, 352, 360
Vaughn, S. R., 110, 117
Venditti, E. M., 68
Vernon, D. T., 353
Villapando, R., 106, 107
Vitulano, L. A., 124
Von Frey, M., 344
Voth, H., 318, 324
Vye, C., 253
Vygotsky, L., 6, 11, 27, 355

Wachtel, P., 25
Wagner, B., 167
Wagner, E. E., 297
Wahler, R. G., 105
Waite, R. R., 272
Walker, H., 95, 98, 105, 213
Walker, W., 259
Wall, P., 345, 347, 355, 359
Wall, S. M., 79
Walsh, T., 348

Wanerman, L., 376, 379, 386
Ward, J., 350
Waters, V., 296
Watts, J. C., 352
Webb, R., 36
Wegner, C., 350
Wehrspann, W., 96, 101, 109
Weinberg, R. A., 122, 123
Weiner, B., 4, 102
Weiner, J., 36
Weinrott, M., 215
Weisenberg, M., 348
Weishaar, M., 298
Weiss, D. S., 96
Weissberg, R., 15, 48, 101, 117, 210, 214, 216
Weissbrod, C. S., 98
Welch, L., 122
Wellman, H., 32
Wells, K. C., 124
Wenar, C., 27
Werry, J. S., 120
West, D., 259
Westby, S. D., 32
Whalen, C., 9, 50, 76, 234, 241, 253
Whatmore, G. B., 294
White, M. J., 50
White, P. E., 117
White, S. H., 194
Whitman, P. B., 126
Wilchesky, M., 215
Wilcox, L., 50, 51, 95, 98, 99, 100, 103, 240, 244, 253
Wilcoxon-Craighead, L., 3, 7, 18
Wilkinson, M. D., 122, 238
Williams, C. L., 149

Williams, J., 294, 303, 304, 309, 310
Williamson, D. A., 106, 107, 118, 213
Wilson, G. T., 2, 5
Wilson, R., 149
Wilson, T. D., 355
Winston, A. S., 75
Wirt, R., 45
Wisniewski, J. J., 125
Wisocki, P., 9
Witt, J. C., 289, 293
Wixted, J. T., 127
Wojnilower, D. A., 67
Wolf, M. M., 93, 105
Wolfe, V. V., 97
Wolfer, J., 358
Wolff, J., 361
Wolinsky, F. G., 351
Wolpin, M., 353
Wood, M. E., 108
Wood, R., 118, 119, 207, 208
Wright, J., 107, 108
Wurtele, S. K., 386

Yahraes, H., 374
Yeager, R., 323, 329, 335
Young, R. D., 376
Yussen, S., 31, 32

Zahn-Waxler, C., 34, 36, 108
Zajonc, R. B., 383
Zatz, S., 259
Zimet, S., 207, 208
Zimmerman, B., 27, 28, 31, 40, 41
Zupan, B. A., 99, 100, 109, 115, 117, 251

Subject Index

Absolutes, view of world in, 335
Abstraction, selective, 299
Academic achievement
anxiety and, 259
MFF performance and, 236
Accuracy, in self-monitoring, 72–73
Achievement
academic (*see* Academic achievement)
need for, impulsivity and, 238
Actions, evaluation of, moral reasoning in, 39 (*see also* Moral reasoning)
Activity(ies)
daily ratings graph of, 302
depression and, 302, 304
Activity groups, in social skills training, 215–216
Addiction (*see* Drug abuse)
ADHD (*see* Attention deficit-hyperactivity disorder)
Adjustment, social (*see* Social adjustment)
Adolescence (*see also* specific topics)
assessment in, 54
developmental variables in (*see* Developmental variables)
drug abuse in (*see* Drug abuse)
moral reasoning in, 43 (*see also* Moral reasoning)
psychotherapy in, 372–390 (*see also* Psychotherapy)

suicide in, 291
Adolescent Activity Checklist, 294
Adult Coping with Depression Course, modification of, 303–305
Adults
approaches used with, childhood approaches versus, 8
young people and, differences between, 375–379
Affective disturbances (*see also* Depression)
assessment of, 124–128
social skills and, 211
Affective factors, in anger arousal, 170
Affective role taking
assessment of, 110
social behavior and, 37
Age-related changes (*see* Developmental variables)
Aggression, 148–201 (*see also* Fighting)
anger and, 150 (*see also* Anger)
cognitive factors in, 151
physical, social skills training and, 206–228 (*see also* Social skills training, with physically aggressive children)
physical distance and, 221–222
reinforcement of, 209
self-control training and, 149–150 (*see also* Anger management; Stress inoculation training)
Alcohol (*see* Drug abuse)

Alcoholics Anonymous, 328
Alternative-solutions thinking, 114–115
in stress inoculation training, 199
Alternative thinking
assessment of, 45
training of, 47
Ambiguity, in directed learning, 13
American Journal of Psychiatry, 291
Amplification, in psychotherapy, 388–390
AMT (*see* Anxiety management training)
Analogue measures (*see also* Role play)
in social skills assessment, 212–213
Anger, 150 (*see also* Aggression)
adaptive/maladaptive function of, parameters for assessment of, 162
arousal of (*see also* Provocation)
coping with, 172–173, 175
determinants of, 170–171
assessment of, 152–163, 169
cognitive-behavioral interview in, 154–155, 156
general issues in, 162–163
interviews and ratings by others in, 156–161
role-play techniques in, 161–162
self-report measures in, 155–156, 157

drug abuse and, Rational Self-Analysis and, 334–335
forms of cognitive thought influencing, 162–163
maladaptive expression of, 193
physiological response to, 193
Anger management, 163–201 (*see also* Stress inoculation training)
case study of, 178–192
foundation for, 167–168
session-by-session guidelines for, 169–177
Anger-situation hierarchy, 171–172
Antecedent, in circular model of depression, 303
Antisocial behavior, role taking and, 37
Anxiety
arousal of, in anxiety management training, 268, 269
assessment of, 124–126
social skills and, 211
types of, 259–266
Anxiety control, coping skills for, 257–284 (*see also* Anxiety management training (AMT); Stress inoculation training, in anxiety management)
in adults, 258–259
approaches to, 258–266
general fears and phobias and, 264–266
guidelines for, 266–283
medical and dental procedures and, 261–264
structured 16-session treatment program of, 265
in test and evaluation anxiety, 259–261
Anxiety management training (AMT), 258, 266–269
for diabetic patients, 263
introduction of, 267
nature of anxiety and, 266
outline of sessions in, 267–269

Appearance, drug abuse and, 319
Appraisals, anger arousal and, 162
Arbitrary inference, 299
Arm placement, physical distance and, 222
Arousal (*see* Anger, arousal of; Anxiety, arousal of)
Assertiveness
anger management and, 176
assessment of, 118–119
Assessment, 90–129 (*see also specific assessment instruments*)
of anger, 152–163, 169
of anxiety, 124–126, 271–272
of attention and impulsivity problems, 119–123, 234–237
of attention and retention, 31
of attributions, 102–104
baseline, for stress inoculation training, 271–272
beginning of, 91–92
behavior rating scales in, 95–101 (*see also* Behavior rating scales)
caution about, 128
clinical interview in, 92–93
in anger assessment, 154–155, 156
cognitive-functional, 52–54
social skills and, 214
of depression, 126–128, 289–290, 292–295, 306
in developmentally based intervention plan, 51–54
of drug abuse, 317–319
conceptual foundation for, 320–323
global techniques in, 92–95
of interpersonal problem solving, 45–46, 53, 112–117
of mood and affect problems, 124–128
of moral reasoning, 39–40
observational, 93–95

of peer interaction, 105–107
of social skills, 212
of pain, 349–351, 354–358, 363
pregroup, problem-solving approach to stress inoculation and, 195–196
of problems in social relationships, 104–119
projective-cognitive, 54
recommendation for, 129
role play in (*see* Role play, in assessment)
of role taking, 34, 53, 107–112
self-monitoring in, 70–74
self-report measures in, 101–104, 117–119
in anger assessment, 155–156, 157
"shotgun" approach to, 52
of social cognition, 107–112
of social skills deficits, 211–214
"test" orientation of, 128–129
time spent in, "cost-benefit ratio" of, 90–91
"Troubles with School" strategy in, 53–54
of verbal self-regulation, 48–49
Attention (*see also* Distractibility)
diversion of, in pain management, 361
problems in, assessment of, 119–123
retention and, 31–34
selective, 209–210
to tasks, developmentally based intervention in, 57
Attentional focusing, assessment of, 120–121
Attention deficit-hyperactivity disorder (ADHD) (*see also* Impulsive children)
assessment of, 119–123
attentional focusing in, 120–121
problem-solving style in, 121–123
Attributional styles, assessment of, 102–104

Attributions, role of, in children's cognitive and behavior patterns, 18
Attribution training, in depression, 302
Attrition retraining, 10 (*see also* Cognitive restructuring)
Automatic behaviors, drug abuse and, 331
Aversive techniques (*see also* Punishment)
  in developmentally based intervention plan, 55
Awareness
  cognitive abilities and, 378–379
  in drug abuse intervention, 325–327
  interpersonal, assessment of, 110
Awfulizing, 335

"Barbs," in application training, 167
BAT-C (Behavioral Assertiveness Test for Children), 106, 213
Beck Depression Inventory (BDI), 127, 293, 308
Beck's Cognitive Therapy, 295, 298–301
  basic principles of, 298–300
  efficacy of, 306, 307, 308
  treatment components of, 300–301
Behavior(s) (*see also specific type*)
  anger and, 171
  cognitions and, reciprocity of, 7
  context of, HSQ and SSQ and, 100
  drug abuse and, 318–319, 322, 323 (*see also* Drug abuse)
  moral, relationship of moral reasoning to, 41–44
  social (*see also* Social behavior)
    developmentally based variables related to, 26–31
  verbal control of, 11–13

Behavioral Assertiveness Test for Children (BAT-C), 106, 213
Behavioral exposure (*see* "Dry run" practice)
Behavioral interventions, cognitive-behavioral therapies versus, 15–16
Behavioral observations, 93–95
  of peer interaction, 105–107
  in depression assessment, 293–294
Behavioral rehearsal, in anxiety control, for bone marrow aspiration, 264
Behaviorism (*see also* Cognitive-behaviorism)
  methodical, 3
  radical, 3
Behavior rating scales, 95–101 (*see also specific scales*)
  for anxiety assessment, 272
  Child Behavior Checklist, 95–96
  for depression assessment, 292–293
  Health Resources Inventory, 100–101
  Home Situations Questionnaire, 100
  individually tailored, in anger assessment, 160–161
  MFF performance and, 235–236
  for pain assessment, 350
  School Situations Questionnaire, 100
  Self-Control Rating Scale, 98–100
  for social skills assessment, 213–214
  Walker Problem Behavior Identification Checklist, 98
Belief systems (*see also* Irrational beliefs)
  social skills and, 210
Belleview Index of Depression (BID), 293, 308
Bibliotherapy, in psychological preparation,

as pain intervention, 351–352
Biological markers, in depression assessment, 294
Bone marrow aspiration, anxiety control and, 263–264
Booklets, in psychological preparation, as pain intervention, 351
Borke's Interpersonal Awareness measure, 110
Brain damage, MFF performance and, 235
Brainstorming, in stress inoculation training, problem-solving approach and, 199
Bystander cartoon measure, 108–109

CABS (Children's Assertive Behavior Scale), 118–119
CAI (Children's Assertiveness Inventory), 119
"Can't" thinking, 335
Cards, visual reminder, in impulsivity training, 243
Carelessness, impulsivity versus, 234–235
CASQ (Children's Attributional Styles Questionnaire), 103
CATS (Children's Action Tendency Scale), 118
Causal thinking, assessment of, 46
CBCL (*see* Child Behavior Checklist)
CDI (*see* Children's Depression Inventory)
CDS (Child Depression Scale), 128
Chandler bystander cartoons, 108–109
Change, process of, psychotherapy and, 386–390
Charts, self-monitoring, 72, 73
Child Assessment Schedule, 293
Child Behavior Checklist (CBCL), 95–96, 213, 294

anger assessment and, 158, 169

efficacy of depression therapy and, 307

teacher report form of, 96–98

Child Depression Scale (CDS), 128

Children (*see also* Cognitive-behavioral interventions, childhood applications of; *specific topics*)

approaches used with, adult approaches versus, 8

cognitive style of, 14–15 (*see also* Cognitive style)

development of cognitive-behavioral procedures with, 11–15

historical perceptions of, 372–375

pairing of, in impulse control training, 250–251

psychotherapy with, 372–390 (*see also* Psychotherapy)

self-efficacy expectations of, 17–18

self-regulation of, 13–14

Children's Action Tendency Scale (CATS), 118

Children's Assertive Behavior Scale (CABS), 118–119

Children's Assertiveness Inventory (CAI), 119

Children's Attributional Style Questionnaire, 18

Children's Attributional Styles Questionnaire (CASQ), 103

Children's Comprehensive Pain Questionnaire, 350

Children's Depression Inventory (CDI), 127, 293

efficacy of therapy and, 307

Children's Depression Scale, 128, 293

efficacy of therapy and, 307

Children's Hostility Inventory, 156

Children's Inventory of Anger, 155, 157, 162, 169, 180

Children's Manifest Anxiety Scale (CMAS), 125, 294

Children's Perceived Self-Control Scale (CPSCS), 103–104

Circles Game, in stress inoculation training, 200

Classical conditioning, role of cognitions in, 3–4

Classroom setting (*see also* Teacher *entries*)

self-management techniques in, 77–79

Clinical interview, 92–93

in anger assessment, 154–155, 156

in depression assessment, 292, 293

Clinician (*see* Therapist)

CMAS (Children's Manifest Anxiety Scale), 125, 294

Cocaine, 315 (*see also* Drug abuse)

Cognition(s)

behaviors and

aggressive, 151

reciprocity of, 7

depression and, 298–299, 304

emotions and, development of, 383–384

pain and, 355

psychotherapy and, 378–379, 381

role of

in behavior and behavior change, 4

in operant and classical conditioning, 3–4

social, assessment of, 107–112

social skills and, 209–211

types of, 153

Cognitive-behavioral assessment, 90–129 (*see also* Assessment)

Cognitive-behavioral interventions (*see also* Training; *specific interventions and related topics*)

for anxiety control, 257–284 (*see also* Anxiety control)

childhood applications of (*see also* Intervention plan(s); *specific applications*)

developmental variables and, 25–59 (*see also* Developmental variables)

development of, 11–15

direction of, 17–18

efficacy of, 15–17

defined, 5–11

for depression, 295–310 (*see also* Depression)

general characteristics of, 6

historical considerations of, 2–5

theoretical basis of, 2–3, 4 (*see also* *specific theories*)

typology of, 8–11

Cognitive-behavioral interview (*see* Clinical interview)

Cognitive-behaviorism

forces providing impetus for, 3–5

origin of, 2–3

Cognitive Bias Questionnaire for Children, 18

Cognitive coping methods, pain and, 360–362

Cognitive deficits, problem solving and, anger control and, 193–194

Cognitive developmental theory, 27–28

Cognitive distortion, depression and, 299–300

Cognitive efficiency factor, in Porteus Maze Test, 123

Cognitive events, 153

Cognitive-functional assessment, 52–54

"shotgun" approach versus, 52–53

social skills and, 214

Cognitive mediation, anger and, 194

Cognitive modeling, 9, 11

in anger management, 174–175

in anxiety management, 275–276, 280

Cognitive modeling, (*cont.*)
exemplary modeling
versus, 32
verbal self-instructions
and, 244, 248
Cognitive perspective taking, 35–36
Cognitive preparation, in
stress inoculation
training (*see* Stress
inoculation training,
cognitive preparation
in)
Cognitive problem solving,
10
individual differences in, 15
Cognitive processes, 153
Cognitive regulation, in
stress inoculation
training (*see* Stress
inoculation training)
Cognitive restructuring, 10
in depression treatment,
306
Cognitive self-instruction,
for impulse control,
233–254 (*see also* Im-
pulse control)
Cognitive skills (*see* Cogni-
tion(s); Skill levels)
Cognitive structures, 153
drug abuse and, interven-
tion in, 328–335
psychotherapy and, 377
Cognitive style, of children,
14–15
assessment of, 121–123
impulsivity and, 234–235
(*see also* Impulse
control; Impulsivity)
Cognitive Therapy (*see*
Beck's Cognitive
Therapy)
*Cognitive Therapy and Re-
search*, 257
Cognitive thought, forms
of, influencing anger
arousal, 162–163, 170
Cognitive triad, in Beck's
cognitive theory of
depression, 299
Commitment stage in drug
abuse treatment,
327–328
Communication
verbal, anger control and,
193–194
voice tone in, social skills
training and, 218–219

Compliments, response to,
in social skills train-
ing, 227
Conceptualization phase, of
stress inoculation
training (*see* Stress
inoculation training,
cognitive preparation
in)
Conceptualizations, goals
and, reciprocal rela-
tionship between, 30
Conceptual labeling, con-
crete labeling versus,
in self-instructional
training, 50–51, 244
Conceptual tempo (*see* Cognitive style)
Concrete labeling, conceptual labeling versus,
in self-instructional
training, 50–51, 244
Conditioning, covert, 9
Conditioning techniques
application of, to private
events, 4
cognitions and, 3–4
Conflict situations (*see*
Provocation)
Confrontation, impact and,
in anger manage-
ment, 172, 174
Consequences (*see* Punishment; Reinforce-
ment; Self-
consequation)
Consequential thinking
assessment of, 46
training of, 47
in stress inoculation
training, 199
Context
of behaviors, HSQ and
SSQ and, 100
imaginative transforma-
tion of, in pain man-
agement, 361
Contingent reinforcement,
in social skills train-
ing, 215
Control
locus of (*see* Locus of
control)
self- (*see* Self-control *entries*)
Cooperative behavior, role
taking and, 37
Coping imagery, 10 (*see also*
Imagery)

Coping skills
anger management and,
168
for anxiety control, 257–
284 (*see also* Anxiety
control)
for pain management,
257–284 (*see also*
Pain)
Coping techniques, goals of,
258
Coping with Depression
Courses, 303–305
efficacy of, 309
Correspondence training,
stress inoculation
training and, for anx-
iety management, 282
Cortisol levels, depression
and, 294
Counselor (*see* Therapist)
Counters, in self-monitoring, 71
"Countoons," 71
Covert conditioning tech-
niques, 9
Covert modeling, 9, 11
Covert self-instructions
in anger management,
176–177
in anxiety management,
277–278
Covert speech, overt speech
versus, drawing task
and, 155, 156
CPSCS (Children's Per-
ceived Self-Control
Scale), 103–104
Crime
drug abuse and, 319 (*see
also* Drug abuse)
juvenile, 148 (*see also* Aggression)
Criticism, response to, in
social skills training,
224
Cues
in anger management, 168
saliency of, development
and, 33
in self-monitoring, 78

DAP (Draw-A-Person)
drawings, pain man-
agement and, 364–
365, 366
Darkness, fear of, 264–265
Delinquent behavior (*see*
Aggression)

Denial, drug abuse and, 336
Dental procedures, anxiety
    related to, 261–262
  pain management and,
    362–367
Depression, 289–311
  assessment of, 126–128,
    289–290, 292–295,
    306
  biological markers in,
    294
  direct observation in,
    293–294
  initial phase of, 292
  related constructs in,
    294
  circular model of, 303
  cognitive-behavioral inter-
    vention models of,
    295–310
    Beck's, 298–301
    efficacy of, 305–310
    Ellis's, 295–298
    Lewinsohn's, 302–305
    Rehm's, 301–302
  cognitive theory of, 5
  diagnostic criteria for,
    289–290, 292
  drug abuse versus, 317–
    318
  future research needs for,
    310
  literature on, 291
  nontransient nature of,
    291
  prevalence of, in children
    and adolescents, 290–
    291
  social skills and, 211
  suicide and, 291
Desensitization
  self-control, for general
    fears, 265
  systematic, 8, 11
    in test anxiety, 260
Determinism, reciprocal, 7,
    28, 354
Development, theories of,
    27–29
Developmental variables,
    25–59
  Beck's Cognitive Therapy
    and, 300
  impulsivity and, 237
  intervention plan based
    on, example of, 51–
    58
  psychotherapy and, 377–
    378

cognitions and, 378–
    379, 381, 383–386
  emotions and, 379,
    383–386
  self-instructional training
    and, 253
  self-monitoring and, 70–
    71
  social act evaluation and,
    34–51
    interpersonal problem
      solving and, 45–48
    moral reasoning and,
      39–45
    role taking and, 34–39
    verbal self-regulation
      and, 48–51
  social behavior and, 26–
    31
  social information com-
    prehension and, 31–
    34
  social skills and, 210–211
Devereux Scale, 38
Dexamethasone suppression
    test (DST), in depres-
    sion assessment, 294
Diabetic patients, diabetic
    control in, anxiety
    management training
    and, 263
Diary, in anger manage-
    ment, 171
Diazepam (Valium), coping
    skills versus, in anxi-
    ety control for bone
    marrow aspiration,
    263–264
Dichotomous thinking, 299
Differences, individual (see
    Individual differ-
    ences)
Differential Emotions Scale,
    294
Dilemmas, open-ended, in
    interpersonal under-
    standing assessment,
    111–112
Directed-learning paradigm,
    13–14
Direct observation, in as-
    sessment, 93–95
  of depression, 293–294
  of social skills, 212
Discipline (see also Punish-
    ment)
  inductive, 45
Discrepancy principle, 30–
    31

Discrimination training, in
    depression, 302
Discussion program, in
    moral reasoning
    training, 44–45
Disease-related pain, 348
    (see also Pain)
Dishonesty, drug abuse and,
    318
Dissonance, in drug abuse
    treatment, 338
Distance, physical, in social
    skills training, 221–
    222
Distortion, cognitive, de-
    pression and, 299–
    300
Distractibility (see also At-
    tention)
  group treatment and,
    195–196
Distraction, self-generated,
    in pain management,
    361
Dot-to-dot drawings, impul-
    sive children and,
    242–243
Drawings
  Draw-A-Person, pain
    management and,
    364–365, 366
  in impulsivity training,
    242–243
Drawing task, in anger as-
    sessment, 155, 156
Drug abuse, 315–342
  assessment of, conceptual
    foundation for, 320–
    323
  behavioral consequences
    of, 322, 323
  denial and, 336
  diagnosis of, 317–319
  motivation for, 321
  myths about, 316–317
  problem of, recognition
    of, 317–319
  treatment of, 323–339
    awareness stage in,
      325–327
    commitment to objec-
      tives in, 327–328
    conditions for success
      in, 324
    dissonance in, 338
    follow-up in, 338–339
    identification of dys-
      functional thoughts
      in, 328–338

Drug abuse, treatment of, (*cont.*)
  identification of repetitive styles of thinking in, 335–337
  L.I.F.E. program for, 339–342
  Moral Inventory in, 328–329, 330–331
  progression through phases in, 337–338
  Rational Self-Analysis in, 332–335
"Dry run" practice
  in pain assessment, 356
  in stress inoculation training
    for anger management, 200
    for pain management, 362
DSM-III-R
  aggression in, 152
  depression criteria of, 290, 292
DST (dexamethasone suppression test), in depression assessment, 294

Egocentric viewpoint, 35
Elaboration, exploration and, in psychotherapy, 386–387
Ellis's Rational Emotive Therapy (*see* Rational Emotive Therapy (RET))
Emotional development
  cognitive development and, 383–386
  psychotherapy and, 379
Emotional states (*see also* Mood disturbances; *specific type*)
  drug abuse and, 322 (*see also* Drug abuse)
  impulsivity and, 235
  social skills and, 211
Enablers, drug abuse and, 326
Environment (*see also* Classroom setting; Hospital setting)
  for anger management, 168
  for drug abuse treatment, 326

  for impulse control training, 246
  inductive, moral reasoning and, 45
  manipulations of, 7
Ethology, 27
Evaluation (*see also* Assessment)
  anxiety related to, 259–261
Exemplary modeling, cognitive modeling versus, 32
Expectations
  anger arousal and, 162–163
  of psychotherapy, 376–377
Explicit modeling, social behavior and, role taking and, 36
Exploration, elaboration and, in psychotherapy, 386–387
External events, provoking anger, 162, 170
External guidance, overt
  in anger management, 175–176
  in anxiety management, 276–277
  in impulse control training, 248
External reinforcement, self-management and, 78

Fairness
  moral reasoning about, 42
  social skills and, 224
Family (*see also* Parent(s))
  in anger assessment, 156–158, 160
  drug abuse and
    myths about, 317
    relationships and, 319
  moral reasoning and, 45
Family Environment Scale, 294
Fear(s)
  anxiety and (*see also* Anxiety)
  assessment of, 124–126
  general, coping skills for, 264–266
Fear Survey Schedule for Children-Revised (FSSC-R), 125–126
Fighting (*see also* Aggression)

intervention in, developmentally based, 56–57
Flexibility
  rigidity and, maturational fluctuations in, 377–378
  in stress inoculation training, 279
Focusing, attentional, assessment of, 120–121
"Friendship therapy," 112
FSSC-R (Fear Survey Schedule for Children-Revised), 125–126

Gate control theory of pain, 345–348
Generalities, abuse of, 335
Generalization
  operant procedures and, 4–5
  promotion of, in anger management, 168
  self-instructional training and, 240–241
  of social skills training, 217, 227–228
  of stress inoculation training, for anxiety management, 282–283
Global assessment techniques, 92–95
Goals
  commitment to, in drug abuse treatment, 327–328
  conceptualizations and, reciprocal relationship between, 30
Goal setting, in stress inoculation training, problem-solving approach and, 199–200
Graph, of mood and activities, 302
Gratitude, expression of, in social skills training, 227
Group approach
  in anger-management program, 168, 177 (*see also* Anger management; Stress inoculation training)
  problem-solving procedures and, 195–196
  in self-instructional training, 251

in self-management program, case study of, 81–86
in stress inoculation training
  for anger management, 168, 177
  for anxiety management, 281–282
Guidance, overt (*see* Overt guidance)

"Habitual" moral reactions, 44
Hamilton Depression Rating Scale, 293
Health Resources Inventory (HRI), 100–101
Home environment (*see* Environment; Family)
Home Situations Questionnaire (HSQ), 100
Honesty, drug abuse and, 318
Hopelessness Scale for Children, 294
Hospital setting, anger assessment in, 158, 160–161
Hostility (*see also* Anger)
  in voice tone, 218–219
"How" questions, in psychotherapy, 386–387
HRI (Health Resources Inventory), 100–101
HSQ (Home Situations Questionnaire), 100
Humor, in anger management, 168
Hyperactivity, 119 (*see also* Impulsive children; Impulsivity)
Hyperactivity rating scale, impulsivity and, 240–241

Imagery, 10
in anxiety management training, 267
extensive, 8, 11
in pain assessment, 355–356, 363
in pain management, 360–362
Rational Emotive, 338
Imagery/distraction, in anxiety control, for bone marrow aspiration, 264

Immaturity (*see also* Developmental variables)
group treatment and, 195–196
impulsivity and, 237
Impact and confrontation, in anger management, 172, 174
Impulse control, cognitive self-instruction for, 233–254
child's level of involvement and, 253
current research on, 252–254
development of, 234–242
generalization and, 240–241
outcome studies of, 253–254
pairing of children in, 250–251
response-cost component in, 245, 247–248
session-by-session procedures for, 246–252
setting for, 246
training materials in, 242–243
verbal self-instructions in, 244–245
Impulsive children (*see also* Impulse control; Impulsivity)
motivation in, 239, 245
reflective children versus, 14–15, 238
  construct validity of MFF and, 236–237
  externalization of symptoms in, 235
  treatment implications for, 237
  verbal control of, 12
  verbal self-regulation in, 49–50, 237
  training materials for, 242–243
Impulsivity (*see also* Impulse control; Impulsive children)
aggression and (*see* Aggression)
carelessness versus, 234–235
emotional disturbance and, 235
problems in, assessment of, 119–123, 234–237

Individual differences
in children's cognitive problem solving strategies, 15
in cognitive developmental theory, 28
Inductive discipline, 45
Inductive environment, moral reasoning and, 45
Inference, arbitrary, 299
Information
in psychological preparation, as pain intervention, 351–353
social, comprehension of, 31–34
Information processing, 27
Inpatient setting, anger assessment in, 158, 160–161
Insight, pattern development as replacement for, in psychotherapy with children and adolescents, 387–388
Interaction, peer, behavioral observation of, 105–107
Interactional model, of moral conduct and developing thought, 42–43
Interpersonal Awareness measure, 110
Interpersonal problem solving, 45–48 (*see also* Problem solving)
assessment of, 45–46, 53, 112–117
  MEPS in, 115–117
  miscellaneous measures in, 117
  PIPS in, 113–115
defined, 45
developmental changes in, social behaviors and, 46–47
role taking and, 38
skills in, anger control and, 194–195
training in, 47–48
Interpersonal understanding measure, 111–112
Intervention plan(s) (*see also* Cognitive-behavioral interventions; *specific type*)

Intervention plan(s), (*cont.*)
developmentally based
assessment in, 51–54
example of, 51–58
implementation of, 54–
58
positive reinforcement
in, 57–58
punishment in, 55–57
teacher/parent model-
ing of appropriate
strategies in, 58
Interview(s) (*see also* Clinical interview)
with others
in anger assessment,
156–161
in depression assess-
ment, 292
Interview Schedule for Children (ISC), 290, 293
Invitations, in social skills
training, 227
Irrational beliefs
aggression and, 210, 227
depression and, Rational
Emotive Therapy
and, 295–296
drug abuse and, 322
treatment of, 328–337
identification of, criteria
for, 331–332
ISC (Interview Schedule for
Children), 290, 293

*Journal of Abnormal Child
Psychology*, 291
*Journal of Clinical Child
Psychology*, 291
*Journal of Consulting and
Clinical Psychology*,
291
*Journal of the American
Academy of Child
and Adolescent Psy-
chiatry*, 291
Justice, moral reasoning
about, 42
Juvenile crime, 148 (*see also*
Aggression)

Keep Cool Rules, 226
K-SADS (*see* Schedule for
Affective Disorders
and Schizophrenia
for School-age Chil-
dren)

Labeling, concrete versus
conceptual, in self-in-

structional training,
50–51, 244
Language (*see also* Speech;
Verbal *entries*)
choice of, repetitive styles
of thinking and, 335
Law breaking (*see* Crime)
Learned Helplessness
Model, 295
Learning, 7–8
modeling and (*see* Modeling)
observational, develop-
mental variables and,
33–34
Leiter International Performance Scale, 243
Lewinsohn's model of de-
pression, 295, 302–
305
basic principles of, 302–
303
treatment components of,
303–305
efficacy of, 307, 308
Life Events Checklist, 294
Life Is For Everyone
(L.I.F.E.) program,
339–342
Locus of control, 102
assessment of, 102–104
impulsive cognitive style
and, 237–238

Magnification, in cognitive
distortion, 299
Maintenance (*see also* Generalization)
operant procedures and,
4–5
Major depressive disorder,
290 (*see also* Depres-
sion)
Marijuana, 315 (*see also*
Drug abuse)
Matching Familiar Figures
(MFF), 12, 14, 121–
123
academic achievement
and, 236
behavior ratings and,
235–236
construct validity of, 236–
237
impulsivity and, 234–237
locus of control and, 237–
238
Matson Evaluation of Social
Skills with Young-

sters (MESSY), 117–
118, 213
Maturation (*see also* Developmental variables;
Immaturity)
fluctuations due to, psy-
chotherapy and, 377–
378
Mazes, impulsive children
and, 242
Means–Ends Problem-Solv-
ing Test (MEPS),
115–117
Means–end thinking, assessment of, 46
Mediation
cognitive, anger and, 194
peer, in social skills training, 215–216
verbal, 50
Mediational viewpoint, 7
Medical conditions
drug abuse and, 319
pain and (*see* Pain)
Medical procedures
anxiety related to, 261–
264
pain related to, 348 (*see
also* Pain)
psychological preparation
for, 351–353
Medications (*see* Drug
abuse; *specific medi-
cation or type of
medication*)
MEPS (Means–Ends Prob-
lem-Solving Test),
115–117
MESSY (Matson Evaluation
of Social Skills with
Youngsters), 117–
118, 213
Methodological behavior-
ism, radical behavior-
ism versus, 3, 7
Methylphenidate, self-in-
structional training
and, 254
MFF (*see* Matching Familiar
Figures)
Minimization, in cognitive
distortion, 299
Model(s), selective attention
to, aggression and,
210
Modeling
cognitive (*see* Cognitive
modeling)
covert, 9, 11

in developmentally based intervention plan, 58
exemplary, cognitive modeling versus, 32
explicit, role taking and, 36
overt, faded, 244, 248
in pain assessment, 357
in psychological preparation, as pain intervention, 352–353
of self-statements
in anger management, 176
in anxiety management, 270–271
social skills and, 209, 216
criticism and, 224
fairness and, 224
name calling and, 224
physical distance and, 222
response to complements and, 227
Modeling videotape (*see* Videotape)
Mood, daily ratings graph of, 302
Mood disturbances (*see also* Anxiety; Depression; Emotional states)
assessment of, 124–128
social skills and, 211
Moral behavior, relationship of moral reasoning to, 41–44
Moral Inventory, in drug abuse intervention, 328–329, 330–331
Moral reactions, "habitual," 44
Moral reasoning, 39–45
assessment of, 39–40
defined, 39
developmental trends in, 40–41
interactional model of, 42–43
relationship to moral behavior of, 41–44
stages of, 40
training in, 44–45
Motivation
for drug abuse, 321–322
in impulsive children, 239, 245, 247–248
Motor behavior, verbal self-regulation of, 49

Multidimensional Measure of Children's Perceptions of Control, 104
Muscle tension, depression and, 294
Mutual role taking, 35

Name calling, response to, in social skills training, 224
National Institute of Drug Abuse, 315
Naturalistic observation
of attentional focusing, 120–121
of social skills, 212
Negative reinforcement, drug abuse and, 321
Negative view, in Beck's cognitive theory of depression, 299
Nighttime fears, 264–265
Novaco Anger Scale, 162
Nowicki-Strickland Internal-External Scale for Children, 102–103

Objectives (*see* Goals; Goal setting)
Observation(s)
behavioral, 93–95
in depression assessment, 293–294
of peer interaction, 105–107
naturalistic
of attentional focusing, 120–121
of social skills, 212
self-, in stress inoculation training, 151
Observational learning
training programs, attention and retention and, developmental variables and, 33–34
Open-ended dilemmas, in interpersonal understanding assessment, 111–112
Open Middle Test, 117
Operant conditioning
failure of, to produce generalization and maintenance, 4–5
role of cognitions in, 3–4
in stress inoculation training, 280

Organic pain (*see also* Pain)
psychogenic pain versus, 348
"Ought" thinking, 335
Outcome studies, of self-instructional training, for impulse control, 253–254
Overanxious Disorder, structured treatment program for, 265 (*see also* Anxiety control)
Overgeneralization, in cognitive distortion, 299
Overt guidance
external
in anger management, 175–176
in anxiety management, 276–277
in impulse control training, 248
self-
in anger management, 176
in anxiety management, 277
verbal self-instructions and, 244
Overt modeling, faded, 244
in impulse control training, 248
Overt speech, covert speech versus, drawing task and, 155, 156

Pain, 344–367
assessment of, 349–351, 354–358
behavioral response to, 350
coping process associated with, 353–354
defined, 344–349
disease-related, 348
gate control theory of, 345–348
imaginative transformation of, 360–361
intervention in (*see* Pain management)
medical procedures causing, 348
multidimensional model of, 345–348
organic versus psychogenic, 348
pattern theory of, 345

Pain, *(cont.)*
  physiological indicators
    of, 350
  preparation for, 351–353,
    360
  psychological signs of,
    350–351
  recurrent, 348
  specificity theory of, 344–
    345
  unidimensional model of,
    344–345
Pain management, 351–354
  cognitive-behavioral strat-
    egies for, 353–354
  assessment and, 354–
    358
  stress inoculation, 358–
    367
  psychological preparation
    in, 351–353
Palkes, Stewart, and Ka-
    hana training aids,
    243
Parent(s) *(see also* Family)
  behavioral ratings by, 95–
    96, 100
  impulsivity and, 235–
    236
  Child Behavior Checklist
    and, 95–96
  drug abuse awareness
    and, 326
  Home Situations Ques-
    tionnaire and, 100
  interpersonal problem
    solving and, 48
  interview with, 92
    in depression assess-
    ment, 292
  involvement of, in im-
    pulse control train-
    ing, 252
  Rational Emotive Ther-
    apy and, 298
  self-reward and, 76
Parent modeling *(see* Model-
    ing)
Parent reports, behavior rat-
    ing scales and, 95
Parent training, in anxiety
    control, 258
  fear of the dark and, 264–
    265
  presurgical, 262–263
Pattern development, in
    psychotherapy, 387–
    388
Pattern theory of pain, 345

Peer group
  aggression reinforcement
    by, 209
  in anger assessment, 156–
    158, 159–160
  drug abuse and, 321
    treatment of, 326
  interaction with, behav-
    ioral observation of,
    105–107, 212
  moral reasoning and, 44
  self-monitoring and, 71
  in social skills training,
    215–216
  values placed on relation-
    ships with, social
    skills training and,
    210
Peer Nomination Inventory
  of Anger, 158, 159–
    160
Peer nomination rating, in
    social skills assess-
    ment, 211–212
Peer rejection, social skills
    deficits and, 207–208
Peer teaching, self-instruc-
    tional, 250–251
Perceptions, psychotherapy
    and, 380–381
Perceptual role taking, so-
    cial behavior and,
    37
Personal constructs theory,
    2
Personality changes, drug
    abuse and, 319
Personalization, in cognitive
    distortion, 299
Perspective taking
  attention to, in punish-
    ment, 55–56
  role taking and, develop-
    mental trends in, 35–
    36
Phobias *(see also* Anxiety)
  coping skills for, 264–266
Physical aggression, social
    skills training and,
    206–228 *(see also* So-
    cial skills training,
    with physically ag-
    gressive children)
Physical appearance, drug
    abuse and, 319
Physical distance, in social
    skills training, 221–
    222
Physical pain *(see* Pain)

Physiological response to
    anger, 193
Physiological response to
    pain, 350
Pictures *(see also* Drawings)
  TAT-like, in pain assess-
    ment, 357
PIPS (Preschool Interper-
    sonal Problem-Solv-
    ing Test), 113–115
Play, sociodramatic, 37–38
Play therapy, 375
  in psychological prepara-
    tion, as pain inter-
    vention, 352
Porteus Maze Test, 12, 123
  impulsive children and,
    242
Positive practice procedures,
    in punishment, 56–57
Positive reinforcement *(see
    also* Reinforcement)
  in developmentally based
    intervention plan,
    57–58
Praise *(see also* Reinforce-
    ment)
  response to, in social
    skills training, 227
Preoperative anxiety con-
    trol, 262–263
Preschool Interpersonal
    Problem-Solving Test
    (PIPS), 113–115
Private events, application
    of conditioning tech-
    niques to, 4
Private speech, anger
    arousal and, 163, 194
Problem solving
  cognitive *(see* Cognitive
    problem solving)
  in depression treatment,
    304
  interpersonal *(see* Inter-
    personal problem
    solving)
  stress inoculation ap-
    proach to, 192–201
    (see also Stress inoc-
    ulation training,
    within problem-solv-
    ing framework)
  style of
    assessment of, 121–123
    impulsive children and,
    238
Procedural Behavioral Rat-
    ing Scale-Revised, 350

Project Aware
  interpersonal problem
    solving and, 47–48
  role taking and, 38
Projective-cognitive assess-
    ment technique, 54
Projective techniques, in
    pain assessment, 350,
    357
Prosocial behavior
  moral reasoning and, 41
  role taking and, 37
  social skills training and,
    226–227
Provocation
  anger reactions to (*see
    also* Anger)
    assessment of, 162
    self-statements and,
      223–225, 226
  cognitive processing and,
    193–194
  dissection of, into se-
    quence of stages,
    164–165
  preparation for, 172, 174
  reflection on, 173, 175
Psychiatric hospital setting,
    anger assessment in,
    158, 160–161
Psychoeducational tasks,
    for impulsive chil-
    dren, 242–243
Psychogenic pain (*see also*
    Pain)
  organic pain versus, 348
Psychological measures of
    pain, 350–351
Psychological preparation,
    in pain intervention,
    351–353
Psychopathology, develop-
    mental processes and,
    26–27
Psychotherapy
  with children and adoles-
    cents, 372–390
  amplification in, 388–
    390
  change process in, 386–
    390
  cognitions and, 378–379
  conceptual framework
    for, 381–386
  differences from adults
    and, 375–379
  elaboration and explo-
    ration in, 386–387
  emotions and, 379

expectations and, 376–
    377
  givens in, 380–381
  goals of, 379–380
  historical perspective
    on, 372–375
  intervention process in,
    383, 384
  maturation and, 377–
    378
  pattern development in,
    387–388
  second-order effects of,
    381
  drug abuse and, 323
Punishment (*see also* Disci-
    pline)
  covert, 9
  in developmentally based
    intervention plan,
    55–57
  self- (*see* Self-consequa-
    tion)
Puppet therapy, in psycho-
    logical preparation,
    as pain intervention,
    352
Purdue Elementary Prob-
    lem-Solving Inven-
    tory, 117

Radical behaviorism, dissat-
    isfaction with, in de-
    velopment of
    cognitive-behavior-
    ism, 3, 7
RADS (Reynolds Adoles-
    cent Depression
    Scale), 293, 308
Rapport
  anger management and,
    168, 169
  Beck's Cognitive Therapy
    and, 300
  Rational Emotive Ther-
    apy and, 297
Rating scales (*see* Behavior
    rating scales)
Rational Emotive Imagery,
    338
Rational Emotive Therapy
    (RET), 5
  basic principles of, 295–
    297
  depression and, 295–298,
    305
  efficacy of, 305, 306
  social skills training and,
    223

treatment components of,
    297–298
Rational Self-Analysis
    (RSA), in drug abuse
    intervention, 332–335
RCDS (Reynolds Child De-
    pression Scale), 293
RCMAS (Revised Children's
    Manifest Anxiety
    Scale), 125–126
Reasoning
  moral (*see* Moral reason-
    ing)
  systematic errors in, de-
    pression and, 299–
    300
Reciprocal determinism, 7,
    28, 354
Reciprocity
  of cognitions and behav-
    iors, 7
  of cognitive skills and sit-
    uational variables,
    30–31
  of goals and conceptualiz-
    ations, 30
Recurrent pain syndromes,
    348 (*see also* Pain)
Reflective children, impul-
    sive children versus,
    14–15, 238 (*see also*
    Impulse control; Im-
    pulsivity)
  construct validity of MFF
    and, 236–237
  externalization of symp-
    toms in, 235
  treatment implications
    for, 237
  verbal control of, 12
  verbal self-regulation in,
    49–50, 237
Rehabilitation, drug abuse
    (*see* Drug abuse,
    treatment of)
Rehearsal (*see also* "Dry
    run" practice; Stress
    inoculation training,
    skill acquisition in)
  behavioral, in anxiety
    control, 264
  social skills and, 209
Rehm's self-control theory,
    295, 301–302 (*see
    also* Self-control the-
    ory of depression)
Reinforcement (*see also*
    Punishment; Re-
    ward(s))

Reinforcement, (*cont.*)
  in anger management, 168
  contingent, in social skills training, 215
  covert, 9
  external, self-management and, 78
  impulsivity versus reflectivity and, 239
  negative, drug abuse and, 321
  positive, in developmentally based intervention plan, 57–58
  self- (*see* Self-consequation; Self-reinforcement)
  social, self-instructional training versus, 50
  social skills and, 208–209, 217
  in stress inoculation training, for anxiety management, 280
Reinforcement criteria, self-imposed versus experimenter-imposed, 14
Rejection, social skills deficits and, 207–208
Relationship therapy, 376
Relaxation procedures
  in anxiety management training, 266–269 (*see also* Anxiety control; Anxiety management training (AMT))
  in depression treatment, 304
  cognitive-behavioral therapy versus, 308–309
  in stress inoculation approach, 165, 173
Relaxation review, 267
Response-cost, impulsivity and, 239–240, 241, 245, 247–248
Response style (*see* Cognitive style)
Responsibility, insulation from, thinking style and, 336
Responsiveness, of therapist, anger management and, 168
RET (*see* Rational Emotive Therapy)

Retention
  attention and, 31–34
  selective, 209–210
Revised Children's Manifest Anxiety Scale, 294
Revised Children's Manifest Anxiety Scale (RCMAS), 125–126
Revised Problem Behavior Checklist, 158, 213
Reward(s) (*see also* Reinforcement)
  impulsive children and, 239–240
  moral reasoning and, 42, 43
  self- (*see* Self-consequation)
Reynolds Adolescent Depression Scale (RADS), 293, 308
Reynolds Child Depression Scale (RCDS), 293
Rigidity, flexibility and, maturational fluctuations in, 377–378
Role play, 37–38
  in assessment
    of adolescents, 54
    of anger, 161–162
    of peer interaction, 106–107
    of social skills, 212–213
  in depression treatment, 306
  moral reasoning and, 44
  in social skills training, 219–220, 221, 222–223, 225, 227
  in stress inoculation training, problem-solving approach and, 198–199
Role reversal, 38
  in impulse control training, 250
Role taking, 34–39
  affective, social behavior and, 37
  assessment of, 34, 53, 107–112
  defined, 34
  developmental trends in, 35–36
  moral reasoning and, 45
  mutual, 35
  perceptual, social behavior and, 37
  punishment and, 56

  self-reflective, 35
  social and conventional system, 35
  social behavior and, 36–37
  social-informational, 35
  training in, 37–38
RSA (Rational Self-Analysis), in drug abuse intervention, 332–335
"Running a movie," as interview technique, in anger assessment, 154–155

Scanning, visual, verbal self-instructions versus, 241–242
Schedule for Affective Disorders and Schizophrenia for School-age Children (K-SADS), 289–290, 293
  prevalence rate of depression and, 290–291
Scholastic achievement (*see* Academic achievement)
School, behavior pattern and, drug abuse and, 318
School Situations Questionnaire (SSQ), 100
SCRS (*see* Self-Control Rating Scale)
Selective abstraction, 299
Selective attention, 209–210
Selective retention, 209–210
Self-consequation, 9 (*see also* Self-reinforcement)
  directed-learning paradigm and, 13
  moral reasoning and, 42, 43
  reinforcement criteria and, 14
  social learning paradigm and, 13
Self-control deficits, 149
Self-control desensitization, for general fears, 265
Self-Control Rating Scale (SCRS), 98–100
  CPSCS and, 103
Self-control theory of depression, 295, 301–302
  basic principles of, 301

treatment components of, 301–302
efficacy of, 307–308
Self-control training (*see also* Self-regulation)
aggression and, 149–150 (*see also* Stress inoculation training)
Self-efficacy, 17–18
Self-evaluation, 74–75 (*see also* Self-management techniques)
depression and, 301
Rational Self-Analysis in, 332–335
Self-generated distraction, in pain management, 361
Self-guidance, overt
in anger management, 176
in anxiety management, 277
verbal self-instructions and, 244
Self-initiated relaxation, in anxiety management training, 268
Self-instruction(s), 10
covert
in anger management, 176–177
in anxiety management, 277–278
Self-instructional training, 6 (*see also* Self-statements; Stress inoculation training; Verbal self-instructions)
development of, 12
for impulse control, 233–254 (*see also* Impulse control)
pairing of children in, 250–251
social reinforcement versus, 50
tasks and, 57
verbal self-regulation and, 50
Self-management techniques, 67–86 (*see also specific type, e.g.,* Self-evaluation)
case studies of, 79–86
group, 81–86
individual, 79–81
classroom application of, 77–79

theoretical considerations of, 68–69
Self-monitoring, 70–74 (*see also* Self-management techniques)
cues in, 78
depression and, 301
self-evaluation and, 75
Self-observation, in stress inoculation training, 151
Self-punishment (*see* Self-consequation)
Self-reflective role taking, 35
Self-regulation (*see also* Self-control *entries*; Self-management techniques)
in children, 13–14
efficacy of, 16
verbal, 48–51
Self-reinforcement, 75–77 (*see also* Self-consequation; Self-management techniques)
depression and, 301, 302
pain and, 360
theory of, 68–69
Self-report measures, in assessment, 101–104, 117–119
of anger, 155–156, 157
of depression, 293, 306
of pain, 357
Self-rewarding (*see* Self-consequation; Self-reinforcement)
Self-statements (*see also* Verbal self-instructions)
in anger management, 174–175
problem-solving approach and, 198
anxiety and (*see also* Anxiety control)
test-related, 259, 260–261
maladaptive, 210
modeling of, in anger management, 176
pain and
assessment of, 356
coping with, 360
social skills and, 210, 223–225, 226
Self-talk (*see also* Self-statements)

drug abuse and, 337
in impulsive versus reflective children, 237
maladaptive, story telling for revealing, 273–274
verbal control of behavior and, 12
Selman's interpersonal understanding measure, 111–112
Sensory information, coping skills compared with, dental anxiety and, 262
Setting (*see* Environment)
Sexual behavior, drug abuse and, 319
Sharing, in social skills training, 227
"Shotgun" assessment approach, cognitive-functional approach versus, 52–53
"Should" thinking, 335
Situational variables, age-related cognitive skills and, reciprocal nature of, 30–31
Skill acquisition (*see also* Social skills)
in stress inoculation training (*see* Stress inoculation training, skill acquisition in)
Skill levels (*see also specific skills*)
development of, social learning theory and, 28–31
situational variables and, reciprocal nature of, 30–31
Social acts (*see also* Social behavior)
evaluation of, developmental variables and, 34–51 (*see also* Developmental variables, social act evaluation and)
Social adjustment
assessment of, 123
interpersonal problem solving and, 46–47
interpersonal understanding and, 111
verbal self-regulation and, 49–50

Social and conventional system role taking, 35
Social behavior (*see also* Social acts)
developmentally based variables and relation of, 26–31
role taking, 36–37
observation of, 105–107
Social cognitive skills, 15
assessment of, 107–112
Social events, discrepancy principle and, 30–31
Social information, comprehension of, 31–34
Social-informational role taking, 35
Social learning theory, 2, 13–14
depression and, 304
view of development in, 27, 28–31
Social problem solving (*see* Interpersonal problem solving)
Social reinforcement, self-instructional training versus, 50
Social relationships, problems in, assessment of, 104–119
Social skills
assessment of, self-report measures in, 117–118
cognitive variables and, 209–211
defined, 207
emotional variables and, 211
modeling and, 209
rehearsal and, 209
reinforcement variables and, 208–209
stimulus variables and, 209
Social skills deficits
assessment and identification of, 211–214
etiology of, 208–211
rejection and, 207–208
Social Skills Test for Children (SST-C), 213
Social skills training
assessment for, 211–214
defined, 207–208
in depression, 304
etiology of deficits and, 208–211

with physically aggressive children, 206–228
approaches to, 214–216
contingent reinforcement in, 215
generalization of, 227–228
length of sessions in, 217
manual for, 216–228
modeling in, 216
outline of sessions in, 216–227
peer-mediated approaches to, 215–216
phases of, 217
relationship establishment in, 218
treatment packages in, 216
target behaviors for, selection of, 214
Society for the Prevention of Cruelty to Children, 375
Sociodramatic play, in role-taking training, 37–38
Sociometric measures, of social skills deficits, 211–212
Solutions, alternative, 114–115
in stress inoculation training, 199
Somatic process, in anger arousal, 163
Specificity theory of pain, 344–345
Speech (*see also* Verbal *entries*)
choice of language in, repetitive styles of thinking and, 335
covert versus overt, drawing task and, 155, 156
private, anger arousal and, 163, 194
S-R formulations, inadequacies of, 3
SSQ (School Situations Questionnaire), 100
SST-C (Social Skills Test for Children), 213
Staff, in anger assessment, 156–158, 160–161
Stage theories of development, 27–28

State-Trait Anxiety Inventory for Children, 272
impulsivity and, 237
test anxiety and, self-statements and, 260–261
Stimulants, self-instructional training and, 253–254
Stimulation, search for, drug abuse and, 321
Stimulus
to anger (*see* Provocation)
variables relating to, social skills deficits and, 209
Storybooks, in psychological preparation, as pain intervention, 351
Story-telling technique, in stress inoculation training, for anxiety management, 273–274
Stress, anger as reaction to, 150
Stress inoculation training, 151
in anger management, 164–167 (*see also* Anger management)
in anxiety management, 258, 269–283 (*see also* Anxiety control)
baseline assessment for, 271–272
"booster" programs for, 282
cognitive capacity and, 281
cognitive modeling in, 280
correspondence training and, 282
flexibility and, 279
generalization and, 282–283
group sessions for, 281–282
nature of anxiety and, 266
outline of sessions in, 271–279
phases of, 270–271, 281
recommendations for, 279–283
reinforcement and, 280

application training in
  anger management and,
    166–167, 177, 200–
    201
  anxiety management
    and, 271, 278–279,
    281
  pain management and,
    362
  problem-solving ap-
    proach and, 200–201
behavior change in, three-
  stage process ac-
  counting for, 151
cognitive preparation in
  anger management and,
    165–166, 169–173,
    196–198
  anxiety management
    and, 270, 272–276
  pain management and,
    358–359, 363
  problem-solving ap-
    proach and, 196–198
educational phase of (*see*
  Stress inoculation
  training, cognitive
  preparation in)
generalization of, 282–
  283
in pain management, 358–
  367
  case study of, 362–367
  phases of, 358–362
within problem-solving
  framework, 192–201
  application training
    phase in, 200–201
  cognitive preparation
    phase of, 196–198
  pregroup assessment
    for, 195–196
  problem-solving tech-
    niques and, 192–195
  skill acquisition phase
    of, 198–200
  social skills training
    and, 225–226
relaxation procedures in,
  165, 173
coping statements and,
  282
skill acquisition in
  anger management and,
    166, 174–177, 198–
    200
  anxiety management
    and, 270–271, 276–
    278, 281

  pain management and,
    359–362, 363–367
  problem-solving ap-
    proach and, 198–200
  social skills training and,
    225
  verbal self-instructions in,
    164–165, 166, 270–
    271
Structured verbalizations,
  retention and, 32
Substance abuse (*see* Drug
  abuse)
Suicide, adolescent, 291
Suicide Ideation Questionnaire, 294
Summary, retention and,
  32–33
Surgery, anxiety before,
  coping techniques
  and, 262–263
Symbolic coding, 33
Systematic desensitization,
  8, 11
  in test anxiety, 260

Tasks, attention to, developmentally based inter-
  vention in, 57
TAT-like approaches, in
  pain assessment, 357–
  358
Teacher(s) (*see also* Classroom setting)
  in anger assessment, 156–
    158, 160–161
  WPBIC and, 98
Teacher modeling (*see* Modeling)
Teacher rating scale, impulsivity and, 240–241
Teacher Report Form
  (TRF), of Child Be-
  havior Checklist, 96–
  98
Test anxiety, 259–261, 277,
  278–279
Test Anxiety Scale for Children, 272
Thanks, expression of, in
  social skills training,
  227
Theoretical basis of cognitive-behavioral inter-
  ventions, 2–3, 4 (*see*
  also specific theories)
Therapist
  in anger assessment, 156–
    158, 160–161

  child's relationship with
    (*see also* Rapport)
  anger management and,
    168
  in depression assessment,
    292, 293
Think-aloud methods
  in pain assessment, 357
  in stress inoculation train-
    ing, for anxiety man-
    agement, 272–273
Thinking
  alternative
    assessment of, 45
    training of, 47
  causal, assessment of, 46
  consequential
    assessment of, 46
    training of, 47, 199
  dichotomous, 299
  dysfunctional, drug abuse
    and, 322, 324–325,
    328–337
  irrational (*see* Irrational
    beliefs)
  means–end, assessment
    of, 46, 115–117
  repetitive styles of, 335–
    337
Thought processes
  behavioral influence of, 3
  drug abuse and, 324–325
  intervention in, 328–335
  influencing anger arousal,
    162–163
  interpersonal problem
    solving and, 113
  moral reasoning and (*see*
    Moral reasoning)
Thumbsucking, self-man-
  agement of, case
  study of, 79–81
Token economy system, 234
  self-management tech-
    niques and, 78 (*see*
    also Self-manage-
    ment techniques; *spe-*
    cific technique)
Tone of voice, in social
  skills training, 218–
  219
Toys, in psychological preparation, as pain inter-
  vention, 351–352
Training (*see also specific*
  type)
  impulse control (*see also*
    Impulse control)
  materials for, 242–243

Training, (*cont.*)
 in interpersonal problem
  solving, 47–48
 in moral reasoning, 44–45
 in role taking, 37–38
 self-control (*see* Self-control training; Stress
  inoculation training)
 self-instructional (*see* Self-
  instructional training)
 in verbal self-regulation,
  50–51
Treatment packages, in social skills training,
 216
TRF (Teacher Report
 Form), of Child Be-
 havior Checklist, 96–
 98
"Troubles with School" assessment strategy,
 53–54
Trying-versus-doing, 335
"Twenty Questions," impulsivity and, 252

Understanding
 cognitive abilities and,
  378–379
 interpersonal, assessment
  of, 111–112

Valium, coping skills versus,
 in anxiety control for
 bone marrow aspira-
 tion, 263–264
Verbal communication
 skills, anger control
 and, 193–194
Verbal control of behavior,
 11–13 (*see also* Self-
 instructional training)

Verbal labels, retention and,
 32–33
Verbal mediation, 50
Verbal self-instructions (*see
 also* Self-instructional
 training; Self-state-
 ments)
 conceptual versus con-
  crete, 244
 impulsivity and, 238, 241,
  244–245 (*see also* Im-
  pulse control)
 motivation and, 245
 response-cost and, 240
 in stress inoculation approach
  to anger management,
   164–165, 166
  to anxiety management,
   270–271
 visual scanning versus,
  241–242
Verbal self-regulation, 48–
 51
 assessment of, 48–49
 defined, 48
 developmental trends in,
  49
 relationship to social adjustment of, 49–50
 training in, 50–51
Verbal style, anger management and, 169
Videotape
 of "dry run" practice
  anger and, 200
  pain and, 356
 in pain assessment, 356,
  357
 of role play, in anger assessment, 161–162

 in stress inoculation training
 for anger management,
  197, 200
 for anxiety manage-
  ment, 280, 283–284
Violence, 148–149 (*see also*
 Aggression)
Virginia Treatment Center
 for Children, 235
Visual reminder cards, in
 impulsivity training,
 243
Visual scanning, verbal self-
 instructions versus,
 241–242
Voice tone, in social skills
 training, 218–219

Walker Problem Behavior
 Identification Check-
 list (WPBIC), 98, 213
"What" questions, in psy-
 chotherapy, 387
"When" questions, in psy-
 chotherapy, 387
"Where" questions, in psychotherapy, 387
"Which One Doesn't Fit?"
 task, in impulse con-
 trol training, 247
"Why" questions, in psychotherapy, 386, 387
WISC Performance IQ, 12
WPBIC (Walker Problem
 Behavior Identifica-
 tion Checklist), 98,
 213

"Yes, but" thinking, 335